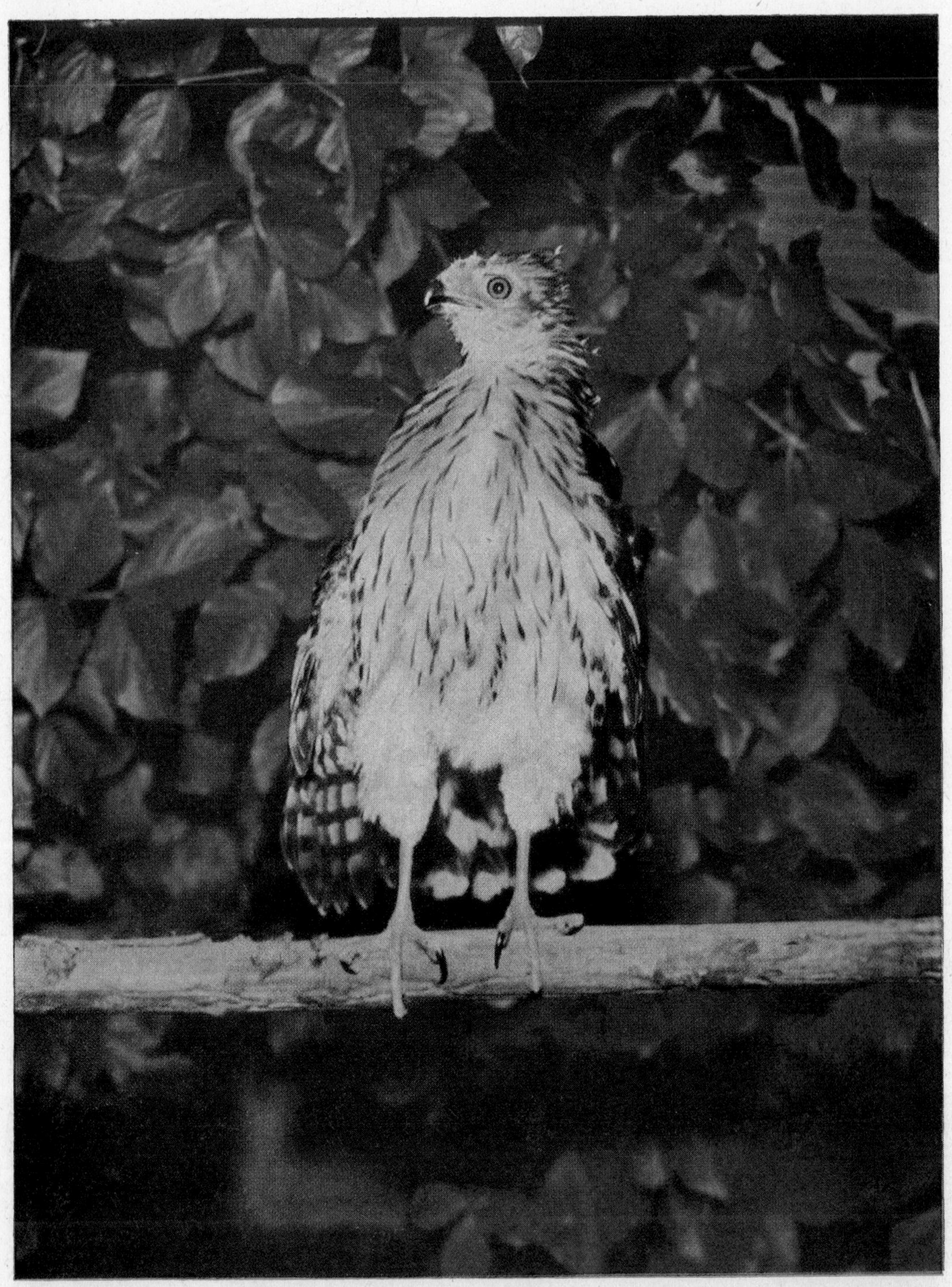

YOUNG COOPER'S HAWK 38 DAYS OLD (*Accipter cooperi*). Length: 14 to 20 inches. Male and female: color above, slatish blue; below, white. Has round tail. Immature: upperparts brown edged with faint rufous tinge. Shoulders and rump show faint white spots. Dull white underparts prominently striped with reddish brown. Range: throughout most of America, north to southern Ontario. Winters north to northern states. Voice: a rapid *kek kek kek kek* etc.

Hal H. Harrison

AMERICAN BIRDS IN COLOR

Land Birds

by

HAL. H. HARRISON

With 192 Four-color Photographs

1948

Wm. H. Wise & Co., Inc.

New York

WISE books are trademarked

Look for the *WISE* old bird!

Manufactured in the United States of America

To

Rene W. Leonhardt

who builds realities
out of my dreams!

CONTENTS

LIST OF COLOR PLATES

INTRODUCTION

In the preparation of this book, the author has been motivated by one overwhelming desire: that he may offer here sufficient inspiration to cause others to find in wild birds a fascinating, exciting, all-absorbing hobby; one that will prove physically, mentally and spiritually uplifting. If it accomplishes this, the book's short-comings will be of little import.

The author is not a scientist; he is a bird watcher (please, not a bird "lover"). In that capacity he has found life out of doors exciting at all times, for birds are everywhere. Although only a few of his adventures have been told here, they are all events that the reader himself may experience time and again when he becomes a bird watcher.

To the uninformed, the thought poses certain logical questions: "How can I become a bird watcher? What must I do? What do I need? Can I spare the time?" Let us answer the last question first.

One of the finest things about bird watching as a hobby is that it demands nothing more than you care to give it. There are no rules. You are in complete charge of the amount of time you devote to it. You may enjoy it at dawn, in the evening, week-ends, vacations, holidays, or going and coming from work. Indeed, one of my closest friends, a keen observer of wild birds, enjoys two hours of bird watching five days a week as his train travels both morning and evening through salt marshes, over rivers and harbors, through coniferous and deciduous woods, across meadows and all kinds of wonderful bird country. What might be a boring ride twice a day is an anticipated adventure.

Another friend of mine travels a great deal for a large corporation. He always disliked the long, tiresome trips by train or bus from one part of the country to another. He became a bird watcher. I talked with him recently after a business trip which took him from Pennsylvania south through Texas. He was on a bus one full day while traveling through parts of Oklahoma and Texas. It was a happy, exciting day, he told me, as he showed me a bird list written on both sides of an envelope; birds that he had been able to identify and observe from the bus window. He beamed with enthusiasm as he told me about it. Bird watching had made the difference.

Tragedy struck a friend of mine. He developed lung trouble and his doctor ordered him to Arizona. He was depressed. In Arizona he became acquainted with a group of bird watchers. As he became interested in bird watching, his thoughts were transferred from his own trouble into his hobby. The last time I heard from him he felt fine and was never happier. In fact, he has secured a position in the west and has no desire to come east to live.

A life-long cripple lives in the country not far from my home. He is confined to a wheel chair. A few years ago, he became interested in the Hummingbirds that visit the flowers in his garden. With red bottles filled with sugar water he enticed these tiny wild creatures to come to his hand. With his eyes he followed the females and discovered their nests. He studied their behavior day after day throughout the summer until they left him in September. Today, he is an authority on the life history and the habits of the Ruby-throated Hummingbird. He has contributed excellent papers to scientific publications, telling of his own observations. Bird watching has made life very interesting for him.

Such stories are endless. I even know a man who is much happier living with a nagging wife because he escapes Saturday afternoons and Sundays to watch the birds. Many men take their wives and families with them on bird watching trips. Youngsters are keen observers.

Now, how can you become a bird watcher? What do you need? You can become a bird watcher all by yourself if you wish, but it is most helpful both in learning about the birds and in retaining your enthusiasm if you have company. In most parts of the country, there are local Audubon societies or bird clubs. Affiliate yourself with one of these if at all possible. In these clubs, you will associate with wonderful people with the same interest and enthusiasm that you have. You will learn faster and your interest will not wane because of lonesomeness.

The first problem facing the new bird watcher is that of identifying the birds he sees. Although binoculars are not absolutely essential, they help immeasureably. Indeed, many birds cannot be identified without glasses. It may be encouraging to know, however, that binoculars are the only expensive piece of equipment required. Buy the best glasses that you can afford. If you know nothing about the optical advantages or disadvantages of certain binoculars, seek the advice of a bird watcher who does. In this regard, I should like to offer one suggestion: Be sure your glasses have a central focusing wheel and that each eyepiece does not focus individually.

An essential but inexpensive piece of equipment for the beginner is a good bird guide that may be slipped into the pocket and taken along on field trips. Roger Tory Peterson's "Field Guide to the Birds" and "A Field Guide to Western Birds" are standard works that have proved invaluable to beginners and seasoned bird watchers alike. Recently, however two new guides to eastern birds have appeared, and these should be investigated: "Audubon Bird Guide to Eastern Land Birds," written by Richard H. Pough and illustrated by Don Eckelberry; and Putnam's "Field Book of Eastern Birds" by Hausman. For Pacific Coast bird watchers, Ralph Hoffmann's "Birds of the Pacific Coast" is a classic.

For study at home, the many photographs with their text in the book you are now reading should prove valuable supplementary material for your trips afield. In the pocket guides, the plates and the text must necessarily be brief and concise. For more leisure time, the material contained in this book, as well as in others covering life history studies, will add interest to bird watching. If a state or regional guide is available for your home area, it will be helpful too.

The birds in this book have been arranged by families, in the order accepted by the American Ornithologists' Union and used in their Check-List. The division of species and subspecies is that of the latest corrections to the A.O.U. Check-list at the time of writing. The reader may question the inclusion of a few birds such as the Woodcock and Upland Plover which belong to families not otherwise included in the present book. Since these species are primarily land birds, found at a goodly distance from water, it has been felt that they belong in this volume, although their close relatives do not.

Bird watching may well start in your own back yard. I know a housewife who never goes afield to study birds, but she keeps one eye on her yard and the other on her housework day after day. In the course of one year, she identified forty-two different birds around her urban home, and had a grand time watching the nesting activities of House Wrens, Robins, Mourning Doves, Catbirds and Song Sparrows. In the winter, she attracts birds to her feeding stations. There is no humdrum existence for this housewife. The days are too short.

A middle-aged couple that I know have made their suburban grounds into a bird sanctuary. They have planted trees and shrubs with a thought to their value as bird food, shelter or nesting sites. They have erected bird houses, they maintain feeding stations, and they have provided several bird baths. Now, they do not have to go afield to study birds. Cape May Warblers bathe in the water pedestals; White-crowned and White-throated Sparrows stop off each spring for scratch feed; a Woodcock brought her little brood to feed under the grape arbor; Orioles swing their nests from the maples; Thrashers scowl from the thickets; and in early May, a dozen different kinds of Warblers forage daily through the trees and shrubs. In the winter, Bob-white and Ring-necked Pheasants come into the yard for grain. To these folks, bird watching is a thrilling game every day in the year.

Birds are identified chiefly by sight or by sound. In the beginning, you will find it impossible to identify all the birds you see or hear. Experience will gradually make identification easier, but bird watching never becomes so matter of fact that it is always easy. Even the experts occasionally run into more than they can handle (Fall Warblers, Empidonax Flycatchers and Sparrows in juvenile plumage for example). Birds are often heard before they are seen. Be sure to trace every new song to the singer and to tie that song to that particular bird, so that the two will eventually become synonymous. A notebook should be carried at all times, and observations kept for future reference.

Many of my friends confine their bird watching merely to keeping lists of the birds they are able to identify. These are carefully dated and preserved, to be checked later against similar lists to be made at the same place. Their greatest interest appears to be that of adding new names to their "life list." Well, one of the nice things about bird watching is that you may do it the way you want to. But I feel that the hobby offers so much more than just keeping a list. It is impossible for me in this limited space to discuss in detail the many ways that bird watching may be made more fascinating. Important, however, are life history studies of various species. This phase is attracting more and more students. There is much to be learned about every bird you observe. Science is a long way from knowing all the answers. In seeking a greater knowledge of bird behavior, the bird watcher goes far beyond the mere listing of birds seen; he becomes intimately acquainted with his subjects; he tries to learn how birds live. An excellent discussion of the opportunities awaiting the bird watcher is presented in Joseph J. Hickey's book, "A Guide to Bird Watching."

Another angle of bird watching that is luring followers constantly is bird photography. The picture-minded bird watcher soon finds himself wanting to catch his subjects on film, especially color film. This branch of bird watching has proved most interesting to the author. From years of experience, I have learned that the successful bird photographer needs three fundamental things: 1. a thorough knowledge of birds in the field; 2. adequate camera equipment and a knowledge of how to use it; and 3. patience. And the greatest of these is patience.

Finally, there is an indirect result from bird watching that cannot be ignored when one contemplates it as a hobby. It is the physical and spiritual value to you, a benefit that comes unconsciously, perhaps, but one that is there nevertheless. The very nature of the hobby demands outdoor exercise, the best kind of exercise, too, for it is acquired incidentally, rather than purposefully. Long hikes in woods, swamps and fields are not nearly as tiring when always ahead there is a new bird to be checked or an old one to be studied.

The spiritual value is an individual matter. One person is more impressionable and is influenced more by the wonders of the natural world than another. But all who pursue a hobby in nature are exposed to the fact, so abundantly apparent, that life on earth does not just happen. Bird watching will constantly confirm one's belief in God, but it also has a tendency to turn one away from dogmatism. The experience may well result in a more tolerant, peace-loving, broader-minded individual.

But let's be bird watchers for the joy of it! Birds are alive, beautiful, elusive, mysterious, ever-interesting, ever-fascinating. A life-long hobby awaits you, regardless of your age, your financial condition, your religion, your race or your color. Bird watchers meet on common ground. They form a great international fraternity whose initiation fee is your interest in birds. Come, won't you join us?

HAL H. HARRISON

April, 1948
Tarentum, Penna.

VULTURES

Family Cathartidae

The Vultures are an American family whose scientific name comes from a Greek word meaning "cleanser." And they are "cleansers" in that they feed on dead and decaying animal matter. Mainly tropic, three members of the family range north to temperate United States. The Vultures are distinguished by small heads without feathers. They build no nests, laying their eggs on the ground. Their flight is majestic; they soar in wide circles high in the sky. On the ground they walk rather than hop, as do most other birds, with an appearance of extreme listlessness.

TURKEY VULTURE ON NEST (*Cathartes aura*). Length: 30 inches. Male and female: naked, bright red head and neck. Body blackish with feathers edged with grayish brown. Range: western America; winters from California and southern Arizona, south. Voice: soft hissing and grunting sounds.
Samuel A. Grimes

TURKEY VULTURE

(Cathartes aura)

"Vultures are the garbage cans of Mexico" was the way a friend of mine described the status of these big birds of prey after he had spent several months traveling in that country. His poignant remark might well have been applied to the Buzzard's role in many parts of our own country where it serves as chief scavenger.

Unable to kill its own prey, the Buzzard has been forced to seek its livelihood among the dead. Since such food is not always available in a freshly-killed or recently-dead condition, the bird's fare is often eaten in a badly decomposed state. The search for carrion is conducted from high in the air where the Buzzard soars in graceful circles, ever watchful, ever alert, with eyes many times more keen than those of humans.

Admiration gained by the Turkey, or Red-headed, Vulture for its grace and beauty on the wing is lost when the bird is seen on the ground. Here it is ungainly, hopping about clumsily with its great wings folded against its slim body. Here, too, the ugly bare reddish head is conspicuous. The Vulture's body is black with grayer wings.

The Turkey Vulture lays its two eggs in a cave, a hollow log, a stump, in dense shrubbery, or some similar place. The young are in the nest about two months, and are fed by regurgitation on decomposed animal matter.

BLACK VULTURE *(Coragyps atratus)*. Length: 24 inches. Male and female: naked head and neck, black. Rest of body, blackish. Whitish patch on lower surface of wing. Range: western Texas and occasionally southern Arizona.
Samuel A. Grimes

The Black Vulture is the bird most likely to be confused with the larger Turkey Vulture. Although the latter's size might cause one to identify it as an Eagle, the Buzzard's small head, slim tail, and habit of soaring with wings extended above the horizontal are distinguishing marks.

The breeding range of the Turkey Vulture extends from southern British Columbia, Saskatchewan, Manitoba, southwestern Ontario, southern New York, and New Jersey, south throughout the United States into Mexico. It winters from California and Nebraska south.

RED TAILED HAWK *(Buteo jamaicensis)*. Length: 19 to 25 inches. Male and female: upperparts dark brown; beneath whitish streaked with dark brown. Rufous red upper side of tail, whitish lower. Yellow legs and feet. Immature: dark gray tail streaked with black. Black streaks on abdomen forming a broad band. Range: dry woodland from Newfoundland to Florida. Winters in Iowa, Maine and Ohio. Voice: a rasping *keer-r-r*.

Samuel A. Grimes

BLACK VULTURE

(Coragyps atratus)

Black Vultures are much more gregarious than their larger relatives, the Turkey Vultures. They feed in small flocks and roost in large flocks; while feeding a pack of them will drive away a Turkey Vulture that tries to join them in their feast of carrion.

This species is distinguished from the Turkey Buzzard by its smaller size (about six inches shorter), by its shorter, square-ended tail, and by large white areas near the tips of the wings which are noticeable in flight. At any distance, the Black Vulture may be recognized by its peculiar manner of flight—alternately sailing and rapidly beating its wings. At close range, the black head of the Black Vulture identifies it from the Red-headed Vulture, although the young of the latter have black heads and must not be confused with the other species.

The Black Vulture is a southern bird, ranging from western Texas, southern Illinois and southern Maryland south into Mexico and Central America.

CALIFORNIA CONDOR

(Gymnogyps californianus)

Approximately one hundred individuals are said to represent what is left today of the rare California Con-

TAME CONDOR ON HIS PERCH (*Gymnogyps californianus*). Length: 45 to 55 inches; wingspread 8.5 to 10.5 feet. Male and female: sooty black or brownish, with naked yellow or reddish head and neck. Under wings are pure white. Range: extremely rare; what few birds exist live in the mountains of southern California. Voice: none.

Wm. L. Finley and H. T. Bohlman from National Audubon Society

dor, or California Vulture, a magnificent big bird of the mountains and deep canyon country of southern California. No bird of prey has a more restricted range.

With a wingspread of 8½ to 9½ feet, it is larger than any other North American bird. It is much larger than the Turkey Vulture, a close relative which it resembles in form, but the latter's wingspread is only about 6 feet.

A study of the life history of the Condor quickly indicates that there are several unusual factors involved in the decline in numbers of this enormous Vulture. The female lays a single egg, and it is doubted if nesting occurs annually since the young bird, when hatched after more than a month's incubation, is in the nest or dependent upon the parents for about six more months. This unusually low rate of reproduction, combined with the encroachments of civilization on its wilderness haunts, has placed the bird's future decidedly in the balance.

After an interruption due to the war, the University of California and the National Audubon Society in 1947 undertook to complete an intensive field study of the life habits of the Condor to determine how the preservation of the bird may be assured.

KITES

Family Elaninae

In America the Hawk-like birds lost the distinction which is maintained in the Old World between Hawks, Eagles, Falcons, and Harriers. The American Hawks are divided into six families, the Kites, Short-winged Hawks, Buzzard Hawks (which include the Eagles), Harriers, Caracaras, and Falcons. The Kites are southern birds, and except for the Everglade Kite, have long pointed wings.

WHITE-TAILED KITE

(Elanus leucurus majusculus)

Another on the list of America's "vanishing birds" is the White-tailed Kite, a Hawk of the river valleys of south central California. In recent years various estimates have been made of the number of White Hawks left in America, and a very liberal estimate seems to be about fifty pairs.

The extermination of this bird will remove from our avifauna one of the loveliest of the birds of prey. It is characterized by its soft colors: white head, breast, and tail, and pale gray back. A black patch on the bend of the wing is evident in flight and when the bird is perched. The immature birds have a broad rust-colored band on the breast and their tail is

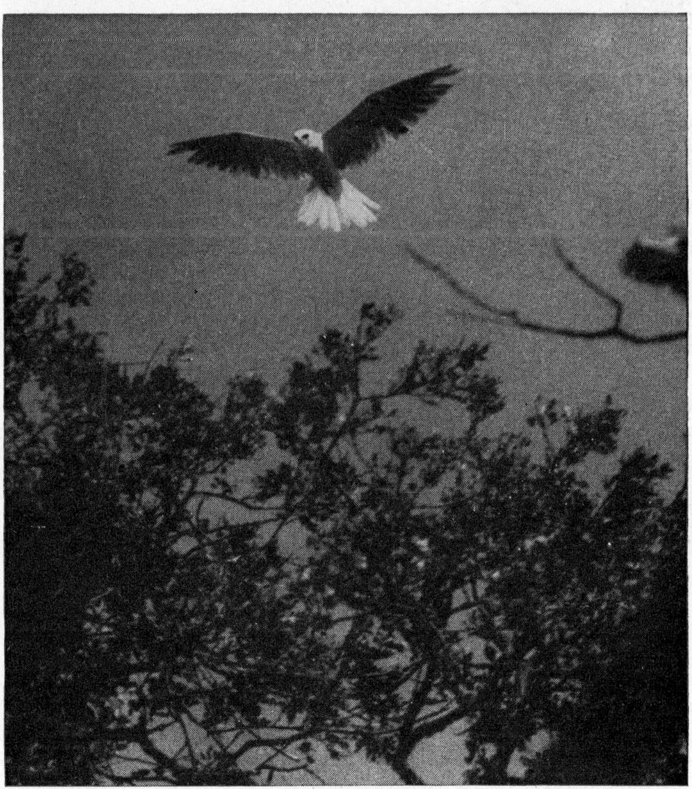

WHITE-TAILED KITE (*Elanus leucurus majusculus*). Length: 15.5 inches. Male and female: light gray, with white head, tail and underparts, and a *large, black patch* toward fore edge of wing. Immature: rusty breast-band and pearly gray tail. Otherwise similar to mature bird. Range: now accidental in east, formerly in Florida. Still found in south Texas.

Gayle Pickwell

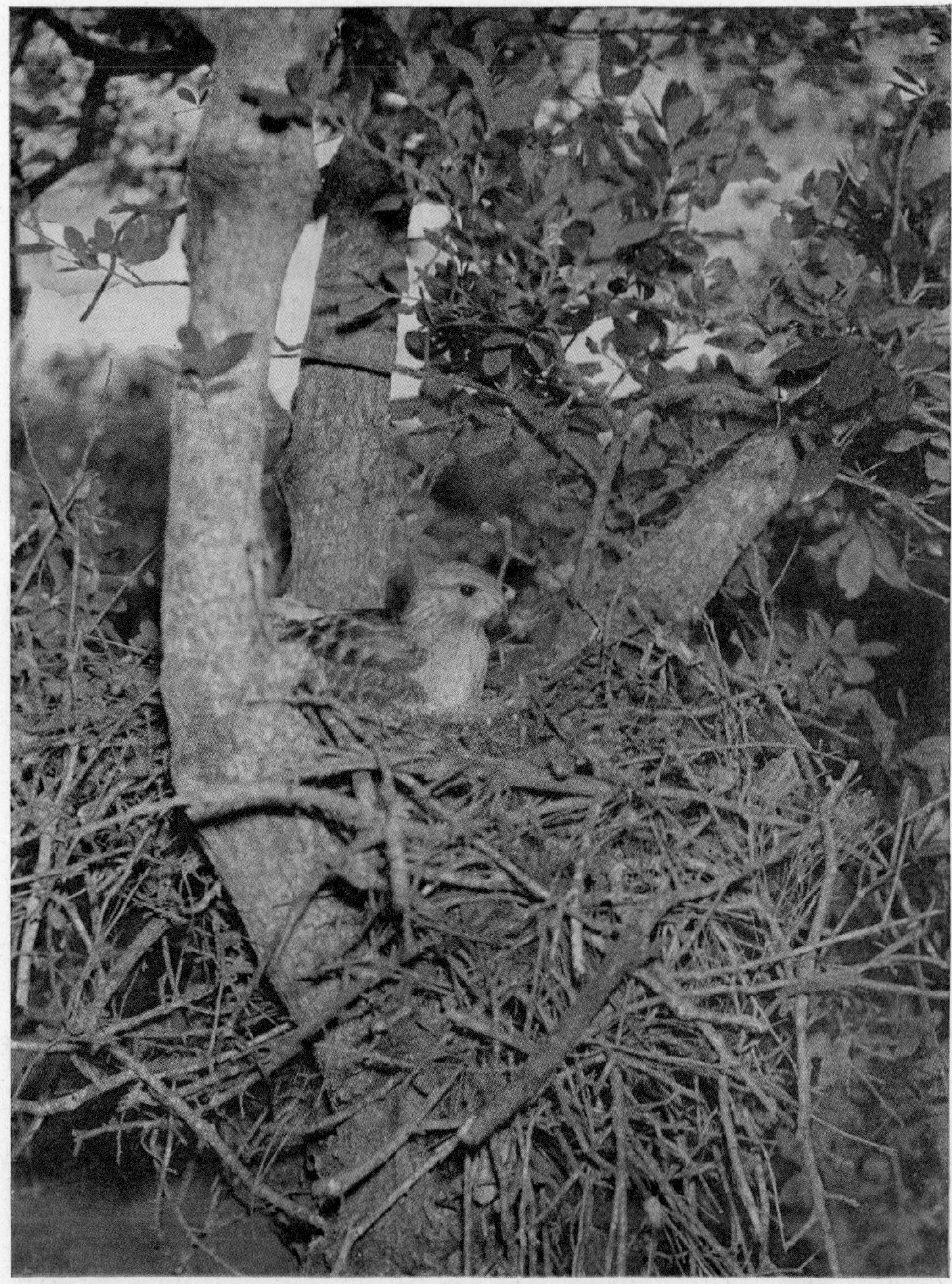

RED-SHOULDERED HAWK (*Buteo lineatus*). Length: 18 to 24 inches. Male and female: upperparts reddish brown; below, lighter reddish brown streaked with light ash and white. Light colored wing-patch near tip. Heavy blackish bands on tail. Range: from Canada to Florida and west to Great Plains. A few winter north to northern United States. Voice: a piercing whistle *kee-yes*.
Samuel A. Grimes

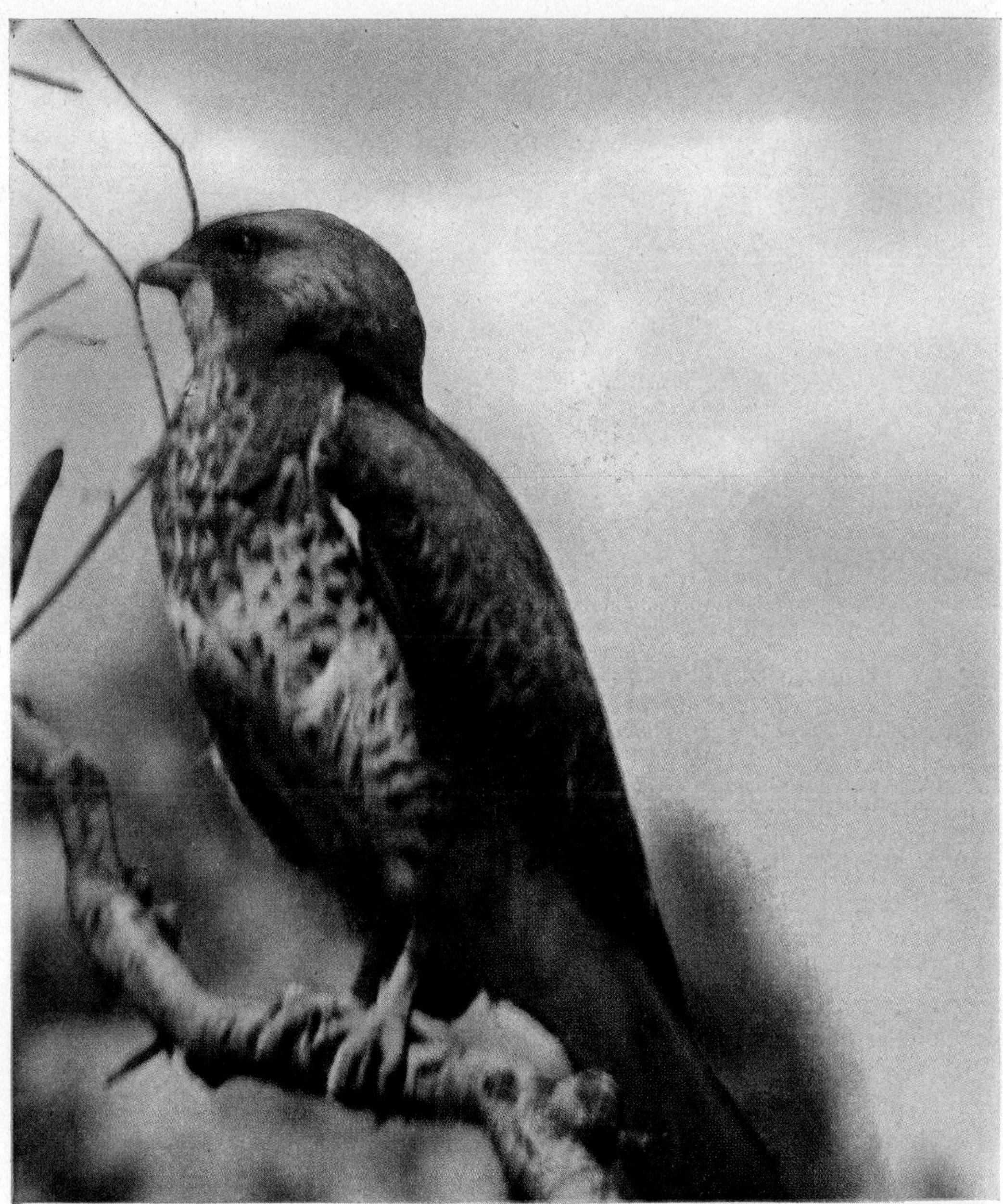

SWAINSON'S HAWK *(Buteo swainsoni)*. Length: 19.5 to 22 inches. Male and female, light phase; above dark grayish brown. Tail faintly barred with white. Upper breast chestnut brown. Rest of underparts tan barred with brownish. Chin, throat and forehead, white. Dark phase; entire plumage deep dusky brown. Both phases, wide dark breast band, and unmarked buffy wing-lining. Range: western North America, breeding east to Great Plains. Winters in Argentina. Voice: shrill whistle *kree-e-e-e.*

William L. and Irene Finley

EVERGLADE KITE AT NEST *(Rostrhamus sociabilis plumbeus)*. Length: 17.5 to 18 inches. Male: completely black except for white patch at base of square tail, legs red, hooked bill. Female: heavily streaked with dark lines on buff body, white line over eye and white tail patch. Immature: brownish black with a chalky cast on back. Range: fresh-water marshes of Florida.
Allan D. Cruickshank, National Audubon Society

The largest of the Kites (24 inches long), it was once widely distributed over the United States. Now it is confined to the river swamps of Florida, South Carolina, and Louisiana, where it builds its nest in the tops of tall trees. Its two or three buff colored eggs are richly mottled with cinnamon and brown. The young birds resemble their parents, but have black streakings over the white parts. The food of this Kite consists of small snakes and other reptiles, frogs, and insects, which it eats on the wing in a graceful maneuver.

tipped with gray. The adult bird is about 15½ inches long.

The White-Tailed Kite nests in the tops of trees, building a typical Hawk nest of sticks and twigs. The three to five eggs are dull white, almost entirely covered with reddish brown splotches. Its food is composed of insects, small birds, field mice, lizards, and other small reptiles. It is rare and accidental in the southeast.

SWALLOW-TAILED KITE

(Elanoides forficatus forficatus)

A striking looking bird, the Swallow-tailed Kite is unmistakable for its white head and underparts, black upperparts, and long forked tail. In grace and beauty of flight, it resembles the much smaller Barn Swallow.

MISSISSIPPI KITE

(Ictinia misisippiensis)

About the same size as the White-tailed Kite (15½ inches), the Mississippi Kite is uniformly bluish gray in color, with the front of the head silvery white. The tail is dark, almost black, without bars or markings. When the wings are spread, an obvious mark is a large pale patch or stripe on the rear edge of the underside. Young birds are streaked with brown below, but have the characteristic black tail.

Its nest is built in a high tree top; often it takes over an old nest of some other species. Its two or three eggs are pale bluish green, usually without markings. Its diet is primarily lizards, frogs, grasshoppers, and other insects.

The Mississippi Kite ranges from the Gulf States north to Kansas.

EVERGLADE KITE

(Rostrhamus sociabilis plumbeus)

Birds with specialized diets are decimated more rapidly by the constant encroachment of civilization than any others. The Everglade Kite lives on a freshwater snail of the genus Pomaces. These snails are grasped in the bird's talons and extracted with the sharp, deeply hooked bill which is specially adapted for the purpose.

GOLDEN EAGLE (*Aquila chrysaetos canadensis*). Length: 30 to 40 inches. Male and female: body evenly sooty black; white tail with dark band at end. Legs feathered to feet. Golden patch on back of neck. Range: mountainous regions of western United States.

George M. *Bradt*

The Everglade Kite may be distinguished from the Marsh Hawk which it resembles in appearance and in its habit of flapping and sailing low over the marshes, by its combination of all-over black, white rump, and broad tail. The Marsh Hawk is gray, with a white rump, and a narrow tail. The immature Everglade Kite is brownish-black with yellowish streakings and markings.

The Everglade Kite builds its nest of sticks and grasses in a bush, small tree or even in a clump of grass. The two or three eggs are dingy white with irregular brownish markings.

As the range of this bird becomes more and more restricted, it looms more prominently on the list of America's "vanishing birds." Today it may be found in this country only in certain fresh-water marshes in Florida.

SHORT-WINGED HAWKS

Family Accipitrinae

The Short-winged Hawks are woodland birds with long tails and short rounded wings. They do not soar like the Buzzard Hawks, but fly with several quick wing beats followed by a sail. In general, female Hawks are larger birds than the males.

AMERICAN GOSHAWK

(Accipiter gentilis)

If we may call the Sharp-shinned Hawk a small edition of the Cooper's Hawk, then let us call the Goshawk a large edition of Cooper's. The Goshawk may be distinguished in the adult form by its pearly gray breast and white stripe over the eye, as well as by its larger size. Cooper's Hawk is 14 to 20 inches long; the Goshawk is 20 to 26 inches long, with a wingspread of almost four feet.

It is winter before we look for the Goshawk to leave its heavily forested home in Canada and come south to the United States. However, scattered pairs annually nest as far south as the mountains of Pennsylvania and western Maryland. Some winters, apparently when its northern food supply is inadequate, the Goshawk enters this country in such great numbers as to be termed an invasion. At such times, this fierce, bold, big blue darter is capable of considerable damage in rural areas where it feeds on poultry, game birds, and game animals. In some states a bounty is paid on this bird.

IMMATURE GOSHAWK (*Accipiter gentilis*). Length: 20 to 26 inches. Male and female: upperparts, uniform slate gray, black crown and black stripe behind the eye. White stripe over the eye. Long tail, wide sturdy wings. Immature bird: above dark brown, heavily streaked with rust. Buff on back and shoulders. Underparts, yellowish white. Light stripe over the eye. Range: breeds in Canada to Michigan, winters irregularly to Missouri, Kentucky and Virginia. Voice: loud, penetrating cry.
Alfred M. Bailey, National Audubon Society

That this big Accipiter's food habits are not favorable to man, there can be no doubt, but in that regard, I like Herbert Ravenel Sass' comments in his story, "Kings of Winter." He writes: "We do not live by bread alone. Beauty and courage, swiftness and strength mean something to us; and we shall find these qualities in high degree in the Hawks of the Accipiter clan. Especially is this true of the largest and strongest of them, the Goshawk, one of

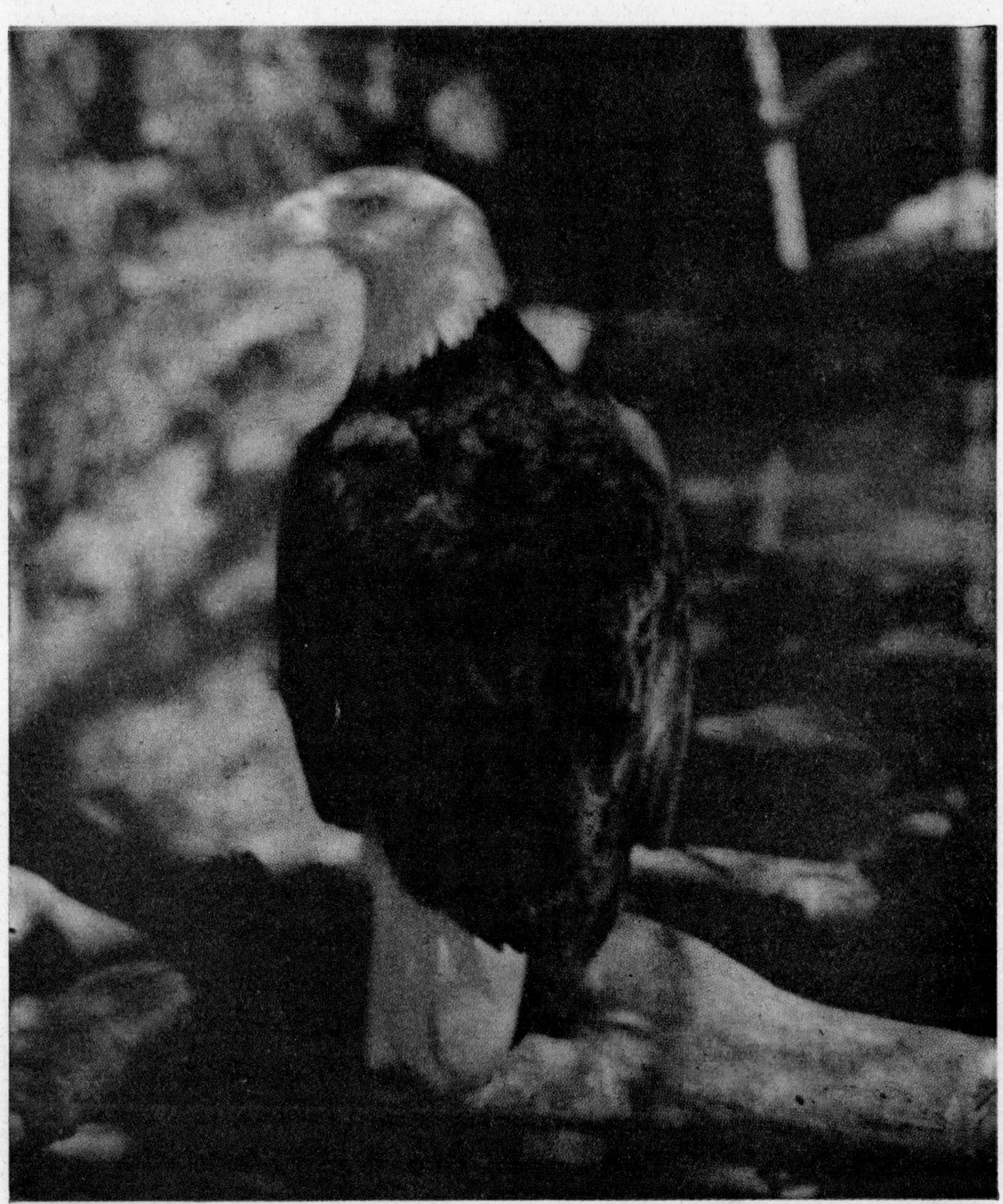

BALD EAGLE (*Haliaeetus leucocephalus*). Length: 30 to 31 inches. Male and female: sooty brownish plumage with head, neck and tail pure white. Has yellow bill, and feet. Immature: head and neck mainly black. May have base of tail whitish but never has contrasting blackish band. Range: from Canada to Mexico. Voice: male; high, clear call *cac-cac-cac*. Female: harsh, broken cry.

William L. and Irene Finley

the deadliest, handsomest, bravest birds of prey in the world."

The Goshawk is pale gray below and blue gray above, with a black crown, and white streak over the eye. The young birds are streaked brown. The tail is rounded. The Goshawk builds its nest high in a conifer, and lays two to five bluish white eggs.

Two races of the Goshawk are recognized; the Eastern Goshawk (*A. q. atricapillus*) and the Western Goshawk (*A. q. striatulus*) which show no field differences

SHARP-SHINNED HAWK (*Accipiter striatus vellox*). Length: 10 to 14 inches. Male and female: upperparts slaty gray; square-tipped tail. Range: breeds from Canada to California, Arizona and New Mexico. Winters through most of western United States.
Alfred M. Bailey, National Audubon Society

SHARP-SHINNED HAWK

(Accipiter striatus velox)

Although somewhat smaller than its relative, the Cooper's Hawk, the Sharp-shinned Hawk matches the fierceness of its big brother. Because of its smaller size, from 10 to 14 inches long, it probably is not often guilty of stealing full grown poultry as is the Cooper's, or Chicken Hawk, but the Sharp-shinned is fond of young poultry and all kinds of song birds from doves and robins to the smallest warblers and sparrows.

The life history of the Sharp-shin parallels that of the Cooper's Hawk. Indeed, it is often referred to as a small edition of that species. The two are marked almost identically, being bluish gray above and barred brown and white below, but the smaller size and the squared (not rounded) tail of the Sharp-shin are the most reliable field marks. Immature birds are brown, much streaked. The Sharp-shin is similar in size to the small Falcons (Sparrow and Pigeon Hawks) but may readily be distinguished by its short rounded wings. Falcon's wings are long and pointed.

The Sharp-shinned Hawk builds a large nest of sticks in trees, and lays four or five dull bluish or greenish eggs which are marked with large brown splotches. Its range covers most of North America.

COOPER'S HAWK

(Accipiter cooperi)

Color Plate, Frontispiece

The Cooper's Hawk is *the* chicken Hawk. It is principally this bird of prey that has given all Hawks an undeservedly bad reputation, but the Cooper's, the real culprit, is rarely shot. The Hawks that pay the penalty are the big, soaring Buteos, or Buzzard Hawks, like the Red-shouldered, Red-tailed, Broad-winged, and Swainson's, for they are the ones that are most often seen and thus the easiest to kill.

It is the Chicken Hawk's method of hunting that helps it escape the man-inflicted punishment intended for it. This Accipiter sits quietly concealed in a tree awaiting an opportunity to strike out an swift wings to swoop up its prey in its sharp talons. Never does it soar lazily in the open where an irate farmer might have an opportunity to shoot it.

Cooper's Hawk does not live on chickens alone. Indeed, the principal source of its food is wild birds, mostly song birds. Small mammals are often taken, as are frogs, lizards, and insects. Its short rounded wings and long tail give the Cooper's Hawk marvelous control of its flight. It is able to dart in and out among forest trees, pursuing its prey with surprising skill.

Like the Sharp-shinned Hawk, Cooper's Hawk is bluish gray above and barred brown and white below. The best field mark, apart from its greater size, is its rounded tail. Immature birds are brown, heavily streaked.

The Cooper's Hawk conceals its nest high in a forest tree. The structure is built principally of sticks and twigs, arranged firmly and hollowed out for the three to five pale bluish eggs. Newly hatched young are covered with thick white down. Young birds in the nest are of different ages because the eggs are laid over a somewhat extended period. The young are in the nest for over a month.

Adult birds become bolder as nesting continues. At a nest which I studied throughout its occupancy, the adults kept out of sight when incubation was interrupted by my intrusion. With young in the nest, they came closer, delivering a piercing cry of *cuk-cuk-cuk-cuk*. By the time the young were three weeks old, the female (always a larger bird than the male) was swooping at me and intimidating me in a fierce manner.

Not until these young Hawks were twenty-three days old was a chicken feather found in the nest. Previous to that, I am convinced their diet was entirely song birds and small mammals. It was interesting to note that other birds in the immediate vicinity of the nest were never disturbed. I counted twenty-three different species of birds singing close by the nesting tree.

The Cooper's Hawk is a migrant in the northern part of its range and permanent resident southward. It breeds from southern British Columbia, southern Quebec, and Nova Scotia south through the United States to northern Mexico. It winters south to Costa Rica.

BUZZARD HAWKS or BUTEOS

Family Buteoninae

The Buteos, which include the Eagles, are large Hawks with broad wings and broad round tails. Their flight is typically soaring. Much confusion exists in many of the species because of the existence of darker plumaged birds, and a number of the subspecies are hardly more than color phases which it takes an expert to distinguish.

RED-TAILED HAWK

(Buteo jamaicensis)

Color Plate Page 3

No Hawk is more widely distributed nor better known than the Red-tailed. And no Hawk has been more unjustly maligned than this big Buteo, which has been working for the American farmer ever since the first settlers erroneously cried "Chicken Hawk" as they saw it soaring over their farms, its keen eyes alert for the movements of meadow mice in the fields below.

To say that a Red-tail never stole a chicken would be incorrect. But Dr. A. K. Fisher who made an intensive study of the food habits of the Hawks, reported that, on the examination of 562 stomachs, the diet of the Red-tail consisted 85 per cent of rodents. As a result the Red-tailed Hawk is protected throughout most of its range.

In addition to its habit of soaring over the open fields watching for food, the Red-tail often sits in an exposed position, usually at the top of an old tree at the edge of a field, watching for likely prey upon which it may pounce.

Like all Buteos, the Red-tail has large broad wings and a round, fan-shaped tail. The upper side of the tail is rufous and the underside is clear and unbarred, in contrast with the conspicuously barred tail of the similar Red-shouldered Hawk. The underparts are whitish with dark streaks on the belly and flanks. The Red-shoulder is uniformly colored below. The immature Red-tail has a dark gray tail which may be banded. The adult bird is from 20 to 25 inches long, the female being the larger bird.

The call of the Red-tail is a forced, complaining scream of *keeeeeeerrrr*. I have always detected an explosive quality, or at least a forced tone to the opening *kee* of the call. The cry of the Red-shouldered Hawk is a piercing double note, *kee-yoo*.

The Red-tail nests as early as February in some parts of its range, although March is the usual month. The nesting site is invariably the top of one of the tallest trees in a small grove of heavy timber. The birds are believed to mate for life, and may return year after year to the same woodlot. The nest is a huge structure of sticks, lined with soft materials. The white or bluish white eggs usually number two.

In the northern part of its range, the Red-tail is migratory, although it is common to find a few wintering individuals here and there. Fall flights of Red-tails are spectacular, and large flights may be viewed from vantage points, sailing southward, riding the air currents. The bird's breeding range, taken as a species with its five geographic races, extends from Alaska through central Canada to Nova Scotia, and south through the United States.

The Eastern Red-tail is *B. j. borealis.* The Florida Red-tail *(B. j. umbrinus)* is darker with a broad black band at the tip of the tail. Krider's Red-tail *(B. j. krideri)* varies from the standard coloration to almost white, with a pale tail the best distinguishing mark. The Western Red-tail *(B. j. calurus)* is generally more rufous.

HARLAN'S HAWK

(Buteo harlani)

A black Buteo of the prairies, this species was formerly believed to be a sub-species of the Red-tailed Hawk. It is distinguished from the dark-phased Red-tails by the lack of red in the tail,

WESTERN MARSH HAWK *(Circus cyaneus hudsonius).* Length: 18 to 24 inches. Male: foreparts and upperparts light gray; white abdomen, white rump-patch. Female: brown upperparts and breast. Both sexes have imperfect ruff around face. Range: Canada south to southern California and New Mexico. Winters from Oregon and Montana to Mexico. Voice: sharp cries, *geg geg geg.*

R. T. Congdon

AUDUBON'S CARACARA (*Polyborus cheriway auduboni*). Length: 22 inches. Male and female: wings and back blackish. White tail, barred with black and having broad black tip. Bare face is reddish orange. Head has black crown and small crest. Underparts have whitish throat and breast and a black belly. In flight, whitish patches at wing tips are conspicuous. Range: Mexican border of Texas, New Mexico, and Arizona. Voice: hoarse, raucous call.
Samuel A. Grimes

which instead is white with a finely mottled black terminal band. It breeds in western Canada, and migrates south to the Gulf States.

RED-SHOULDERED HAWK

(*Buteo lineatus*)

Color Plate Page 6

When the Red-shouldered Hawk is called by its inappropriate name of "Chicken Hawk," it is just as much maligned as the Red-tailed Hawk which shares this unjust name. Despite the fact that scientists have proved that the diet of the Red-shoulder contains 65 percent small rodents against 2 percent poultry, farmers and hunters continue to shoot this big Buzzard Hawk and brag about their accomplishments. Of 220 stomachs examined by the United States Biological Survey, 3 contained poultry while 102 contained mice. The Red-shoulder enjoys legal protection throughout most of its range, but enforcing the law among the ignorant seems to be difficult.

Although commoner in some localities than the Red-tailed Hawk, the Red-shoulder is probably not as well known generally for it is not so open in its habits as the other. It is characteristic of this bird to sit concealed in a tree at the edge of a field, waiting for an opportunity to pounce upon its prey. Like other Buteos, the Red-shoulder is a soaring Hawk, and its graceful flight is always a joy to bird-watchers.

The Red-shouldered Hawk is strongly attached to its nesting site, returning year after year to nest in the same watered woodland in open farm country, or to the wooded river bottoms. The nest is firmly built of sticks, securely placed high in a tree, the choice of tree depending only upon what tall tree is available. Although a new nest is usually constructed each year, a pair of these Hawks sometimes returns to repair and use an old nest after a lapse of several seasons. Three or four eggs are laid, usually three, which are dull or bluish white spotted with brown.

The adult Red-shoulder (18 to 24 inches long) may be identified by its plain, ruddy underparts and by the conspicuous barring on the underside of the tail, absent in the Red-tailed Hawk. A good field mark for the Red-shoulder is the two translucent spots or "windows" on the underside of the wings near the tips and at the base of the primaries. The reddish brown shoulder of this species is seldom visible from the ground, and thus is not usually a useful field mark. Immature birds are streaked below, as in most other species.

The cry of the Red-shoulder is a piercing *kee-yoo,* very similar to one of the Blue Jay's calls. Indeed, unless one is very familiar with the slight difference, it is well to investigate all Jay-like calls when in Red-shoulder country.

Individual Red-shouldered Hawks often spend the winter in the northern portion of their range, but generally the species is migratory. The Red-shoulder, including its five subspecies, ranges over North America, exclusive of the Rocky Mountains, from southern Canada south to Mexico. It ranges throughout the eastern part of the country west to Nebraska, Kansas, and central Texas, and reappears on the Pacific coast as the Red-bellied Hawk *(B. l. elegans)* which has rather brighter rust underparts.

The other subspecies, among which there is little field difference, are the Northern Red-shoulder *(B. l. lineatus)*; the Florida Red-shoulder *(B. l. alleni)* which is smaller and has a whiter head; the Insular Red-shoulder *(B. l. extimus)* which is restricted to the Florida Keys and is the smallest of the Red-shoulders; and the Texas Red-shoulder *(B. l. texanus)*.

BROAD-WINGED HAWK

(Buteo platypterus platypterus)

So weak and unhawklike is the call of the Broad-winged Hawk, that the first time I heard it, I did not believe it, although the Buteo was in plain sight, perched high in a tree not far from its nest in a thick wooded ravine. I thought I was hearing an off-sounding call of a Wood Pewee, and not until the Hawk moved to another perch and again uttered its high-pitched, plaintive call, was I convinced. Since then, however, I have decided that there is a resemblance between the soft *p-wee-e-e* of the Broad-wing and the screaming *keeerrrrrrr* of its larger relative, the Red-tail, the difference being one of modulation.

The Broad-wing is a woodland Hawk. It is quiet, and, compared with others of its tribe, it is gentle. Although it complains when one molests it in the vicinity of its nest, yet there is seldom any of the intimidation and aggressiveness that usually characterize the other birds of prey.

Placed moderately high in dense woodland, the nest of the Broad-wing is a loose structure of twigs. Two eggs is the usual number. Both sexes incubate, and hatching requires about three weeks, or a few days longer. A characteristic of this Hawk is its habit of daily decorating its nest with sprigs of fresh green foliage.

That the Broad-wing is a Buteo may be told at once by its chunky body, broad wings, and broad rounded tail. It is considerably smaller (14 to 18 inches) than either the Red-tailed or Red-shouldered Hawks. When soaring overhead, the Broad-wing may be distinguished by its white throat, brown barred underparts, and tail barred with three black and three broad white bands.

Broad-wings are migratory and leave their northern range in early fall. They usually travel in flocks of large size. As many as ten thousand Broad-wings have been counted in autumn migration (4,078 in one day, September 24, 1938), passing south along the Kittatinny Ridge of the Alleghenies at Hawk Mountain Sanctuary in northeastern Pennsylvania.

Like the other Buzzard Hawks, its food is mainly insects, small mammals,

BROAD-WINGED HAWK AT NEST (*Buteo platypterus platypterus*). Length: 14 to 18.5 inches. Male and female: broad black and white banding on tail. Bird is dark grayish brown. Underparts streaked with light reddish brown. Young: dark tail bands in greater number, stubbier tail, shorter wings. Range: Texas and Gulf Coast to New Brunswick. Winters in Tropics and Florida. Voice: high-pitched piercing whistle. A plaintive *p-wee-e-e-e-e*.

Samuel A. Grimes

snakes, frogs, and toads. According to Dr. A. K. Fisher, the Broad-wing is especially fond of the caterpillars of the large moths which feed on the leaves of trees.

The Broad-wing is an eastern Hawk, breeding from central Alberta, New Brunswick, and Nova Scotia, south to the Gulf States, and west to central Texas. It winters in Mexico, Central America, and south into South America. A few individuals remain in southern Florida.

SWAINSON'S HAWK

(Buteo swainsoni)

Color Plate Page 7

Swainson's Hawk is a common Buteo of the western plains, prairies, and deserts, a bird of the wide open spaces, highly beneficial, and unusually trusting for a Hawk. No other Buteo will permit such close approach by man as the Swainson's, not only as it perches in characteristic fashion on an exposed pole or fence post, but in the vicinity of its nest. It is one of the tamest of all Hawks.

No other Hawk can offer a better record of food habits than this species. Its diet is almost entirely rodents and insects; indeed, there is no evidence that this Hawk ever attacks poultry. Any small birds it may take are negligible in comparison with its economic value to the western farmer.

Identification of Swainson's Hawk is not always an easy matter, for it is complicated by a light and dark phase, as well as birds in intermediate stages. Ralph Hoffman suggests that "the best mark by which a Swainson's Hawk in any plumage can be recognized is the considerable unmarked buffy area on the underside of the wing." It is about the size of a Western Red-tail and a Red-bellied Hawk (20 to 22 inches), but its wings are longer and more pointed than these species. In a typical bird, the wide brown band on the breast is distinctive, but lighter phases do not show this band. Its tameness and its sluggish lazy flight are aids in identification. Its voice is a shrill whistle, *kreeeee*.

Swainson's Hawk usually builds its nest in a tall tree, placed well out on a branch, but it will nest on the ground or in bushes. The two to four eggs are greenish, or buff white usually spotted with reddish brown.

This Hawk migrates south of the United States for the winter. Spectacular flights both spring and fall are often observed, large flocks of these birds moving together to and from their breeding range. In the summer, the birds are found nesting throughout the dry regions of the west from British Columbia, Great Slave Lake, and Manitoba south to northern Mexico.

ZONE-TAILED HAWK

(Buteo albonotatus)

This black Buteo may be taken for a Turkey Vulture by the uninitiated, but the whitish tail bands distinguish it. The three slate-colored bands increase in width and distinctness toward the tip; from below the stripes are almost pure white. In the immature bird the tail bandings are more numerous and less regular. It is somewhat more slender than the other Buteos; its length is 19 to 22 inches.

The Zone-tail builds its nest in trees along the banks of streams. The two to four eggs are dull white, spotted with brown at the large end. Its range is

DUCK HAWK (PEREGRINE FALCON) (*Falco peregrinus anatum*). Length: 15 to 20 inches. Male and female: upper parts slate gray; below yellowish barred with black; unmarked white throat and breast. Face has heavy dark mustache-shaped patches. Range: breeds chiefly on cliffs from Arctic south to northern Georgia and northern Louisiana. Winters from northern United States to Gulf of Mexico. Voice: a rasping *cack cack cack;* repetitious *we'chew* and a wailing cry.
Hal H. Harrison

SENNETT'S WHITE-TAILED HAWK (6 WEEKS OLD) *(Buteo albicaudatus hypospodius).* Length: 23 to 24 inches. Male and female: clear white underparts and white tail with black band near its tip. Upperparts, bluish gray slate color. Immature: quite blackish, somewhat spotted with white on the breast. Range: southern Texas.
James O. Stevenson

confined to the mountainous country along the Mexican border of Texas, New Mexico, and Arizona.

SENNETT'S WHITE-TAILED HAWK

(Buteo albicaudatus hypospodius)

Another Mexican Buteo that enjoys only a limited range in the United States is Sennett's White-tailed Hawk, a long-winged Buteo with white underparts and white tail. The tail is banded near the tip with black. A chestnut shoulder patch breaks the gray upperparts.

The White-tail occurs only in southern Texas where it is generally distributed over bushy lowlands, especially the coastal prairies. Sand ridges covered with yucca and cactus are its favorite nesting sites. It builds its nest in low trees or bushes and lays two or three dull white eggs, faintly spotted with brown.

SHORT-TAILED HAWK

(Buteo brachyurus)

This small Buteo which is only about 17 inches long, is confined to south Florida and the Florida Keys, where its two color phases are readily distinguishable. The black phase shows a black belly and black underwings; while the white phase shows white in the same areas. At close range the black phase shows a conspicuous white patch near the bill. In Florida no other Hawk has plain black or white underparts.

AMERICAN ROUGH-LEGGED HAWK

(Buteo lagopus s. johannis)

The American Rough-legged Hawk is a winter resident in the United States, migrating from its summer home in the far north. Members of the Rough-legged group differ from the other Buteos by having their legs feathered to the toes, a protection, no doubt, from the extreme cold of their northern territory.

The Rough-leg is somewhat larger than the other Buteos, 20 to 24 inches long, with a longer tail and longer wings. It is a bird of the open country, hunting somewhat in the manner of the Marsh Hawk. I have found the best field identification for this Hawk to be its habit of hovering with beating wings, like a Sparrow Hawk.

Two color phases are recognized. In the light phase, the black belly and white tail with a black band at the end are distinguishing marks. Sometimes the belly is light with a mottled black band. In the dark phase, the black body with a great deal of white in the flight feathers are field marks.

The young birds of the light phase have a grayish brown tail with a white tip. The underparts are heavily marked with black, and the band across the belly is solidly dark. In the dark phase, the young birds are also sooty black. The adult bird is 20 to 24 inches long.

FERRUGINOUS ROUGH-LEGGED HAWK (*Buteo regalis*). Length: 23 to 24 inches. Male and female: rusty colored above and whitish below with whitish tail. Dark feathers on legs form V overhead in flight. Range: western North America. Voice: relatively none.
Rudolph Hindemith, American Museum of Natural History

The Rough-legged Hawk builds its nest in large trees and lays two or three dingy white eggs sprinkled with dark brown. In the winter, it ranges from southern British Columbia, and southern Ontario south to southern California, Texas, and North Carolina.

AMERICAN ROUGH-LEGGED HAWK (*Buteo lagopus s, johannis*). Length: 20 to 23.5 inches. Male and female: black phase; entire bird black. Light phase: upperparts dark grayish brown, underparts vary from white to reddish buff streaked with black. Black belly. Prominent black patch at the wing wrist. Range: breeds in Canada. Winters from North American border to California and New Mexico. Voice: relatively silent.
Alfred M. Bailey, National Audubon Society

FERRUGINOUS ROUGH-LEG

(*Buteo regalis*)

One of the most beneficial of all western Hawks is the majestic Ferruginous Rough-leg. Soaring high above its favorite haunts, the arid plains and prairies, it hunts for ground squirrels, prairie dogs, and meadow mice. Or, one may find it perching quietly on a fence post or small tree, or even on the ground, watching for prey.

Like its close relative, the American Rough-legged Hawk, the Ferruginous (24 inches long) is found in two color phases—light and dark. In all plumages, its best field mark are its plain, light-colored tail and the distinct white areas on the upper side of the wings. Its coloration in the light phase is ruddy above and whitish below. The legs are feathered in dark chestnut. In the dark phase, this bird resembles the American Rough-leg, but is usually more rusty.

The breeding range of this Buteo extends from southern Canada to northeastern California, Nevada, and New Mexico. Although it may be found in winter in any part of its breeding range, the Ferruginous Rough-leg is essentially migratory, and its winter range extends into Mexico.

HARRIS'S HAWK

(Parabuteo unicinctus harrisi)

A fairly large black Buteo (22 inches long), Harris's Hawk is found in southeastern California and through the southern parts of Arizona, New Mexico, and Texas. It shows patches of rich chestnut color on the wings and legs. Its rump and tail tip are white.

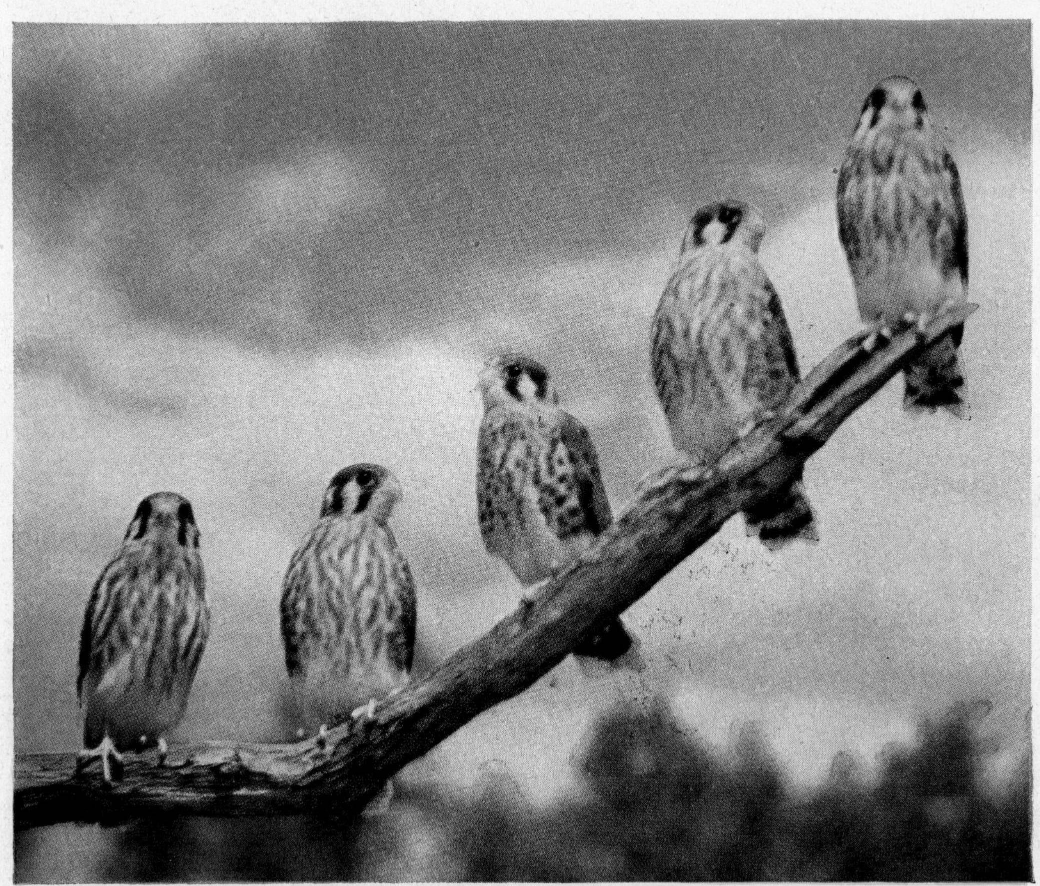

SPARROW HAWKS (YOUNG) *(Falco sparverius)*. Length: 9 to 12 inches. Male and female: color above, cinnamon brown, below rust and white; rufous red tail; black and white patterned face. Male: blue gray wings. Range: Florida to Quebec; winters north to southern Ontario. Voice: high, quick, *klee klee klee* or *killy killy killy*.
Hal H. Harrison

Although it somewhat resembles the female Marsh Hawk, it is more dumpy in appearance and, in flight, it can be seen the white completely encircles the base of the tail.

It builds its nest in cactus or mesquite and lays from two to four greenish white eggs which are faintly spotted. The young birds are more brownish than the adults and streaked. The white on the tip of the tail is less distinct than in the adult.

MEXICAN GOSHAWK

(Buteo nitida maxima)

A Buteo in fact and in proportions, but an Accipiter in name and in coloration—that is the Mexican Goshawk which reaches the United States along the streams of the border valleys of Arizona and New Mexico, and along the lower Rio Grande in Texas. It is a graceful bird, 16 to 18 inches long, swift of flight, and adept at sailing and maneuvering through the mesquite forests.

The plumage of the Mexican Goshawk is handsome; a mantle of ash gray, the breast closely barred with gray and white, the tail boldly banded with black and white and tipped with gray. In tail markings and general proportions, it resembles somewhat the Broad-winged Hawk of the east.

This Mexican bird moves into the wild country of our southwest border in late spring, and retires south again in early fall. The nest of green twigs is placed in trees. Two eggs are usual. The principal food of the species is lizards, but large insects and rodents are also taken. It eats a few small birds, but not to an extent to make the Hawk a menace.

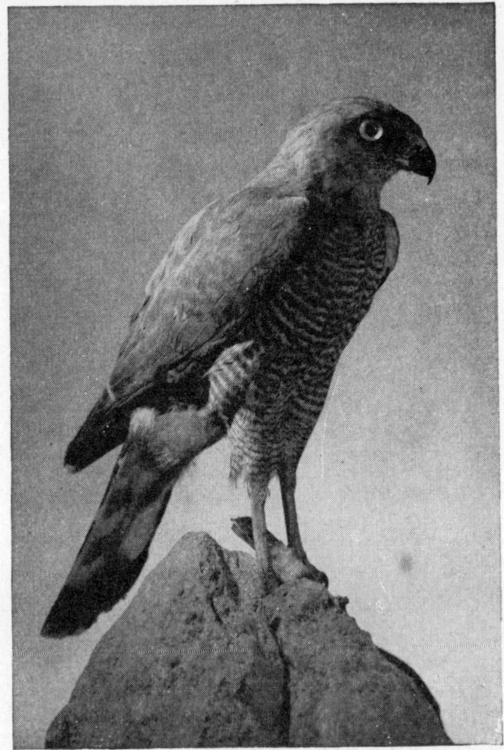

MEXICAN GOSHAWK (*Buteo nitida maxima*). Length: 16 to 18 inches. Male and female: gray back, gray and white streaked underparts. Black tail banded with white. Range: Mexican border of Arizona, New Mexico and Texas. Voice: none.
Rudolph Hindemith, American Museum of Natural History

MEXICAN BLACK HAWK

(Buteogallus anthracinus anthracinus)

The range of the Mexican Black Hawk is very limited and local in the United States, since it occurs only from the lower Rio Grande valley in Texas to southern Arizona. It is found in heavily wooded canyons or river bottoms, where it is a summer resident. In autumn, it retires into Mexico and Central America.

The Mexican Black Hawk is a coal black Buteo, 20 to 23 inches long, much heavier and with broader wings than the Zone-tailed Hawk with which it might be confused. From below, the

Mexican bird is entirely black with a single wide white band across the tail.

GOLDEN EAGLE

(Aquila chrysaëtos canadensis)

Color Plate Page 9

The Golden Eagle, King of Birds, is a mighty hunter, lacking almost entirely the scavenger habits of its relative, the Bald Eagle. Once widely distributed, this magnificent bird is now rare east of the Rockies in the breeding season. Today, one finds it in the wild mountainous country of the west, nesting high in lofty crags in inaccessible cliffs, or at the tops of giant trees.

Many stories have been told of the Golden Eagle's prowess as a hunter. It is this bird that is reported on occasions to have carried off babies, but such reports have invariably proved false. It is capable of hunting and killing large prey, although the size of the quarry that it can lift successfully from the ground is far less than some reports would indicate. Large prey is eaten where it is killed. A list of mammals

RUFFED GROUSE ON NEST *(Bonasa umbellus)*. Length: 16 to 19 inches. Male: reddish brown upperparts streaked with black. Sides of neck have large tufts of glossy greenish or bluish black feathers. Fan-shaped tail has broad black terminal band. White underparts streaked with blackish brown and buffy throat. Female: almost no neck tufts and is smaller. Range: Canada south to New Jersey and Appalachian Mountains. Also south to Mississippi Valley and west ot Michigan, Wisconsin and northeast Iowa. Voice: male, muffled drumming *bup bup bup bup bup bup bup up rrrrrr.*
Hal H. Harrison

WHITE TAILED PTARMIGAN *(Lagopus leucurus)*. Length: 12 to 13 inches. Male and female in summer: most of wing, tail and lower abdomen, pure white. Rest of plumage brown. Male and female in winter: pure white except for black eyes and bill. Range: Rockies from Montana to northern New Mexico. Cascade mountains of Washington. Voice: during mating season, hoarse and loud.
Alfred M. Bailey

that this bird is known to have killed ranges from deer, antelope, calves, and lambs, to pocket gophers, mice, and moles. The list of bird victims is just as varied, ranging from Great Blue Herons, Turkeys, and Red-tailed Hawks to Meadowlarks and Thrushes.

The flight of the Golden Eagle is powerful and graceful. Its great wing-spread (often over seven feet) is surpassed only by the California Condor among the birds of prey. The adult eagle is a dark brown bird. In favorable light, the golden brown head and hind neck may be seen. Unlike the Bald Eagle, its legs are feathered to the toes. The brown immature Bald Eagle might be confused with the Golden Eagle, but their ranges overlap only occasionally during migration.

To a great extent, the Golden Eagle is a resident bird wherever found, but certain northern individuals are annually forced south in their search for food. At such times, records of the bird's appearance far from its breeding range are not uncommon.

The nest of the Golden Eagle is usually built on inaccessible cliffs, or sometimes in large trees. The birds use the same nest year after year, adding to it until the nest becomes a large structure four or five feet in diameter. The two eggs are white, with splotches of chestnut, brown, and purple.

The period of incubation lasts a month. The newly hatched eaglets are covered with white down through which black pin-feathers appear in about a month.

BALD EAGLE

(Halioeetus leucocephalus)

Color Plate Page 12

My first experience at the nest of a Bald Eagle, our national bird, was a disappointment. It was on a morning in early June that I approached the eyrie high in a dead stub on a remote island deep in the Pymatuning refuge of the Pennsylvania Game Commission. I poled my boat, loaded with camera equipment, through a sea of mud and old stumps and snags. From a distance, I could see the white headed male perched on a stub near the nest. At the side of the nest stood the immature female. In the nest were two young.

MEXICAN BLACK HAWK (*Buteogallus anthracinus anthracinus*). Length: 20 to 23 inches. Male and female: unusually wide wings. Broad white band across tail center. Body very dark slate gray. Range: along streams, near Mexican border of Arizona, New Mexico and Texas.
Rudolph Hindemith, American Museum of Natural History

While I was still far away, the male flew into the swamp and did not appear again that morning. The female stayed until the boat was about two hundred yards from the island, then she glided off the nest, circled the island twice, emitting a few screams, and then she, too, flew off into the swamp and did not return again. When my companion climbed to the nest while I waited in vain for pictures, the old Eagles made no effort to protect their young. What a contrast to a Duck Hawk or an Osprey!

In 1782, when Congress declared the Bald Eagle our national bird, the act received considerable opposition, especially from Benjamin Franklin who called the Eagle a "lousy bird." His choice was the Wild Turkey. Congress overruled Franklin by citing the Eagle's courage, striking appearance, great size, and its dominant position in the bird world.

It seems almost incredible that after naming the Eagle our national bird, Congress failed to offer it any protection for 158 years. Indeed, it was not until June, 1940, that a national law was passed offering it sanctuary in the entire United States. This act provided for a fine of $500 and six months' imprisonment for molesting the Eagle.

Complete protection did not come too soon. The Eagle has been decreasing in numbers for years, and in many regions where its great cry was a familiar sound, it is now entirely gone. In only a few places may the Eagle now be called common. Along the coasts of Florida, Alaska, and British Columbia, it is still found in goodly numbers.

Where Eagles nest, they are practically nonmigratory. During the winter they may disappear from their usual haunts, especially if food becomes scarce, but they soon return to start nesting in March. The nest, like the bird, is big. It is made of sticks, placed high in the crotch of a huge tree, sometimes eighty feet or more from the ground. By adding to the structure and making annual repairs, Eagles have been known to use the same nest as long as thirty-five years. Eagles mate for life. If one dies or is killed, the other seeks a new mate.

Two eggs are usual, but three or four are not rare. Incubation requires about a month, and the young are in the nest about ten weeks. It takes three or even four years for an Eagle to reach maturity. During the first year it shows none of the white feathers on the head, neck, or tail. In fact, young Bald Eagles closely resemble the western Golden Eagle which is entirely dark brown.

The adult Bald Eagle is dark brown, with a striking white head, neck, and tail. First-year birds are mainly black but with the body feathers white beneath the surface. During the second and third years the feathers become increasingly mixed with black, brown, and gray. The head and tail are still dark, however. The cry of the male is a high clear *cak-cak-cak*. That of the female is shriller and more broken and has been likened to a maniac's laugh.

Economically, the Bald Eagle is not of any great importance to man. It feeds largely upon fish and carrion, varying its diet with birds, small mammals, and reptiles. To a great extent, it is a scavenger. Although capable of fishing for its own food, it often prefers to eat dead fish which have been washed ashore.

Two races are recognized: the Northern Bald Eagle *(H. l. washingtoniensis)* and the Southern Bald Eagle *(H. l. leucocephalus)* which show no field differences.

HARRIERS

Family Circinae

The Harriers are slender Hawks with long wings. They build their nests on the ground in marshes or similar locations. It has been said that when the male brings food to the incubating female Harrier, she leaves the nest, he drops the prey, and she catches it in mid-air. The only American Harrier is the Marsh Hawk.

MARSH HAWK

(Circus cyaneus hudsonius)

Color Plate Page 16

Gracefully, buoyantly, and tirelessly the Marsh Hawk flies low over the fields, marshes, and prairies, head bent down, watching for meadow mice on the ground below. The bird veers suddenly to the side, and we see plainly the white rump, the distinguishing field mark worn in all plumages. We note that while the tail is long and Falcon-like, the wings are not pointed like a Falcon's, yet they are much longer than those of an Accipiter. We note, too, that the wings are held above the horizontal, except when soaring, in a manner suggestive of the Vulture's flight.

The male Marsh Hawk is gray, the lightest of the common Hawks. The larger female is brown. They are slim birds 18 to 24 inches long, never found far from the ground from which they glean a livelihood of rodents and other small mammals, frogs, snakes, insects, and small birds. Their diet is highly beneficial to man.

The hunting method is a harrying (thus the family name of Harrier) performed by beating the long wings close to the ground, quartering the prairies and meadows, tirelessly searching for prey. When a victim is sighted, the bird stops quickly, flutters or hovers above, and then drops swiftly to seize it in its talons.

The Marsh Hawk nests on the ground, building a platform of weed stalks, grasses, and twigs in tall vegetation in marshes, along the margins of prairie sloughs and open grassy places, usually in wet surroundings. The four to six eggs are pale greenish or bluish, usually unmarked. At nesting time the male performs his famed courtship flight, a series of aerial dips and somersaults, a delight to all bird watchers. The Marsh Hawk's cry is a weak *pee-pee-pee.*

Marsh Hawks are migratory over much of their range, most individuals spending the winter in the southern states or south of the Mexican border. The breeding range of the bird extends from northwestern Alaska, central Quebec, and Newfoundland south to northern Lower California, southern Texas, and southeastern Virginia.

CARACARAS

Family Polyborinae

The Caracaras are carrion-feeding Vultures of Central and South America, of which one species reaches the United States. All are primarily black and white, and have long bare legs. The feathers in the crown can be raised into a crest. Their flight is strong, direct, and rapid.

AUDUBON'S CARACARA

(Polyborus cheriway auduboni)

Color Plate Page 17

Audubon's Caracara is a Falcon, looks like an Eagle in flight, and acts like a Vulture on the ground. It is a South American Hawk that reaches the northern limits of its breeding range in Florida, Texas, and Arizona.

This "Mexican Eagle" is a bird of the prairie country. In Florida it reaches its greatest numbers on the Kissimmee Prairie where it nests in the tops of the cabbage palmettos. In the desert regions of the southwest, it often nests in the branches of the giant cactus. In Texas it places its nest in mesquites, oaks, and other trees.

In flight, Audubon's Caracara may be identified by the white patches on the primaries and the white tail tipped with black. In the air, its pose is Eagle-like. The throat and breast are whitish; the belly is black. At close range the Eagle-like beak and red face are conspicuous. The bird is very much at home on the ground where its long legs serve it well in walking or running.

Although the Caracara catches much of its own prey, especially fish and frogs, it is also a scavenger which feeds on carrion.

The Brazilian name of Caracara came from its cackling cry.

FALCONS

Family Falconinae

The Falcons are the Hawks which were used in the ancient sport of Falconry. When hawking was at its height in England, the rank of the sportsman could be told from the kind of Falcon he used—the Gyrfalcon for royalty, the Peregrine Falcon for a nobleman, the Goshawk for a yeoman, and the Kestrel for a servant. The Falcons are slim Hawks with long pointed wings and long tails. Their bill is hooked, as are their extremely sharp talons.

GYRFALCON

(Falco rusticolus obsoletus)

Until recently the black and white color phases of the Gyrfalcon, a huge Arctic Falcon, were believed to represent different races. Intensive study in the taxonomy of the Gyrfalcon has recently led ornithologists to the conclusion that the North American subspecies of *Falco rusticolus* listed in the 1931 edition of the A. O. U. Check-List are in fact only one species, with the color phases often occurring in the same brood.

In the United States, the Gyrfalcon is a rare winter visitor, and the bird watcher who can include it in his "life list" is to be envied indeed. It is considerably larger (20 to 25 inches) than a Duck Hawk, which it resembles in its black and gray phases. In the white phase, it might be mistaken for a Snowy Owl, but the long pointed wings and the characteristic Falcon flight distinguish it.

In times past, the Gyrfalcon was sought eagerly by falconers because of the bird's swift flight and great endurance. In its home in the far north be-

GREENLAND GYRFALCON *(Falco rusticolus obsoletus)*. Length: 20 to 25 inches. Male and female: grayish brown above and white below, varying in color phases from almost pure white to black birds. Range: Arctic North America; in winter occasionally reaching the northern United States. Voice: none.
W. R. Spofford, National Audubon Society

yond the limit of trees, the Gyrfalcon subsists largely on the bird life of the area. It nests on ledges and cavities of cliffs, and lays two to four whitish eggs which are often so heavily spotted with brown as to appear solidly brown.

PRAIRIE FALCON ON NEST (*Falco mexicanus*). Length: 17 inches. Male and female: ashy brown above, spotted white below, showing blackish patches under the wings in flight. Range: western North America to the eastern border of the Plains. Voice: a rattling *ker-r-r-r* or whining *kruk*. Also a cry of *wert-wert-wert-wert-wert*, rather less harsh than that of the other hawks.
Alfred M. Bailey, National Audubon Society

PRAIRIE FALCON

(Falco mexicanus)

The western hills, plains, prairies, and brushy deserts from Canada to Mexico are the favored haunts of this Falcon, a pale brown Hawk that very closely resembles the Duck Hawk when coloration is not distinguishable. The upperparts of the Duck Hawk are dark gray; the back of the Prairie Falcon is sandy. Sparrow Hawks and Pigeon Hawks, both typical Falcons, are noticeably smaller than the Prairie Falcon which is about 17 inches long.

Like its close relative, the Duck Hawk, this Falcon usually selects a ledge or small cave on the perpendicular side of an inaccessible cliff for its nest. The three or four buffy eggs, marked with splotches of reddish brown and chocolate, are lighter than the eggs of the Duck Hawk. The Prairie Falcon's diet is made up principally of small birds, although game birds, particularly quail, are taken frequently. Its cry is a mellow *wert-wert-wert-wert-wert-wert-wert*.

This Falcon is related to the European and Asiatic Lannerets and like them is a bold and fearless hunter in pursuit of its prey.

DUCK HAWK

(Falco peregrinus anatum)

Color Plate Page 21

The Duck Hawk is the American representative of the world-wide race of noble birds, the Peregrine Falcons. Sixteen races are recognized in various parts of the world. With its subspecies, the Peale's Falcon of the Pacific northwest, the Duck Hawk is the only Peregrine inhabiting North America. It breeds from beyond the limit of trees in the Arctic, southward to the southern states. It is found from the Atlantic to the Pacific, and in winter as far south as South America.

For a species with such a wide range and a bird that seems to have no enemies except man, it is surprising how rare this majestic Falcon is, over its entire range. Bird watchers everywhere consider the sight of a Duck Hawk an outstanding event during a day afield.

As in other parts of the world, the Peregrine is sought in America as a

SHARP TAILED GROUSE (*Pedioecetes phasianellus*). Length: 17.5 inches. Male and female: upperparts yellowish brown sprinkled with black. Head is slightly crested. Color below, whitish. Has short pointed tail which appears white in flight. Range: prairie brushland and open woodlands from Canada south to central Nebraska, Minnesota, and western Wisconsin. Voice: a cackling *cac-cac-cac-cac-cac* etc. Courting note, a single coo.
Alfred M. Bailey

bird to be trained in the ancient art of falconry. It has been said of the American devotees of the sport, "They are a breed of super-sportsmen, the most exclusive in the world—one falconer to a million of population is a generous estimate."

Two methods of securing wild birds are employed by falconers; taking a young bird from its nest and hand-raising it; and trapping a bird in migration, known as a "passage Hawk." The latter makes the better hunter.

A prerequisite to securing nestling birds (aside from the all-important state and federal permit) is the ability to climb mountains, for Duck Hawks are cliff dwellers. In addition, robbing the nest involves braving the wrath of the female bird, and that alone is not a job for the timid. A falconer once told me that the nests of this Hawk are so well studied and checked that American falconers have charted the eyries throughout the country. Histories of these nesting sites are kept accurately and religiously.

The Duck Hawk is a bird killer. It obtains its prey by striking it while on the wing. The usual approach is to rise in spiraling flight high above its quarry, then, with terrific speed, to power dive directly upon the luckless bird. Seldom does it miss. Any size bird from a Warbler to a Duck is taken. Shore birds are particular favorites. During the winter, a Duck Hawk will often establish itself in a city and spend

BOB-WHITE. MOTHER BIRD ON NEST *(Colinus virginianus)*. Length: 8.5 to 10.5 inches. Male: reddish brown back and wings, gray tail. White line over eye bordered with jet black. White throat. Upper breast conspicuously banded with black bar. Lower breast and abdomen white, barred with black. Female: similar to male but no black on breast and buffy line over eye. Range: western states. Voice: whistled *Bob-white*, or *Poor Bob-white*.
Samuel A. Grimes

several months gleaning an easy living from the city's semi-domestic pigeons.

The maximum speed attained by this swift bird is estimated at from 150 to 200 miles an hour in a power dive. Its ordinary flight is one of grace and agility as it progresses with quick, powerful strokes.

One may distinguish the Duck Hawk from other birds of prey by its characteristic Falcon flight, its long pointed wings, and long tail. The adults are slate-backed and barred below. The immature birds are brown and heavily streaked below. The adult has unmistakable black "mustaches." It may be distinguished from other Falcons by its size; while the Sparrow Hawk and Pigeon Hawk are about the size of a Robin, the Duck Hawk is the size of a Crow. Its cry is a repeated *we-chew*, and a rapid, rasping *cack-cack-cack*.

Peale's Falcon *(F. p. pealei)* is distinctly darker in color. It is migratory, and a winter visitor to the northwest Pacific coast.

APLOMADO FALCON

(Falco fusco-coerulescens septentrionalis)

A rare, medium-sized Falcon (15 to 18 inches long) of the desert regions along the Mexican border, this handsome bird has dark wing linings and a black belly which contrast strikingly with its white breast. Its thighs and under-tail are orange brown. It is somewhat larger than the Sparrow Hawk and a little smaller than the Duck Hawk. Its food is mainly insects and reptiles, with some small birds and mammals.

PIGEON HAWK

(Falco columbarius)

Not that it would be innocent of such a practice, but the name "Pigeon Hawk" was not given to our American Merlin because it kills pigeons. This little Falcon, only 10 to 13½ inches long, was so named because of its Pigeon-like attitude which it displays at times and also because of certain mannerisms of flight which resemble those of a Pigeon. Generally, however, the flight of the Pigeon Hawk is typically that of a Falcon—swift and dashing.

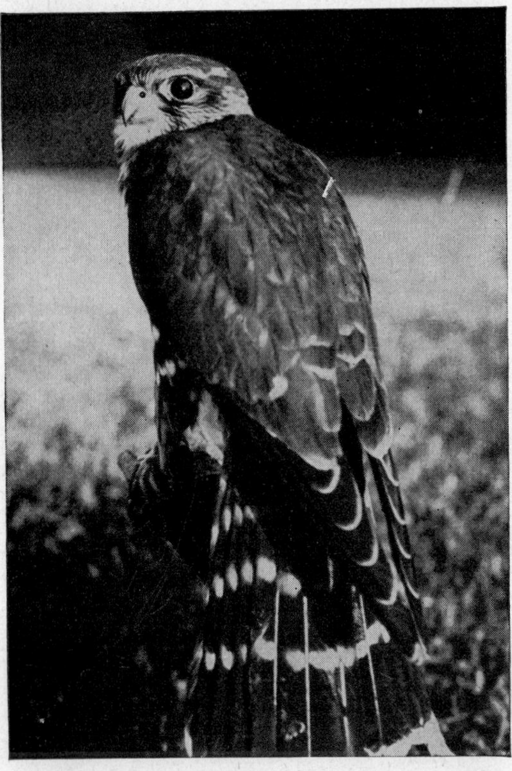

PIGEON HAWK (MERLIN) *(Falco columbarius)*. Length: 10 to 13.5 inches. Male: bluish gray above, with broad bands on the tail. Female and young: dusky brown. Range: breeds in Great Plains region from Canada south to northern Montana. Winters south through Colorado, New Mexico and western Texas.
Edward Prins

The Pigeon Hawk has been described as a miniature Duck Hawk, which it resembles in coloration and mannerisms. Because of its small size, however, it is more likely to be confused with the Sparrow Hawk. However, the slate blue back of the male and the dark brown back of the female are drab beside the gayly colored Sparrow Hawks.

The Pigeon Hawk builds its nest on ledges or in trees, or twigs and grasses, and lays four or five white eggs which are splotched with brown.

Despite its wide distribution throughout North America, the Pigeon Hawk is nowhere considered common. Since its principal food is small birds, perhaps this is a happy situation. Four races of this Falcon are currently recognized: one eastern race, the Eastern Pigeon Hawk *(F. c. columbarius)*; and three western races, the Black Pigeon Hawk *(F. c. suckleyi)* which is considerably darker, Richardson's Pigeon Hawk *(F. c. richardsoni)* which is pale above, and the Western Pigeon Hawk *(F. c. bendirei)* which has a very dark crown.

SPARROW HAWK

(Falco sparverius)

Color Plate Page 24

American Kestrel would have been a more appropriate name for the smallest of all our North American Hawks, the Sparrow Hawk. Early Americans named it for a British bird of the same name, but our American Sparrow Hawk is a Falcon; its European namesake is an Accipiter. Its closest English relative is the Kestrel.

The Sparrow Hawk ranges throughout most of North America and is probably the Hawk best known to the casual observer. Surely no other bird of prey is seen more often by the American motorist, for one of its favorite perches is the top of roadside telegraph poles, particularly those bordering open fields.

From this lofty perch, the little Falcon scans the countryside in search of food. Suddenly it strikes out, its long pointed wings beating powerfully as it veers one way and then another. In a flash, the sweeping flight is arrested. The bird faces the wind and hovers, body tilted upward, wings beating lightly. Food has been sighted, a grasshopper probably, and the Hawk drops to the ground. Up it goes quickly and back to the watch tower on the pole. Alighting, it dips its long tail and abruptly folds its wings. Holding its prey in its sharp talons, the bird begins to tear it apart with its hooked bill.

The Sparrow Hawk is not much larger than a Robin (9 to 12 inches). The male has blue-gray wings; both sexes have rufous backs and a characteristic black and white face pattern.

Along the roadside, the only bird with which the Sparrow Hawk might be confused is the Mourning Dove, but the Hawk's large head and thick neck distinguish it. The Sparrow Hawk may be distinguished from the slightly larger Pigeon Hawk by its reddish brown back and tail. Although similar in size to the Sharp-shinned Hawk which has short rounded wings, the long pointed wings of the Sparrow Hawk should differentiate it.

Unlike others of its kind, the Sparrow Hawk hides its four or five spotted eggs in a natural cavity in a tree, old woodpecker holes, bird boxes, hollowed out cacti, or even in the towers of city buildings. Young Sparrow Hawks in juvenile plumage are unique in that the sexes are readily distinguishable at that age, resembling the adults of like sex.

The commonest note of the Sparrow Hawk is a shrill, ringing *killy, killy, killy, killy,* from which it received the name of Killy Hawk in the south.

The food habits of this little Falcon are often questioned, but its diet varies considerably according to the season and locality. In the summer, when grasshoppers are plentiful, the bird at times feeds on them almost exclusively. Other insects, mice and other mammals, reptiles, amphibians, and small birds are also eaten. In the winter, especially in the northern states, birds make up a large part of its bill of fare. Twice I have watched a Sparrow Hawk swoop down on a surprised Titmouse at my own feeding station.

Three geographic races of the Sparrow Hawk are recognized in the United States: the Eastern Sparrow Hawk *(F. s. sparverius)*, the Desert Sparrow Hawk *(F. s. phalaena)*, and the Little Sparrow Hawk *(F. s. paulus)*, which show no apparent field differences.

CURASSOWS and GUANS

Family Cracidae

The Curassows and Guans are game birds of Central and South America. They are about the size of a Turkey, arboreal in habits, and feed on fruit, seeds, and insects. Some of the members of the family are handsomely colored, and all are excellent eating.

CHACHALACA

(Ortalis vetula mccalli)

Northernmost and least handsome of a family which includes a number of beautifully colored South American birds, the Chachalaca is confined to the lower Rio Grande Valley. It is a brown bird, about two feet long, resembling a half-grown Turkey. Its head is small, and its tail long and rounded.

Not often seen because of its liking for deep woods, it can be heard in the early morning and sometimes before rain when its raucous *cha-cha-lac* is unmistakable. The bird is arboreal, nesting in trees, but comes down to the ground to scratch for nuts, seeds, and insects. It lives in small flocks.

BLUE QUAIL (SCALED) *(Callipepla squamata)*. Length: 10 to 12 inches. Male and female: pale grayish blue plumage. Breast appears scaled. Lower abdomen buffy. Short white crest on crown. Range: Arizona, Colorado, New Mexico and Texas. Voice: *chek-ah.*
Fred Bashour

GROUSE

Family Tetraonidae

The Grouse include the larger members of the Chicken-like game birds. Their plumage is generally brown, red, and gray, with the male usually brighter than the female. Generally they depend upon their coloration for concealment, staying still on the ground until almost walked upon, when they take off with a great whir of wings. The courtship performances of the male are often spectacular, consisting of strutting and dancing, and in the case of the Ruffed Grouse, the typical drumming. They are ground birds, feeding on insects, seeds, berries, and suchlike. Their roughly fashioned nests are constructed of leaves and twigs.

CALIFORNIA QUAIL (*Lophortyx californica*). Length: 9.5 to 10.5 inches. Male: above, dusky brown, deep chestnut stripes along sides of back. Crest, black. Back of head has olive brown patch. Short plume curving forward from crown. Underparts; throat is black bordered with white. Abdomen is scaled. Female: grayish brown general tone. Head lacks black and white markings. Abdomen is also scaled. Range: native in southern Oregon and California. Voice: cry, *qua quer go*.

Alfred M. Bailey

DUSKY and SOOTY GROUSE

(Dendragapus obscurus)

The "Blue Grouse" of the Rocky Mountains have been divided by ornithologists into three races (the Fleming's Grouse, *D. o. flemingi,* having been recently declared synonymous with Richardson's Grouse). They are the Dusky Grouse *(D. o. obscurus)* which is the southern race, and Richardson's Grouse *(D. o. richardsoni)* the northern form. Recently, a third race of the Dusky Grouse group was recognized. It is called the Oregon Dusky Grouse *(D. o. pallidus)*, and it occurs in south central British Columbia to eastern Washington and northeastern Oregon.

Although grayer and considerably larger (18 to 21 inches long) than the Franklin's Grouse, these Blue or Dusky Grouse might easily be confused with that species which also ranges through the Rocky Mountains. Franklin's Grouse has much darker underparts than the Dusky species, and where the latter show a yellow patch over the eye, Franklin's Grouse shows a red one.

RICHARDSON'S GROUSE *(Dendragapus obscurus richardsoni)*. Length: male, 21 inches; female, 18 inches. Male: dusky gray body, yellow or orange patches over the eyes. Black underparts. Female: smaller than male, brownish patches over the eyes. Range: northern Rockies from Canada south to Wyoming, and central Idaho. West to eastern Oregon and Washington. Voice: male in courtship gives a series of five or six 'hoots'.
Karl H. Maslowski, National Audubon Society

Since there is considerable intergrading in the *obscurus* group, it is most difficult to distinguish between the Dusky and the Richardson's Grouse in the field. Geographic location is probably the best identifying factor, although this cannot be relied upon positively. Yellowstone National Park, for example, is on the borderline between the ranges of the two. Each form is present, and also all degrees of gradation between them, making field identification next to impossible.

High in the mountains along the Pacific coast, from Alaska to southern California, one encounters other members of the Blue Grouse group, called Sooty

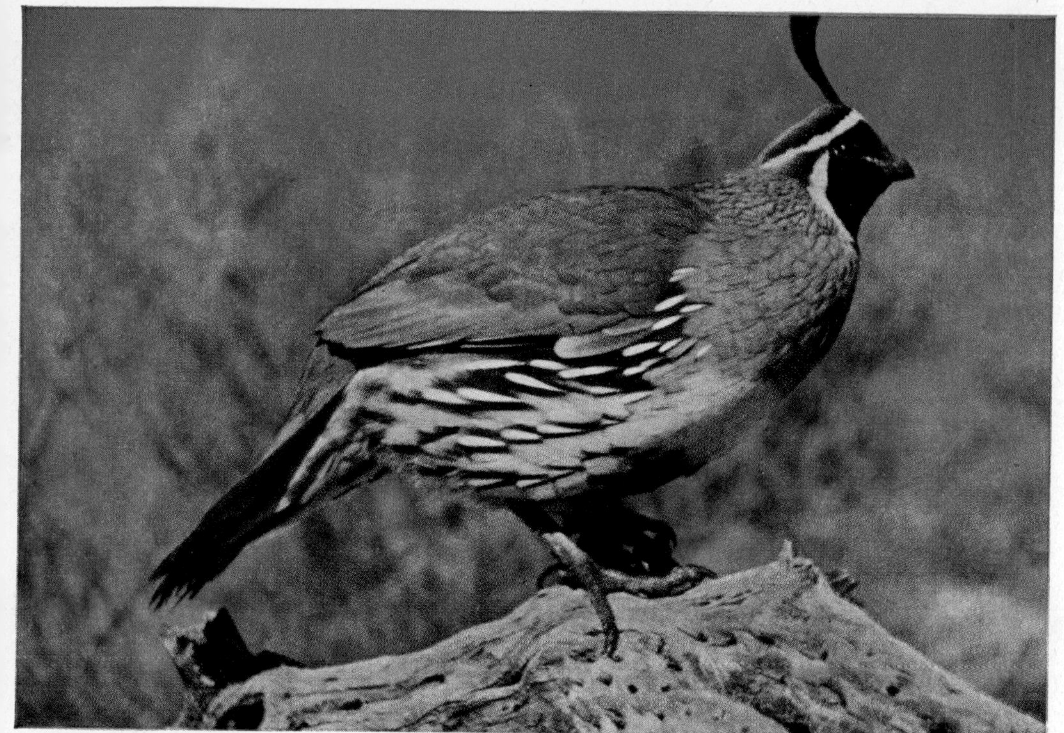

GAMBEL'S QUAIL (*Lophortyx gambellii*). Length: 10 to 11 inches. Male: upperparts bluish gray. Reddish brown crown, black crest. Forehead and throat black with white border. Large black patch on light belly. Female: unmarked brownish gray head. Buffy throat streaked with dark brown. Unmarked buff abdomen. Range: southwestern United States. Voice: *kway-o* and call *chi-quer-go.*
Ross and Florence Thornburg

Grouse, and until recently considered a separate species. These are large dark gray birds, 16 to 19 inches long, with a light band across the tip of the tail.

Although the female places her nest on the ground, fir trees are the bird's home and its refuge, for here it spends much of its life. Plumage coloration that matches its surroundings so perfectly makes the Sooty Grouse most difficult to see when it is perched against the trunk or sitting lengthwise on a branch. These Grouse are so confident of their camouflage that they often pay little attention to an observer on the ground.

The "hooting" of the male in his lofty tree top perch is a characteristic utterance during the courtship of the Sooty. The "hoots" are a series of low muffled notes, comparable to the call of the Great Horned Owl. This vocal rendition is accompanied by drooping wings, spreading tail, and inflation of the yellow air sacs on the neck.

Four races of the Sooty Grouse are recognized; the Sooty Grouse *(D. o. fuliginosus)*, the Sitka Grouse *(D. o. sitkensis)*, the Sierra Grouse *(D. o. sierrae)*, and the Mount Pinos Grouse *(D. o. howardi)*.

SPRUCE GROUSE

(Canachites canadensis)

A bird of the northern wilderness, the Spruce Grouse is found in the spruce forests of Canada south to northern New England, New York, and Minnesota. It is completely fearless and too trusting for its own good, even allowing itself to be taken by hand.

The male bird is black and gray above, and splotched black and white below. The female is browner and dull whitish below, thickly barred with black. In distinction from the Ruffed Grouse, she lacks the black band at the end of the tail, and is barred, not spotted. The Spruce Grouse is 15 to 17 inches long.

The nest is built on the ground, well concealed in spruce thickets or brush. The eight to fourteen eggs are buff colored, splotched with darker brown.

There are two geographic races of the Spruce Grouse: the Hudsonian Spruce Grouse *(C. c. canadensis)*, and the Canada Spruce Grouse *(C. c. canace)*, which show no field differences. Only the Canada Spruce Grouse reaches the northern border of the United States.

FRANKLIN'S GROUSE

(Canachites franklini)

While a number of gallinaceous birds are commonly called "Fool Hen," (Mearn's Quail, for instance) because of their habit of sitting tight instead of flying at the approach of danger, none deserves the name more than the Franklin's Grouse, a dusky gray Grouse of the mountainous interior of the northwestern states and southwestern Canada. In the case of Franklin's Grouse, however, the name comes from the bird's misplaced confidence rather than its instinctive ability to hide. Stories are told of persons who picked one up or hit it with a stick, or even emptied a gun in its direction while the bird watched curiously to see what was going on.

A handsome bird, the Franklin's Grouse is the western counterpart of the Spruce Grouse of the east. Indeed, so close is the relationship that some ornithologists cite the possibility of its eventual reduction to a subspecies of

SOOTY GROUSE *(Dendragapus obscurus)*. Length: 16 to 19 inches. Male: dark gray with light band at tip of tail. Female: browner than male. Range: high mountains of Pacific States. Voice: in courting; six or seven low hooting notes.
John E. Schwartz

the Spruce Grouse. The only conspicuous difference between the two is the buffy colored tail tip of the Spruce Grouse which is absent in Franklin's. They are about the same size, 15 to 16 inches long.

Franklin's Grouse is nonmigratory, but it is rarely seen in the winter when it takes to the trees and shuns the ground. Its food is largely conifer needles which are said to give the flesh a resinous flavor.

FRANKLIN'S GROUSE (*Canachites franklini*). Length: 15 to 16 inches. Male: upperparts striped black and gray. Black underparts, black and white bars on the sides of the rump. Red patches over the eye. Female: blackish above. Tail coverts and tail, white-tipped. Range: Rocky Mountain section. Voice: a series of five or six 'hoots' in courtship.
H. R. Flint

RUFFED GROUSE

(Bonasa umbellus)

Color Plate Page 26

To thousands of hunters the Ruffed Grouse is the unrivaled king of North American game birds. In the south it is called "Pheasant." In the north it is a "Partridge." But whatever you call it, or wherever you find it, the Ruffed Grouse is a smart, wary bird.

No bird demands of the hunter more skill and patience, more experience and intelligent study. None gives more of a challenge to the ratio of birds killed to shots fired. It takes a top-notch Grouse hunter to put one bird in his game pocket for every three shots fired.

The famous drumming of the Ruffed Grouse is at its height during the mating and nesting season. The drumming is done entirely by the male from an elevated spot, such as a fallen log or a rock. Drumming serves a twofold purpose; to notify females that the drummer is now available, and also to warn other males that he is now at home on his territory and that means "keep out."

For years this muffled drumming or hollow booming role that reminds one of giant heart beats was the source of great controversy among naturalists as well as sportsmen. Four different methods of producing the sound have been advanced as authentic: beating the wings against the body, beating the wings together, beating the perch, and beating the air with the wings. The last is correct. With its tail flattened against the drumming perch, the bird beats its wings forward and upward to produce the drumming sound. The actual performance requires only about eight seconds.

The male Grouse takes care of none of the menial domestic duties. His services are reserved for breeding only, and after mating is accomplished, the female goes alone to handle the details. These include selecting the nesting site, always on the ground and usually at the base of a tree; laying the nine to twelve buff colored eggs; incubating the eggs for three weeks, or a few days longer if the weather is cold and wet; and finally caring for the downy little chicks that hatch all ready to leave home.

To the hunter accustomed to hearing the Ruffed Grouse leave the woodland floor with a roar of wings (usually with a tree or bush between it and the hunter), it may be a surprise to learn that this loud noise is intended to alarm and disconcert its would-be assassin. A Grouse can fly away noiselessly if it chooses. The Ruffed Grouse is a red-brown or gray-brown bird 16 to 19 inches long, with a broad black band near the tip of the fan-shaped tail. Two color phases are recognized: red birds with ruddy tails, and gray birds with gray tails.

Grouse are quite sedentary. Undisturbed, an individual may spend its entire life within the confines of one restricted area. In its various geographic forms, the Ruffed Grouse ranges from Labrador to Alaska, and south to Pennsylvania, Tennessee, Colorado and northern California. In the Appalachians it reaches northern Georgia.

The races of the Ruffed Grouse are not clearly defined, but at present five

MEARNS'S QUAIL *(Cyrtonyx montezumae mearnsi)*. Length: 8 inches. Male: pale brown back with streaks and bars of black and white. Black and white head markings. Underparts speckled white on slate gray sides, and dark brown abdomen. Female: duller and without face marks. Range: central Arizona, central New Mexico, western Texas, and south. Voice: a rolling cry.

William L. Finley

are recognized. These are the Eastern Ruffed Grouse (*B. u. umbellus*), the Canada Ruffed Grouse (*B. u. togata*), the Nova Scotia Ruffed Grouse (*B. u. thayeri*), the Gray Ruffed Grouse (*B. u. umbelloides*), and the Hoary Ruffed Grouse (*B. u. incanus*). There are no obvious field differences.

WILLOW PTARMIGAN, MALE IN SPRING PLUMAGE (*Lagopus lagopus*). Length: 15 to 17 inches. Male, summer: brownish rufous above, barred with black and white below. Females, summer: tawny brown above, and below spotted and barred with black. In winter both sexes are white. The feet are completely feathered. Range: Arctic regions of North America south to Gulf of St. Lawrence, central Ontario and south Saskatchewan.
A. A. Allen

WILLOW PTARMIGAN

(Lagopus lagopus)

The bird watcher who would study the Willow Ptarmigan must travel far to the north, and in the summer, even beyond the limit of trees onto the moss-covered tundras of the Arctic. Finding it there is not an easy matter, for the summer plumage of chestnut brown blends well with the ground covering where it nests. In winter only its beady black eyes and black bill are conspicuous, as its white feathers blend into the snowy background. Few birds have a more complete and perfect camouflage throughout the year.

This alpine Grouse is very similar to its close relative and neighbor, the Rock Ptarmigan. In winter, the male Rock Ptarmigan has a black line joining its bill with its eye, but in summer the brown plumage is practically indistinguishable from the Willow Ptarmigan. The bird is 15 to 17 inches long.

In winter the Willow Ptarmigan migrates south of its breeding range, but seldom farther than the central Canadian provinces and southern Alaska. It is a rare visitor to our northern borders.

The food of this Ptarmigan consists of insects and berries in the summer, and in the winter it eats the twigs and buds of the alder and willow. Its nest is made in a depression in the ground, lined with leaves or feathers. The seven to twelve eggs are reddish or yellowish brown with dark spots.

The geographic races of this Grouse are of little interest to casual students for they are indistinguishable in the field.

ROCK PTARMIGAN

(Lagopus mutus)

In habits and appearance, the Rock Ptarmigan closely resembles its relative, the Willow Ptarmigan. As the names imply, however, the Rock Ptarmigan haunts the barren rocky slopes and mountain tops, while the Willow Ptarmigan prefers the valleys and tundras.

In winter plumage the Rock Ptarmigan shows a black line from the bill to the eye. At close range the bill of the Rock Ptarmigan is more slender than that of its relative.

WHITE-TAILED PTARMIGAN

(Lagopus leucurus)

Color Plate Page 27

The only one of the three species of Ptarmigan that reaches the United States and the smallest (12 to 13 inches) is the White-tailed Ptarmigan, a resident of the barren country above the timberline in the Rocky Mountains. It is a grayish brown, Grouse-like bird that changes its summer plumage for snow white feathers when winter comes. In winter, the only parts of the bird that are not white are its black eyes and bill, unnoticeable in this perfect camouflage against the white world in which it survives.

Because of its remote habitat, so difficult to visit, the White-tailed Ptarmigan is little known to bird watchers. Those who have met it on its home grounds find it fearless and trusting of humans, permitting close approach.

Like the other Ptarmigans, it makes its nest on the ground and lays from ten to sixteen eggs which are buff or rusty brown, heavily spotted with brown. Young birds have a gray tail.

Five closely related races are recognized throughout its range in the high mountains from Alaska and the Mackenzie River to New Mexico.

GREATER PRAIRIE CHICKEN

(Tympanuchus cupido)

Thanks to the outlawing of market hunters, and thanks to the wise management of state governments in maintaining rigid supervision over its hunting in recent years, the Greater Prairie Chicken, most important upland game bird of the middle west, has been checked on its road to extinction. Indeed, in some favored areas, it has even shown a slight increase in its numbers. But no matter how encouraging the picture may be, the fact remains that only a few exist today.

ROCK PTARMIGAN IN SUMMER AND WINTER PLUMAGE *(Lagopus mutus)*. Length: 15 to 17 inches. Male and female: small Arctic Grouse. Changes brown summer plumage for white feathers when winter sets in. In winter, the Rock Ptarmigan has a *black mark* from the bill, through the eye. Range: Arctic regions of North America south to Gulf of St. Lawrence, Labrador and Newfoundland.

Alfred M. Bailey

GREATER PRAIRIE CHICKEN (*Tympanuchus cupido*). Length: 18 inches. Male and female: upperparts yellowish brown spotted with black. Below, white barred with dusky brown. Has short rounded tail. Range: Great Plains west to eastern Colorado and northeast Montana. Found occasionally in eastern Wyoming.
Charles W. Schwartz, National Audubon Society

Regarding its dwindling population, Charles W. Schwartz, in his excellent life history "The Prairie Chicken in Missouri" writes of the bird in that state: "Less than seventy-five years ago, the resonant booming call of the Greater Prairie Chicken could be heard each spring throughout the prairies of Missouri and even on the open ridges of the Ozarks. Today this species occupies only about twenty-five hundred square miles, or one-tenth of its original range in the state. The population has likewise dwindled from countless numbers to approximately thirteen thousand birds."

Most characteristic of the Prairie Chicken is its spring courtship, performed by the male birds on ancestral booming grounds. The display opens with the cock bird stamping his feet rapidly on the ground. As he dances up and down, orange shaped and orange colored air sacs on the sides of the neck become inflated, wings are drooped, tail fanned out, pointed neck feathers erected, and orange eyebrows are puffed out. In this spectacular stance, the bird suddenly utters a hollow booming sound and expels the air from the inflated sacs. A nearby male (the booming grounds are a community affair) accepts the challenge and goes through the same performance.

Schwartz describes the booming thusly: "The quality of the booming is like that of the lower notes of an ocarina or the sound made by blowing across the neck of a bottle. In the fully developed call there are three notes, rising at even intervals of a quarter- or half-tone." He states that the three notes together last two or three seconds and might be written as *oo-loo-woo*. He adds, "The call often has a curious ventriloquial character and may be heard easily a mile away on a calm day."

The Prairie Chicken, which is about 18 inches long, may be distinguished from the Sharp-tailed Grouse by its short, rounded black tail and its heavily barred underparts. The female has a dark colored barred tail. Sage Hens have black bellies and spikelike tail feathers.

The Prairie Chicken makes its nest in open prairie country in tufts of grass, or low bushes. Its eight to twelve eggs are dull buff, usually without markings. Its food is primarily insects and grasshoppers which makes it a valuable bird to the farmer.

KILLDEER COMING ON NEST (*Oryechus vociferus vociferus*). Length: 9 to 11 inches. Male and female: olive brown upperparts, white below. Two black bands on head, two on breast. Golden red tail visible in flight. Range: breeds from Canada to Mexico; winters in Pacific States and from Colorado south. Voice: loud, emphatic *kill-deer* or *kill-dee* or *dee-ee*.
Hal H. Harrison

The now extinct Heath Hen (*T. c. cupido*) was a member of this race which now includes two species: the Greater Prairie Chicken (*T. c. pinnatus*), and Attwater's Prairie Chicken (*T. c. attwateri*). The latter is a vanishing species found only in Texas. Census figures taken in 1937 estimated the total population of Attwater's Prairie Chicken at only 8700 birds.

LESSER PRAIRIE CHICKEN

(*Tympanuchus pallidicinctus*)

In the Great Plains from Kansas and Colorado to central Texas and eastern New Mexico, the bird watcher will find a dwindling race of small, pale grouse known as the Lesser Prairie Chicken. Although its decline appears to have been checked in recent years, the bird has disappeared from many sections where it was once abundant.

The habits of the Lesser Prairie Chicken are similar to its larger cousin, the Greater Prairie Chicken. It, too, resorts to ancestral booming grounds for courtship display in the spring. In this species the air sacs on the neck are red instead of yellow or orange. The booming notes differ in tone. The coloration of the bird is paler in tone, and it is about two inches smaller.

WOODCOCK (*Philohela minor*). Length: 10 to 12 inches. Male and female: above brown, below pale orange brown. Almost neckless. Has extremely long bill. Range: breeds from Florida and Louisiana to Canada. Winters north to New Jersey and Ohio Valley. Voice: low, nasal *beezp* or *peent*.

Hal H. Harrison

LESSER PRAIRIE CHICKEN *(Tympanuchus pallidicinctus).* Length: 16 inches. Male and female: pale brown hen-like bird with short rounded tail. Range: Great Plains west to eastern Colorado and northeast Montana, east Wyoming, limited area in southwest Kansas, western Oklahoma, northern Texas and northeast New Mexico. Voice: similar to Greater Prairie Chicken, but weaker.
Rudolph Hindemith, American Museum of Natural History

SHARP-TAILED GROUSE

(Pedioecetes phasianellus)

Color Plate Page 34

In parts of its range on the western prairies, the Sharp-tailed Grouse, an important game bird, may be confused with the similar Prairie Chicken and the Sage Hen. Its short pointed tail identifies it from the former which has a short rounded black tail, while Sage Hens have black bellies and are much larger birds than Sharp-tails. Female Ring-necked Pheasants have pointed tails, but they are much longer than the Sharp-tails'. The Sharp-tailed Grouse is a light speckled brown, and averages about 18 inches in length.

The breeding range of this Grouse has become more and more restricted as cultivation of the prairie country has been extended. It is to be sought in the thickets and scattered woodlands of the prairies rather than in the wide open country, home of the Prairie Chicken.

Like other Grouse, the Sharp-tail has a spectacular courtship display which is performed on ancestral mating grounds on prairie knolls. Several weeks each spring, the males resort to these "dancing hills" where they fight, strut, stamp, and dance to the accompaniment of a booming sound produced by expelling air from inflated sacs on the sides of the necks.

The nest is on the ground. From 10 to 13 eggs are laid in a hollow which is scantily lined with prairie vegetation. Incubation is performed by the female and requires about three weeks. So well camouflaged is a sitting hen that she will not flush until an intruder is about to step upon her. Young birds leave the nest when hatched.

In its six geographic forms, the birds breed from the Great Plains west to the foothills of the Rockies, and north to Alaska and the Mackenzie River. They appear again in the Great Basin region.

SAGE GROUSE or SAGE HEN

(Centrocercus urophasianus)

Dawn is breaking over a western prairie. We have been in a well camouflaged blind for almost an hour, listening to a strange sound in the darkness around us. Now that it is getting light, we can see what we have been hearing—the most spectacular of bird courtship performances, the strutting of the Sage Grouse.

We count eight Sage Cocks in view now. They are strutting about with their spike-like tail feathers erect and spread like little Turkey gobblers. The air sacs on the neck of one big bird are greatly extended. His neck and breast look like a huge balloon. Suddenly the bird tosses the sacs up and down. The stiffened feathers of the breast grate against the wing feathers, producing a rasping sound. The act is concluded when the cock expels the air from the sacs, creating a new series of sound and rumblings.

In the distance, we see other cocks strutting. We are in the midst of a great avian pageant that occurs each spring, a pageant that is becoming more and more rare each year as the Sage Grouse or Sage Hen, the largest member of the Grouse family, continues to disappear from ancestral haunts. Those haunts are now the favored locations in the sagebrush plains east of the Cascades and Sierras from southeastern Washington and Montana south to eastern California, Nevada, Utah, and northern Colorado.

SAGE HEN (*Centrocerus urophasianus*). Length: male, 28 inches; female, 22 inches. Male: large, gray brown body, yellow whitish below. Black belly and spike-like tail feathers. Female: tail shorter, with narrower feathers than male. Considerably smaller size on the whole. Range: sagebrush plains east of Cascades and Sierras from southeast Washington, and Montana south to eastern California, Nevada, Utah and north Colorado. Voice: cock has a sharp cackle, *kek, kek, kek,* which voices its alarm when flushed.

Alfred M. Bailey

The male Sage Grouse is identified by its large size (28 inches long), its black belly, and its long sharp tail feathers. Females are smaller (22 inches) but have the distinguishing black belly.

These birds nest among the sage bushes, scratching out a slight depression in the ground where the seven to nine olive or greenish eggs with brown spots are laid. The baby birds can run about fifteen minutes after they hatch. By fall, the young birds are full grown but are lighter in color than the adults. Their food is mainly sage leaves and insects.

QUAILS, PARTRIDGES, and PHEASANTS

Family Phasianidae

The true Pheasants are birds of the Old World, and their American representatives are the Quail and the introduced European pheasants. All are handsome birds, with the most colorful being the western birds. They are small Chicken-like birds which have actually increased in numbers with the spread of the farmlands. Their principal food is insects and certain weed seeds, so that they are of great value to the farmer.

EUROPEAN PARTRIDGE

(Perdix perdix perdix)

This gray Partridge has been introduced from Europe into various sections of the eastern United States, most successfully in open farming country in the upper Mississippi valley. It is between a Grouse and a Bobwhite in size (12 to 14 inches long), plump, with a short ruddy tail. It is marked with a dark spot on the belly and by chestnut

UPLAND PLOVER *(Bartramia longicauda)*. Length: 11 to 12.5 inches. Male and female: mixed black and buffy brown upperparts. Outer tail feathers streaked with black, white and chestnut. Buffy breast streaked with black; white abdomen. Range: Canada to northeastern Utah, and occasionally to eastern Oregon, Colorado and New Mexico. Voice: *kip-ip-ip-ip*.
Fred Bashour

bars on the flanks. Its voice is a loud *kar-whit, kar-whit.*

BOBWHITE

(Colinus virginianus)

Color Plate Page 35

No North American game bird has so endeared itself to the populace at large than the Bobwhite. Whether you know it in the spring, when its whistled *bob-white* love call rings across the open fields, or whether you know it best in the fall when it becomes the hunted "Quail" of the north and the "Partridge" of the south, the Bobwhite is an admirable bird without a single fault to condemn it to the human race.

The Bobwhite has a dual personality. In the spring it is tame. Then it seeks rather than avoids the haunts of man as it comes into gardens, yards, and nearby fields. Here the Quail sings its love song, performs its courtship rites, and finally builds its nest. The familiar call of *bob-bob-white,* or *bob-white,* or just *white* serves a double role as a courtship song and as a song of defiance to other males that dare to encroach upon occupied territory.

Although a very simple structure, the Bobwhite's nest is so well hidden and camouflaged, and the bird is such a close sitter, that comparatively few nests are found. To build their home, the birds excavate a hollow in the ground. This is lined with grasses and other vegetation, and an arch is formed over the cup by skillfully weaving surrounding vegetation with introduced materials. An opening is left on the side, and through this the birds enter and leave. Through this opening the sitting bird watches as it incubates. Twelve to twenty white eggs are laid. The chicks leave the nest as soon as they are dry.

In the autumn, the Bobwhite presents another side to its personality as the birds form wild flocks or coveys, haunting the woods and fields, seeking food and shelter. Now they are wary and alert. No more do we hear that cheery *bob-white* call, for now protection from their annual autumn enemy —the man with the gun—becomes of prime importance. The Quail's rare combination of lying well to a dog, flying swiftly when flushed, and making a delicious table food has made it a much hunted game bird, particularly in the south.

At this time of year, the coveys which are composed of families or flocks of several families, hold very close together. When flushed, they scatter, only to reassemble when danger has passed. The regathering is accomplished by answering a "gather call," a two-part whistle slurred together. At night, a covey roosts in characteristic fashion—on the ground in a tight circle, each bird facing out, and each bird set at all times to spring away in a different direction should danger surprise the flock.

The food habits of the Bobwhite have been studied extensively, and it is sufficient to say here that the bird's diet has been found to be entirely beneficial to man. Indeed, the Bobwhite is so highly respected and desired by some farmers that they place a self-imposed restriction on hunting them on their lands.

Although the Quail reaches its peak of abundance in the southeastern states, it has been introduced successfully in many western and northern states, and is now found from coast to coast.

The sexes are distinguished by the male's white throat and eye stripe, which are buffy in the female. The birds are 9 to 11 inches long.

SCALED QUAIL

(Callipepla squamata)

Color Plate Page 38

In the vast arid regions of the southwest, widely scattered over rough desert plains that are covered with thorny underbrush, or on rocky foothills where hunting is difficult, one finds the Scaled, or Blue, Quail, a grayish bird, identified by the scaled appearance of its breast and its bushy white crest. The latter gives rise to another common name, Cotton Top.

The Scaled Quail is decidedly terrestrial, preferring to run rather than fly when molested. Its powerful legs serve it well, and its running speed is amazing. The Scaled Quail does not lie for a dog, but flushes at a distance, disappearing through the thick brush without even hesitating long enough for an opportune shot from the pursuer.

The call is a two-noted *chek-ah,* rather like a Guinea Hen.

The Arizona Scaled Quail *(C. s. pallida)* and its close relative, the Chestnut-bellied Scaled Quail *(C. s. castanogastris)* are found only in the arid regions of central and southern Arizona, southern Colorado, New Mexico, and west, central, and southern Texas.

CALIFORNIA QUAIL

(Lophortyx californica)

Color Plate Page 39

If one comes upon them suddenly and unexpectedly, one may hope to see a covey of California, or Valley Quail take to their wings with a loud whirr, but the more common view is that of a little flock of gaily plumed, ashy brown birds making off through the chaparral as fast as their swift little legs will carry them. They are chunky birds, active, wary, and always alert. When forced to fly, they will take to the air for only a short distance, then set their wings and scale down.

In California the Valley Quail is the most important upland game bird. In years past it was remarkably abundant, and reports of as many as 100,000 birds being marketed in San Francisco in a single season were not unusual. Today it is still common, but not abundant.

The chief field marks of the California Quail which is about 10 inches long are the male's black plume which curves forward from the crown over the forehead, the black throat encircled with white, the bluish gray breast, chestnut patch in the middle of a buff colored belly, and white stripes on the sides and flanks. The female has a shorter plume and is generally duller. The Mountain Quail has a straight plume, sloping backward. The Gambel's Quail, although generally similar, has a black patch on its buffy belly.

The call of the California Quail is a three-noted *qua-quer-go.*

There are three subspecies: the California Quail *(L. c. californica),* the Valley Quail *(L. c. vallicola),* and the Catalina Quail *(L. c. catalinensis),* which show no field differences.

GAMBEL'S QUAIL

(Lophortyx gambeli)

Color Plate Page 41

Gambel's Quail, Arizona Quail, or Desert Quail, is a game bird of the arid

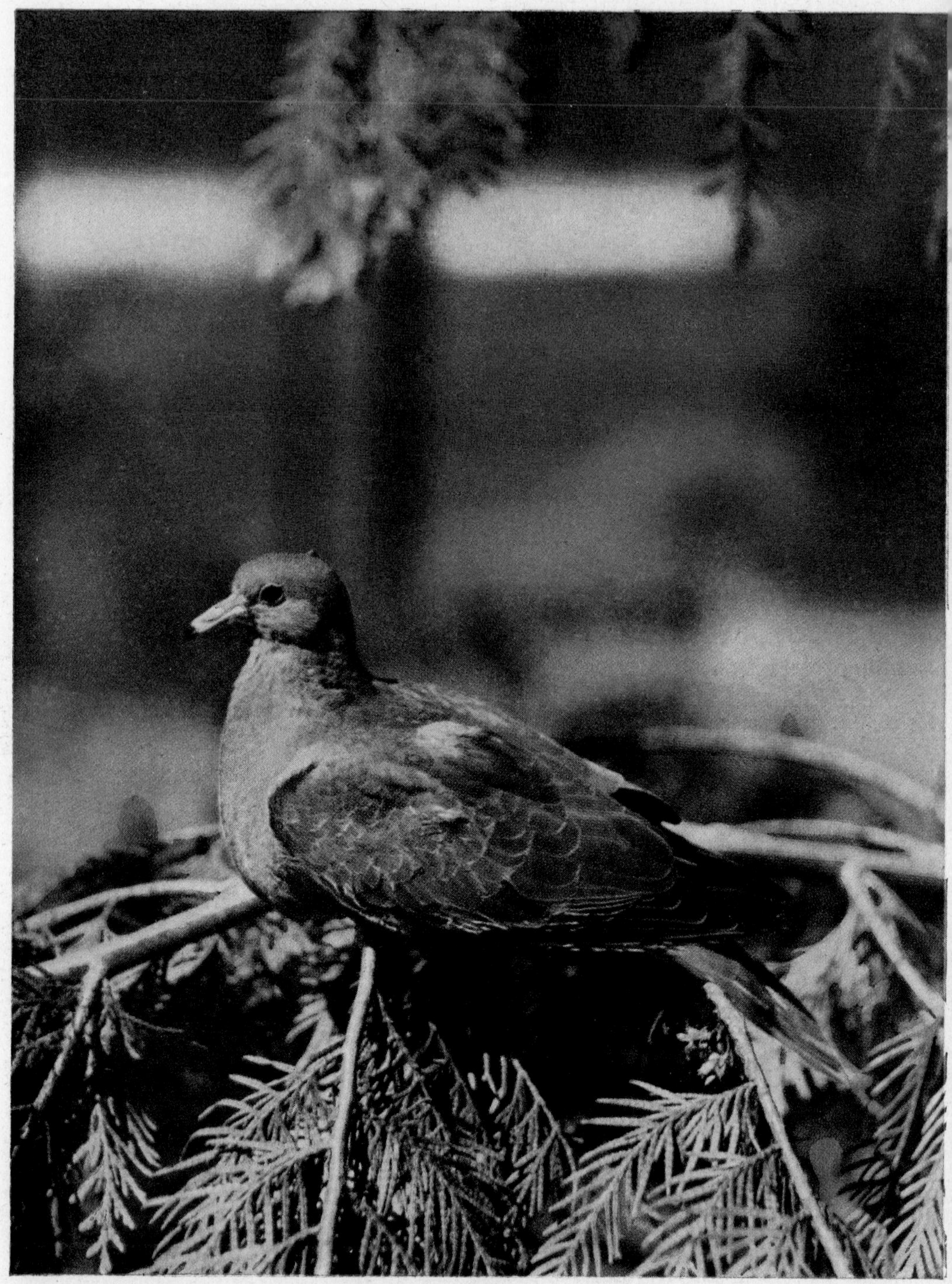

BAND-TAILED PIGEON (*Columba fasciata*). Length: 15.5 inches. Male: iridescent brownish upper back; bluish gray underparts. White crescent on back of neck. End of tail has broad pale gray band bordered above by black. Female: duller, grayer, often lacking neck patch. Range: Pacific States, also in Arizona, New Mexico, Colorado and western Texas. Winters in southwest United States. Voice: owl-like oo-*whoo* or *whoo*-oo-*whoo*.

William L. and Irene Finley

southwest. In this region it replaces the California Quail which it resembles in coloring and size. In the western part of its range, Gambel's Quail associates with the Valley Quail. The two may be distinguished, however, by the large black patch on the light belly of the male Gambel's. Both birds sport the gay plume that curves forward from the head, and both are strikingly colored in combinations of blue, gray, chestnut, and black. Its three-noted call is rather more drawling than that of the California Quail.

Although its reputation as a runner does not quite equal that of the Blue, or Scaled, Quail of the desert, yet Gambel's Quail commands the respect of those who hunt it. Many a sportsman will attest to its ability to outrun its pursuer. The bird will not lie to a dog, and when flushed in open country, it is a fast flier. Those who enjoy this delicious fowl on the table usually more than earn their reward. In spite of the Gambel's attraction for the hunter, they are able to maintain themselves because of their rapid reproduction; as they lay ten to twelve eggs.

There are two subspecies recognized: Gambel's Quail *(L. g. gambeli)* and the Olathe Quail *(L. g. sanus)*.

YOUNG MOUNTAIN QUAIL IN NEST *(Oreortyx picta)*. Length: 11 inches. Male and female: upperparts deep olive brown. Crest black. Top of head bluish gray. Throat and flanks, rich chestnut brown. Long straight head plume of two feathers about two inches long. Range: mountains of southwest Washington, Oregon, southern Idaho, western Nevada, and southern California. Voice: a loud, mellow cry, *wook?* repeated at infrequent intervals by male in breeding season. Both sexes have alarm whistles uttered rapidly and tremulously.

H. D. Wheeler, National Audubon Society

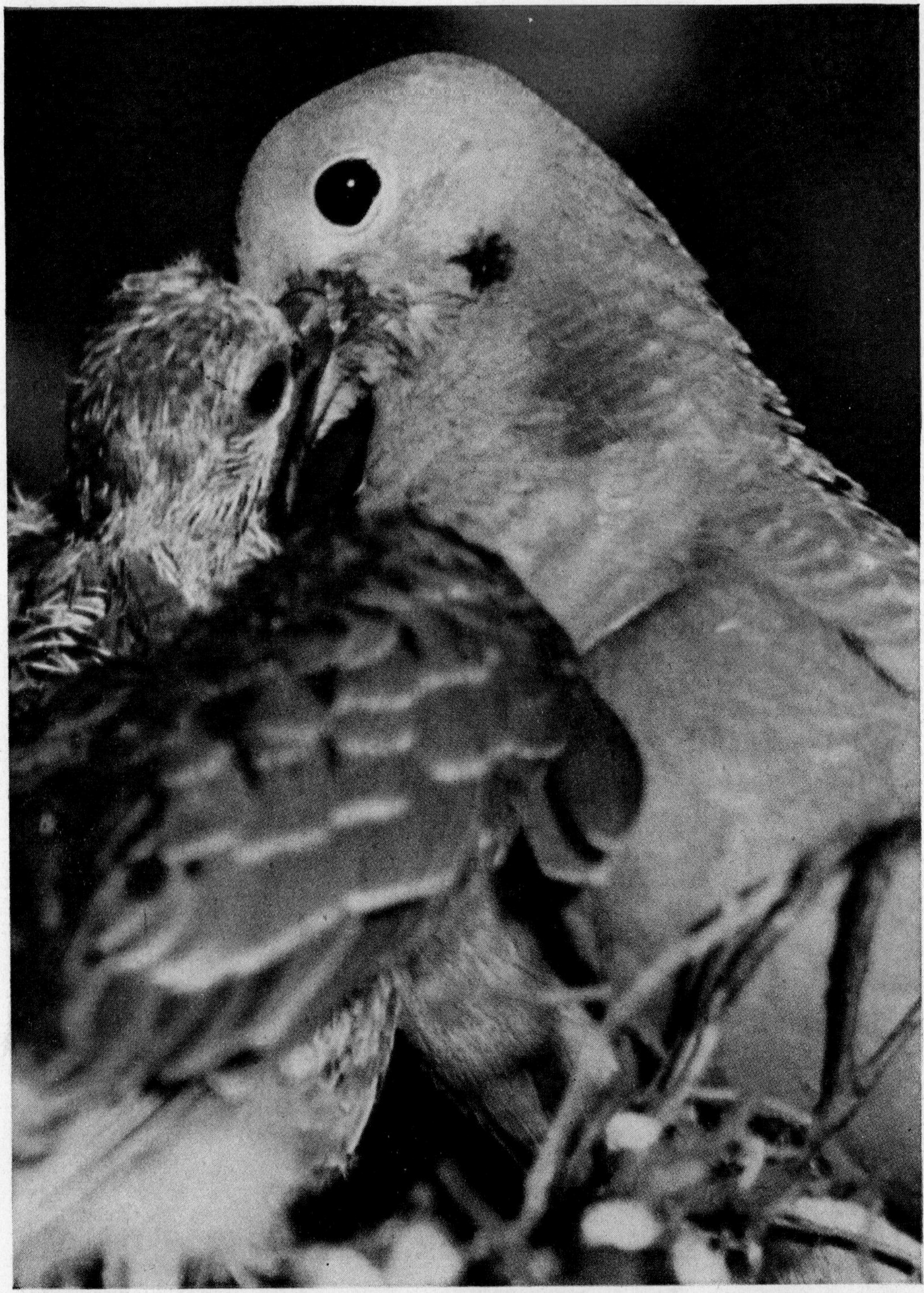

MOURNING DOVE (*Zenaidura macroura*). Length: 11 to 13 inches. Male and female: brown body. Pointed tail with white patches visible in flight. Range: breeds throughout the United States from Canada to Mexico; winters from southern Oregon, southern Colorado, northern Ohio and North Carolina to Panama. Voice: a mournful *coah*-cooo-cooo-coo.

Hal H. Harrison

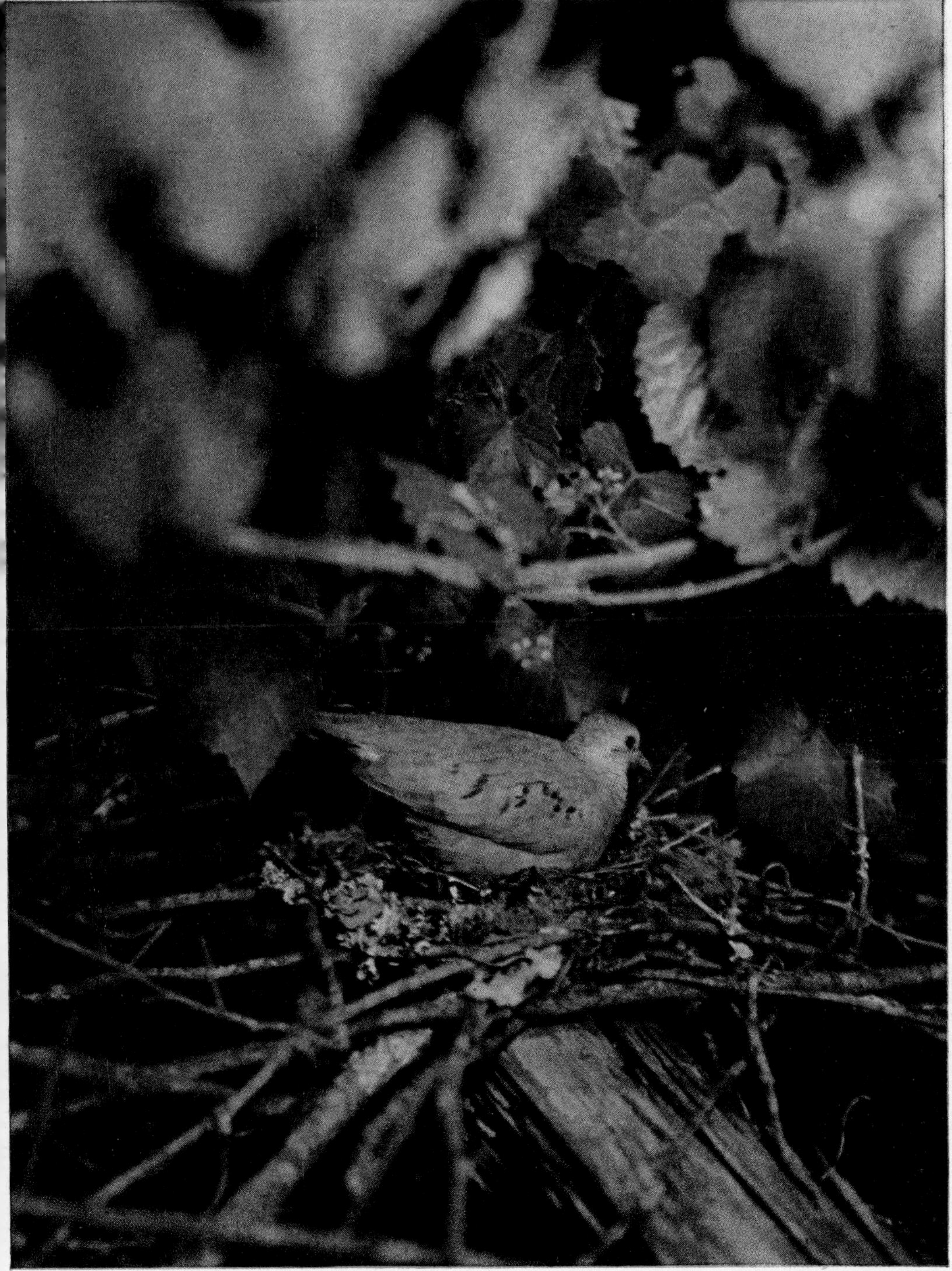

GROUND DOVE (*Columbigallina passerina*). Length: 6.75 inches. Male and female: small dove, above grayish brown; below grayish red. Has stubby black tail and round wings. Range: resident of low country from South Carolina to Texas. Occasionally found in North Carolina. Voice: a moaning repeated *woo-oo, woo-oo, woo-oo.*

Samuel A. Grimes

MOUNTAIN QUAIL

(Oreortyx picta)

Largest of the North American Quail (11 inches long), the Mountain, or Plumed, Quail is a Partridge of the higher mountains of southwestern Washington, Oregon, southern Idaho, western Nevada, and California. It is indeed a handsome bird, with its chestnut throat and belly, gray breast, and jaunty long straight head plume. The sexes are similar, but the female's plume is shorter and her coloration generally duller. The Mountain Quail may be distinguished instantly from the California or Valley Quail by its straight plume; that of the latter curves forward. The voice of the Mountain Quail is a melodious *wook, to-wook.*

The nest is a typical Quail nest, and the eggs are usually seven to twelve in number, but may be as many as eighteen or twenty. When the young are first hatched they are striped and streaked with yellow, brown, and black. The plume does not show for a few days, and then it begins to develop as a sort of "top knot." The Mountain Quail feeds mainly on seeds and berries of various sorts.

Two subspecies are recognized in the United States: the Mountain Quail *(O. p. palmeri)* and the Plumed Quail *(O. p. picta)*.

MEARN'S QUAIL

(Cyrtonyx montezumae mearnsi)

Color Plate Page 44

"Whoso calls this the 'Fool Quail' writes himself down a bigger fool than the bird, who has been taught his lesson of concealment by Mother Nature herself." Thus wrote H. W. Henshaw to Florence Merriam Bailey after witnessing the remarkable confidence that the Mearn's Quail places in its protective coloration. The name of "Fool Quail" was earned by this bizarre bird of the grassy valleys and bushy mountain slopes of Arizona, New Mexico, and Texas because of its habit of freezing instead of running or flying when danger approaches.

The oddly marked black and white face of the Mearn's Quail gives it a clownlike appearance. The upperparts are brown, barred with black; the sides of the breast and flanks are black dotted with white; the median underparts are dark brown and black. Females lack the facial stripes and are generally duller. Smallest of the Quails, it averages 8 inches in length.

The low call of this Quail is said to suggest the wavering cry of a Screech Owl. It has a ventriloquistic quality, which results in considerable exasperation for the bird watcher who attempts to trace the call to the bird.

RING-NECKED PHEASANT

(Phasianus colchicus torquatus)

We have no true Pheasants native to America. The Grouse is called a Pheasant erroneously. The Ring-necked Pheasant, America's number one game bird, is of Asiatic origin and was introduced into Europe at a very early date. The first successful introduction into the United States occurred in 1881 when Judge O. N. Denny, our Consul General in Shanghai, China, sent thirty Ring-Necked Pheasants to Oregon. Twenty-six survived and were released in the Willamette Valley. In the east, the first successful liberation occurred in 1887 when Rutherford Stuyvesant brought a number of Pheasants from England and liberated them on his estate in Allamuchy, New Jersey.

The Ring-neck has proved a hardy bird, and today it is the most numerous game bird in the area it occupies. And it occupies a big slice of the country, roughly the northern half. The center of density seems to be South Dakota, termed the "Pheasant Capital of the World," where millions of birds are shot annually.

During most of the year, the Ring-neck lives a quiet existence. Its homeland is cultivated fields and bushy pastures, swamps and moist thickets. The cock bird with its extravagant hues and white band about the neck needs no introduction. The hen lacks all this grandeur and might be mistaken for a Grouse except for her longer tail.

The courtship "song" of the cock Pheasant sounds more like the crowing of a little bantam rooster than the sound one would expect from such a magnificent fellow. But it seems to get results.

The Ring-neck hen builds her nest on the ground, often in a grain field.

RING-NECKED PHEASANT ON NEST (*Phasianus colchicus torquatus*). Length: male, 33 to 36 inches; female, 20.5 inches. Large hen-like birds. Male: head and neck greenish with purplish iridescence, white ring around neck. Reddish bronze breast. *Long, sweeping, pointed tail.* Female: mottled brown with shorter tail than male. Range: mainly north of Mason and Dixon line and north only as far as deep snows will allow. Voice: courting males utter loud, double squawk.

Allan D. Cruickshank, National Audubon Society

She lays from six to fourteen eggs, usually ten or twelve. On her nest the hen is much more concealed than the clutch of olive buff eggs that is exposed when she flushes.

Unquestionably the hunters of Quail and Grouse are indebted to the Ring-neck for diverting sportsmen from their own favorites. And since the Ring-neck thrives in our temperate zone, and since game farms have been most successful in propagating the bird, it is likely that the Ring-necked Pheasant will continue as America's most popular game bird for a long, long time.

TURKEYS

Family Meleagrididae

The Wild Turkeys are a typical American bird, the only species being found in North and Central America. Once plentiful in the United States, they are now restricted to a few ranges in the east and to parts of the west. The type is confused by the fact that Wild Turkeys will mate with strayed domestic birds, thus confusing what little difference there is between the species.

WILD TURKEY

(Meleagris gallopavo)

Most people, I believe, have the idea that their annual Thanksgiving Turkey is a descendant of our native Wild Turkey. It is not; the domestic species is a descendant of the Mexican Turkey, and it arrived here in a rather roundabout way. From Mexico it was taken to Europe by the Spaniards early in

WHITE WINGED DOVE (*Zenaida asiatica*). Length: 11 to 12.5 inches. Male: upperparts brownish shading to bluish gray on lower back. Underparts soft fawn brown to grayish white on abdomen. Large white patch on wings, and rounded tail, tipped with white bar. Female: smaller and duller. Range: occasional in southern Florida, Louisiana, and south central Texas. Voice: loud and emphatic *coo-uh-cuck-oo.*

Ross and Florence Thornburg

MERRIAM'S TURKEY (*Meleagris gallopavo merriami*). Length: male, 48 inches; female, 36 inches. Naked head and neck different shades of red with upright growth on forehead. Body is predominantly iridescent copper bronze, with whitish tips to tail feathers. Range: mountains of southern Colorado, Arizona, New Mexico and western Texas. Voice: similar to *gobble-gobble* of domestic Turkey.

Rudolph Hindemith, American Museum of Natural History

the sixteenth century. From Spain it was taken to England, and it arrived in the United States when the English colonists brought it with them.

Wild Turkeys have vanished as civilization encroached on many parts of their former range, particularly in New England. Today they are found only in remote mountainous areas, heavily wooded forests, and inaccessible swamps. Although the Turkey is the largest and probably the finest of all game birds, relatively few sportsmen ever enjoy hunting it because of its scarcity and because of stringent hunting laws imposed by the states in an effort to save it from extermination. Because the Wild Turkey is nonmigratory, it lacks federal protection, and its destiny is entirely in the hands of the various state game commissions.

In a wild state, the habits of the Wild Turkey are much like other gallinaceous birds. In the spring, the adult male struts and gobbles before the hens. The old gobbler is polygamous. His hens make their nests in secluded places on the ground where a bit of earth has been scratched out to create a hollow for the eight to fifteen buff colored, spotted eggs. Young Turkeys follow the hen until fall. The males flock together, feeding on foot by day, flying into trees to roost by night.

Four races of the Wild Turkey are recognized throughout its breeding range from Pennsylvania and Colorado to Florida and Mexico. The Eastern

Wild Turkey has chestnut tips to its tail feathers. Merriam's Turkey *(M. g. merriami)* of the southwest has whitish tips, as does the domestic Turkey. Male Turkeys are about four feet long and females three feet.

The various subspecies are confused by the fact that Turkeys sometimes stray from the barnyard and interbreed with the wild birds, giving rise to hybrids which are difficult to assign to any species.

PLOVERS and TURNSTONES

Family Charadriidae

The Plovers and Turnstones are a family of small shore and wading birds, of which eight species occur in North America. Of these, one, the Killdeer, is also found on completely dry land, miles from any water. It particularly likes freshly plowed fields where it runs along the furrows feeding on grubs and other insects.

Plovers run energetically about on their relatively long legs. Their wings are long and pointed; their necks and tails, short. They lay their eggs on the ground in shallow depressions.

KILLDEER

(Oxyechus vociferus vociferus)

Color Plate Page 48

Kill-dee, kill-dee, kill-dee.

Is there a farmer from the Atlantic to the Pacific or from Mexico to northern Canada who is not familiar with the piercing cry of the swift flying Killdeer across the fields of his farm throughout the spring and summer?

The Killdeer, a Plover, undoubtedly is the most widely distributed and best known of all the shore birds. But un-

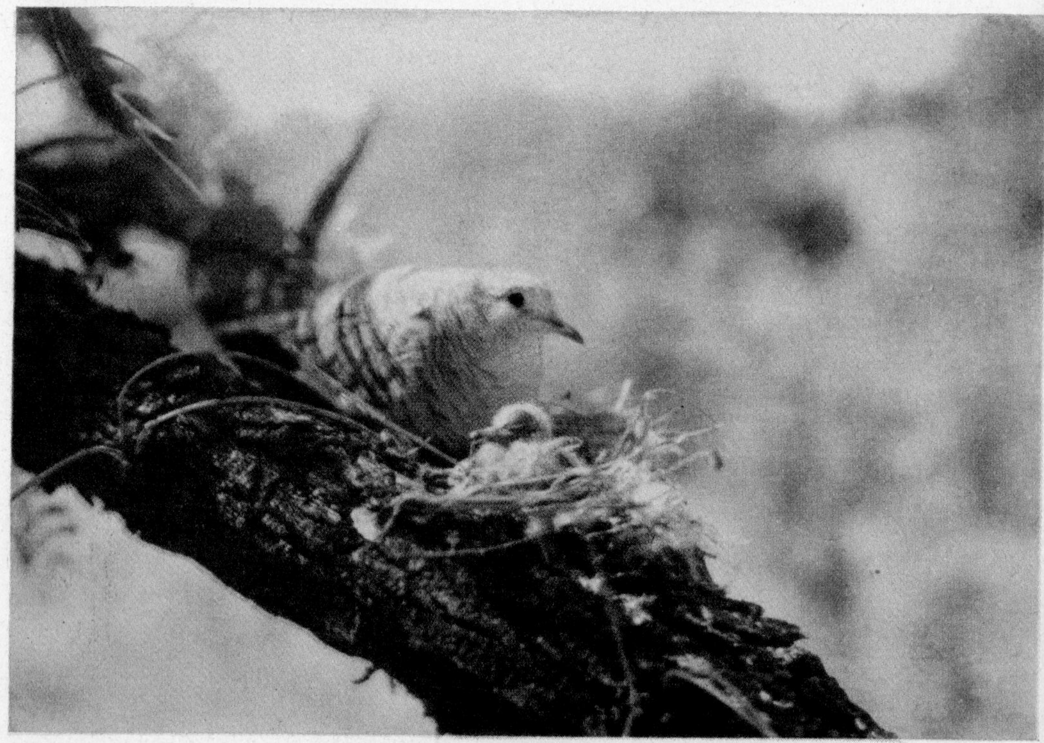

INCA DOVE *(Scardafella inca)*. Length: 8 inches. Male and female: upperparts, grayish brown; below grayish red and buff. Has longish square-ended tail with prominent white sides. Range: Arizona, southern New Mexico, and southern Texas. Voice: *coh-coo.*

Fred Bashour

like most members of that family, it delights in placing its eggs in the open windswept fields. The edges of gravel roads, cinder piles, railroad tracks, and similar places are also selected. Wherever the four splotched eggs are placed, points in like the pieces of a pie, they blend well with their surroundings. Since a very scant nest, if any, is attempted, and the eggs are always exposed, their protective coloration must hide them.

This Killdeer Plover is the farmer's friend. It consumes great quantities of insects. Government reports show that "in all, 97.2 percent of the Killdeer's food is composed of insects and animal matter. The bird preys upon many of the worst crop pests and is a valuable economic factor."

The pattern of the Killdeer's body is a good example of eruptive markings that serve as a camouflage. One would think that the white ring around the neck and the two black bands across the white breast would make the bird conspicuous. In flight the tail shows golden red. But when the Killdeer remains motionless, or freezes, these markings serve to break the form into a number of pieces that are no longer birdlike. In this way the Killdeer often escapes detection. The bird is 9 to 11 inches long, with a long tail.

When one enters a field where a Killdeer's nest is located, both birds call wildly in what always seems to me to be a pathetic tone. They flutter on the ground, pretending to have broken wings, inviting the intruder to follow. When the birds are engaged in this ruse, the nest is quite a distance away, for you may depend upon it, the Killdeer is never noisy in the immediate vicinity of the nest—unless the intruder actually finds the eggs.

Incubation requires twenty-seven to twenty-eight days. The young are hatched in an advanced stage of development and leave the nest as soon as they are dry. Young Killdeers are not fed by their parents, but are shown where food may be secured. Because their flight feathers develop slowly, the young are almost fully grown before they can fly. During this growing period, they depend upon their protective coloration to hide them from enemies. A baby Killdeer has only one black ring across the breast.

The Killdeer was once an American game bird. Because of its swift flight and the skill required to shoot it on the wing, it was hunted enthusiastically. Today these valuable insect destroyers enjoy full protection throughout the year in all parts of the country.

Although migratory, the Killdeer remains in the north late in the fall and returns early in the spring. It winters throughout the southern states and south to Peru.

WOODCOCK and SNIPE

Family Scolopacidae

The Woodcock and Snipe are also small shore or wading birds, some of whose members are habitually found on dry land miles from water. They differ from the Plovers in having long slender bills, and are usually more plainly colored.

WOODCOCK

(Philohela minor)

Color Plate Page 49

One April morning a couple and their son found a Woodcock incubating its eggs in an open field. That afternoon, I asked the boy to show me the nest. He searched for over an hour and was unable to find it. His father scoffed at him when we returned. He would show me the nest. But he experienced the same difficulty. Finally the mother, indicating that her family must be losing its eyesight, undertook to find it for me. I haven't seen that nest yet.

This experience is not unusual, for nature offers no finer example of camouflage than a sitting Woodcock. And that is no secret to the bird either, for this Timberdoodle of the autumn woods will sit on its nest so closely that many persons have touched its back before it flushed.

The Woodcock's irregular flight from the nest is always accompanied by the whistling notes so familiar to hunters who tramp the upland swales in October. The whistling is not vocal. It is produced by the rushing of the wind through the three outer primary feathers of each wing.

The Woodcock is classified as a shore bird, a member of the Sandpiper family. Unlike most shore birds, it seeks the alder thickets and the willow bottoms as nesting sites. Here, in true shore bird fashion, the Woodcock lays four buffy eggs, spotted with rufous, and laid points in like the pieces of a pie. Its nest is a slight depression in the ground lined with dead leaves. The adult bird is 10 to 12 inches long, with coloration and pattern resembling dead leaves.

The availability of food is a prerequisite for the Woodcock in choosing a nesting territory. Since the bird's diet is almost one hundred percent earthworms, it must live near moist ground into which it can probe with its long prehensile bill. This bill is a special gift of nature, for it is ideally suited for its work of securing earthworms. The tip of the upper mandible is flexible. Thus, when a worm is located, the bird need only open the tip of its bill to grasp it. Some observers contend that the Woodcock first locates the worms by feeling with its sensitive feet.

Those who fail to locate the Woodcock in the spring on its singing grounds miss one of his most spectacular performances—the courtship sky dance. My first experience came on a clear, moonlight night in April, on a country road bordering an alder-cat-tail swamp.

I brought my car to a sudden stop as the clear nasal *peent* of a Woodcock rose from the swamp. Suddenly the regularly spaced calls stopped. A whistling of wings followed as the Timberdoodle took to the air. In great spirals he flew up and down toward the moon. All the while, his wings whistled a love song to a female hidden in the bog below.

Reaching the peak of his flight high above the earth, the Woodcock started his spectacular drop. The regular whistling of the long climb into the sky changed now to an irregular whistling interspersed with a soft melody. Down he came in a power dive, faster and faster. Nearing the earth, the bird checked his descent by spreading his wings. He alighted very close to where he had taken off a few minutes before. And again—*peent!*

Woodcocks breed from Manitoba and Nova Scotia to northern Florida. They are migratory and practically all of them spend the winter along the Gulf of Mexico near the delta of the Mississippi River.

WILSON'S SNIPE

(Capella gallinago delicata)

Once a plentiful game bird of the northeast, Wilson's Snipe has almost disappeared from much of its former range. It is 11 or 12 inches long, and generally brown in color. The bill is extremely long and slender.

The Snipe prefers the borders of streams and marshy meadows, and when flushed takes off in a zigzag, in contrast with the straight flight of the Woodcock. In flight it shows a short orange tail. When flushed it utters a rasping *scape-scape.*

The eggs which number three or four are olive gray spotted with brown, and are laid with the points in.

Wilson's Snipe breeds from Newfoundland and Manitoba south to northern Pennsylvania, Illinois, and South Dakota. In winter it moves south to the Gulf of Mexico, some birds remaining north to Pennsylvania or even further.

UPLAND PLOVER

(Bartramia longicauda)

Color Plate Page 61

The Upland Plover is not a plover; it is a Sandpiper and was formerly known as the Bartramian Sandpiper. In years past, it was a popular game bird, but today, under the protection of the federal government, the bird has been saved from inevitable annihilation at the hands of market gunner.

Although anatomically a Sandpiper, and thus classed as a shore bird, the Upland Plover is truly a field Plover which scorns water and makes its home in grassy fields and prairies. It nests on the ground, laying four slightly glossy eggs. They are less pointed than the eggs of most shore birds, and are buffy with brownish spots.

The Upland Plover may be identified by its size and shape easier than by its rather nondescript buffy brown plumage. It is slender, graceful in form, and larger (about 12 inches long) than a Killdeer. Its long neck, small head, short bill, and long tail are characteristic. In flight, its long pointed wings, dark rump, and barred

YELLOW-BILLED CUCKOO *(Coccyzus americanus).* Length: 11 to 12.5 inches. Male and female: grayish brown above, white below. Slate black upper mandible of bill, yellow below. Legs and feet gray. Rufous color in wings visible in flight. Range: breeds from New Brunswick, Quebec and southern Ontario south to Florida and Mexico. Winters in South America. Voice: a rapid *ka ka ka ka ka ka ka ka ka ka ka ka ka kow kow kowp kowp kowp kowp.*
Hal H. Harrison

whitish outer tail feathers are distinguishing marks. In lighting, the Upland Plover holds its wings high before folding them at its sides. In flight its call is a rolling cry. Its song opens with an ascending trill, ending with a descending whistle.

Although it was once abundant throughout most of the country during the breeding season, the Upland Plover is now gone from much of its former range, and is now more or less local in distribution. Within its local range it is not uncommon.

PIGEONS and DOVES

Family Columbidae

There is no true distinction between the Pigeons and Doves, which belong to a family almost world wide in its distribution. The young birds are fed at first by a liquid secreted in the crop of the parent, and later by regurgitation. The voice of all Pigeons and Doves is a cooing which varies in characteristic among the various species. Both sexes build the nest, incubate the one or two eggs and take care of the young, which are born naked.

WHITE-CROWNED PIGEON

(Columba leucocephala)

This wild Pigeon of south Florida and the Keys is similar in size (13½ inches) and build to the Domestic Pigeon. In color it is entirely dark, with a shining white crown. Its voice is Owl-like, consisting of a low *wof, wof, wo, co-woo.* Its eggs are either unmarked white or buff colored. It is rather rare in Florida.

BLACK-BILLED CUCKOO (*Coccyzus enthropthalmus*). Length: 11 to 12 inches. Male and female: olive brown above, white below. Narrow red eye-ring and black bill. Range: breeds from southern Manitoba south to Arkansas and North Carolina. Winters in South America. Voice: a fast, rhythmic *cu cu cu, cucucu, cucucu, cucucu, cucucu* etc.

Hal H. Harrison

BAND-TAILED PIGEON

(Columba fasciata)

Color Plate Page 56

If you should flush a little flock of heavily built Pigeons from an oak grove in the Pacific coast states; if their tails are broad and rounded, not pointed like a Mourning Dove's; and if you should see a wide band of gray across the end of the tail, bordered above with black, you have most assuredly found Band-tailed Pigeons. They are fairly large, 15½ inches long, and are more likely to be confused with domestic Pigeons than with any of the wild Doves.

At one time, the Band-tailed Pigeon was well on its way to join its relative, the Passenger Pigeon, in extinction. Like the latter, it was widely slaughtered for market, and only wise legislation in time saved it. The fact that this Pigeon usually lays but one egg, making reproduction a slower process than than in most birds, also would have hastened its extinction. Today, the hunting of Band-tails is regulated by federal law.

The Band-tailed Pigeon ranges from southern British Columbia and Montana to western Texas. It winters in the southwestern states and Mexico.

RED-BILLED PIGEON

(Columba flavirostris flavirostris)

A large Pigeon of the lower Rio Grande Valley, the Red-billed Pigeon may be distinguished from others by its size (13 inches) and its dark coloring. Its tail is broad and rounded, and in good light its foreparts show deep maroon. Its call is a drawn out cooing, rather high-pitched. It is a shy bird.

ROCK DOVE

(Columba livia)

The Rock Dove of the rocky coasts of Europe is the parent stock of our domesticated Pigeons, many of which have become naturalized in various sections of the United States. In general, it needs no description except to differentiate it from the Band-tailed Pigeon. The Domestic Pigeon has red legs and a conspicuously pale rump. Its voice is the familiar cooing.

MOURNING DOVE

(Zenaidura macroura)

Color Plate Page 58

Perhaps you belong to the affirmative side of the debate: "Resolved that the Mourning Dove is a song bird." Or, perhaps you have done a bit of Dove shooting in the south and are sold on the argument that the Mourning Dove is a real sporting bird, fast on the wing and tough as blazes to hit.

But there is one point upon which bird lovers and hunters agree; that the Mourning Dove, also called Turtle Dove, Wild Dove, Wood Dove, and Carolina Dove, is a most interesting personality. It is, first of all, an individualist, and it is a good thing that it is for it might otherwise have followed its brother, the Passenger Pigeon, down the road to extinction. Mourning Doves pair off and nest in their own private territories, not in huge flocks like the Passenger Pigeons.

It is not much of a nest each pair builds, just a flimsy platform of twigs lined with a few grasses, but what they lack in quality they make up in quantity. In the northern states where Doves are summer residents, they have at least two broods each year, often

ROADRUNNER *(Geococcyx californionus)*. Length: 20 to 24 inches. Male and female: upperparts brownish and white, streaked darkest on wings. Long tail, shaggy prominent crest. White streaks on chest. White abdomen. Range: California, Utah, and Colorado south to Mexico. Voice: a song composed of a series of dove-like coos.
Alfred M. Bailey

three; while in the south, where they are permanent residents, they have as many as five or six. The Mourning Dove is the only game bird that breeds in every one of the United States, and there is some evidence of breeding somewhere in every month of the year.

The only visible difference in the sexes is the male's somewhat brighter coloring. Both are brown, 11 to 13 inches long, and inconspicuous against the soil of an open field where they often feed. The tail is pointed and shows white spots when the bird is in flight. The wings produce a whistling sound when the Dove flies.

The male is a devoted husband and father. He gathers nesting material and delivers it to his mate. She places it on the horizontal limb of a tree, very often an evergreen. There is no rush about the job. The birds work a few hours each morning, and the project takes six or seven days.

The female lays two eggs, rarely three. They are always pure white. Both birds incubate, and the young hatch in fourteen to fifteen days. Young Doves are helpless, but they grow rapidly, doubling their hatching weight the first day. They remain in the nest eleven or twelve days.

One of the most unusual things about Doves is their manner of feeding the young by regurgitation of a glandular fluid called "pigeon milk" produced in the crops of both parents. The feeding process is quite a sight. Each youngster takes its place at the side of the parent bird and pushes its bill inside the bill of the adult. In this position, the old bird actually pumps the "pigeon milk" into the mouths of the nestlings. Each feeding requires five or six minutes.

The Mourning Dove's name comes from its "song," a low toned moaning *coo-ah coo, coo, coo.* It is one of the first bird songs of spring. Weed seeds are the Dove's main source of food. Ordinarily, it eats waste kernels rather than ripe heads.

The Eastern Mourning Dove *(Z. m. carolinensis)* is the only wild member of the Pigeon family in the northeastern part of the country. Our smallest Dove, the Eastern Ground Dove, is not found north of South Carolina. A somewhat paler form of the Mourning Dove *(Z. m. marginella)* is found in the west.

PASSENGER PIGEON

(Ectopistes migratorius)

The Passenger Pigeon is gone. Millions of them were killed to satisfy man's lust for the money their flesh brought in the markets. It is a sad story of man's ruthlessness in dissipating our natural resources, but I have often thought the Passenger Pigeon did not die in vain, perhaps, after all.

PASSENGER PIGEON, MOUNTED GROUP *(Ectopistes migratorius).* Length: 16.30 inches. Male: bluish slate color upperparts; back and sides of neck iridescent purple bronze. Tail has broad white band at tip. Underparts, reddish beige. Female: duller than male, brownish olive, fading to white on abdomen. Range: formerly North America to the Hudson Bay. Now extinct. Voice: a mournful *ooah, cooo, cooo, coo.*

L. W. Brownell

The extermination of no species of animal has ever received the vast publicity, nor has any other incident been pointed out so consistently and constantly as an example of what man's greed can do to our natural resources, as the example so clearly shown in the extermination of the Wild Pigeon. It is still the conservationists' greatest forte—"where millions darkened the skies, now there is none."

The story of this great slaughter is fresh in everyone's mind: the night raids on the great communal roosts; the slaughter at the nest with thousands of young left to die, or eggs left to rot; the trainloads of barrels of dressed Pigeons sent daily to market. It will remain forever a dark spot on American conservation. But surely the Passenger Pigeon, the Carolina Paroquet, the Great Auk, the Heath Hen, the Eskimo Curlew, and the Labrador Duck, now extinct from our fauna, surely these have had a tremendous influence on the protective laws that have made repetition of these tragedies impossible.

Not since 1904 has a report of a Passenger Pigeon in the wild been accepted as authentic. The end of the species occurred in the Cincinnati Zoo when the last remaining individual died on September 1, 1914. Since then, innumerable reports from persons claiming to have seen Passenger Pigeons have been scouted and declared "mistaken identity."

The Band-tailed Pigeon of the west, which is often mistaken for a Passenger Pigeon, has a square, not pointed, tail. The smaller Mourning Dove often has been erroneously identified as a Wild Pigeon, but the much larger size and the blue-gray head of the latter were distinctive. The flight of the Passenger Pigeon was silent; the wings of the Mourning Dove whistle.

CHINESE SPOTTED DOVE (*Streptopelia chinensis chinensis*). Length 12.5 inches. Male and female: brown, darker above, with a collar of black and white spots on the back of the neck. The square-tipped tail has white in the corners. Range: introduced around Los Angeles where it is common. Voice: typical cooing.
T. M. Blackman, National Audubon Society

GROUND DOVE

(*Columbigallina passerina*)

Color Plate Page 59

The Ground Dove, erroneously called "Mourning Dove" in many parts of the south, is our smallest dove. It is a dainty little bird, about the size of a Bluebird (6 or 7 inches long) that has grown quite tame throughout its range where it is afforded complete protection. In Florida, where it is common, it is a bird of the dooryard, walking quickly on short legs, with a graceful nodding motion of the head as it searches for food.

The male's upperparts are soft grayish brown, its tail blackish and squared, and its forehead and underparts a delicate pink to purplish brown. The female is similar, but her forehead and underparts are pale brownish gray. When disturbed, the birds rise on whistling wings, displaying characteristic reddish brown in the under wings.

This species nests on the ground, in low bushes or trees, and on stumps. The two eggs are pure white. The bird's call is a series of soft, mournful *coos*

The Eastern Ground

BARN OWL (*Tyto alba pratincola*). Length: 15 to 20 inches. Male and female: white heart shaped face, golden brown upperparts; whitish underparts. Long legged with large head. Range: from Washington and Colorado south to Mexico. Voice: a rasping snore or hiss.
John S. Dunning

Dove *(C. p. passerina)* ranges along the coastal plains from South Carolina to southeastern Texas. The paler Mexican Ground Dove *(C. p. pallescens)* ranges through southeastern California, southern Arizona, New Mexico, and western Texas.

CHINESE SPOTTED DOVE

(Streptopelia chinensis chinensis)

The Chinese Spotted Dove is an exotic species which has been introduced, or which has escaped, and is now abundant in the Los Angeles region of California. The bird's range is gradually extending eastward, and my latest information is that it has established itself as far east as Redlands in Riverside County, California.

It is most likely to be confused with the Mourning Dove, although the Chinese Spotted Dove is a larger bird, and has a rounded or squared tail. Like the Mourning Dove, the white tail feathers are conspicuous in flight. A collar of black and white spots on the back of the neck is one of the bird's best field marks.

RINGED TURTLE DOVE

(Streptopelia risoria)

This species is non-native, but is now apparently well established in Los Angeles. Certain individuals have been reported as "wild" in Sacramento County.

It is described as larger and paler than a Mourning Dove, which it resembles. A black ring encircling the back of the neck is its best field mark.

WHITE-WINGED DOVE

(Zenaida asiatica)

Color Plate Page 64

The voice of the White-winged Dove has been variously described as resembling the crowing of a young rooster, the rendering of one of the common notes of the Barred Owl, a harsh cooing, and notes that may be

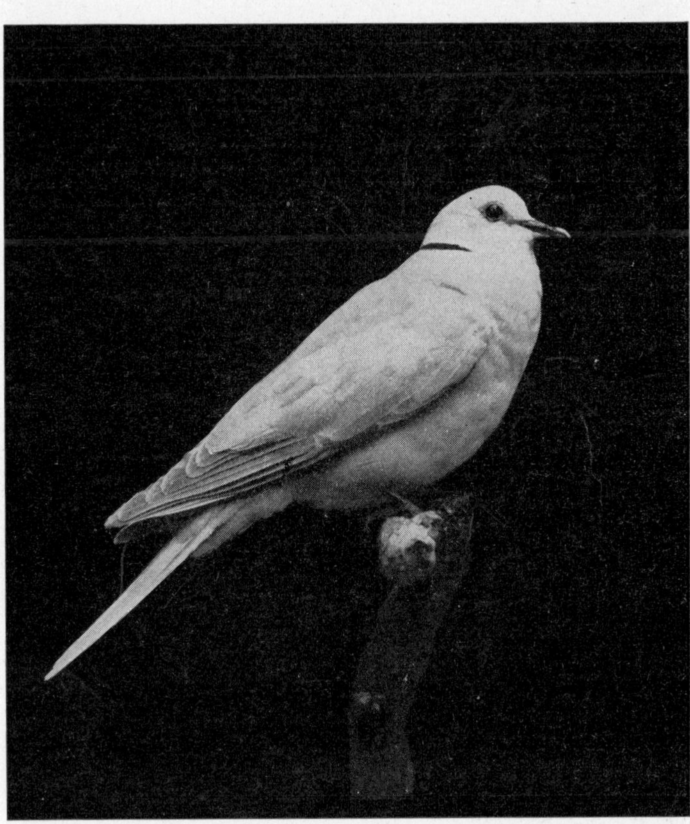

RINGED TURTLE DOVE *(Streptopelia risoria)*. Length: 11 inches. Male and female: pale ashy brown, lighter underneath. Neck is completely encircled with black collar. Tail is long and rounded with white in the corners. Range: introduced around Los Angeles. Voice: typical cooing.
Chicago Museum of Natural History

translated as *Who cooks for you?* One writer remarks that the call is "given with rather insulting emphasis."

White-wings are game birds under federal protection. They look very much like heavy Mourning Doves (11 to 12½ inches), but may be identified from that species by the large white patches in the wings. The rounded tail is tipped with large white spots on all but the central feathers, which appear in flight like a white band across the tail.

This species is a bird of the cactus deserts and mesquite regions of southeastern California, southern Arizona, southwestern New Mexico, and southern Texas. Nests are frail platforms of twigs, often placed in colonies in mesquite or other trees and shrubs. Its two eggs are creamy white. The whirring flight of the White-winged Dove make it one of the best known of the southwestern birds.

WHITE-FRONTED DOVE (*Leptotila verreauxi angelica*). Length: 12 inches. Male and female: dark brown above, with metallic sheen on back of head and back. Tail is blackish, tipped with white. Forehead and throat white, breast pale pink. Range: lower Rio Grande Valley. Voice: a low, *oo-whooooo*; at a distance only the *whooooooo* is audible.
Rudolph Hindemith, American Museum of Natural History

INCA DOVE

(Scardafella inca)

Color Plate Page 66

The diminutive Inca Dove of southern Arizona, New Mexico, and Texas was a bird of the mesquite and cactus before man moved west. Now it is semi-domesticated, feeding along roadsides and in yards and gardens, cooing from telephone wires, and nesting in shade trees and city shrubbery. It is gentle and unafraid.

Monotonous is the general description given to the Inca's constant cooing notes, which are mournful rather than soft and soothing like the call of the Western Mourning Dove. "The song is really more suggestive of a funeral procession than of a wedding journey," wrote W. L. Finley.

The Inca's best field mark is its long tail which is about half the bird's entire length of 8 inches. The tail has white edges. The body feathers have a scaled appearance due to the dark outlines of their edges. The wing coverts are chestnut brown, a mark to be looked for when the bird is in flight.

WHITE-FRONTED DOVE

(Leptotila verreauxi angelica)

In the lower Rio Grande Valley in Texas, secluding itself in the tall timber, one may confidently look for the White-fronted Dove, a species similar to the White-winged Dove, but lacking the conspicuous white wing patches of that bird. In flight, the white tipped tail and the reddish wing linings are noticeable. Its underparts are light or whitish.

The call of this Dove is described as exceedingly deep toned. It can be identified instantly by its characteristic utterance, a low ghostly *whooooo.*

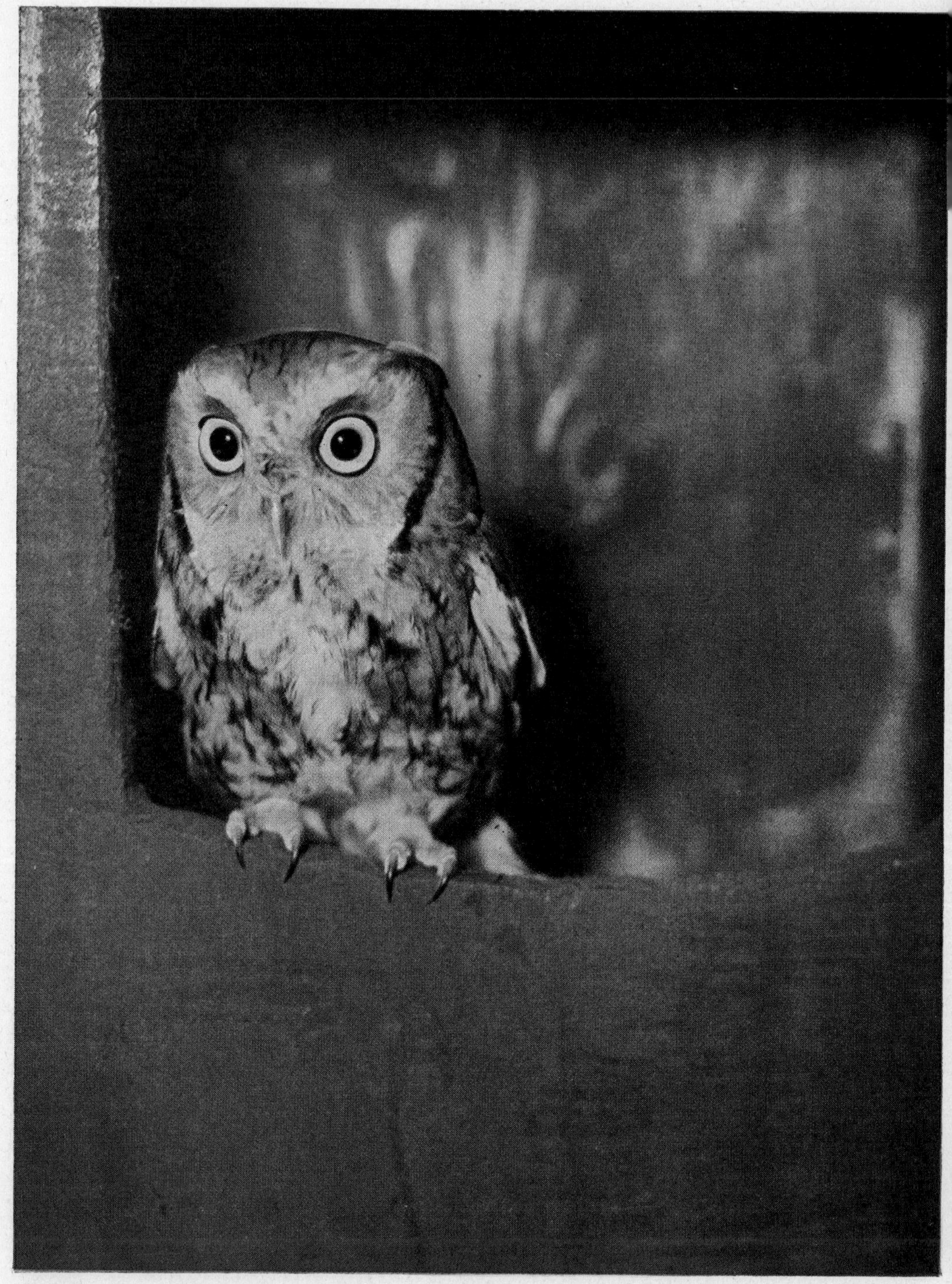

SCREECH OWL, RED PHASE (*Otus asio*). Length: 8 to 10 inches. Male and female: upperparts chestnut rufous; face, light cinnamon rufous. In this picture the ear tufts are flattened on head. Underparts white with spots of innamon rufous. Range: resident from Canada to Mexico. Voice: mournful wail running down scale.

Hal H. Harrison

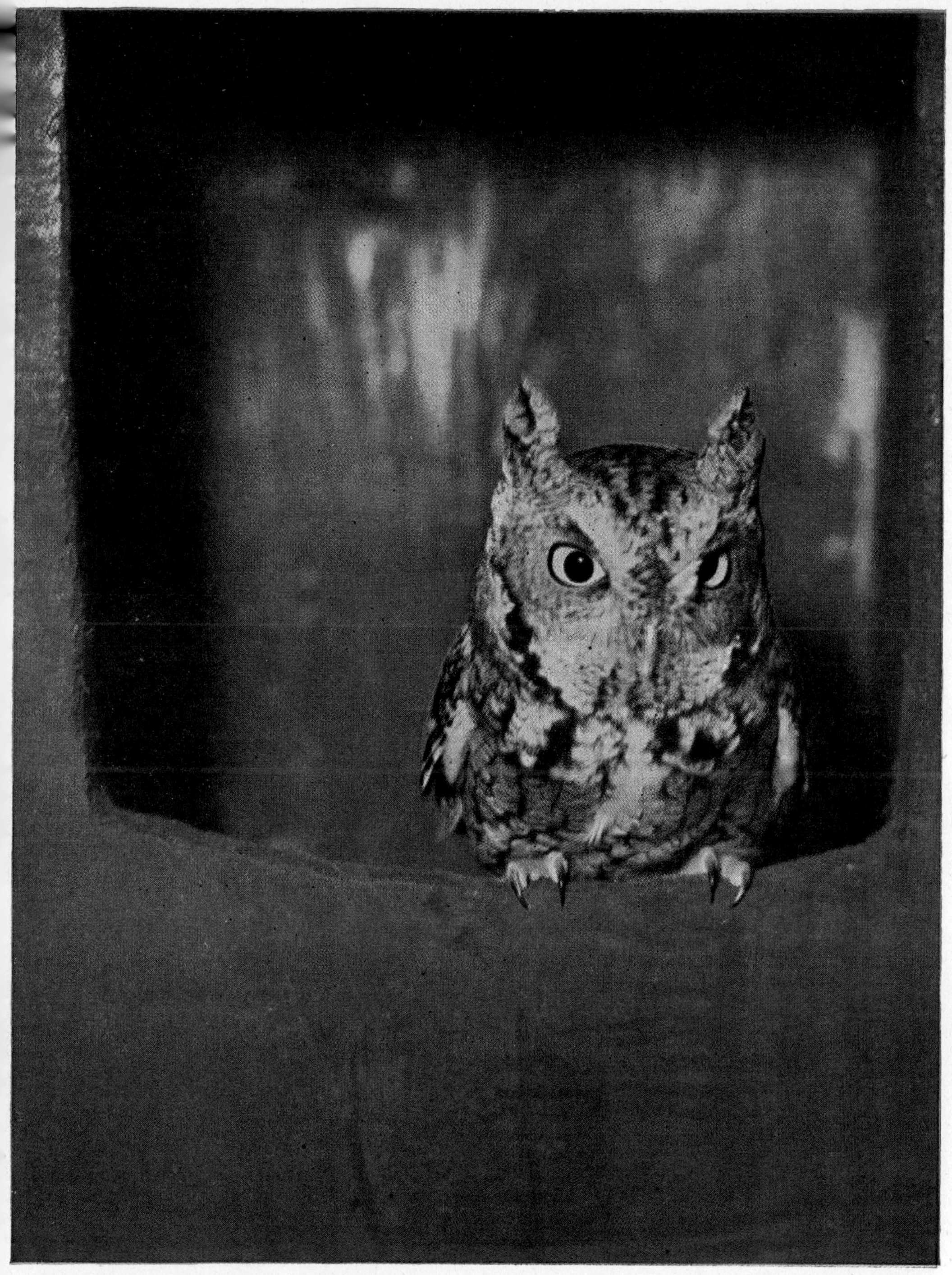

SCREECH OWL, GRAY PHASE (*Otus asio*). Length: 8 to 10 inches. Male and female: upperparts brownish gray streaked with black. Underparts white with broad streaks of black. Prominent ear tufts. Range: resident from Canada to Mexico. Voice: a mournful wail running down scale.
Hal H. Harrison

PARROTS

Family Psittacidae

Of the exotically colored Parrots which are found in the tropics and subtropics around the world, only two reach the United States, and one of those is probably extinct. The Parrots are characterized by their thick hooked beak and their strong feet which enable them to climb and grasp food.

CAROLINA PAROQUET

(Conuropsis carolinensis)

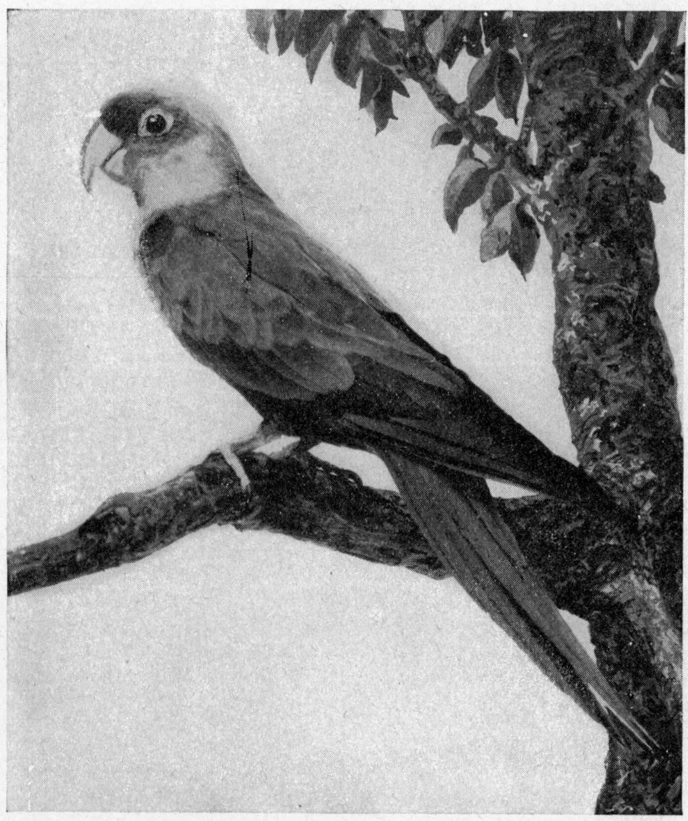

CAROLINA PAROQUET *(Conuropsis carolinensis)*. Length: 13 inches (tail, 7). Male and female: size of Mourning Dove. Bright green body with yellow head, becoming orange colored about base of bill. Range: formerly along coastal region from Florida to Virginia, but now nearly extinct. Voice: sharp, rolling call.
Chicago Natural History Museum

With the passing of the Carolina Paroquet, the United States lost its only native parrot. Except on rare occasions when the Thick-billed Parrot wanders from its home in Mexico into the mountains of southern Arizona and New Mexico, no wild Parrots are known today in this country.

In early days, the Carolina Paroquet *(C. c. carolinensis)* with its paler more western race, the Louisiana Paroquet *(C. c. ludovicianus)* ranged throughout the Gulf coast northward along the Atlantic coast to Pennsylvania and New York; in the Mississippi Valley north to Wisconsin and Ontario and westward to Colorado. Man's encroachment narrowed the bird's range until it was last seen in Florida in 1920. Rumors persist even now, however, that some individuals still reside in certain inaccessible swamps in South Carolina. It is remotely possible that the bird may not be extinct.

The Carolina Paroquet is the size of a Mourning Dove, bright green with a yellow head, and with orange at the base of the bill. A similar Mexican species, *Aratinga holochlora,* which might occur in southern Florida, is entirely green.

THICK-BILLED PARROT

(Rhynchopsitta pachyrhyncha)

Unless unknown individuals of the Carolina Paroquet still exist in remote areas of the southeast, the Thick-billed Parrot is the only Parrot that now occurs in the United States. The irregular appearance of these heavy-billed birds across the Mexican border in Arizona and New Mexico is our only claim for including this species in our American list. However, there have been instances when from seven hundred to a thousand birds have been observed in the Chiricahua Mountains.

THICK-BILLED PARROT *(Rhynchopsitta pachyrhyncha).* Length: 16.5 inches. Male and female: a sturdy bird, green with red on head, bend of wing and thigh. Has very heavy black curved bill. Immature: white bill and less red. Range: mountains of southeast Arizona, especially Chiricahua Mountains. Voice: harsh, confused, clattering sounds.
Rudolph Hindemith,
American Museum of Natural History

This species is about the size of a small Crow (16½ inches long). Its plumage is green except for a poppy red forehead. The bill is black, and tough and is used by the bird to extract pine seeds.

CUCKOOS and ANIS

Family Cuculidae

This family comprises the Cuckoos, the Ground Cuckoos or Roadrunners, and the Anis which bear little outward resemblance to the other members of the family. The American Cuckoo is not parasitic as are several of the European members of the family. Almost without exception the Cuckoos, certainly those of America, are dull colored birds with long tails.

YELLOW-BILLED CUCKOO

(Coccyzus americanus)

Color Plate Page 70

Unlike the famous European Cuckoo whose parasitic habits resemble those of our American Cowbird, the Yellow-billed Cuckoo and its close relative, the Blackbilled Cuckoo, build nests of their own and rear their own young. At times, however, both species are guilty of laying their eggs in each other's nests and even in the nests of other species of birds.

Both the Yellow-billed and the Black-billed cuckoos are notoriously poor nest builders, with the former being the worst. The nest is placed in shrubbery or in a tree four to ten feet above the ground. It is a shallow, frail platform of twigs, often so poorly lined that the eggs inside may be seen from beneath. I once found the nest of a Yellow-billed Cuckoo by first finding a broken egg on the ground beneath a wild grape tangle. The bird in leaving the platform nest had probably dislodged the egg.

The Yellow-billed Cuckoo lays three or four greenish blue eggs. The eggs are laid at infrequent intervals and incubation starts before the laying of the last egg. Thus it is not uncommon to find young of different ages, or even to find young and eggs together in the same nest. I found a nest in a thorn tree three and a half feet from the ground containing one young Cuckoo covered with quills and two young Cuckoos entirely feathered.

Cuckoos are hatched almost naked. They are repulsive black little creatures. As they grow, they sprout quills or feather sheaths. In approximately a week, these quills split open and feathers emerge. An observer watching the splitting of the sheaths wrote that "this process took place with such rapidity that it reminded me of the commotion in a corn popper or a rapidly blooming flower."

On the roofs of the mouths of nestling Cuckoos are large white spots. These are papillae or discs, arranged systematically, and apparently used as suction cups to grasp the smooth tapering bills of the feeding adults. When the young are in the quill stage, they are quite noisy, emitting a loud buzzy hiss, and beating their wings rapidly at the slightest disturbance.

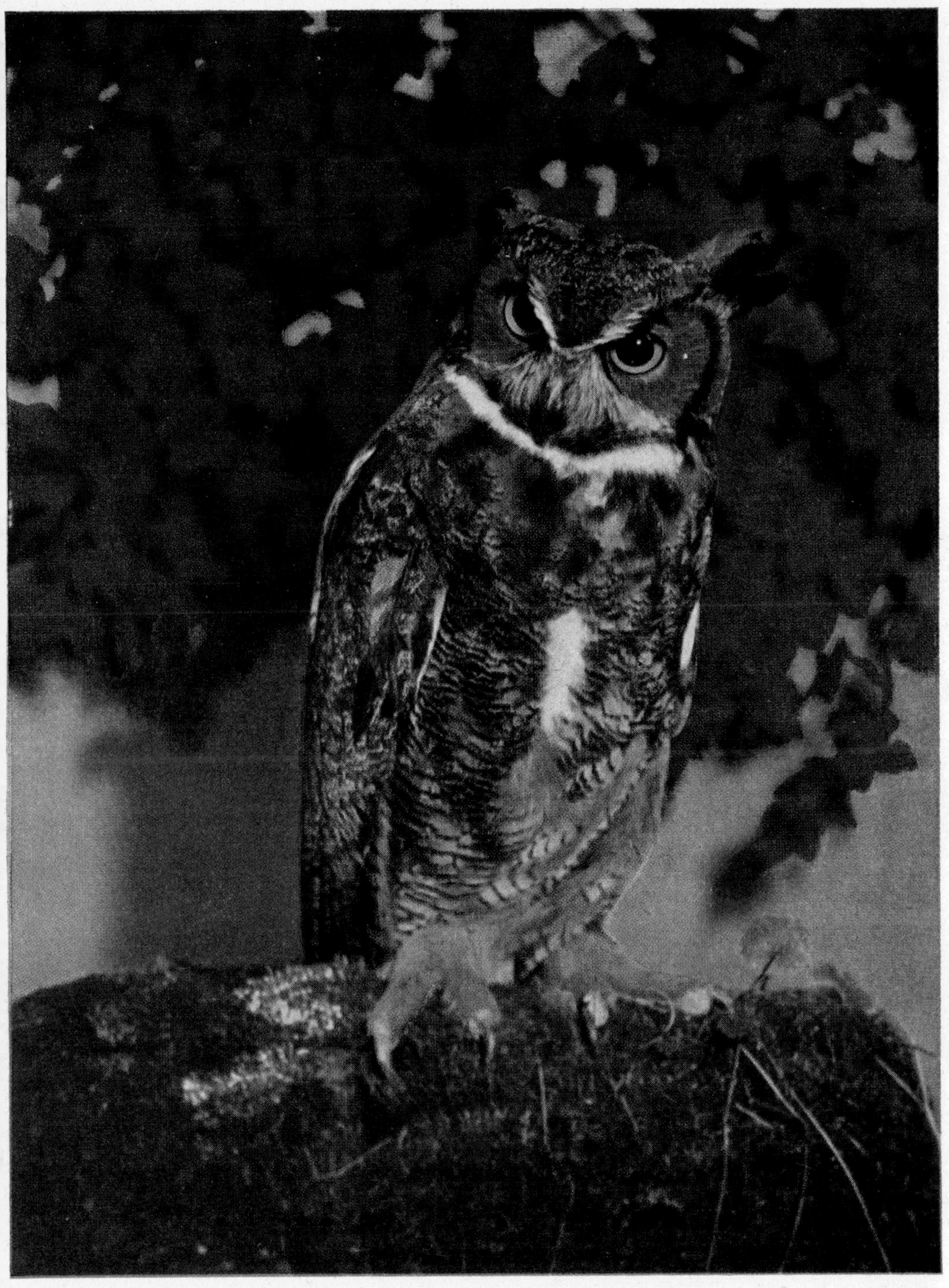

GREAT HORNED OWL (*Bubo virginianus*). Length: 24 to 33 inches. Male and female: upperparts mottled brownish, yellowish, white and black. White throat. Underparts whitish barred with dark. Ear tufts about two inches long; fully feathered toes. Range: Canada to Mexico. Voice: hooting; *hoo, hoo-oo, hoo, hoo.*

Hal H. Harrison

Shortly after the metamorphosis of quills into feathers, the young birds leave the nest and climb among the branches of the nesting tree. This stage is entered long before the young can fly, and the adults continue to feed them wherever they happen to be in the vicinity.

A complete discussion of the identification of the Yellow-billed Cuckoo and the Black-billed Cuckoo, both by appearance and song, is contained in the article on the Black-billed Cockoo. Both birds are known in rural areas as Rain Crows.

Both species are famous as destroyers of caterpillars, which most birds shun. Examination of the stomachs of 121 Cuckoos disclosed 2771 caterpillars, or an average of 23 for each bird. Tent caterpillars and fall web worms, both common pests, are relished by both Cuckoos.

The California Cuckoo *(C. a. occidentalis)* is a western form of the Yellow-billed Cuckoo *(C. a. americanus)*. The latter form is the more widely distributed and nests from North Dakota and New Brunswick to northeastern Mexico and Florida.

MAYNARD'S CUCKOO

(Coccyzus minor maynardi)

The Black-eared, or Maynard's, Cuckoo is a breeding bird of Florida and the West Indies. It is readily distinguished from the Yellow-billed Cuckoo by the buff color of the underparts and the black mark or "ears" on the gray head. Even young birds which do not have the ear marking can be distinguished by the buff underparts. Its voice is more deliberate than the Yellow-billed, being a deep *gaw-gaw-gaw.*

BLACK-BILLED CUCKOO

(Coccyzus erythropthalmus)

Color Plate Page 71

Bird watchers do not have much difficulty identifying a Cuckoo; the big problem is, which Cuckoo is it—the Yellow-billed or the Black-billed?

From their names, one might imagine that it is just a matter of glancing at the color of the bill of the bird in question, and so it is, if you happen to be a few feet away. But most observers never get that close to a shy and retiring Cuckoo. Even under such favorable circumstances, it must be remembered that only the lower mandible of the Yellow-billed Cuckoo is yellow; the upper mandible is black, as are both mandibles in the Black-billed species. Both birds are about the same size, 11 to 13 inches long.

More noticeable in the field, however, are the rufous wing feathers of the Yellow-billed Cuckoo, entirely lacking in the Black-bill. Then, if the bird under observation is at rest and the under tail feathers are in view, the Black-bill may be distinguished by the narrow white tips of the gray brown feathers. In the Yellow-bill, large white spots appear at the tips of the black tail feathers.

One has to be close enough to check the mandibles to be able to note also that the eyelids of the Black-billed Cuckoo form a red ring around the eye, while the ring in the Yellow-billed Cuckoo is yellow.

There is one means of identification which the experienced observer considers conclusive—the songs of the two birds. To the inexperienced, this method is not easy for, although the songs are different generally, all parts of the songs are not. Both birds emit

SMOOTH-BILLED ANI (*Crotophaga ani*). Length: 12.5 inches. Male and female: black, with iridescent bronze and green coloring. Range: Louisiana and southern Florida. Voice: a whining whistle.
New York Zoological Society

phrases that are so much alike that no one can distinguish them, but anyone can learn to identify the birds after hearing their entire songs.

The song of the Black-bill is prefaced with a gutteral gargling note, followed by a series of *kow-kow-kow* notes given in couplets or triplets, one syllable in each set being accented, and each set given in regular measured time, not retarded at the end. The song of the Yellow-bill, on the other hand, is a prolonged series of rapid syllables, *kuk-kuk-kuk-kuk-kuk,* ending with a series of retarded notes, *kowp-kowp-kowp-kowp,* becoming slower and slower as the song runs down the scale.

The breeding range of the Black-billed Cuckoo extends over the northern half of the United States and southern Canada, east of the Rockies. It is decidedly a bird of the woodlands.

Although its nest is flimsy, it is usually more substantial than that of its relative. It consists of a platform of twigs lined with soft material. Two or three blue-green eggs are laid. These are somewhat darker and a bit smaller than the eggs of the Yellow-bill.

Both sexes incubate, and the young hatch in ten or eleven days. The unusual feeding habits of the young, described fully under the Yellow-billed Cuckoo, apply to this species also.

Like the Yellow-billed the Black-billed Cuckoo is sometimes parasitic on other birds. It is known to have laid its eggs in the nests of the Chipping Sparrow, Yellow Warbler, Wood Pewee, Cardinal, Cedar Waxwing, Catbird, Wood Thrush, and the other Cuckoo.

Although the complete winter range of the two common Cuckoos is not definitely charted, both birds are known to migrate to South America.

ROAD-RUNNER

(*Geococcyx californianus*)

Color Plate Page 73

The Road-runner, or Chaparral Cock, is known to many who have never seen this funny bird of the southwest. Its odd appearance and its unusual habits, especially that of eating whole snakes and lizards, has gained for this strange member of the Cuckoo family a reputation that extends far beyond its range in California, Utah, and Colorado south into Mexico.

Like so many other birds of the desert or semi-arid regions, the Road-runner always prefers to run rather than to fly from danger. Its reputation in that regard is well founded, for it has been clocked by motorists as fast as fifteen miles per hour. Dr. George M. Sutton, who knows the bird well, declares that for a short distance the bird can exceed even that speed.

In appearance, the Road-runner, which the Mexicans call *Paisano,* or fellow countryman, is long and slender (20 to 24 inches) with a shaggy crest, a tail as long as its body, short rounded wings, and large strong feet. The upperparts are conspicuously streaked with brown and white; the underparts are whitish, with the chest streaked with black. A naked area about the eyes is colorful—light blue and orange red.

The Road-runner's diet of lizards and snakes is another of its characteristics that has been advertised far and wide. Its menu is by no means specialized, however, for it is also fond of insects, especially grasshoppers, rodents, small birds, fruits, and seeds.

Regarding the Road-runner's song, Dr. Sutton, who has heard it many times at dawn, describes it thusly: "Here (the eastern rim of a mesa, a dead tree, or high cactus), directing his bill downward until it almost touches his toes, he begins to coo. *COO, COO, COO, OOH, OOH, OOH, OOH, OOH,* he calls, pumping out the syllables in a hoarse, throaty voice, his head rising a little with each *COO* until the bill points upward, the pitch of the song meanwhile dropping gradu-

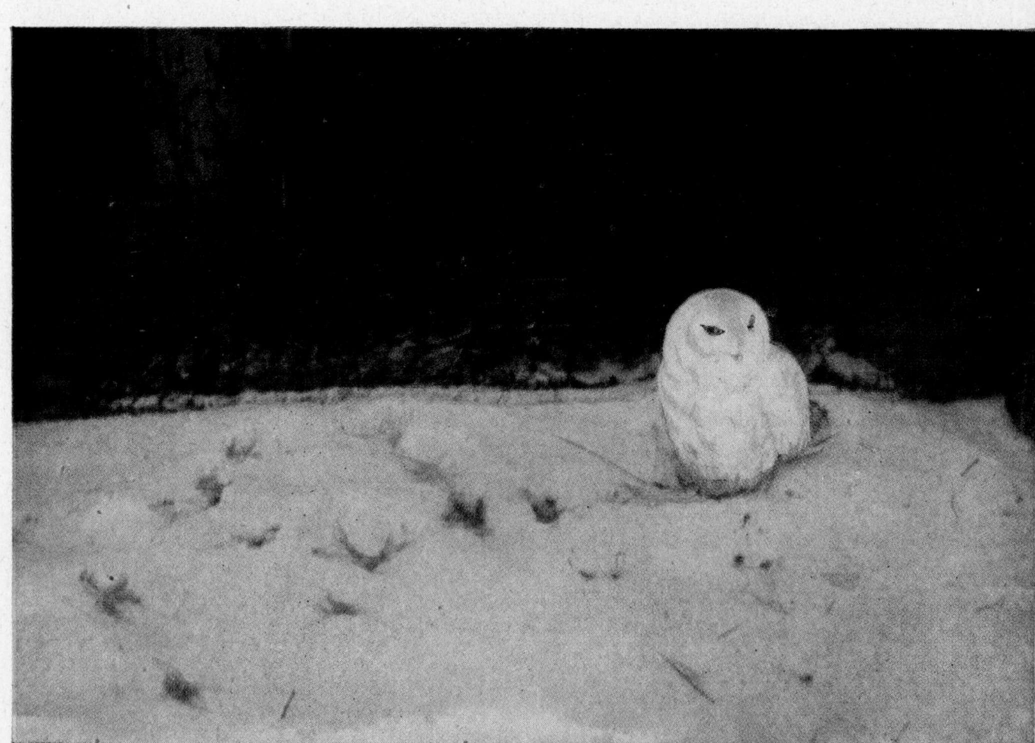

SNOWY OWL *(Nyctea scandiaca).* Length: 20 to 26 inches. Male: pure white body speckled with brown on crown, shoulders, back and tail. Lacks ear tufts. Female: similar to male but more heavily barred. Range: Arctic, wintering to Middle States. Voice: shrill plaintive note.
Helen Cruikshank

ally lower. So he starts with head low and coo high, and ends vice versa. Cattlemen say that before he begins his song he 'lays his beak on the rock.' "

SMOOTH-BILLED ANI

(Crotophaga ani)

The Smooth-billed Ani is a West Indian bird which is occasionally found in southern Florida and Louisiana. It is coal black, about 12 inches long, resembling a Grackle except for its huge curved bill which gives it a peculiar Parrot-like appearance. It is loose jointed and ungainly in flight. Its voice is a long drawn, whiny whistle.

The birds live in flocks, often building community nests which are rough structures of sticks. Several females lay their three to five bluish eggs in one such nest. The Ani feeds on insects, lizards, and berries, and follows cattle from which they pick off the ticks and insects.

GROOVE-BILLED ANI

(Crotophaga sulcirostris sulcirostris)

Similar in appearance to the Smooth-billed Ani, the Groove-bill is distinguished by three grooves in the upper mandible, which are not readily discernible in the field. The Groove-bill's range is the lower Rio Grande Valley, with an occasional appearance in Arizona. Its voice and habits are like the Smooth-bill.

OWLS

Families Tytonidae and Strigidae

The Owls are nocturnal birds of prey which swallow their victims whole, disgorging the indigestible portions in the form of pellets. The two families are divided generally by the shape of the face, the Barn Owls having a rather heart shaped face, and the other Owls having round faces.

The nests of Owls are usually built in holes or they may take over the abandoned nests of Hawks or Crows.

BARN OWL

(Tyto alba pratincola)

Color Plate Page 76

As I write this, I have fresh in my mind a Barn Owl's nest that I visited yesterday afternoon. It is in an old Pigeon loft fastened to the inside of a barn near the roof. Six white eggs are in the process of incubation, and these are laid on the floor of the box with no

BURROWING OWL *(Speotyto cunicularia).* Length: 9 inches. Male and female: small and brown spotted above with whitish, below light gray barred with brown. Range: western prairies to Minnesota and western Iowa and Louisiana. Also prairies of central and southern Florida. Voice: a shaky chuckling call; high mellow night song; *coo-co-hoo* or *coo-hoo.*

Helen Cruikshank

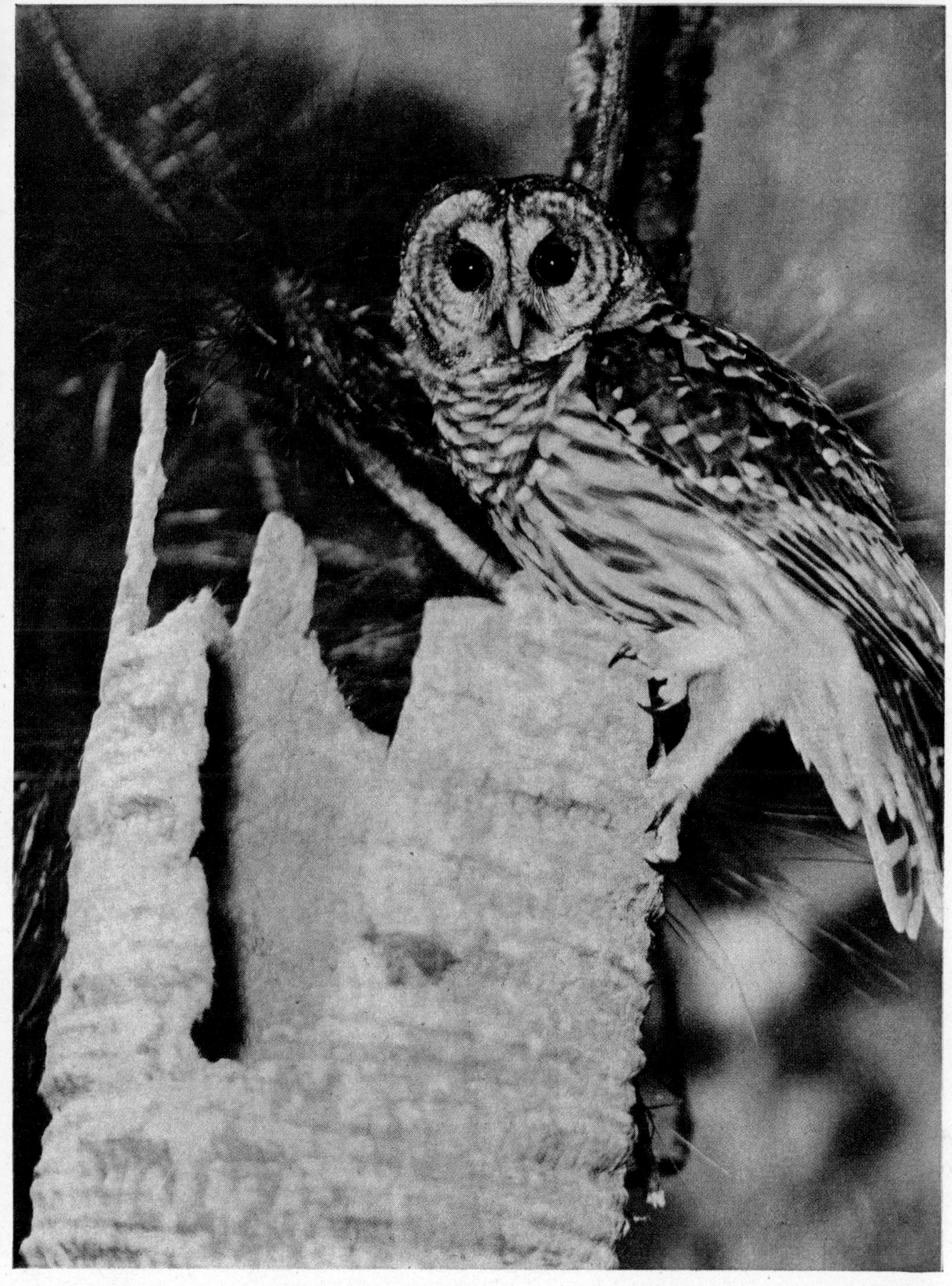

BARRED OWL (*Strix varia*). Length: 18 to 22 inches. Male and female: brown upperparts spotted with white. Brown eyes. Light gray underparts streaked lengthwise on belly and crosswise on breast with dark brown. Range: Canada to Gulf of Mexico, Florida and Texas. Voice: eight accented hoots in two groups of four, *hoohoo-hoohoo . . . hoohoo-hoohooaw.*

Samuel A. Grimes

semblance of a nest except a litter of broken pellets that the owl has gathered in that spot. In the corner, not more than a foot from the eggs, I counted the bodies of eight freshly killed mice which, I presume, were stored there for consumption during the day.

The finding of these dead mice (an experience duplicated by other observers) plus the skulls of many rodents found in the pellets or castings disgorged by these owls, are a key to the bird's economic importance. Fortunate is the farmer who gives shelter to a pair of these valuable birds. He has, indeed, found a "better mouse trap."

This Owl chooses a wide variety of nesting sites, but all are located in or adjacent to open country where the birds may hunt at night for mice, rats, shrews, moles, and gophers. Birds form a very small percentage of the food taken. The Barn Owl nests in such sites as silos, water towers, barns, deserted buildings, church towers, hollow trees, mine shafts, and burrows in clay banks.

The Barn, or Monkey-faced, Owl can be mistaken for no other. Its white heart shaped face is sufficient to identify it, but also evident are its long legs and its golden brown upperparts combined with whitish underparts. Like other Owls, its flight is silent and mothlike, the head appearing large and out of proportion to the body. The bird is 15 to 20 inches long.

The common note of this Owl is a harsh hissing, often uttered while in flight. A rasping scream that pierces the night air is a rather frightening cry to many. A snapping, clicking noise, made with the bill, is characteristic of adults and young alike.

Young Barn Owls are in the nest for over two months, and many bird watchers have found them interesting as well as amusing subjects for study as they grow up. In addition to their queer antics, they utter an assortment of sounds, such as hissing, whining, screaming, and snoring.

The Barn Owl is a bird of worldwide distribution. In the United States it breeds from coast to coast, and south from Massachusetts, southern Ontario, Minnesota, and southern British Columbia. Although this Owl is migratory, wintering individuals are not uncommon in the northern states. For two winters, I studied the castings from a Barn Owl that was a permanent resident in a small cave high in a Pennsylvania cliff.

SCREECH OWL

(Otus asio)

Color Plates Pages 80 and 81

Screech Owls do not screech. They emit a wavering, tremulous cry, an eerie, ghostly sound that carries well through the still night. To many superstitious folks, this call is a bad omen from which many fantastic stories have arisen. In parts of the south, it is claimed that when an Owl lands on the gable of a house, someone in the house will die before morning unless everyone turns his pockets inside out, turns the left shoes upside down, and throws some salt in the fire.

The Screech Owl is the smallest Owl with "horns" or tufts on its head. Many believe that these feather tufts are the bird's ears, but they are only ornaments. The outer openings of the true ears are located at the borders of stiffly feathered eye discs.

In the east, this little Owl (8 to 10 inches long) may be found in either of two color phases—red or gray. This is called dichromatism, and science can offer no satisfactory explanation for it. The birds mate indiscriminately with no regard for color. A red and gray mating may produce all gray young, all red young, or some of each. There appears to be no eugenic formula for the condition. Western Screech Owls, strange to say, are not dichromatic, and are all gray.

In feeding, the adult Owl swallows its prey whole or in large pieces. If the meal happens to be a small bird or a mouse, the fur, feathers, and bones are all swallowed. Later the indigestible parts are expelled from the stomach in the form of pellets. By examination of these castings, biologists may ascertain quite accurately the bird's animal diet. Screech Owls, it has been discovered, are guilty of killing a large number of small birds. Included in their diet, however, are many insects, crayfish, mammals, fish, spiders, and reptiles. The bird-killing habit is excused by Dr. Arthur A. Allen of Cornell University on the grounds that it is a powerful factor in the balance of nature. He points out that a single pair of Robins in five years might increase to over 15,000 birds if all their youngsters lived and reproduced.

Like most Owls, the Screech Owl is much commoner than the average person realizes, but because of its nocturnal habits, it is not often observed. Owls can see in the daytime, but it is instinctive for members of this group to hunt at night. They spend the day sleeping inside cavities or sunning in the open.

Screech Owls are cavity nesters, laying four or five white eggs. On occasion they will accept man-made nest boxes. Nesting occurs from March to May. The young are cared for in the nest until they are about a month old. They are then taught by the parent birds to hunt their own food.

The Screech Owl is a resident bird wherever found. With its many geographic forms, it is generally distributed over most of North America.

FLAMMULATED SCREECH OWL

(Otus flammeolus flammeolus)

The Flammulated Screech Owl is a rare western species that is very locally distributed in high mountains from eastern Washington and Idaho south to Mexico. It is much smaller than a Screech Owl (6½ to 7 inches) and has short rounded ear tufts, dark chocolate brown eyes, and a variegated pattern of browns and grays.

FLAMMULATED SCREECH OWL *(Otus flammeolus flammeolus)*. Length: 6.5 to 7 inches. Male and female: much smaller than Screech Owl, largely gray with tiny rounded ear-tufts. *Only western Owl having brown eyes.* Range: high mountains from Mexico to eastern Washington and Idaho. Voice: a single gentle hoot, repeated steadily at intervals of two or more seconds.
Chicago Natural History Museum

SPOTTED SCREECH OWL (*Otus trichopsis aspersus*). Length: 8.5 inches. Male and female: upperparts dark gray mixed with black, gray and tan; large white spots on underparts. Range: in canyons between 4000 and 6500 feet in mountains of southern Arizona. Voice: four notes; *booobooboo-boo, booobooboo-boo,* etc. (three notes, a pause, and a fourth note). At times, a repeated four-syllabled *choo-oo-coo-coo;* also series of four to seven quick, evenly spaced notes, *boo boo boo boo boo boo boo.*
Chicago Natural History Museum

The song of this tiny creature is said to be two notes, *boo-boot,* with the second note louder than the first. Given at regular intervals, the utterance becomes monotonous.

SPOTTED SCREECH OWL

(*Otus trichopsis aspersus*)

Finding the Spotted Screech Owl in the canyons of the southern Arizona mountains is an easier job by night than by day. Its call of *boot-boot-boot-boot-boot-boot* repeated rapidly is one of its best field marks. In a variation of this call, the *boots* are given in a series of four notes, the last note in each series being slightly delayed.

To recognize by sight this permanent resident Owl of the Huachuca Mountains, look for the large white spots on the lower hind neck, scapulars, and greater wing coverts. The larger black spots on the underparts are also distinguishing marks. The facial feathers have greatly developed bristly tips.

GREAT-HORNED OWL

(*Bubo virginianus*)

Color Plate Page 85

What Hawks are to the daylight hours, Owls are to the night. Where the Hawks leave off, the Owls begin. Together the two families of birds present a twenty-four-hours-a-day vigil against many of man's enemies, particularly rats and mice.

The feeding habits of most of the Owls have been ascertained through the analysis of their castings, and biologists have proved conclusively that as a family the owls are highly beneficial to man. This information has led to the legal protection of most Owls. The Great-horned Owl is a notable exception, however.

The feeling of resentment against the Great-horned Owl is so great, especially among hunters, that some states offer a bounty as a reward for killing both the adults and the nestlings. The attitude in such cases seems to be that this big Owl is trespassing upon man's private property when it feeds upon rabbits and game birds. Such bounty systems are always subjects of much debate wherever they are in force.

The Great-horned Owl has a ravenous appetite. It attacks and eats most any living thing, excepting the larger mammals, but including skunks and house cats. Its food depends largely upon what prey is accessible in its territory. Some individuals develop a taste for poultry and these, most assuredly, should be controlled. In other cases, however, the feeding habits of individuals have been found to be more beneficial to man.

The Great-horned Owl is the only large Owl with ear tufts or "horns." It has a wingspread of over four feet, and is about two feet in length. The similar Long-eared Owl is much smaller, and has its horns set close together, not far apart as in the Great-Horned. The Long-eared Owl is streaked lengthwise below, while the Great-horned is barred crosswise.

None of our native birds nest earlier than the Great-horned Owl. February is the usual time for laying the two or three white eggs in a renovated nest of a Red-tailed Hawk or Crow. Occasionally, the Owl will nest in a tree cavity. During the twenty-eight day incubation period, the eggs must be protected at all times against freezing, and it is not uncommon to find the female on her nest covered with snow. The young remain in the nest for about two months after hatching, and during that time the adults are vicious in the protection of their charges. Intruding

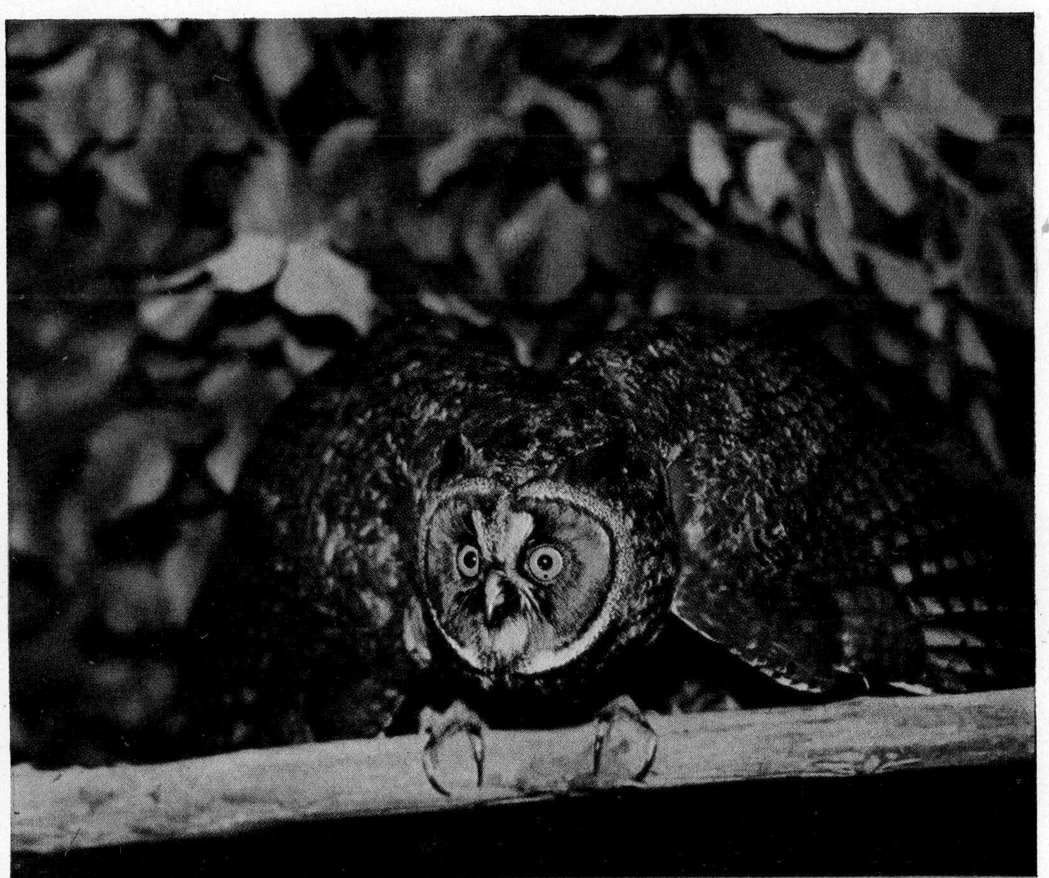

LONG-EARED OWL (*Asio otus wilsonianus*). Length: 13 to 16 inches. Male and female: upperparts grayish brown streaked with white and yellowish brown. Breast grayish white streaked with grayish brown. Ear tufts are blackish and close together. Range: Newfoundland and Ontario south to Virginia and northern Texas, winters from southern Canada to Gulf of Mexico. Voice: mournful *hoo, hoo, hoo.*

Hal H. Harrison

HAWK OWL *(Surnia ulula caparoch)*. Length: 15 to 17 inches. Male and female: upperparts dark brown speckled with white; below, white, barred with brown. No ear-tufts. Poorly developed facial disk. Range: northern North America; breeding northward to tree limits of Alaska. Voice: varied series of whines, whistles and screams. Flight-call sounds like *pi-reek, pi-reek*.
Chicago Natural History Museum

humans are sometimes subject to actual attack.

The Great-horned Owl is considered a "five-hooter," the Barred Owl, an "eight-hooter." The common call consists of five notes, thus: *hoo-hoo, hoo; hoo-hoo*. Three hoots or six hoots are also given, but never eight. The Barred Owl renders its hoots in two groups of four.

The range of the Great-horned Owl extends from the limit of trees in North America to South America. Ten geographic races of the bird are recognized in North America, some of the more northern races being much paler in color.

SNOWY OWL

(Nyctea scandiaca)

Color Plate Page 88

The average bird watcher in the United States must wait for an "Owl year" before he may hope to have the rare privilege of seeing the great white Owl of the north, the Snowy Owl. Although wandering individuals may be found in the northern states any winter, it is only at intervals of four or more years that a mass invasion occurs, referred to as an "Owl year." It is the failure of the Snowy Owl's food supply in the Arctic that causes it to fly south in search of sustenance.

This beautiful creature, arriving in our country legally unprotected, is wantonly slaughtered by gunners who proudly display their trophies, gallant birds reduced to a mass of blood-stained white feathers. At home on the Arctic tundra the Snowy Owl feeds on lemmings, Arctic hares, and snowshoe rabbits. Forced south, it is compelled by circumstances to find its food as best it can. At that time, rabbits, rodents, and birds comprise the greater part of its diet.

The male Snowy Owl is almost pure white; the larger female's white plumage is flecked with dusky bars. The bird ranges in size from 20 to 26 inches. The round head is tuftless. On its breeding grounds in the Arctic, the bird places its nest on the open tundra.

HAWK OWL

(Surnia ulula caparoch)

A daylight hunting Owl of the far north, the American Hawk Owl, like its larger cousin, the Snowy Owl, enters the United States as a winter visitor only when forced south by a failing food supply. Its visits are not as regular as those of the Snowy, nor does it ever invade the States in as great numbers.

The name of Hawk Owl comes from the bird's general appearance and its manner of hunting. Its body is slender, more Hawklike than Owl-like. It perches conspicuously in the open, watching for prey in a Hawklike attitude. It has a habit of jerking its long rounded tail in the manner of a Sparrow Hawk, and its flight is reminiscent of the Falcons. Despite these Hawklike traits, it still has the noiseless flight of an owl.

Other distinguishing characteristics of this Arctic visitor are its medium size, 15 to 17 inches long (smaller than a Crow), rounded head without tufts, and its gray-brown back and cross barred breast and abdomen. The facial disc is white, bordered on the sides with black. The legs are feathered to the toes.

PYGMY OWL

(Glaucidium gnoma)

In the forested mountain ranges of western United States, the Pygmy Owl, smaller than a Robin (about 7 inches long), lives throughout the year. Two color phases occur, one gray, one reddish. It is an "earless" Owl with a black-striped breast and a tail longer in proportion to the bird than in any other Owl. The perky angle at which the tail is held while the bird is perched is unusual for an Owl.

Another un-Owl-like characteristic of the Pygmy is its flight. While all the other members of the Owl tribe fly noiselessly like big moths, the Pygmy's flight sounds like that of any ordinary bird. Its manner of flight has been described as both like the Sparrow Hawk and the Shrike. The latter comparison arises from its habit of dropping on prey with folded wings, and then beating the wings rapidly to regain its perch.

Regarding the feeding habits of this Owl, it is admitted that during the nesting season, it often preys on small birds, but during the remainder of the year, the food taken is largely insects, small mammals, and reptiles. For such a small creature, the Pygmy shows unusual courage and fearlessness in its hunting habits. It often hunts in broad daylight.

The usual call note of this Owl has been likened by many observers to the cooing of a Mourning Dove. Others detect in it a cuckoolike utterance. Hoffmann describes it as "a soft whistle,

PIGMY OWL *(Glaucidium gnoma)*. Length: 7 to 7.5 inches. Male and female: very small, 'earless' Owl; rusty brown or gray brown with a striped breast. A black patch on each side of hind neck is a good mark when seen. Range: Canada south to southern California, southern Arizona and New Mexico. Voice: mellow, whistled notes ending with two or three slow, deliberate notes as *too-too-too-too-too-too-too-too-too-took-took-took*. Commonest note, a single *took* uttered every two to three seconds.

Joseph S. Dixon

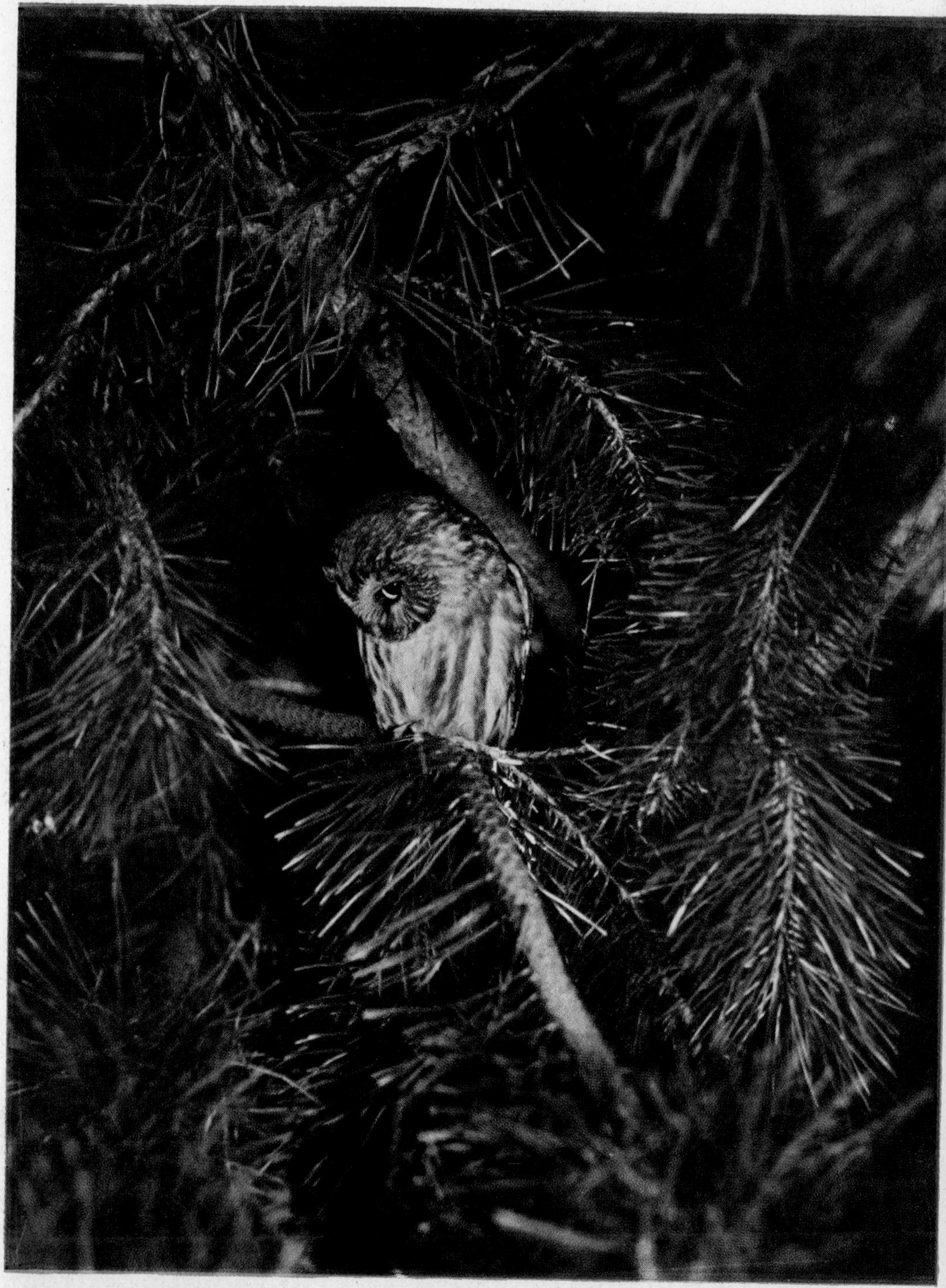

SAW-WHET OWL (*Aegolius acadia acadia*). Length: 7 to 8.5 inches. Male and female: dark brown upperparts sprinkled with white. Underparts whitish striped with brown. *Immature in summer:* chocolate brown with *blackish* face and white patches forming V between the eyes. Range: from Canada to Indiana and West Virginia. Winters south to Louisiana and Virginia. Voice: mellow whistled repetitious note, *too too too too too too* etc.

R. T. Congdon

repeated either singly or in a rapid succession of staccato notes, suggesting the syllables *kew, kew, kew, kew;* the note is frequently heard during the day."

Throughout its extensive western range, nesting occurs in forested areas in tree cavities, usually abandoned Woodpecker holes. Several geographic forms of the Pygmy Owl are recognized, two of which occur in the United States. They are the Coast Pygmy Owl (*G. g. grinelli*) and the California Pygmy (*G. g. californicum*).

ELF OWL IN GIANT CACTUS (*Micrathene whitneyi whitneyi*). Length: 6 inches. Male and female: very small, with no ear-tufts, having white eyebrows. In gray phase, the upperparts are brownish gray spotted with yellowish, and underparts a mixture of gray, white and light brown. In brown phase the upperparts are tobacco brown. Range: southeast California, southern Arizona, southwest New Mexico and southwest Texas. Voice: a series of quick, high, notes, *whi-whi-whi-whi-whi-whi,* often becoming chattery, or *chew-chew-chew-chew-chew* or *teeok-teeok-teeok-teeok*, etc. rapidly uttered.
Karl H. Maslowski

FERRUGINOUS PYGMY OWL

(*Glaucidium brasilianum cactorum*)

While the range of the Ferruginous Pygmy Owl is confined to the delta of the Rio Grande and southern Arizona, it is best distinguished from the more widely distributed Pygmy Owl by its preference for low-lying river valleys.

Its breast is brown striped rather than black, and it has a habit of jerking its tail. It is slightly smaller than the Pygmy Owl. The call is a *chu-chu-chu,* repeated many times, so that it has been said to sound like a small steam engine chuffing.

ELF OWL

(*Micrathene whitneyi whitneyi*)

In abandoned Woodpecker holes in giant Saguaro cacti of the south west lives our tiniest Owl, the Elf Owl. It is no larger than a Sparrow, considerably smaller than the Screech Owl, and at least an inch smaller than the Pygmy Owl, from which it may be recognized by its shorter tail. The Elf Owl is earless. Like the Screech Owl, it is dichromatic, being found in both red and gray plumage phases.

The Elf Owl is largely nocturnal in its habits, flying across the desert at night in search of the insects upon which it feeds almost entirely. During the daytime this dwarf Owl is sometimes seen sitting in the entrance to its cavity in a giant cactus.

The Elf Owl lays two to three spotless white eggs. The young are similar to the adults but lack the cinnamon buff on the face.

BURROWING OWL

(Speotyto cunicularia)

Color Plate Page 90

Burrowing Owls are small brown Owls of the open prairies, round headed without ear tufts, long legged, and short tailed. They are about 9 inches long. They are usually found on the ground in the daytime as well as at night. A curious bobbing habit is characteristic of the species.

Old burrows of prairie dogs and other mammals are the usual homes of the Burrowing Owls, although on occasions they dig their own burrows. They nest in these holes as well as use them for shelter throughout the year. The alarm note of the Burrowing Owl, often heard as it makes a quick dash for the safety of its burrow, is a *cack, cack, cack, cack.* Its song is a series of mournful *coos.*

The Western Burrowing Owl *(S. c. hypugaea)* breeds from British Columbia and Manitoba south to western Iowa and Louisiana. The Florida Burrowing Owl *(S. c. floridana)* is found in the prairies of central and southern Florida.

BARRED OWL

(Strix varia)

Color Plate Page 91

Of all the so-called "Hoot Owls," the Barred Owl is the most proficient hooter. From the depths of the deepest forests, especially the wooded swamps, hemlock groves, and pine woods, comes the Barred Owl's eight hoots—*hoo-hoo-hoo-hoo—hoo-hoo-hoo-tohooah,* the last note greatly emphasized. The calls are varied, however, and are not always in perfect order of eight. The hooting is at its height during the early part of the evening and before sunrise. During the day, this Owl retires to the seclusion of its forested retreat.

The Barred is a large gray Owl, 18 to 22 inches long, almost the size of the Great-horned Owl, with a large round puffy head lacking horns or ear tufts. Unlike most Owls, whose eyes are yellow, the Barred Owl's eyes are brown. The underparts are barred crosswise on the breast, and streaked lengthwise on the belly.

Early in the spring, the Barred Owl starts to

SPOTTED OWL ON NEST *(Strix occidentalis)*. Length: 19 inches. Male and female: large, dark brown owl with round puffy head. The heavily spotted and barred underparts, and large dark eyes will distinguish the bird. Range: mountains from Mexico to southern Colorado, Arizona and Cascades of central California. Also coast belt from California to Washington. Voice: a high-pitched hooting. Usually given in groups of three: *hoo, hoo, hoo,* or four, *hoo-whoowhoo-whooo.*

J. S. Ligon

GREAT GRAY OWL *(Strix nebulosa nebulosa)*. Length: 24 to 33 inches. Male and female: dusky grayish brown body and underparts striped with grayish white lengthwise. The eyes are yellow and the bird is earless. Large facial disks. Young: downy, buffy white. Range: Arctic North America, wintering south in our most northern states. Voice: similar to Screech Owl.
William H. Carrick

nest, often in a hollow tree, but just as often in the open in an old nest of a Crow or Hawk. Two to four pure white eggs are laid. Incubation requires from three to four weeks. Young are hatched blind and remain in the nest for well over a month.

The food of the Barred Owl is varied, but includes many rodents, birds, reptiles, amphibians, fish, and insects. The type of food is determined largely by what is available in the area. In its hunting, the Barred is less ferocious than the Great-horned, its talons being incapable of killing prey as large as that of the Great-horned.

The Barred is one of the commonest eastern Owls, breeding east of the Rockies and south of Hudson Bay. It is nonmigratory. Three geographic races are recognized.

SPOTTED OWL

(Strix occidentalis)

The Spotted Owl is the western representative of the Eastern Barred Owl, and is often called the Western Barred Owl. Although the colors of the two races are similar, the bars of the Barred Owl's plumage are replaced with spots in the western species.

No other western Owl resembles this large (19 inches) round faced, earless bird of the deep woods. It also differs from other Owls in its fearlessness (or stupidity) in allowing humans to approach it closely.

The A. O. U. Check-list recognizes three races of the Spotted Owl. These are the California Spotted Owl *(S. o. occidentalis)*, the Northern Spotted Owl *(S. o. caurina)*, and the Mexican Spotted Owl *(S. o. lucida)*. The species breeds from Mexico north to southern Colorado, Arizona, central California, and along the coastal belt from Mariposa County, California to Washington.

GREAT GRAY OWL

(Strix nebulosa nebulosa)

Largest of the North American Owls, the Great Gray Owl of the far

CHUCK-WILL'S-WIDOW (*Caprimulgus carolinensis*). Length: 11 to 13 inches. Male and female: brown general tone, streaked with black, plain brown throat, broken whitish band across upper breast and stiff bristles around base of bill. Range: Florida north to Maryland, Ohio, Indiana, and Kansas. Winters from Florida south. Voice: *chuck-will-wid'ow*, accented on second and third syllables.
Helen Cruickshank

north is a rare visitor to the United States. Like the more common Snowy Owl, it is sometimes driven south by failure of its food supply in the Arctic.

The Great Gray resembles its close relative, the Barred Owl, in its rounded head without ear tufts, but it is larger (24 to 33 inches), grayer, and has yellow eyes, not brown. It is dusky gray in color, with its underparts striped lengthwise. It has a noticeable black chin spot.

The Great Gray Owl builds its nest high in conifers, of sticks and twigs, warmly lined with feathers. The two to four white eggs are unusually small for such a large bird. The cry of the Great Gray is like that of the Screech Owl, or a booming *whoo-oo-oo-oo*, repeated at intervals.

LONG-EARED OWL

(*Asio otus wilsonianus*)

Color Plate Page 95

Because Owls are so nocturnal in their habits, few persons ever get to know them intimately. Even the little Screech Owl that lives in your town is a sleepy bird when surprised during the day by someone who may recognize its barklike form against a tree trunk.

Most nocturnal of the family is the Long-eared Owl, so this one is among the least known. I had been studying wild birds for many years before I had any intimate contact with it. But that event was memorable.

A Boy Scout found a nest for me on May 3rd. It was in a woodland crabapple tree, 35 feet from the ground. The structure was a huge mass of sticks, an old Crow's nest remodeled. It contained five very disturbed downy young whose wing feathers were just developing.

The female flew noiselessly from the nest as we approached, and then did something that I have never known a bird of prey to do. She flew to the ground and executed a broken-wing act as cleverly as any Killdeer or Mourning Dove. Still fluttering piteously, she disappeared into the underbrush.

As we climbed to the nest, the female flew at us viciously. The male perched at a distance, but his protests were confined to vigorous bill snapping and an occasional cry that sounded like a puppy dog's whine. To our surprise, both birds disappeared shortly after their initial demonstration and did not return again during the hour or more that we were photographing the young.

The three largest youngsters kept crawling out of the nest and climbing about in the tree. I was concerned about this behavior until I learned later that young Long-eared Owls leave the nest weeks before they can fly. The old Owls continue to feed them wherever they perch in the tree tops. The difference in size among the young is due to the fact that the female starts to incubate when her first egg is laid. This results in a five to ten day difference in the ages of the youngest and the oldest.

The Long-eared Owl is the size of a Crow (13 to 16 inches). The Great-horned Owl, with which it is often

WHIP-POOR-WILL (*Caprimulgus vociferus*). Length: 9 to 10 inches. Male: a mixture of black, gray, buffy brown and yellowish brown above. Black throat and upper breast, the latter crossed by white band. Buffy abdomen speckled with black. Female: has buffy breast band. Range: Canada to Georgia and Louisiana; winters from South Carolina and Gulf Coast south. Voice: *whip-poor-will*, often repeated.

John S. Dunning

SHORT-EARED OWL ON NEST (*Asio flammeus flammeus*). Length: 13 to 17 inches. Male and female: upperparts light yellowish brown, heavily streaked with black. Underparts light straw color streaked with dark brown. Large buffy wing-patches show in flight. Range: open country from Canada south to Colorado. Winters from Washington and Montana south to Mexico. Voice: a sneezy *kee-yow!*
A. Dawes Dubois, National Audubon Society

mistaken, is nearly two feet long. The ears of the former are situated close together toward the center of the forehead. On the Great-horned Owl these tufts are far apart. In flight, the ear tufts are pressed flat against the head. The coloration of the Long-eared Owl is generally dark, with lengthwise streaks underneath. The facial disc is reddish-brown, bordered with black.

Economically, the Long-eared Owl is most valuable and is deserving of legal protection at all times. A report by A. K. Fisher states that this Owl "is preeminently a mouser, but it also destroys some insects and probably some batrachians and reptiles." Of 107 stomachs examined by this scientist, 84 contained mice.

The Long-eared Owl is migratory, particularly in the northern part of its range, which extends from British Columbia and southern Quebec to southern California and Virginia. In winter it ranges south to southern Florida and Mexico.

SHORT-EARED OWL

(Asio flammeus flammeus)

Indicative of the Short-eared Owl's economic importance to man is the fact that this semidiurnal bird of prey must migrate from its northern range each fall in order to continue uninterrupted its search for rodents, its favorite food. Yet, due to the fact that it often hunts by day, it has been wantonly destroyed by hunters who never question the righteousness of their deed, and who brag ignorantly of their killing this useful bird.

The Short-eared Owl is the Harrier of the Owl family. It hunts in the manner of a Marsh Hawk, flying low over the fields and prairies, dropping suddenly to the ground to seize its prey in its talons. Like a Marsh Hawk, it nests on the ground, often in a marsh, where the five to seven white eggs are laid in a slight depression sparsely lined with grasses. Lest the Hawk and the Owl be confused, it is well to rememɔer that the Marsh Hawk flashes a conpicuous rump spot in flight, and that his streaked buffy-brown Owl has a arge round neckless head and a much horter tail. The short ears of this Owl ıre really short. Only under very favɔrable circumstances can the feathered ufts be seen at all. The Short-eared Owl is 13 to 17 inches long.

The call of this Owl has been described as a "shrill barking call like the *Ki-yi* of a little dog" (R. H. Lawrence). Another description refers to it as a "subdued noise, muffled and short, half sneeze, half bark" (Mabel Densmore). The courtship song is a long series of low pitched *hoots*.

The Short-eared Owl breeds from northern Alaska and Greenland to California, Kansas, and New Jersey. It winters from the northern states south to Florida, the Gulf states, and Central America.

RICHARDSON'S OWL

(Aegolius funerea richardsoni)

"Phillip-pile-tshish" is one of several Indian names for the Richardson's, or

NIGHTHAWK INCUBATING EGGS ON GRAVEL ROOF *(Chordeiles minor)*. Length: 8.5 to 10 inches. Male and female: upper and lower parts and two middle tail feathers, a streaked mixture of grays, black and buffy browns. Rest of tail feathers are tipped with black and crossed near tips by a white band. Wings are crossed by broad white patch. Bill is short, mouth gaping and surrounded by bristles. Range: breeds from Newfoundland, southern Quebec and northern Manitoba south to the Gulf of Mexico. Winters in South America.

Hal H. Harrison

RICHARDSON'S OWL (*Aegolius funerea richardsoni*). Length: 9 to 12 inches. Male and female: upperparts grayish brown, spotted with white. Underparts white streaked with dark. The facial disks of this *earless* owl are *framed with black* and the bill is yellowish. Range: breeds in Canada. Found occasionally in winter, south to Oregon and Colorado. Voice: a low, liquid note.
Chicago Natural History Museum

Boreal, Owl, a rare visitor in the United States. The name means "water dripping bird" and is applied to this Arctic Owl because its common call note resembles the sound of water dripping.

Only when heavy snows make hunting for prey impossible in its northern haunts does this relative of the Saw-whet Owl venture south across the Canadian border. Its home is the vast wilderness between eastern Canada and Alaska, where, despite long summer days, it is strictly nocturnal in its habits. As yet, there are no records of its nesting in this country.

The Richardson's is smaller than a Screech Owl (9 to 12 inches long) and lacks ear tufts. It is larger than a Saw whet from which it may be distin guished by its yellow bill (the Saw whet's is black) and by the blac outline of the facial disc. The tip of it head is spotted, not streaked, and th back is conspicuously marked wit large white spots.

SAW-WHET OWL

(Aegolius acadica acadica)

Color Plate Page 98

The trusting little Saw-whet Ow was named for one of its many calls which sounds like the rasping noise of saw being filed. Included in the bird' repertoire of utterances, however, are variety of whistles, squawks, and note like the ringing of a bell.

This resident of the forested areas i entirely nocturnal in its habits. During the day, it is so sleepy and dull that i may be approached closely and even lifted from its perch. The usual nesting site is an abandoned Woodpecker hole

Smallest of the eastern Owls, th Saw-whet is considerably smaller than a Screech Owl (7 to 8 inches long). The upperparts are brown, spotted with white. The head is streaked with white and lacks ear tufts. The white underparts are striped with rich brown. The facial disc is gray, and the eyes yellow.

The Saw-whet Owl breeds from southern Alaska, Alberta, and Nova Scotia to California, Arizona, and Mexico; and in the east to the northern United States as far south as western Maryland in the mountains.

GOATSUCKERS

Family Caprimulgidae

The name of Goatsucker was derived from the old European superstition that these birds were able to milk goats. Actually they seek the insects which are found in the animals' vicinity. The Goatsuckers are nocturnal birds which spend their days lying hidden, in which they are aided by their protective coloration. They catch their food, largely insects, on the wing.

CHUCK-WILL'S-WIDOW

(Caprimulgus carolinensis)

Color Plate Page 102

To most southerners, the Chuck-will's-widow is a voice in the night, not a bird. It is something to listen to, not to see. And although thousands from Maryland to Kansas and south to Florida and the Gulf coast and Texas are familiar with the summer cry of this largest member of the Goatsucker family, relatively few have ever seen the bird.

The call is in four parts with the accent on the third syllable. It calls *chuck, will's WID-ow*. Although the opening *chuck* may be heard clearly for a much greater distance than the same note in the Whip-poor-will, yet it is given in a low tone and is sometimes lost when the call comes from a great distance. Then it sounds like *will's WID-ow*. The bird is a persistent singer, especially when it first returns from its winter home in southern Florida and southward. Alexander Sprunt, Jr. counted 834 consecutive calls of the Chuck one evening in June near Charleston, South Carolina.

Resting by day and hunting its insect food by night, the Chuck-will's-widow lives about the same as other members of its family. The habit of placing its two brown and purple blotched eggs on the floor of the woods with no attempt at nest building is the same as that of the Whip-poor-will. The bird's flight is silent and mothlike.

In addition to its larger size (11 to 13 inches) and its characteristic call, the Chuck-will's-widow may be distinguished from the Whip-poor-will by its brown throat and ill-defined white throat band. Both species may be told from their close relative, the Nighthawk, by the absence of the broad white patch across the wing which is clearly visible when the Nighthawk is in flight.

WHIP-POOR-WILL

(Caprimulgus vociferus)

Color Plate Page 103

There are those who dread the call of the Whip-poor-will as an eerie voice in the twilight gloom. To me, it has always been a restful, soothing call, one to be listened for with keen anticipation in late April and early May in the northern states. And so it comes to me from off in the hills or from the shelter of a nearby woodlot, that persistently whistled call of *whip-poor-will*, piercing the evening stillness. Surely it is spring when this nocturnal bird returns from its winter sojourn in the Gulf states or in Central America.

One must be quite close to a singing Whip-poor-will before he is able to distinguish the fourth note in the call. It is a very low *cluck* that is uttered between each *whip-poor-will*. Generally the *cluck* is not heard and the song is described as a three syllable utterance, with the *will* accented and carrying farthest.

As a member of the Goatsucker family, the Whip-poor-will is closely related to the Nighthawk, but it is a different species entirely. Early American settlers identified the call of the Whip-poor-will as the voice of the Nighthawk and were oblivious to the former's existence.

Generally, the Nighthawk is a city dweller; the Whip-poor-will is its country cousin. When perched, the Whip-poor-will's wingtips do not reach the end of its rounded tail whereas the Nighthawk's wings extend beyond its forked tail. The Nighthawk's sides are barred; the Whip-poor-will's are not. In flight, the Nighthawk shows a conspicuous white patch on the underside of each wing. These are absent on the Whip-poor-will. The Whip-poor-will is about 9 or 10 inches long.

Whip-poor-wills nest on the ground laying their two blotched white eggs in the open, often on dead leaves. No

CHIMNEY SWIFT (*Chaetura pelagica*). Length: 5 to 5.5 inches. Male and female: above sooty black, lighter below. Range: eastern United States, rarely to eastern Montana and eastern Wyoming. Voice: joyful twittering.
Hal H. Harrison

nest is attempted, but an indentation occurs where the female sits during incubation. The eggs are well camouflaged by their surroundings, and from these invisible eggs hatch invisible little Whip-poor-wills that look for all the world like dead leaves.

The eastern species *(C. v. vociferus)* breeds from New Brunswick and Manitoba southward to the Gulf states and westward to the Great Plains. It winters south from South Carolina and the Gulf states. In the west it is replaced by Stephen's Whip-poor-will.

NUTTALL'S POOR-WILL *(Phalaenoptilus nuttallii)*. Length: 7 to 8 inches. Male and female: plumage a mixture of gray, brown, buff and black. White tipped tail. Range: chiefly in arid country from Canada to Mexico, and from Rogue River Valley, Oregon, to lower California. Voice: a loud, repeated *poor-will, poor-will.*
Karl H. Maslowski, National Audubon Society

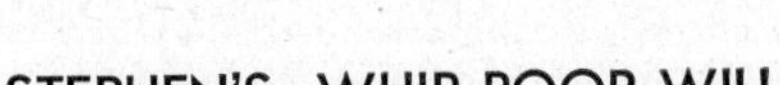

STEPHEN'S WHIP-POOR-WILL

(Antrostomus vociferus arizonae)

The Whip-poor-will of the west, this bird is found in the mountains of southern Arizona, New Mexico, and Texas. Its voice is heard only at night and is a *whip-poor-will,* more rolling than that of the eastern bird.

It is a larger bird (9 to 10 inches) than the Poor-will, and has more conspicuous white patches on the tail. Its wings are wholly brown, without the white bars of the Pauraque or Nighthawk.

POOR-WILL

(Phalaenoptilus nuttallii)

Suddenly from the ground at our feet a grayish brown bird with long pointed wings sailed into the air with mothlike silence, zig-zagged over the desert brush, and came to earth somewhere ahead. We easterners who had never seen a Poor-will remarked that it looked very much like our own Whip-poor-will, but that its tail was noticeably shorter. The absence of white wing patches eliminated the possibility of its being a Nighthawk.

Such an incident is uncommon, for the Poor-will is so completely nocturnal in its habits that we know it best by its characteristic call of *poor-will,* repeated over and over again. It is smaller than a Nighthawk (7 to 8 inches), gray-brown in color, with a white-tipped tail.

Four races of this Goatsucker occur in the western states: Nuttall's Poor-will *(P. n. nuttallii)* from southeastern British Columbia and North Dakota to eastern Kansas, southern Arizona, and eastern California; the Dusky Poor-will *(P. n. californicus)* in California west of the Sierra Nevadas and south to Lower California; the Desert Poor-will

(P. n. hueyi) in the valley of the lower Colorado; and the Sonora Poor-will *(P. n. adustus)* in southern Arizona.

MERRILL'S PAURAQUE

(Nyctidromus albicollis merrilli)

Largest of the western Goatsuckers (12 inches long), the Pauraque is confined to the Gulf coast of Texas and the lower Rio Grande Valley, where it can be differentiated from the Whip-poor-will and the Chuck-will's-widow by the triangular black markings on its shoulders and the white bands across the wings. It has much more white in the tail than does the Nighthawk. Its voice, heard only at night, is a hoarse *pur-we-eeeeer,* rolled out emphatically.

NIGHTHAWK

(Chordeiles minor)

Color Plate Page 105

The birth of a baby at our local hospital is rarely important news. It happens many times a day. But when a wild bird decides to have her young at the hospital, and when that expectant mother is able to command the attention of a staff of doctors and nurses, it adds up to an unusual story.

A doctor was the first to break the news to me, and when I arrived at the hospital, I found the "patient" was a Nighthawk incubating her two blotched eggs on a gravel roof. The bird blended so well with the roof that it could easily escape detection. It flushed only when I stooped to touch it. In leaving the nest, it turned to intimidate me with wings spread wide and with its hissing mouth opened menacingly. Did I say "nest"? There was no sign of a nest. The eggs were entirely exposed, but they, too, blended perfectly with the surroundings.

Nurses and doctors, working in the operating rooms overlooking the roof, were intensely interested in developments. They promised to keep me informed as incubation progressed. That was on May 20th.

It was not until early June that the blessed event occurred. One of the doctors called to say that the eggs had hatched and the young were doing nicely. Father Nighthawk had been observed pacing the ledge around the roof that morning.

Arriving at the hospital, I was escorted by the supervising nurse of the operating department, who showed me the two downy youngsters with no less pride than she would have shown me the twins born to a human mother. And from that day until the entire family glided off the roof for the last time, they had professional nursing service twenty-four hours a day.

Gravel roofs are a common nesting site for the Nighthawk throughout its range from Newfoundland to the southern Yukon and south to Mexico, the Gulf coast, and Florida. Its natural nesting habitat, however, is on the ground in wooded areas, hillsides, and farm country. The Nighthawk, or Bull Bat, as it is also called, is misnamed. It is not a Hawk at all, but a member of the same family as the Whip-poor-will.

I think everyone knows the Nighthawk best as it gathers insects over our towns and cities on summer evenings. Here, in company with fast flying Swifts and fluttering bats, this grayish bird which is 9 or 10 inches long, flies high overhead on long pointed wings, scooping insects into its cavernous mouth. Here we can note the big white patches under each wing, marks that distinguish it quickly from the Whip-poor-will. Here, too, we hear the familiar nasal cry of *peent*.

In the mating season, the male executes a spectacular power dive. From high in the air, he suddenly rockets to earth with wings partly closed. Just as a crash seems inevitable, he spreads his wings, and with a booming noise, zooms upward. The booming is created by the sudden rush of air through the wings.

In late August, flocks of Nighthawks head south in leisurely flight. Many of them travel as far as Argentina.

TEXAS or LESSER NIGHTHAWK

(Chordeiles acutipennis texensis)

Somewhat smaller (8 to 9 inches) than the other Nighthawk, the Texas bird is browner and has the white wing stripe nearer the tip. However, it is best identified by its voice which is a low *chuck-chuck* or purring sound, and by its habit of flying low over the ground rather than high.

In the breeding season it prefers the lowlands, while its larger relative prefers the mountains. Its range is southwestern United States, north to central California, southern Nevada and Utah, and central Texas.

SWIFTS

Family Apopidae

The Swifts are highly beneficial insect-eating birds which are unable to perch as do most birds. Instead they cling to vertical surfaces, using their tail for support as do the Woodpeckers. Another peculiarity of the Swifts is their well developed salivary glands, the excretion from which is used in making their nests. American Swifts use it to glue together twigs and branches. One Oriental species builds its nest entirely of this substance; these are the nests used by the Chinese in making "bird nest" soup.

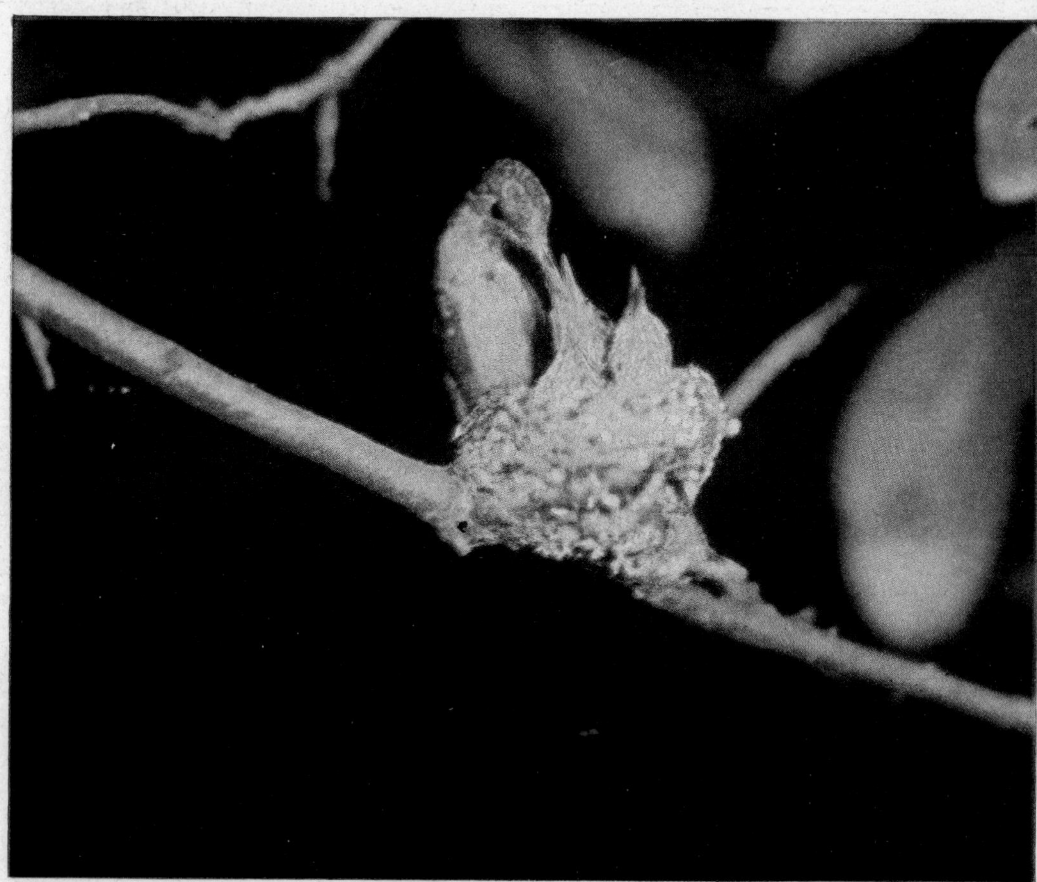

FEMALE RUBY THROATED HUMMINGBIRD FEEDING YOUNG (*Archilochus colubris*). Length: 3 to 3.75 inches. Male: upperparts metallic green, darker green wings, ruby colored throat; underparts, grayish white. Female: duller, with white throat. Range: Gulf of St. Lawrence to Gulf of Mexico. Winters from Florida, south.

Hal H. Harrison

BLACK-CHINNED HUMMINGBIRD *(Archilochus alexandri)*. Length: 3.75 inches. Male: upperparts greenish, underparts grayish white; black throat and brilliant purple blue patch on lower throat; white collar beneath this. Sides of body are washed with green. Female: greenish above, whitish below. Range: western United States from Mexico to Canada, east to Montana and Texas; winters in southern California, south. Voice: none.
Fred Bashour

BLACK SWIFT

(Nephoecetes niger borealis)

Its all-black color, its larger size (7 inches), and its slightly forked tail, which it fans while in flight, are the field marks that distinguish the Black Swift from others of the family. The batlike flight and the long slim wings of the Black Swift should eliminate confusion with the similar Purple Martin.

This fast flying, big Swift of the Pacific coast breeds in remote areas. Not until 1901 was the first nest found on a sea cliff west of Santa Cruz in California. Later it was discovered nesting inland in the Yosemite Valley. It is still a rare western breeder.

CHIMNEY SWIFT

(Chaetura pelagica)

Color Plate Page 108

While the coming of the white man to America has decimated the ranks of many native birds, there are notable instances where his arrival actually has benefited certain species. The pampered little House Wren most assuredly is one. The Robin has thrived. And the Chimney Swift has found a nesting Utopia in the millions of chimneys that man has erected. Indeed, chimneys have practically replaced the ancestral nesting sites in hollow trees.

No bird offers the city dweller a more spectacular migration spectacle than the Chimney Swift. Its custom of mass roosting in huge chimneys while enroute north and south has been enjoyed by thousands. Favorite chimneys are revisited year after year by flocks that often number several thousand individuals.

The flock's entrance into the chimney at dusk is a dramatic presentation of a weird ritual. The birds assemble in a funnel-like formation above the building, the narrow end of the funnel just above the chimney. Then, as the flock moves in spiral flight, birds at the tip of the funnel drop rapidly into the opening. Other birds take their places, and they, too, drop away, constantly reducing the size of the funnel until the last bird is away for the night. Inside, the Swifts cling to the sides of the bricks in uniform rows.

BLACK SWIFT (*Nephoecetes niger borealis*). Length: 7.25 inches. Male and female: sooty black upperparts; paler underparts; black bill. Slightly forked tail and long slim wings. Range: migrates and breeds at scattered points along Pacific coast and inland in mountains. Voice: a light twitter.
Chicago Natural History Museum

The roosting habit has made it possible for ornithologists to band hundreds of thousands of Swifts by trapping them at night. It was this banding that eventually solved the mystery of where Swifts spend the winter. They were discovered wintering in Peru in 1944.

As great flocks of Chimney Swifts move north in the spring, mated pairs break away and start nesting. Only one pair nests in a chimney, but the birds feed together in their communal dining room in the sky. Their diet is entirely insectivorous.

The Chimney Swift's nest is remarkable although crude. It is built entirely of twigs which the bird gathers by snapping them from trees with its feet. These are glued to the side of the chimney and to each other by the bird's sticky saliva which hardens when exposed to air. Into this slightly concave structure are laid four or five white eggs.

The quill-covered young know instinctively to cling with their sharp claws, and thus they remain in the chimney until their feathers are fully developed. The hissing of the young in the nest, especially when the old birds enter to feed, has been heard with misgivings by many housewives. It sounds like escaping steam.

The Chimney Swift is blackish in color, about 5 inches long, and has such a short tail that it is apparently tailless. Its wings are narrow, and it frequently sails between wing beats.

The Chimney Swift breeds from southern Canada to the Gulf, and from the Atlantic seaboard to eastern Texas, Montana, and central Alberta.

VAUX'S SWIFT

(Chaetura vauxi vauxi)

Vaux's Swift replaces the Chimney Swift on the Pacific coast where it is found from Santa Cruz north to Alaska. Very slightly smaller, it is of the same general coloration, sooty black above and paler below. It appears tailless except when the tail is spread, since the tail is only half the length of the wings. Like the Chimney Swift, it prefers the dark for hunting its diet of insects. Vaux's Swift winters in Mexico and Central America.

WHITE-THROATED SWIFT

(Aeronautes saxatalis saxatalis)

The White-throated Swift breeds on inaccessible cliffs in the western states from Canada to Mexico. Characteristically it is a Swift, but unlike the other members of its family, it does not hesitate to come out during the daytime.

It is uniformly brownish black, marked by white spots on each side of the rump above, and by white on the cheek, chin, throat, and center of the breast. It builds its nest on cliffs or caves, or in holes in limestone cliffs.

HUMMINGBIRDS

Family Trochilidae

The Hummingbirds are the jewels of the bird kingdom. Very small birds, the males are brilliantly colored, with an iridescence that is dazzling. The females and young birds are less colorful, and often very difficult to differentiate in the field. The Hummingbird's bill is long and needlelike to enable it to sip nectar from flowers, but they also eat insects. The Hummingbird beats its wings so rapidly in flight that they become only a blur. It has the ability to remain stationary in the air, supporting itself on beating wings. Some male Hummingbirds make distinctive sounds which are the result of their wings beating the air. The Hummers are American birds of which only a few species reach the United States; of these, only one, the Ruby-throat, is common in the east.

LUCIFER HUMMINGBIRD

(Calothorax lucifer)

A rare Hummer of southern Arizona and western Texas, the male Lucifer has a purple throat and rusty sides, with a bill curved slightly downward. Like most Hummers, the female is greenish above and whitish below, almost impossible of field identification.

A small Hummingbird, only 3½ inches long, the Lucifer may be found feeding among the agave plants in the Chisos Mountains.

RUBY-THROATED HUMMINGBIRD

(Archilochus colubris)

Color Plate Page 112

The mighty midget of our garden is a tiny mite of a bird, the Ruby-throated Hummingbird, smallest bird in eastern North America, and the only Hummingbird to invade that part of the continent. The bird's lopsided distribution is emphasized when we realize that almost five hundred kinds of Hummingbirds have been described in the Western Hemisphere. Practically all of them are residents of South America, only seventeen species having been recorded in the United States at any time.

The Ruby-throat's incredible power of flight is just one phase of a many-sided personality. It is hard to believe that such a diminutive creature, with a wingspread of only a little more than four inches, could drive itself forward a mile a minute. Helicopter engineers would do well to study the Hummingbird, for it is the only land bird that can fly backwards, and one of few to rise straight up in the air.

Hovering before a flower from which it is sipping nectar or searching for spiders or aphids, the Ruby-throat drops its body from a normal flight position to one almost vertical; thus, the wing beats are practically back and forth instead of up and down. By using the vibrations of a violin note as a basis for computation, it has been estimated

BROAD-TAILED HUMMINGBIRD (*Selasphorus platycercus platycercus*). Length: 4.5 inches. Male: metallic green above, tail bronzy black, underparts whitish. Bright rose red throat patch. Female: upperparts bronzy green. Whitish underparts. Whitish throat spotted with dark. Range: Rocky Mountain Region. Voice: a *shrill trilling* produced by wing motions in flight.
Alfred M. Bailey

that a Hummingbird's wings will complete as many as two hundred beats per second. More conservative estimates range from six hundred to one thousand strokes per minute.

But whatever the speed, one is constantly impressed with the bird's dynamic energy. It is attracted naturally to the brightly colored garden flowers, especially red and blue, but it is possible to attract more Hummingbirds by placing little red vials of sugar syrup here and there about the grounds. I paint pill bottles red and wire them to plant stakes.

The well known brilliance of the male Hummingbird is an iridescent thing, depending upon reflected light to display the fiery red throat and brilliant green back. The ruby throat gorget is lacking entirely in the female.

Those who attract Hummingbirds to their garden may be rewarded with the sight of the male's spectacular "pendulum dance." With a preening female as the object of his courtship, the male sweeps before her in great pendulumlike arcs, displaying to best advantage his flaming throat, and chattering like a little mouse.

The male's devotion is short lived, however, for the female assumes entire responsibility for the nest, incubation of the eggs, and feeding the young. The male never visits the nest at any time, but judging from his mate's reputation as a nest building artist, she does not seem to need him. Her one-inch cup is constructed of the finest cottony plant down, tied together with spider webbing, and covered with delicate lichens. It is saddled to a horizontal limb where it looks like a knot. The two white eggs are the size of navy beans.

Even migrating to its winter home in Mexico and Central America, the Ruby-throated Hummingbird is dramatic, for its five hundred mile non-stop flight across the Gulf of Mexico to Yucatan is a constant source of wonder to all who remember that the bird is just three and a half inches long.

BLACK-CHINNED HUMMINGBIRD

(Archilochus alexandri)

Color Plate Page 113

Easterners who are bewildered by the various species of Hummingbirds they find in the gardens of southern California, will have a nostalgic reminder of their beloved Ruby-throat in the pendulum dance of the closely related Black-chinned Hummingbird. The sweeping flight of the Black-chin takes the shape of a narrow figure 8, with the heavy droning of the wings quite audible. As in the eastern species, the Black-chin's performance is presented for the approval of a perching female.

COSTA'S HUMMINGBIRD ON NEST *(Calypte costae)*. Length: 3.25 inches. Male: body greenish bronze, throat and forehead purple. Female: greenish above, underparts whitish. Range: breeds in low country of southwest United States. Voice: high, shrill, hissing sound.
Lewis W. Walker

Identification of the male Black-chinned Hummingbird is not difficult. The male is about 3½ inches long. His squared black throat is separated from the dusky underparts by a white band. In favorable light it will be seen that what appeared to be an all black gorget is really a black chin with the lower throat bluish purple or violet.

The female Black-chinned, green above and white below, offers more difficulty in field identification. While the female Anna's Hummingbird may be known by its larger size, the female Costa's is certainly not distinguishable from the female Black-chinned. The greater amount of green in the tail of the female Black-chin is offered as an aid in separating the two species, but I do not feel that this is much help to the average bird watcher.

The Black-chinned Hummer breeds from southern British Columbia and western Montana to northern Mexico and western Texas. It favors the dry foothills and canyons.

COSTA'S HUMMINGBIRD

(Calypte costae)

Except the diminutive Calliope Hummingbird, no bird in the United States is smaller than the three-inch long Costa's Hummingbird of the arid southwest (southern California, Utah, Nevada, and Arizona). To many observers, no Hummingbird surpasses it in beauty. Like a blazing helmet its crown and throat glow in the sun—now violet, now purple, now amethyst, and now black, as the reflecting light changes. The elongated sides of the gorget, called ruffs, are diagnostic, although the larger Anna's Hummingbird displays similar but shorter red ruffs.

Females of the Costa's, Anna's, and Black-chinned Hummingbirds are practically indistinguishable in the field. With practice, the Anna's may be recognized by her larger size, but experienced California ornithologists agree that it is impossible to recognize the female Costa's from the female Black-chinned under ordinary field conditions.

ANNA'S HUMMINGBIRD

(Calypte anna)

Californians are more familiar with the large red-throated and red-crowned Anna's Hummingbird than with any other species. It and the non-migratory Allen's Hummingbird are the only members of the family that are strictly resident species. Occasionally the Anna's wanders from its normal range west of the Sierras, but it is considered by ornithologists to be non-migratory.

Anna's Hummingbird makes itself more conspicuous than other Hummers by preferring the thickly populated areas as its habitat, feeding in gardens and parks throughout the year. Its larger size (4 inches long), the absence of rufous in the plumage, the red gorget and crown, and the gorget's lower gray border serve to identify the male Anna's from other Hummingbirds of the area. The female resembles the female Costa's more than any other. Identifying marks for the female Anna's are its larger size, darker gray underparts, and the usual scattering of red spots on the female's throat.

ANNA'S HUMMINGBIRD ON NEST *(Calypte anna)*. Length: 4 inches. Male: red throat and red forehead. Body greenish. Female: dark greenish color throat, heavily spotted with red dots. Range: California, west of Sierras. Voice: squeaking and grating notes.
William L. Dawson, National Audubon Society

Nesting occurs before the arrival of migrant Hummers, sets of eggs being usual in January and February. Since this species normally has two broods, nesting continues into late spring.

BROAD-TAILED HUMMINGBIRD

(Selasphorus platycercus platycercus)

Color Plate Page 117

The Broad-tailed Hummingbird, with its rose pink throat patch and its green crown and back, is one of the most abundant birds of the Rocky Mountains. It breeds from Montana and southern Idaho south to Mexico and west to the Sierra Nevadas, reaching California in the eastern mountains.

Characteristic of this species, and a point that makes the male quickly distinguishable, is the insectlike buzzing of its wings, a sound that might be likened to the shrill notes of a cicada. The sound is made only when the bird is in direct flight. As it hovers about a flower, its wings hum in true Hummingbird fashion.

In general appearance, the Broad-tail suggests the Ruby-throat of the east, but since their ranges do not coincide, this does not present a problem. The rose pink gorget, combined with the green crown, distinguishes the male from other western Hummingbirds. The Rufous Hummingbird has a red gorget, but its rufous back is distinctive.

The three rufous colored outer tail feathers may aid in distinguishing the female Broad-tailed from the other species which she resembles. Closest to the Broad-tail in appearance is the female Calliope, but the former is over an inch longer (4½ inches long) than the Calliope.

The Broad-tailed Hummingbird migrates in winter to Guatemala.

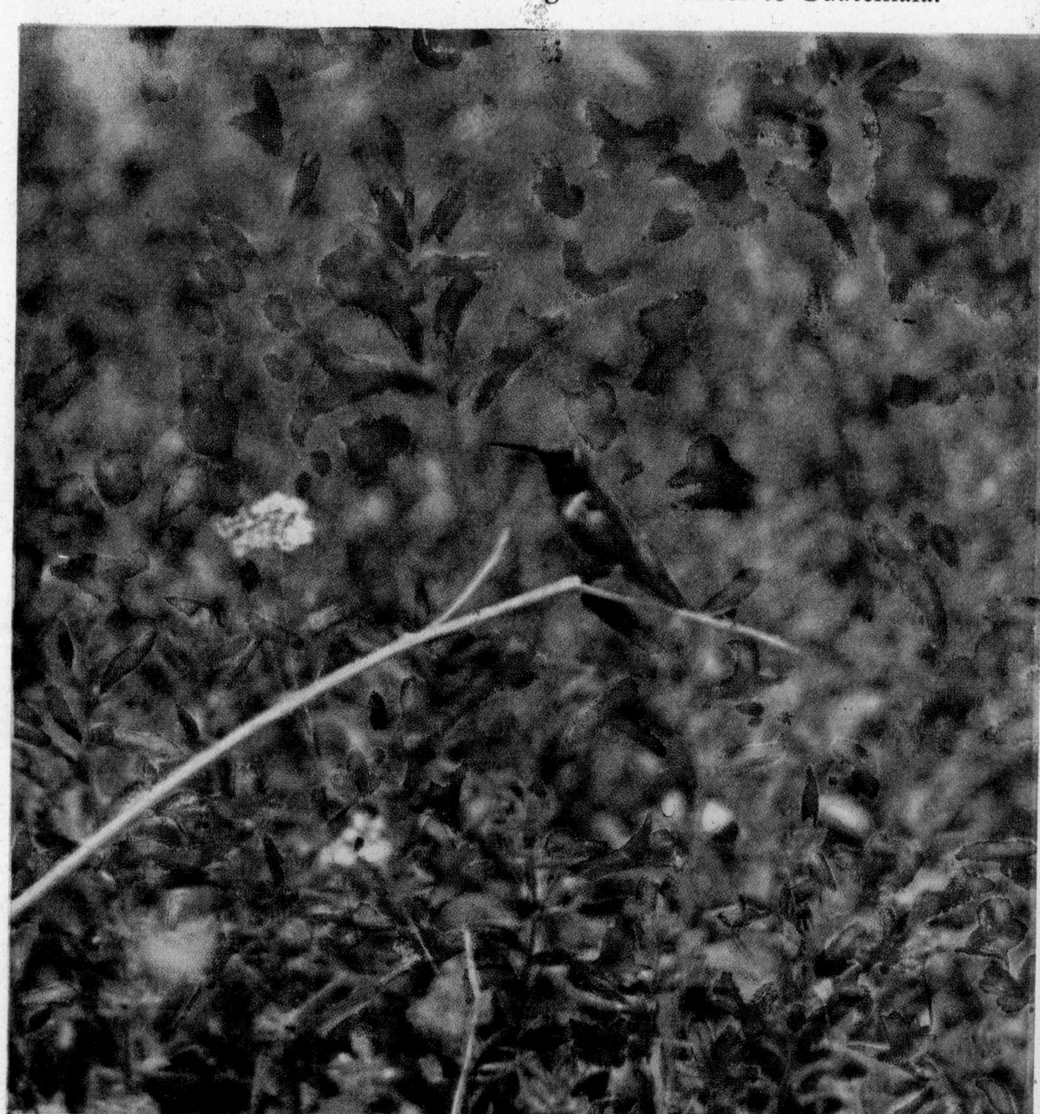

RUFOUS HUMMINGBIRD (*Selasphorus rufus*). Length: 3.5 inches. Male: upperparts bright rufous color, whitish abdomen. Flame red throat. Female: upperparts bronzy touched with rufous on rump and tail, underparts white; sides reddish brown. Range: western America. Winters in southern Mexico.

Harlan E. Eckler

RUFOUS HUMMINGBIRD

(Selasphorus rufus)

Color Plate Page 120

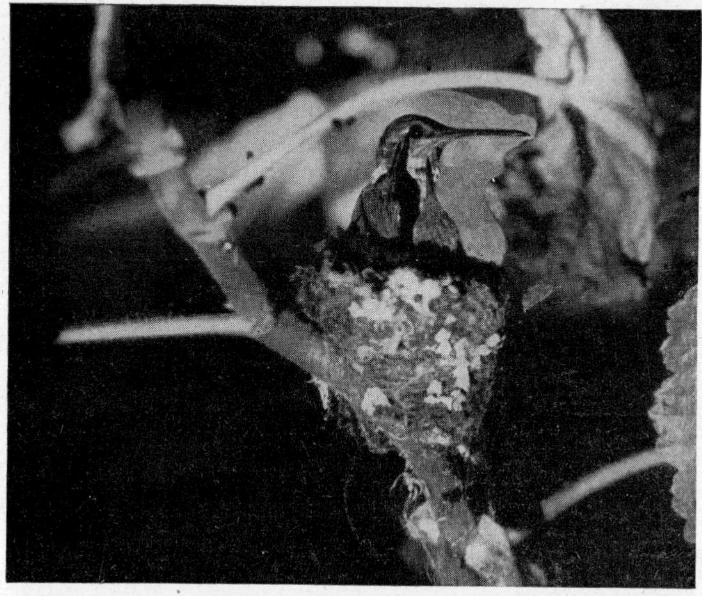

ALLEN'S HUMMINGBIRD, FEMALE AND TWO YOUNG IN NEST *(Selasphorus sasin)*. Length: about 4 inches. Male: metallic green back, rufous rump, bright red throat, abdomen reddish brown. Female: tail tips black and white, whitish belly, reddish brown sides. Range: California; some winter in Santa Barbara Islands.
Laidlaw Williams, National Audubon Society

The male Rufous Hummingbird, probably the most abundant of the western Hummers, and certainly one of the spectacularly colored of all its tribe, may be recognized by the large amount of rufous on the crown, back, and tail. Indeed, no other Hummingbird has a rufous back. Allen's Hummingbird has a rufous rump, but its back is green.

In other ways, the Rufous and the Allen's Hummingbirds are similar. They are practically the same size (3½ inches long), and both have flaming scarlet gorgets. At certain angles, the gorget of the Rufous appears pure burnished gold. The females of the two species are indistinguishable in the field. Some rufous on the rump or tail feathers of the female Rufous may aid in distinguishing it from other females.

The male Rufous has a fiery temper that matches his fiery appearance. He is most pugnacious and seems to delight in fighting with other birds, not only in the vicinity of the nest, but while feeding, flying, or just perching. His emotions are none the less violent when it comes to love-making, for the courtship flight of this Hummingbird is dazzling. From high in the air he rockets to earth, checking his flight a few inches from a perching female.

The Rufous Hummingbird breeds from Oregon and southwestern Montana into Canada and as far north as Alaska. No other Hummingbird breeds that far north. In migration it is abundant throughout the Rocky Mountain region. It winters in southern Mexico.

ALLEN'S HUMMINGBIRD

(Selasphorus sasin)

The brilliant male Allen's Hummingbird may be distinguished from the male Rufous Hummingbird by the large amount of green on its back (the back of the Rufous Hummer is entirely rufous), but the females of the two species are almost indistinguishable in the field.

In the breeding season, Allen's Hummingbird is found only in a narrow coastal district of California extending from the Oregon line south to San Clemente and Santa Catalina Islands.

In winter some individuals remain in California. These are called the non-migratory Allen's Hummingbird *(S. s. sedentarius)*. Those that move southward are the migratory Allen's Hummingbird *(S. s. sasin)*.

CALLIOPE HUMMINGBIRD

(Stellula calliope)

The smallest of the United States Hummingbirds (barely 3 inches long), the Calliope lives in the high mountains of the west from Canada to southern California. The male has a white throat with red rays. The female can be told from the female Rufous by the lack of rust color on the center of the rump.

RIVOLI'S HUMMINGBIRD

(Eugenes fulgens aureoviridis)

Color Plate Page 122

To observe the Rivoli's Hummingbird in the United States, the bird watcher must travel into the mountain canyons of New Mexico and Arizona. Its general range lies through Mexico and Central America to Nicaragua.

It is the largest of the North American Hummers (5 inches long), although the Blue-throated Hummingbird looks just as large in the field. It is with this species that the Rivoli's is most likely to be confused, but the latter has a green gorget, while that of the Blue-throat is blue; also, the Blue-throat's tail has distinctive white spots.

At a distance, the Rivoli's Hummingbird looks all black. In favorable

RIVOLI'S HUMMINGBIRD (*Eugenes fulgens aureoviridis*). Length: 5 inches. Male: upperparts metallic green; below, black, green and gray. Black and white streaks through eye, green throat. Female evenly gray below, white marks on face, greenish tail with small grayish white spots at the corners. Range: southwestern United States.

Ross and Florence Thornburg

BELTED KINGFISHER (*Megaceryle alcyon*). Length: 11 to 14 inches. Male: grayish blue above. White collar around hindneck. White spots before eye and wings tipped with white. Feathers of head frequently raised, forming crest. Underparts white with grayish blue band across the breast. Female: cinnamon colored sides and breast bands. Range: Manitoba to Gulf of Mexico. Winters north to Illinois, Ohio and New England. Voice: high rattle.
Don L. Jacobs

light the purple crown and the green throat may be seen. The female is greenish above and greenish or dusky below. She can be told from the female Blue-throat by her spotted throat and mottled underparts.

BLUE-THROATED HUMMINGBIRD

(Lampornis clemenciae)

From its principal breeding range in Mexico, the Blue-throated Hummingbird crosses our border in Arizona, New Mexico, and Texas, thus making it one of our American birds.

Arthur Cleveland Bent, in his "Life Histories," writes of this Hummer's field marks: "This large Hummer (5 inches long) is not likely to be confused with any other Hummingbird except the almost equally large Rivoli's. The most conspicuous field mark of the Blue-throated is the long, broad tail, with the prominent white tips of the three outer rectices, recognizable in both sexes and at all ages; only the female Rivoli's has light tipped outer rectices, and these are gray rather than white. The blue throat of the male is not conspicuous, except at short range and in good light, but the white postocular and rictal stripes are more easily seen at short distances, especially the former."

There are two geographical subspecies of this Hummingbird which show no obvious field differences.

BUFF-BELLIED HUMMINGBIRD

(Amazilia yucatanensis chalconota)

Limited in its range to the Rio Grande delta of Texas, this Hummingbird is unmistakable for its green throat and coral or pink bill with a black tip. The underparts are buff, and unlike most Hummingbirds, the female is similar in coloring to the male and thus easy to recognize.

The Buff-bellied Hummingbird builds its nest in a shrub or small tree in open woodlands and on the edge of thickets. It is quite noisy, uttering shrill twittering squeaks.

BUFF-BELLIED HUMMINGBIRD ON NEST *(Amazilia yucatanensis chalconota)*. Length: 4.5 inches. Male and female: upperparts light greenish bronze. Underparts buff colored, throat green, coral-billed. Range: Rio Grande Delta, Texas. Voice: shrill, noisy cries.
Olin S. Pettingill, Jr.

WHITE-EARED HUMMINGBIRD

(Hylocharis leucotis leucotis)

Limited to the mountains of southeast Arizona, the White-eared Hummingbird is recognizable in both sexes by the broad white stripe behind the ear, and the pink bill with black tip. The male has greenish underparts, a blue and green throat, and a purple forehead. The female lacks the metallic head and throat patches.

BLUE-THROATED HUMMINGBIRD *(Lampornis clemenciae)*. Length: 5 inches. Male: black and white streaks through eyes, and blue throat. White spots in tail. Female: evenly gray underparts, large blue black tail with exceptionally large white spots at the corners. Range: southwest Texas, New Mexico, Arizona.
Rudolph Hindemith, American Museum of Natural History

BROAD-BILLED HUMMINGBIRD

(Cynanthus latirostris)

Occurring in much the same range as the White-eared Hummingbird, the Broad-billed can be distinguished by the lack of the white ear stripe, having only a tiny spot of white behind the eye. The male is greenish with a metallic blue throat, and with a bright red or pink bill with a black tip. The female has pink at the base of the bill, and an unmarked pearl gray throat and underparts. She can be distinguished from the female white-eared Hummingbird by the lack of the white eye-stripe.

TROGONS

Family Trogonidae

The Trogons are tropical birds of splendid plumage. One, the Quetzal of Guatemala, is even more beautiful than the Bird of Paradise, and was revered by the Aztecs, only chieftains being permitted to wear its plumage. One member of the family enters the United States, and it is rare.

COPPERY-TAILED TROGON (*Trogon elegans*). Length: 11.5 inches. Male: head and upperparts metallic bronze green; underparts, *bright rose red* separated from the dark head by a white band. Bird has moderately long, square-tipped tail and stout bill. Face and throat are black, and there is a white crescent on the breast. Female: similar, but brown above, and duller underparts. Range: mountains of southern Arizona. Voice: a series of low, coarse notes: *kowm, kowm, kowm, kowm, kowm, kowm, kowm.*
Chicago Natural History Museum

COPPERY-TAILED TROGON

(Trogon elegans)

A rare Mexican visitor to the United States in the mountains of southern Arizona and in the valley of the lower Rio Grande in Texas is the gorgeously colored Coppery-tailed Trogon. Like the Parrots that it resembles, the Trogon nests in hollow trees.

The adult male is about 12 inches long, metallic green above and geranium red below. Separating the dark head and the rosy underparts is a white crescent. The tail is broadly tipped with black, the outer feathers are white, and the middle feathers coppery-bronze. The female is similar, but brown above and not so bright red beneath.

The call note of this Trogon is said to suggest that of a hen Turkey. It is delivered while the bird sits upright on the limb of a tree, with its tail hanging straight down.

KINGFISHERS

Family Alcedinidae

The Kingfishers are found world wide, but only a few species belong to the New World, and only two reach the United States. The Kingfisher, as the name implies, catches fish which form its principal food. It builds its nest in cavities in banks along the streams. The family name *Alcyones* is derived from the Greek legend concerning Halcyon who was turned into a Kingfisher together with his wife for incurring the wrath of the gods. As the legend went, no winds blew during the days of their brooding, whence the expression "halcyon days."

BELTED KINGFISHER

(Megaceryle alcyon)

Color Plate Page 123

The high pitched rattling call of a Kingfisher flying ahead of me along a winding creek; the fluttering wing beats of this picturesque blue and white bird as it hovered above a pool before diving to snare a luckless chub; the pounding of its newly caught prey on a dead limb of an overhanging tree, and the toss into the air with the fish landing in the bird's beak head first; the torpedo-like dive into or out of the nesting burrow; the shaggy crest; all these are the boyhood memories of Kingfishers that I cherish.

I have always wondered how a man who calls himself a sportsman, a devout follower of Izaak Walton, could kill this grand bird with so flimsy an excuse as the fact that it, too, is a fisherman. As Arthur Cleveland Bent so ably puts it: "The most serious enemies of the Kingfisher are the selfish fisherman, who wants all the fish for himself and begrudges the poor bird an honest living, and the proprietor of a trout hatchery, who is unwilling to go to the trouble and expense of screening his pools to protect his fish. The former shoots every Kingfisher he can with misguided satisfaction; the latter either shoots or traps any that visit his pools."

The irony of this situation is that the Kingfisher is not guilty of doing any measurable damage to game fish in the streams where fishermen might vie with it for a catch. Indeed, in the defense of this wilderness bird, one might even prove that the species is actually beneficial to its human predators. In the examination of 313 stomachs of Kingfishers collected in widely different sections of the country, the U. S. Biological Survey showed that less than half the fishes taken were of kinds usually eaten by man. Many of the fishes sought by this bird are noted enemies of sporting varieties because they feed on the spawn of the species prized by man.

The Kingfisher can be confused with no other bird, except possibly the Blue Jay. It is 11 to 14 inches long, blue-gray above with a ragged crest, a large

EMALE FLICKER FEEDING (*Colaptes auratus*). Length: 13 to 14 inches. Male and female: upperparts rayish brown, barred with black; underparts violet brown and yellowish; black crescent on breast, hite rump, red patch on nape of neck. Male has black mustache. Range: eastern North America om Canada to Florida and Gulf of Mexico; winters north to Great Lakes. Voice: song, a loud *wick wick wick wick wick* etc. Notes: *klee-yer* and *flick-a, flick-a* etc.

Hal H. Harrison

head, and a heavy long pointed beak, and small comparatively weak feet. The male has one wide blue band across its white breast; the female has two, the lower one brown. The loud rattling call is unmistakable.

The Kingfisher nests in a self-constructed burrow in a perpendicular bank. Digging is done with the bill; the dirt is removed by the feet. The tunnel extends inward for three to six feet, sloping gradually upward. Often the burrow makes an abrupt turn at the inner end where the five to eight white eggs are laid. The young, when hatched, are blind, naked, helpless, and thoroughly ugly. They remain in the nest about four weeks.

Although migratory, some individual Kingfishers remain each winter in the north where they find sufficient open water to afford them a livelihood. The two races of the Belted Kingfisher, Eastern *(M. a. alcyon)*, and Western *(M. a. caurina)*, range throughou North America from Alaska south t northern South America.

TEXAS KINGFISHER

(Chloroceryle americana septentrionalis)

Smaller than the Belted Kingfishe (7 inches long) and without the hea crest, the Green Kingfisher is limite to southern Texas and Arizona.

The male is dark metallic bronz green above with white spots, and broad chestnut band across the whit chest. The female has no chestnut coloring, but wears two bands of greenis black spots across the chest.

Like its larger relative, this Kingfisher nests in holes in the banks o streams, and is as jealous a fisherman. Its call is a much weaker edition of the rattle of the Belted Kingfisher, hardly more than a clicking noise.

WOODPECKERS

Family Picidae

As their name implies, the Woodpeckers hunt their food on the bark and in crevices of trees. For this reason, their bill is sharp and very strong. They are able to go up and down the trunks and branches, supporting themselves on their strong legs and balancing by means of their tails. The Woodpeckers nest in hollows in trees which they often dig out themselves with the aid of their beak. Because of the great number of insects and grubs consumed, they are economically very beneficial.

FLICKER

(Colaptes auratus)

Color Plate Page 127

During the years that I have written a nature column, there is one question concerning the identification of birds that has been asked me more than any other one. It is this: "What is the big brown bird that hops awkwardly over my lawn, digging in the grass with its bill?" The answer is: "A Flicker."

Our best known Woodpecker is a rebel in the family ranks, for the Flicker does most of its feeding on the ground, searching for its favorite food —ants. Thus, the Flicker, our only brown Woodpecker, attracts a great deal of attention. Folks are impressed by its large size (13 to 14 inches long, larger than a Robin) and its beauty: black bars on a brown back; black crescent on the breast; scarlet band on the back of the head; golden linings to the wings and tail; and a white rump spot, quite noticeable as the bird bounds away in undulating flight.

A second glance will disclose that some Flickers have a mustache and others do not. Quite appropriately, the male sports this black adornment running from his bill across the throat on each side of the head; it is absent in the female. Knowing this rule of sexes, observers are often surprised to find a nesting cavity filled with little "male Flickers," all wearing mustaches. The fact is that all baby Yellow-shafted Flickers wear mustaches. The rule applies only to adults.

That the Flicker is not entirely at home on the ground is evident by its awkward hopping. Anatomically, it is still built for tree climbing like others of the family. But unlike other Woodpeckers, its bill is slightly curved and pointed. Its tongue is different, too, for while a typical Woodpecker tongue is barbed for spearing wood borers, the Flicker's tongue is smooth, long, and very sticky. Ants that adhere to it remain to be eaten.

In its nesting, the Flicker is true to Woodpecker traditions. It excavates a cavity in a tree trunk and at the bottom, in a bed of chips, it lays its six to ten pure glossy white eggs. Both sexes incubate. The young hatch in about

PILEATED WOODPECKER (*Hylatomus pileatus*). Length: 17 to 19.5 inches. Male: body slate black and white; head with prominent red crest, and red crown. Black line through eye bordered with yellowish white above and below. Female: similar to male but forehead and front half of crown grayish brown or olive. Range: Canada, south to Florida and Gulf of Mexico. Voice: common call *kuk—kuk—kukkuk—kuk-kuk* etc.

Hal H. Harrison

sixteen days and are in the nest from three to four weeks. During their last few days of confinement, young Flickers are very noisy and often give away an otherwise unsuspected nesting site. Flickers feed their young by regurgitation, pumping partly digested food into their crops.

When Flickers return to the north in early spring, they engage in lively specacular and often amusing courtship ntics. Franklin L. Burns, in his mono- ;raph on the species, describes the ac- ions of the male as "bowing, hopping, rancing, dancing, strutting, flirting is wings, as he pleads and urges his ase with flickering, wacuping, and ickupping notes; finally he sidles up o her, she coyly sidles away, and per- aps takes wing, followed by the one r more suitors to another tree, where he whole performance is repeated."

Throughout its wide range, the Flicker is said to have no less than 125 common names. The eastern species is est known as Yellow-shafted Flicker, r Yellow Hammer. Three races are ecognized: the Northern Flicker *(C. ı. luteus)*, the Southern Flicker *(C. a. uratus)*, and the Boreal Flicker *(C. a. borealis)*.

RED-SHAFTED FLICKER AT NEST-HOLE *(Colaptes cafer)*. Length: 13 to 14 inches. Male and female: brown back, conspicuous white rump. A black crescent across the breast. Salmon-red under wings and tails. Male has red mustache. Range: throughout western United States. Voice: song, a low *wick, wick, wick, wick, wick*. Notes, a loud *kew*, or *kee-yer* and a *flick-a, flick-a*.
Alfred M. Bailey, National Audubon Society

RED-SHAFTED FLICKER

(Colaptes cafer)

Except for a marked difference in coloration (but not in pattern), and a difference in breeding ranges, the life histories of the Red-shafted Flicker and its eastern relative, the Yellow-shafted, or Northern, Flicker, are almost identical. Although they are different species in the genus *Colaptes*, the two Woodpeckers indicate their close relationship by intergrading where their ranges overlap. In such areas a great many confusing hybrids result.

The most conspicuous difference between the Red-shafted and the Yellow-shafted Flickers is the color of the wing and tail linings—in the one, red; in the other, yellow. Both sexes of the Yellow-shafted have a red crescent on the back of their heads which is entirely missing in the Red-shafted. And while males of the Yellow-shafted sport a black mustache, the males of the Red-shafted species are adorned with a red one. It is also of interest to note that while the young of both sexes of the eastern species have black mustaches, only the young males of the Red-shafted Flicker have red mustaches.

The voice of the Red-shafted Flicker is similar to the Yellow-shafted. Both are described by Peterson as a loud *wick-wick-wick-wick-wick*. The notes are a low *kew*, and *flick-a, flick-a*.

The Red-shafted Flicker breeds throughout western United States and winters through most of its range. Two subspecies are recognized: the Red-shafted Flicker *(C. c. collaris)*, and the Northwestern Flicker *(C. c. cafer)*. There are no field differences.

MEARN'S GILDED FLICKER

(Colaptes chrysoides mearnsi)

If it were possible to change the mustache of the common Flicker of the east from black to red, and then remove the red crescent on the nape of both sexes, we should have a Gilded Flicker. We should also have the head markings of the western Red-shafted Flicker, but the yellow wing and tail linings give it the body of the eastern species. In size and voice, it is like the other two Flickers.

MEARN'S GILDED FLICKER *(Colaptes chrysoides mearnsi)*. Length: 13 inches. Male: brown-backed, yellow wing and tail linings. Red mustache mark. Female: similar but lacks red mustache mark. Range: deserts of southern California and Arizona. Voice: typical Flicker notes. Song, a loud, *wick, wick, wick, wick, wick.*
Chicago Museum of Natural History

Mearn's Gilded Flicker is a deser Woodpecker of southeastern Califor nia and southwestern Arizona. It is on of three geographic races of the Gilde Flicker, the other two being confine to Lower California.

PILEATED WOODPECKER

(Hylatomus pileatus)

Color Plate Page 130

Excepting the nearly extinct Ivory-billed Woodpecker of the deep south the Pileated Woodpecker is the larges member of the family in North America. Despite its large size (17 to 2c inches, about the size of a Crow), th bird is relatively unknown to the average bird watcher because of its shy anc retiring nature.

The Pileated (the preferred pronunciation is "pile-" not "pill-"eated, although either is correct) is a handsome bird of the big timber, breeding from the Atlantic coast to the Rocky Mountains throughout the Transition and Canadian faunal areas. Its unmistakable markings include a bright red crest, black body with a narrow white stripe on the side of the head and neck, and a conspicuous white patch on the wing. The male has a red forehead and a red streak on the sides of the cheek, like a mustache.

Residents of Florida or Louisiana where an Ivory-billed Woodpecker might be seen, will recognize it by its larger size, its ivory-white bill, and the very large white wing-patches. The crest of the male Ivory-billed is red, that of the female is black.

Not only does the Pileated Woodpecker elude its would-be observers by its constant wariness and its alert attitude, but during much of the year t is silent. In the spring, however, like ts relative, the Flicker, the Pileated enters into some clownlike courtship antics, which include much bowing and uttering of the *wuck-a-wuck* notes. One call of the bird resembles the *flick-a, flick-a* notes of the Flicker, but much louder and more raucous.

I found a nest of a Pileated Woodpecker thirty-five feet from the ground in a dead white oak stub in early May. At my approach, the incubating or brooding female left the nesting hole and flew noisily to another tree about a hundred yards away. The beating of its great wings was surprisingly audible. Clinging to the side of the tree, the bird made a terrific clucking racket, the woods fairly ringing with her cries. The male appeared, but did not join in the disturbance. When I retired some distance away, the female returned to the nest.

Late in May, when I again visited this nesting tree, two young Pileated Woodpeckers were spending most of their time at the entrance to the nesting cavity, stretching their necks and calling in a rasping voice. While I hid in a blind, the old birds fed the young. The method was plainly by regurgitation.

The Pileated Woodpecker's chief source of food is ants, which it seeks by ripping great oblong holes in the trunks of standing or fallen timber. With its hammerlike bill, the bird drives to the heart of the tree to invade colonies of great carpenter ants. As many as 2600 ants have been found in the stomach of one bird.

The Log-cock, Cock-of-the-woods, Lord-god, or Black Woodpecker, as the Pileated is locally called, is a permanent resident wherever it is found, although it wanders over a large territory.

Four geographic races of the Pileated Woodpecker are recognized: the Southern Pileated *(C. p. pileatus)*, the Northern Pileated *(C. p. abieticola)*, the Florida Pileated *(C. p. floridanus)*, and the Western Pileated *(C. p. picinus)*. The breeding range of the species extends from Nova Scotia, southeastern Quebec, the southern Mackenzie, and British Columbia south to Florida, the Gulf Coast, and west to southeastern Texas. Although the bird is not found in the south Rockies and the Great Basin, it appears again from central California north.

RED-BELLIED WOODPECKER

(Centurus carolinus)

Color Plate Page 134

The name of the Red-bellied Woodpecker is misleading so far as field identification of the bird is concerned, for the name comes from an inconspicuous wash of crimson on the bird's lower belly. For field purposes, it is more important to remember that the Red-bellied Woodpecker has a pronounced zebra-like back, barred crosswise with black and white. The male's crown and nape are crimson; the female has red on the nape and back of the head, but the crown is gray. The underparts are gray in both sexes. The bird is 9 to 10½ inches long.

The Red-bellied Woodpecker is decidedly an eastern species, reaching its greatest abundance in the southern pine barrens, swampy bottomlands, and deciduous woods. It is not particularly shy and often is a common inhabitant of the southern plantations, nesting in self-made cavities in dead trees.

From its characteristic call of *chad*, it gets its common name in the south.

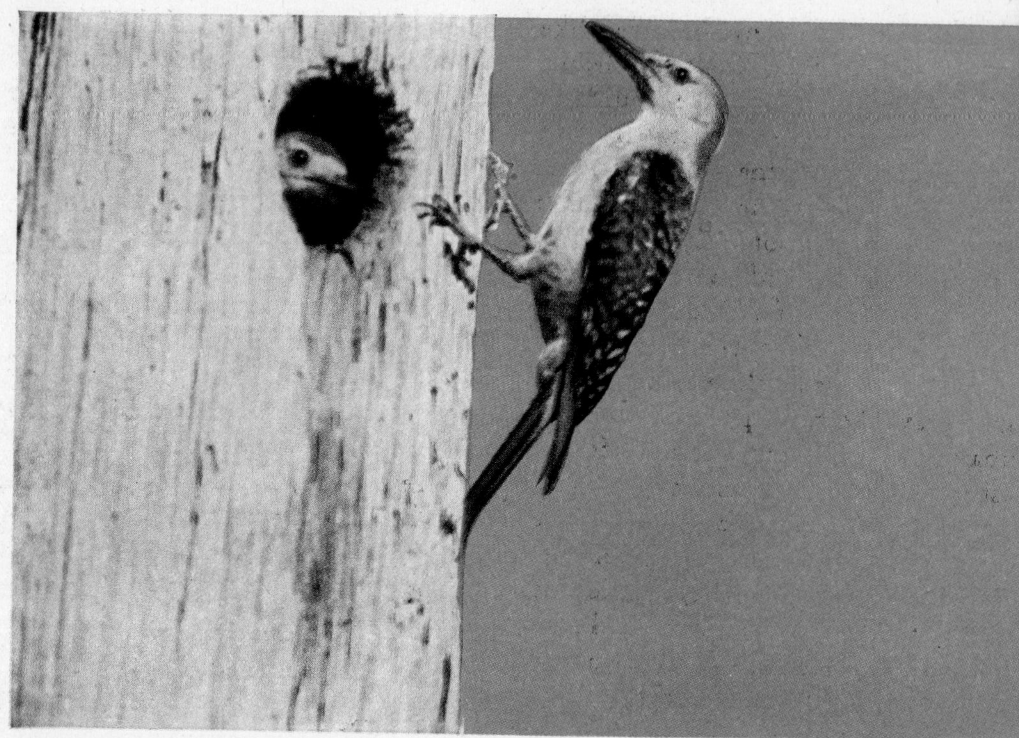

RED-BELLIED WOODPECKER (*Centurus carolinus*). Length: 9 to 10.5 inches. Male: red crown and nape; back barred with black and white. Underparts, sides of throat and cheeks ashy white. Female: similar to male but has ashy gray crown instead of white. Range: resident of Florida and Gulf of Mexico north to Delaware, Lake Erie, Minnesota and South Dakota. Voice: note, *churr* or *chaw* also *chiv-chiv*.
Samuel A. Grimes

Zebra bird, or Zebra Woodpecker are other rather appropriate names. Its habits are generally quite Woodpecker-like in all respects.

GOLDEN-FRONTED WOODPECKER

(*Centurus aurifrons aurifrons*)

Color Plate Page 135

The range of the Golden-fronted Woodpecker in the United States is confined to Texas, where it is unevenly distributed from the north central part of the state, south to Mexico.

In appearance and habits it is very much like its close relative, the Red-bellied Woodpecker, and is about the same size (9 to 10 inches). In the western extremity of its range, the Red-bellied sometimes occupies the same regions as the Golden-fronted. Both are zebra-backed, but the Golden-front shows a conspicuous white rump. The head of the male Red-bellied is red from the forehead to the hind neck, while in the male Golden-front three areas of color appear on the head: yellow forehead, red crown, and an orange-yellow band on the nape. The female has no red on the head.

The voice of the Golden-front is a rolling *churr*.

GILA WOODPECKER

(*Centurus uropygialis*)

Color Plate Page 137

The zebra-backed Gila Woodpecker is a noisy, conspicuous, and common resident of the southwest desert coun-

GOLDEN-FRONTED WOODPECKER (*Centurus aurifrons aurifrons*). Length: 9.5 inches. Male: yellow forehead, red crown, orange nape, barred black and white upperparts, grayish brown below. Female: similar to male but lacks crown patch and has prominent yellow patch on back of neck. Range: Texas south to Valley of Mexico. Voice: a rolling *churrr*.
Fred Bashour

try, reaching its greatest abundance in the desert mesa of southern Arizona. It is the carpenter of the desert, for not only does it build homes for itself in the giant saguaro cacti, but it unknowingly builds homes for a number of other desert creatures that occupy the abandoned cavities of the Gila. Among the birds to which the Gila Woodpecker is a benefactor are the Desert Sparrow Hawk, Saguaro Screech Owl, Elf Owl, Ferruginous Pygmy Owl, Martins, Ash-throated Flycatchers, and the Arizona Crested Flycatchers.

The Gila Woodpecker is easily identified as a medium-sized Woodpecker (8 to 10 inches long, about the size of a Hairy), with a black and white back, barred crosswise, and a grayish brown head, neck, and underparts. In flight, a white patch on each wing is conspicuous. The male's red crown-patch can be seen only at close range.

Its voice is much like that of the Golden-fronted.

RED-HEADED WOODPECKER

(*Melanerpes erythrocephalus erythrocephalus*)

Color Plate Page 140

Over some of its extensive range in southern Canada and the United States east of the Rockies, the brightly colored Red-headed Woodpecker has practically disappeared. Many who formerly knew it well are conscious of its absence, and the one factor blamed most for this condition is the European Starling.

I question this conclusion. Although the Starling may be a factor, I doubt if it is a major one. The Red-headed Woodpecker is a pugnacious bird, and in most cases, I believe it is capable of holding its own when vying with Starlings for nesting sites. Rather, I would blame the destruction of desirable habitat as the principal reason for the disappearance of this Woodpecker from many areas where it was formerly abundant.

When one sees a pair of Red-heads holding on to an oak grove for years and then vanishing when the woodlot is finally cleared, the hypothesis seems logical. Lumbering, I dare say, has also caused many resident individuals in the northern states to move south in the winter in search of food. Those that do not migrate are rather dependent upon acorns and beechnuts for winter food. Observers throughout the country are agreed that food supply, not temperature, is the deciding factor in the bird's winter range.

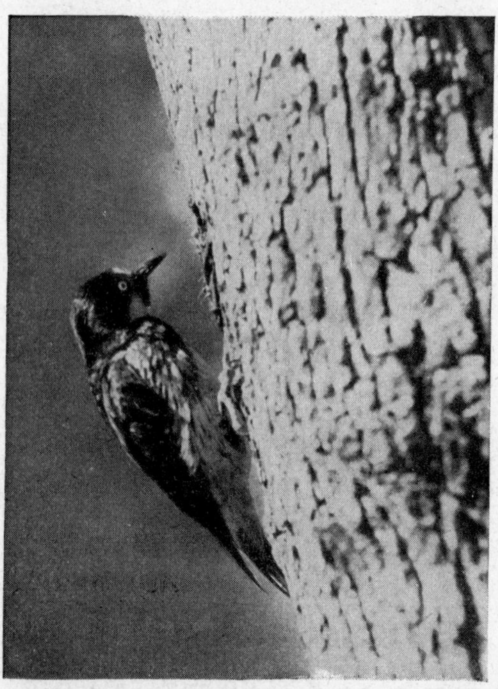

CALIFORNIA (ACORN) WOODPECKER *(Balanosphyra formicivora)*. Length: 9.5 inches. Male and female: upperparts black, with black and white streaked face, and red crown. Rump patch, and patch in each wing, white. Pale sulphur yellow lower throat and foreneck. Breast band solid black. Abdomen, bluish white streaked with black. Range: southwest Oregon, California, Arizona, New Mexico and western Texas. Voice: *whack-up, whack-up, whack-up* or *ja-cob, ja-cob, ja-cob.*

Ross and Florence Thornburg

Fortunately, Red-heads are adaptable. With natural habitat constantly diminishing, individual pairs have gradually accepted what man has offered as a substitute—telephone poles, for instance. The Red-headed Woodpecker is very often one of the common birds of the roadside, surveying its territory from the tops of poles, making its home in cavities within the pole. Unlike some members of its family, this Woodpecker does not shy from human habitation. Indeed, the natural color photograph on page 140 was taken at a nesting hole three feet from the ground in a post erected for swings in a school playground. A less private place would be hard to find.

The Red-headed Woodpecker has been nicknamed "Uncle Sam," for it sports the red, white, and blue colors of that mythical gentleman. The blue is bluish black, however. Many species of Woodpecker have red patches on their heads, but this is the only species with the entire head and throat red. In flight it shows characteristic patches of white on the dark wings and rump. The sexes are indistinguishable, but young birds have brown heads which they wear until fall. Adults are 8½ to 9½ inches long.

The Red-head is a noisy bird with a vast repertoire of indescribable utterances. A common call note is *queer, queer, queer.*

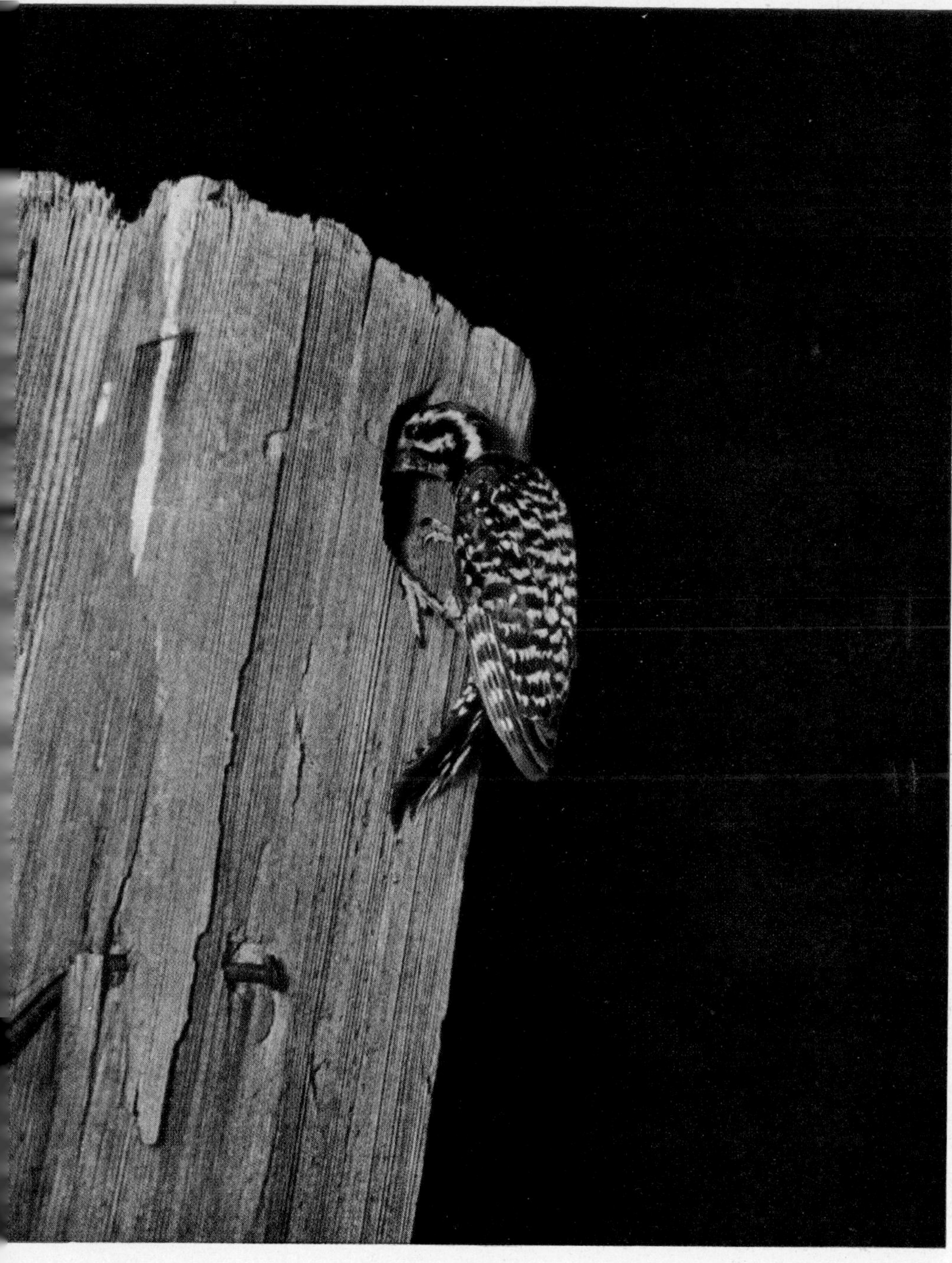

GILA WOODPECKER (*Centurus uropygialis*). Length: 8 to 10 inches. Male: head and underparts dull brownish gray, upperparts striped black and white. White patch in each wing shows in flight. Round scarlet patch on crown. Female: similar to male but lacks red spot. Range: along Colorado River in California, Nevada, and through Arizona to New Mexico. Voice: a rolling *churr* and a sharp *pit*.

George M. Bradt

Like the Flicker, it often feeds on the ground, and like the California Woodpecker, it often stores acorns for winter use. While the western bird wedges them in holes in the bark, the Red-head places its store in cavities.

The summer diet of this bird is made up of fruits and berries as well as much animal matter. The fruit stealing habit of some individuals has gained for the Red-head a bad reputation in some areas.

CALIFORNIA WOODPECKER

(Balanosphyra formicivora)

"California Acorn-storing Woodpecker" is an appropriate name that has been suggested for the California Woodpecker, for it designates one of the bird's outstanding characteristics—that of storing acorns in holes prepared for that purpose in the bark of trees. Thousands of acorns have been found in the trunk of a single tree, each wedged tightly into an individual hole by this bird.

The conspicuous markings of the California Woodpecker set it apart from all others. In flight it appears all black with a white rump and a white patch on each wing. Facing an observer, its clownlike face, white abdomen, and broad band across the chest are distinctive. Its call is described as *whack-up, whack-up.*

Four races of this species are recognized in North America, two of them in the United States. These are the Ant-eating Woodpecker *(B. f. formicivora)*, found in Arizona, New Mexico, and Texas; and the California Woodpecker *(B. f. bairdi)*, a breeding bird of the Pacific coast from Oregon south to Lower California.

LEWIS'S WOODPECKER

(Asyndesmus lewisi)

Color Plate Page 141

Lewis's Woodpecker is a rebel fro the family ranks, the most un-Wooc pecker-like of all the Woodpeckers. I the air, the bird does not fly in the ur dulating bounds so characteristic of i family, but flies evenly with flappin wings like a Crow or a Jay. Indeed, is called Crow Woodpecker in parts c its range, which extends from souther Canada southward to Arizona an New Mexico, and from the mountair of southern California to South Da kota and Kansas.

In its feeding habits, it is most lik a Flycatcher, flying out from a favo ite perch to snare passing insects. I feeds on the ground a great dea searching for crickets, beetles, an other insects. Unlike other Woodpeck ers, it does not bore in trees for a liveli hood, but does glean some food fror the bark and leaves of trees. Like th California Woodpecker, it often stor acorns for future consumption.

Since it is not a "hammering" Woodpecker, it prefers to use an aban doned hole of another Woodpecker a its nesting cavity. While it is charac teristic of Woodpeckers to land agains the sides of tree trunks, Lewis's is jus as like to land on a limb and perch side wise. And finally, unlike other Wood peckers, Lewis's gather in flocks lik Blackbirds during certain seasons.

Lewis's Woodpecker should be mis taken for no other. It is a large bird, 1 inches long. Its rosy underparts, gra upper breast, red face, and black bac and tail are distinctive. From a distanc it looks entirely black. The sexes ar similar. Its voice is a harsh *churr* dur ing the breeding season. At othe imes of the year it is ilent.

YELLOW-BELLIED SAPSUCKER

(Sphyrapicus varius varius)

YELLOW-BELLIED SAPSUCKER *(Sphyrapicus varius varius)*. Length: 8 to 8.5 inches. Male and female: upperparts black barred with brownish white; lower parts, red, black and yellow. Longitudinal white patch on black wing, and red forehead patch distinguish bird. *Males* have red throats, *females*, white. Immature bird is sooty brown. Range: eastern North America. Winters from Pennsylvania, Ohio Valley, and Indiana to North Carolina mountains. Voice: a squealing cat-like or jay-like mewing note.
Rudolph Hindemith, American Museum of Natural History

Most bird watchers re familiar with the 'ellow-bellied Sapucker as a migrant beween its winter home n the Gulf states, Mexco, the West Indies, and 'anama, and its summer ome in the Canadian .ife Zone. It is the most nigratory of the Woodecker tribe, and may be bserved in spring and 'all from Iowa to New England southward.

Its habit of drilling for sap in living rees is a black mark on the Yellowellied Sapsucker's reputation, for in his way it does considerable damage to imber. It also eats many harmful inects, especially those attracted to the ap oozing from newly made holes, perlaps in return for its damage.

This Woodpecker, which is about 8 nches long, may be distinguished by ts red forehead patch. Males also have ed throats, but the female's throat is vhite. The back is black, irregularly arred with whitish, and a long white atch on the closed black wing is disinctive in all plumages. The upper reast is black, the sides of the abdomen lack and white, and the underparts ale yellow.

Its voice is like the mewing of a cat, or sometimes like a Jay. Its drumming s rhythmic, several rapid thumps folowed by slow rhythmic ones.

RED-NAPED SAPSUCKER

(Sphyrapicus varius nuchalis)

Color Plate Page 144

The Red-naped Sapsucker is the western race of the eastern Yellow-bellied Sapsucker, and its appearance and habits are essentially the same as that species. It ranges in summer through the Rocky Mountains, east of the Sierra Nevada and Cascades, from central British Columbia and Alberta to western Texas and Arizona.

In autumn, the Red-naped Sapsucker leaves its summer home in the high altitudes and migrates to the lowlands where it spends the winter.

RED-BREASTED SAPSUCKER

(Sphyrapicus varius subspecies)

Like the Red-naped Sapsucker, the two races of the Red-breasted Sap-

RED-HEADED WOODPECKER (*Melanerpes erythrocephalus erythrocephalus*). Length: 8.5 to 9.5 inches. Male and female: red head, neck, throat and upper breast. Bluish black back. Large square white patches on rear edge of wing visible in flight. White lower parts. Immature: head, neck, and upper chest brownish gray spotted with black; black shoulders, back and wing coverts. Underpart whitish. Range: Gulf of Mexico to New England, New York and Ontario, Michigan, Minnesota and Manitoba. Voice: a loud *querr* or *queeoh*.

Hal H. Harrison

EWIS'S WOODPECKER (*Asyndesmus lewisi*). Length: 11 inches. Male and female: greenish black above; gray and red underparts. Has wide gray collar around breast and back of neck; and ed face-patch. Range: from Canada throughout western America. Voice: generally silent. A harsh *churr* in breeding season.

Ross and Florence Thornburg

sucker are western forms of the typical Yellow-bellied Sapsucker. While very little field difference can be detected between the Red-naped and the Yellow-bellied, the Red-breasted Sapsucker is unusual for a subspecies because it shows a marked difference in coloration. Indeed, there is considerable controversy among taxonomists regarding the exact status of this form.

The entire head and breast of the Red-breasted Sapsucker are red, while only the forehead and throat are so colored in the closely related Red-naped Sapsucker. In other respects, however, the two birds are similar, and the same size, about 9 inches long.

The Northern Red-breasted Sapsucker *(S. v. ruber)* breeds from southern Alaska to western Oregon. The

Southern Red-breasted Sapsucker *(S. v. daggetti)* nests in the mountains of California.

WILLIAMSON'S SAPSUCKER

(Sphyrapicus thyroideus)

Color Plate Page 145

Williamson's Sapsucker *(S. t. thyroideus)* and its subspecies, Natalie's Sapsucker *(S. t. nataliae)* are the only American four-toed Woodpeckers that have no red in the head or nape in either sex. And unlike other North American woodpeckers, there is a vast difference in the plumage of the sexes. Indeed, for many years, the female was named the Brown-headed Woodpecker and was considered to be another species entirely.

RED-BREASTED SAPSUCKER *(Sphyrapicus varius subspecies)*. Length: 8.5 to 9 inches. Male and female: entire head and breast are bright red. Long white wing-patch. Range: breeds in higher mountains of California, southern Oregon, western Oregon, and western Washington. Winters in nearby valleys and south along California coast to Monterey.
Chicago Natural History Museum

The western mountains are the habitat of this Sapsucker, and it breeds from southern British Columbia and Montana to central Arizona and New Mexico. In winter it is found south as far as Texas and Lower California.

The male is black on the upperparts crown, and chest, with a white shoulder patch and two white stripes cutting the black face and crown. The chin and throat are red, the belly yellow. In flight, the white rump patch and the white shoulder patch flash against the black back and tail. The bird is about 9½ inches long.

The female can be confused with no other Woodpecker in her range. She is zebra-backed, brown headed, with a yellow belly and barred sides. The white rump shows in flight.

HAIRY WOODPECKER

(Dendrocopus villosus)

Color Plate Page 149

One might easily confuse the Hairy Woodpecker with its smaller counterpart, the Downy Woodpecker. On rare occasions, when the two species are seen together, the larger size of the Hairy (8½ to 10½ inches) is quite noticeable. Seen separately, however, a large Downy may be named a Hairy, while a small Hairy may be misidentified as a Downy.

I have always found that the bills of the two birds are their best identifying marks. The bill of the Hairy is as long as its head; the bill of the Downy is not. Indeed, it is comparatively stubby.

If the observer is close enough to see the white outer tail feathers as they are

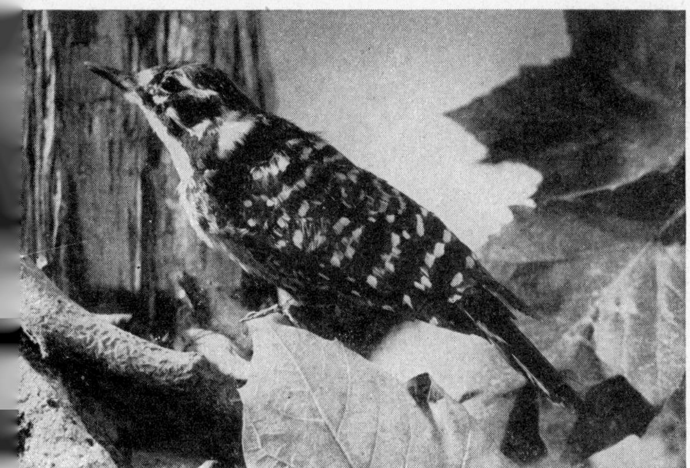

NUTTALL'S WOODPECKER *(Dendrocopus nuttalli).* Length: 7 inches. Male: upperparts black and white striped, with red cap; white underparts with black spotted sides. Female: lacks red cap. Range: foothills of California. Voice: high rattling cry, and loud *prrit.*
Rudolph Hindemith, American Museum of Natural History

pread against the tree runk while the bird is feeding or hitching its way up the tree, it may be noted that in the Hairy these feathers are pure white, while in the Downy they are spotted with black. Still another identifying mark, if it can be observed, is the fact that the red spot on the back of the Hairy's head is divided, while the spot on the Downy is in one piece.

Although it will not serve for positive identification, it helps to know that the Hairy Woodpecker is more likely to be found in big timber, while the Downy is fond of orchards and shade trees. The Hairy is much shyer than its smaller cousin and less likely to become a regular visitor to the suet feeder in the garden. Its call is louder than the Downy, being a sharply uttered *peek.* The Downy calls *pik.*

The habits of the two Woodpeckers are similar. Many geographic forms of the Hairy, some differing slightly in size and coloration, are widespread throughout North America. The Hairy of the Canadian forests is considerably larger than that of our southern states.

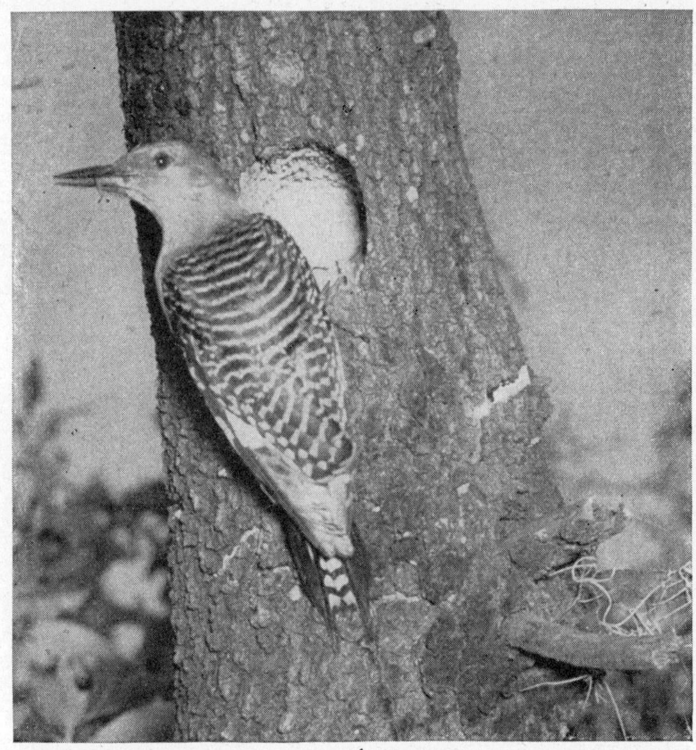

LADDER-BACKED WOODPECKER *(Dendrocopus scalaris).* Length: 7.5 inches. Male: upperparts black and white, underparts white. White line disjointed by black, down back. Has red cap. Female: similar to male but lacks red cap. Range: California, Arizona, New Mexico, Colorado, Oklahoma, and Texas. Found in dry country. Voice: rattling series of notes. Note, a sharp *pick.*
Samuel A. Grimes

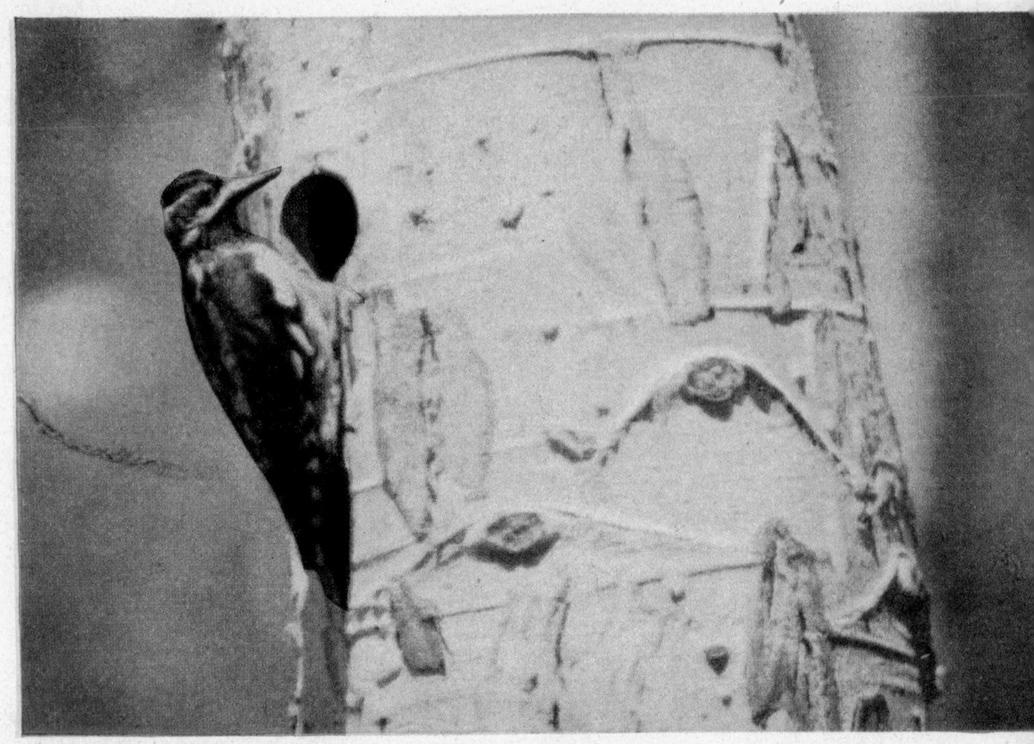

RED-NAPED SAPSUCKER (*Sphyrapicus varius nuchalis*). Length: 8 to 8.5 inches. Male: back barred with pale yellow and black. Black wing feathers have white patch. Red forehead and throat patch. Underparts pale yellow. Female: similar to male but with white throat. Range: mountains from eastern Washington and Montana south to northeast California, Arizona, central New Mexico and western Texas. Winters south into Mexico. Voice: nasal *cheerrrrr*.
Alfred M. Bailey

DOWNY WOODPECKER

(Dendrocopus pubescens)

Tap, tap, tap! Tap, tap, tap! Not a loud tap, just a muffled little tapping that is quite distinct on a frosty morning in January. On a bleak winter day, with the world so still and quiet, we are grateful for such a commonplace thing as the diligent hammering of a Downy Woodpecker's bill against a piece of frozen suet in our garden.

When the summer birds went south last fall, a handful of hardy ones stayed behind, determined to forage for their winter food where they had spent the summer. Thus, at our winter feeding station, we find such guests as the Cardinal, White-breasted Nuthatch, Chickadee, Tufted Titmouse, Blue Jay, and our very good friend, the Downy Woodpecker.

That "very good friend" is not sentiment. It's a fact. This little black and white mite, the smallest of our Woodpeckers (6½ to 7 inches long), is an important guardian of our orchards and shade trees. Over seventy-five percent of its diet is animal matter, gleaned from the bark crevices where larva and their eggs lie hidden.

How well equipped is the Downy for seeking its livelihood! Its bill is pointed like a carpenter's chisel. Its skull is thick and heavy, adding great force to the hammering of its bill.

WILLIAMSON'S OR NATALIE'S SAPSUCKER (*Sphyrapicus thyroideus*). Length: 9.5 inches. Male: jet black above. White double stripes on side of the head. White rump and shoulder patch. Black throat and breast; red throat-patch. Yellow belly. Female: zebra-backed with brown head, white rump and striped sides. Range: Canada south in mountains to California, central Arizona, and New Mexico. Winters into Mexico. Voice: nasal *cheeer* or *que-yer*.
Alfred M. Bailey

Then, as additional equipment, sharp barbs are attached to the Downy's tongue. The latter may be extended about two inches from the end of the bill. Even the deeply hidden wood borers do not escape the Downy's search.

Then there are its special climbing feet. The usual arrangement of toes on a perching bird's foot is three in front and one behind. The Woodpecker has two in front and two behind, making it possible for the bird to clamp itself to the side of a tree. A sharp strong tail, which may be used against the tree like a camp stool, is also helpful.

Have you ever noticed that some Downies that visit your garden feeding station have red spots on the backs of their heads, while others are just plain black and white? The red spot is worn only by the males. Like the Hairy, the Downy has a white back.

In the spring, Downies forsake the wandering flocks of winter birds, establish a territory, and enter into courtship which culminates in nest building. Since the Woodpecker does not have a beautiful song with which to woo a mate, it beats a tattoo on a hollow limb. This is called "drumming." A loudly repeated note, *wick, wick, wick, wick,* is also part of the courtship. This is accompanied by wing spreading and a display of the red occipital patch. The male pursues the female from tree to tree in great undulating bounds.

Like other members of its tribe, the Downy lays pure white eggs at the bottom of a cavity drilled in a tree. A few chips serve as a nest. Both birds incubate. The young are hatched blind and naked. When they leave the nest, they are taught by the parents to bore for insects. Unlike most birds, the Downy will eat caterpillars.

The Downy is one resident bird that insists on a warm bed during the long winter nights. This winter home is usually a cavity, much like a nesting hole, which the bird chisels and drills for that purpose. One winter, a Downy used a Wren box in my garden as its hotel. The entrance hole was too small, so the Woodpecker drilled it to correct size.

The geographic races of the Downy Woodpecker inhabit most of the timber country of North America, from Alaska to Florida.

ARIZONA WOODPECKER (*Dendrocopus arizonae arizonae*). Length: 8 inches. Male: upperparts, brown; nape, red, bordered by conspicuous white patches. Has striped face and heavily barred sides. Underparts are white, thickly spotted with brown. Female: similar, but lacks red on head. Range: oak belt of mountains in southeast Arizona and southwest New Mexico. Voice: a sharp *spik* or *tseek*.
Ross and Florence Thornburg

LADDER-BACKED WOODPECKER

(Dendrocopus scalaris)

Two races of the Ladder-backed Woodpecker, which might well be called the Downy Woodpecker of the arid southwest, are recognized in the United States, although fifteen subspecies are found throughout the western hemisphere.

The Texas Woodpecker *(D. s. symplectus)* and the Cactus Woodpecker *(D. s. cactophilus)* are the two that range through the desert country of southeastern California, Arizona, New Mexico, southeastern Colorado, western Oklahoma, and Texas.

Since no other Woodpeckers with ladder backs and striped faces occur in that area, these two species should be confused with no other birds. The very similar Nuttall's Woodpecker occurs in California west of the Sierra Nevada. The Ladder-back is about 7½ inches long, black and white in coloring. The male has a red cap. Its call is similar to the Downy Woodpecker.

NUTTALL'S WOODPECKER

(Dendrocopus nuttalli)

West of the southern Cascades and the Sierra Nevadas, from southern Oregon to northwestern Lower California, the Nuttall's Woodpecker is at home. The very similar races of the Ladder-backed Woodpeckers do not occur in the same areas as the Nuttall's, thus eliminating considerable confusion for bird watchers. Indeed, the Nuttall's is the only Woodpecker with

RED-COCKADED WOODPECKER (*Dendrocopus borealis*). Length: 8.5 inches. Male: black crown with red tufts of feathers on sides of head behind eyes, black and white striped back and wings, and white cheeks. Underparts, white. Female: lacks red feathers, but otherwise the same. Range: pine woods of southern states. Voice: a rasping *sripp* or *zhilp*.
Samuel A. Grimes

a barred black and white back and a striped face that occurs west of the Sierras. Males have a red cap. The Downy Woodpecker may be recognized instantly by the lack of bars and the presence of a broad white stripe on its back. The Nuttall's is partial to groves of live oaks.

ARIZONA WOODPECKER

(Dendrocopus arizonae arizonae)

With the exception of the Flicker, the Arizona Woodpecker is our only brown backed Woodpecker, and is about 8 inches long. The sides are barred and the face is striped. Males have a red patch on the nape of the neck.

This bird is found in the United States only in the mountains of southeastern Arizona and New Mexico. It is a Mexican species that only occasionally crosses the border. In winter it moves down from the higher parts of the mountains to lower levels.

RED-COCKADED WOODPECKER

(Dendrocopus borealis)

Although there is nothing unusual about the appearance of the Red-cockaded Woodpecker, a zebra backed bird of the open pine country of the South Atlantic and Gulf states, it certainly is interesting because of its unusual habits.

WHITE-HEADED WOODPECKER AT NEST HOLE (*Dendrocopus albolarvatus*). Length: 9 inches. Male: white head; crown and nape bright red; body black. Female: similar, but lacks red. Range: Washington to California, west to Nevada. Voice: a sharp *chick*, sometimes *chick-ik-ik-ik*. Also a rattle occasionally.
Gayle Pickwell

ARCTIC THREE-TOED WOODPECKER (*Picoides arcticus*). Length: 9 to 10 inches. Male: upperparts, shiny black with heavily streaked sides and yellow crown. Underparts white. Female: similar to male but lacks crown patch. Range: Quebec south to northern New York, New England and Minnesota. Voice: '*a short, sharp cruck or crick*'.
Joseph S. Dixon

Unlike the Downy Woodpecker, with which it might be confused except for its conspicuous white cheeks, the Red-cockaded shuns habitation and frequents the yellow pine woodlands where it is found in company with others of its kind. Several nesting pairs often share the same pine area when the trees are not too close together.

Characteristic of this bird is its habit of puncturing the bark around its nesting hole until the entire area is sticky with oozing resin. Also characteristic is the bird's uncanny accuracy in choosing for its nesting site a living pine with a decaying heart. Wise lumbermen shun trees where the Red-cockades have already advertised the poor timber value.

Young males in their first plumage have red crown patches which they lose with the first molt. When they acquire adult plumage, the males have a red streak on each side of the occiput. The crown is then black. The call is a rasping *zripp*.

WHITE-HEADED WOODPECKER

(*Dendrocopus albolarvatus*)

A black Woodpecker with a white head and white wing patch is a White headed Woodpecker. Males have a red patch on the nape. It can be confused with no other species.

The White-head is about the size of a Hairy Woodpecker (9 inches long). It inhabits the conifers of the Pacific coast and feeds largely on pine seeds. Its voice is a sharp *chick*.

Two races are recognized: the Northern White-headed Woodpecker (*D. a. albolarvatus*) and the Southern White-headed Woodpecker (*D. a. gravirostris*). They are indistinguishable in the field.

ARCTIC THREE-TOED WOODPECKER

(*Picoïdes arcticus*)

Male Three-toed Woodpeckers are the only Woodpeckers with yellow crowns. Females lack this marking. In the Arctic Three-toed, or Black-backed, Woodpecker, the back is solid black. In the similar American Three-toed Woodpecker, the back is transversely banded with white or "ladder-backed." Both birds measure 8 to 10 inches in length.

The Arctic Three-toed is a bird of the conifers where wood-boring beetles constitute the greater portion of its diet. It is generally tame and unsuspicious, often permitting close approach by an observer.

This Woodpecker is not strictly an Arctic resident as its name might imply, although it does breed farther north than any other Woodpecker except the American Three-toed. In the United States, the Arctic Three-toed reaches the northern sections of California, Montana, Wyoming, Minnesota, Michigan, New York, Vermont, New Hampshire, and Maine. It is a winter resident throughout most of its breeding range. Even in the depths of winter it is able to find, beneath the bark of the trees, the grubs on which it subsists, and thus has no need to migrate.

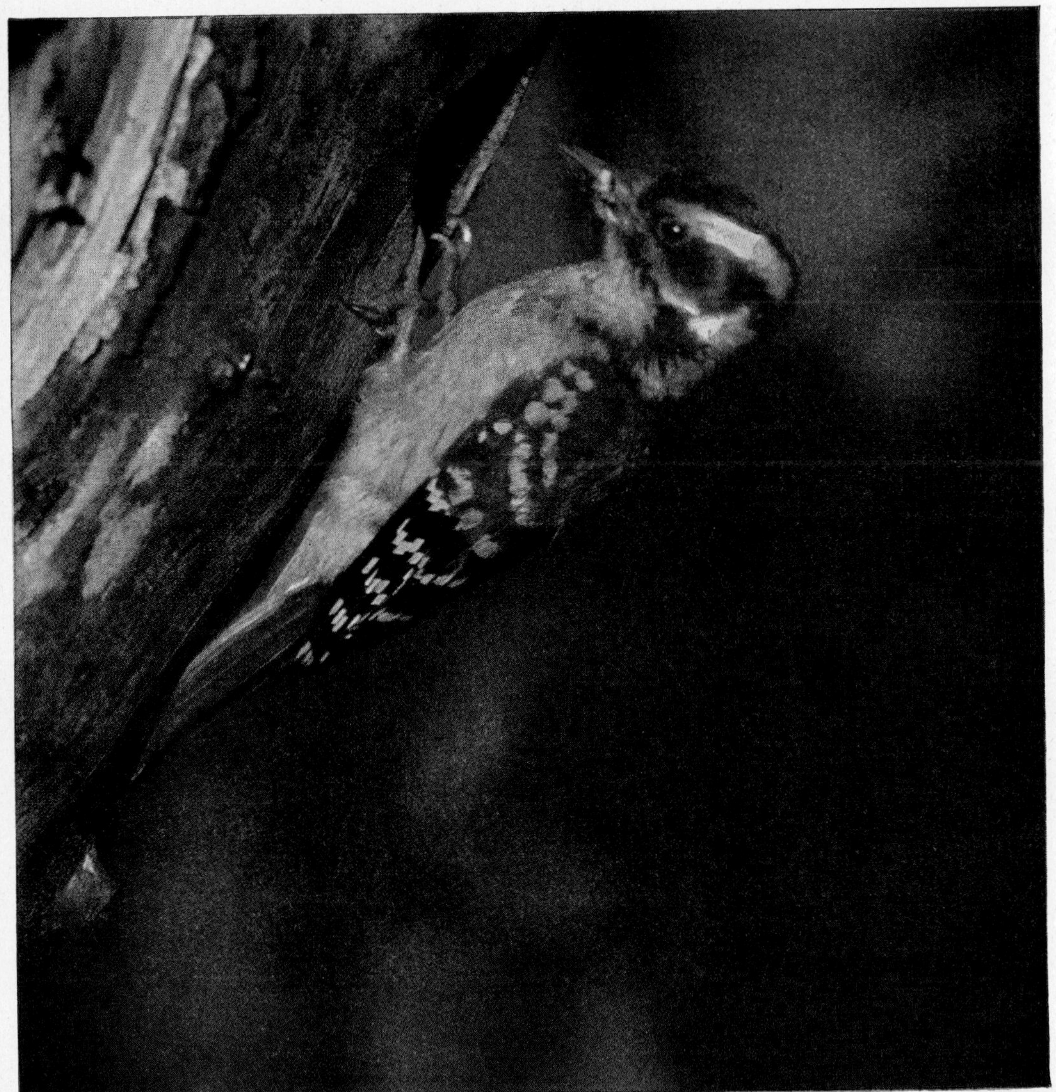

HAIRY WOODPECKER (*Dendrocopus villosus*). Length: 8.5 to 10.5 inches. Male: black and white upperparts; white underparts. Small red patch on back of head. Females lack patch but otherwise are similar. Range: forests from Canada to Mexican mountains. Voice: a rattle; note, *pleek*.
Hal H. Harrison

AMERICAN THREE-TOED WOODPECKER

(Picoïdes tridactylus bacatus)

Another Woodpecker of the extreme north, the American Three-toed covers much the same range as the Arctic, and the males of both species have yellow caps. However, it is distinguishable from its close relative by the barred back, which is a distinguishing feature of the female as well. The bird nests in evergreens, and is considered to be almost nonmigratory. Even in the dead of winter, it is able to find beneath the bark of the trees, the grubs on which it subsists.

IVORY-BILLED WOODPECKER

(Campephilus principalis)

In 1939, James T. Tanner, after three years' intensive study of the Ivory-billed Woodpecker on a project sponsored by the National Audubon Society, estimated the total population of Ivory-bills as twenty-four individual birds. These, Tanner discovered, were confined to not more than five areas in Louisiana, Florida, and possibly South Carolina. It probably is North America's rarest bird and well on the way to extinction.

If this largest of North American Woodpeckers does become extinct (and it seems more than likely that it eventually will), it will be due principally to the loss of the bird's specialized food supply through logging operations. Tanner wrote: "An Ivory-bill can find food only in some dead trees or parts of trees, and once these have passed a certain stage of decay, the Ivory-bill can no longer secure food there."

IVORY-BILLED WOODPECKER *(Campephilus principalis)*. Length: 20 inches. Male: upperparts black. White stripes from eyes along sides of neck joining in middle of back. Bright red crest. Large white wing-patches, and ivory white bill. Underparts black. Range: reported last in Louisiana, but close to extinction. Voice: a single, loud tooting note.

A A. Allen, National Audubon Society

Virgin or primitive forests are demanded by the Ivory-bill for sustenance. The complete lumbering of such habitat will doom the bird, but the permanent preservation of tracts of such highly valuable timber is a difficult piece of conservation to sell to business interests. Yet, on such a thin thread, rests the future of this magnificent big bird, which measures 20 inches in length.

Reports of Ivory-bills being seen almost anywhere throughout the country are common. A recent report was addressed to me from eastern Ohio. These, of course, are Pileated Woodpeckers, a bird as large as a Crow, but still smaller than an Ivory-billed Woodpecker. The Pileated has a dark bill; the Ivory-billed's is white. The best field mark, however, is the large white patch on the wing of the Ivory-billed, visible when the bird is perched. The Pileated, when perched, shows no white on its black back.

The voice is very different from that of the Pileated, being a single tooting note, whereas that of the Pileated is more Flicker-like.

DOWNY WOODPECKER (*Dendrocopus pubescens*). Length: 6.5 to 7 inches. Male: black and white above, white below. Bright scarlet nape. White stripe above and below eye. Female: similar to male but lacks red patch. Range: resident from Gulf of Mexico to Canada. Voice: rapid descending notes. Note, a flat *pick*.

Hal H. Harrison

COTINGAS

Family Cotingidae

The Cotingas, or Chatterers, are ·illiantly colored birds of tropical merica. Only one, the Becard, reaches e United States as an accidental visor. The family includes the Cock-ofe-Rock, and the Bell Birds among its embers in Central and South America.

XANTHUS'S BECARD

(Platypsaris aglaiae richmondi)

The Rose-throated Becard is accintal along the Mexican border. It rembles a Flycatcher in appearance and bits, and prefers deep open woods. Its diet consists of flying insects and wild berries.

The male (6½ inches long) is gray with a dark, bushy, erectile crown and dark cheeks, and a rose colored throat. The heavy crown and short tail give the bird a heavy headed appearance. The female is brown with a rust colored tail, dark gray cap, and a buff collar. Her underparts are buff white.

The nest is a mass of woven fiber about a foot long and nine inches in diameter, suspended from the tip of a branch. The entrance is in the side. The female lays five eggs which are white with brown spots.

FLYCATCHERS

Family Tyrannidae

The Tyrant Flycatchers are American birds, of which a number of species are found in the United States. On the whole they are dull colored birds. They catch their prey by sitting still on a perch until a hapless insect flies by. Then they dart out with amazing speed, often executing complicated maneuvers, to seize the insect on the wing, usually with a loud click of the bill, and then return to their perch.

EASTERN KINGBIRD

(Tyrannus tyrannus)

Color Plate Page 154

If you have never watched a King bird harrying a Hawk or a Crow or Vulture that has invaded its sacred ter ritory, you have not spent much tim afield. The sight is one that alway stops even the most seasoned bir watcher, for it is the re-enaction o

KINGBIRD (*Tyrannus tyrannus*). Length: 8.5 to 9 inches. Male and female: upperparts gray becomin black on crown and upper tail coverts. Crown crested with partially concealed patch of orange red White band at tip of tail. Underparts, grayish white. Range: Nova Scotia to Gulf of Mexico Winters in tropical America. Voice: a rolling *pi-teer-rrry* or *pe-cheer-ry*.

John S. Dunning

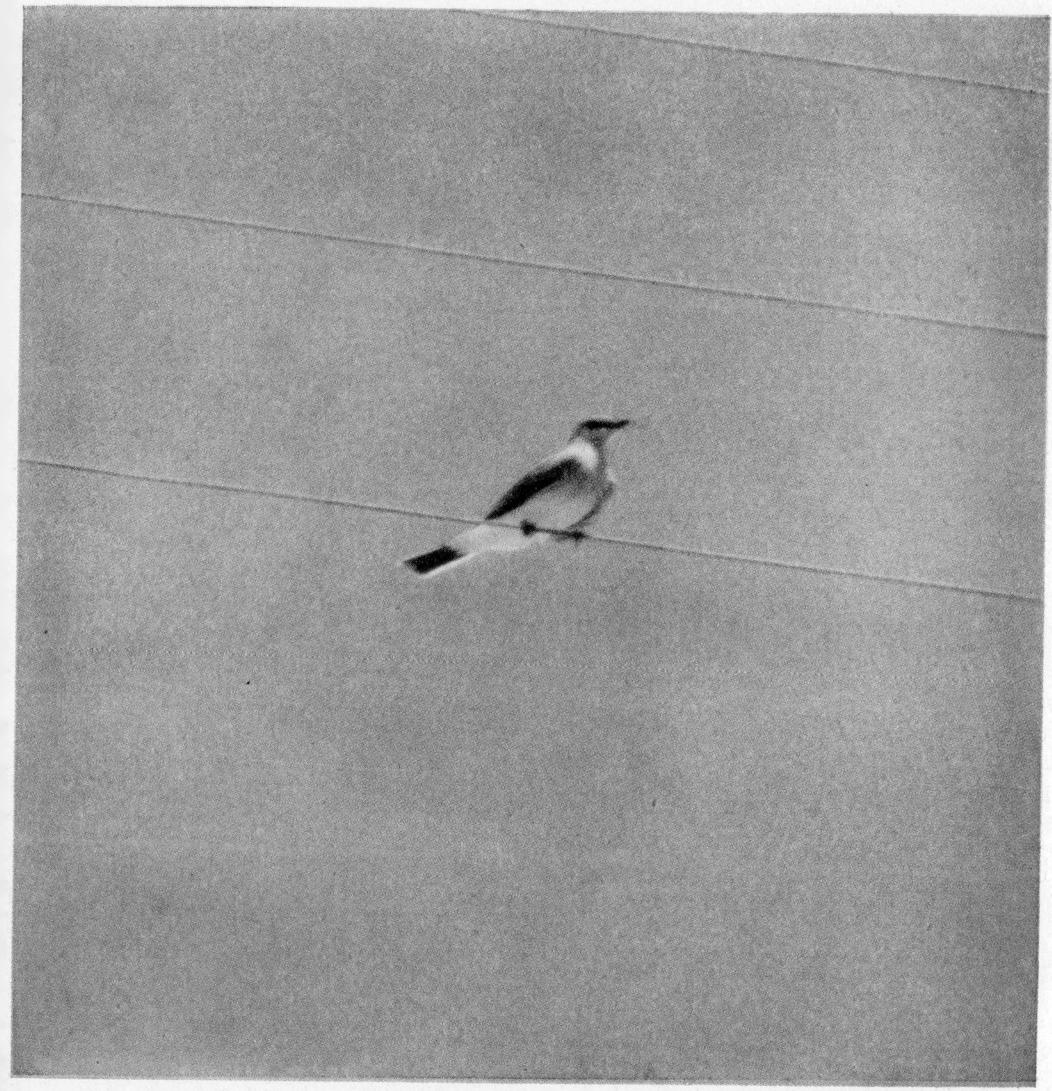

WESTERN KINGBIRD *(Tyrannus verticalis)*. Length: 8 to 9.5 inches. Male and female: upperparts, light ashy gray; underparts, gray breast and yellowish abdomen. The black tail is edged with white. Male has partially concealed crown patch of orange red feathers. Range: western United States. Breeds east to Kansas. Voice: shrill bickering call; also sharp *whit*.

Harlan E. Eckler

that ever popular and timeless theme, "little fellow beats big bully."

From a tree top, a fence post, or a telephone wire, the black and white Kingbird surveys his domain while keeping a constant watch for passing insects. He snares the latter with typical Flycatcher precision—a quick dart into the air, a snap of the bill, and a return to the perch on fluttering wings. As it alights, the Kingbird fans its black tail, showing clearly the white band across the tip. The concealed red patch on the crown is seldom seen in the field. The bird is about 9 inches long.

The Kingbird's reputation for fearlessness is universal. Although other small birds attack larger ones when their territories are invaded (Red-wings habitually attack Crows), none is more aggressive than the Kingbird. Indeed, a Kingbird was reported as repeatedly attacking a low-flying airplane. On the other hand, one observer reported a Kingbird as "beating a hasty retreat from the onslaughts of an angry Yellow Warbler."

COUCH'S KINGBIRD (*Tyrannus melancholicus*). Length: 9.5 inches. Male and female: olive back, yellowish abdomen, gray head. Tail deeply forked. Range: Texas and southern Arizona. Voice: a high, nasal *queer* or *chi-queer;* also scolding series of notes.
Rudolph Hindemith, American Museum of Natural History

"Bee Martin" is an unfair name given to the Kingbird by those who claim the bird feeds extensively on bees. Professor F. E. L. Beal states: "The Biological Survey has made an examination of 281 stomachs (of Kingbirds), collected in various parts of the country, but found only 14 containing the remains of honeybees. In these 14 stomachs there were in all 50 honeybees, of which 40 were drones, 4 were certainly workers, and the remaining 6 were too badly broken to be identified as to sex."

The Kingbird's habitat is varied. Throughout much of its range it is a bird of the orchards and the open farm country. It invariably avoids heavy forests. Apple trees are often chosen as nesting sites. In other places, the Kingbird shows an evident fondness for water by nesting in marshes and along rivers and lakes. In these situations, the nest is often directly over water. Two Kingbird nests that I found one summer offer a good example of extremes in nesting sites. One was in the fork of a willow two feet above the water of a marsh; the other was sixty feet from the

GRAY KINGBIRD ON NEST (*Tyrannus dominicensis dominicensis*). Length: 9 to 9.5 inches. Male and female: pale, washed-out gray color, conspicuously notched tail. Very large bill. Range: east and west coasts of Florida. Winters in West Indies.
Samuel A. Grimes

ground in the top of an oak tree in an open farm woodlot.

The Kingbird's nest is usually rather bulky, but the lining is a neat, compact cup of grasses, rootlets, and hair. Three is the usual number of eggs—creamy white marked with brown and gray. The call of the Kingbird is a series of high rasping notes. It is found from central Canada to South America.

GRAY KINGBIRD

(Tyrannus dominicensis dominicensis)

A typical Kingbird, noisy, pugnacious, and fired with energy, is the Gray Kingbird, a summer resident of Florida and the Keys. It closely resembles the common Kingbird, but is lighter than that species (pale gray) and has a notched tail with no white in it. It is somewhat larger, 9 to 9½ inches long. Its call is a rolling three syllables, less strident than the Eastern Kingbird.

It winters in the West Indies and northern South America after a short breeding season.

COUCH'S KINGBIRD

(Tyrannus melancholicus)

Couch's Kingbird *(T. m. couchii)* is the common Kingbird of the lower Rio Grande Valley in Texas. It is a northern race of a species widely distributed through Central and South America.

Although Couch's Kingbird closely resembles both the Arkansas Kingbird and Cassin's Kingbird, its tail is forked, and is entirely brown, bearing no white edging whatever. Its back is olive, the head gray, and the belly yellowish.

Its voice is high and nasal, and it also utters a scolding series of notes.

Another race of this species, the West Mexican Kingbird *(T. m. occidentalis)* is evidently a rare breeding bird in southern Arizona in the vicinity of Tucson.

WESTERN or ARKANSAS KINGBIRD

(Tyrannus verticalis)

Color Plate Page 155

What has been said regarding the fearlessness of the Eastern Kingbird in attacking its enemies, the Hawks,

CASSIN'S KINGBIRD AT NEST *(Tyrannus vociferans vociferans)*. Length: 9 inches. Male: upperparts olive gray, yellowish underparts, and dark mark through the eye. Resembles Arkansas Kingbird, but no white sides on the tail. Range: breeds from central California, Utah and southern Wyoming, to Mexico. Winters from central California to Mexico. Voice: a low nasal *queer*, or *chi-queer* or *chi-bew*, also an excited *ki-dear, ki-dear, ki-dear*, etc.
Hustace H. Poor, National Audubon Society

Crows, and other big birds that invade its territory, may be repeated with emphasis in regard to the Western or Arkansas Kingbird. It is just as aggressive and just as noisy as its eastern cousin.

The appearance of the two species, although similar, need not be confusing. Since the Arkansas Kingbird is quite evidently extending its range eastward (in the Great Plains area the ranges of the two Kingbirds overlap), it is well to remember that it differs from the Eastern Kingbird by having a yellow belly and no white tips on the tail feathers. Its tail is bordered on the sides with white. Indeed, it is more likely to be confused with the Crested Flycatcher which it resembles, than the Eastern Kingbird. The Crested Flycatcher's rufous tail is its best field mark, however.

DERBY FLYCATCHER AT NEST (*Pitangus sulphuratus texanus*). Length: 10.5 inches. Male and female: upperparts brown with rust colored wings and tail, bright yellow underparts and crown patch, and black and white patterned face. Range: lower Rio Grande Valley, Texas. Voice: a loud, *git-a-hear!* Also *wheep!*
Olin S. Pettingill, Jr.

The Western Kingbird's call consists of various shrill twitterings and bickerings.

Ranging throughout the western states, the Arkansas Kingbird breeds east of Minnesota, Iowa, Kansas, and Oklahoma. In migration, stragglers are found each year as far east as the coast. It winters from Mexico to northern South America.

CASSIN'S KINGBIRD

(Tyrannus vociferans vociferans)

Cassin's Kingbird, a breeding Flycatcher from central California and central Montana south to Mexico, looks so much like the Western or Arkansas Kingbird that it is difficult to separate the two in the field. Ralph Hoffmann offers the following suggestions:

"To distinguish the two Kingbirds in the country where both occur, chiefly in southern California, note the distinct white throat of the Cassin contrasting with its dark breast. The light gray of the Western Kingbird fades to an almost white throat directly under the bill, but does not offer a marked contrast to the surrounding gray. The back of the Cassin Kingbird is also darker gray with an olive cast. The Cassin in winter and spring shows a very narrow light edging at the tip of all the tail feathers, evident when the bird sits low on

SCISSOR-TAILED FLYCATCHER (*Muscivora forficata*). Length: 11.5 to 15 inches. Male: pale gray body, reddish crown patch, salmon pink sides and wing-linings. The deeply forked long scissor-like tail is conspicuously marked with black and white. Female: similar to male but duller in color with shorter tail. Range: breeds in Texas, Oklahoma, Kansas and southern Nebraska, occasionally east to western Louisiana and southwest Missouri. Winters in Central America. Voice: a harsh *keck* or *kew*.
Samuel A. Grimes

a wire with its back to the observer; later in the season the edging becomes worn and is not conspicuous. If a Kingbird shows a prominent white outer feather in the outspread black tail, it is a Western Kingbird."

The call of Cassin's Kingbird is very different from the Western, being, according to Peterson, a low nasal *queer*, or *chi-queer*, and an excited *ki-deer, ki-deer, ki-deer.*

SCISSOR-TAILED FLYCATCHER

(Muscivora forficata)

Color Plate Page 159

Travelers through Texas, particularly the southern part of the state, are always impressed and delighted with the delicately colored, long tailed, Scissor-tailed Flycatcher, the "bird of paradise" of the Lone Star State, a rather common bird of the open country. It is one of the most striking of all Ame ican birds; picturesque when perchin graceful in flight, and possessed of fiery personality rivaled only by its re atives, the Kingbirds.

The only other bird with which t Scissor-tail might be confused is t Fork-tailed Flycatcher *(Muscivora t rannus)*, but the latter is a tropical sp cies which has been recorded only ca ually in the United States. The ex tremely long swallow-tail, the strikin combination of colors—gray, pin white, and black, with a wash of sa mon pink under the wings and on th sides—sets the Scissor-tailed Flycatch apart from all others. It is a good size bird, 11½ to 15 inches long.

When perched on pole or telephone wir the long tail is tightl closed. In casual fligh the streamers trail be hind. In the sprin when the male zoom into the sky for h courtship gymnastics, h proves himself an aeri acrobat without a pee It is then that the grace ful swallow-tail i opened and closed lik giant white scissors a the bird zig-zags an seesaws to the tune of hi own piercing scream and shrieks.

Although recorde outside its normal rang on many occasions, th Scissor-tailed Flycatche is a bird of south centra United States, rangin south to Panama. I breeds from centra Kansas to southern Texas

MEXICAN CRESTED FLYCATCHER *(Myiarchus tyrannulus nelsoni)*. Length: 9 to 9.5 inches. Male and female: upperparts grayish olive brown, yellow belly. Two grayish white wingbars and grayish white throat. Range: lower Rio Grande Valley, Texas, and deserts of southern Arizona. Voice: a vigorous, bold *pwit*, and rolling *pureeeet*.

Eliot Porter

ASH-THROATED FLYCATCHER AT NEST HOLE (*Myiarchus cinerascens*). Length: 8 to 8.5 inches. Male and female: back is gray brown with trace of olive. It has two white wingbars, a white throat, a pale yellow abdomen and rusty colored tail, and black beak. Range: breeds from Oregon, Washington, Utah and south Wyoming into Mexico. Prefers dry country. Voice: *Pwit*, also a rolling *prrrit* and *ke-wherr*.
George M. Bradt

DERBY FLYCATCHER

(Pitangus sulphuratus texanus)

A large (10½ inches) heavy Flycatcher of the lower Rio Grande Valley, the Derby is unmistakable for its rufous wings and tail, with intensely yellow crown and underparts. Its face is patterned in black and white. The female is colored like the male.

One of the most interesting habits of this bird is its fishing, in which it behaves like a Kingfisher, but its dive is not so deep nor clean. The major portion of its diet is large flying insects, and occasionally, fruit. Its nest is a bulky structure, preferably high in a thorny tree The entrance is in the side. The four creamy eggs are spotted with brown around the large end.

The native name of *Chio* is derived from the bird's call note. It is generally noisy and conspicuous.

SULPHUR-BELLIED FLYCATCHER

(Myiodynastes luteiventris swarthi)

The Sulphur-bellied Flycatcher likes the sycamore trees of the mountains of southeastern Arizona. It is a medium sized Flycatcher (8 inches long) with yellowish underparts streaked with black, a rufous tail, white stripe over the eye, and a yellow crown. The back is streaked. The female is similar. It is the only Flycatcher to have a streaked yellow breast. The rump is a reddish brown.

OLIVACEOUS FLYCATCHER (*Myiarchus tuberculifer olivasceus*). Length: 7.25 inches. Male and female: upperparts olive brown, underparts olive grayish, yellow-bellied with gray throat and rusty-colored tail. Range: breeds in mountains of southeast Arizona and is also found in Mexico and southwest Texas. Voice: a mournful, drawling whistle, slurring downward, *peeur;* very characteristic.
Rudolph Hindemith, American Museum of Natural History

CRESTED FLYCATCHER (*Myiarchus crinitus*). Length: 8 to 9 inches. Male and female: upperparts olive brown, with rufous tail. Crown feathers form crest. Underparts gray with yellow belly. Range: breeds from New Brunswick south to Florida. Winters in southern Florida, eastern Mexico and Central America. Voice: whistled *wheeeep* and *prrrreet* deep in throat.
Hal H. Harrison

Its voice is a high penetrating *kee-zee-ick* which has been compared with the creaking of a wheelbarrow.

CRESTED FLYCATCHER

(Myiarchus crinitus)

Color Plate Page 162

If you have spent any time at all near the summer domain of the Crested Flycatcher, you will agree heartedly with John Burroughs who called it "the wild Irishman" of all the Flycatchers.

In a family that includes the pugnacious bullying Kingbird, the title is hardly a compliment to the nature of the bird. But when one observes the fierce and aggressive manner of the bird in ruling its woodland kingdom; when one is startled by that sudden shrill whistled *wheep, wheep, wheep;* and finally, when one catches sight of that tousled crest as the bird surveys the intruder from a lofty perch, then a "wild Irishman" seems appropriate.

It is little wonder that other woodland creatures are silenced momentarily by that shrill *wheep* of the Crested Flycatcher. Many times it has brought me up with a start as the bird fired it at me from close range. But all is forgiven when I see him perched regally overhead, gray throat and breast pushed out, sulphur yellow belly gleaming in the sun, cinnamon tail spread below; for here is one of the highlights of the day's bird watching.

From that lookout on a dead stub, the bird checks the parade of passing ısects for a choice victim. Spotting ne, it dashes into the air, snaps it up vith a "click" of its broad flat bill, and ıils back to its perch. Perhaps the next ılly will find it hovering on vibrating innamon wings. Again, like a Blue ay, it may sail from one perch to another with wings and tail spread wide.

The nest of the Crested Flycatcher s placed commonly in a natural cavity n a tree, but the bird is not limited to uch a site. In one summer, I found pairs nesting in two different bird boxes, a hole in a telephone pole, and in n abandoned Woodpecker hole on the underside of the limb of an ancient pple tree. It will place its nest from ix to fifty feet up.

A great deal has been written about his bird's habit of placing a cast-off nakeskin in its nest. Many contend hat the bird does this deliberately to care away predators. To me, the idea is bsurd. To begin with, the snakeskin, vhen used (and it isn't always), is very often woven into the nest deep in the dark cavity where a predator would never see it. But principally, I cannot ascribe to any bird the intelligence necessary to know in advance that, in case of an attack by a predator at some later ime, that predator might be frightened away by the cast-off snakeskin now being placed in the nest. Nor do I believe that the inanimate sloughed kin of a snake would frighten a woodand creature if it did see it. The fact hat the Crested Flycatcher often substitutes onion skins, waxed paper, strips of cellophane, and the like for a snakeskin should eliminate the "scare crow" theory at once.

Deep in the feathered cup of a Crested Flycatcher's nest are laid five unusually marked and very beautiful eggs, covered with large blotches of reddish brown interspersed with scratches of brown or black. After an incubation period of almost two weeks, the adults feed the young in the nest for another two weeks, or even longer. Nestlings are restless and noisy. The constant *peeping* may be heard throughout the day. These birds are more often heard than seen.

The Crested Flycatcher eats many injurious beetles and weevils.

Crested Flycatchers breed from southern Canada to Florida and west to Texas. They winter in Mexico, Central America, and South America. Two races are recognized: the Northern Crested *(M. c. boreus)* and the Southern Crested *(M. c. crinitus)*.

YOUNG BLACK PHOEBE *(Sayornis nigricans semiatra)*. Length: 6.5 inches. Male and female: upperparts sooty black, underparts, white. Range: resident in western Texas, southern New Mexico, Arizona, southern Utah, southern Nevada and north through California. Voice: song, a thin, *fi-bee, fi-bee, fi-bee,* the first two notes rising, the last two falling; note, a sharp *kip.*
James Murdock, National Audubon Society

MEXICAN CRESTED FLYCATCHER

(Myiarchus tyrannulus nelsoni)

Very similar to the Ash-throated Flycatcher, except for differences of size and degree of coloration, the Mexican Crested is limited to the lower Rio Grande valley and the deserts of southern Arizona, which region also belongs to the Ash-Throated.

The Mexican bird is about an inch longer (9 to 9½ inches) with a deeper yellow breast and a deeper olive back. Both Flycatchers have a rufous tail. The voice of the Mexican Flycatcher is a sharp *pwit* and a rolling *purrett,* much more raucous than the Ash-throated.

The Mexican Flycatcher lays its three to five creamy buff eggs in a nest of fibers, feathers, or hair, in natural cavities and Woodpecker holes, often in giant cactus.

YELLOW-BELLIED FLYCATCHER (*Empidonax flaviventris*). Length: 5 to 5.5 inches. Male and female: decidedly yellow from throat to belly. The eye-ring is also yellow. Upperparts, dark, olive-greenish-gray. Range: eastern North America north to Newfoundland, Quebec, Manitoba, Michigan, Minnesota; migrates through United States to Central America. Voice: a lifeless *per-wee* or *chu-wee.*
Chicago Natural History Museum

ASH-THROATED FLYCATCHER

(Myiarchus cinerascens)

Like its eastern relative, the grea Crested Flycatcher, the Ash-throate Flycatcher of the arid southwest nes in holes. Favorite sites are knots in tree old Woodpecker holes, abandoned nes of the Cactus Wren, and occasionall in odd situations, such as the exhau pipe of an abandoned oil engine.

Since the ranges of the easter Crested and the Ash-throated do no overlap, confusion in that regard eliminated for the bird watcher. Th rufous tail distinguishes it from th black-tailed Kingbirds, and its large size (8 to 8½ inches) and white throa distinguish it from the gray-throate Olivaceous Flycatcher. Its voice is *pwit,* or rolling *prrrrit.*

The Ash-throated Flycatcher range from Washington and Colorado t eastern Texas south into Mexico in th lowlands and foothills of dry countr

OLIVACEOUS FLYCATCHER

(Myiarchus tuberculifer olivascens)

The range of the Olivaceous Flycatcher in the United States is restricted to the mountains of souther Arizona. It is the smallest of its genu (7 inches long), and may be distinguished from the larger but simila Ash-throated Flycatcher by its gra throat. The former has a white throat Like others of the family, it has a rufous tail and a yellow belly. Its voic is distinctive, being a mournful drawling whistle, and is its best identification in the field. Its song is typicall loud and joyful. It breeds in the mountains of southeastern Arizona and casually in the Chicos Mountains of Texas

EASTERN PHOEBE

(Sayornis phoebe)

Color Plate Page 166

Fond memories carry us back through the years to happy summer days spent "out at grandma's." Many bird watchers can date accurately their interest in nature to early days spent on a farm. And because this impressionable period was spent in close association with rural birds, certain ones have been indelibly preserved in our minds as "farm birds."

As the beautiful Bluebird, the chattering House Wren, the raucous Crow, and the graceful Barn Swallow fit so nicely into that category, so does the gentle little Phoebe bring back memories of a springhouse with its dark, damp interior, and the nest of Phoebes on the ledge below the roof on the south side. The folks at grandma's called them "pewees," and they said that every year they came back in the spring to nest again. One year the cat got the young, but as grandpa said, "We gave her a trouncin' that she'll never forget."

The male had a favorite perch on a projecting dead twig of an old apple tree at the edge of the orchard. When he arrived in April, he spent a great deal of time repeating his name, over and over again. Sometimes he would say it *FEE-bee*, and other times, just to break the monotony, I suppose, he would say it *fee-BEE.* His appearance was just as plain as his song—a gray brown Flycatcher about 7 inches long, with white underparts but no wing-bars and no eye-ring; just nothing to distinguish it except a conspicuous habit of wagging its tail.

From that dead twig, he carried on much of his never ending search for passing insects (insects constitute almost ninety percent of the Phoebe's diet). Light on the wing, the bird

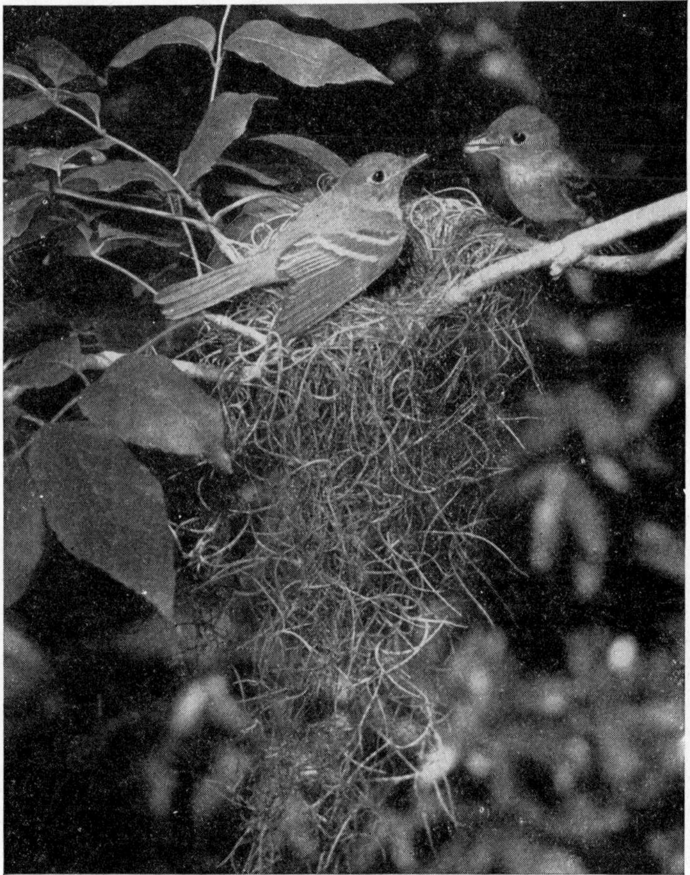

ACADIAN FLYCATCHER, MALE AND FEMALE AT NEST (*Empidonax virescens*). Length: 5.5 to 6.75 inches. Male and female: grayish olive green with yellowish sides. Has conspicuous light eye-ring and two white wingbars. Range: breeds in Southern and Central States. Voice: a sharp, explosive, *wee-see!* or *spit-chee!* Also a thin *peet.*

Samuel A. Grimes

PHOEBE AT NEST AT ENTRANCE TO A COAL MINE (*Sayornis phoebe*). Length: 6.5 to 7 inches. Mal and female: upperparts gray brown, whitish below. Black bill. Range: Canada south to Texas northern Mississippi, and Georgia, winters throughout southern United States, north to Virginia Voice: *phoe-be* or *fi-bree*.
Hal H. Harrison

darted out swiftly, snapped up a bug, twisted gracefully in midair, and sailed back to its favorite twig to await another chance to sally forth again. Its diet is made up of such injurious insects as boll-weevils, cucumber beetles, locusts, moths and caterpillars.

None of the Flycatchers accepts a wider choice of nesting sites than does the Phoebe. Although common about farms where they place their nests of mud and mosses in outbuildings, over windows, on ledges in barns, and similar places, they are just as likely to place their nest under a bridge on a supporting beam. Many Phoebes still return to ancestral nesting places on rocky cliffs.

During the past seven years I have studied such a nest plastered to the side of vertical rock at the entrance to an abandoned coal mine. Here the birds have raised two broods each year, the second being raised in the same nest after a few repairs were made following the departure of the nestlings. These birds arrive in late March, start rebuilding the nest in early April, and lay their four or five white eggs soon after.

The Eastern Phoebe ranges from the Mackenzie River and Nova Scotia to eastern New Mexico and Georgia. In winter it ranges from Virginia south to the Gulf states and Mexico. The only bird with which it might be confused is the Wood Pewee, but the latter has two white wingbars and does not have the Phoebe's habit of wagging its tail. The white underparts of the Eastern

SAY'S PHOEBE (*Sayornis saya saya*). Length: 7 to 8 inches. Male and female: brownish upperparts, black tail. Rusty breast and brown abdomen. Range: western United States. Voice: a plaintive *pee-ur*.
George M. Bradt

Phoebe distinguish it instantly from its western relatives, the black-breasted Black Phoebe and the rusty-breasted Say's Phoebe.

BLACK PHOEBE

(Sayornis nigricans semiatra)

A most welcome member of the Flycatcher family around ranches, parks, yards, and homes in the southwestern states is the Black Phoebe, a strikingly marked permanent resident over much of its range. Its white belly shows in sharp contrast to its sooty black breast, head, and upperparts, the only Flycatcher so marked. Its diet is almost one hundred percent insectiverous, making it one of our most economically valuable birds.

While the Black Phoebe and the Say's Phoebe occupy much of the same range, each shows a decided preference for its own particular type of habitat. The former is more likely to be found in watered areas in the vicinity of streams, irrigation ditches, gardens, and ponds. Say's Phoebe, on the other hand, prefers open barren country.

The Black Phoebe's call note is a sharp *tsip*. The song is an indefinite repetition of two pairs of notes, *ti wee, ti wee* (Hoffman).

SAY'S PHOEBE

(Sayornis saya saya)

Color Plate Page 167

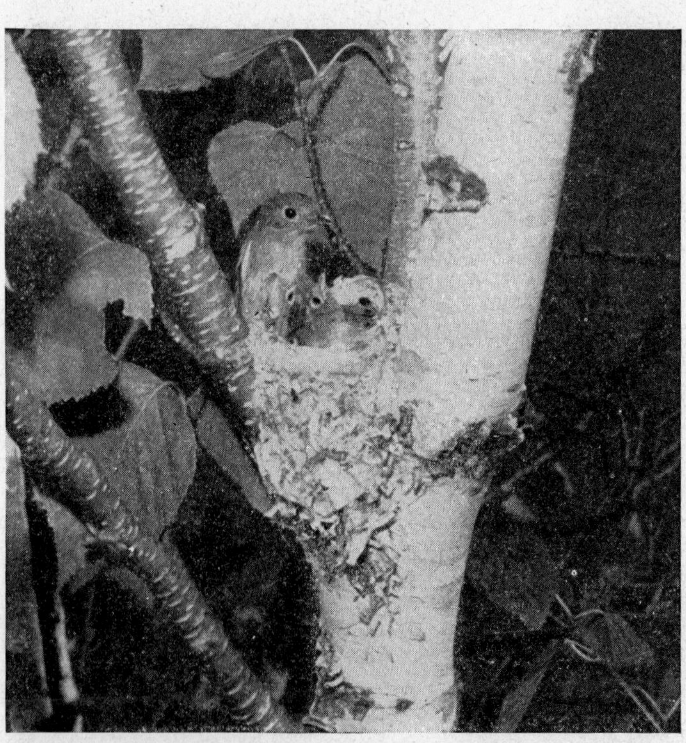

LEAST FLYCATCHER AT NEST *(Empidonax minimus)*. Length: 5 to 5.75 inches. Male and female: underparts whitish to yellowish white belly. Upperparts brownish olive; two grayish white bars on wings. Range: breeds in eastern North America to central Montana and eastern Wyoming. In winter it is found in Central America. Voice: jerky, repeated *che-bec*, accenting the last syllable.

B. W. Baker

The common eastern Phoebe has its western counterpart in Say's Phoebe, not in appearance, but in habits. Say's Phoebe is a common resident of the arid regions where it is just as much at home on the ranches and in the towns as it is in the sagebrush plains, the foothills, or the rocky canyons. Like its eastern relative, it delights in placing its nest about houses, where it will return year after year.

Say's Phoebe, which is 7 or 8 inches long, is distinguished by its rust colored underparts, brown back, black tail, and its habit of flicking its tail when it alights. From a low perch, the

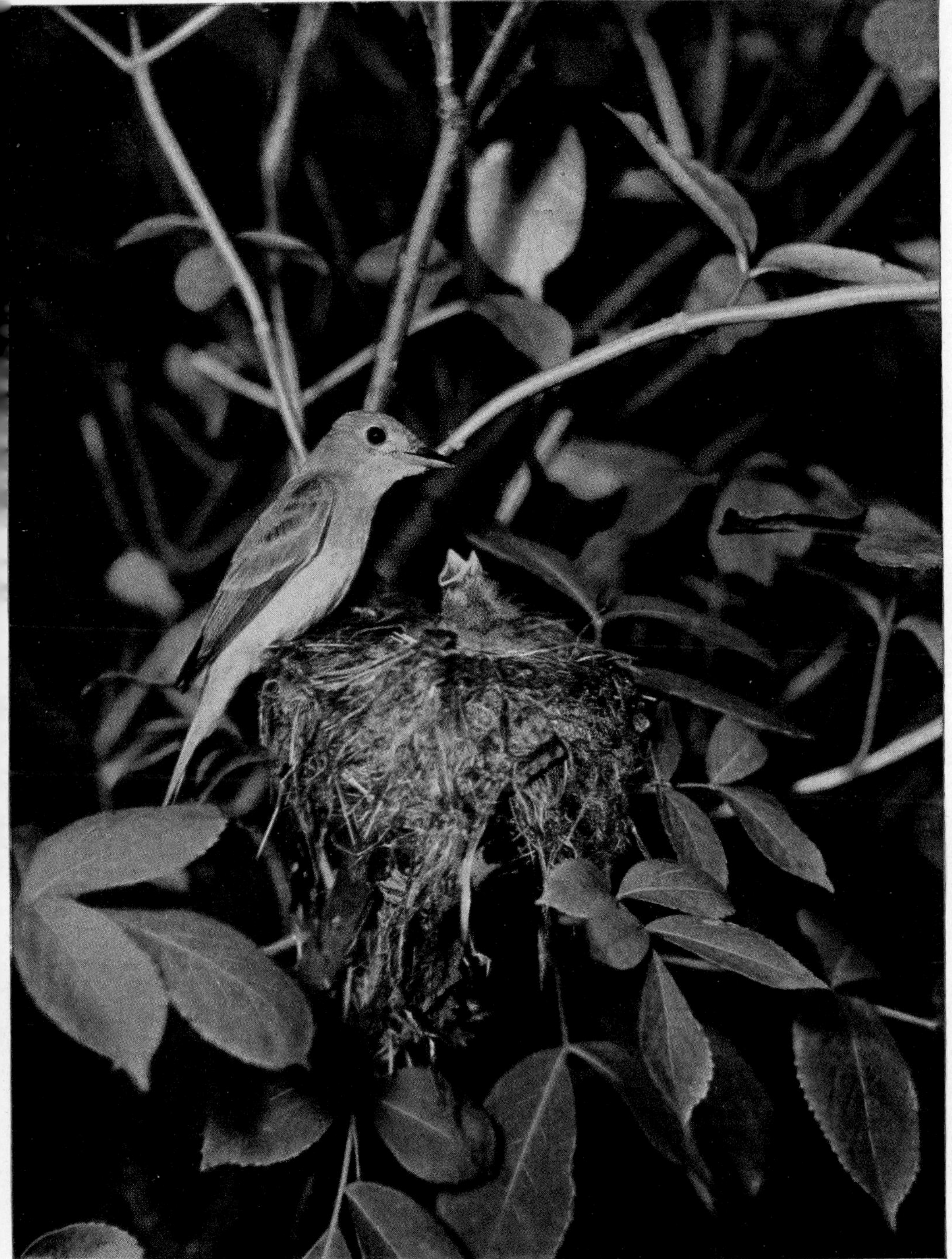

ALDER FLYCATCHER (*Empidonax traillii*). Length: 5.25 to 6 inches. Male and female: upperparts dark olive green. Light eye-ring and two white wingbars. Underparts white with yellowish abdomen. Range: from Manitoba south to northern New Jersey and west to central Arkansas. Voice: song, varied, according to section bird inhabits. Northeast bird sings, hoarse *wee-be-o*. Ohio bird; *fitz-bew* or *witch-brew*. Note, *pep* or *pit*.

Hal H. Harrison

bird continually sails into the air in pursuit of passing insects, catching them with a click of its bill. Besides the smaller winged insects, this species also eats the larger forms, such as large grasshoppers and locusts.

Unlike the *phoebe* note of the eastern Phoebe, Say's Phoebe utters a soft sweet *phee-eur*. It has been described as similar to the call of the Wood Pewee.

Say's Phoebe breeds from Canada to Mexico and east to the Great Plains. It is absent in the humid Pacific coast belt where its place is taken by the Black Phoebe. Say's Phoebe winters south from New Mexico, Arizona, and central California.

YELLOW-BELLIED FLYCATCHER

(Empidonax flaviventris)

The Yellow-bellied Flycatcher is not included among the confusing *Empidonax* Flycatchers of the east because its yellow breast distinguishes it instantly. However, it is known to most bird watchers only as a spring and fall migrant since its summer home is in the coniferous bogs of Canada. It reaches the United States only in suitable habitat in a few of the northern states.

During migration and on its nesting grounds, the Yellow-bellied is a shy bird, very difficult to approach. It is silent during migration, and its courtship song is described as similar to the song of the Wood Pewee. Unlike other Flycatchers, this species nests on or near the ground, usually in mossy hummocks.

It is a small bird, 5 or 5½ inches long, uniformly yellow from throat to belly. The upperparts are greenish yellow, and it has a yellow eye-ring.

WRIGHT'S FLYCATCHER ON NEST *(Empidonax wrightii)*. Length: 5.25 to 6 inches. Male and female: upperparts brownish gray, the wings with whitish double bars. Whitish ring around the eye. Underparts light grayish white. Range: over entire Rocky Mountain zone, southward to Arizona and New Mexico. Winters in California and southern Mexico. Voice: series of three notes *see-pit, serzel, pee-ee*. The *serzel* is a low double note.
William L. Dawson, National Audubon Society

ACADIAN FLYCATCHER

(Empidonax virescens)

During the summer when birds are nesting, southerners have little trouble identifying the Acadian Flycatcher, for, of the three troublesome species (Acadian, Least, and Alder Flycatchers), only the Acadian is a breeding bird. North of the Mason and Dixon Line, however, bird watchers do have trouble, for here the breeding ranges of the three overlap.

The Acadian is a quiet, shy species of the deep woodland. If its nest is found, it will serve to identify the bird. The structure is a frail shallow basket, built like a hammock on horizontal twigs. The nests of the Alder and Least Flycatchers are neat cups in upright forks.

WESTERN FLYCATCHER AT NEST (*Empidonax difficilis*). Length: 5.5 to 6 inches. Male and female: upperparts yellowish cast olive-brown, underparts washed with yellow, including throat, wingbars whitish, with white eye-ring. Range: breeds from Canada, south to Mexican border. Voice: a penetrating *ps-seet* with rising inflection.
Ross and Florence Thornburg

The Acadian Flycatcher is greenish in color, with a yellow wash on the sides, but it cannot be definitely identified by coloring. Its song, according to Peterson, is a sharp *wee-see*, or *spitchee*, and a thin *peet*.

For a more complete discussion of this difficult group of Flycatchers, see the Alder Flycatcher.

ALDER FLYCATCHER

(Empidonax traillii traillii)

Color Plate Page 169

No group of birds anywhere has given bird watchers more headaches in field identification than the members of the *Empidonax* genus of the Flycatcher family. Within the range of the eastern form of the Alder Flycatcher, also called Traill's Flycatcher, which is pictured on page 169 in natural color, there are three species with which it is confused: the Yellow-bellied, Acadian, and Least Flycatchers. Like many a more skilled observer before me, I concluded long ago that sight identification alone is never positive for these four birds.

The western bird observer has exactly the same problem trying to separate in the field the Traill's, Hammond's, Wright's, Gray, and Western Flycatchers. Indeed, reliable ornithologists are prone to scoff at any attempt to separate the Hammond's from the Wright's, even when the songs are heard.

Fortunately these little Flycatchers do not all sing alike, build nests alike, lay eggs alike, nor choose the same type of habitat. In these individual peculiarities, then, the bird watcher has his forte. But in general appearance, these birds are all alike—about 5 or 6 inches long, olive green above, with conspicuous eye-rings and double wingbars.

WOOD PEWEE AT SIDE OF NEST *(Contopus)*. Length: 6 to 6.5 inches. Male and female: upper parts olive gray, lower parts whitish. No eye-ring. Has two prominent white wingbars. Range breeds from Florida north to Canada. Winters in Central and South America. Voice: drawling whistled *pee-a-wee*. Also *pee-ur*.
Hal H. Harrison

Various shades of brown, greenish brown, olive, gray, etc., are offered as identifying characteristics, but none is adequate for positive sight identification by the amateur bird watcher.

A possible exception among the eastern forms is the Yellow-bellied Flycatcher which shows considerable yellow below; it is the only species with a decidedly yellow throat. Its call of *per-wee*, rising on the second note, is somewhat similar to the call of the Wood Pewee. The bird is a recluse of the northern evergreen forests, and the only Flycatcher known to nest on the ground.

The Acadian Flycatcher will be found along the small streams that traverse heavily shaded woodlands and ravines. Its song is interpreted as an abrupt *ka-reep*, with the accent on the second syllable. The call note is a short *peet*.

There is considerable variation in the song of the Alder Flycatcher, but a common interpretation is *way-be-o*, with the accent on the middle syllable. Dr. Sutton offers an interpretation of *becky-weer*. The call is a liquid *pip*. This species is a resident of the alder thickets and damp bottomland, often found at the edge of swamps.

The Least Flycatcher ; more helpful since it ıngs its common name, *he-bec*. A Flycatcher esting in an orchard ·ill more surely be this pecies.

Members of the *Em-*·*idonax* genus breed hroughout North America. All of the astern species winter outh of the United tates.

BUFF-BREASTED FLYCATCHER (*Empidonax fulvifrons pygmaeus*). Length: 5 inches. Male and female: dull grayish brown; with *white eye-ring* and wings with double whitish bars. Rich, buff colored breast. Range: breeds in mountains of Arizona and New Mexico. Voice: *chicky-whew*.
Rudolph Hindemith, American Museum of Natural History

LEAST FLYCATCHER

(Empidonax minimus)

Bird watchers can be ;rateful that this little ·lycatcher habitually calls its popular ıame *che-bec*. By this note it may be dentified on its breeding grounds rom the Mackenzie River and Quebec o Oklahoma and the mountains of North Carolina. In spring and fall nigration, however, it is practically mpossible to distinguish it from the Alder and Acadian Flycatchers.

The Least is a bird of the orchards nd open woodlands, and this habitat vill assist in separating it from the Acadian Flycatcher, a bird of deep lamp woodlands, and the Alder Fly-:atcher, which prefers the alder and villow thickets of marshes and stream dges.

For a more complete discussion of he characteristics of the confusing *Empidonaces*, see the Alder Flycatcher.

HAMMOND'S FLYCATCHER

(Empidonax hammondii)

Almost impossible to distinguish in he field from Wright's Flycatcher, Hammond's is differentiated by its preference for high conifers in mountainous areas. Both birds are olive above, with yellowish underparts and a gray band across the chest. Hammond's Flycatcher has the colors somewhat more intense, but this is impossible to tell in the field. Their songs are so similar that only an expert can tell them apart. Hammond's breeds from Canada south to central California and Colorado.

WRIGHT'S FLYCATCHER

(Empidonax wrightii)

While eastern bird watchers sweat over the identification of the Alder, Acadian, and Least Flycatchers, westerners have more trouble with five confusing members of this genus: Traill's, Western, Gray, Hammond's, and Wright's Flycatchers.

Ornithologists are frank to admit that Wright's and Hammond's cannot be distinguished in the field by color alone. Their songs are similar too, but some help is afforded during the breeding season in the fact that Hammond's is a bird of the high conifers in mountainous areas, while the Wright's is a breeding bird in the foothills and the chaparral covered slopes of the same territory.

WESTERN WOOD PEEWEE ON NEST *(Contopus richardsoni)*. Length: 6 to 6.5 inches. Male and female: olive brown above and whitish below. Has *two conspicuous wingbars* but lacks *eye-ring*. Lower mandible of bill is yellow. Range: western United States. Voice: differs in quality and inflection from eastern bird; the single syllable suggesting the word *deer*, or *tweer*.
R. T. Congdon

The Gray Flycatcher is also similar to Wright's, but here again its preferred habitat of sagebrush plains and other arid regions helps distinguish it. Traill's Flycatcher is the Alder Flycatcher of the east, and like it prefers the willows and alders along the streams and shuns dry country.

The Western Flycatcher, which shows much more yellow coloring than the Wright's, prefers groves of trees near habitation or in canyons.

Wright's Flycatcher breeds from Canada south to southern California, northern Arizona, northern New Mexico, and western Texas.

COUES' FLYCATCHER *(Contopus pertinax pallidiventris)*. Length: 7.75 inches. Male and female: upperparts deep smoke gray, underparts yellowish white and smoke gray. Range: breeds in mountains of central and southeast Arizona and southwest New Mexico. Voice: a wistful whistled *ho-say, re-ah*, or *ho-say, ma-re-ah*. Its note is a low pip.
Rudolph Hindemith, American Museum of Natural History

GRAY FLYCATCHER

(Empidonax griseus)

Another of the western Flycatchers which is almost impossible to identify in the field is the Gray Flycatcher.

Again its breeding habitat is the surest dentification since it picks the sage-brush country of eastern Oregon and he arid pinyons and junipers of Utah. t is very slightly larger than Wright's Flycatcher and grayer on the back. Its ong is difficult to tell from the pre-eding two birds.

WESTERN FLYCATCHER

(Empidonax difficilis)

Another headache for the western ird watcher is the Western Flycatcher, which is very similar to Traill's, Wright's, and Hammond's Flycatchers.

The Western is widely distributed, hiefly from the Rocky Mountains westward, from Alaska to southern California and Texas. Its preferred reeding habitat is open areas in the hade of tall tree groves near habita-ion, and in canyons.

Peterson describes its voice as a sharp isping *ps-seet,* with rising inflection, nd its song as three thin colorless notes, *z-zeek trip seet!*

BUFF-BREASTED FLYCATCHER

(Empidonax fulvifrons pygmaeus)

It is unusual for any of the *Empi-donax* Flycatchers to offer bird watch-rs any help in distinguishing among hem, especially in coloration, but the Buff-breasted Flycatcher, smallest of he North American members of the genus (5 inches long), is an exception o the rule. While the majority of this confusing family have varying mounts of yellow wash on their un-derparts, the present species stands lone with a warm buffy breast with-out any yellow.

Unfortunately, most bird watchers are never able to take advantage of this easy means of distinction, for few ever see this diminutive Flycatcher that reaches the United States only in the mountains of southern Arizona.

COUES'S FLYCATCHER

(Contopus pertinax pallidiventris)

Another Mexican Flycatcher that reaches its northern limits just over the

OLIVE-SIDED FLYCATCHER *(Nuttallornis borealis).* Length: 7.25 to 8 inches. Male and female: upperparts, dark olive, grayish brown. Large bill, white throat and *dark chest-patches,* nearly separated by a narrow strip of white from throat to belly. Near the back behind wings are tufts of white. Range: from Alaska through Rocky Mountains to Mexico. Winters in South America. Voice: song, a lively whistle, *hip-three-cheers!* or *whip whee! wheer!* The alarm notes are a piercing *pip-pip-pip.*
Rudolph Hindemith, American Museum of Natural History

VERMILION FLYCATCHER *(Pyrocephalus rubinus)*. Length: 5.5 to 6.5 inches. Male: head and underparts brilliant red. Upperparts and tail blackish brown with black line running through eye to bill. Female: upperparts dark brown; wings and tail darker. Breast white streaked with dark brown and black. Under tail coverts and belly, pinkish. Range: along Gulf Coast from Texas to western Florida. Voice: twittering *zi-breee* or *p-p-p t-zeee.*
Harlan E. Eckler

border of the United States is Coues's Flycatcher, which is found only in the mountains of Arizona and New Mexico.

It is a large Flycatcher, about 8 inches long, with a gray breast and sides, and a whitish chin. In coloration, it is similar to the Wood Pewee, but in shape, size, and actions it resembles an Olive-sided Flycatcher.

Its voice is a whistled *ho-say, re-ah,* or *ho-say, ma-re-ah,* whence its local name of José Maria.

WOOD PEWEE

(Contopus virens)

Color Plate Page 172

If you have never been in the woods on a summer morning during the hour before dawn when wild creatures arouse themselves to start another day, you have missed the morning twilight song of the Wood Pewee, a song that artist Edmund Sawyer describes as "the sweetest, most soul-searching voice in nature."

It is an impressive experience in a charming setting. On the tip of a dead limb high in an oak tree, this nondescript little Flycatcher alights to whistle its plaintive song, *pee-a-wee, pee-o, ah-di-dee.* Writing it is so inadequate, for the notes blend in such continuous harmony that the song becomes a sweet, slow, gliding rhythm.

Of the Wood Pewee's song, Dr. Frank M. Chapman wrote: "His pensive gentle ways are voiced by his sad sweet call. The notes are as musical and restful, as much a part of Nature's hymn, as the soft humming of a brook." On the subject of this lovely wildwood voice, Dr. Wallace Craig wrote an entire book, "The Song of the Wood Pewee," published by the University of the State of New York.

Members of the Flycatcher family throughout the world number over 700, but only 40 of these inhabit the United States. They are scientifically classified as "songless, perching birds." To those of us who have thrilled to the song of the Wood Pewee, that classification has never been entirely clear.

The Wood Pewee is about the size of a Sparrow (6 to 6½ inches long), olive brown above, and whitish below. Two white wingbars distinguish it from the Phoebe. Also, the Pewee does not wag its tail like a Phoebe. The Pewee's lack of a conspicuous eye-ring distinguishes it from the smaller Flycatchers.

From its winter home in Central America and northern South America, the Wood Pewee arrives in the north at the height of the Warbler migration in early May. Although the bird often chooses a woodland for its nesting habitat, it is not averse to orchards and open groves. For several years I found Wood Pewees nesting in a pear tree in a neighbor's yard.

The bird prefers to saddle its beautifully constructed nest to a horizontal dead limb high in a tree. The lowest nest I have ever found was the one in the pear tree, twelve feet from the ground. The color picture on page 172 was taken at a nest forty feet from the ground.

The nest itself is a masterpiece of bird architecture. It is constructed to resemble a natural growth on the limb to which it is attached. It is built of mosses, rootlets, and fine grasses, covered with lichens and reinforced with spider webs. It reminds one of a large edition of a Hummingbird's nest. Three is the usual number of eggs. They are white with a wreath of markings about the larger end.

The Eastern Wood Pewee breeds from Nova Scotia, southern Ontario, and southern Manitoba south to Florida, the Gulf Coast, and southern Texas, and west to central Oklahoma, eastern Kansas, and North Dakota.

WESTERN WOOD PEWEE

(Contopus richardsoni)

The same wide range enjoyed by the Eastern Wood Pewee in the eastern part of the country is enjoyed by the Western Wood Pewee in the remaining half of the continent. Although some ornithologists believe that the two are merely races of the same species, others believe that there are sufficient differences, especially in song and nesting habits, to warrant full specific rank for both. They are listed as two species by the A.O.U.

The Western Wood Pewee's song is a monotonous *pee-ee* repeated throughout the breeding season. The utterance is harsh and has even been likened in quality to the rasping note of the Nighthawk. This, of course, makes it a much different song from the sweet plaintive song of the Eastern Wood Pewee.

In appearance, the Western Wood Pewee is slightly larger (6 to 6½ inches long) than the other small Flycatchers with which it associates. The sides of the breast are dusky and are divided by a narrow light line. No eye-ring is evident, making it readily distinguishable from the *Empidonaces.*

The Western Wood Pewee likes orchards for its nest, which is a deeper cup than that of the eastern bird and is not covered with lichens.

OLIVE-SIDED FLYCATCHER

(Nuttallornis borealis)

In my experience with the Olive-sided Flycatcher as a migrating bird, I have found the two cottonlike tufts of white feathers on the lower back above the wings to be its best field mark. These have been evident to me when other field marks were lacking. Its erect position while perching, the short neck, and large head are also distinctive. At close range, a front view discloses a white abdomen which narrows between the dark olive sides of the breast. This pattern suggests "a dark jacket unbuttoned down the front."

On its breeding grounds in coniferous forests from Newfoundland and Alaska south in the mountains to North Carolina, western Texas, central Arizona, and Lower California, the Olive-sided may be detected by its characteristic noisy song, a three-syllabled utterance. It has been interpreted in words as *look three deer, quick three beers,* or *come right here.* The emphasis is on the middle syllable, and the last is slurred downward.

VERMILION FLYCATCHER

(Pyrocephalus rubinus)

Color Plate Page 176

In the springtime, brilliantly colored flowers hold the spotlight in the western deserts. Somber colored birds move in the background. To this rule, the brilliant Vermilion Flycatcher must be regarded as a notable exception, for when spring comes to the desert, nothing surpasses this feathered ball of fire in its bid for attention.

Those who have had the rare privilege of watching the male Vermilion Flycatcher perform his courtship flight, give an enchanting account of their experiences. Charles William Beebe writes:

"Up shoots one from a mesquite tree, with full, rounded crest, and breast puffed out until it seems a floating ball of vermilion—buoyed up on vibrating wings. Slowly, by successive upward throbs, the bird ascends, at each point of vibrating rest uttering his little love song—a cheerful *ching-tink-a-le-tink! chink-tink-a-le-tink!* which is the utmost he can do. When at the limit of his flight, fifty or seventy-five feet above our heads, he redoubles his efforts, and the *chings* and the *tinks* rapidly succeed each other. Suddenly, his little strength exhauted, the suitor drops to earth almost vertically in a series of downward swoops, and alights near the wee gray form for which he at present exists."

The head and underparts of the Vermilion Flycatcher are vermilion red; the upperparts and the tail are brown. The bird is 5½ or 6½ inches long. The female is dark brown above with streaks on her white breast, and a salmon wash on her belly and undertail coverts.

The species ranges throughout the arid regions of the southwest from Utah and southern New Mexico to Texas and California.

Its home is the cottonwoods and willows along streams, although it is also partial to oak groves. Its nest is a typical Flycatcher nest.

BEARDLESS FLYCATCHER

(Camptostoma imberbe)

A small Flycatcher of southern Texas and Arizona, the Beardless resembles a Kinglet or Vireo more than a Flycatcher. It is olive gray above, and dingy white below, with indistinct wingbars and eye-ring. Its bill is small and dark. But it takes an expert to distinguish it from Bell's Vireo which has rather more yellowish sides, or the immature Verdin which has a bill strongly yellow at the base.

The Beardless Flycatcher's song is distinctive, being a series of gentle notes increasing in volume in the middle, or otherwise described as three long slow notes followed by a trill.

It builds its nest in forest growth or thick second growth. The three white eggs are finely speckled with brown. Although the bird is primarily an insect-eater, it also feeds on small fruits.

LARKS

Family Alaudidae

The Larks are almost entirely birds of the Eastern Hemisphere; only one, the Horned Lark is native to North America. They are terrestrial in their habits, nesting on the ground, and are generally brownish, streaked and spotted to blend with their surroundings.

They travel in flocks except during the breeding season. More than two hundred and fifty Larks are known. These birds walk rather than hop.

MALE PRAIRIE HORNED LARK (*Eremophila alpestris*). Length: 7 to 8 inches. Male and female: upperparts pinkish brown streaked with dark brown. Pale yellow throat with black collar and two single black horns. Dark tail; underparts, white. Range: breeds and winters from Canada to Mexico. Voice: tinkling twitter, high in pitch. Note *tee* or *tee-titi*.

Hal H. Harrison

VIOLET-GREEN SWALLOW (*Tachycineta thalassina lepida*). Length: 5.5 inches. Male and female: violet green upperparts, white below. Two white patches over tail base. Range: breeds from Canada south to Mexico.

William L. and Irene Finley

HORNED LARK

(Eremophila alpestris)

Color Plate Page 180

Perhaps you will never realize a cherished desire to listen to the song of the famed European Skylark, so popular in Old World song and story. But while you are waiting for that dream to come true, you will be delighted with the lovely flight song of our only true American Lark. . . . The Horned Lark.

The best known of the many geographic forms of the Horned Lark in America is the Prairie Horned Lark *(Eremophila alpestris)*, and it was this one that I watched rising from a golf course one March morning to climb into the sky to offer his love to a female hidden somewhere below.

Leaving the ground, the bird mounted higher and higher in large sweeping circles, all the while delivering a series of sweet twittering notes. Higher and higher it mounted until it became a speck in the blue. My companion lost it with his naked eyes. I watched through binoculars. Suddenly, far above the earth, the bird checked its ascent, hovered a few moments, and then closed its wings and started earthward. Downward it shot, faster and faster, gaining momentum every second. And just as it seemed that it must surely crash, the Lark opened its wings and glided to a graceful landing.

Larks are notoriously early nesters. Long before most summer birds have returned to their northern breeding grounds, Horned Larks are feeding their young. The first of several broods is started in March, sometimes as early as February. The nest is built on the ground in the open with no protection other than a slight indentation. It is lined with grasses. It is characteristic of these birds to build a "platform" of mud and tiny stones in front of the nest.

Because of the habit of the incubating female known as "abandonment concealment," the finding of a Horned Lark's nest is a difficult task. Long before an intruder is near the nest, the female slips away quietly. To flush her at the nest is thus impossible. To find the tiny hollow with its three or four grayish speckled eggs on several acres of barren land is truly a "needle-in-the-haystack" undertaking.

To find it without the aid of the feeding parents is still more difficult when the nest contains the protectively colored young birds which freeze low in their hideaway. Young Larks leave the nest before they are able to fly, following the parents about the field. At this stage, the male takes charge, leaving the female free to start her next brood.

Horned Larks are well named, for both sexes wear little black feathered adornments on the sides of their heads that may be raised to look like horns. The male's black markings are more vivid than the female's and his horns are more conspicuous. The bird is 7 or 8 inches long.

Another well-distributed member of the family is the Northern Horned Lark *(E. a. alpestris)*. The eye-line of this species is yellow. In the Prairie Horned Lark it is white. The breast of the former is more yellowish than the Prairie's. The Meadowlark is not a member of the Lark family, but of the Blackbirds.

Horned Larks breed throughout Canada and the United States, except the South Atlantic and Gulf states.

SWALLOWS

Family Hirundinidae

The Swallows are represented all over the world, with a number of species being native to America. Their wings are extremely long, reaching to the tail or beyond when closed. Like the Swifts, their legs and feet are very weak, being useful only for perching. Their food is insects which are captured and eaten on the wing.

VIOLET-GREEN SWALLOW

(Tachycineta thalassina lepida)

Color Plate Page 181

The two conspicuous white rump patches on the iridescent green and purple back of the Violet-green Swallow spare bird watchers a great deal of confusion trying to distinguish this species from the very similar Tree Swallow. Both have pure white underparts and both have slightly notched tails. Only in favorable light may one see the blue-black or green-black iridescence of the Tree Swallow's back. The Violet-green is about 5½ inches long. This strictly western bird breeds from Alaska south to Mexico and eastward only to South Dakota and Nebraska. It nests in natural cavities in trees, abandoned Woodpecker holes, holes in crevices in rocky cliffs, and in a great variety of similar places.

In the winter, the Violet-green retires to Mexico and Central America. A few individuals winter each year in the Imperial Valley in southern California, in the lower Colorado Valley and in northern Lower California.

TREE SWALLOW

(Iridoprocne bicolor)

Color Plate Page 184

When I think of the Tree Swallow and the associations with which I have always found the bird, there comes to mind a northern marsh with its Redwings, Swamp Sparrows, Alder Flycatchers, Marsh Hawks and Virginia Rails; its spatterdock, duckweed, swamp roses, pickerel weed, arrowhead and cattails; its painted turtles, tree frogs, water snakes, muskrats and raccoons; those are the natural companions of the Tree Swallows where I have come to know them best.

In late March and early April, the Tree Swallows move up the Atlantic coast, the first of their family to head north in the spring. It is the only Swallow that habitually winters in the southern United States, and thus its average migration hop is a shorter one, although for the individuals that breed as far north as Point Barrow in northern Alaska, their journey is longer than some of the other Swallows that winter in South America and nest in the United States.

Despite the fact that the Tree Swallow's diet is not as completely insectiv-

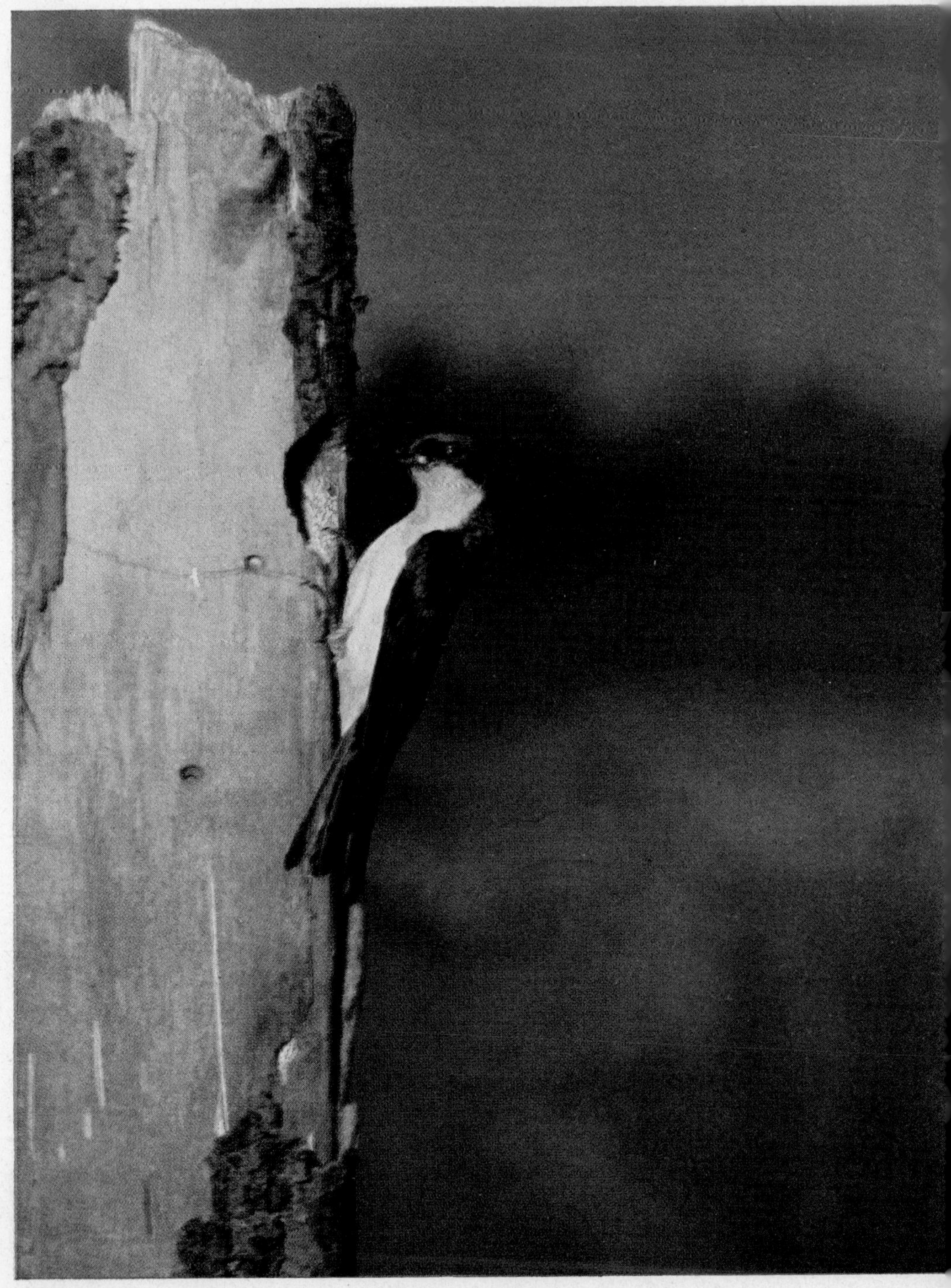

TREE SWALLOW (*Iridoprocne bicolor*). Length: 5 to 6 inches. Male and female: greenish steel blu upperparts, white underparts. Range: Quebec to Virginia, Arkansas, and Kansas. Winters alon coast from Florida to North Carolina. Voice: *cheet* or *chi-veet*.
Hal H. Harrison

erous as the other members of the tribe, and it is able to subsist at times on vegetable matter, especially the fruit of the bayberry, still droves of Tree Swallows sometimes starve to death when caught suddenly in a late spring cold snap in the north, or die in an unexpected freeze in the south during the winter.

The ancestral nesting sites of Tree Swallows are natural cavities in trees or abandoned Woodpecker holes, but like its larger relative, the Purple Martin, many Tree Swallows have accepted man-made nesting boxes as their homes. An outstanding example of what can be done to attract these birds is the result obtained on Cape Cod where ninety-eight wooden boxes were placed in favorable sites one year. The nesting population jumped from four pairs to sixty. The following year, with four hundred boxes available, the breeding population soared to one hundred and thirteen pairs. An experiment well worth trying.

Unlike the Purple Martin, Cliff Swallow and Bank Swallow, the Tree Swallows show no tendency to nest in colonies, but prefer to breed in isolated pairs. The nest itself is made of dry grasses and is invariably lined with a great many feathers. Research done at the Cape Cod project disclosed the fact that 3,300 feathers were used by the Swallows in lining the nests in forty-six boxes. Ninety-nine percent of the feathers were those of the Herring Gull. The birds show a decided preference for white feathers and will travel far to get them. Four to six pure white eggs are laid.

Depending upon the number of young in a brood, and thus the amount of food that the parents can bring daily to their offspring, young Tree Swallows remain in the nesting cavity from sixteen to twenty-four days. Like little frogs with immaculate white throats, the young ones perch at the entrance hole awaiting the arrival of the old birds with food. An adult zooms past and calls *silip*. Little necks are stretched far out and yellow mouths are held wide open to receive the meal of insects.

The Tree Swallow which is 5 to 6 inches long will be confused with no other Swallow in eastern United States, for it is the only one with pure white underparts. The back is greenish blue, iridescent in favorable light. In the west, it may be mistaken for the Violet-green Swallow, which also has a white belly, but the two white patches at the base of the tail of the Violet-green will always distinguish it.

BANK SWALLOW

(Riparia riparia riparia)

Color Plate Page 186

During road construction work near a large swamp in northwestern Pennsylvania, steam shovels carved out a large sand and clay bank. The excavated earth was hauled away, and when the project was completed, there was left a high perpendicular bank of clay. Here was an ideal nesting site for Bank Swallows, and a colony of these fleet-winged birds promptly moved in.

The Bank Swallow, also called Sand Swallow or Sand Martin, is a small, brown-backed bird (5 to 5½ inches long) with a distinct band across its white breast. Our only other brown-backed Swallow, the Rough-winged Swallow, lacks this distinct band across its breast. In flight, when the band is difficult to see, the Bank Swallow may

BANK SWALLOW (*Riparia riparia riparia*). Length: 5 to 5.5 inches. Male and female: above plain grayish brown; white throat, chin, cheeks and underparts. Wide band of grayish brown across chest. Range: Quebec, Alaska, south to Virginia and northern Alabama, and Texas; winters in South America. Voice: a dry rattle *brrt* or *bjit*.
Hal H. Harrison

be distinguished from the Rough-wing by its whiter underparts. The tails of both species are just slightly forked, not deeply forked like the swallow-tail of the Barn Swallow.

The flight of the Bank Swallow is irregular and zig-zagged. Its voice is weak and its song is a few simple twittering notes. The alarm note is a harsh *te-a-r-r*. An intruder in the immediate

ROUGH-WINGED SWALLOW (*Stelgidopteryx ruficollis serripennis*). Length: 5 to 5.75 inches. Male and female: grayish brown, paler below. The barbs on the feathers are curved giving wings rough feel. Range: Gulf of Mexico north to Massachusetts, New York, Ontario, Minnesota, and North Dakota. Winters in Central America. Voice: a rough *trit-trit*.
Hal H. Harrison

vicinity of a nesting colony evokes a constant twittering and chattering from the adults fluttering overhead.

Using its rather weak feet and its bill, the Bank Swallow digs its own nesting burrow. The openings are about as large as one's fist, flat on the bottom and arched on top. The depth of the burrows ranges from fifteen to forty-seven inches, with twenty-eight inches about average.

The tunnels are begun with the bird clinging to the side of the bank, picking with its bill until a ledge is formed. It uses its tail in Woodpecker-fashion, as a support. When a ledge is secured, the Swallow then uses its bill and its feet for digging. The wings are often used to throw dirt from the tunnel. Both sexes excavate.

Burrow digging occurs about mid-May. Since Bank Swallows are gregarious, large colonies are generally the rule. About fifty pairs made up the colony that I studied and photographed. The bank contained over seventy burrows, however. The birds enter and leave their tunnels on the wing, rarely stopping or even hesitating at the entrance, making photography very difficult.

The nests themselves are flimsy affairs of grasses, rootlets, straws and the like, placed near the inner end of the tunnel. After the four or five pure white eggs are laid, feathers are often added to the lining of the nest. Incubation requires from fourteen to sixteen days, and the young are in the nest from eighteen to twenty-two days. Before leaving their burrows, the young appear at the entrances for several days, begging for food.

Although this bird's range is limited locally to where it finds banks suitable for mating, its general range is wide and varied. In America, breeding colonies occur from northern Alaska and northern Quebec south to southern California, Texas, central Alabama, and Virginia. It winters in Brazil and Peru, migrating through Mexico and Central America. It also occurs in Europe, Asia, and northern Africa.

ROUGH-WINGED SWALLOW

(Stelgidopteryx ruficollis serripennis)

Color Plate Page 187

Despite its close relationship to the highly gregarious Bank Swallow, the Rough-winged Swallow is a confirmed individualist. Although it usually nests in burrows in sandy banks as does the Bank Swallow, the Rough-wing does not nest in colonies nor does it dig its own burrow.

The old nesting tunnels of Bank Swallows and Kingfishers are the usual nesting places for Rough-winged Swallows, but they are by no means confined to these sites. I found a pair nesting in an old drain pipe in a stone wall along a creek. Crevices in rock ledges or around bridges and old buildings are often chosen. At the very edge of a colony of fifty pairs of Bank Swallows I found a lone pair of Rough-winged Swallows nesting in an old burrow.

At this latter site, I had a fine opportunity to study the two similar species together. The principal field mark, of course, is the distinct band across the white breast of the Bank Swallow, entirely lacking in the dusky breast o[f] the Rough-winged. The Rough[-]winged Swallow is somewhat larger (to 5¾ inches long) than the Ban[k] Swallow. In flight, it does less zig-zag[-]ging and more gliding than the Bank and the wing beats are slower. In th[e] air, the Bank Swallow is noticeabl[y] lighter in color beneath than th[e] Rough-wing.

The voices of the two species ar[e] similar, although the alarm note of th[e] Rough-winged seems more harsh. Th[e] bird's song is a faint twittering, give[n] on the wing.

The nest of the Rough-winge[d] Swallow is a pile of grasses and twig[s] placed at the end of the burrow. Th[e] six or seven eggs are pure white. In on[e] nest that I studied, I found seven well-feathered youngsters at the end of a tunnel in a clay bank. The nest was just beyond arm's length from the burrow entrance.

At this burrow, I took the natural color picture on page 187, but only after an interesting experiment. I found that pictures of the adults entering or leaving the tunnel were impossible, for they came in on the wing and left without the slightest hesitation at the mouth of the burrow. Finally I placed a handkerchief loosely bunched just inside the tunnel, making the Sparrows' entrance impossible (I thought).

For awhile, the old birds shied from the burrow. They returned innumerable times with food, fluttered about in the air, but refused to alight. Eventually one bird overcame its fear and landed. It contemplated the handkerchief for a moment and then grabbed it in its bill and started tugging. The handkerchief became dislodged enough to permit the bird to enter the burrow.

Feeding was resumed. These birds became so tame that they used my camera as a landing perch before entering the nesting burrow.

The Rough-winged Swallow nests from the Atlantic to the Pacific and south into Mexico. It winters in Mexico and Central America. Recently a sub-species was recognized in the southwest, ranging from Guerro to Texas, southern Arizona and southern California. It is the Sonora Rough-winged Swallow. *(S. r. psammochrous)*.

BARN SWALLOW

(Hirundo rustica)

Color Plate Page 190

It is an ill-advised farmer, indeed, who discourages Barn Swallows from choosing his barn or other out-buildings as their summer home. Discounting the beauty of their shiny steel-blue backs and rufous underparts; ignoring the graceful flight that adds so much to the beauty of a country landscape; considering these fork-tailed Barn Swallows for their economic worth as insect-eaters alone, the farmer has a staunch friend.

With a diet that demands nothing but insects, the Barn Swallows sweep the country side from morning until night, gleaning a livelihood from guests unwelcome on the farm. The Swallow's large mouth and short, flat, triangular bill are especially adapted to its manner of feeding on the wing. This constant use of the wings with its resultant disuse of the feet has had its affect on the bird's anatomy. Wings have evolved strong and streamlined; feet have grown weak, fitted only for perching.

The Barn Swallow may be distinguished from other swallows by its deeply forked tail. It really has a "swallow tail." It is the bird people refer to when they say just "the Swallow." Its flight song may be interpreted as a series of twittering notes, *kittick, kittick.*

The building of a Barn Swallow's nest is interesting to observe, and one is impressed with the patience of the birds as they make trip after trip, hour after hour, day after day, until thousands of tiny mud pellets have been placed and shaped to make the circular cup. Grasses and straws are added to the mud for reinforcement and the lining is padded with a thick blanket of soft feathers. The four to six white eggs are marked with reddish brown spots.

The adults work harmoniously in building the nest. They share the incubation of the eggs and are both devoted to the young. Barn Swallows that I have observed have had two broods, the second occurring in July. In all cases, the birds used the same nest for both broods. Other observers have found that where the birds returned to last year's nest, two broods were raised, while birds that built new nests raised only one brood that season.

I am always amused at the way little Swallows hang their heads over the side of the nest, each eager to be first with its mouth open when the old birds return with food. They learn quickly that the one that stretches the farthest and opens its mouth the widest is the one most likely to eat regularly.

Ranging over most of North America in the summer, the Barn Swallow migrates south to Mexico and South America for the winter. It returns to the northern states in April, remaining until August or early September when mixed flocks of old and young birds start their leisurely flight southward. Migration is by day, never by night.

CLIFF SWALLOW

(Petrochelidon pyrrhonota)

Color Plate Page 191

Before the white man settled America and built his barns, Cliff Swallows were appropriately named, for then they built their mud nests on the perpendicular sides of cliffs. Today, the common name of "Eaves Swallow" is more appropriate, for these colorful birds have, for the most part, forsaken their ancestral haunts for the eaves on the outside of barns. Here, in colonies, they build their clever bottle or gourd-shaped homes of mud and straw, lined with feathers.

The Cliff Swallow is usually found in close association with Barn Swallows, which often build their open nests on ledges about barns, usually inside the buildings. The Cliff Swallow's best field mark at all times is its conspicuous buffy rump patch. It is square-tailed, distinguishing it instantly from the

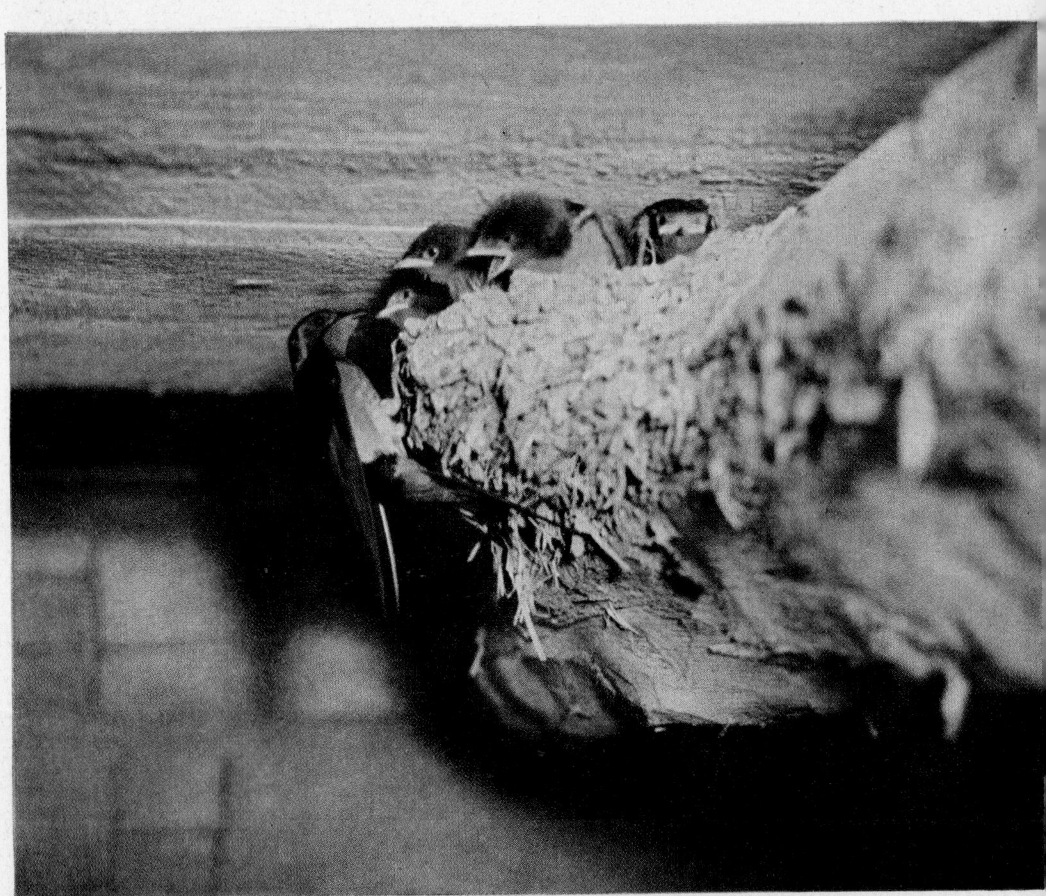

BARN SWALLOW AT NEST. YOUNG FULLY FEATHERED ARE READY TO LEAVE THE NEST (*Hirundo rustica*). Length: 6 to 7.5 inches. Male and female: steel blue upperparts, chestnut below. Long forked tail with white spots on it. Range: breeds from central Quebec and southern Manitoba south to North Carolina, north Alabama, Tennessee and Arkansas. Winters from Mexico to Brazil. Voice: a soft *wit* or *kwik-kvik, wit-wit*. Around nest, ee-*tee*.

Hal H. Harrison

CLIFF SWALLOW (*Petrochelidon pyrrhonota*). Length: 5 to 6 inches. Male and female: steel blue upperparts; chestnut and whitish below. Has buffy rump and dark throat patch. Range: Gulf of St. Lawrence, Ontario and Manitoba south to West Virginia, Alabama and Texas. Voice: squeaky and husky.
Harlan E. Eckler

swallow-tailed Barn Swallow in flight. A dark throat patch and a pale buff forehead are also diagnostic. It measures 5 to 6 inches in length.

Although distributed throughout most of North America, breeding colonies of Cliff Swallows are decidedly localized. Throughout much of its range it is uncommon, particularly in the central states. It is highly migratory, spending the winter as far south as Argentina.

COAHUILA CLIFF SWALLOW

(Petrochelidon fulva pallida)

Limited in the United States to south central Texas, this Swallow is like the Cliff Swallow, but with a pale rust or buff throat, which is readily apparent in the field.

PURPLE MARTIN

(Progne subis)

Color Plate Page 194

While everyone has heard of the Swallows that return each spring to Capistrano, only a few people know of the Swallows that return just as regularly each year to Saxonburg near my home. The difference is a good press agent! The first Purple Martin colony was established in this little Pennsylvania village in the days of Christian Stuebgen who came from Germany well over a hundred years ago. The Martins have been returning to Saxonburg during the first week of April ever since.

This historic fact can be paralleled in scores of other cities and hamlets throughout America where this largest of all our Swallows has returned each spring to nest in the houses provided for it by the townspeople. An advance guard of several males (a friend of mine calls them "room clerks") arrives first. They are joined later by the main flock.

The adult male Purple Martin can be mistaken for no other Swallow. It is uniformly deep bluish black, both above and below. The females are dark above, but their underparts are dingy gray. Immature males are much like adult females, except that they show more blue on the underparts. The adult plumage is not acquired until the end of the second summer, but birds breed in immature dress. The Martin is the largest Swallow, being 7½ to 8½ inches long.

In the air, the Purple Martin exhibits all the grace and beauty for which the Swallow family is noted. Characteristic of the bird's flight is its habit of alternately flapping and sailing. Passing overhead, glossy sable wings outstretched, the bird calls a harsh *keerp*. The "song" of the Martin is not a specific rendition, but rather a "loud, rich chirrupping," with a number of lower guttural notes interspersed.

The Purple Martin has been a favorite with mankind for many generations. The early Indians attracted them to their villages by placing hollow gourds at the ends of cross sticks on poles. The Negroes continued the custom on southern plantations, and today, thousands of Martin houses, many elaborate, others simple, are erected for these birds throughout their North American breeding range. A pole with a colonial-type Martin house at the top makes a center-piece for many American gardens.

The communal nesting habit of the Martin makes possible the attraction of large flocks. The bird is an early spring migrant, and the females follow closely the vanguard of males to the northern states in early April. Nesting material is carried into the house compartments chosen by the pairs. Four or five pure white eggs are laid. Both parents feed the young, which are in the nest from three to four weeks.

In late summer and early fall, large flocks of Martins assemble before and during the southern migration. Flocks numbering as many as 100,000 birds have been reported. The autumnal flight of the Martins takes them to South America for the winter.

From a purely economic standpoint, persons who attract Martins to their gardens are amply repaid for their troubles. The bird's diet is one hundred percent insectiverous, and the numbers of obnoxious insects consumed by a colony of Martins in a season would be fantastic.

Martins breed from southern Canada and Alaska south into Mexico and the West Indies.

CROWS and JAYS

Family Corvidae

The Crow and Jay family is almost world-wide in its distribution, with the greatest number of species occurring in temperate regions. They are mostly large birds, some of which are brilliantly colored, and can by no means be called "song birds."

CANADA JAY

(Perisoreus canadensis canadensis)

Color Plate Page 198

Call him what you will, "whiskey jack," "camp robber," "moose-bird," "grease-bird," or even some unprintable names that you may have tossed his way in a moment of exasperation, the Canada Jay is still an inimitable personality, an integral part of the Canadian woods. He will steal anything you may be careless enough to leave lying around, such as a box of matches, a bar of soap, a pack of cigarettes, a bass plug, or a wrist watch. If he can get to your food cache, so much the better, but he seems mischief-bent most of the time.

The Canada Jay is a crestless bird about 11 or 13 inches long that has been fittingly described as a "magnified Chickadee." It is gray with a black hood and white forehead. Its fluffy plumage exaggerates its size. The only gray bird of the north woods with which it might be confused is the Northern Shrike, a bird with black wings and tail.

The apparent lack of fear and the sociability that characterizes the Canada Jay most of the time disappears when the bird starts to nest in March and April. Quietly it retires to a remote area where a nest of twigs is hidden in a dense conifer. The four, brown-spotted, grayish eggs are laid in a warm fur-and-feather-lined cup.

The bird has a large repertoire of vocal utterances, many harsh and jay-like, others soft and melodious.

The breeding range for the Canada Jay starts from the northern limit of conifers, from Labrador to British Columbia, and southward to northern Minnesota and Maine. The species is generally sedentary.

Western sub-species of the Canada Jay include the Rocky Mountain Jay *(P. C. capitalis)*, which is larger and lighter in color; Alaska Jay *(P. C. fumifrons)*; Oregon Jay *(P. C. obscurus)*; Gray jay *(P. C. griseus)*; and the Pacific Canada Jay *(P. C. pacificus)*.

BLUE JAY

(Cyanocitta cristata)

Color Plate Page 199

"The trouble with the Blue Jay is that we all fall in love with him in the winter when he is being good, but lose sight of him in the spring and summer when he is practicing his villainies," wrote W. L. Dawson in "Birds of Ohio."

The bad reputation acquired by the Blue Jay long ago has remained with it through the years. The "villainies," it seems, are confined principally to the jay's alleged fondness for the eggs and young of other birds. It has been called "a cunning, mischievous, thieving, cruel, boastful, quarreling, treacherous wanton." And if a bird is all those things he is a bad, bad bird indeed!

I don't believe it. To me, the Blue Jay is a dashing bird, an integral part of the American forest, and I am sorry that it is unprotected in so many states. While it makes more than its share of noise, it also carries more than its share of beauty in the bird world.

Since the Jay's diet is about 75 per-cent fruit, grain, and nuts, and the remainder almost entirely insects and small animals, it is likely that the bird' bad qualities have been over-empha sized.

The pugnacious nature of the Jay i evident to even the most casual ob server. There is no doubt of it to one who decides to examine a Jay's nest especially one containing young. Botl adults fly viciously at the intruder often striking with their wings. A luckless Owl caught napping during the day often falls target to a roving band of Jays that harass it amidst a great uproar.

For some unexplained reason, Blue Jays are particularly localized. They may be abundant where you live, but twenty miles away, folks may consider them quite rare. Where they are abundant, they are usually fearless. Jays

PURPLE MARTIN (*Progne subis*). Length: 7.5 to 8.5 inches. Male: entirely blue black. Female: upperparts dark brown; back, black. Throat and breast gray, abdomen whitish. Range: breeds from Canada south to Mexico. Voice: sweet song *peeyou, peeyou, peeyou.*

Hal H. Harrison

ROCKY MOUNTAIN JAY ON NEST *(Perisoreus canadensis capitalis)*. Length: 11 to 13 inches. Male and female: gray with white crown, unkempt appearance. Young: dark, slate-colored. Range: Rocky Mountain region. Voice: a gentle, whistled *whee-ah*.
Alfred M. Bailey, National Audubon Society

will come into the yard where they delight in raiding garbage cans. Surprised at their pilfering, the birds fly off with indignant cries of *jay, jay, jay*.

The Blue Jay's nest is a bulky affair of sticks, often placed in an evergreen tree. The eggs, four to six, are olive color with irregular spots. Both birds build the nest, both incubate the eggs, and both are very attentive to the young. The Blue Jay is 11 or 12 inches long, bright blue above and whitish below, with a prominent crest.

In photographing Blue Jays, I have found that they are rather easy subjects if the photographer is willing to withstand the attacks and terrific scoldings that he must undergo while setting up equipment and preparing for pictures. Operating my camera by remote control, I have always been able to escape the onslaught by hiding in my bird blind at a distance from the nest.

Blue Jays migrate erratically. Although it is not uncommon to find them at northern feeding stations throughout the winter, many do travel southward in the fall.

It is always a surprise to the uninformed to learn that the Jay's closest relative in eastern United States is the common crow. Certainly they look nothing alike, but sometimes the raucous call of the Jay seems to indicate a relationship. Ravens and Magpies are also in this family.

In several geographic forms, the Blue Jay occurs from Newfoundland, Quebec, northern Manitoba, and Southern Alberta south to Florida and the Gulf Coast, west to central Texas, and eastern Colorado.

STELLER'S JAY

(Cyanocitta stelleri)

Color Plate Page 204

The Steller's Jays, including all seven geographic races, are the crested Blue Jays of the vast coniferous forest area of western North America, ranging from Alaska southward to Central America and from the Pacific coast to the Rocky Mountains. Here they replace the familiar Blue Jay of eastern North America as the only Jays with crests.

The long crest and entire foreparts of the Steller's are black or dark brown. The wings, tail, and underparts are deep blue. Steller's is a large Jay, 12 to 13½ inches long. The California Jay whose range overlaps that of the Steller's in some areas, is a crestless Jay of the oak woods. Steller's prefers the conifers.

The Steller's is Jay-like in its habits, even its bad ones. Its call is a loud harsh *shaack, shaack, shaack,* similar to but lower pitched than the call of the California Jay. Other calls are interpreted as *kweesch, kweesch, kweesch,* and *klook, klook, klook* and many others.

The geographic races of this species are Steller's Jay *(C. s. stelleri)*; Queen Charlotte Jay *(C. s. carlottae)*; Coast Jay *(C. s. carbonacea)*; Blue-fronted Jay *(C. s. frontalis)*; Black-headed Jay *(C. s. annectens)*; Long-crested Jay *(C. s. macrolopha)*; and the Nevada Crested Jay *(C. s. percontatrix)*.

FLORIDA JAY

(Aphelocoma coerulescens coerulescens)

Color Plate Page 201

To the residents of Florida and to the northern folks whc migrate to that state each winter, where the nonmigratory Florida Jay is found exclusively, the bird is better known as the Scrub Jay. Either name is descriptive, for this crestless Jay is found nowhere else but Florida, and almost nowhere else in Florida except the "scrub" areas. This latter is typically Floridian, too, for it consists of a type of vegetation peculiar to that state—mostly sand pine and shrubby oak.

The Florida Jay is about the size of a Blue Jay (11½ inches long) but may be recognized instantly by its more slender build, longer tail, and crestless head. The wings and tail are blue with no black and white markings. Although not as noisy as the Blue Jay, the Scrub Jay has a loud, harsh call. A song of this bird is said to be a mixture of "low, sweet-toned calls, high in pitch."

The Scrub Jay is a rather isolated species. Its closest relatives are the western crestless Jays of the *Coerulescens* group.

CALIFORNIA JAY

(Aphelocoma coerulescens)

In the case of the California Jay, one might do well to remember that bit of philosophy that suggests "if you cannot say something good about a man, say nothing." The evidence against this *Blue Jay* of California seems to be overwhelmingly on the wrong side of the ledger as far as the bird's economic habits are concerned. There seems to be little doubt that it is a nest robber and a fruit thief.

This oak-inhabiting Jay may be recognized by its blue head, wings and tail, its brownish back, pale gray underparts, and dark band across the breast. The absence of a crest distinguishes it instantly from the Blue Jay and the Steller's Jay, even when coloration is not discernible. The color pattern is similar to that of the Blue Jay, however, and it is about the same size (12 inches long).

California Jays are noisy birds, much bolder than Blue Jays. A familiar cry is *tschek, tschek, tschek* uttered in a higher tone than the call of the Steller's Jay. Another note is *ker-wheek.*

The bird's noisy demeanor is evident throughout the year, except when the birds pair off for nesting. Then they become surprisingly silent.

A number of geographic races of the California Jay are recognized, including the Woodhouse's Jay *(Aphelocoma coerulescens woodhousei)* which was formerly considered a distinct species. Variations in size and color warrant the subspecies, but these are indistinguishable in the field.

SANTA CRUZ JAY

(Aphelocoma insularis)

Limited to Santa Cruz Island, off the coast of California, this Jay is considered a distinct species. It is similar to the California Jay, but somewhat larger (12 inches long) and more vividly colored. It is crestless.

ARIZONA JAY

(Aphelocoma ultramarina arizonae)

The Arizona Jay is a Mexican species that reaches the United States in Arizona and New Mexico. It is a crestless Jay with uniformly dull gray underparts, dull blue head, and bluish gray back, wings and tail. It lacks the breast band of the California Jay (Subspecies, Woodhouse's Jay) with which it might be found. It is 11½ to 13 inches long.

Its voice is quite different from that of the California Jay, being a querulous *chenk*. Another geographic form of this Jay, Couch's Jay *(A. u. couchi)*, also reaches the United States and is found in the Chisos Mountains of Texas.

GREEN JAY

(Xanthoura luxuosa glaucescens)

A Jay of the lower Rio Grande Valley, its color makes it unmistakable. Both male and female have the back, shoulders, rump, tail and wings, green. The cheeks, crown, and back of head are blue, and the throat black. The bird is 11 or 12 inches long. It builds its nest of thorny twigs in dense thickets and lays four to seven grayish or greenish eggs, spotted with brown or lavender. The Green Jay has a variety of calls, sometimes a dry throaty rattle. Its main call is *chek, chek, chek, chek*. Like its relatives, it is fond of robbing garbage pails for scraps of meat.

PIÑON JAY

(Gymnorhinus cyanocephalus)

A small Jay, 10 or 11 inches long, uniformly grayish blue and without a crest, the Piñon Jay lives in piñon and juniper woods through the Rocky Mountains area from Washington to western Texas. The throat is streaked with grayish white. The tail is square

ARIZONA JAY *(Aphelocoma sordida arizonae)*. Length: 11.5 to 13 inches. Male and female: upperparts dull blue, back grayish. No crest. Underparts dull grayish white. Range: Arizona, New Mexico, Texas. Voice: a harsh *drenk*, or *jenk*.
Ross and Florence Thornburg

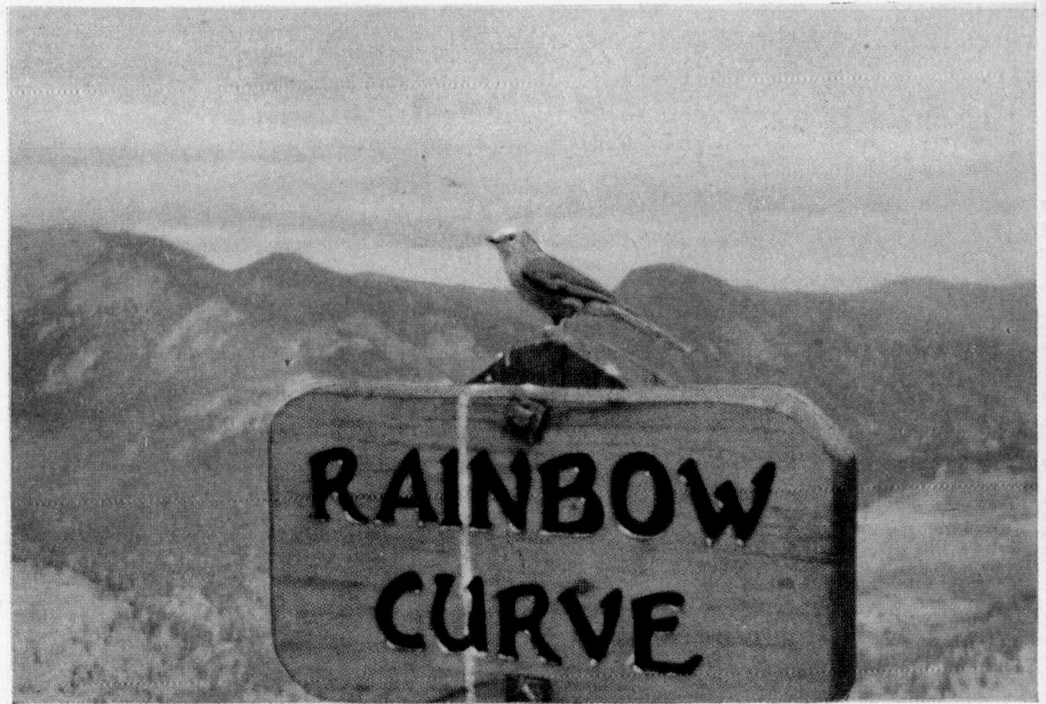

CANADA JAY (*Perisoreus canadensis canadensis*). Length: 11 to 13 inches. Male and female: upperparts gray. Has dark patch on back of head, white crown and no crest. Tail tipped with white. Underparts light gray. Range: Newfoundland to Nova Scotia south throughout northeastern United States west to Minnesota. Voice: a whistled *whee-ah*.
Alfred M. Bailey

and much shorter than the wings. The female is similar to the male, but smaller and duller.

The Piñon Jay is a sociable bird, acting more like a Crow than a Jay. It moves along in flocks, feeding on piñon nuts and juniper berries, and even nests in colonies. Its large, bulky but compact nest is built in piñon pines or juniper bushes and the three to five eggs are bluish white, thickly spotted. The common call note is a shrill querulous *peek peek*, or *whee whee*, but it also makes various other Jay-like sounds. While feeding on the ground a group of these Jays keep up a shrill chattering.

After the young are out of the nest, the birds join large groups again, and troupe around the country.

AMERICAN or BLACK-BILLED MAGPIE

(*Pica pica hudsonia*)

Color Plate Page 209

The beautifully marked black and white American Magpie is one of the characteristic birds of the sparsely wooded or treeless regions of western North America, especially in areas where open, low-growth vegetation predominates. Graceful in flight, with its long iridescent tail feathers leveled off behind, and its white patches flashing with every wing beat, the Magpie is a handsome fellow. It is a hardy creature, too, and like its relative, the Crow, seemingly well able to withstand the buffeting it receives from those who would destroy it. But whether one dislikes it for its bad habits or admires it for its more virtuous qualities, the Magpie is well-known to all who live within its range. It is a large bird, 17½ to 21½ inches long, with a tail which is half the length of the bird. Its plumage is an iridescent black, with white on the shoulders and abdomen.

The nest of the Black-billed Magpie is a large well-constructed affair, often placed in an impenetrable thorn tree. It is generally conspicuous even at a distance, but its thorny location usually makes it safe from molestation. Sometimes the birds use the same nest from year to year. Seven is the usual number of greenish gray eggs, blotched with brown.

Although ordinarily wary and suspicious, Magpies are easily tamed and make interesting pets. They are noisy birds, flocking together after the nesting season, roaming the countryside. Large roosts of Magpies are not uncommon.

Much has been written concerning the food habits of the Magpie. In this regard it has earned for itself a bad reputation, especially among stockmen. The bird sometimes proves injurious to cattle, sheep, and newly-born stock. About three-fifths of its diet is animal

BLUE JAY ON NEST (*Cyanocitta cristata*). Length: 11 to 12 inches. Male and female: upperparts bright blue, with crested crown. Lower parts, white. Black necklace around throat. Range: Gulf of St. Lawrence to Gulf of Mexico. Voice: harsh *jeeah* or *jay*.

Hal H. Harrison

YELLOW-BILLED MAGPIE (*Pica nutalli*). Length: 16 to 18 inches (tail 9.5 to 10.25 inches). Male and female: large black and white land birds with long sweeping iridescent tails and large white patches on wings. Yellow bill. Range: valleys of central California. Voice: *cheh cheh cheh cheh,* also dry rattle in throat.
Chicago Natural History Museum

matter. This includes many kinds of insects, carrion, and small mammals, mainly rodents.

The Black-billed Magpie ranges from Alaska and Manitoba to New Mexico.

YELLOW-BILLED MAGPIE

(Pica nutalli)

The Yellow-billed Magpie looks exactly like the American or Black-billed Magpie, except that the former has a yellow bill and the latter, as its name indicates, has a black bill. It is also somewhat smaller, being 16 to 18 inches long.

The range of the Yellow-billed Magpie is greatly restricted compared to that of its relative. The Yellow-billed is found only in the valleys of central California, west of the Sierra Nevadas, chiefly in the Sacramento and San Joaquin Valleys.

RAVEN

(Corvus corax)

Color Plate Page 213

As man has advanced his civilization, the Raven has retreated before him. Today, this big member of the Crow family has disappeared from much of its former range and is rare in a large part of the territory it still inhabits. No bird is more a part of the remaining American wilderness than the Raven. It can be looked for confidently only in wild mountainous country, inaccessible sea cliffs, virgin forests, bleak desert mesas, and the vast, treeless tundra. In certain sections of Alaska and the far north, however, Ravens have lost much of their wildness and enter villages in the role of scavengers, appearing quite fearless.

Although one of the most omnivorous birds, the Raven is to a great extent a scavenger. It does catch and kill some of its own food, but it generally prefers to live on the flesh of dead animals and fishes. On some oceanic islands among bird concentrations along coastal cliffs, Ravens often glean an easy living by preying on the eggs and young of nesting sea birds.

The Raven is considerably larger than a Crow, 21½ to 26½ inches long, but may be mistaken by the casual observer. Its wingspread is over four feet while that of a Crow is less than three feet. The bird's croaking notes are entirely different from the Crow's cawing, and voice is the best

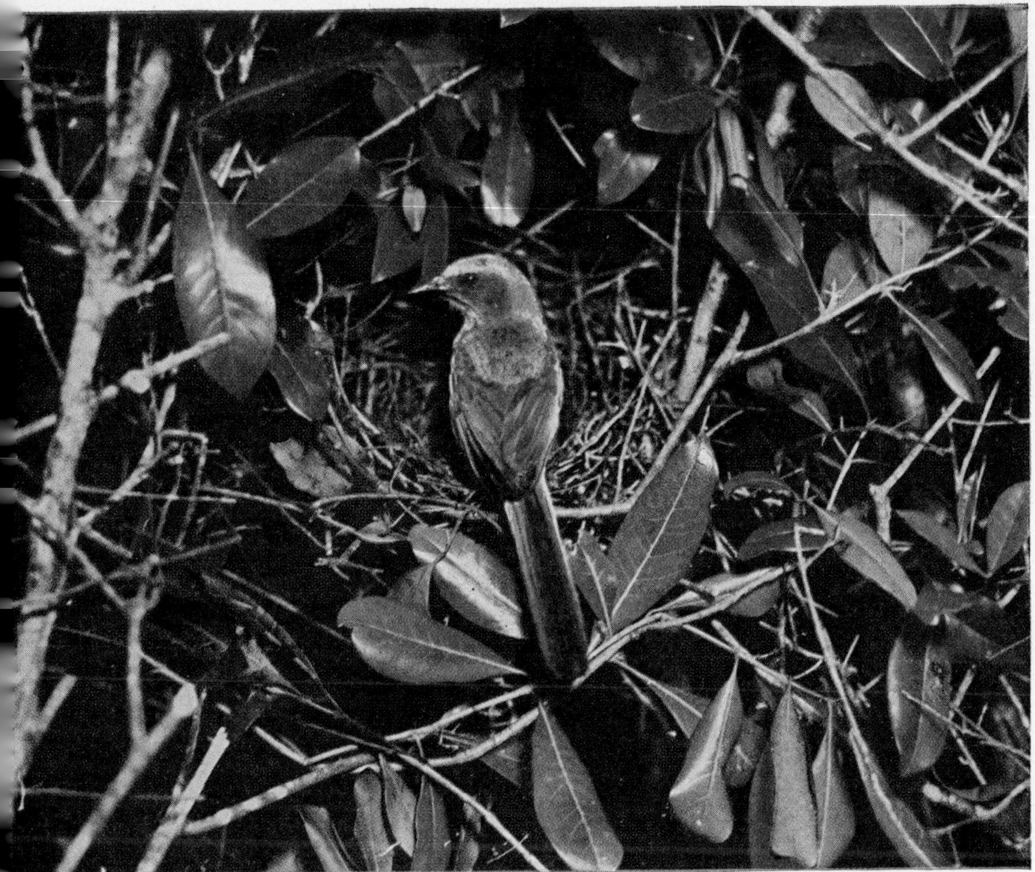

FLORIDA OR SCRUB JAY *(Aphelocoma coerulescens coerulescens)*. Length: 11.5 inches. Male and female: back brownish gray. Wings and tail unmarked blue, underparts grayish white. Head is not crested. Range: scrub oak regions of Florida. Voice: hoarse *kwesh kwesh kwesh*. Also a rasping *zhreek zhrink*.
Samuel A. Grimes

field mark, when it can be heard. In flight the two birds differ, the Raven being more Hawk-like, alternating its flappings with soarings on wings held horizontally. It frequently veers from side to side in flight.

The Northern Raven *(C. c. principalis)* is found from the Arctic circle southward to the most northern states, and in the mountains to Georgia. The American Raven *(C. c. sinatus)* is the Raven of the west, occurring eastward to North Dakota and southward to Central America. The Southwestern Raven *(C. c. clarionensis)* inhabits southwestern California.

WHITE-NECKED RAVEN

(Corvus cryptoleucus)

Don't be surprised if you fail to see the white neck of a White-necked Raven, for the white bases of its neck feathers are seldom visible. A fortunate gust of wind which might ruffle the plumage of a perching bird will afford the observer his best opportunity but, generally, bird watchers will find only an all-black bird (19 to 21 inches in length), larger than a Crow and smaller than an American Raven.

Fortunately, the White-necked Raven can be identified usually by a

WHITE-NECKED RAVEN (*Corvus cryptoleucus*). Length: 19 to 21 inches. Male and female: black, the feathers in good light showing a metallic bluish sheen. The base of the feathers on the neck and breast of this species is white. It has stout feet. Range: deserts of southeast Arizona, southern New Mexico, southeast Colorado, southwest Oklahoma, and western and southern Texas. Voice: a hoarse *krack*.

E. R. Kalmbach

process of elimination. In this species' haunts on the deserts of the southwestern states and Mexico, both the Crow and the American Raven are absent; the latter preferring the mountains, and the Crow's range overlapping only on the north and east boundaries of the White-necks range in Oklahoma and Texas. It may be distinguished from the Crow, however, by its low-pitched, guttural voice.

CROW

(Corvus brachyrhynchos)

Color Plate Page 216

No wild bird has received more persecution and condemnation from man than the Crow, and none has stood up under constant pressure more successfully than this "black marauder." There are no "fool hens" among the Crows or they would have been extinct long ago. Indeed, conservationists who oppose the complete annihilation of any species regardless o[f] its habits, have lon[g] since stopped worryin[g] about the Crow. It ca[n] take care of itself!

That the Crow [is] wary is unquestione[d] and its craftiness [is] recommending it mo[re] and more as a game bir[d] to American hunter[s:] not as a table bird, bu[t] as one that offers th[e] sportsman a test of ski[ll] in out-smarting i[t.] Many nimrods, wh[o] condemn the wholesal[e] slaughter of Crows b[y] bombings, are finding fair sport in the use o[f] blinds, decoys (particularly Owls, the Crows' sworn enemies) and Crow calls, to entice "Corvus" within gun range. Since the bird i[s] unprotected, and hunting can be enjoyed at all seasons, Crow shoots ar[e] likely to increase in popularity.

The Crows that one sees in nois[y] flocks throughout the fall and winte[r] suddenly become quiet recluses i[n] April. The flocks break up and th[e] birds pair, and any Crows that are seen in May are silent and alone as they g[o] and come from their woodland homes. It is the breeding season, and high in a tree crotch the Crow fashions a well-built nest of sticks, neatly lined with a deep cup of grasses and fibers.

Four to six handsome ovate eggs are laid. They vary greatly in shade, but green is the usual ground color. They are marked with irregular blotches of browns and grays. Incubation requires eighteen days, and normally, the young are in the nest five weeks, but may leave earlier if disturbed.

This otherwise crafty bird has one very vulnerable spot as far as human predators are concerned. A gregarious instinct causes these big black birds to roost together in fall and winter. Roosts with populations up to two hundred thousand individuals have been reported. Here the Crow leaves itself wide open for slaughtering. In one famous case in a midwestern state several years ago, 328,000 Crows were killed in one season by dynamite bombs placed in the roost during the day and exploded at night.

Through generations of experience, Crows are very wary of man, yet, young Crows, taken from the nest at the right time, make interesting pets. They show great confidence in humans under these circumstances but are inclined to be mischievous.

Needless to say, the Crow's voice is not one of its virtues. Its raucous cawing is known to everyone throughout the bird's vast range. Variations of the *caw* are common, and it is evident to those who have studied the bird's vocal moods that it is versatile.

In the extreme northern parts of its range, the Crow is migratory. In the breeding season, it ranges throughout most of North America in one of its four geographic races. These forms are: Eastern Crow *(C. b. brachyrhynchos)*; Southern Crow *(C. b. paulus)*; Florida Crow *(C. b. pascus)*; and Western Crow *(C. b. hesperis)*. The Northwestern Crow *(Corvus caurinus)*, like the Fish Crow, is now considered a full species.

FISH CROW

(Corvus ossifragus)

To identify a Fish Crow, depend upon its voice as your most reliable field mark. Although this black bird of the Atlantic and Gulf coasts is a bit smaller than its close relative, the Common Crow, the difference is not great enough to be a safe identifying mark, unless the two species are seen together. The Fish Crow is 16 to 20 inches long.

Bent describes the voice of the Fish Crow as "quite different from that of our Common Crow; shorter, less prolonged, more nasal, staccato, and not so

FISH CROW *(Corvus ossifragus)*. Length: 16 to 20 inches. Male and female: glossy black with blue iridescence above and green below. Range: the Atlantic coast from southern New England to Florida and along the Gulf of Texas; winters in southern portion of range. Voice: a more high-pitched nasal *car* than the common Crow.

Allan D. Cruickshank, National Audubon Society

STELLER'S JAY (*Cyanocitta stelleri*). Length: 12 to 13.5 inches. Male and female: upperparts grayish black. Lower back, abdomen, upper tail coverts blue. Head, crested. Range: Canada south to Mexico. Voice: a loud *shook-shook-shook* or *shack-shack-shack* or *wheck-wek-wek-wek-wek-wek* or *kwesh kwesh*.
R. T. Congdon

loud; it is hoarser, as if the bird had a sore throat or cold. I wrote it in my notes as *cor* or as an exact pronouncing of the word *car*. The hoarse voice of the Fish Crow might be confused at times with a similar note uttered by young Common Crows just out of the nest.

The Fish Crow ranges from southern New England southward along the coast to Florida, and west along the Gulf coast to eastern Texas. It is seldom found far from coastal marshes and beaches except in Florida where it follows the rivers inland. Its general habits are similar to the Common Crow, even its bad reputation. In Florida, the Fish Crow is guilty of raiding heronries where it steals the eggs of nesting birds.

CLARK'S NUTCRACKER

(Nucifraga columbiana)

Color Plate Page 218

"Camp robber" is not a name earned exclusively by the gray, crestless Jays of the north *(Perisoreus)*, for Clark's Nutcracker, another member of the family which inhabits the high mountains from Canada south to southern

California, Arizona, and New Mexico, has gained for itself the same title. Indeed, it is often found in company with Jays, foraging for food around habitation, although it is not as guilty of pilfering personal belongings nor is it quite as fearless as the "whisky jacks."

Clark's Nutcracker (named for its discoverer, Captain William Clark, of the Lewis and Clark expedition) walks about much in the manner of a small Crow. It has a light gray body with black wings and tail. Conspicuous white patches in the wings distinguish it at all times from the Jays whose general coloration is similar. The Nutcracker's noisy, boisterous habits and its general behavior are quite Jay-like. It builds its typical Crow-like nest in evergreens and lays from three to five eggs which are spotted with brown and purple.

The voice of Clark's Nutcracker is harsh and grating. Its call is a squawking *char-r-r-r-r*, repeated several times.

TITMICE

Family Paridae

The Titmice, which includes the Chickadees, Verdins, and Bush-tits, are small birds distinguished by their cone-shaped bills. Their coloring is uniformly gray or brown, although they may have variously colored head patches. Economically they are very beneficial, for they feed on minute insects and insect eggs which are passed over by larger birds. A family characteristic is their ability to hang upside down while searching for food.

BLACK-CAPPED CHICKADEE

(Parus atricapillus)

Color Plate Page 219

All night long the snow fell in great white flakes. The wind howled around the house and we were grateful for a warm fire. It certainly wasn't a night to be out.

When morning came, the wind had ceased. The snow clouds had emptied their cargo, and the world lay before us, a fairyland of frosty crystals. No sign of life outdoors this morning. But wait! What is that cheery note? It calls *chicka-dee-dee-dee.*

Here is winter's sunniest disposition—a Black-capped Chickadee, a little fluffy ball of black, white and gray feathers that fears no snows and gives not a hoot for zero weather. If you are among the thousands who maintain feeding stations for the birds, you need no introduction to this little acrobat with the black skull cap, for no bird is friendlier toward human beings than the Chickadee. And inquisitive too! How he cocks his head on the side and peers with beady black eyes toward that bag of sunflower seeds, waiting for its contents to be scattered over the morning table.

The Chickadee's bill is sharp and adept at probing under tree bark for insect eggs and larvae. It has a Woodpecker-like ability to cling to trees while feeding. Beef suet helps attract them to the garden, and sunflower seeds rank high on the Chickadee's list of favorite foods. Its bill is not thick and strong like a Finch, so instead of cracking seeds in Cardinal-fashion, the Chickadee places them between its toes and cracks them with a series of thrusts with its bill.

It is a rather safe rule that where you find one Chickadee you will find others, for they travel in little bands in the fall and winter, often joining with other birds to forage for food. These roving bands usually consist of the Chickadee's cousin, the Tufted Titmouse, Nuthatches, Downy Woodpeckers, Kinglets, and occasionally a Brown Creeper.

With the first warm days of approaching spring the Chickadee utters his true song, a plaintively whistled *phee-bee.* Courtship is a tender performance. The male takes great delight

MEXICAN CHICKADEE (*Penthestes sclateri eidos*). Length: 5 inches. Male and female: gray, with black cap and bib, the black of the bib spreading across the upper breast; the sides are dark gray, and the cheeks white. Range: mountains of southeast Arizona and southwest New Mexico, south into Mexico. Voice: *chick-a-dee-dee-dee*, similar to the Black-capped Chickadee.
Rudolph Hindemith, American Museum of Natural History

a feeding his prospective mate. With wings fluttering, she awaits his arrival with the choicest morsels he can find for her approval. Often he will fluff his feathers until he looks like a little ball of gray and white down.

Chickadees make their home in a rotted tree or stump where they can peck out a cavity with their not-too-strong bills. Sometimes they adopt a Woodpecker's abandoned hole, or a natural cavity in a tree. A nest of mosses, grasses, and feathers is built to hold the six to nine speckled eggs. Both birds incubate. The young have ravenous appetites which keep the adults busy from dawn to dusk carrying food.

Sexes are alike, about 5 inches long, and Chickadees wear the same color plumage the year around. Young birds look like their parents.

The Black-Capped Chickadee is a resident bird throughout its range. Eight geographic forms occur from central Quebec, Nova Scotia, and northern Alaska, south to New Jersey, Kansas, northern New Mexico, and northwestern California.

CAROLINA CHICKADEE

(*Parus carolinensis*)

Color Plate Page 226

The Carolina Chickadee and the northern Black-capped Chickadee are so much alike that field identification is very difficult. The former is slightly smaller (4¼ to 4¾ inches long) and has a shorter tail and a larger bill with less white in the wing due to the absence of the narrow white feather edgings.

Many observers feel that the two specimens are differentiated most easily by their calls. The Carolina's *chickadee* call is rendered more rapidly and on a higher pitch than the Black-capped's.

The greatest vocal difference between the species is in the spring song, commonly called the *phoebe* song.

Saunders describes the Black-capped's song as a simple *fee-bee*, while the Carolina's song is interpreted as *sufee-subee* or else *feesu beesu*. This is an aid in distinguishing the species.

The nesting habits of the two species are similar, so what has been said in the chapter on the Black-capped, may be applied to the present species also. Despite the close relationship between the two, the ranges of each are quite definitely defined and hybrids are considered rare.

CALIFORNIA BLUE JAY (*Aphelocoma coerulescens*). Length: 11.5 to 12 inches. Male and female upperparts blue; shoulders and middle of back, brown; underparts white, dark band across chest. No *crest*. Range: western United States from Washington to Mexico; west to coast; and in Rockies. Voice: a hoarse *check-check-check-check* also *kwesh kwesh kwesh*.
Harlan E. Eckler

Including the four geographic races that make up this species, the range of the Carolina extends from central New Jersey, central Ohio, central Missouri, and northern Oklahoma, south of Florida and the Gulf coast to central Texas.

MEXICAN CHICKADEE

(*Parus sclateri eidos*)

In the highest parts of the mountains of southeastern Arizona and extreme southwestern New Mexico, the Mexican Chickadee enters the United States. It is similar to the common Black-capped Chickadee, but is larger, its coloration is darker, its sides and flanks are olive gray, and the black of the throat fans out over the chest.

MOUNTAIN CHICKADEE

(*Parus gambeli*)

Color Plate Page 227

To recognize the Mountain Chickadee, an inhabitant of the western mountains, look for the white line over each eye, cutting the black cap. This eyebrow line distinguishes it from all other members of the family. Peterson says of its song, "*Chickadee* notes huskier than those of the Black-capped Chickadee; *chuck-a-zee-zee-zee*."

Six geographic forms of the Mountain Chickadee are recognized breeding from northern British Columbia and Montana to northern Lower California and western Texas.

The Mountain Chickadee nests in a Woodpecker hole or a natural cavity.

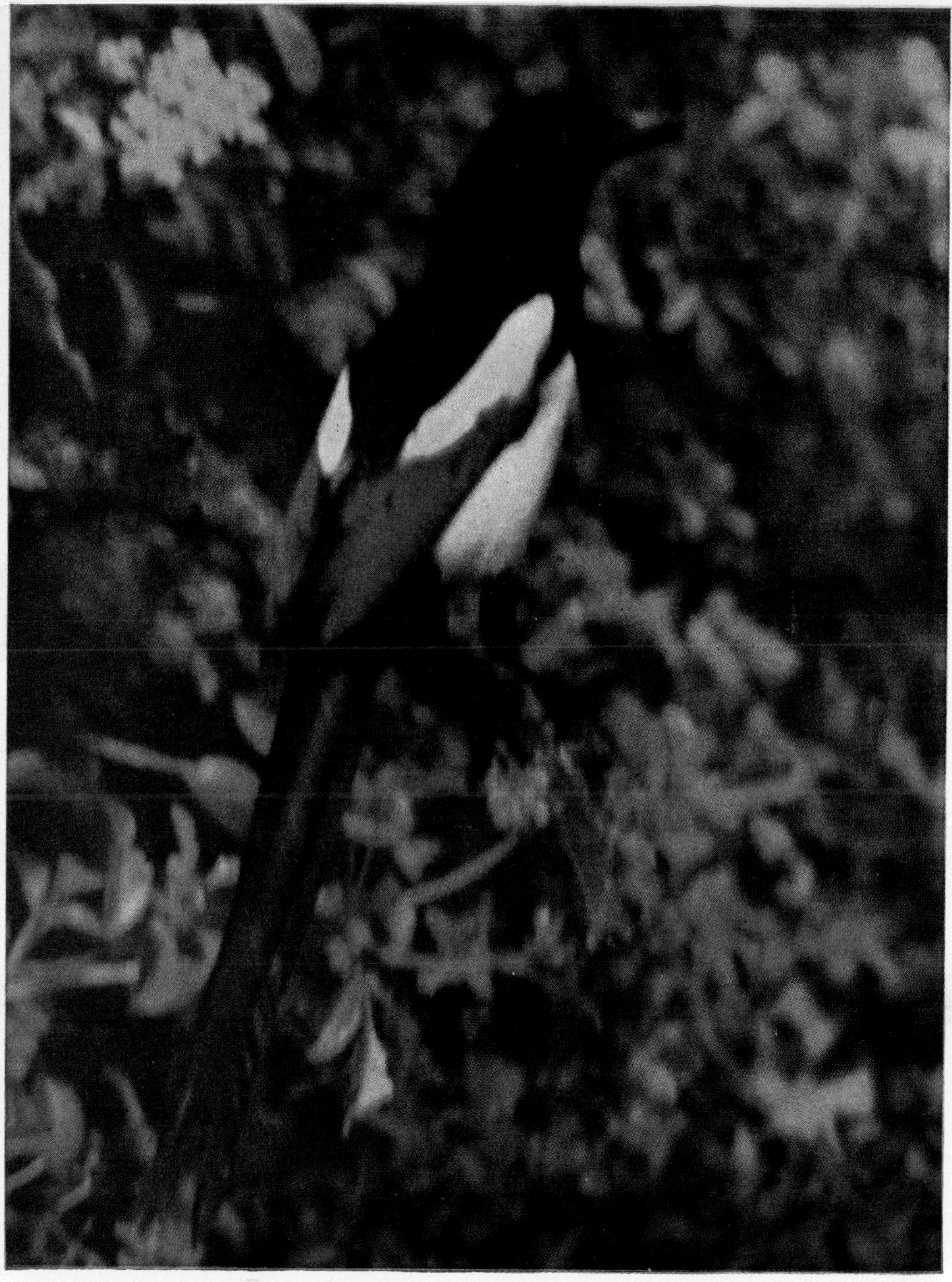

MAGPIE (*Pica pica hudsonia*). Length: 17.5 to 21.5 inches; tail, 9.5 to 12 inches. Male and female: abdomen and wing patches pure white, rest of body black. Long sweeping tail, iridescent in flight. Black bill. Range: Rocky Mountain region and west to eastern Washington, California and Oregon. Voice: a rapid *cheq cheq cheq cheq*. Also a querulous *maaag* or *maa-maa*.

William L. and Irene Finley

HUDSONIAN, ACADIAN or BROWN-CAPPED CHICKADEE

(Parus hudsonicus)

Only along the extreme northern borders of the United States will we find the Brown-capped Chickadee, which, in the east is called the Acadian Chickadee *(P. h. littoralis)*, and in the west is the Hudsonian Chickadee *(P. h. hudsonicus)*, the Columbian Chickadee, or the Cascade Brown-headed Chickadee *(P. h. casadensis)*.

But wherever one is fortunate enough to see it, this energetic little bird is a most welcome addition to any bird list.

This race is similar to the common Black-capped Chickadee, but it is brown instead of gray, with a dark brown cap instead of a black cap. Brewster describes the notes of the Brown-cap as a "sharp *che-day, day*, very different from any note of the common Chickadee."

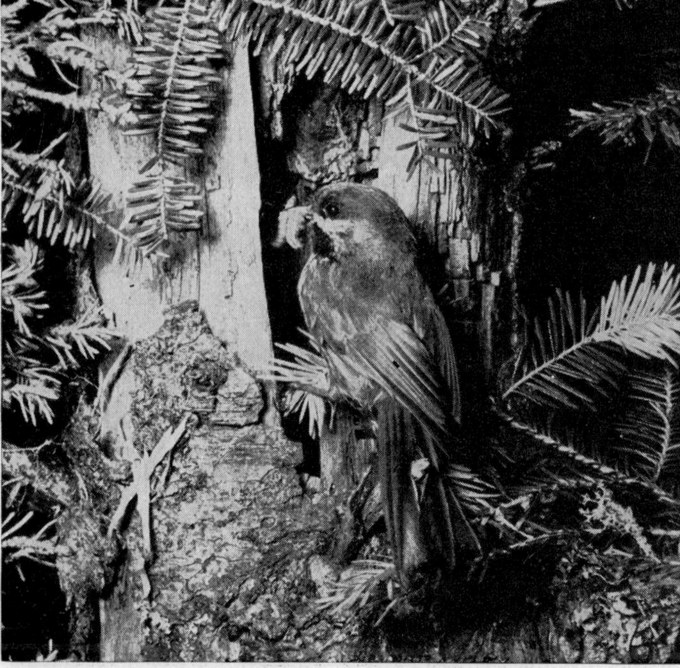

BROWN-CAPPED CHICKADEE AT ENTRANCE TO NEST *(Parus hudsonicus)*. Length: 5 to 5.5 inches. Male and female: generally brown, with a brown cap. Range: breeds in the spruce forests of northern New England, and New York west to Minnesota; occasionally found in the winter south to northern New Jersey and Pennsylvania. Voice: a slow wheezy *chick, chee-day-day*.
Eliot F. Porter, National Audubon Society

CHESTNUT-BACKED CHICKADEE

(Penthestes rufescens)

Like the other Chickadees, the Chestnut-backed has a black cap, black bib and white cheeks; however, it is distinguished immediately by its chestnut back and rump. It is 4½ to 5 inches long.

Its distribution is limited to the Pacific Coast, south to northern California, and while it prefers the coniferous forests, it is not adverse to visiting civilization, and will make its home in bird houses. Ordinarily its nest is built in a high dead stump, and the five to seven eggs are white, usually unmarked. Its call is the same as the Black-capped Chickadee, *chick-chick-a-dee-dee*, but more rasping. It apparently has no whistled call, according to Peterson.

BLACK-CRESTED TITMOUSE

(Parus atricristatus)

The jaunty black crest of the Black-crested Titmouse identifies this little gray bird instantly.

In southern Texas and in the Rio Grande Valley, it is the only Titmouse found.

The Black-crested Titmouse is 5 to 6 inches long, gray above and whitish below, with rufous sides. The slender crest is black. Its notes are like a Chickadee. Peterson adds that it also has a rapidly whistled call *peter, peter, peter, peter*.

BLACK-CRESTED TITMOUSE (*Parus atricristatus*). Length: 5 to 6 inches. Male and female: small bird with gray upperparts, thin black crest of head, white underparts and rusty sides. Range: lowland of Texas. Voice: Chickadee-like notes, also a rapidly whistled *peter-peter-peter*, or *hear, hear, hear, hear*.
Rudolph Hindemith, American Museum of Natural History

PLAIN TITMOUSE

(*Parus inornatus*)

Just as plain as its name is this active little brownish gray Titmouse that ranges through the oak woods from Oregon and southwestern Wyoming to lower California and western Texas. It is a likable little bird, 5 to 5½ inches long, with a jaunty crest, a beady black eye, and a spritely manner. Its voice is very Titmouse-like, following the pattern of other members of its family and closely resembling the *dee-dee* notes of the Chickadee. In the spring, its song is a whistled *Twitt-y, witt-y, witt-y* or, *ti-wee-ti-wee, ti-wee*. (Hoffmann).

Ten geographic races of the Plain Titmouse are now recognized by the A.O.U.; eight in the United States and two in Lower California. All are alike in the field.

TUFTED TITMOUSE

(*Parus bicolor*)

Color Plate Page 230

Peto, peto, peto. When that loud, clear whistle rings through the woods in March and late February, it is like a breath of spring, for indeed, it is the spring song of the Tufted Titmouse. All winter long this little gray bird with the crest has been a daily visitor at the feeding station. With its brother, the Chickadee; its southern relative, the Cardinal; and its traveling companion, the White-breasted Nuthatch, the Titmouse has enjoyed the sunflower seeds.

The winter notes of the Tufted Titmouse are harsh and scolding. Its occasional *day-day-day-day* although reminiscent of the Chickadee, is uttered in a wheezy, coarse, peeved tone. It takes the first warm days of late winter to inspire the hurried, clear, *peto* whistle. Over and over again it is repeated as the busy Tomtit forages among the trees of the deciduous woodland.

The Tufted Titmouse is a pioneer among birds. Like the Carolina Wren, the Cardinal and the Mockingbird, it is of southern affinity, but certain individuals have been extending the range of the species northward, until now the Tufted Titmouse appears as a perma-

PLAIN TITMOUSE *(Parus inornatus)*. Length: 5 to 5.5 inches. Male and female: upperparts, brownish gray, with prominent crest; underparts, gray to grayish white. Range: southern Oregon and Idaho, and southwestern Wyoming, south to southern California, southern Arizona, southeastern New Mexico and central Texas. Voice: *tchick-a-dee-dee*, similar to notes of Chickadee. In spring an emphatic, whistled chant, *weet-y weety weety* or *tee-wit, tee-wit, tee-wit.*

Ruth and H. D. Wheeler, National Audubon Society

nent resident in central Iowa, southern Wisconsin, southern Michigan, southern Ontario, New York, and northern New Jersey. The bird appears in a new area during the winter. When it stays to breed, the range of the species is thus extended.

In the winter, the Tufted Titmouse often joins one of the wandering flocks of birds that band together to forage for food. In April, when they break away in pairs, the Titmice are on the lookout for a nesting site in a tree cavity. I have found them nesting high and low, in live and dead trees, but always inside, never in the open. At times they accept man-made nest boxes, such as the one shown in my natural color illustration on page 230.

Although a great variety of materials is utilized in the cavity-nest, Titmice invariably use hair in the lining. One afternoon in late April, my son left his bicycle on the front porch of our home. To the handlebars was attached a "coon tail," a popular bike adornment among the youngsters. I happened to glance out of the window just as a Tufted Titmouse was flying away with a beakful of this hair. It returned again and again, much to my son's disgust when he finally saw his bedraggled prize. I followed the bird to a natural cavity in an apple tree in a neighbor's yard.

Five or six finely spotted eggs are incubated for twelve days. The young are in the nest at least two weeks, and when they leave, the family remains together for some time. I have encountered these noisy little parties during summer hikes through the woods. I do not believe the Tufted Titmouse has more than one brood each season.

The crest and brown flanks of the Tufted Titmouse are its best field marks. No other mouse-gray bird in the east has a crest. Its length is 6 to 6½ inches. The range of the Black-crested Titmouse *(Parus atricristatus)* overlaps that of the Tufted Titmouse in parts of Texas. This bird may be distinguished by its black crest and white forehead. His appearance is snappy and his lively manner and cheerful disposition are similar to that of his relative the Eastern Chickadee.

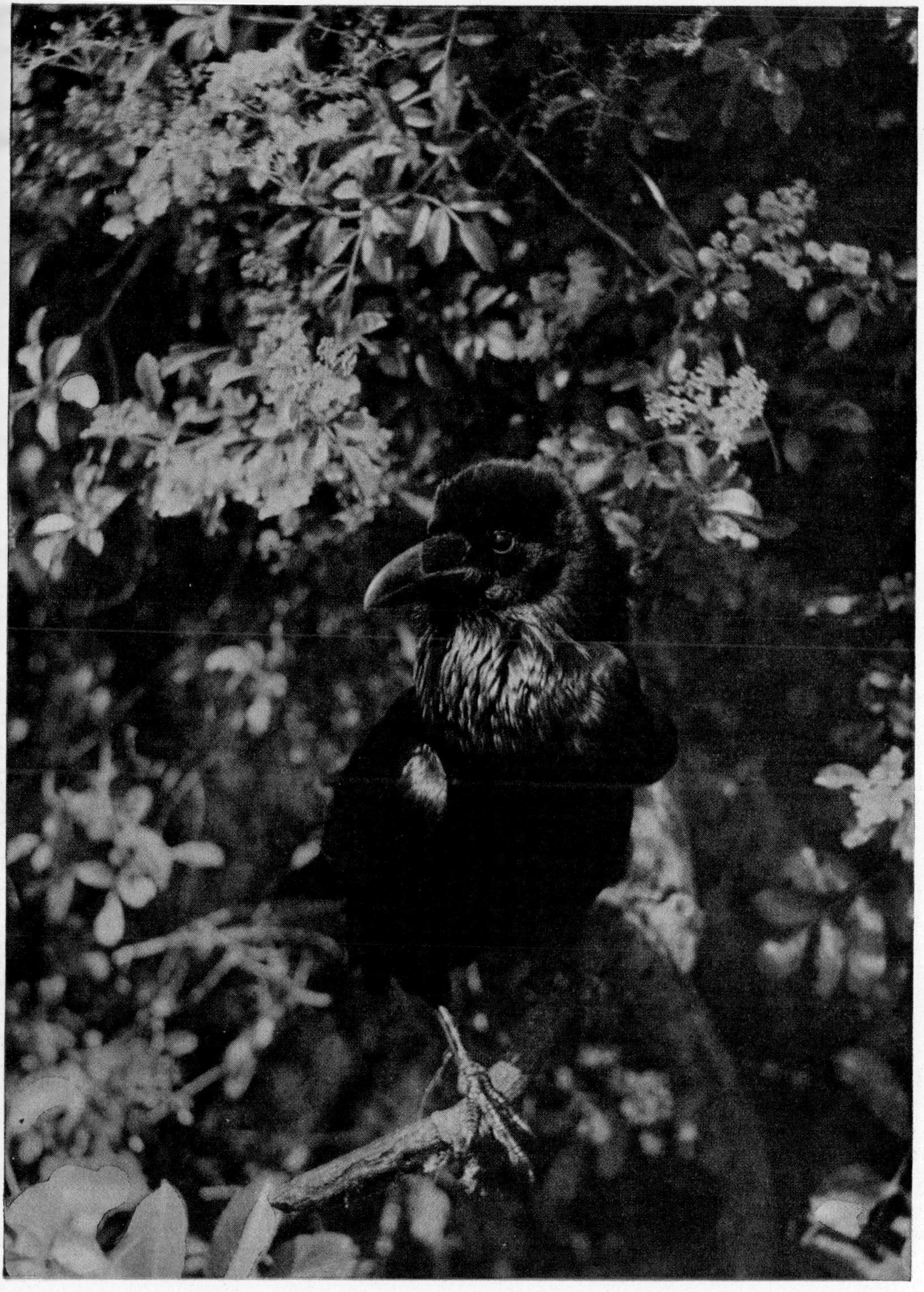

RAVEN (*Corvus corax*). Length: 21.5 to 26.5 inches. Male and female: black plumage; long feathers at throat. Range: western United States. Voice: *cr-r-ruck*.
William L. and Irene Finley

BRIDLED TITMOUSE

(Parus wollweberi annexus)

Like the Black-crested Titmouse, the Bridled Titmouse is a Mexican species that reaches its northern limits across our southern border in Arizona and New Mexico. Its distinctive black and white striped face is a conspicuous field mark. Its behavior is similar to that of the Chickadees and other Titmice.

BUSH-TIT AT ENTRANCE TO NEST (*Psaltriparus minimus*). Length: 4 to 4.5 inches. Male and female: gray above, brownish white below. Range: the western slope of the Rockies from Washington to Mexico. Voice: lisping, chipping notes constantly uttered.
Chicago Natural History Museum

VERDIN

(Auriparus flaviceps)

Color Plate Page 231

The tiny Verdin (4 to 4½ inches) is the Chickadee of the desert. Unmindful of heat or thirst, this little olive-gray bird with the yellow head and neck, and chestnut shoulder patches, spends its entire year in the arid regions of southern Texas, Arizona, and New Mexico, southwestern Utah, southern Nevada, and California.

BRIDLED TITMOUSE (*Parus wollweberi annexus*). Length: 4.5 to 5 inches. Male and female: upperparts deep olive gray and black; underparts, pale olive gray and black; black crest feathers, sides of head bridled with black. Range: oak regions of mountains of southeast and central Arizona, and southwest New Mexico. Voice: rapid notes, *tsick-a-dee-dee-dee-dee* etc.
Rudolph Hindemith, American Museum of Natural History

The Verdin's home is really its castle, for the globular mass of thorny twigs, leaves, and stems, woven together and lined with feathers is not only a nest for eggs and young, but a winter shelter for the adult birds. The nest is usually placed in a thorny tree or bush at the end of the limb. The tiny opening is on the side.

The alarm note of the Verdin is a chattering. Its song is a series of whistles written *tswee, tswee, tswee.*

BUSH-TIT

(Psaltriparus minimus)

Tiny mites of birds even smaller than Chickadees, Bush-tits are energetic, active, woodland sprites that we find flocking together the year 'round, except during the breeding season when they are in pairs. Bush-tits like the oak and piñon covered hillsides where they are on the move throughout the day, feeding in acrobatic positions, lisping softly to each other as they forage. Their coloring is nondescript—tiny gray birds (4 or 4½ inches long) with long tails.

The Bush-tit constructs a most unusual nest, a marvelous piece of avian architecture. It is a long, gourd-shaped hanging pocket, constructed of soft materials and carefully camouflaged. The usual length is from seven to ten inches deep, but one was found twenty-one inches long.

Four geographic races are now recognized within our borders; the Coast Bush-tit *(P.m. minimus)*, which ranges along the Pacific Coast from southwestern British Columbia through California to Mexico; the California Bush-tit *(P.m. californicus)*, found in the interior from south central Oregon, south to Kern County, California; and the Lead-colored Bush-tit *(P.m. plumbeus)*, which may be distinguished from the other two by its brown cheeks, ranges in the Rockies from eastern Oregon and western Wyoming south to Texas; and the little San Bernadine Bush-tit *(P.m. sociabilis)* a new California race. Lloyd's Bush-tit is now considered a subspecies of *Psaltriparus melanotis (lloydi)*. It is found in southern New Mexico and western Texas.

NUTHATCHES

Family Sittidae

The Nuthatches are immediately recognized by their ability to climb down tree trunks headfirst, a feat which no other tree climbing bird attempts. All the family are small birds, plainly colored, with long bills and short tails which they do not use to brace themselves as other climbing birds do. Although classified by the ornithologists as song birds because they possess vocal cords, their voices are actually nasal and trumpet-like and most unmusical.

WHITE-BREASTED NUTHATCH

(Sitta carolinensis)

Color Plate Page 233

The White-breasted Nuthatch is the little bluish gray bird with a black cap and white breast that defies the law of gravity by walking down tree trunks headfirst. It's a topsy-turvy, upside-down bird with a characteristic nasal call of *yank, yank, yank.*

If its tail were a bit longer, the Nuthatch would be about the size of a

CROW *(Corvus brachyrhynchos)*. Length: 16 to 20 inches. Male and female: entire body deep black Long, pointed wings. Immature: head, neck and body grayish black. Range: Newfoundland south to Florida and Texas. Winters north to Great Lakes and southern Maine. Voice: a loud *caw.*
Helen Cruikshank

Sparrow. As it is, it is 5 to 6 inches long. But unlike the Woodpecker's tail which is used like a camp stool in hitching up tree trunks, the Nuthatch's tail is short and square. A careless observer might confuse the Nuthatch with the Black-capped Chickadee in which company it is often found during the winter, but aside from the black caps, the two birds have little in common in their appearance or behavior.

The White-breasted Nuthatch is a permanent resident wherever it is found, and with all of its nine geographic races included, the bird's range includes the United States, Canada, and Mexico. In the northern portion of its range, it is one of the common winter birds at dooryard feeding stations. Beef suet, placed as a substitute for its highly insectivorous diet, is a grand decoy.

Sunflower seeds are also relished by the Nuthatch. In this regard, it is interesting to observe how differently birds of close association are equipped to eat the same food. Take for example, a Cardinal, a Chickadee and a Nuthatch at a sunflower feeder. The Cardinal will take each seed in its big strong beak and crack it, extracting the inner seed. The Chickadee will carry the seed to a favorite limb where it will grasp it in its claws and hammer it open with its bill. The Nuthatch's beak is not as strong as the Cardinal's, nor as short as the Chickadee's, so it wedges the seed into a crevice in the bark and then cracks it open with quick thrusts of its bill. Indeed, it was this manner of feeding that gave the bird its common name of "Nuthatch."

It has been suggested, logically enough, that the Nuthatch's method of feeding while coming down a tree trunk headfirst may be nature's way of making sure that many of the tree borers, insect eggs, and larvae overlooked by the Woodpeckers and Creepers enroute up the tree are taken by the Nuthatch coming down.

BLACK-EARED NUTHATCH (PYGMY) *(Sitta pygmaea).* Length 4.5 inches. Male and female: very small. *Gray brown cap coming down to the eye.* A whitish spot sometimes visible on the nape of the neck. Range: from Washington and Montana south to Mexico, and from Rockies west to Cascades and Sierras. Also along coast and southern California. Voice: a metallic piping *kit-kit-kit* and a high *ki-dee* constantly repeated sometimes becoming an excited twitter or chatter.

Ross and Florence Thornburg

CLARK'S NUTCRACKER *(Nucifraga columbiana)*. Length: 12 to 13 inches. Male and female: light gray body, white patches in tail and wings. Wings blackish gray. Range: mountains from Canada to southern California, Arizona and New Mexico. Voice: a rasping caw, *khaaa* or *khraa*.
Ross and Florence Thornburg

As the birds pair off in the spring, the male starts to sing his high, shrill, maniacal laugh: *ha, ha, ha, ha, ha, ha.* The nesting site is usually an old Woodpecker hole or a natural cavity. Occasionally Nuthatches will use man-made nest boxes, as did the bird in the natural color illustration on page 233. Although this bird accepted a box of plain boards, a house camouflaged by a natural bark covering is more likely to be occupied.

The six creamy eggs are finely speckled with reddish brown. Both birds incubate, and the young hatch in less than two weeks. The parents feed the youngsters for some time after they leave the nest, and bird watchers are likely to run across little families of Nuthatches feeding together in the woods in the summer.

RED-BREASTED NUTHATCH

(Sitta canadensis)

Color Plate Page 236

I remember my first Red-breasted Nuthatch. It was in a woodland where White-breasted Nuthatches are common throughout the year, where the nasal *yank* of that bird is an ever present voice. Without recognizing it as the call of a Red-breasted Nuthatch, I was attracted to a tree where the voice of a Nuthatch did not sound right. So marked was the difference in the note that I was conscious of it before I had made the identification. Although similar, the *yank* is more nasal and higher pitched.

In appearance, the Red-breast may be distinguished from its commoner relative by its buffy underparts, the

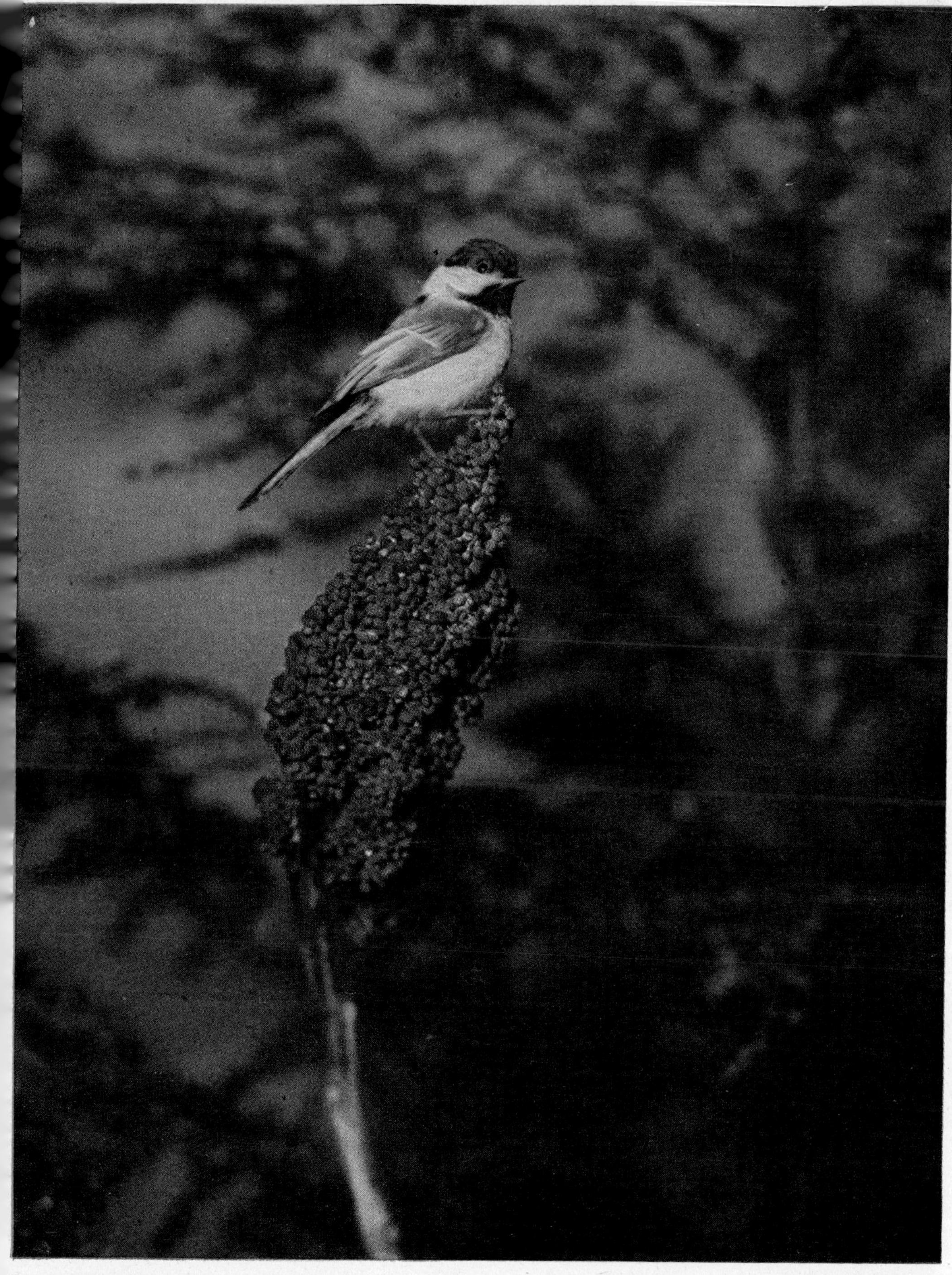

BLACK-CAPPED CHICKADEE FEEDING ON FRUIT OF STAGHORN SUMAC IN WINTER (*Parus atricapillus*). Length: 4.75 to 5.5 inches. Male and female: gray back, wings and tail, black crown and throat. Buff flanks. Range: resident from Ontario and Newfoundland south to Kansas, Missouri, Illinois, Ohio, Pennsylvania, northern New Jersey, and North Carolina mountains. Voice: song, *chick-a-dee-dee-dee-dee* or *dee-dee-dee-*. In spring, *fee-bee*, or *fee-bee-ee*.
Hal H. Harrison

white line over the eye and its smaller size (about 4½ inches). It is a bird of the conifers, nesting in the Canadian evergreen forests and in the higher mountains of the United States south to North Carolina in the east and California and New Mexico in the west. In migration, it sometimes reaches as far south as the Gulf States and Florida.

BROWN-HEADED NUTHATCH

(Sitta pusilla)

Color Plate Page 240

The Brown-headed Nuthatch, smallest of the eastern Nuthatches, is a bird of the southern pines. It ranges from southern Delaware to southern Missouri and south to the Gulf coast and eastern Texas.

The distinguishing field marks of this species are its small size (4 to 5 inches) and the cinnamon-brown head, and white nape spot. The back is bluish gray; the underparts, white. The bird's voice is nasal like other members of the family, but its calls are many and varied. Little bands of these birds forage together throughout the year, except during the nesting season, and while together carry on a ceaseless chattering.

The Gray-headed Nuthatch *(S. p. caniceps)* a race of the Brown-headed, occurs in Florida. In this form the head is brownish gray.

PYGMY NUTHATCH

(Sitta pygmaea)

Chattering and scolding as they feed, flocks of Pygmy Nuthatches are conspicuous birds of the yellow pine forests in mountainous regions of western United States. The Pygmy, or Black-eared, Nuthatch resembles the Brown-headed Nuthatch of the southeast with its brownish head and blue-gray back. Its gray-brown cap comes down to the eye. This characteristic as well as its stubby tail and general smaller size (4½ inches) will distinguish it from other Nuthatches within its range to which it bears a strong family resemblance in its habits.

Four geographic races are recognized: Pygmy Nuthatch *(S. p. pygmaea)*, Black-eared Nuthatch *(S. p. melanotis)*, the White-naped Nuthatch *(S. p. leuconucha)*, and the Nevada Nuthatch *(S. p. canesiens)*. All look alike in the field.

CREEPERS

Family Certhiidae

The Tree Creepers are small dull birds, which creep up the trunk, usually in a spiral, seeking grubs and insects in the bark. They use their long pointed tails as props to aid their climbing. So nondescript is their coloring that they are often indistinguishable from the bark of the trees on which they are climbing.

BROWN CREEPER

(Certhia familiaris)

Color Plate Page 241

We know the Brown Creeper best as a little mouselike bird that creeps quietly up a tree trunk to the first branches, then glides lightly to the base of a nearby tree to repeat the performance. Sometimes it spirals as it ascends, and sometimes, if we listen carefully, we can hear the faint lisping call of *seep seep,* so thin and so weakly delivered that an inattentive listener might miss it entirely.

All through the winter day, the industrious Brown Creeper works incessantly, never stopping to rest, but always searching the bark of tree trunks for insects, insect eggs and larvae. Its thin, curved bill is ideally suited for probing; its long, sharp claws are just right for climbing; and its pointed, stiffened tail feathers are grand assistants in hiking up the trees in Woodpecker fashion.

It has been suggested that the Brown Creeper be called the "bark bird," for its entire life is spent near the bark of trees. From the bark it gleans a livelihood, and under the bark it builds its nest. It even looks like a piece of bark, streaked grayish brown above; grayish white beneath. It is 5 or 6 inches long and quite inconspicuous.

The common breeding range of the five North American forms of the Brown Creeper is in northern forests, but it is found occasionally breeding in mountainous regions to the south and elsewhere where typical Canadian faunal areas exist. Few persons have ever found its nest, which is carefully hidden under a loose piece of bark attached to the trunk of a tree. Into this location, the birds carry twigs, strips of bark and mosses. Here are laid the six or seven white eggs sparsely spotted with brown.

I spent an afternoon early one June in Cook Forest Park in northwestern Pennsylvania, following a male Creeper through a pine and hemlock forest, hoping he would lead me to a nest. He didn't, but I was able to study its song, which is seldom given except on the breeding grounds. It was a high pitched, weak trilling, quite Warbler-like in general form. The bird's actions were the same here as on its wintering territory—a constant creeping up one tree after another, apparently never tiring and definitely never resting.

The lisping call that one hears during the winter is not unlike the call of a Golden-crowned Kinglet. It even has a bit of the lisping quality of the Cedar Waxwing's notes, yet it may be distinguished easily from the calls of either of these birds.

It has been my experience with this feathered Brownie that it is not particularly interested in offerings of suet at the winter feeding stations. If it happens to be enroute up a tree where suet has been placed, it will feed there momentarily and then go on. It seldom visits the suet deliberately and regularly as do the Woodpeckers and Nuthatches.

Four geographic forms of the Brown Creeper occur in the west, but all are indistinguishable in the field. They are: Rocky Mountain Brown Creeper *(Certhia familiaris montana)*, Sierra Nevada Brown Creeper *(Certhia familiaris zelotes)*, the Tawny, or California Brown Creeper *(Certhia familiaris occidentalis)*, and the Mexican, or Sierra Madre Brown Creeper *(Certhia familiaris albescons)*.

WREN-TIT

Family Chamaeidae

The Wren-tits are limited to North America, and consist of only one species. Intermediate between the Titmice and the Wrens, they are small birds with long tails. Their short bill has the upper mandible curved downward.

WREN-TIT

(Chamaea fasciata)

Intermediate between Titmice and Wrens, is the family of Wren-tits, a single genus with six subspecies inhabiting the Pacific coast area from Oregon south into lower California and east to the interior of California. They are secretive little brown birds with long tails, favoring the chaparral-covered hillsides.

About 6½ inches long, the Wren-tit is more often heard than seen. It is generally brown, with the back dusky and the underparts buffy cinnamon; streaked faintly. The eye is conspicuously white.

Its song is a series of ringing notes which Mrs. Bailey writes *keep, keep, keep, keep, keep-it, keep-it, keep-it*. It sings all year around.

It builds a compact nest of bark, roots, grass, and hair, in low bushes. The four eggs are pale bluish green.

Four subspecies are recognized in the United States: the Coast Wren-tit *(C. f. phaea)*, the Ruddy Wren-tit *(C. f. rufula)*, Gambel's Wren-tit *(C. f. fasciata)*, and the Pallid Wren-tit *(C. f. henshawi)*. There are no apparent field differences.

DIPPERS

Family Cinclidae

Although the Dippers are distributed over a wide section of the world, only one species is found in the United States. The family is found only in mountainous areas where it lives near the swift mountain streams. Its food consists of water insects and the larvae of fish. The Dipper is able to move underwater, propelling itself by its wings. The nests are usually placed behind small waterfalls where the moisture reaches them.

DIPPER or WATER OUZEL

(Cinclus mexicanus unicolor)

No true water bird loves the water more than the Dipper or Water Ouzel. This slate-gray bird of the Rockies and the mountains of California walks in water, swims in it, dives in it, and once every year practically builds its nest in water. Since its habits are the same both winter and summer, one might say that the Dipper is all wet the year 'round—except that it never really gets wet. Its plumage is heavy and thick with underdown, permitting it to live its semi-aquatic life in comfort.

The Water Ouzel's short tail and short, rounded wings give it a chunky appearance like a large Wren, although it is almost as long as a Robin (7 to 8½ inches). Its habit of bobbing up and down is characteristic. The Dipper's haunts are the mountain torrents, the waterfalls and the cascades, and here it searches for underwater insects, larvae, and small fish. Its mossy nest is built on the shelf of a rock, often so close to a waterfall that it is sprayed continually. The entrance to the domed structure is on the side.

The Dipper's clear, ringing song is not affected by the weather any more than its aquatic habits. It will plunge into an ice-choked stream and come out singing just as readily as it sings in summer. All who know it agree that the Dipper is a bird with a dynamic personality.

WRENS

Family Troglodytidae

Almost worldwide in its distribution, and known for its fine songsters, the Wren family received its family name of "one who creeps into holes" from its preference for nesting in hollows and cavities. The Wrens are small birds, never gaily colored, and are economically of much benefit because of the quantities of insects they consume.

HOUSE WREN

(Troglodytes aëdon)

Color Plate Page 245

Every child has heard the story of Jenny Wren. And Johnny Wren, too, for it is the male House Wren that attracts so much attention with his incessant bubbling song. Jenny doesn't sing.

House Wrens are one of the commonest, best known, best loved, and most economically valuable of our summer birds. No other wild bird has taken so completely to man-built bird boxes as this little bird whose friendliness to man is evidenced in its constant desire to live near him in complete domesticity.

Male Wrens arrive from the deep south at their northern breeding grounds in late April and early May. Females do not arrive for another week or longer. Upon arrival, the male stakes his territorial claim, fills all the avail-

WREN-TIT AT FEEDING STATION *(Chamaea fasciata)*. Length: 6.5 inches. Male and female: grayish brown body and long tail. Underparts cinnamon brown with faint dusky streaks; eye, *white*. Range: California and coast belt of Oregon. Voice: short, quick ringing notes on the same pitch.

Laidlaw Williams, National Audubon Society

able nesting sides with sticks and then pours out his bubbling song all day long.

When Jenny arrives, her mate takes her on an inspection tour of the "dummy" nests he has crudely started. She chooses one that suits her, pulls out all the twigs that Johnny has placed and starts all over again to build the kind of nest that she wants. The other desirable cavities are left plugged with sticks, no doubt to give the impression

CAROLINA CHICKADEE (*Parus carolinensis*). Length: 4.25 to 4.75 inches. Male and female: similar to Black-capped Chickadee, with grayer wings not margined with white, and smaller in size. Range: from New Jersey, Ohio, Missouri and Oklahoma to Gulf of Mexico. Voice: high-pitched and rapid *chick-a-dee-dee-dee* and song, *fee-bee, fee-bay.*

Samuel A. Grimes

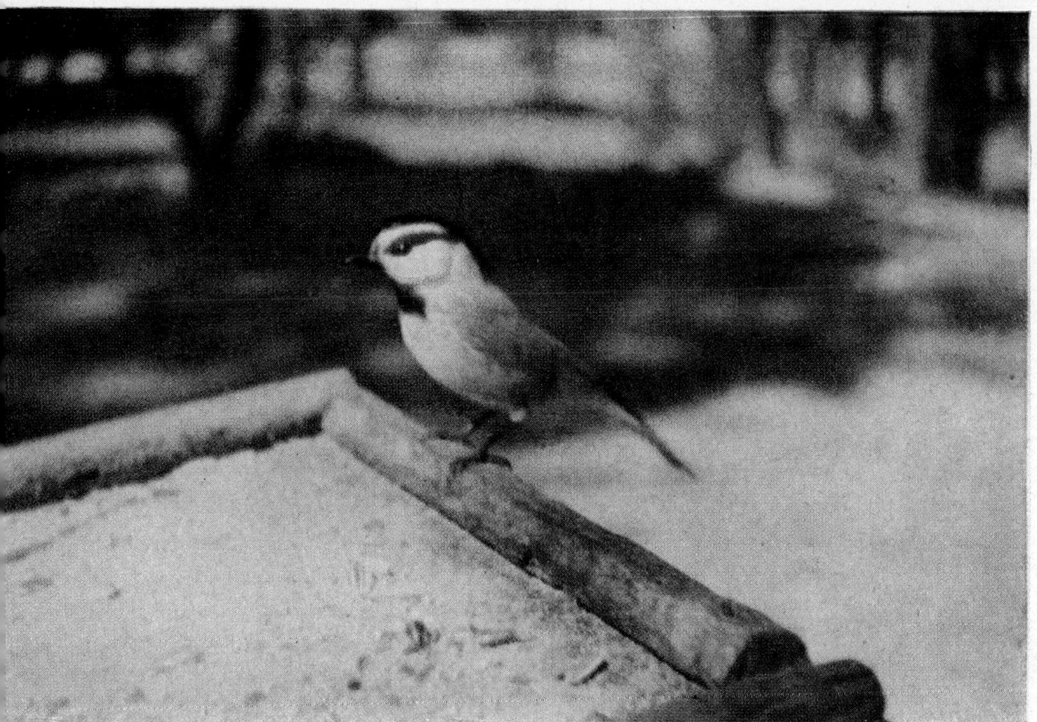

MOUNTAIN CHICKADEE (*Parus gambeli*). Length: 5 to 5.75 inches. Male and female: similar to Black-capped Chickadee but black cap broken by white line over each eye. Range: mountains from Canada to western Texas, New Mexico, Arizona, and southern California. Voice: notes of song more distinctly separated than that of Black-capped's. The three high notes of *fee-bee-bee*, are whistled.
Ross and Florence Thornburg

of occupied nests to other prospective home-seekers.

It is not selfishness (interpreted in the human sense) that prompts a pair of House Wrens to guard their territory so jealously. It is necessity. The Wren's diet is about ninety-eight per cent insects and twelve to sixteen young may be raised in a summer. Since Wrens feed their young about every two minutes throughout the day, it is imperative that a tremendous quantity of insects be available in the immediate vicinity at all times. To share this food supply with another Wren family might prove disastrous to both.

Because of this strict territorial instinct of the House Wren, it is useless for persons to place a great many Wren boxes in a small area.

Jenny Wren is a terrific scold. She fusses and she fumes. And if there ever was a hen-pecked bird it is Johnny. Just let him relax too long from his domestic duties as a husband and father, and Jenny is after him, scolding in no playful manner.

The House Wren is 4½ to 5 inches long, gray-brown in color, and lacking any of the facial striping of some of the other species.

Wrens lay from six to eight mottled pinkish brown eggs. They hatch in about two weeks. At least two broods are attempted each season. The natural home of the House Wren is in cavities in trees, stumps and suitable niches most anywhere, but man made boxes have proved ideal, and the majority have deserted their ancestral nesting sites.

DIPPER (*Cinclus mexicanus unicolor*). Length: 8 inches. Male and female: uniformly slate colored. Range: mountains of western North America from Canada to southern California. Voice: a sharp *zeet*. Song is high and clear, rather Wren-like.
Alfred M. Bailey and R. J. Niedrach

Stories of freak sites for Wrens' nests are common. I have found them nesting in a pair of swimming trunks, in the pocket of a bathrobe, in the leg of a pair of trousers, in the radiator of an automobile, in old shoes, tin cans, hats, etc.

The Eastern House Wren *(T. a. aëdon)* is replaced in the west by the Western House Wren *(T. a. parkmanii)*. A third race, the Ohio House Wren *(T. a. baldwini)* has recently been recognized.

WINTER WREN

(Troglodytes troglodytes)

The Winter Wren, smaller than the common House Wren, is a tiny brown midget that bobs through the woodland tangles with its diminutive tail held far over its back. Its nervous disposition is evident in its hurried dives out of sight and in its alarm notes.

To most of us, the Winter Wren is a winter visitor or a migrant, for the bird's summer home is in the coniferous forests, rocky ravines, cool swamps, and mountainous areas of Canada, south to northern United States. Those who have heard its song on its breeding grounds describe the Winter Wren's voice as one of the finest in the northern forests.

The very short tail and the dark barred belly are this Wren's best field marks. In winter one often hears its sharp note of *kip*, which sounds quite similar to the alarm note of a Song Sparrow. Excepting the Short-billed Marsh Wren, it is the smallest member of the family, being only 4 inches long.

Two eastern forms, a western race and light resident races in Alaska are recognized.

BEWICK'S WREN

(Thryomanes bewickii bewickii)

Bewick's Wren is distributed in a number of geographical races over most of the United States south of central Pennsylvania, southern Michigan and Washington. It behaves much like the House Wren showing a perky inquisitiveness and building its nest in all sorts of odd corners. Like the House Wren it nests in bird-boxes.

It is distinguished from the Rock Wren by its darker color above and its whiter throat and breast. The song varies among the different subspecies, but usually resembles that of the Song Sparrow but rather thinner. It builds its nest like the House Wren and lays from four to seven dull white eggs, spotted with chestnut.

CAROLINA WREN

(Thryothorus ludovicianus)

Color Plate Page 248

I have before me some notes on the song of the Carolina Wren which I made in Pennsylvania on a day in April. The same Wren changed its song three times while I listened. My interpretations were written: *yer weet-chiter, weet-chiter, weet-chiter, weet,* and *yur tardy, yur tardy, yur tardy* and *tee-dirty, tee-dirty, tee-dirty, tee-dirty.* Looking through the literature on the Carolina Wren, I have discovered that dozens of other interpretations could be added to mine, indicating that the bird is a versatile singer. I have heard it sing every season of the year, sometimes in pairs, or duets, one male answering another.

The Carolina is the largest of the eastern Wrens (5½ to 6 inches long), rusty brown above and buffy below with a white line over the eye. The Bewick's Wren has a white-tipped tail; the Long-billed Marsh Wren has a striped back.

The natural habitat of the Carolina Wren is the woodland thickets, dense tangles and brush piles. Ancestral nesting places include cavities in trees, beneath logs, in the roots of fallen trees, and near the ground in matted vegetation. Like some others in its family, however, it has taken kindly to civilization, and often nests about old buildings or even in bird boxes.

The typical species of the Carolina Wren *(T.l. ludocicianus)* ranges from Nebraska and Connecticut to northern Florida and the Gulf States. Three other races are recognized: the darker, larger Florida Wren *(T.l. miamensis)*, the Lomita Wren *(T.l. lomitensis)* of the Rio Grande Valley in Texas, and Burleigh's Carolina Wren *(T.l. burleighi)* a Gulf race.

CACTUS WREN

(Campylorhynchus brunneicapillus)

Color Plate Page 250

If you have spent any time at all on the desert, you have discovered that the cholla cactus is one to be avoided. Its spines cling tenaciously to the careless. The Cactus Wren seems to

WINTER WREN *(Troglodytes troglodytes)*. Length: 4 to 4.25 inches. Male and female: reddish brown upperparts; buffy line over the eye. Underparts, light brown; belly heavily streaked with black and white. Range: Canada, south to Minnesota and New York, and northern Georgia; winters south to Texas and Florida. Voice: high warbles and trills, long sustained song.

Rudolph Hindemith, American Museum of Natural History

TUFTED TITMOUSE AT NEST (*Parus bicolor*). Length: 6 to 6.5 inches. Male and female: upperparts slate gray, tufted crest, rusty flanks; underparts whitish. Range: from Florida, north to northern New Jersey and west to Nebraska. Voice: clear whistled chant, *peter, peter, peter,* or *here, here, here, here.*

Hal H. Harrison

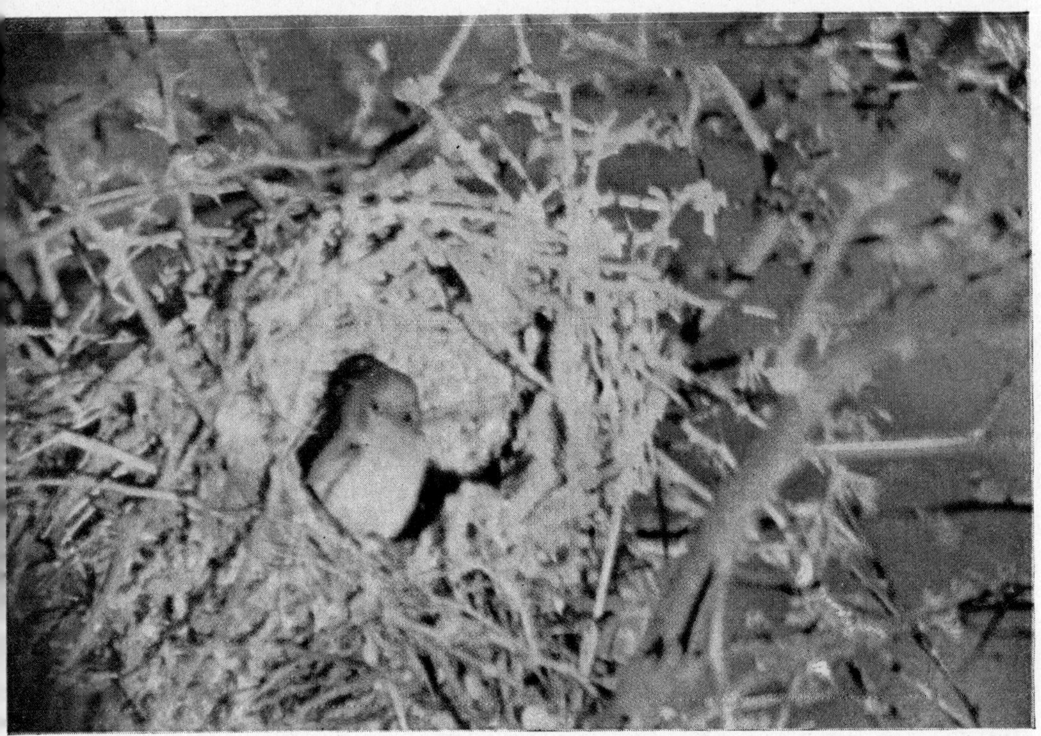

VERDIN (*Auriparus flaviceps*). Length: 4 to 4.5 inches. Male and female: yellow head, brownish white underparts. Wing bend, rufous. Range: deserts of California, Nevada, Utah, Arizona, New Mexico and Texas. Voice: *see-lip* or *see*. Song, a whistled *weet*.
Harlan E. Eckler

have learned that the cholla is shunned, and it may feel safe; for it is a favorite nesting place for that bird of the desert country.

Held firmly in the protecting thorns, a globular nest of grasses, with an opening on the side, is built by this cactus-loving species. Unwren-like as it is in many respects, the male displays a trait of some of its relatives by building dummy nests; thus, a number of unused and partly built structures may be expected in one area.

This species is a large Wren (7 to 8½ inches long) with a heavily spotted throat and breast; a long, slightly rounded tail barred on the edges with white; a white stripe over the eye, extending to the bill; and a slightly curved bill.

Of the Cactus Wren's song, Florence Merriam Bailey writes: "His song, which he sings with abandon—head thrown back and tail hanging—seems as shorn of adornment as the cactus, but, grating and monotonous as it is, harmonizes so well with his surroundings that he seems, indeed, to sing the song of the desert." The song has been interpreted as an unbirdlike *Chur-cha-ra, chur-cha-ra, chur-cha-ra*. Although not so noisy in winter, the bird sings throughout the year.

The food of this Wren consists mainly of insects.

The Cactus Wren is a resident bird of the deserts of southern California, southern Nevada, southern Utah, Arizona, New Mexico, and southern Texas.

LONG-BILLED MARSH WREN

(Telmatodytes palustris)

Color Plate Page 251

"Marshy" was the affectionate name we gave him—that vibrant male Long-billed Marsh Wren that we heard day after day singing from the tops of swaying cattails along a roadside marsh at Pymatuning. He was there any time of the day, always bubbling with effervescence that actually seemed to be contagious.

It was early June when we found him. That day, between his regular trips to the top of the cattails to render his rasping song, he was occupied with that typical Marsh Wren activity of building a dummy nest. His song sounded like the action of a sewing machine that needed oil. He delivered it with his head thrown back and his stubby tail thrown forward until they almost met. His rendition completed, he grabbed a mouthful of down from a dead cattail bob and flew away to add it to the coconut-shaped structure he was building among several cattail stalks. The next day, when we passed "Marshy's" territory, he had forsaken the nearly completed nest of the day before, and was now engaged in getting another one underway about ten feet from the first.

It is not unusual for certain male members of the Wren family to build these "cock" nests that are never used by the female. The Cactus Wren of the west builds them. House Wrens build them regularly in any number of bird boxes on their territories, but Long-billed Marsh Wrens are really demons for this eccentric activity. One observer found fifteen such nests within a twenty-foot circle.

SHORT-BILLED MARSH WREN (*Cistothorus platensis stellaris*). Length: 4 to 4.5 inches. Male and female: upperparts, brown streaked with black and white; underparts, buffy. Range: breeds from Canada south to northern Delaware, Indiana, Missouri, and eastern Kansas; winters from southern Illinois and New Jersey to the Gulf of Mexico. Voice: song, a dry chattering—*chap chap chap chap chap chapper - rrrr*. Call-note, *chick* or *chap*.
Eliot F. Porter, National Audubon Society

The nest of the Marsh Wren is globular with a small opening on the side. It is strongly constructed of grasses and leaves and lined with down. It is well camouflaged by surrounding marsh vegetation which supports it. After considerable search, I found the female incubating the five brownish eggs in a nest forty feet from where her mate was so busy building more nests. Here, then, was the true nest, built by

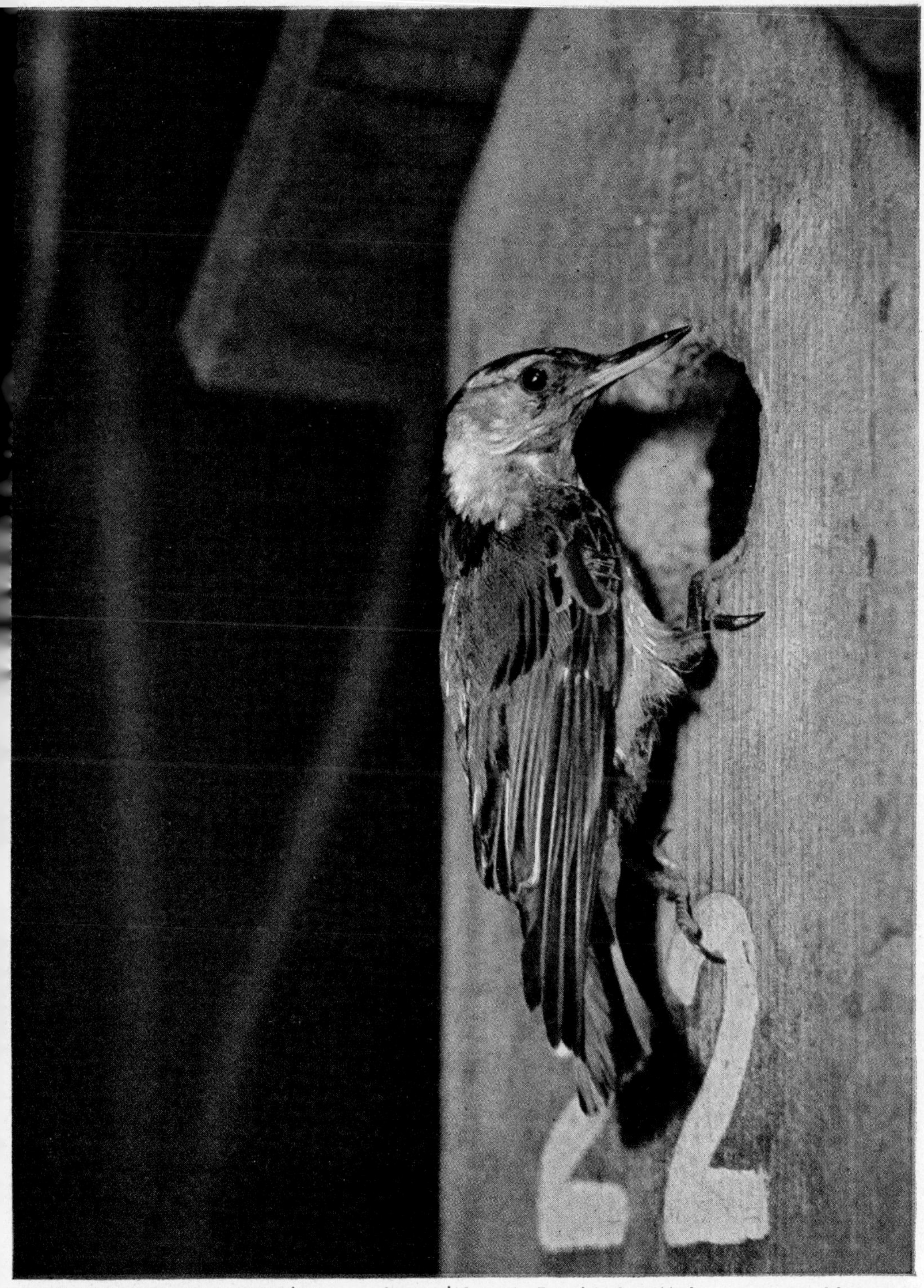

WHITE-BREASTED NUTHATCH (*Sitta carolinensis*). Length: 5 to 6 inches. Male: upperparts blue gray. Tail edged with white; black crown and nape, and white underparts. Female: similar but blue gray wash replaces black in male. Range: from Quebec and northern Minnesota south to Florida and Gulf of Mexico. Voice: low nasal whistled song, *whi, whi, whi, whi, whi, whi, whi, whi,* or *who who who who* etc. Note, nasal *yank.*

Hal H. Harrison

the female who apparently was not interested at all in the others.

Why are these dummy nests constructed? Some ornithologists say that they are built to draw attention from the occupied nest. Others claim that the male builds them as roosting places. A more recent theory contends that the practice is a substitute for courtship, an outlet for the male's abundant sexual energy. I do not know the answer, but I do know that this little bird is motivated by some powerful instinct that compels him to build one nest after another. It is one of those birdland mysteries still unanswered. The Long-billed Marsh Wren is 4½ to 5½ inches long with a black and white striped back and a solid brownish black crown. The white eye stripe is conspicuous. The underparts are whitish.

Another Wren that we encountered at Pymatuning was the less common Short-billed Marsh Wren. Although the two may be distinguished in the field by appearance and song, their habitat also differs greatly. The Short-billed Marsh Wren avoids the cattails and prefers the drier parts of the marsh the high grass, the reedy edges.

Ten geographic races of the Long-billed Marsh Wren breed throughout the United States, ranging much further than the more eastern Short-billed Marsh Wren. Both species winter in southern United States, the Long-billed migrating as far south as Mexico.

SHORT-BILLED MARSH WREN

(Cistothorus platensis stellaris)

The Short-billed Marsh Wren may be distinguished from the closely related Long-billed Marsh Wren by its streaked crown, its light under-tail covers and the absence of a white line over the eye. It is also slightly smaller, 4 or 4½ inches long. In addition, the Long-billed is a Wren of the cattails; the Short-billed prefers the sedge marshes and the damp grassy meadows. The song of the Short-billed is a rapidly repeated *chap, chap, chap, chap, chap, chap,* markedly different from the Long-billed's gurgling rattle. Like the Long-billed, the male builds a number of dummy nests.

The breeding range of the Short-billed

CANON WREN AT NEST *(Catherpes mexicanus)*. Length: 5.5 to 5.75 inches. Male and female: upperparts reddish brown, with *white breast* and *throat*. Deep chestnut belly. Range: western United States from Washington to Mexico. Voice: a cadence of clear notes *te-you, te-you, te-you, tew tew tew tew tew*, etc., or *tee tee tee tee tew tew tew tew*, etc.
Gayle Pickwell

Marsh Wren extends from southeastern Saskatchewan, southern Ontario, and southern Maine to eastern Kansas and southern Maryland. It winters from south Illinois and southern New Jersey to Florida and the Gulf of Mexico.

CAÑON WREN

(Catherpes mexicanus)

Cañon Wren is a most appropriate name for this bubbling little creature of the western cañons, gulches, and rocky valleys, for there it is at home among the jagged rocks and crevices. Its deep chestnut belly which contrasts with its white breast identifies it instantly from its neighbor and close relative, the Rock Wren. Its color is reddish brown and its throat is conspicuously white. It is a large Wren, between 5½ and 6 inches long.

"From the bare grim walls of rock the Cañon Wren pours out a cascade of sweet liquid notes, like the spray of a waterfall in sunshine" (Hoffmann).

ROCK WREN

(Salpinctes obsoletus)

Color Plate Page 254

The Rock Wren is a bird to be watched for in the mesa, the open mountain slopes and the rimrock regions of the west from Canada south to Mexico and east to western North Dakota, central Nebraska and central Texas. It is a Gray Wren, 5¼ or 6¼ inches long, with a finely streaked breast; whitish line over the eye; buffy patch at the end of the tail; and dingy white underparts. The Cañon Wren has a white breast and throat, passing into reddish brown underparts.

The song of the Rock Wren is a harsh *kra-wee, kra-wee, kra-wee.* The call note is *tick-here.* This species nests in crevices in rocks, where it often forms a pavement of small stones at the entrance to the nest.

MOCKINGBIRDS and THRASHERS

Family Mimidae

This exclusively American family, often called the Mimic Thrushes, is noted for the fine songs of some of its members. The birds are closely related to the Thrushes, and like them wear brown and gray colors. Their tails are usually long, and their slender bills are curved downward. Their nests are open above and generally are built of twigs, lined with rootlets Their eggs are speckled or plain greenish.

MOCKINGBIRD

(Mimus polyglottos)

Color Plate Page 255

"Listen to the Mockingbird" is excellent advice, for this Mimic Thrush of our southern states has gained its worldwide reputation as a songster strictly on its merits. And the Mocker is never reluctant to pour out its torrent of notes; sweet, clear, sharp, grat-

RED-BREASTED NUTHATCH *(Sitta canadensis)*. Length: 4.25 to 4.75 inches. Male: upperparts slate blue with black head. Underparts buffy. *Broad black line* through the eye, and white above it. White throat. Female: bluish gray replaces black in male. Underparts light orange brown. Range: Canada to Michigan and east to New England. In Appalachians to North Carolina. Voice: high, nasal *yank-yank*.
Helen Cruikshank

ing, harsh, high, low or hushed; day or night, spring, summer, fall, or even in the dead of winter. Indeed, it seems to live to sing!

The name "Mockingbird" is well chosen, for no other bird is so adept at imitating the songs of other birds. Its habit of repeating its phrases three or more times is often the best clue to the fact that one is listening to a Mockingbird and not the real owner of the particular song being rendered. Its call note is a loud *smack*.

Thickets, hedges, and low trees are favorite meeting sites of these 9 to 11 inch long, slender, long-tailed gray birds which show white patches on wings and tail, especially in flight. Here they place their bulky, loosely constructed nest of sticks. The three to five greenish to buff colored eggs are blotched with brown. The Mockingbird's favorite habitat is the suburban areas where it lives in gardens, shady streets, parks and shrubby countrysides.

The breeding range of the Eastern Mockingbird *(M. p. polyglottos)* occurs from Maryland, Ohio, Illinois, southern Iowa, and Nebraska, south to the Gulf of Mexico. Occasionally, the Mockingbird is found as far north as the Great Lakes and New England.

The western race of the Mockingbird *(M. p. leucopterus)* breeds from central California and western Kansas south to Mexico. It winters south from central California and Arizona.

CATBIRD

(Dumetella carolinensis)

Color Plate Page 258

"Let us bear in mind the needs of the Catbird when we care for our grounds, and leave him a corner in which he may find a shady thicket sufficiently dense to be congenial. It would be to me a poor gardener indeed that did not have some retreat from which I could hear that harsh complaining cry of the Catbird, when I chanced to stroll by."

Those words of wisdom for gardeners came from Dr. Witmer Stone, and those who heed them will enjoy saucy Catbirds all summer, for failure to attract this "black Mockingbird" is usually due to a lack of its favorite haunts —garden shrubbery, dense undergrowth, berry tangles, and thick vines.

Not that the Catbird spends all of its time in such dark, secluded places. Far from it. But it is there that the female conceals her coarse nest of

SENNETT'S THRASHER *(Toxostoma longirostre sennetti)*. Length: 10.5 to 12 inches. Male and female: upperparts rich reddish brown. Underparts white, breast heavily streaked with black. Long bill. Range: southern Texas. Voice: song, a series of notes and phrases. Call note, *too-ree.*
Rudolph Hindemith, American Museum of Natural History

twigs, leaves, and grapevine bark, neatly lined with rootlets. Here she lays her four unmarked bluish green eggs, darker and smaller than those of the Robin or Wood Thrush.

While his mate is busy with domestic duties, the male Catbird entertains with his conglomeration of notes, phrases, and calls. Whoever said that the Catbird "sings Chinese" was a keen listener. Yet, with all its harsh, unmusical notes, the bird manages to render a fair share of pleasant ones too.

Describing the Catbird's song, Schuyler Mathews observed that "the yowl of the cat is thrown in anywhere, the gutteral remarks of the frog are repeated without the slightest deference to good taste or appropriateness, and the harsh squawk of the old hen, or the chirp of the lost chicken, is always added in some malapropos manner. All is grist which comes to the Catbird's musical mill, and all is ground out according to the bird's own way of thinking." Other birds' notes are more or less perfectly reproduced.

Those who have attracted Catbirds to their gardens are familiar with that saucy flick of the tail as the bird peers inquisitively from the edge of the shrubbery; the spritely gait as it runs lightly across the lawn; the sudden lunge into the air for a passing insect; the catlike cry of *meow* when it is disturbed; and the snatches of other birds' songs recognized in the Catbird's varied musical program.

The Catbirds, Mockingbirds and Thrashers, all members of the Mimic Thrush *(Mimidae)* family, are closely related to the Wrens. In the Catbird's actions, I detect something Wrenlike in its nervousness, the flicking of the tail, the quivering of the wings, and the saucy, erect position in which the tail is often carried. These traits remind me in many respects of Jenny Wren!

No other bird in America possesses the same combination of colors as the Catbird. Its all over slate-gray plumage is broken only by a black cap and chestnut under-tail coverts. It is an inch shorter than a robin, (8½ to 9 inches). Sexes are indistinguishable in the field.

Catbirds arrive in the northern states and southern Canada in late April and early May. They migrate during the night from their winter home in the Gulf States and south to Panama.

BENDIRE'S THRASHER *(Toxostoma bendirei)*. Length: 9.5 to 10.5 inches. Male and female: upperparts grayish brown, underparts buffy white with streaks of dark. Range: deserts of southwest United States. Voice: song, a *continuous* musical warble. Note, *tirup.*

Rudolph Hindemith, American Museum of Natural History

BROWN THRASHER

(Toxostoma rufum)

Color Plate Page 262

A family that had resided for many years

in Texas came to western Pennsylvania to live. One day, the woman said to me:

"We were so surprised to find a Mockingbird singing near our new home. We enjoyed them so much in Texas, but we never dreamed that we would find them here."

The woman had not heard a Mockingbird, for this beautiful songster is decidedly a southern species. She had enjoyed the song of a Brown Thrasher, a member of the same family as the Mockingbird and Catbird.

A more careful listener would have detected the difference between the song of the Thrasher and the Mockingbird. While the former renders each phrase of its song twice, the Mockingbird usually repeats several times. The Catbird does not repeat at all. The song of the Mockingbird is much more varied than that of the Thrasher, but the form is similar. Indeed one of the Thrasher's common names is Brown Mockingbird.

I like the interpretation of the bird's song which gained for it another common name, the "planting bird." The rendition is written thus: *plant-a-seed, plant-a-seed; drop-it, drop-it; cover-it-up, cover-it-up; pull-it; eat-it-all, eat-it-all; chew it, chew-it.*

Still another common name for the Thrasher is Brown Thrush, and here, again, the bird is mistaken for another—the Wood Thrush. The long tail, streaked breast, yellow eye, and downward curve of the bill are characteristics of the Thrasher. This 10½ to 12 inch bird is rufous red above. The Wood Thrush is smaller with a shorter tail and a spotted breast. The Brown Thrasher has wing bars.

The Brown Thrasher is the only song bird that ever actually struck me in

CALIFORNIA THRASHER (*Toxostoma redivivum*). Length: 11.5 to 13 inches. Male and female: a dull, grayish brown bird with cinnamon brown belly. Sickle-shaped bill. Range: California, north along coast through San Francisco Bay region. Voice: long-sustained variety of phrases, some clear, and musical, others harsh. Low-pitched and leisurely. Note, a sharp *weeek*.
Chicago Natural History Museum

defence of its nest. Many birds will feign attack, but my experience with the Thrasher is that it is not fooling; it really means it. Along with the physical attack, the intruder is struck with a barrage of verbal bombshells which include loud hissings, clickings and a *smack* note like a loud kiss. A three note whistle *tee-ola* is thrown in for good measure.

The Thrasher's large, bulky nest is placed in briars, brush piles, and thorn trees. A few nests that I have found were on the ground. The four eggs (occasionally three) are thickly and uniformly covered with fine brown dots.

Despite its vicious defence of its nest, and its habit of singing from a conspicuous perch, the Brown Thrasher is by nature a shy bird; much more so than either the Catbird or the Mockingbird. We find it inhabiting the dry thickets, bushy pastures, and cut-over wastelands. For such a large bird, it is able to conceal itself remarkably

BROWN HEADED NUTHATCH (*Sitta pusilla*). Length: 4 to 5 inches. Male and female: upperparts grayish blue, brown crown to eye, white underparts. Range: from Gulf of Mexico to coast of Delaware and southern Missouri. Voice: a rapid *kit-kit-kit*, or squeaky *ki-day* or *ki-dee-dee*, repeated over and over.
Samuel A. Grimes

well, dodging in and out of thickets with ease.

Like the Catbird, the Thrasher is accused of eating much domestic fruit, but analysis shows that sixty-five percent of its diet is insectiverous. The fruit eaten is mostly wild, and the damage to cultivated fruit is exceedingly small. The Brown Thrasher is an aid to the farmer, for the groves where it lives and feeds are the breeding grounds of harmful insects. It eats beetles, grasshoppers, caterpillars and spiders, which certainly makes it of economic value.

The Thrasher family is represented in the east only by the Brown Thrasher (*T. r. rufum*) which winters in southern United States. A subspecies, the Western Brown Thrasher (*T. r. longicauda*) has recently been recognized.

SENNETT'S THRASHER

(*Toxostoma longirostre sennetti*)

Sennett's Thrasher, or Long-billed Thrasher, is a bird of limited range in the United States, being confined to southern Texas in the Lower Rio Grande Valley and the Gulf Coast district. It is quite similar to the Brown Thrasher, about the same size (10½ to 12 inches) with the back less reddish brown than the latter. The breast streaks are black, not brown.

BENDIRE'S THRASHER

(*Toxostoma bendirea*)

Of the several species of Grayish-brown Thrashers that inhabit the des-

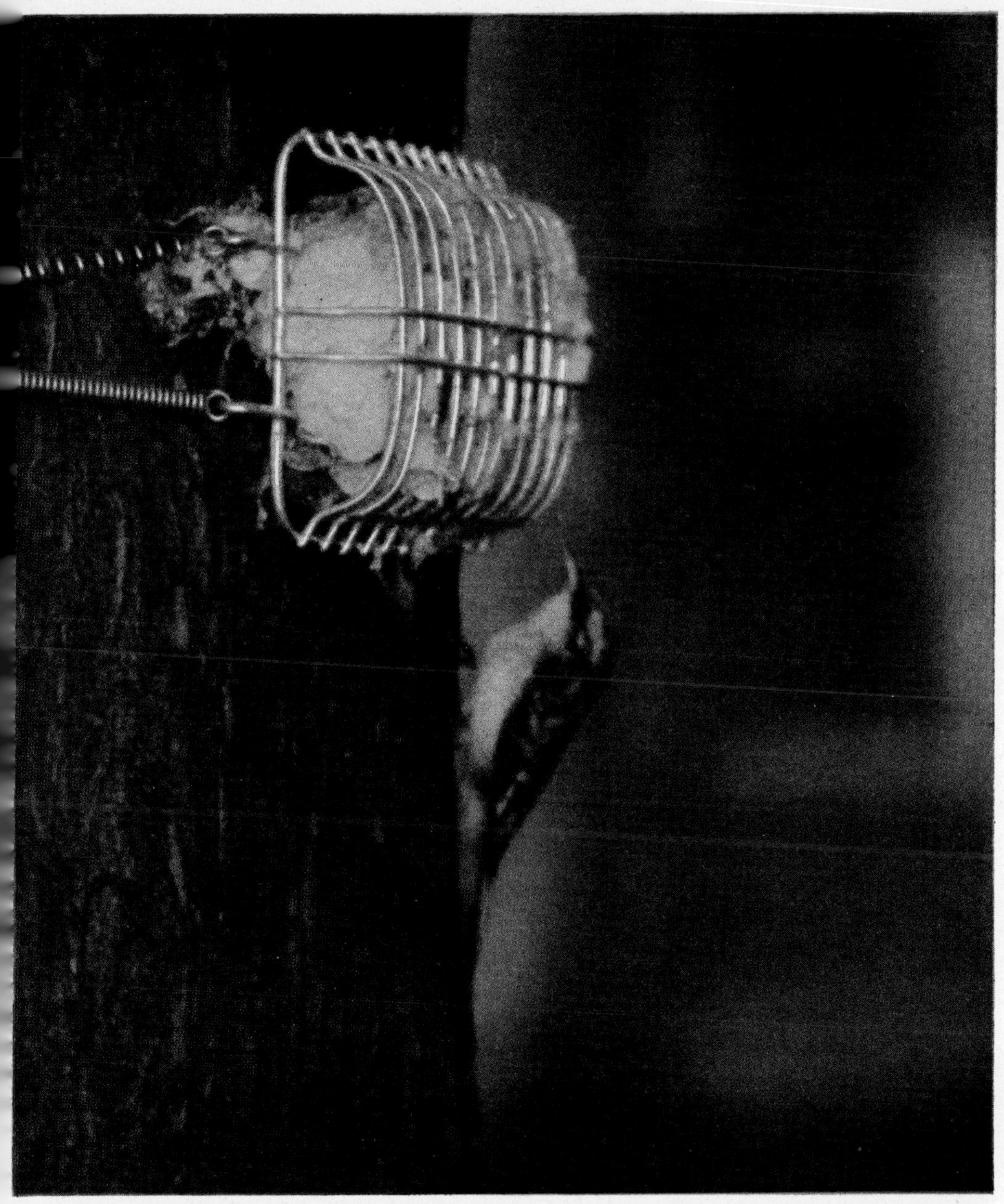

BROWN CREEPER (*Certhia familiaris*). Length: 5 to 5.75 inches. Male and female: upperparts brown streaked with grayish white; underparts dull white. Bill is curved and thin. Range: breeds from southern Quebec, central Ontario and northern Manitoba south to northern parts of United States. Winters to Texas and Florida. Voice: song; weak clear notes *see-ti-wee-tu-wee* or *see-see-see ti-ti-see.*

Hal H. Harrison

erts of the southwest, Bendire's Thrasher is probably the most uncommon. It may be distinguished from the other Thrashers by its comparatively short, straight bill. Also, it is somewhat smaller, 9½ to 10½ inches long. It is similar to the Palmer's Thrasher in having a faintly spotted breast, but the latter has a deeply curved, sickle-like bill. Bendire's Thrasher has a yellow

LECONTE'S THRASHER AT NEST *(Toxostoma lecontei).* Length: 10.5 to 11 inches. Male and female: upperparts pale grayish brown; tail tipped with light gray. Underparts, white, faintly washed with creamy brown. Range: deserts of southern and western Arizona, southern California south into northwestern Mexico. Voice: infrequent snatches of song, heard usually in early morning.
James Murdock, National Audubon Society

eye. Its song is a continuous warble, not broken into phrases as are those of the other Thrashers.

PALMER'S or CURVE-BILLED THRASHER

(Toxostoma curvirostre)

Color Plate Page 263

One of the richest songs of the southwest desert country is that of the Palmer's, or Curve-billed, Thrasher. Its quality rivals that of its close relative, the Mockingbird. Its two-syllabled call note is a sharp *whit-whit*.

At home in the sage and mesquite country of southern Arizona, New Mexico, western Oklahoma, and southern Texas, the Palmer's Thrasher may be distinguished from other Thrashers of the area by its spotted breast and sides and its decurved bill. It is medium sized—10½ to 11½ inches long. The Crissal and Leconte's Thrashers have deeply curved bills but both have plain breasts. Bendire's Thrasher has a spotted breast but its bill is short and straight.

The nest of the Curve-bill is made of twigs and thorns and is lined with grasses. The structure is usually placed in a thorn bush, cactus, or yucca. The eggs are thickly spotted.

Three races are recognized, all indistinguishable in the field: Palmer's Thrasher, *(T. c. palmeri)*, Curve-billed Thrasher *(T. c. celsum)*, and Brownsville Thrasher *(T. c. oberholseri)*.

CALIFORNIA THRASHER

(Toxostoma redivivum)

Over much of its range in the southwest, the California Thrasher is the only Thrasher with a deeply curved bill. Where its range overlaps that of Leconte's Thrasher, the latter may be distinguished by its much lighter coloration.

On the chaparral covered slopes, west of the deserts and Sierras, one can look for this shy bird. Its song is very like the Mockingbird but it lacks the rapidly repeated phrases of the Mocker. Observers are reluctant to attribute to the California Thrasher the brilliant vocal performance possessed by the Mockingbird. The California Thrasher is a large Thrasher, 11½ to 13 inches long, dull gray-brown in color with pale rufous on its belly and under tail coverts.

Unlike the Sparrows and Chewinks which scratch for insects with their feet, the California Thrasher probes his needle-like bill into the ground.

LECONTE'S THRASHER

(Toxostoma lecontei)

The 100-yard dash champion of the desert is Leconte's Thrasher. This bleached-looking gray bird prefers to use its legs rather than its wings in fleeing from impending danger. In this regard it rivals such larger birds as the Road-runner and the Scaled Quail which also run from danger.

Home for Leconte's Thrasher is the hottest of hot desert country where man often finds conditions intolerable. Here, this Thrasher with the sharply decurved bill, plain breast, and dark tail spends its days, skulking on the floor of the desert, avoiding detection whenever possible, and flying only when forced by a faster-footed pursuer. Its pale gray plumage blends well with the desert sand. It is much lighter colored than the Crissal Thrasher, and may be distinguished from the Curve-billed Thrasher by its plain breast. It is 10½ or 11 inches long.

In one respect only is Leconte's Thrasher a conspicuous bird: when it sings. Its song is a beautiful rendition, loud and clear and may be heard far away. It often sings at night. The savage heat of the bird's habitat seems to have no affect on its joyful disposition. The nest is built in the center of a cholla cactus or mesquite and is bulky.

The Desert Thrasher *(T. l. arenicola)* is a subspecies of Leconte's Thrasher *(T. l. lecontei)*.

CRISSAL THRASHER

(Toxostoma dorsale dorsale)

A shy Thrasher of the Western Deserts, the Crissal Thrasher may be distinguished from the Curve-billed Thrasher by its plain breast and the deep rust on the underside of its tail. It is darker than Leconte's Thrasher and again the deep rust beneath the tail is characteristic. It is 10½ to 12 inches long. Its song is like that of the other Thrashers, perhaps not quite so loud and vigorous. The nest is built in bushes, and is loosely constructed. The three eggs are perfectly plain pale bluish green.

SAGE THRASHER

(Oreoscoptes montanus)

None of the Mimic Thrushes resembles its close relative, the Mockingbird, more than the Sage Thrasher. In-

SAGE THRASHER ON NEST *(Oreoscoptes montanus)*. Length: 8 to 9 inches. Upperparts grayish brown; underparts, buffy white with dark streaks. White spots at the tip of the tail. Range: breeds in sagebrush country from eastern Washington and Montana, south to California and New Mexico. Winters in southern New Mexico, southern California and southern Arizona. Voice: song, a series of clear ecstatic warbled phrases.

Alfred M. Bailey, National Audubon Society

deed, Florence Merriam Bailey has suggested that it might be called the "Mockingbird of the Sagebrush," for its habits as well as its song, combine the characteristics of Thrashers and Mockingbirds.

The heavily streaked breast of the Sage Thrasher immediately eliminates any possibility of confusing it with the Mockingbird, although its gray back, white spots on the tail-tips, and its habit of elevating its wings at intervals are like the Mockingbird. It is 8 to 9 inches long. The song is a low warbling, rapidly and beautifully delivered. It rarely repeats its phrases.

The Sage Thrasher breeds in arid sagebrush country from British Columbia to central California and eastward to Nebraska. It winters from southern California and central Texas southward.

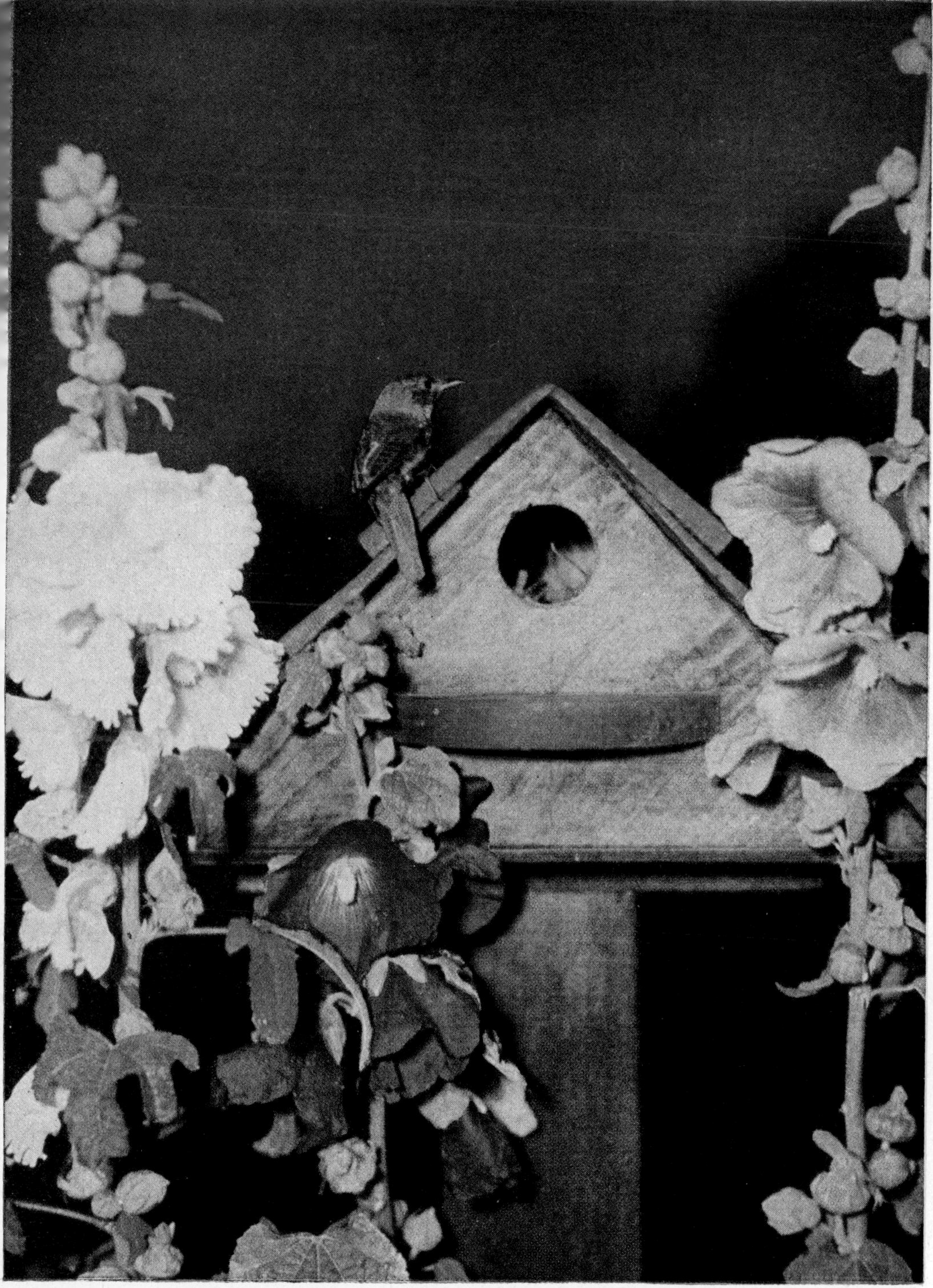

HOUSE WREN (*Troglodytes aedon*). Length: 4.5 to 5.25 inches. Male and female: gray brown above, white and gray brown below. No evident facial markings. Range: Canada to Virginia, Kentucky, Missouri and Texas. Winters in southern Atlantic and Gulf States. Voice: gurgling song.
Hal H. Harrison

THRUSHES

Family Turdidae

The Thrushes are songbirds, which present a widely varying appearance in their adult plumage. The relationship is betrayed in the young birds, all of which have their underparts spotted. The family has almost worldwide distribution, the European Nightingale being one of the best songsters in the family. The American representatives include the Thrushes, the Robin, and the Bluebirds.

ROBIN

(Turdus migratorius)

Color Plate Page 265

Everybody knows the Robin! Like the Bluebird, it is heralded as a harbinger of spring in the northern states when it starts to arrive in late February and March. The Robin's red breast has been a theme for song and story for generations, although much of the early literature was written about a different bird, the English Robin Redbreast. Robin's-egg-blue is a highly publicized pastel shade for feminine wear. In fact, the Robin is so well known throughout America that we take it for granted and feel that, well—everybody knows the Robin!

Yet, most people think the Robin is listening for worms when it cocks its head on the side on the lawn; not everyone could tell you why young Robins have spotted breasts while the adults do not; many people are puzzled when a Robin spends days flying at a cellar window or pecking at the hub-cap of an automobile; it would be news to thousands to learn that Robins often winter as far north as New England; and how many people could explain the phenomenon of certain Robins building as many as 26 nests in a row and using only one of them to raise a family!

In answer to that first point: It is generally conceded by ornithologists that the Robin is looking for worms when it cocks its head on the side. Since its eyes are on the sides of its head, it is necessary to turn the head in order to put one eye above a close object.

The Robin is a big migratory Thrush. True Thrushes have spotted breasts, but in the evolution of the Robin, the adults have lost their spots. Young Robins, however, show the family trait. This is true also of young Bluebirds. They are Thrushes too. The adult Robin is about 9 inches long, with a dark gray back and brick red breast. The female is paler in color than the male.

No bird is more zealous in protecting its nesting territory against intruders than the robin. Fights between male Robins are common in every town and hamlet in America throughout the spring. When a male Robin suddenly discovers its own reflection in

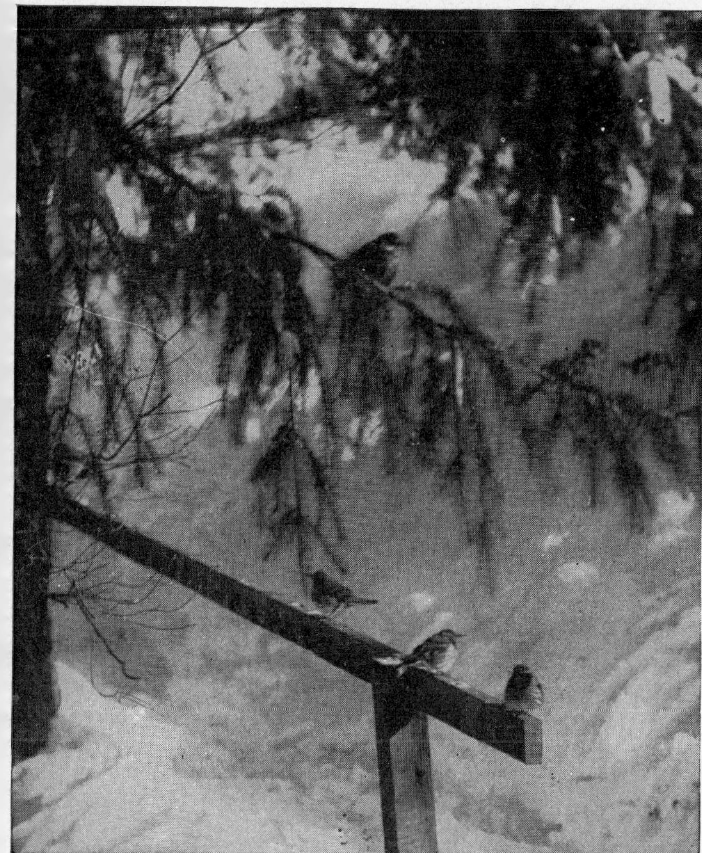

VARIED THRUSHES (*Inoreus naevius*). Length: 9 to 10 inches. Male: upperparts slate color; underparts tawny and white, with an *orange eye-stripe, orange wingbars,* and a *black band* across the rusty chest. Female: much duller than male, with breast-band gray. Immature: breast-band imperfect or spotted with orange. Underparts speckled with dusky gray. Range: evergreen forests of northwestern California, Oregon, Washington, Idaho, and northwestern Montana. Winters along California coast and in central California. Voice: a long, eerie, quavering, whistled note, followed by one on a lower or higher pitch.

William L. and Irene Finley

a glass window or any shiny surface, like an automobile hub cap, it immediately starts to fight the "other Robin." To stop the commotion, the glass should be soaped, for when the reflection disappears, the fight is over.

Robins spend the winter in the southern states. Often, however, a small flock may find shelter and abundant food in a favorable northern valley, swamp, or thicket, and spend the winter there. Robins reported in northern states in January are wintering Robins, not migrants with news of an early spring.

The multiple-nesting building stunt is a lack of orientation on the part of the female. It is the result of the bird's confusion, caused by the similarity of form in the nesting location. The confusion lasts until the bird forms a habit of flying to one spot. Until then, it continues to build in a number of adjacent places.

Nesting habits of Robins are too well known to demand repetition here. The bird's appearance and its caroling song are so well known that it is undoubtedly America's best known bird.

Six varieties are recognized throughout the Robin's breeding range, which extends from coast to coast, north to the limit of trees and south to Mexico.

VARIED THRUSH

(Ixoreus naevius)

Although it is a fairly abundant bird in the Pacific northwest, nesting records of the Varied Thrush, or Alaska Robin, are not numerous. In summer it is a resident of the heavy coniferous forests, and, regarding the scarcity of nesting records in Oregon, Gabrielson and Jewett write: "The endless miles of fir forests in the state make finding a nest either a lucky accident or the happy ending of a painstaking search that takes time few of us have to give."

The Varied Thrush is Robin-like in appearance, and size. Its rusty brown breast is crossed by a black band. The side of the head is black, crossed above by an orange-brown stripe. The wings are banded and edged in orange-brown. The female is generally duller with a gray breast band.

The bird has an unusual haunting note, a sort of monotone song that is a combined voice and whistle note.

The Varied Thrush winters in the valleys of the Pacific northwest.

Two races are recognized: Pacific Varied Thrush *(I. n. naevius)*, and Northern Varied Thrush *(I. n. meruloides)*.

WOOD THRUSH

(Hylocichla mustelina)

Color Plate Page 268

For many years long before I heard the song of a Hermit Thrush, I considered the Wood Thrush's song the most beautiful of all bird music. There were many to agree. Then I heard the Hermit singing in a hemlock forest at twilight. Since then, I have never been quite sure what I think.

When I listen to a Wood Thrush at dawn, pouring out its liquid notes in a dew-drenched forest glade, pausing between short, flutelike soprano phrases only long enough to rewind his instrument for the next set of notes, I am sure that no bird could render more heavenly music. Indeed it is not until the ethereal contralto phrases of the Hermit Thrush come drifting

CAROLINA WREN *(Thryothorus ludovicianus)*. Length: 5.5 to 6 inches. Male and female: upperparts rufous red with broad white line over the eye. Buffy underparts. Range: Rhode Island, lower Hudson River, Pennsylvania, Ohio, Iowa and Nebraska south to Florida, Gulf Coast and Texas.
Samuel A. Grimes

OLIVE-BACKED THRUSH AT NEST (*Hylocichla ustulata*). Length: 6.5 to 7.5 inches. Male and female: uniform gray, buffy eye-ring and buffy cheeks. Range: breeds in spruce belt from northern Manitoba and Newfoundland south to northern Michigan, New York, northern New England, and in Appalachians to West Virginia. Migrates through southern United States; winters in South America. Voice: Song is composed of melodious, breezy, flute-like phrases, each phrase rising. Note, *whit*. Migrants at night a short *heep*.
Ross and Florence Thornburg

through the evening gloom of a coniferous forest that I am convinced again that here is the master of all feathered songsters.

For those who have heard only the Wood Thrush, the answer is obvious: here is America's number one singer. True, the Mockingbird is a talented artist, a clever musician, possessing a repertoire of notes and musical phrases unequalled anywhere. But the Mockingbird's notes pour from its throat; the melody of a Wood Thrush is released from its heart!

From its winter home in Central America, the Wood Thrush returns to the eastern and central states in late April, and early May. Arriving on home territory, the male immediately starts to sing, and that familiar *a-olee* is heard constantly until the molt in late July.

Although generally a bird of the damp woodland, the Wood Thrush is constantly accepting man-made habitats. It often nests in gardens, especially those where thick shrubbery is provided, and city parks are common nesting sites. The bird builds a typical Thrush nest of wet muddy leaves with a lining of rootlets and grasses. It is placed from four to fifteen feet from the ground. Paper and rags are often added to the outside of the cup, and in recent years, I have found the birds using cellophane.

The Wood Thrush's eggs are typical Thrush eggs—plain bluish green. They are smaller than those of the Robin, but larger than the Veery's. The female Wood Thrush incubates the eggs, but both sexes share in feeding. Young Wood Thrushes are in the nest about twelve days. Most pairs have two broods. A visitor to the nest of a Wood Thrush will be met by the bird's alarm note . . . *pit-pit-pit-pit*.

The Wood Thrush is the largest (7½ to 8½ inches) of the five typical spotted Thrushes of the east (Veery, Wood, Hermit, Olive-backed and Gray-cheeked). Its white breast, completely covered with big brown spots is the most heavily spotted of these

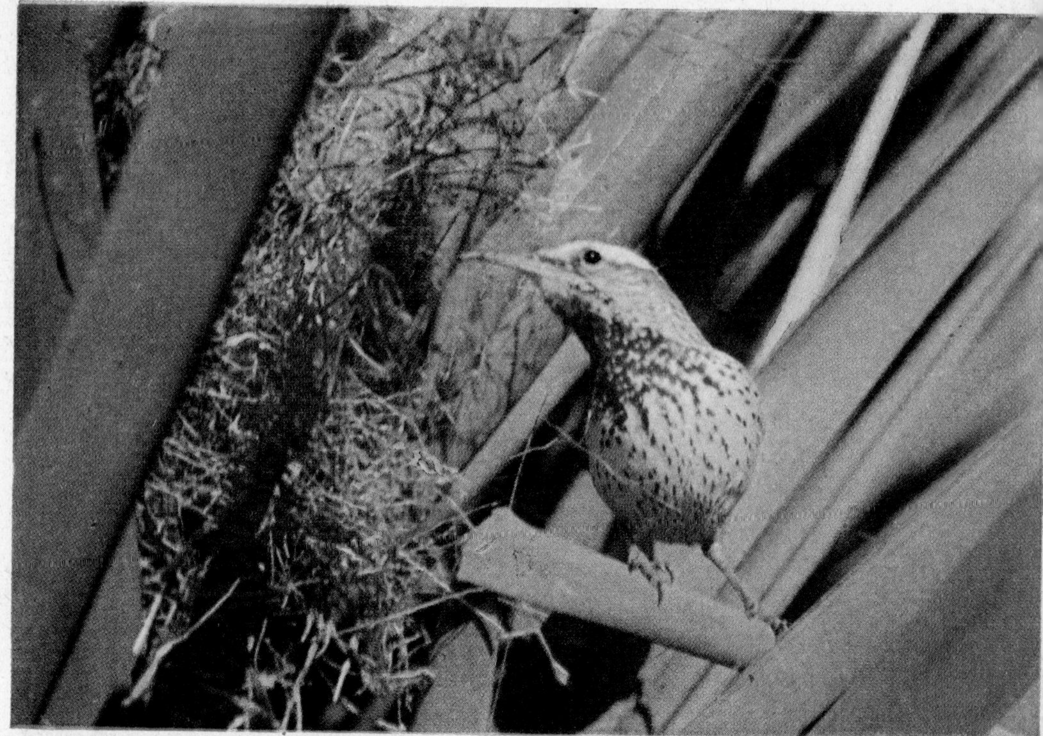

CACTUS WREN *(Campylorhynchus brunneicapillus)*. Length: 7 to 8.5 inches. Male and female: brown above, back streaked with white. Conspicuous white line over the eye. White spots in outer tail-feathers. Throat and breast white, heavily spotted with black. Range: desert regions of California, Nevada, Utah, Arizona, New Mexico and Texas. Voice: a rapid *cheh-cheh-cheh-cheh* or *chug chug chug chug chug chug chug.*

Fred Bashour

species. The Veery, with which the Wood Thrush might be confused is smaller and is the least spotted of the family. At a distance, its breast seems almost clear. The back of the Wood Thrush's head is reddish brown, contrasting with its otherwise plain brown back. The Hermit has a reddish brown tail.

Distinguishing marks between the Wood Thrush and the Brown Thrasher are discussed under the latter bird.

The breeding range of the Wood Thrush extends from central New Hampshire, southeastern Ontario, central Minnesota, and South Dakota, south to northern Florida, Louisiana, and eastern Texas. It winters from Florida southward.

HERMIT THRUSH

(Hylocichla guttata)

Color Plate Page 272

A famous nature writer recently set down his wishes for his last day on earth. Among the final sounds, he declared, should be "the voice of a Hermit Thrush far in a darkening wood at evening."

Those of us who have had the privilege of standing quietly in a hemlock woods at twilight, listening reverently to the hymnlike strains of a Hermit Thrush ringing through the stillness like a benediction, will extend to that writer a sincere: "So be it!"

Many inspired authors before him, and many yet to come will try with

LONG-BILLED MARSH WREN (*Telmatodytes palustris*). Length: 4.5 to 5.5 inches. Male and female: upperparts brown and black with white streaks; underparts white and pale brown. White line over eye. Range: Canada and New England to Florida and Gulf Coast. Winters in southern United States. Voice: reedy, becoming throaty rattle, *cut-cut-turrrrr-ur*.

Hal H. Harrison

GRAY-CHEEKED THRUSH (*Hylocichla minima*). Length: 6.25 to 8 inches. Male and female: dull gray brown above, gray cheeks. Inconspicuous eye-ring. Range: spruce forests from near tree limits in Newfoundland, central Quebec and northern Manitoba, south in high northeastern American mountains. Winters in South America. Voice: thin, nasal song; often rises abruptly at close, *whee-wheeoo-titi-whee*. Note, *vee-a* or *quee-a*, uttered by migrants at night.
Chicago Natural History Museum

all the power of words to tell of the feeling of peace and contentment, the upsurging of spiritual emotion, that came as he listened to glorious song.

John Burroughs in "Wake-Robin" writes of the Hermit: "His instrument is a silver horn which he winds in the most solitary places." "American Nightingale" is one of many names earned by the Hermit. "Swamp Angel" is another. F. Schuyler Mathews, eminent authority on wild bird songs, describes the Hermit's offering as "the grand climax of all bird music."

A true spotted Thrush of the genus *Hylocichla*, the Hermit is closely related to the Wood Thrush, Veery, Olive-backed Thrush, and Gray-cheeked Thrush. The casual observer might confuse any of the five, for generally they look alike—brown backs with spotted breasts. But there are two characteristics exclusive of its song, that make identification of the Hermit quite easy. One is its reddish tail, conspicuous in contrast with its olive-brown back. The second is its habit of slowly raising or tilting its tail, especially when it alights. It is smaller than the Wood Thrush, being 6½ to 7½ inches long.

Many birds are notoriously misnamed. Not the Hermit. It is a recluse of the deep forests and swamps, and one may hear its song many times before he sees the bird. It slips silently away to another part of its territory long before the searcher has reached it.

The Hermit's nest is usually placed on or near the ground, although the nest at which the photograph on page 272 was taken was nine feet up in a leaning Hemlock. The nest is constructed of moss, twigs, bark, leaves, and ferns. It is lined with rootlets, sometimes with pine needles. The eggs in true Thrush style, are greenish blue, three to five in number.

It is late autumn before the Hermit leaves for the south. The other true Thrushes have all gone before. But the Hermit is the only one that winters in the United States. The others migrate to Central and South America. In the spring, it is the Hermit that leads the way back to its beloved forests. By early May, when the Wood Thrushes are still arriving from the south, the Hermit's ethereal music is already spread across the cool stillness of the northern woods. Including its seven subspecies, the Hermit Thrush inhabits much of North America during the nesting season. It ranges from central Alaska to California in the west, and from northern Manitoba and southern Quebec to the mountains of Virginia in the east.

RUSSET-BACKED or OLIVE-BACKED THRUSH

(Hylocichla ustulata)

In the identification of the spotted Thrushes of eastern North America, it is generally conceded that the principal difficulty occurs distinguishing between the Olive-backed Thrush *(H. u. swainsoni)* and the Gray-cheeked Thrush *(Hylocichla minima)*. The others, the Wood Thrush, Hermit Thrush and Veery do not offer bird watchers any serious problems in recognition.

Peterson offers the following advice: "When we come upon a Thrush that lacks any warmth of color in its plumage and is uniformly gray-brown or olive-brown above, then we have found one of two species. If the bird also has a conspicuous buffy eye-ring and buffy cheeks, it is the Olive-backed Thrush. If the cheeks are gray and the eye-ring indistinct or lacking, then it is the Gray-cheek, (but see them well and be cautious, especially in the fall)." The Olive-back is about the size of the Hermit Thrush (6½ to 7½ inches long).

In most parts of the country, bird watchers see both birds as migrants, for their breeding range is in the spruce forests of the north. In this capacity, both are shy and neither sings while enroute through the states. A close view is not always possible, so I have learned a rule that is most helpful; at least it is a good point from which to start. It is this: in migration, Olive-backed Thrushes move through the trees, often high up, while Gray-cheek Thrushes stay close to the ground.

WESTERN BLUEBIRD *(Sialia mexicana)*. Length: 6.5 to 7 inches. Male: upperparts cobalt blue with chestnut on the upper back; underparts chestnut and bluish. Female: Gray above with brown on back and blue tail; underparts, grayish cast with brown and rufous. Range: breeds in the Rockies east to Idaho and western Montana south to Mexico; winters in the Pacific states to western Texas. Voice: a short *pew*, also a chattering note. Song is very similar to Eastern Bluebird.

Rudolph Hindemith, American Museum of Natural History

ROCK WREN (*Salpinctes obsoletus*). Length: 5.25 to 6.25 inches. Male and female: grayish brown upperparts speckled with black and white. Light brown rump. Underparts whitish streaked with dark. Range: western United States east to Dakotas, Nebraska and Kansas. Voice: a rough chant, *tew, tew tew tew tew tew* or *chr-wee chr-wee chr-wee;* call, a clear *ti-keer*, also a trill.
George M. Bradt

The song of the Olive-backed, although decidedly Thrushlike, is generally conceded to be inferior to that of the Wood or Hermit Thrushes. "It may be distinguished by the fact that all the notes are equal length and there is a gradual rise in pitch in each phrase." (Saunders). The Olive-backed Thrush breeds from Alaska and Newfoundland to northern California and New York and in the mountains to West Virginia.

On the Pacific Coast from Alaska to southern California, the Russet-backed Thrush *(H. u. ustulata)* replaces its eastern form, the Olive-backed. The two races are indistinguishable in the field. In the Rocky Mountain region, a third race is now recognized: Western Olive-Backed Thrush *(H. u. almae)*.

GRAY-CHEEKED THRUSH

(Hylocichla minima)

High in the mountains of New England, deep in the most inaccessible forests, far from the haunts of man, nests a southern form of the Gray-cheeked Thrush, known as Bicknell's Thrush *(H. m. bicknelli)*. To the north, even beyond the limit of trees in the most bleak and desolate areas of North America, breeds the larger northern Gray-cheeked, or Alice's Thrush (*H. m. minima*).

Most bird watchers know the Gray-cheeked only as a migrant to and from its winter home in South America. In migration it is easily confused with the

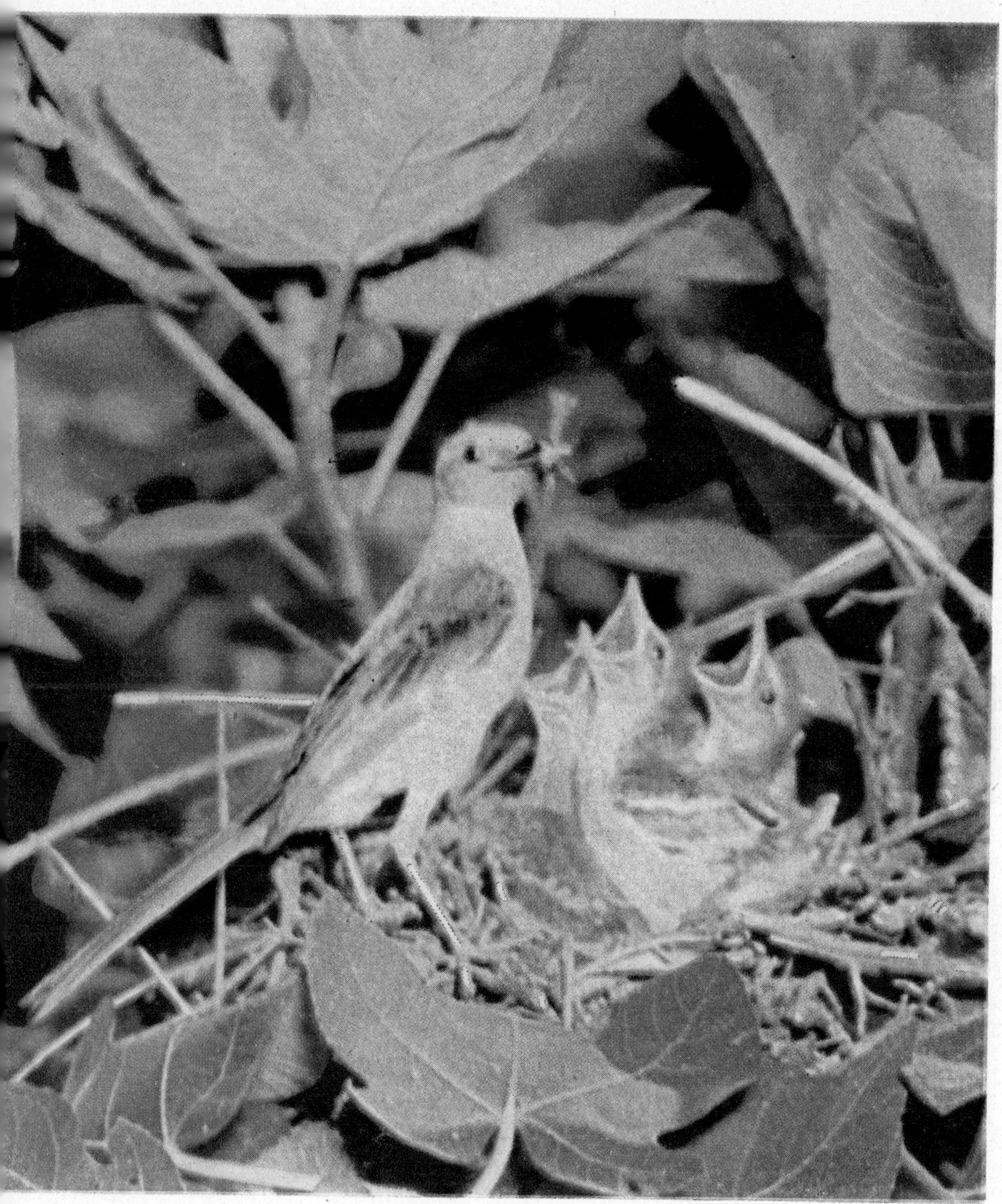

MOCKINGBIRD (*Mimus polyglottos*). Length: 9 to 11 inches. Male and female: upperparts dark gray, longish tail tipped and edged with white. Wings have two white wingbars and white wing patch. Underparts, light gray. Range: Maryland south to Gulf of Mexico; west to Nebraska. Voice: varied songs; imitates noises of neighborhood. Repeats each phrase at least a dozen times before going on to next. Often sings at night. Note, a loud *tchack*.

Samuel A. Grimes

similar Olive-backed Thrush. The Gray-cheeked can be identified when well seen by its gray cheeks and lack of conspicuous eye-ring. Enroute through the States, the Gray-cheeked is silent, shy and retiring.

During the spring the Gray-cheeked Thrush feeds mainly on insects but in the fall it prefers wild fruits and berries such as sour gum, dogwood, poke berries, and frost grapes.

Like other members of the *Hylocichla* group, the Gray-cheeked Thrush has a beautiful voice, but its song has been heard only by those fortunate enough to have visited this recluse on its nesting grounds. The song has been described as resembling the Veery.

MOUNTAIN BLUEBIRD AT ENTRANCE TO NEST HOLE IN TREE (*Sialia currucoides*). Length: 6.5 to 7.5 inches. Male: cerulean blue above, turquoise blue below, with white belly. Female: gray above and brownish below, with bluish wings, tail, and rump. Range: breeds on the eastern side of the Cascade Mountains to the plains from Canada to central Arizona and New Mexico; winters from Oregon south into Mexico. Voice: a low *terr*. Song is high sweet warble, sounding more like a Robin than like the Eastern Bluebird.
A. M. Bailey

VEERY

(Hylocichla fuscescens)

Color Plate Page 273

To many, the Veery is but a voice from the depths of a damp woodland. Shy and elusive, it shuns human companionship, slipping quietly away through the undergrowth when approached.

Dusk is the time of day to search for the Veery, for in the evening, one finds him in grand voice; indeed, in good Veery country at twilight, one may hear several singing and answering in their soft spiraling voice with the enchanting double tone. The latter gives one the impression that an echo follows each note. The spiraling is a downward sweep from the highest note to the lowest, trailing off at the end.

Louis J. Halle, Jr. writing in "Audubon Magazine" has caught the ethereal feeling of the Veery's song: "This voice is merely uncanny and unearthly. It has a soft, reedy double tone such as might conceivably be produced by a violinist drawing his bow across two strings at once; but no mechanical instrument could produce such thin, resonant chords. It has also a windy quality, and perhaps one could give an idea of it by comparing it to the sound produced by blowing across the top of a bottle. The overtone, the resonance, as if the bird carried its own echo within itself, might make one think that the song was actually issuing from inside a bottle. It is a soft, tremulous, utterly ethereal sound, swirling downward and ending, swirling downward and ending again. Heard in the gloom of twilight, back and forth across the marshes, it gives the impression that this is no bird at all but some spirit not to be discovered." The syllables are written *veero, veery, veery,* etc.

The alarm or call note of the Veery, the one you will hear quickly when the bird discovers you listening to its song, is a soft two-syllable utterance that I would describe as *whee-you.* Sometimes, only the *you* is audible.

The Veery *(H. f. fuscescens)* or Wilson's Thrush as it is known to many, returns from its winter home in Central and South America to the northern woods in early May. It nests from the Gulf of St. Lawrence to Ohio and south to New Jersey, and in mountains to Georgia. With territory established, the male begins to sing about a week or so after its arrival. Nesting, on or near the ground, is well underway by late May.

I have found many nests of the Veery, and all have been beautifully constructed in delightful wildwood settings. Some have been in moist ravines with ferns and wild flowers for their setting; some have been on rocky hillsides with mosses abounding; a few were in thick bogs, sphagnum-tamarack, and rhododendrons; and one in particular that I remember was at the side of a trinkling brook, hidden in ferns with the pink blossoms of a wild geranium forming a canopy overhead. Inside the nest were five greenish blue eggs, making the color scheme complete.

The Veery (6½ to 7½ inches) may be distinguished from the Wood Thrush by its uniform tawny-brown upperparts; its lightly spotted breast (least spotted of all the Thrushes) ; and its almost white sides. The sexes are indistinguishable in the field.

The Willow Thrush *(H. f. salicicola)* is a western race of the Veery. A Newfoundland species has been named the Newfoundland Veery *(H. f. fuliginosa)*.

EASTERN BLUEBIRD

(Sialia sialis)

Color Plate Page 277

The return of the Bluebird to our northern states in March with its purported sign of spring is not a bit of American folklore; it is a reality. When we see "the Bluebird, shifting his light load of song from post to post along the cheerless fence," spring cannot be far away. Here, then, is our true avian harbinger of warm days to come, a most welcome arrival at the thawing doorstep of a winter-weary populace.

Each March in my life, and in the lives of thousands who annually watch and wait for the first Bluebird to come north from its sojourn in the snow-free south, the soft notes of that first warbled *tru-al-ly, tru-al-ly,* are among the most satisfying songs of the out-of-doors.

There he sits on a fence post, and we watch with thankful eyes. He wears a blue velvet mantle over his back and rounded shoulders, and his breast reflects the reddish brown earth. Suddenly he darts to the ground, seizes a luckless insect, and returns to his perch. He flicks one wing each time he lands,

CATBIRD (*Dumetella carolinensis*). Length: 8.5 to 9.25 inches. Male and female: slate gray body with blackish crown, wings and tail. *Under tail coverts, chestnut.* Range: breeds from Nova Scotia to Florida and west to Texas; winters in southern United States. Voice: mewing note, similar to cat; song is disconnected series of notes and phrases.
Hal H. Harrison

and sometimes just before he takes off. But the real fluttering of wings occurs a week or so later when the female Bluebirds begin to arrive. Then, on vibrant wings, and to the accompaniment of his own incessant warbling, the male pursues his chosen mate from one perch to another.

Nesting occurs early, for at least two broods are attempted each year. Cavities in trees are natural nesting places, but man-made nest boxes are readily acceptable. A lining of grasses is placed for the four to six pale blue eggs, the lightest of all Thrush eggs.

Like young Robins, young Bluebirds have spotted breasts, displaying a true Thrush characteristic which has been lost in the adults. Young Bluebirds wear the spotted plumage until the late summer molt, after which they closely resemble the adults. The adult Bluebird is 6½ to 7½ inches long, with a solid blue back and a rusty red breast. The female is paler than the male.

Competition for nesting sites is keen among Bluebirds, House Wrens, Starlings and English Sparrows. At times, flying squirrels will usurp nesting holes and among the predators to be guarded against are snakes and mischievous Wrens with egg-puncturing habits. All is not serene in the nest life of a Bluebird!

In the fall, with nesting duties over, Bluebirds become gregarious like Robins and are found about the countryside in wandering flocks. They remain in the northern states until very late autumn when they retire to the south.

Wintering Bluebirds are not uncommon in the north however.

The breeding range of the Eastern Bluebird extends from northern Ontario to southern Florida and west to the Rockies. Two races are recognized: Eastern Bluebird *(S. s. sialis)*, and Florida Bluebird *(S. s. grata)*. Two other birds that are largely blue occur in the Bluebird's range: the Blue Jay, which has a crest and a white breast; and the Indigo Bunting, which has a blue breast as well as a blue back.

TOWNSEND'S SOLITAIRE AT NEST *(Myadestes townsendi)*. Length: 8 to 9.5 inches. Male and female: a gray body with two whitish wingbars, a white *eye-ring*, and *white sides* on the tail. Range: breeds in high mountains from Canada southward to central California. Migrates in nearby country from Canada south to Mexico. Voice: a high, thin, *see-see-see*. Song, a series of thin notes rising up the scale, then dropping into a chatter.

Gayle Pickwell

WESTERN BLUEBIRD

(Sialia mexicana)

Easterners with the sweet, warbling song of their own Bluebird fresh in their memories are invariably disappointed with the song of the Western Bluebird. Although this species replaces the eastern race in appearance and in habits in the far west, its simple song of *chu, chu, chu* in no way rivals the lovely utterance of the other. Its call note is a short "*pew*."

The Western Bluebird is 6½ to 7 inches long, with a deep chestnut back and breast and blue head, wings and tail. Some individuals have blue backs. The Mountain Bluebird has a blue breast. The Lazuli Bunting has two conspicuous white wingbars.

Two varieties of this species are recognized; Western Bluebird *(S. m. occidentalis)*, which breeds from British Columbia to western Montana and south through California, and the Chestnut-backed Bluebird *(S. m. bairdi)*, which ranges in summer from Utah and central Texas southward, following the mountains, into Mexico. It winters in Arizona, New Mexico and western Texas.

MOUNTAIN BLUEBIRD

(Sialia currucoides)

Since the range of the smaller, all-blue Indigo Bunting does not reach as far west as that of the Mountain Bluebird, one has little chance of confusing the latter with any other bird except the Blue Grosbeak. The deep blue of the Grosbeak appears black at a distance. The blue of the Mountain Bluebird is an exquisite cerulean. The Blue Grosbeak has a thick bill and two chestnut bars on its wings.

The Mountain Bluebird is 6½ to 7½ inches long, cerulean blue above and below, with a white belly. The female is dull brown with some blue on the rump, tail, and wings. Its song is a fine warble, higher than that of the Eastern Bluebird and more suggestive of the Robin's song.

WHEATEAR

(Oenanthe oenanthe)

A European bird which has gradually spread to the New World, the Greenland Wheatear belongs to the barren lands of Greenland and arctic America. In migration and in the winter, it reaches as far south as New England, Michigan, and Nebraska. It migrates to Europe and Africa, so that the birds found in the United States are casual strays.

In shape, like a small Bluebird (6¼ inches long), the Wheatear is best recognized by its brownish color, with plain cinnamon-brown underparts. The rump is white, as is the tail which is conspicuously washed with a black inverted T. It stands upright on rather long legs, but seldom stays still, bobbing its tail and hopping about. Its food is mainly insects which it catches by fluttering dashes into the air. It also eats seeds and berries.

The Wheatear breeds in Greenland and arctic America where it builds its nest in rabbit holes or crevices in rocks, etc. The five to seven eggs are pale bluish green and unmarked.

TOWNSEND'S SOLITAIRE

(Myadestes townsendi)

High, high in the mountains of the far west, breeding from Alaska to Mexico and eastward to the Black Hills of North Dakota, lives the Townsend's Solitaire, a slim gray Thrush that looks like a Catbird, feeds like a Bluebird, runs across the ground like a Robin, and sings like a Black-headed Grosbeak. A buffy mark on each wing, white outer tail feathers and a conspicuous white eye-ring are its best field marks. It is 8 or 9 inches long, and gray in color. Its song is a long warble, more rapid than the Black-headed Grosbeak's.

GNATCATCHERS and KINGLETS

Family Sylviidae

The Gnatcatchers and Kinglets are related to the Thrushes, but are distinguished by their much smaller size and by the fact that their young are not spotted. The American members of the family are not accomplished songsters. Economically, they are very valuable, feeding on leaf-eating insect larvae and plant lice.

BLUE-GRAY GNATCATCHER

(Polioptila caerulea)

Color Plate Page 280

Like the Kinglets, Gnatcatchers belong to the family *Sylviidae* and are called Old World Warblers. The Gnatcatchers are represented in America by a single genus *(Polioptila)*, and although eight forms occur in North America, only one, the Blue-gray Gnatcatcher, is found in the eastern United States.

The Blue-gray Gnatcatcher is a tiny bird (4½ to 5 inches long), no larger than a Kinglet, but it has a much longer tail. It is grayish blue above, white below, with a narrow white eye-ring. Males are brighter and have a black line over the eye. The comparatively long tail is black in the middle, white on the sides, and is very often cocked in Wren-fashion.

Blue-gray Gnatcatchers are nervous little mites, always on the move, jerking their tails, drooping or fluttering their wings, peering here and there and uttering wheezy, rasping notes that are very thin and high pitched. In Fly-

PLUMBEOUS GNATCATCHER *(Polioptila melanura)*. Length: 4.5 to 5 inches. Male and female: blue gray above, whitish below with black cap and narrow white eye-ring. Range: deserts of California, Nevada, Arizona, New Mexico, and Rio Grande Valley of western Texas. Voice: a thin querulous peee note. Its song is a thin, wheezy, series of notes.

William L. Finley, National Audubon Society

catcher-style, they often dart into the air to snare a passing insect in a complicated maneuver.

The nest of the Blue-gray Gnatcatcher is a masterful piece of bird architecture. It is constructed of plant fibers and down, decorated with lichens, and held together with spider webbing. It is placed in a crotch or very often saddled to a horizontal limb in the manner of a Hummingbird's nest.

The Western Gnatcatcher *(P. c. amoenissima)* is a geographic race of the Blue-gray Gnatcatcher *(P. c. caerulea)*.

PLUMBEOUS GNATCATCHER

(Polioptila melanura)

In the summer, when the Plumbeous Gnatcatcher wears its glossy cap, it is easily distinguished from the similar Western Gnatcatcher, whose crown is bluish gray. But when autumn comes and the two species meet in migration and spend the winter together on the southwestern deserts, the black cap of the Plumbeous has changed to gray. Then, the call notes of the two are considered better field marks than the different amount of white in the tails. Re-

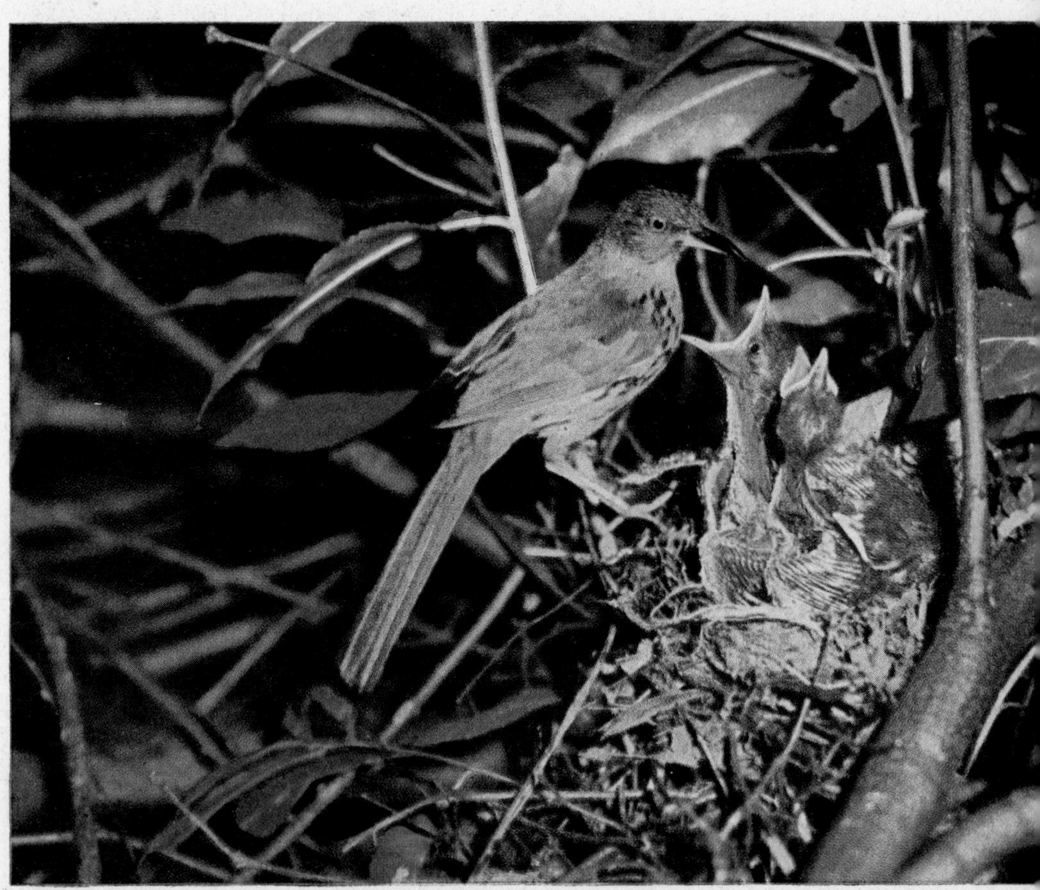

BROWN THRASHER *(Toxostoma rufum)*. Length: 10.5 to 12 inches. Male and female: upperparts brownish rufous, lower parts, buffy, heavily streaked with dark. Has long tail, curved bill, and yellow eyes. Range: breeds in eastern United States west to Rocky Mountains. Voice: song of deliberate notes and phrases.

Hal H. Harrison

URVE-BILL THRASHER (*Toxostoma curvirostre*). Length: 10.5 to 11.5 inches. Male and female: ght brownish gray upperparts. Wings double-barred with white. Blackish tail, tipped with white. nderparts grayish white spotted faintly with dark. White throat. Pale orange eye. Range: klahoma, Texas, New Mexico and southern Arizona. Voice: *whit-wheet*, song made up of notes and phrases.
Alfred M. Bailey

ırding the calls, Hoffmann states that The call of the Plumbeous Gnat-ıtcher is a series of two or three short otes, *chee chee chee*, unlike the single nphatic *pee* of the Western."

The Plumbeous Gnatcatcher (*P. m. elanura*) is 4½ inches long, blue gray oove and whitish below, with a black rown, and less white in the tail than ıe Western. He breeds in the deserts southeastern California, southern evada, Arizona, New Mexico, and ıe Rio Grande Valley in western exas. A subspecies, the Black-tailed natcatcher (*P. m. californica*), hich is dull gray beneath instead of hite, has a very limited range in uthern California. Another, the onora Gnatcatcher (*P. m. lucida*) ranges in southern Arizona and south-eastern California.

GOLDEN-CROWNED KINGLET

(*Regulus satrapa*)

Color Plate Page 282

Excepting the Hummingbirds, the Kinglets are the smallest of our birds. John Burroughs called the Golden-crowned Kinglet "a sort of 'hop-o'-my-thumb bird," and he marvelled that "so small a body can brave the giant cold of our winters."

The eastern race of the Golden-crowned Kinglet breeds in the Canadian fauna and winters southward to Florida. It is hardier than its close relative, the Ruby-crowned Kinglet, and thus is found much farther north during the winter. The Golden-crowned is a bird of the conifers, but in migration it may be found feeding in deciduous woods. As they feed actively among the branches, flitting from one twig to another, Kinglets nervously flick their wings, an identifying characteristic of the family and one that helps distinguish them from Warblers.

The Golden-crowned Kinglet is a chunky little mite, 3½ to 4 inches long, olive green above and grayish beneath, with a conspicuous white and black bordered crown patch. In the male, this patch is orange; in the female, yellow. The Golden-crown has a white stripe over the eye. The call notes, uttered often even in winter, is a three-phrased *tsee, tsee, tsee.* It is similar to the Brown Creeper's single note of *seeee.* The song is not as remarkable as that of the Ruby-crowned It is a series of ascending thin note terminating in a descending chattering. The true song is seldom heard except on the breeding grounds in th Canadian north.

The Eastern Golden-crowned Kinglet *(R. s. satrapa)* is replaced in th west by the Western Golden-crowne Kinglet *(R. s. olivaceus).*

RUBY-CROWNED KINGLET FEEDING AT WELLS DRILLED BY SAPSUCKER *(Regulus calendula).* Length: 3.75 to 4.5 inches. Male: upperparts olive, underparts grayish buff, scarlet crown patch, prominent broken white eye-ring. Female: lacks red crown patch. Range: across Canada from northwest Alaska to New Brunswick. Winters southward in United States. Voice: a husky *ji-dit.* Song: *tee tee tee tew tew tew tew-ti-dadee tidadee-ti-dadee.*

Samuel A. Grimes

RUBY-CROWNED KINGLET

(Regulus calendula)

Everyone who hears the tiny Ruby-crowned Kinglet bubbling over wit its loud, melodious warbling song i struck with the same question: "Ho can he do it?" And the question becomes all the more pertinent when w learn that the Kinglet's lower larynx the sound-producing organ, is no much bigger than a pin's head, an that the muscles that control it ar almost microscopic. Dr. Coues writes "If the strength of the human voic were in the same proportion to the siz of the larynx, we could converse wit ease at a distance of a mile or more."

The Ruby-crown, a summer resident of the Canadian spruce forest from northwestern Alaska to Nev Brunswick and Nova Scotia, and in th high mountains to southern California central Arizona and New Mexico, i known to most of us as a migrant or a winter visitor. Its characteristic song is heard repeatedly as the little mit flutters its way north each spring, feeding nervously from tree to tree as it travels.

The scarlet patch on the male's crown is usually concealed. It is exposed when the bird lifts the crown

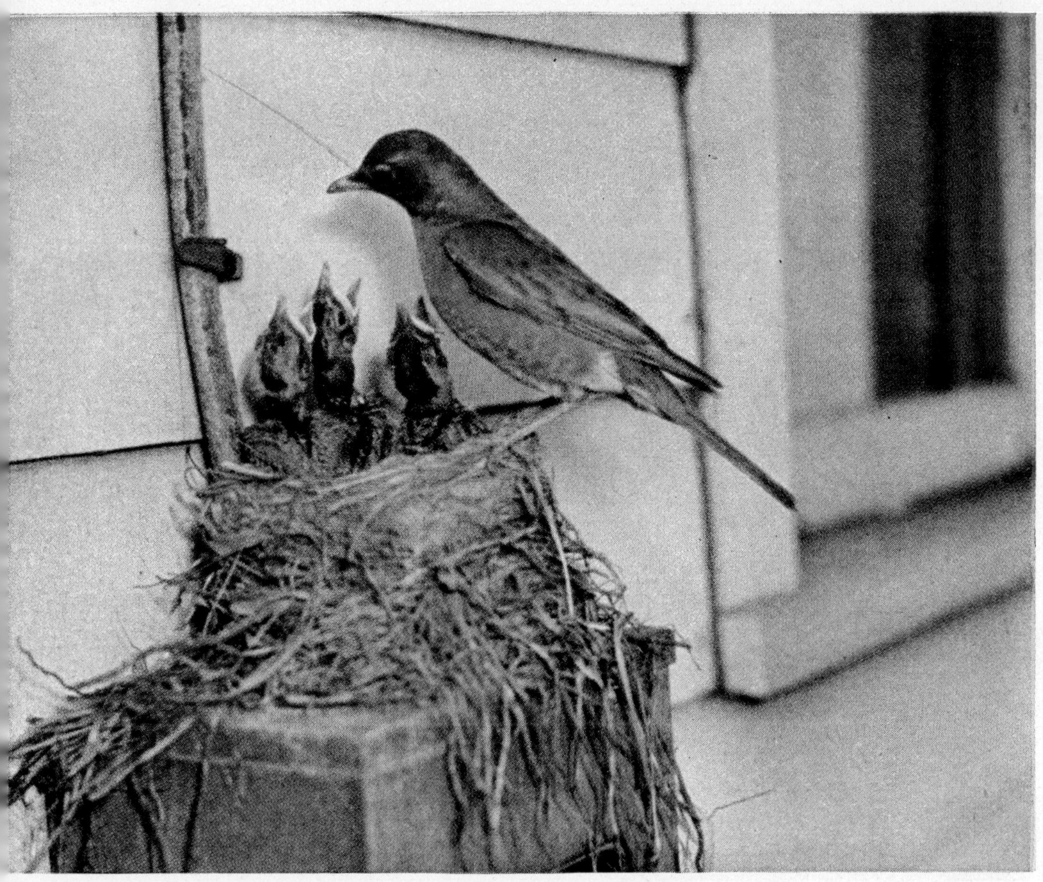

AMERICAN ROBIN (*Turdus migratorius*). Length: 8.5 to 10.5 inches. Male: black head and tail, gray back, *brick-red* breast. Female: paler throughout. Immature: speckled breast. Range: Canada south to Georgia, Mississippi and Louisiana. Winters in southern United States north to Ohio Valley and New England coast. Voice: clear whistled caroling.
Hal H. Harrison

feathers that cover it. In the Golden-crowned Kinglet, however, the crown patches of both the male and the female are always visible. The Ruby-crowned Kinglet's stubby tail and its nervous fluttering distinguish it from the Warblers with which it might be confused.

PIPITS

Family Motacillidae

A family of terrestrial birds which walk and run gracefully on the ground, rather than hopping as do most birds. Only two species are found in the United States. These birds are striped and streaked with brown, so that they appear very like the Larks. Like the Larks, too, they build their nests on the ground.

PIPIT

(Anthus spinoletta)

Color Plate Page 283

In the fall, scattered flocks of Pipits invade the United States on their southward journey from breeding grounds far to the north. It is then that bird watchers commonly get acquainted with this Sparrow-like bird of the meadows, marshes, sand dunes, beaches and plowed fields. Here he will find them walking, not hopping, in little flocks of from a dozen to a hundred, constantly wagging their tails (thus the family name of Wagtail) as they feed. When the flock is flushed, the distinguishing white tail feathers are evident in the undulating flight.

Besides the white tail feathers, there is nothing outstanding in the Pipit's plumage. It is about 6½ inches long, olive brown above with a buffy eye line. The underparts are buffy with streaks on the upper breast and sides. Its slender bill (not conical) is a good field mark if it can be seen. The name "Pipit" came from an interpretation of one of the bird's utterances. Its voice is soft and thin. Like the Skylark, it sings from high in the air during courtship.

The breeding range of the Pipit extends from the Arctic throughout northern and central Canada and along the

SPRAGUE'S PIPIT *(Anthus spragueii)*. Length: 6 to 7 inches. Male and female: upperparts, grayish brown streaked with buff and black; underparts buffy white, streaked with black. Has thin Pipit bill. Range: breeds in prairies of Montana east to mountains. Migrates through eastern Wyoming to Texas. Voice: a thin *jee-jeet*. Sings while soaring overhead.

Rudolph Hindemith, American Museum of Natural History

high mountains to New Mexico. It winters in central and southern United States and Mexico.

SPRAGUE'S PIPIT

(Anthus spragueii)

The head-bobbing, tail-jerking Missouri Skylark is a breeding bird of the Great Plains of North Dakota and Montana, east of the Rockies. Sprague's Pipit, it is called, and it may be distinguished from the more widely distributed American Pipit by its striped back and its lightly streaked breast. During the summer, however, the American Pipit is not found on the prairies but is a nesting bird of higher elevations.

WAXWINGS

Family Bombycillidae

The Waxwings are birds of the northern hemisphere, equipped with vocal chords, though they are not thought of as songbirds, and with the peculiarity of plumage which has given them their name. The coloration is soft, and they carry a long crest. Their food is mainly insects and berries.

Waxwings construct bulky nests which are often built in orchards about twenty feet or so from the ground.

BOHEMIAN WAXWING

(Bombycilla garrulus pallidiceps)

The Bohemian Waxwing is a large edition of the more common and more widely distributed Cedar Waxwing. The Bohemian nests in the Canadian northwest from Alaska south to Alberta. In winter, it is a nomadic wanderer, moving southward and eastward, often with Cedar Waxwings.

WOOD THRUSH (*Hylocichla mustelina*). Length: 7.5 to 8.5 inches. Male and female: upperparts rich brown, underparts white, spotted prominently with black. Reddish head. Range: breeds from central New Hampshire, Ontario, Minnesota and South Dakota, almost to the Gulf of Mexico. Winters from Florida south. Voice: flute-like song, *ee-e-lay*. Call, a rapid *pip-pip-pip-pip-pip*.

Hal H. Harrison

Besides its larger size (7½ to 8½ inches), the Bohemian may be distinguished from the Cedar Waxwings by the white in its wings and the chestnut under-tail coverts. The latter are white in the Cedar bird. The Bohemian lacks the wash of yellow that is evident on the belly of the other species. Its voice is a low trill.

CEDAR WAXWING

(Bombycilla cedrorum)

Color Plate Page 287

Anyone who takes a second glance at a Cedar Waxwing is impressed by the silky lustre of the bird's sleek brown and tan plumage; its refinement and quiet dignity; its unruffled poise and self-restraint even under trying circumstances; and its general demeanor that would instantly stamp a human being, who had the same qualities, as a perfect lady or gentleman.

How well the Cedar Bird's song (or lack of it) blends with its general decorum! There are no loud warblings or raucous callings, just a few high thin lisping notes strung together with a faint ringing quality. Undoubtedly its voice is one of the least developed of all our so-called song birds. It reminds one of the call notes of the Brown Creeper or Golden-crowned Kinglet. There is no particular "song period" in the bird's life, for the unchanging lisping notes are delivered throughout the year.

There is no other bird, except the more northern Bohemian Waxwing, with which the Cedar Waxwing might be confused. The sexes are alike; crested brown birds, 6½ to 8 inches long, with a black mask over the eyes and a broad yellow band at the tip of the tail. Red tips on the ends of the secondary feathers form little spots that look like bits of sealing wax on the folded wings; thus the name "Waxwing." The Bohemian is larger, has white wingbars, yellow-edged primaries, and rich brown under-tail coverts which are white in the Cedar Waxwing.

Like that notoriously late nester, the Goldfinch, the Cedar Waxwing flocks comb the countryside for fruit and berries until mid-June when a few pairs start to nest. The height of the breeding season, however, occurs in late July and early August. Since Cedar Waxwings are double-brooded, it is not

BOHEMIAN WAXWING *(Bombycilla garrulus pallidiceps)*. Length: 7.5 to 8.5 inches. Upperparts brownish gray, darker on wings and tail. Under tail coverts chestnut red. Crested head; neck and underparts beige becoming yellow on belly. Has broad yellow band on end of tail and bright red on tips of secondary wings. Range: breeds in western Canada; winters irregularly to north central states and rarely to northeastern states. Voice: low trill.
United States Fish and Wildlife Service, by O. J. Murie

uncommon to find young in the nest in September. Indeed, the color photograph on page 287 was taken in western Pennsylvania on September 8th.

The Waxwing builds a large nest of grasses, rootlets, and fibrous material. Characteristic of all nests that I have seen are the long streamers of grass that are permitted to hang from the nest and wave in the breeze below. The three or four eggs are bluish gray, spotted with black, brown or lavender.

The sight of a Cedar Waxwing regurgitating cherries or other fruit into the mouths of the young is a memorable one. The adult arrives at the nest with its throat bulging with juicy cargo. The parallel lines of the neck indicate a full gullet. The young begging for food serve as a stimulus for the adults to bring up the food, one berry at a time. Like a fish traveling down the long neck of a heron, each berry may be watched as it descends the youngster's throat. The capacity of an adult gullet seems endless as one berry after another pops out.

The Waxwing is guilty of raids on orchards, especially cherry trees, although much wild fruit is eaten too. Insects also form an important part of the bird's diet. This fact was brought home to me one June day while I was driving along the shore of a winding river. Cedar Waxwings, hundreds of them, were hovering and fluttering like Flycatchers above the water, feeding on insects, possibly newly hatched cadis-flies or May-flies.

The Cedar Waxwing breeds throughout southern Canada and most of the United States, except California.

SILKY FLYCATCHERS

Family Ptilogonatidae

The Silky Flycatchers are limited to Central America. One species only reaches the United States. They are like the Waxwings in general habits. The nests are built in woodlands, and are loosely constructed of twigs and mosses.

PHAINOPEPLA

(Phainopepla nitens lepida)

Color Plate Page 290

The Phainopepla is a tropical Flycatcher that has extended its range to include the mountainous regions of southwestern United States from western Texas to California. It is called the Silky Flycatcher or Shining Crested Flycatcher because of the satin-like sheen of its glossy, blue-black plumage. In flight, white patches are conspicuous in the wings. The crest is slender and pointed. The female Phainopepla is brownish gray with a crest. The bird is 7 to 8 inches long.

The male Phainopepla is almost as unusual as the male Phalarope among the shore birds. He alone builds the nest, a saucer-like structure of plant fibers and twigs placed in a tree. While building, he has been known to drive the female away. The male then does a large share of the incubating and feeding of the young.

The song of this bird is a casual warble; its note is a low *wurp*.

SHRIKES

Family Laniidae

The common name of the Shrikes, Butcher Birds, comes from their habit of impaling their prey of insects, small birds, and mammals upon thorns. Only one genus is found in America, and three species occur in the United States.

NORTHERN SHRIKE

(Lanius excubitor)

The Loggerhead Shrikes have their northern counterpart in the Northern Shrike, a larger bird (9 to 10½ inches)

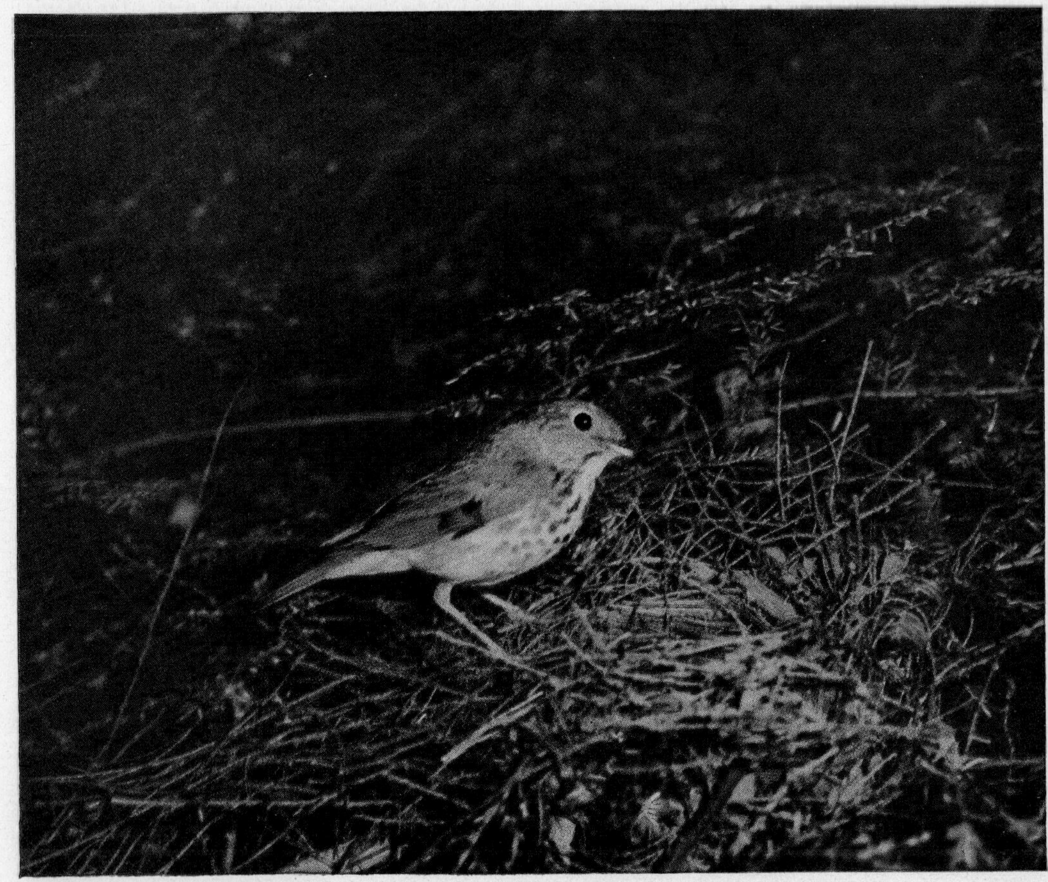

HERMIT THRUSH *(Hylocichla guttata)*. Length: 6.5 to 7.5 inches. Male and female: russet brown upperparts, white underparts spotted with dark. Conspicuous reddish tail. Range: Canada south to California and throughout mountains in western United States. Winters from Oregon, Arizona and New Mexico, south. Voice: clear flute-like song. Note, a low *chuck* or *quilp*; also *tuk-tuk-tuk* and a harsh *pay*.
Hal H. Harrison

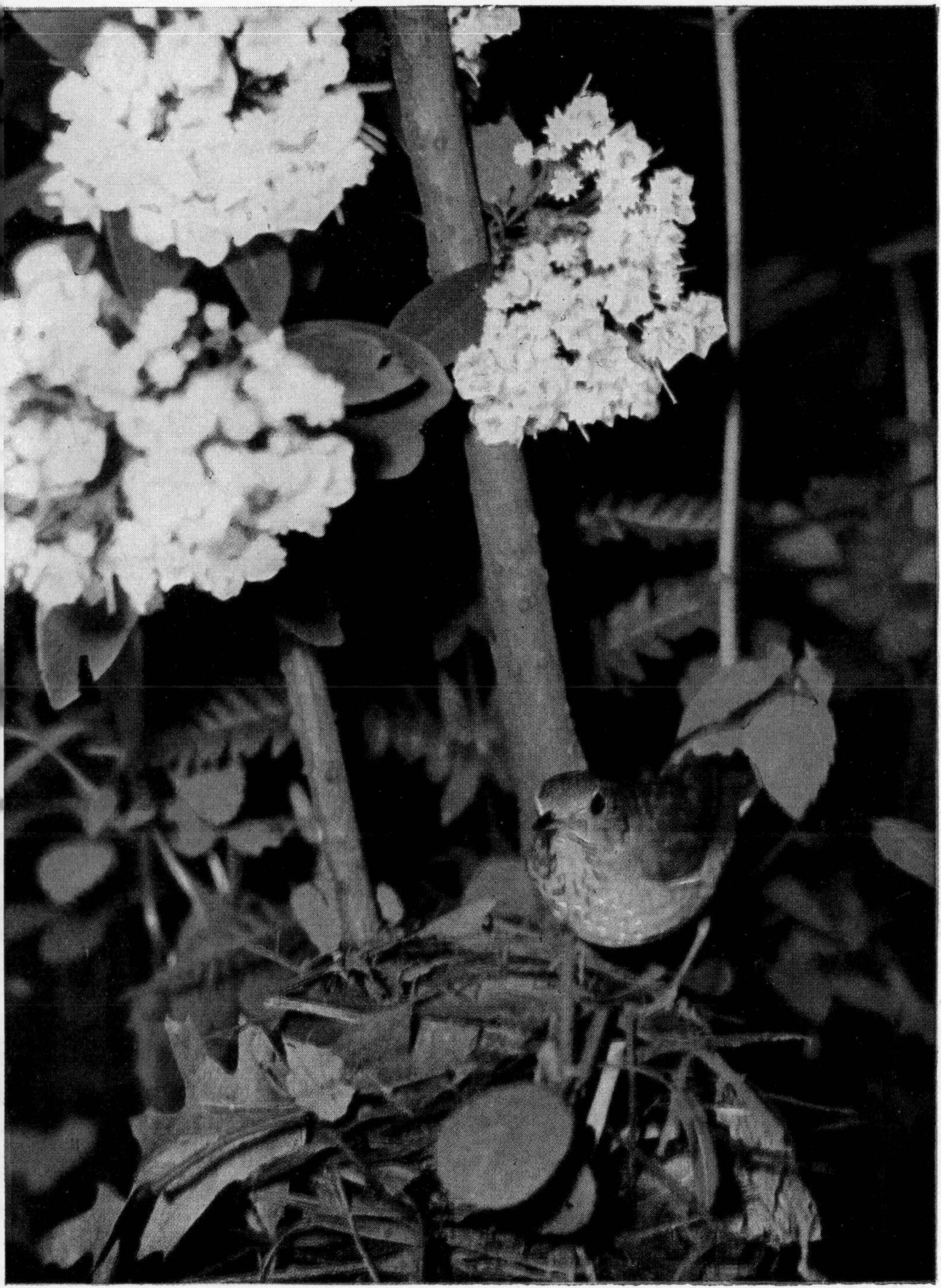

VEERY AT NEST IN LAUREL (*Hylocichla fuscescens*). Length: 6.5 to 7.5 inches. Male and female: upperparts cinnamon brown; underparts buff and white spotted with light brown. Range: Newfoundland to Indiana, New Jersey and Iowa. Migrates through southern United States. Winters in South America. Voice: whistles which coast downward; *vee-ur, vee-ur, veer veer*. Note, *phew* or *view*.
Hal H. Harrison

with dusky gray bars on the breast. The habits of the Northern are very similar to those of the Loggerhead (which see), but the former is more likely to be observed in the United States in winter. Its breeding range is from the limit of trees to southern Canada. In the winter, it moves south as far as central California, Arizona, New Mexico, Texas, Kentucky, and Virginia. Two races are recognized; Northern Shrike *(L.e. borealis)* and Northwestern Shrike *(L.e. invictus)*.

LOGGERHEAD SHRIKE

(Lanius ludovicianus)

Color Plate Page 294

"Butcher Bird" is a common name earned by the Shrike because of its habit of killing more than it needs for food, a condition normally rare among birds. It is a bird of prey among songbirds, a unique position, for as it mingles with other small birds, they do not recognize it as a killer in the evident manner that they fear Hawks and Owls. Its slow, rather clumsy flight, might make capturing its prey difficult were it not for this fact.

Members of the Shrike family have the characteristic habit of impaling their prey upon thorns, barbed wire, and twigs. Although it is generally thought that this habit is merely a matter of storing up food for future consumption, the fact that the Shrike's feet are very weak and unfit for grasping probably had led it to impale its prey to hold it secure while the bird feeds.

NORTHERN SHRIKE *(Lanius excubitor)*. Length: 9 to 10.5 inches. Male and female: Robin-sized. Light gray above and white with gray below. Has *black mask* through eyes. Bill has hooked upper mandible. Range: breeds from tree limits south to southern Ontario and southern Quebec. Winters south irregularly to Kentucky and Virginia. Voice: song is sweet, varied warbled notes, but harsher than the Thrasher's song.

Chicago Natural History Museum

Shrikes hunt from favorite lookouts from which they can fly to seize a bird, grasshopper, lizard, snake, or small mammal. In the manner of birds of prey, Shrikes disgorge indigestible parts of their food in the form of pellets or castings which often advertise their nests.

Wastelands grown up to thorn trees are ideal nesting and hunting grounds for Shrikes. The nest of bark strips, twigs, and vegetable fibers, lined with grasses and feathers, is placed in a thorny tree or bush. Three to five eggs are laid, creamy white, thickly marked with cinnamon-brown or lavender. The male's voice is harsh and unmusical.

Shrikes are chunky birds, gray above, white below, big headed and long tailed. A black mask crosses the eyes. The Loggerhead Shrike is 9 inches long. His black mask extends across the forehead at the base of the bill. This mark is absent in the similar Northern Shrike, a larger bird. The latter also has scaled or barred underparts, absent in the Loggerhead races. A Shrike's flight is characteristic, a series of alternate flappings and sailings with an upward sweep at the end as it comes to rest. In flight, a white area is conspicuous in the black wings.

Loggerhead Shrikes are generally distributed throughout all parts of the United States. The family is divided into nine geographic races, all similar. They are: Loggerhead *(L.l. ludovicianus)*, Migrant *(L.l. migrans)*, White-rumped *(L.l. excubitorides)*, California *(L.l. gambeli)*, Nelson's *(L.l. nelsoni)*, Island *(L.l. anthonyi)*, Sonora *(L.l. sonoriensis)*, Grinnell's *(L.l. grinnelli)*, and Mearns's *(L.l. mearnsi)*.

WHITE-RUMPED SHRIKE

(Lanius ludovicianus excubitorides)

Color Plate Page 295

The White-rumped Shrike, a bird of the arid west, is a race of the Loggerhead Shrike. It is similar to the more common migrant Shrike, but is paler gray. The division between the gray back and the white upper tail coverts is more abrupt. The underparts are whiter.

The common name of Mouse Bird which is applied to this species comes from its beneficial habit of preying upon field mice, shrews and moles. It also captures small birds and occasionally lizards.

Its habits are similar to other members of the family.

STARLINGS

Family Sturnidae

The Starlings are Old World birds, of which one species was introduced into the United States in 1890. It has become naturalized to such an extent that it is considered a nuisance in many localities.

STARLING

(Sturnus vulgaris vulgaris)

Color Plate Page 297

Regardless of what any of us may think about it, the Starling has come to America to stay. The spread of this European immigrant since it was successfully introduced into Central Park in 1890 and 1891, has been phenomenal. Today, it is one of our commonest eastern birds, and its range has been extended to the Rocky Mountains. It is just a matter of time until the Pacific Coast states are invaded as successfully as the rest of the country.

The Starling's success in America has not been popular for three important reasons; the bird's aggressiveness against native hole-nesting species; its depredation of cherries, apples, corn, and garden produce; and its objectionable roosting habits. The public is most conscious of the last, for in many places the communal roostings of these birds present a serious problem.

The deafening noise of a flock of several thousand Starlings at daybreak or in the evening, plus the filth associated with such a huge flock confined to a small area, is decidedly objectionable. Tree roosts are usually abandoned in winter in favor of warmer church steeples, ledges beneath the eaves of city buildings, and similarly protected places.

In April, the flocks break up into mated pairs, and for awhile the roosts are abandoned. Each pair establishes a nesting site in a suitable cavity, and the birds are not fussy about the place chosen. Holes in trees (confiscated from Bluebirds or Flickers, if necessary), nesting boxes, eaves of houses, holes in roofs or gables, church towers, ledges in barns, walls of old buildings, and scores of such places are acceptable.

The cavity is filled with sticks and grasses and lined with feathers and finer grasses. The five or six eggs are pale blue, very similar to Robin's eggs. Both sexes incubate. Young Starlings remain in the nest until they can fly.

The broods are on the wing by mid-June, and flocks begin to assemble again. At this time, the bird's greatest depredations occur, for these wandering flocks descend upon fruit trees and gardens. To the Starling's credit, however, is the fact that the bird also feeds extensively upon grasshoppers, cut worms, various grubs, Japanese beetles, and millepedes.

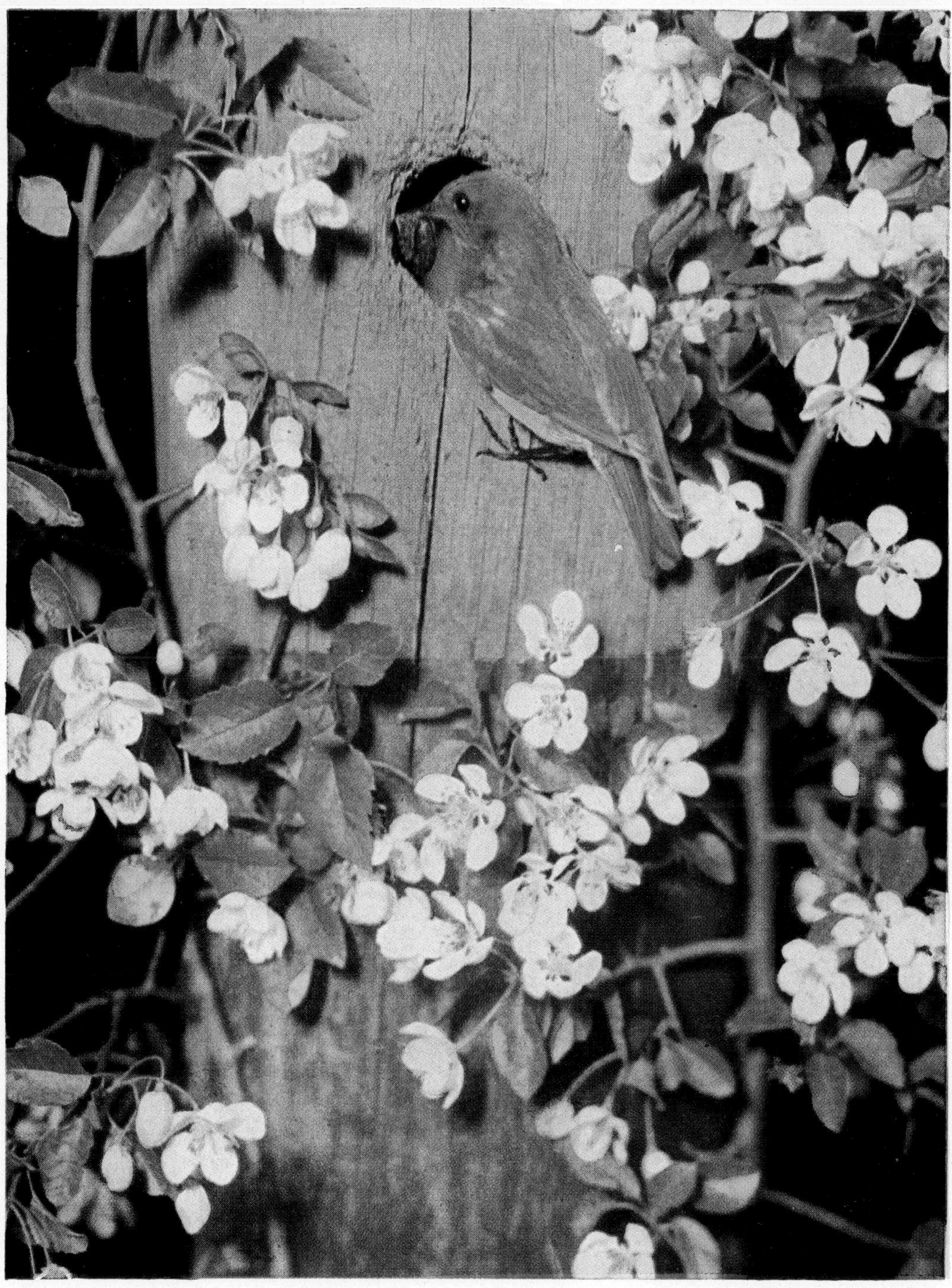

BLUEBIRD IN CRABAPPLE (*Sialia sialis*). Length: 6.5 to 7.5 inches. Male: upperparts bright blue. Underparts: brownish-orange, abdomen and underneath tail coverts, white. Females: duller than male. Immature: grayish, and speckle-breasted. Range: eastern United States from Newfoundland to Gulf of Mexico; winters north to Ohio Valley and occasionally to Great Lakes. Voice: a gurgling song of three or four notes.

Hal H. Harrison

The Starling's breeding plumage is iridescent green and purple. The bill is bright yellow. Starlings have shorter tails, longer bills and more pointed wings than blackbirds; they are 7½ to 8½ inches long. Their flight is swift and flocks appear in the air in compact formation.

In the fall and winter, the Starling's bill is dusky brown and its feathers are flecked with white and buff. Starlings in juvenile plumage are grayish like female cowbirds. In the fall, they acquire the spangled winter plumage of the adults.

The best known call of the Starling is a drawn out whistle. The bird's ability to imitate the songs of other birds was noticeable during a Christmas bird census one year. Several members of our party had already written the name of Bob-white in their notebooks when the Starling imitating the Quail's call was discovered on a fence post across a nearby field. I have often heard it imitate a Killdeer.

VIREOS

Family Vireonidae

The Vireos are residents of America, mainly tropical, but a number of species are found in the United States. They are small birds, very similar, and indeed identification of the individual species is sometimes very difficult. Their family name, meaning "I am green" comes from the general tendency toward an olive or greenish coloring. They are also known as Greenlets. They suspend their nests, which are finely woven, from a forked branch.

BLACK-CAPPED VIREO

(Vireo atricapillus)

Rather more energetic and sprightly than the other birds, the Black-cap breeds in the south-central portion of the United States, locally in Kansas, Oklahoma, and Texas. The bird is 4½ inches long, olive green over the back and wings. Its best identification is the white eye-ring, and the top of the head and neck which is black in the male, and grayish in the female. The breast is whitish, merging into yellowish on the flanks. The wings are conspicuously marked with two bars which are yellow in the male, and whitish in the female,

Its song varies from harsh to sweet and consists of a number of different phrases. Its alarm note is a harsh and unmusical chirp. It builds its nest in thick shrubbery in gullies or canyons. It is a perfectly woven structure of bark strips, grasses, skeleton leaves, spider webs, and caterpillar silk. The four white eggs are unmarked.

HUTTON'S VIREO *(Vireo huttoni)*. Length: 4.25 to 4.75 inches. Male and female: upperparts, dull olive brownish gray, with two broad white wingbars, a partial eye-ring, and a large, light spot between eye and bill. Underparts dull whitish, washed on sides with yellowish. Range: resident in Pacific states and oak belt of mountains of southeast Arizona, southwest New Mexico and western Texas. Voice: a hoarse, double-noted *zu-weep* with rising inflection, also a hoarse *day, de-de-de-de.*

Rudolph Hindemith, American Museum of Natural History

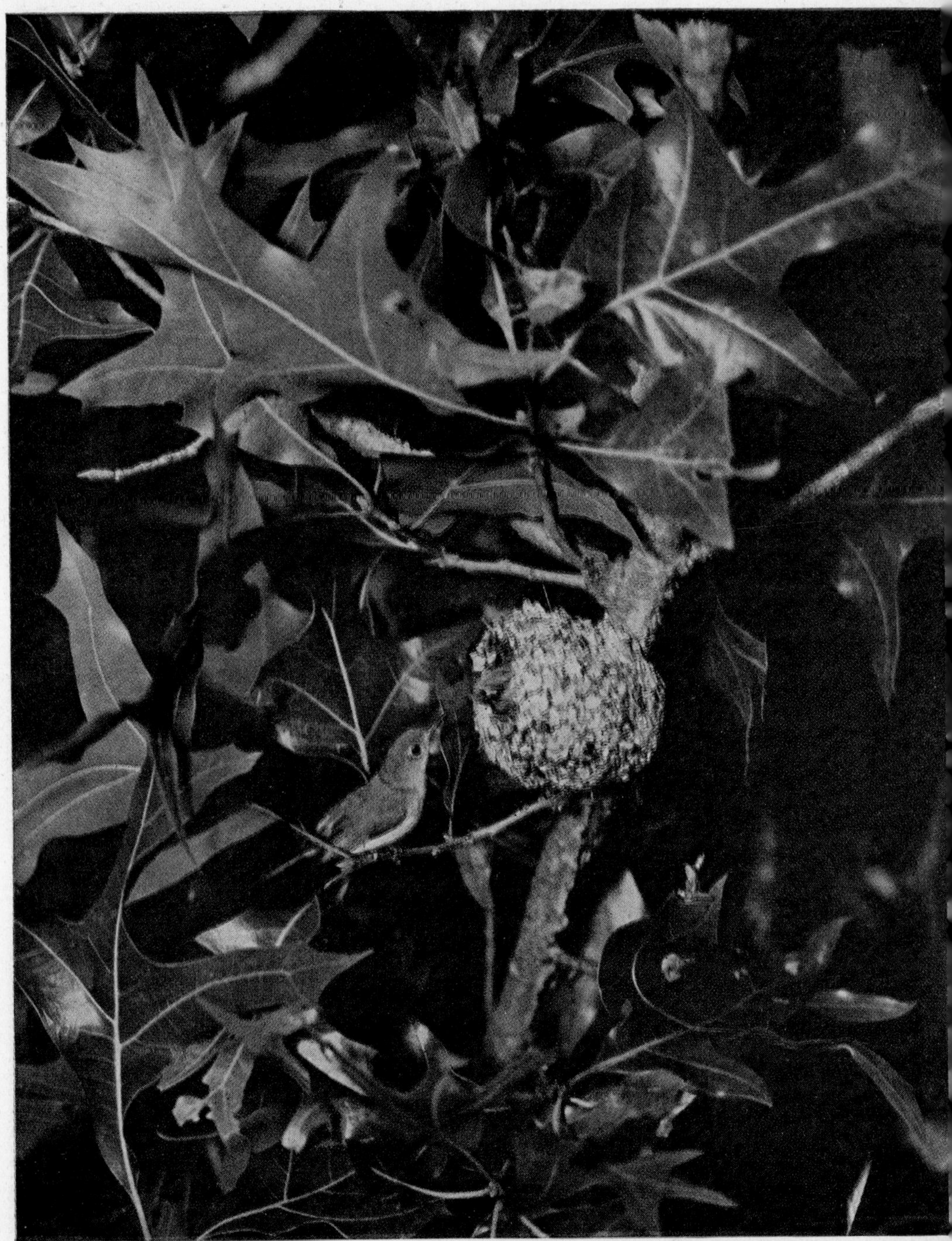

BLUE-GRAY GNATCATCHER (*Polioptila caerulea*). Length: 4.5 to 5 inches. Male: upperparts bluish gray with narrow white eye-ring and U-shaped black mark on forehead. The tail is long and black in center, white on sides. Underparts are grayish white. Female: upperparts brownish gray and lacks U-shaped forehead mark. Range: southern New Jersey, southwest Pennsylvania, extreme southern Ontario, southern Michigan and southern Iowa south to Gulf of Mexico; winters from coastal South Carolina, southern Mississippi and southern Texas south. Voice: song, thin and squeaky. Note *zpee*.

Samuel A. Grimes.

WHITE-EYED VIREO

(Vireo griseus)

Color Plate Page 300

BELL'S VIREO ON NEST *(Vireo belli)*. Length: 4.75 to 5 inches. Male and female: upperparts, olive brown, washed with greenish on the upper tail coverts. Faint white wingbars and narrow light eye-ring. Underparts, dull sulphur yellowish white. Range: breeds in California, southern Arizona, southwest New Mexico, and western Texas, also eastern Colorado. Voice: song, low and husky, *cheedle, cheedle, chee? cheedle, cheedle, chew!*
Donald M. Menke, National Audubon Society

"I have never known bird to change its song nd the tempo of its ng so completely and rapidly as the White-ed Vireo. I detected otes of the Catbird, ouse Wren, Towhee, nd Tufted Titmouse in s repertoire. This bird ossesses Mimic Thrush ualities in its versatile ng." I made that note ne May morning just ter I had listened to feeding White-eyed ireo in a crabapple icket. My observations ave been certified many times by other bservers who consider this pert little rd most loquacious and un-Vireo-ke in its utterances. The White-eyed ireo is smaller than the Red-eyed 4½ to 5½ inches). Its upperparts e olive; eye-ring, yellow; iris of the e, white; wings with two whitish rs; underparts, white; sides, washed ith yellow.

The Yellow-throated Vireo and the lue-headed Vireo both possess wing-rs like the White-eyed, but the dark ayish blue head, combined with pure hite underparts distinguishes the lue-headed; while the Yellow-roated Vireo's bright yellow throat is agnostic.

The White-eyed should be looked for bushes and thickets rather than in ll trees. It breeds from Minnesota and ew Hampshire south to Texas and orida. It winters in Florida, the Gulf oast, Mexico, and Central America.

The geographic races of this species include the Southern White-eyed Vireo *(V. g. griseus)*, Key West Vireo *(V. g. maynardi)*, Bermuda Vireo *(V. g. bermudianus)*, Rio Grande Vireo *(V. g. micrus)*, and Northern White-eyed Vireo *(V. g. noveboracensis)*.

HUTTON'S VIREO

(Vireo huttoni)

Hutton's Vireo *(V. h. huttoni)* is a resident bird throughout its range on the Pacific Coast west of the Sierras and the Cascades, from southern British Columbia south to Baja California. A subspecies, Stephen's Vireo *(V. h. stephensi)* is found in southeastern Arizona, New Mexico, and western Texas.

This is a small (4½ inches long), olive-colored Vireo with white wing-bars and dingy yellow underparts. The

GOLDEN-CROWNED KINGLET (*Regulus satrapa*). Length: 3.5 to 4 inches. Male: upperparts oli gray; underparts, olive white, conspicuous orange crown and *white stripe* over the eye. Fema similar to male but with yellow crown patch. Range: Manitoba throughout northern Americ Winters from southern Canada to Gulf of Mexico. Voice: high call note *see-see-see*. Song seri of high thin notes.
Fred Bashour

whitish eye-ring is incomplete above. Although it is apt to be confused with the Ruby-crowned Kinglet, the more deliberate actions of the Vireo, its heavier bill, and slightly larger size are its best distinguishing marks, especially in winter.

BELL'S or LEAST VIREO

(Vireo belli)

The Bell's, or Least Vireo is the most nondescript of the Greenlet family, being similar to the White-eyed Vireo i general coloration and wingbars, bu lacking the yellow-spectacled eyes c the latter as well as the white eye itsel It is about 5 inches long. Bell's is a bir of the bottomland thicket, willow and streamside bushes, and the thic brush of the arid southwest. Nestin and feeding occur quite low, the bir seldom venturing more than ten fe above the ground.

The song of Bell's Vireo is a jumb of warbled notes, delivered rapidly an without much musical ability.

PIT *(Anthus spinoletta)*. Length: 6 to 7 inches. Male and female: upperparts brownish gray; nderparts buffy streaked with dark, outer tail feathers, white. Range: from Canada south to Oregon and northern New Mexico. Voice: thin *jee jeet* or *pi-pit*.
Harlan E. Eckler

Four geographic races occur in the ;enus. They are generally distributed rom northwestern Indiana, southern outh Dakota, northeastern Colorado, outhwestern New Mexico, southern Arizona and northern California south o central Texas and Mexico. The races are: Bell's Vireo *(V.b. bellii)*, Texas Vireo *(V.b. medius)*, Arizona Vireo *(V.b. arizonae)* and Least Vireo *(V.b. pusillus)*. There are no discernible field lifferences.

GRAY VIREO

(Vireo vicinior)

Arid slopes of southwestern mounains are the favorite habitat of the Gray Vireo, a Greenlet that is very similar to he Least Vireo, except that it lacks wingbars. It is about 5½ inches long. The Least is a bird of the bottomlands and would not be found nesting near the Gray.

Hoffmann says of the song of the Gray Vireo: "The song is divided into three of four separate phrases which follow each other in regular sequence; these are repeated over and over with untiring persistence." Although the song of the Gray resembles the Cassin's Solitary Vireo and the Plumbeous Solitary Vireo, neither would be found nesting in chaparral country. Indeed, no other Vireo's breeding range coincides with the Gray's in much of its habitat.

The Gray Vireo is found nesting in southern California, Nevada, southwestern Colorado, and extreme western Oklahoma, and south into Mexico.

YELLOW-THROATED VIREO

(Vireo flavifrons)

Color Plate Page 304

Like the Warbling Vireo, the Yellow-throated Vireo is often so difficult to see that it is well to be familiar with its song for positive identification. The song is similar to the Red-eyed Vireo's, but it is huskier and lower pitched. It has been suggested that the Red-eyed Vireo's voice is soprano, the Yellow-throated's contralto. The rich notes, slurred together in a Robin-like carol, are much pleasanter than the Red-eyed's song.

The bright yellow throat of this species is distinctive, no other Vireo possesses such brilliant coloring. The bird is 5 to 6 inches long. Its upperparts are olive, the wings have two whitish bars, and its belly is white. Tall deciduous trees in rural areas, in villages, and in parks are the home of this species. Here it feeds and sings; here it builds its typical Vireo cuplike nest.

The breeding range of the Yellow-throated Vireo extends from souther[n] Manitoba, southern Quebec, an[d] Maine, south to the northern portio[n] of the Gulf States. It winters in Mexic[o] and South America.

BLUE-HEADED VIREO

(Vireo solitarius)

Color Plate Page 305

"Tamest Wild Bird I Have Eve[r] Known."

In my notebook, that title belongs t[o] the Blue-headed Vireo. From the firs[t] time I met it on its breeding ground in Cook Forest State Park, Pennsylvania, no other song bird has impresse[d] me as being quite as tame and trustin[g] of human association as this Solitar[y] Vireo.

The first nest I ever found was hun[g] seven feet from the ground on th[e] forked branch of a sapling white pine[.] It was a typical Vireo "basket," heavil[y] covered with bits o[f] paper on the outside. I[t] contained four whit[e] eggs sparsely spotte[d] with black about th[e] large end. One of th[e] parent birds was incubating. (To me th[e] sexes are indistinguishable).

As I set up my ladde[r] and camera equipment[,] I was surprised to discover that my subjec[t] did not move from th[e] nest. Most birds ar[e] gone long before this[.] I focused through th[e] ground glass and flashe[d] my pictures with th[e] Vireo in front of me al

GRAY VIREO (*Vireo vicinior*). Length: 5.5 to 5.75 inches. Male and female: upperparts and sides of head, a dull gray; underparts, dull grayish white. Has *narrow* white eye-ring. Range: breeds from southern California, southern Nevada, southwest Colorado, and extreme western Oklahoma, south into Mexico. Voice: song, a rapid and patchy series of short whistled phrases, with a rising and falling inflection.

Rudolph Hindemith, American Museum of Natural History

the time. Finally, I reached over to touch the bird and was able to stroke its back. The only protest was a rather feeble attempt to peck my hand.

Since then I have found many nests of this bird, and the fearlessness of the adults has always been the same. They seemed to be oblivious to any intrusion. Other observers, however, have found nesting birds that were quite fussy about any human approach. One day, I took a family of four well-feathered young from the nest and placed them in my son's cupped hands. The old birds landed on his hands to feed.

The Blue-headed Vireo (5 to 6 inches long) may be recognized by its bluish gray head, white eye-ring, and pure white throat. These characteristics distinguish it from the Yellow-throated Vireo and the White-eyed Vireo which possess wingbars similar to the Blue-headed.

The song of the Blue-headed Vireo is more pleasing than the song of the more abundant Red-eyed Vireo. Although their songs are similar, the Solitary's offering is much richer and uttered more leisurely. Forbush calls it a "wild, sweet song, a charming cadance of the wooded wilderness."

Bradford Tory writes of its song: "In form its music resembles the Red-eye's, the Philadelphia's, and the Yellow-throat's; but to me it is more varied and beautiful than any of these, though some listeners may prefer the Yellow-throat for the richness and fullness of its 'organ tone.' The Solitary's song is matchless for the tenderness of its cadence, while in peculiarly happy moments the bird indulges in a continuous warble that is really enchanting."

An amusing incident involving this bird's song occurred at Cook Forest. One phrase of the Blue-headed's repertoire reminded a feminine member of our party so much of the war-popular "G.I. whistle" that once she actually turned to see the fresh fellow who was whistling at her!

Geographic forms of the Blue-headed Vireo include the Northern Blue-headed Vireo *(V.s. solitarius)*; Mountain Vireo *(V.s. alticola)* in the south; and Plumbeous Vireo *(V.s. plumbeus)* and Cassin's Vireo *(V.s. cassinii)* in the west.

PLUMBEOUS VIREO

(Vireo solitarius plumbeus)

A race of the Solitary Vireo, the Plumbeous Vireo is a bird of the Rocky Mountain regions from northern Nevada, northern Utah, southern Montana, southeastern Wyoming, and south into Mexico. It is uniformly gray above, and may thus be distinguished from its close relative the Cassin's Vireo which has an olive back. The latter breeds in the Pacific states and closely resembles the type species, the Blue-headed Vireo (which see) of the east.

The Blue-headed Vireo and western species are similar in habits.

BLACK-WHISKERED VIREO

(Vireo altiloquus barbatulus)

A bird of southern Florida, the Black-whiskered Vireo is identical with the Red-eyed except for the narrow black streak, or whisker, on either side of the throat. Its song is made up of various short phrases which suggest its local names, such as *whip-Tom-Kelly*, or *cheap-John-stir-up*. It builds its cuplike nest in mangrove forests, and the three eggs are purplish in color.

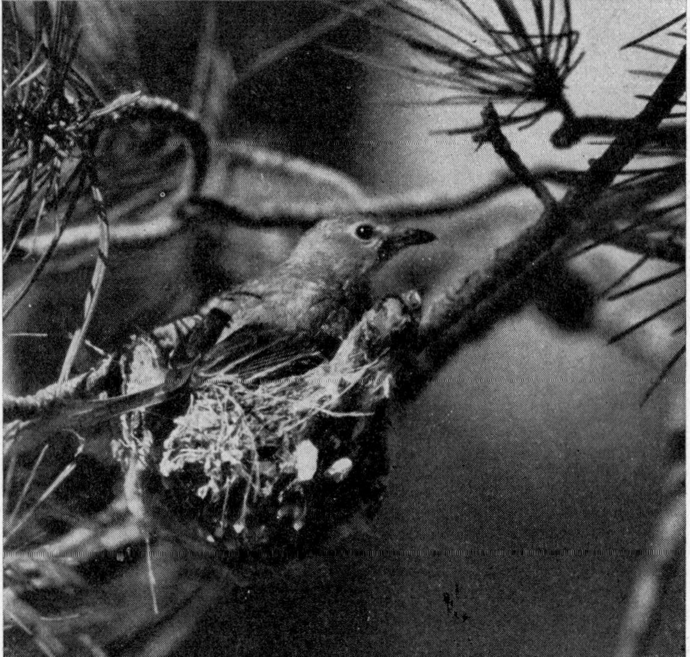

SOLITARY (PLUMBEOUS) VIREO ON NEST *(Vireo solitarius plumbeus).* Length: 5 to 6 inches. Male and female: entire upperparts dark slate gray; sides of the body washed with leaden gray. Has conspicuous white eye-ring, and wingbars. Range: Rocky Mountains from Nevada, northern Utah, southern Montana, and southeast Wyoming south into Mexico. Voice: series of short whistled phrases, with a rising or falling inflection, with short wait between phrases.

Alfred M. Bailey and R. J. Niedrach, National Audubon Society

YELLOW-GREEN VIREO

(Vireo flavoviridis)

The Yellow-green Vireo is considered by ornithologists to be a race of the Red-eyed Vireo, but the A.O.U. gives it specific rank. A bird of Central America, it is occasionally found breeding in southern Texas. It is similar to the Red-eyed Vireo, but is much greener above, and its under-tail coverts are yellow. It is about 6½ inches long. Its voice is like the Red-eyed Vireo, but the phrases are shorter. It nests in thickly leaved shrubs and lays its three white eggs in a deep cup which is often decorated with spiders' egg cases. The bird winters south to northern South America.

RED-EYED VIREO

(Vireo olivaceus)

Color Plate Page 309

No bird sings more than the Red-eyed Vireo. No bird could, for this little Greenlet utters its two, three, and four note phrases continuously from dawn until dusk, day in and day out, from May until September. Like so many questions and answers, depending upon the inflection given each phrase, the Vireo sings *Here I am! Here I am! See me? Don't you see me? Here I am! See me? See me?* and on and on and on in ceaseless repetition. It is somewhat Robin-like in character but it is a broken song not a continuous caroling, made up of deliberate phrases.

As a family, the Vireos are closely related to the Warblers, and, like the Warblers, they are small, tree-inhabiting birds whose diet is largely insectivorous. That they should often be mistaken for Warblers, or vice versa, is excusable. Certain Warblers are colored very much like Vireos (Tennessee, Pine and Nashville, for instance), and in the treetops as they glean their food among the leaves, they often present a challenge to the bird watcher.

Although Vireos are less active than Warblers, less fluttery in their movements, generally duller in coloration, with larger heads and thicker bills, the best field mark is their diagnostic songs. With the exception of the White-eyed

EDAR WAXWING (*Bombycilla cedrorum*). Length: 6.5 to 8 inches. Sleek brown bird with long crest. p of tail broadly banded with yellow and also yellow on abdomen. Range: Gulf of St. Lawrence south to North Carolina, Georgia and Kansas. Voice: thin lisp zeee.
Hal H. Harrison

'ireo, the songs of the Vireos are some-vhat similar and when one learns the notes of the common Red-eyed, he has he basis for identification of the other /ireos.

In appearance, the Red-eyed Vireo's pest field mark is the black-bordered vhite stripe over the eye. The gray cap s not seen often, and the red eye is of little help at a distance. It is 5½ to ½ inches long, olive-green above, vhite below and has no wingbars. The Philadelphia Vireo lacks wingbars too, out it is yellowish beneath. The Warbling Vireo does not have wingbars either, but its head is indistinctly striped.

Like the nests of all members of the family, the Red-eyed's is a neat, beautifully constructed, pendulous cup, attached to the forks of horizontal twigs. Fibers, wood stems, plant down, leaves, and papers are the basis for the nest, which is woven and held together with cobwebs. The materials used in construction serve well as a camouflage in the summer, but the weathered, black nests are very conspicuous hanging in the leafless winter trees. Although most nests are placed low, I have found some thirty feet or higher. Young maples and shads are used extensively. The bird lays four white eggs sparsely spotted with black.

As a bird student who has specialized in getting up in the middle of the night to see what the Cowbird is doing at dawn, I have had more than my share of luck at the nest of the Red-eyed Vireo. This species is a common victim, and I have caught the Cowbird at dawn on two different occasions laying her parasitic eggs in the Red-eyed's nest. In the case of other victims, the Cowbird usually waits until its host has laid one or more of its own eggs, but she often lays the first egg in this Vireo's nest. The little Greenlet then does one of three things: deserts the nest, builds a false bottom over the Cowbird egg, or does nothing at all. The latter course is the common one. In one summer, I studied twelve different nests of this species, ten of which were parasitized by the Cowbird.

The breeding range of the Red-eyed Vireo includes all of eastern United States and southern Canada, and in the northwest to the Pacific coast and southern Mackenzie River. It winters in South America. There are no subspecies.

PHILADELPHIA VIREO

(Vireo philadelphicus)

Although the Philadelphia Vireo is similar to the Warbling Vireo, it may be distinguished by its yellow underparts. This in combination with the lack of bars on the wings should be unmistakable. At close range the dark spot between eye and bill is corroboration. The bird is 4½ to 5 inches long, somewhat smaller than other Vireos.

The Philadelphia Vireo is distributed throughout eastern North America, breeding from Ontario and Manitoba south to northern New England and northern Michigan. It migrates to Cer tral America for the winter.

Its call is like that of the Red-eye Vireo, but higher pitched and mo disconnected. It builds its cuplike ne rather high in a deciduous tree. Th four eggs are white with brown spots.

WARBLING VIREO

(Vireo gilvus)

Color Plate Page 312

It is well to learn the song of th Eastern Warbling Vireo *(V. g. gilvus* for the bird is very difficult to see as i gleans its food from the tops of ta elms, oaks, maples, and other shad trees along village streets. The song i unlike other Vireos, lacking the shor utterances characteristic of the family As its name implies, the song is a war ble, resembling the song of the Purpl Finch, but more languid.

The Warbling Vireo is rather non descript: grayish or olive upperparts whitish underparts, and a faint whit line over the eye. It has no wingbars Two other eastern Vireos lack wing bars: the Red-eyed and the Philadel phia. The Red-eyed may be distin guished by its pronounced black-bor dered white stripe over the eye. Th Philadelphia has yellowish underparts

This species breeds from souther Manitoba, central Ontario, and Nov Scotia, south to northwestern Texas southern Louisiana, and North Car olina. It winters south of the Unite States.

The Western Warbling Vireo *(V. g swainsonii)* may be distinguished from all other common western Vireos, except the Red-eyed, by the absence o an eye-ring. The Red-eyed is the only other western species that lacks both the eye-ring and wingbars, but the well-defined white eye line with its black border distinguished the Red-eyed from the Warbling.

The western Warbling Vireo breeds from Canada south to Mexico. It winters south of the United States. Its call-note is a wheezy *twee*.

WOOD WARBLERS

Family Parulidae

The Wood Warblers form one of the largest of typically American bird families. They are small birds, almost completely insectivorous in their habits, and many of them are expert flycatchers. They are distinguished for their beautiful plumage, which is colorful and attractive, rather than particularly striking. Peterson calls them "the butterflies of the bird world." While the many species are relatively easy to distinguish in the spring when they are in breeding plumage, in the fall when there are many immature birds, and when the adults have assumed their greenish coloring, it is almost impossible to tell many of them apart.

BLACK and WHITE WARBLER

(Mniotilta varia)

Color Plate Page 314

Several weeks later than the Louisiana Water-thrush, right on the heels

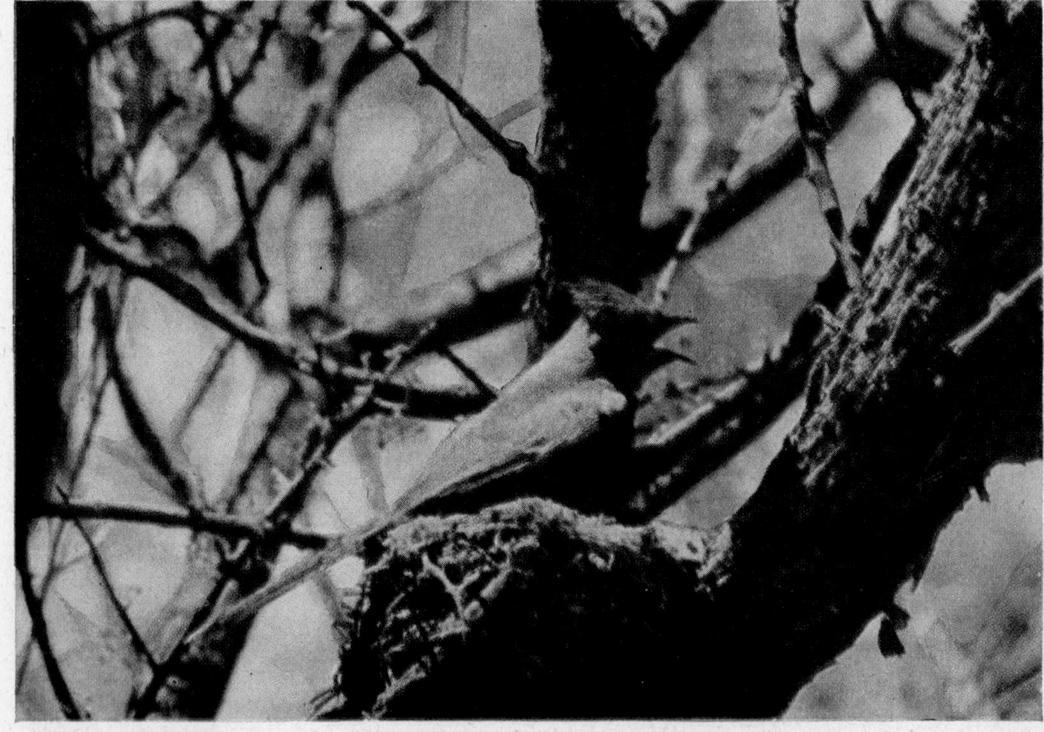

PHAINOPEPLA (*Phainopepla nitens lepida*). Length: 7 to 7.75 inches. Male: bluish black bird with white patch on wing and crested head. Female: dark gray with no wing patches. Range: breeds in southwestern United States. Winters in southern California, Arizona and western Texas. Voice: warbled, weak song; note, *wurp*.

William L. and Irene Finley

of the Myrtle Warbler, and at the same time as the Ovenbird, the Black and White Warbler arrives on its northern breeding grounds, fresh from a winter spent in Florida, Texas, the West Indies, or South America.

WORM-EATING WARBLER AT NEST (*Helmitheros vermivorus*). Length: 5 to 5.5 inches. Male and female: dull olive with black stripes on buffy-head. Range: eastern United States, from southern Connecticut to Georgia and west to southern Iowa. Voice: a thin, rapid buzz.
Samuel A. Grimes

Those who ordinarily have difficulty identifying members of the Wood Warbler tribe, are grateful for this species, for it is unmistakable in its zebra attire of black and white. It has been described as a "pen and ink sketch of a bird." Its characteristic habit of skirting around tree trunks in Nuthatch-fashion, makes identification positive. No other Warbler is black and white, except the more northern Blackpoll, but the latter has a black cap instead of a striped crown. It is more likely to be confused with a Chickadee. The Black and White is 5 or 5½ inches long.

The song of the Black and White Warbler is not difficult to learn. Upon arrival on its nesting territory, it sings incessantly until after nesting is underway. The song is high, thin, and wiry, and is interpreted as *weesy, weesy, weesy, weesy, weesy, weesy, weesy*, usually repeated seven times. It has been suggested that it sounds like a weak echo of the Ovenbird's louder song. Others recognize a similarity to the Redstart's *teetsa* song, but thinner and longer. I have always felt that a violinist could play an exact duplicate.

On the ground at the base of a tree is the usual nesting site of the Black and White Warbler, although it may choose a site under a log, a fallen limb, an upturned root, or a rock. The nest is constructed of dead leaves, strips of grapevine bark, grasses, rootlets and hair. The five eggs are profusely spotted with reddish brown.

When flushed from her nest, the female invariably uses the "injured bird" ruse that is characteristic of some of the other Warblers (Ovenbird and Louisiana Water-Thrush for instance). At a nest at the base of a white oak, a female ran in front of me, her wings fluttering like an injured butterfly. When I failed to follow, she returned close to my feet, and, lying partly on her side, fluttered her wings in what I might have presumed to be her last few gasps before death if I had not known better.

The behavior of the male was entirely different at this nest where I was set up for natural color pictures (see the illustration on page 314). He came

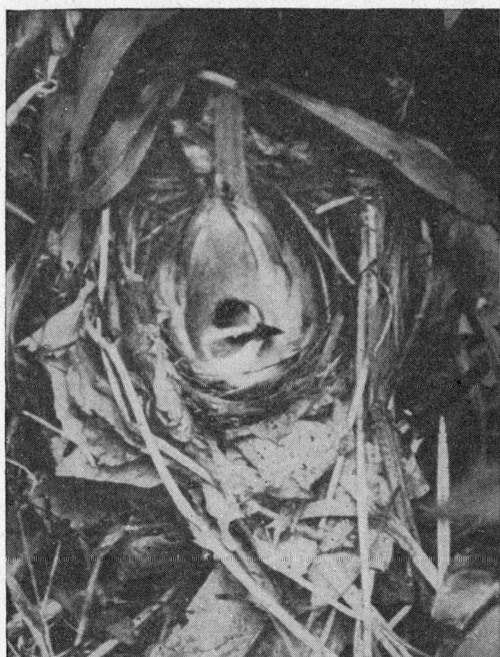

GOLDEN-WINGED WARBLER ON NEST (*Vermivora chrysoptera*). Length: 5 to 5.25 inches. Male: upperparts bluish gray, head crown, bright yellow. Yellow wing-patch and black throat. Underparts, white, or ashy white. Female: similar to male, but black parts replaced by gray, and yellow, dimmer. Range: eastern United States, from northern Vermont to South Carolina. Winters in Central America. Voice: one buzzy note, followed by three in a lower pitch, *bee-bz-bz-bz*.
United States Fish and Wildlife Service

with food at infrequent intervals, flew directly to the tree trunk, came down head first to the nest, fed the young, and was gone in an instant. The female, whose plumage is not as clean-cut black and white as her mate's, never ceased to be highly nervous. She was very reluctant to approach the nest while the camera was near.

It is noteworthy that this Warbler's creeping habit has reflected itself in the bird's anatomy. The bill is long, slender, and slightly decurved, with the upper mandible usually notched at the tip and extending over the lower one. The hind toe, in comparison with the middle toe, is longer and has a stouter nail than in any of the other Warblers. The tail is nearly square and compared with the wing is rather short.

The breeding range of the Black and White Warbler extends from central Manitoba and the Gulf of St. Lawrence to the northern parts of the Gulf States. It is the only species in the genus *Mniotilta*.

PROTHONOTARY WARBLER

(Protonotaria citrea)

Color Plate Page 315

Like a number of other birds of austral affinity, the Prothonotary Warbler is gradually extending its range northward. Although a common bird in many southern swamps, flooded bottomlands, borders of lakes, rivers, and ponds, the Prothonotary has been found nesting as far north as Wisconsin and Minnesota. Always, however, its favorite habitat is a swampy location.

The entire head, neck and underparts of the male are yellowish orange, the undertail coverts are white, and the upperparts, yellowish green. The rump, wings and tail are bluish gray. Females are duller. The bird is 5½ inches long. The Blue-winged Warbler with which it might be confused is not so orangey-yellow, has a black line through the eye, and two white bars on its wings.

Sweet, sweet, sweet, sweet, or *tweet, tweet, tweet, tweet,* is the song of the Prothonotary, delivered in one pitch, and, at a distance, remindful of the call of a Solitary Sandpiper. This Warbler is the only eastern member of the family that nests in cavities, choosing old Woodpecker holes in dead stubs, often surrounded by water. It has been known to accept man-made nesting boxes placed in well chosen locations. The eggs are creamy white, heavily marked with brown.

The winter home of the Prothonotary is Central America to Colombia.

SWAINSON'S WARBLER

(Limnothlypis swainsonii)

Color Plate Page 319

Because of its shy and retiring nature, and because of the inaccessibility of its nesting habitat, the Swainson's Warbler is seldom seen by the average bird watcher. It is a bird of the southern swamps and river bottoms, and usually places its nest in rank growths of cane, not far from water.

The bird is about the size of a Prothonotary Warbler (5 inches long) with which it associates. Both sexes are alike, olive brown above, with the top of the head cinnamon-brown and a yellowish white line over the eye. The underparts are dull yellowish white. The similarly colored Worm-eating Warbler has a striped crown, while the Blue-wing has white wing-bars. Swainson's is somewhat reminiscent of a Vireo in its habits.

Swainson's Warbler is said to sing very much like the Louisiana Water-thrush, but the song is shorter and less vigorous. "It opens with three slurred phrases on the same pitch and closes with two shorter notes on a slightly lower pitch," writes Howell in "Florida Bird Life."

WORM-EATING WARBLER

(Helmitheros vermivorus)

In my Warbler notes, I find the following entry made early one morning in May while listening to the song of a Worm-eating Warbler on a brushy hillside in western Pennsylvania: "The duration of an individual song is two to three seconds. It starts low and increases in volume. It is buzzy and insect-like, and in comparison with the Chipping Sparrow's trill, it is thinner and more wiry, less melodious, and is delivered more hurriedly and in shorter time. It is more like the song of the Grasshopper-sparrow than any other bird, but uttered from the woods, the song could never be that of the latter."

This song is not one to attract much attention, and the bird's modest garb of brown, buff and white certainly is not conspicuous. The prominent black stripes on the buff colored head are diagnostic, and since the bird usually

BACHMAN'S WARBLER *(Vermivora bachmanii).* Length: 4.25 inches. Male: olive green upperparts; face and underparts yellow, black patch on throat and crown patch. Female: upperparts olive green and underparts, yellow; lacks black throat and has grayish crown. Range: southeastern United States from Virginia and southern Indiana, west to Louisiana. Winters in Cuba. Voice: a wiry, buzzing trill.

Rudolph Hindemith, American Museum of Natural History

LOGGERHEAD SHRIKE *(Lanius ludovicianus)*. Length: 9 inches. Male and female: gray above, white below, black mask through eyes. White patches in wing. Range: Canada south into Mexico; winters in California. Voice: song, a collection of musical notes and phrases.
Samuel A. Grimes

feeds on the ground or in low tangles, the head markings are important. The bird is 5 or 5½ inches long.

The Worm-eating Warbler nests on the ground in damp woodlands and hillsides from southern Iowa, northern Illinois, Pennsylvania, and the Hudson and Connecticut river valleys to southern Missouri, Tennessee, Virginia, and the mountains of South Carolina.

GOLDEN-WINGED WARBLER

(Vermivora chyrsoptera)

A droning insect-like utterance that repeats *beeeee, buzz, buzz, buzz* and which comes from the foliage at the top of a bush or small tree, is the song of a golden-winged Warbler. Its close relative, the Blue-winged Warbler, with which it sometimes hybridizes sings *beeeeee-buzzzzzz,* a shorter version of the other song.

The Golden-winged (5 inches long) is the only Warbler that combines a black throat with a yellow wing patch. Additional field marks are gray upperparts, yellow forehead, broad, black stripe through the eye, and a white belly. The female is similar but gray instead of black.

This beautifully marked Warbler is confined to regions east of the Mississippi, breeding in the northern states. It nests near the ground, the structure being supported by weed, grass, or flower stems. The preferred habitat is woodland borders grown over with rank weeds and tangles.

WHITE-RUMPED SHRIKE *(Lanius ludovicianus excubitorides)*. Length: 9 inches. Male and female: gray above, white below. Black mask through eyes, white patches in wing. Range: Canada to Mexico. Voice: repeated notes and phrases.
George M. Bradt

In autumn migration, the Golden-winged leaves the United States by way of the Gulf States and winters from Guatemala to Columbia.

BLUE-WINGED WARBLER

(Vermivora pinus)

Color Plate Page 322

Bird watchers who hope to see the rare hybrids, Brewster's Warbler and Lawrence's Warbler, should investigate the song of every Blue-winged Warbler they hear. These two hybrids are the results of matings between a Blue-winged Warbler and its close relative, the Golden-winged Warbler. Since the colors and patterns of the parents are so different, strikingly marked hybrids result. The songs of the hybrids may resemble either parent or parts of the songs of both.

The head and underparts of the Blue-winged Warbler, which is 4½ to 5 inches long, are yellow with a black line through the eye; the back and tail are olive green; the wings are bluish gray with two white wingbars. The common song of the Blue-wing is an utterance of two notes, which I would interpret as *beeeeee-buzzzzzz* with the first higher pitched than the second. It is similar to the Golden-wing's song, but the latter puts two or even three more *buzzzzzz* notes onto the song.

Although most of my associations with this Warbler have been in swamp forests, swampy thickets, and scrubby woodland edges, it also shows a preference for bushy fields and overgrown pastures. Like the Golden-wing, the Blue-wing places its nest on or near the ground carefully hidden by surrounding vegetation. The five white eggs are speckled with brown.

The Blue-winged Warbler breeds from Rhode Island and southern Massachusetts to southeastern Minnesota and northeastern Kansas, south to northern Georgia and Alabama. It winters from northern Mexico to Columbia.

BREWSTER'S and LAWRENCE'S WARBLERS

(Vermivora leucobronchialis and Vermivora lawrencei)

Ordinarily hybrids do not occur in nature and the most noteworthy exception to this rule among the birds occurs in the cross-breeding of the Golden-winged and Blue-winged Warblers. The bird that results from the initial cross-breeding is like the Golden-winged Warblers but lacks the black throat. Originally it was believed to be a separate species, and was named Brewster's Warbler. There are often other variations such as white or yellow wingbars, or a verging toward yellow on the underparts, but on the whole the black eye mark and whitish underparts are unmistakable.

When two Brewster's Warblers breed, or when an occasional individual inherits the tendency from both parents, a bird with black throat and yellow underparts results, which has been named Lawrence's Warbler. It is much rarer than Brewster's hybrid.

The song varies depending on which parent the bird is most like, and the habits are like those of the dominant parent.

BACHMAN'S WARBLER

(Vermivora bachmanii)

The rarest North American Warbler, and one of the rarest of all North American song birds, is Bachman's Warbler, found most often in the river swamps of the southeast. Its breeding range has been defined as southeastern Missouri, northeastern Arkansas, western Kentucky, northern Alabama, and South Carolina. It is doubtful if a dozen occupied nests have ever been found. It is known only in Cuba during the winter. It migrates through Florida and the Gulf States.

Bachman's Warbler's field marks are a yellow face and belly, a black crown, and long black throat patch. Peterson points out that "it suggests a small Hooded Warbler with an incomplete hood." The bird is about 4¼ inches long. The female lacks the black throat, and is generally greenish, with a yellow forehead and underparts, and a gray crown.

TENNESSEE WARBLER

(Vermivora peregrina)

The well known trill of the Chipping Sparrow has been used as a basis for describing many birds' songs, and here, again, we must use it to describe the song of the Tennessee Warbler. This bird of the Canadian bogs has a

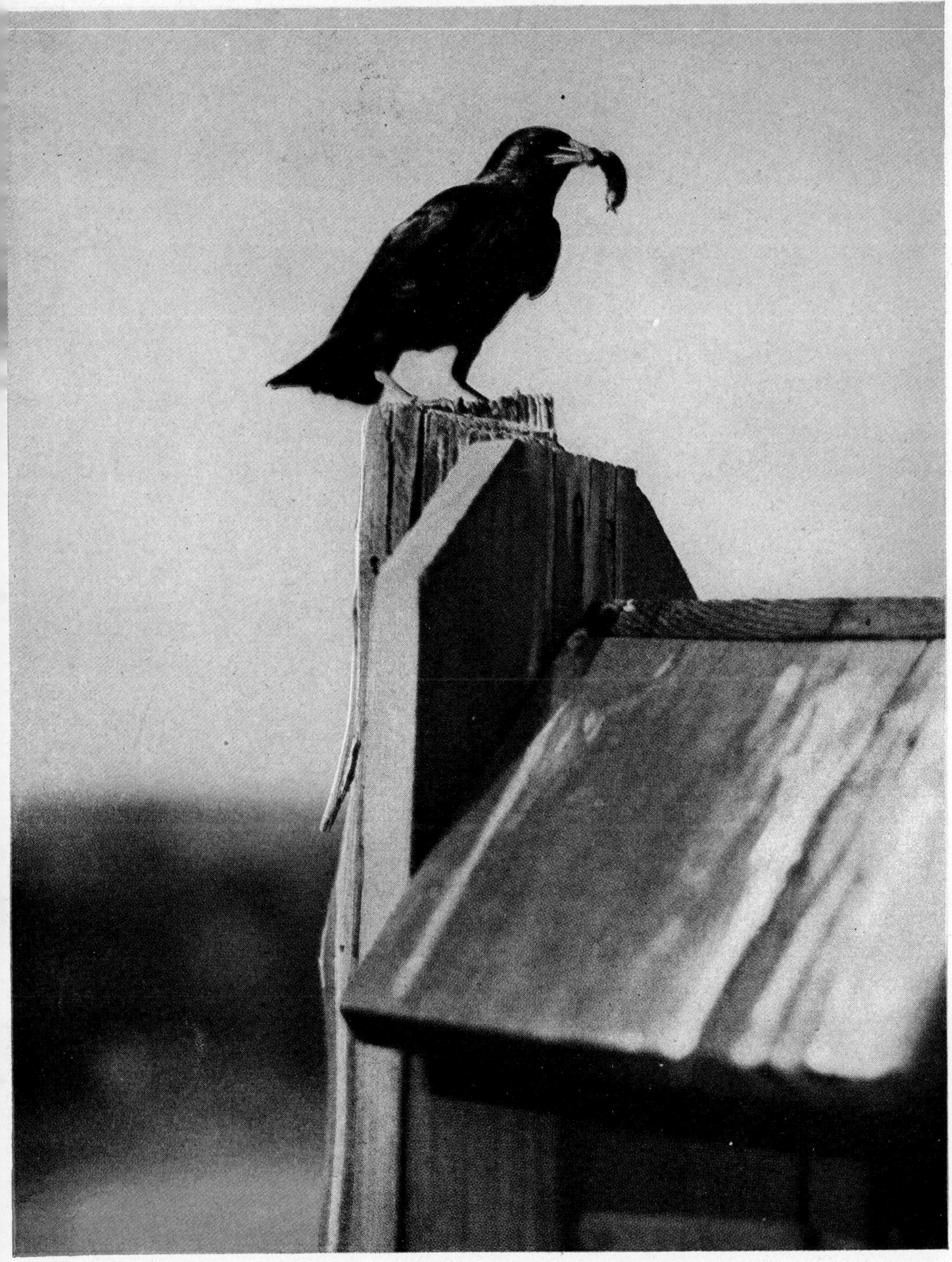

STARLING (*Sturnus vulgaris vulgaris*). Length: 7.5 to 8.5 inches. Male and female: A blackbird glossed in spring with purple and green. In winter, bird is heavily speckled with light dots. Has yellow bill in spring. Range: northeastern United States, but found west to Rockies, north to Gulf of St. Lawrence, and south to Gulf of Mexico. Voice: song of whistled notes. Note, *feee-u.*

Hal H. Harrison

TENNESSEE WARBLER *(Vermivora peregrina)*. Length: 4.5 to 5 inches. Male: upperparts olive green, underparts white. In spring, male is unmarked except for a prominent white stripe over the eye; and gray head. Female: similar to male in spring, but duller. Adults and immatures in autumn: olive green above, yellowish below, yellowish line over the eye. Range: said to breed in mountains of northwest Montana. Migrates through Colorado, Wyoming, and Montana. Voice: two parted song, *teet-see, teet-see, teet-see, teet-see, dee, de, de, de, de, de, de, de.*
Rudolph Hindemith, American Museum of Natural History

variety of utterances, some in two or three parts, but most of them have a Chippy-like trilling quality. The bird sings during migration, for which bird watchers may be thankful; otherwise, its nondescript appearance and its tree-top feeding habits might render it "unknown" on many bird lists.

Spring males have a gray head, a white eye line, olive-green back and whitish underparts. The Tennessee looks very much like a Vireo and is 4½ to 5 inches long, but its quick Warbler movements, its smaller size, and its thin bill are good field marks. The female in spring is like the male, but with less gray on the head, and with yellowish underparts. In the fall, both sexes are greenish above, unstreaked yellowish below, and show a conspicuous yellow line over the eye.

This Warbler breeds in Canada and winters in South America.

ORANGE-CROWNED WARBLER

(Vermivora celata)

The Orange-crowned Warbler breeds in northwestern Canada and crosses the United States in a long diagonal to winter in the South Atlantic and Gulf States. In the Fall it is often found in Massachusetts and the eastern Atlantic states on its way south along the coast.

It is a dingy green olive above, and yellowish below, with faint streakings on the underparts. The orange crown is almost always concealed by the grayed olive tips to the feathers. The bird is 5 inches long.

The song is a varied musical trill, opening slowly and speeding up as the pitch rises. The bird builds its nest on the ground, in clumps of bushes or hidden in leaves. Its eggs are four to six in number, creamy white, spotted with chestnut.

NASHVILLE WARBLER

(Vermivora ruficapilla ruficapilla)

Color Plate Page 323

Many Warblers are olive-green above and yellow below. Details in their plumage are essential to bird watchers who hope to distinguish them. In the Nashville Warbler, it is the gray head with a white eye-ring that sets it apart. A brick-red spot on the bird's crown is of no field importance. Indeed, I remember seeing this mark clearly only once, and that was during migration when a male Nashville happened to be feeding low in a bush ahead of me. The female is duller with a yellowish eye-ring. She may be confused with a female Yellow-throat, but the latter has white beneath her yellow throat, absent in the Nashville female's plain yellow underparts. The bird is 4½ to 5 inches long.

In New England, a favorite habitat of the Nashville Warbler is the abandoned fields and pastures thickly grown over with small birches. Here, on the ground in the club mosses or ferns, the bird builds its nest. Elsewhere it chooses a brushy habitat where no woodland canopy occurs overhead to exclude sunlight, such as open woods, tree bordered fields, and second-growth timber.

The Nashville's song consists of a series of notes on the same pitch, followered by a descending trill. The first part of this two-parted song may be written *weet see, weet see, weet see* trailing off into a Chipping Sparrow trill in the latter half.

New England is the center of abundance of the Nashville, although it breeds north to Quebec and central Ontario and south to Nebraska, northern Illinois, northern New Jersey, and Connecticut. It winters in Mexico principally.

A western race, the Calaveras Warbler *(V. r. ridgwayi)* occurs on the Pacific Coast, in deciduous groves.

VIRGINIA'S WARBLER

(Vermivora virginiae)

The female sex came in for an unusual amount of recognition when certain Warblers were named. There is Grace's, Lucy's, and Virginia's. The latter was named for the wife of its discoverer, Dr. W. W. Anderson.

Although Virginia's is similar to several other Warblers (Lucy's, Colima and Calaveras, the latter a western race of the Nashville), its yellow rump and undertail coverts are diagnostic. Lucy's Warbler has a chestnut rump. The Colima is found only in the Chisos Mountains in Texas where Virginia's occurs only as a migrant. Virginia's Warbler is gray, about 4 inches long, paler below, with the yellow rump and undertail coverts. Its white eye-ring and rusty crown spot can only be seen at close range. Its song is undistinguished, described by Peterson as *chip-chlip-chlip-chlip-chlip-wich wich*. It is a restless nervous little bird.

VIRGINIA'S WARBLER *(Vermivora virginiae)*. Length: 4 inches. Male and female: gray upperparts, with bright yellowish green rump and under tail coverts, and chestnut crown patch, narrow white eye-ring, and touch of yellow on breast. Immature: lack coloring on crown and breast. Range: breeds in Rocky Mountain region. Voice: loose, colorless series of notes, *chip-chilip-chilip-chilip chilp-wick-wick*.

Rudolph Hindemith, American Museum of Natural History

WHITE-EYED VIREO (*Vireo griseus*). Length: 4.5 to 5.5 inches. Male and female: greenish oliv above; whitish below. Yellowish eye-ring. White eyes. Range: breeds from Florida and Gulf o Mexico north to Massachusetts, New York, Ohio and Wisconsin. Winters along coast from Gulf t South Carolina. Voice: clearly pronounced *chick-a-per-weeoo-chick*.
John S. Dunning

Virginia's Warbler breeds in the Rockies from southern Arizona and northeastern New Mexico, north to Nevada, Utah and northern Colorado. It prefers altitudes of about 5,000 feet where it nests on the ground among scrub oaks and willows.

COLIMA WARBLER

(Vermivora crissalis)

A little-known bird of the Chisos Mountains of Texas, the Colima Warbler is similar to Virginia's Warbler, but rather darker in coloring. It lacks the yellow on the breast, but does have yellow at the base of the tail. Its song is a simple trill, rather like the Chipping Sparrow, but shorter and more musical.

LUCY'S WARBLER

(Vermivora luciae)

Lucy's Warbler is an active littl bird (4 inches long) of the Colorad River Valley and its tributaries in Utah New Mexico, Arizona, and southeastern California. It is gray above and yellowish white below. Although the mal sports a chestnut rump and a chestnu crown patch, the latter is difficult t see in the field. The similar Virginia's Warbler has a yellow rump patch.

The song of Lucy's Warbler has been described as "a lively little double tril ending with a *twee*."

One of the most characteristic bird of the mesquite country, Lucy's Warbler often makes its nest in a hole in a giant cactus.

PARULA WARBLER

(Parula americana)

Color Plate Page 326

A lovely, dainty, ever active little Warbler with a characteristic ascending buzzy trill is the Parula Warbler of the southern swamps and northern forests found only where conditions are suitable for nesting. And nesting conditions are generally "suitable" only where hanging "mosses" are abundant — Spanish moss in the south and usnea moss, or "old man's beard," in the north—and in this material the Parula builds its nest by weaving together the strands, and adding other material.

SENNETT'S WARBLER *(Parulapitiayumi nigrilora)*. Length: 4.25 to 4.75 inches. Male: upperparts bluish gray with yellow throat and breast and two white wingbars. Yellowish patch on back. Yellow throat separated from crown by black line. Abdomen, white. Female: duller than male. Range: resident in lower Rio Grande Valley, Texas. Voice: a buzzy trill, which climbs scale.
Rudolph Hindemith, American Museum of Natural History

The Parula is a bluish Warbler about 4½ inches long with a yellow throat and breast, and two white wingbars. A blackish or rufous band crosses the yellow breast. If it can be seen, the large golden-green patch in the middle of the back is diagnostic. In the female the dark chest band is indistinct.

The greenish back patch is more evident than one might suppose in a tree-inhabiting species. The word "parula" means a diminutive "Parus" or "Titmouse" and was applied to this bird because of its Chickadee-like habit of hanging upside down while searching for food.

Two forms of the Parula are recognized: Northern Parula War-

LUCY'S WARBLER AT NEST *(Vermivora luciae)*. Length: 4 inches. Male and female: upperparts mouse gray with chestnut rump-patch and crown. Underparts white. Immature: largely gray with no distinctive markings. Range: deserts of southwest United States. Voice: song, a series of high and rapid notes, *weeta, weeta, weeta, che che che che che* on two pitches.
Eliot F. Porter, National Audubon Society

bler *(P. a. pusilla)* and the typical Southern Parula Warbler *(P. a. americana)*. The latter is described as slightly smaller and lighter in color than the Northern.

SENNETT'S WARBLER

(Parula pitiayumi nigrilora)

Sennett's Warbler, sometimes called Pitiayumi Warbler, is a Mexican species that reaches our border only in the lower Rio Grande Valley in Texas. It is similar to its close relative, the Parula Warbler, but its cheeks are black, the indistinct breast band is lacking, and the white around the eye is absent. The general coloration is bluish above with two white wingbars (shorter than the Parula's), and a yellow throat and breast becoming white on the lower belly. The female is similar, but not quite so distinctive.

The favorite habitat of the Sennett's is in thick woods where Spanish moss abounds, for, like the Parula, it nests in this lichen. Its song is identical with the Parula s, consisting of a buzzy trill, *chipper, chipper, chipper, chip-eeee.*

OLIVE WARBLER

(Peucedramus olivaceus arizonae)

A traveler in the mountains of Arizona or southern New Mexico might identify a *peto, peto* call note as that of a Titmouse only to discover it coming from a spectacular looking Warbler with an orange head and breast, broken by a black cheek patch. This is the Olive Warbler, a Mexican species which is 4½ to 5 inches long, that reaches our country in the open pine forests of those two states. The female is generally gray and yellowish.

The Olive's feeding habits are described as very leisurely and Vireo-like In this regard, it is considered similar to the Pine Warbler. Its song is described by Peterson as a "ringing chant with several variations: *tiddle tiddle tiddle ter*, or *cut-year cut-year cut-year*, or *peter peter peter peter.*"

YELLOW WARBLER

(Dendroica petechia)

Color Plate Page 327

Do all birds accept the parasitic egg of the Cowbird? Most birds do; some do not. The Yellow Warbler, also called Summer Yellow Bird and Wild Canary, is one that is not always willing to find a place in her nest for this large intruding egg. What she does about it is remarkable.

Very often, when the Yellow Warbler finds a Cowbird egg in its nest, it will build a new nest on top of the old one, burying the Cowbird egg. A persistent Cowbird may try again, or another Cowbird may pay the nest a visit. Once more the little Warbler may build another floor on top of the second. Indeed, as many as five or six stories have been built, one on top of the other, each one burying a Cowbird egg. Sometimes the Warbler buries one or more of her own eggs during this period of frustration.

Migration records of this dainty little bird emphasize how little time some of our summer birds actually spend with us in the north. The Yellow Warbler arrives in apple blossom time in April. By May it is nesting. The young are on the wing in June. Where a second nesting follows an unsuccessful first attempt, the young are out of the nest in July. By the end of that month, many Yellow Warblers are already heading south, and by the end of August, the bird has practically disappeared from its breeding range. Four months after its arrival, the Yellow Warbler is returning to its winter home in Central and South America.

We feel that our garden, our shrubbery, our orchard is the real home of the Summer Yellow Bird; that it leaves us of necessity, not by choice. But I wonder if its journey to us in the spring is not the necessary trip, for it hurries away so quickly while food is abundant and long before cold weather arrives.

The song of the Yellow Warbler is considered typical of a number of other Warblers whose songs contain similar *sweet-sweet notes*. A common form of the Yellow Warbler's song may be written: *sweet, sweet, sweet, sweeter, sweetest*. Another is *wee-chee, we-chee, chee, chee*. The songs of the Chestnut-sided, Nashville and Magnolia Warblers are similar, but the one song with which I have always confused the Yellow Warbler's is that of the Redstart. I must always listen carefully to be sure which is which.

No other Warbler builds as neat and compact a nest as the Yellow. It is well woven of fibers and fine grasses and lined with cottony plant down, grasses, and hair. I have found these birds nesting in willows, alders, elderberry bushes, and berry tangles, but the loveliest nesting site I have ever found was in a garden in the crotch of a blossoming crabapple tree. I shall long remember the sight of that bright yellow bird sitting on its silvery nest surrounded by pink blossoms. A color photographer's dream.

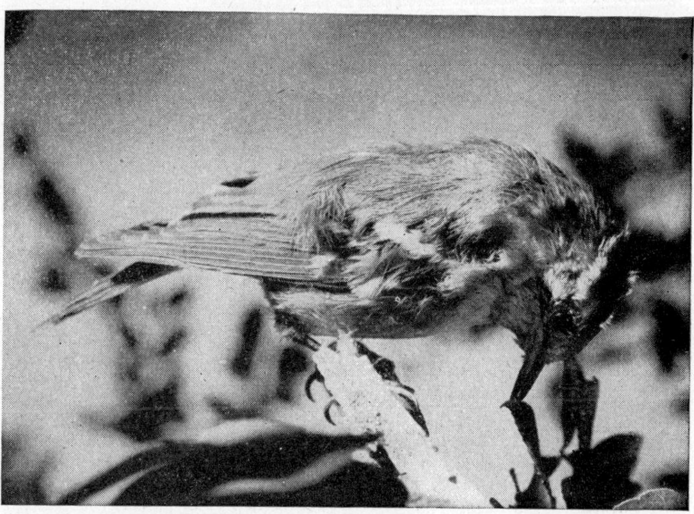

OLIVE WARBLER *(Peucedramus olivaceus arizonae)*. Length: 4.5 to 5 inches. Male: head, neck and upper breast rich chestnut or orange brown, rest of upperparts olive gray. Two white wingbars. *Black cheek patch*. Underparts, whitish. Female: crown and nape olive greenish, dark gray eye-bar, and dusky ear patch. Has yellowish breast and white belly. Range: pine forests of high mountains of southeast Arizona and southwest New Mexico. Voice: a ringing, chant, *tiddle tiddle tiddle ter*, or *cut-year, cut-year, cut-year*, or *peter peter peter peter*.

Rudolph Hindemith, American Museum of Natural History

The Yellow Warbler is our only small bird that appears to be all yellow. It is about 5 inches long. At close range, one sees the reddish brown streaks on the male's breast. On the female, these are quite faint, and her general coloration is duller and greener than the male.

In its various geographic or regional forms the Yellow Warbler breeds from the northern limit of trees and from coast to coast from northern Quebec, Ontario, Mackenzie and Alaska, south to northern South Carolina, Alabama, southern Missouri and southwestern

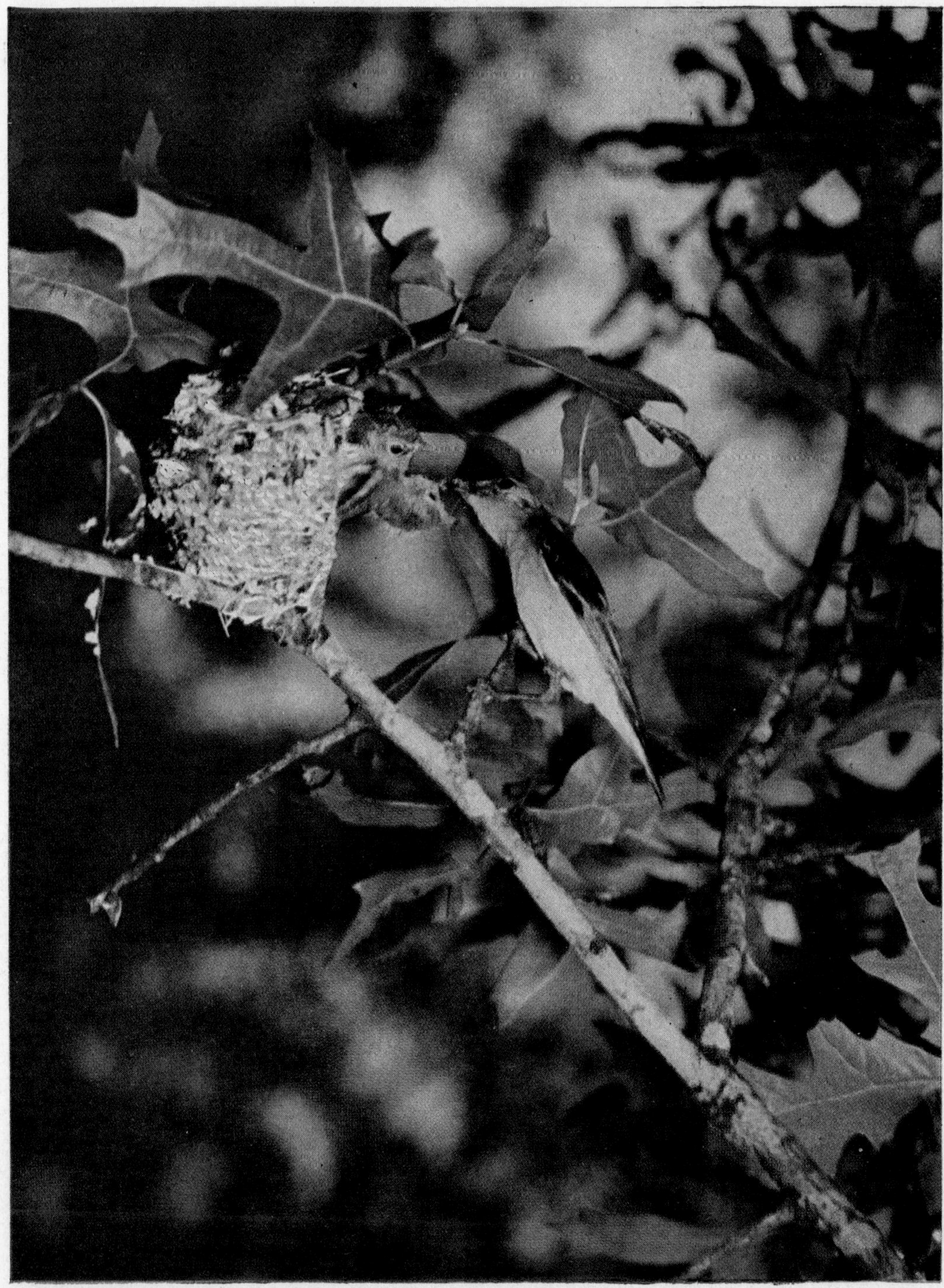

YELLOW-THROATED VIREO *(Vireo flavifrons)*. Length: 5 to 6 inches. Male and female: upperparts olive green with white wingbars, yellow eye-ring and bright yellow throat and breast. Abdomen, whitish. Range: Manitoba, Maine and Quebec to Florida and Gulf Coast; winters from southern Mexico to South America. Voice: musical song with slight roughness occasionally. One distinctive phrase is *ee-yay* or *three-eight*.

Samuel A. Grimes

BLUE-HEADED VIREO (*Vireo solitarius*). Length: 5 to 6 inches. Male and female: slatish blue foreparts, upper body olive green, underparts white. White eye-ring and line to base of upper bill. Has white wingbars. Range: Manitoba and Gulf of St. Lawrence to North Dakota, Minnesota, Michigan and northern New Jersey. Winters in Gulf States and along coast to South Carolina. Voice: a song made up of whistled phrases.
Hal H. Harrison

Texas, and south through Mexico to South America. It also breeds in the Florida Keys and the West Indies.

MAGNOLIA WARBLER

(Dendroica magnolia)

Color Plate Page 329

High on the list of all beautiful birds and near the top of the list of beautiful Warblers must go the black and yellow Magnolia Warbler. The Blackburnian may head the list, and the Cape May and the Parula may run neck and neck in the beauty contest, but none has a more striking all-over pattern than the Magnolia.

The male's yellow plumage is set off in startling fashion by its black and white borders and trimmings. The yellow underparts serve as a brilliant background for the black stripes on the breast and sides; the yellow rump blazes at the base of a black back; the tail, largely white, is crossed by a distinctive black band; a bluish gray crown is framed by black cheeks; and a white patch on the wing coverts is diagnostic. The female's pattern is the same, but uniformly duller. Males, females, and immatures, are similar in the fall, all attired in subdued plumage, brown above and yellowish below. The Magnolia is 4½ to 5 inches long.

Before I knew the Magnolia Warbler, I was quite well acquainted with the Hooded Warbler. I was familiar with its song. When I heard my first Magnolia singing, I was amazed that a Hooded Warbler should be singing in a hemlock forest so far from its normal range. To this day, the songs are similar to my ears. My confusion is not the same as most bird watchers, for it is the Yellow Warbler's song that is generally considered the one closest to the Magnolia.

Two common songs composed of slurred double phrases, are interpreted as *weeta weeta weeeeeeetee* and *weeta weeta weeta.* The ending of the first is high-pitched; the ending of the second descends.

All Magnolia nests that I have found have been in hemlock. Most of them were in young trees within ten feet of the ground. The only nests I have found in old hemlocks were located on low horizontal branches. All nests were uniformly frail structures, loosely built of hemlock twigs and rootlets. The eggs are spotted with reddish brown.

The Magnolia is truly a "Hemlock Warbler." One observer in northern Pennsylvania who observed fifty nests of this species during several seasons reported forty-nine in hemlock. The Magnolia's breeding range lies principally in the Canadian Life Zone, from Newfoundland west to the Rockies. It nests south along the Appalachian highland to Virginia. Winters are spent in Mexico and Central America.

CAPE MAY WARBLER

(Dendroica tigrina)

Color Plate Page 332

It seems to me that so often the most beautiful pictures in nature are the ones my color camera fails to record. I am thinking now of a beautiful May morning when the bird watcher is glad to be afield, when birds are everywhere, especially the Wood Warblers. From an apple tree laden with pale pink blossoms comes a song I have not heard for a year—the thin, buzzy, insect-like *zee, zee, zee, zee* of the Cape May Warbler.

The picture is framed as I look up. There he perches, the gorgeous, male Cape May with his tiger-like pattern, chestnut cheeks, black streaked yellow underparts, and black crown; there he perches, completely surrounded by apple blossoms. He is on his way to the spruce forests of Canada or northern New England, after a winter in the Bahamas and West Indies.

Perhaps I shall see the bird again in the fall, but in much different plumage. The Cape May is one of the brilliant spring Warblers that returns through the United States in autumn, clad in drab feathers. The young resemble the female, which is quite different from the male in spring. The yellow rump and the line over the eye are the best field marks. The female is often very nondescript, lacking the chestnut cheeks. Her breast is whitish with indistinct streakings. The birds are 5 to 5½ inches long.

The Cape May Warbler is another in the long list of misnamed birds. Its only connection with Cape May, N. J., is the fact that a male was taken there in 1809 by George Ord. Later, when Alexander Wilson described the bird from this specimen, he named it.

BLACK-THROATED BLUE WARBLER

(Dendroica coerulescens)

Color Plate Page 336

As a family, the butterfly-like Wood Warblers are my favorite birds. As a species, the male Black-throated Blue Warbler ranks high on my list of "lovely birds." He can be mistaken for no other. His head and back are rich gray-blue. His throat and sides are pitch black. His breast and belly are snow white. As Roger Peterson describes him, he is "very clean cut."

As I now dream of some day recording the brilliant Blackburnian Warbler in true natural color, I used to fancy a Kodachrome of the male Black-throated Blue. That dream came true in a dense rhododendron bog along Thom's Run in Cook Forest State Park, Pennsylvania, where I found three nests in June. All were hidden carefully under the broad rhododendron leaves, and the behavior of the birds at each nest was similar.

I never knew the female Black-throated Blue before that experience. She can be missed so easily among migrating Warblers, for there is nothing to make her conspicuous—plain, brown backed with a light line over the eye and a small white patch at the base of the primaries. That white wing spot, which the male also wears, is quite noticeable in the field, and serves as her best field mark. A blue cast on the "shoulder" of the female's wing is not conspicuous, however. The birds are about 5½ inches in length.

Although the song of the Black-throated Blue Warbler contains the *zwee* notes characteristic of a number of other Warblers, it is husky rather than wiry. The common song goes like this: *zwee-zwee-zwee-zweeeeee*, the last note ascending on the scale. Peterson writes it as *zur zur zur zreee*, husky and lazy. Forbush interprets it as *wee-wee-wee-weep* with downward inflection on the first three and rising on the last note. The full song is not always given. At times, only two or three notes are uttered, and the trailing off at the end is omitted.

In the Cook Forest rhododendron bog, nesting pairs were abundant, territories joining each other for miles. The nests were all constructed similarly—rather bulky exteriors, but neatly

MYRTLE WARBLER AT NEST *(Dendroica coronata coronata)*. Length: 5 to 6 inches. Male in spring: upperparts slate blue, whitish below, with a heavy inverted U of black on the breast and sides, and a patch of yellow on the crown and one in front of each wing and yellow rump-patch. Female in spring: same pattern, but brown instead of bluish. Winter birds: brownish above, white below, streaked with dark. Range: Canada south to Minnesota, Michigan, New York and Massachusetts; winters in southern United States. Voice: summer song, a loose trill; spring song, weak and colorless.

Eliot F. Porter, National Audubon Society

lined and finished. Strips of bark, fiber and rotted wood were used as the basis for the cup. All nests contained four eggs, buff or greenish white, heavily blotched with dark reddish brown.

Nests of this species were difficult to locate, not only because they were exceptionally well hidden under the rhododendron leaves, but because the adults were singularly quiet in the vicinity of their homes. After a nest was located, I was able to watch the incubating female slip away very quietly as I approached. Near hatching time, however, she would freeze on the nest, permitting me to come very near. Even then, when I flushed her, there was no loud chipping and fussing such as characterizes the behavior of many Warblers around their homes. With young in the nest, the adults did repeat a *chip* alarm note when I disturbed them, but beyond this they did not seem to become alarmed.

The Black-throated Blue Warbler *(D. c. coerulescens)* breeds from Minnesota, Ontario, and Quebec to Michigan, Pennsylvania (mountains), and Connecticut. It winters from Key West to the Bahamas through the Greater Antilles and in Guatemala and Colombia.

A subspecies, Cairns's Warbler *(D. c. cairnsi)* described by Elliott Coues in 1897, breeds in the mountains from Maryland to Georgia. It is a darker form.

MYRTLE WARBLER

(Dendroica coronata coronata)

Among the very first Warblers to make their appearance in the northern states in the spring are the Myrtles, also called Yellow-rumped Warblers because of the yellow rump patch that is evident in both sexes in any plumage. The bird's general coloration is blue-gray and white. It is the only Warbler that displays four bright yellow patches: rump, crown, and one in front of each wing. As inverted black U just below the white throat on the breast and sides is also a helpful mark. The females are similar, but are brown instead of blue-black. In the fall both sexes are brownish above and streaked white below. The yellow rump patch is still evident. The bird is 5 to 6 inches long. The song is a Junco-like trill. The call note is a loud *check.*

The breeding grounds of the Myrtle Warbler are the coniferous forests from the limit of trees in northwestern Alaska to the mountains of New England. It winters from Kansas and southern New England to Mexico and southward. In the north, in the winter, it lives on bayberries and cedar berries.

A western race, the Alaska Myrtle Warbler *(D.c. hooveri)* winters to California and Louisiana south to lower California.

AUDUBON'S WARBLER

(Dendroica auduboni)

Color Plate Page 337

Although the breeding ranges of the two birds are different, the Audubon's Warbler and the Myrtle Warbler sometimes occur in the same areas during migration. Then, the uninformed might confuse them, but the yellow throat of the Audubon's (white in the Myrtle) and the large white wing patches (two bars in the Myrtle) are the best field marks. Otherwise, the species are similar; yellow rump, yellow side patches and yellow crown, all

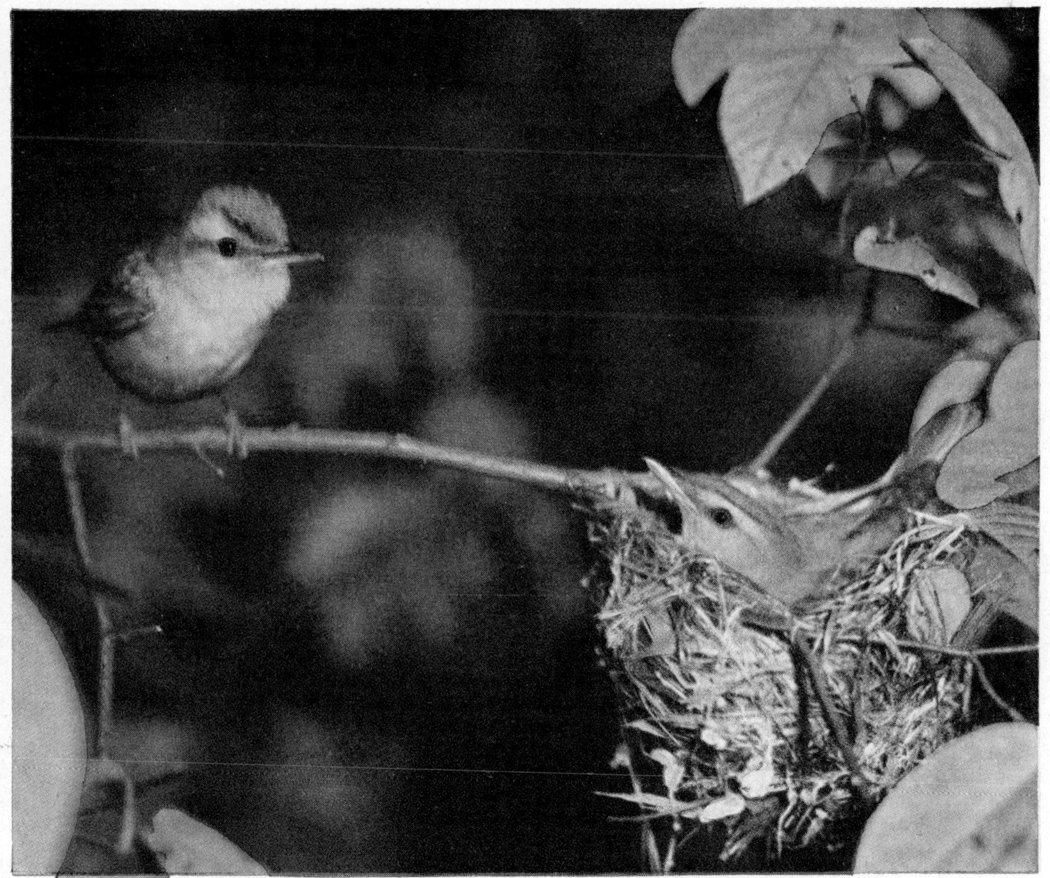

MALE AND FEMALE RED-EYED VIREO AT NEST *(Vireo olivaceus).* Length: 5.5 to 6.5 inches. Male and female: grayish green above, white below. Gray cap and white stripe bordered with black over the eye. Range: Gulf of St. Lawrence, and central Manitoba south to the Gulf Coast and Florida. Winters in South America. Voice: series of clipped boring phrases. Note, a nasal *chway.*
Hal H. Harrison

BLACK-THROATED GRAY WARBLER *(Dendroica nigrescens).* Length: 4.5 to 5 inches. Male: head and throat black, broad stripe of white over ear, back to side of nape; another from base of bill along sides of throat. Upperparts, gray; underparts, white. Female: lacks black throat but retains black eye and crown patches. Range: breeds from western Colorado, Washington, Nevada, northern Utah, south to southern California, southern Arizona and southern New Mexico. Voice: *dzeer dzeer dzeer tseetsee.* The first three wheezy, followed by two quick higher pitched notes.
Rudolph Hindemith, American Museum of Natural History

conspicuous against the gray, black and white pattern. In drab fall plumage, both species are distinguishable from others by the yellow rump patches and from each other by the throat color. Audubon's Warbler is about 5 inches long.

In feeding, Audubon's Warbler is often like the Flycatchers in its aerial sallies. Its call note is a *tchip*. The song is a loose trill, preceded by a series of high-pitched notes, *tsit, tsit, tsit*.

Two races of this Warbler are recognized: Audubon's Warbler *(D.a. auduboni)* which breeds from Canada south to the mountains of southern California, Arizona and New Mexico. It winters in the Pacific States, lower Rio Grande valley, and Texas, south to Mexico and Guatemala. The other race is the Black-fronted Warbler *(D.a. nigrifrons)* which breeds in the mountains of southeastern Arizona. It has a greater area of black on its breast.

BLACK-THROATED GRAY WARBLER

(Dendroica nigrescens)

A black crown cap, a black and white striped face, and a black throat distinguish the Black-throated Gray Warbler (4½ to 5 inches), a breeding bird of the west from southern British Columbia, Nevada, northern Utah, and western Colorado, south to southern California, Arizona, and New Mexico. The Chickadee has white cheeks; the Black and White Warbler has a striped crown; Townsend's Warbler is similarly patterned, but is yellow where the Black-throated Gray is white; and the Black-poll Warbler lacks the black throat. The female Black-throated Gray does not have a black throat, but her black and white facial markings, which are similar to the males, distinguish her.

In its feeding and nesting habits, the Black-throated Gray shows no outstanding preference, but inhabits a variety of situations from undergrowth in open fir forests to valley growths of oak and scrub. Its cupped nest which is firmly anchored to the twigs and leaves has been found from ground level to fifty feet up in conifers.

The Black-throated Gray's song is a lazy, buzzing *zee*-type song, low-pitched, and rolling. Mrs. Bailey has noted the "quiet woodsy quality" of the song, reminiscent of the Black-throated Green and the Black-throated Blue.

TOWNSEND'S WARBLER

(Dendroica townsendi)

Bird watchers in the northwestern states who are fortunate to catch an occasional glimpse of the Townsend's Warbler as it forages in the tops of tall pines and firs will confuse it with no other bird. Its black throat and bright yellow cheeks and its yellow underparts striped with black are distinctive. The female is similar with the yellow throat. The bird is 4½ to 5 inches long.

The song of Townsend's Warbler is similar to that of the Black-throated Gray Warbler. Hoffmann states that the song "has less of the drawling inflection in the opening notes than the Black-throated Gray's and often ends with a prolonged *ee-zee*. Easterners will note a similarity between the Townsend's song and that of the Black-throated Green Warbler.

In summer, the Townsend's Warbler is at home in the mountains from Montana and western Oregon north to Alaska. It winters on the Pacific coast from Washington to California and south to Nicaragua.

BLACK-THROATED GREEN WARBLER

(Dendroica virens)

Color Plate Page 341

The first bird's song that I ever tried to describe in words was that of the Black-throated Green Warbler. I remember the incident so well for I had spent over an hour trying to find the singer among the trees of a deciduous woods during migration in late April. How that bird eluded me! Years later, I read that other bird watchers had detected a ventriloquistic quality in the song of this Warbler, an observation to which I can heartily subscribe.

No matter in which direction I walked, the song seemed to be coming from elsewhere. I became quite exasperated. This had never happened to me before. Finally, I decided to jot down what the bird seemed to be singing, my only hope of identification later. I wrote *dee, dee, dee, dee, dirt.* Then I noted the fact that the bird said *dirt* in a lower pitch and in a minor key.

As I finished writing, I saw a bright yellow and black Warbler flitting about in a sapling maple a few feet ahead. It was a new bird for me. As I watched, I heard a soft, plaintive call of *dee, dee, dee, dee, dirt.* For a moment I did not realize that this bird so

TOWNSEND'S WARBLER *(Dendroica townsendi).* Length: 4.25 to 5 inches. Male and female: upperparts greenish olive, *black-and-yellow* striped head and striped yellow underparts. Range: breeds from Canada, south to northwestern United States; winters along coast from Washington to California. Voice: *Dzeer, Dzeer, Dzeer, tseetsee,* wheezy, buzzy quality.

Rudolph Hindemith, American Museum of Natural History

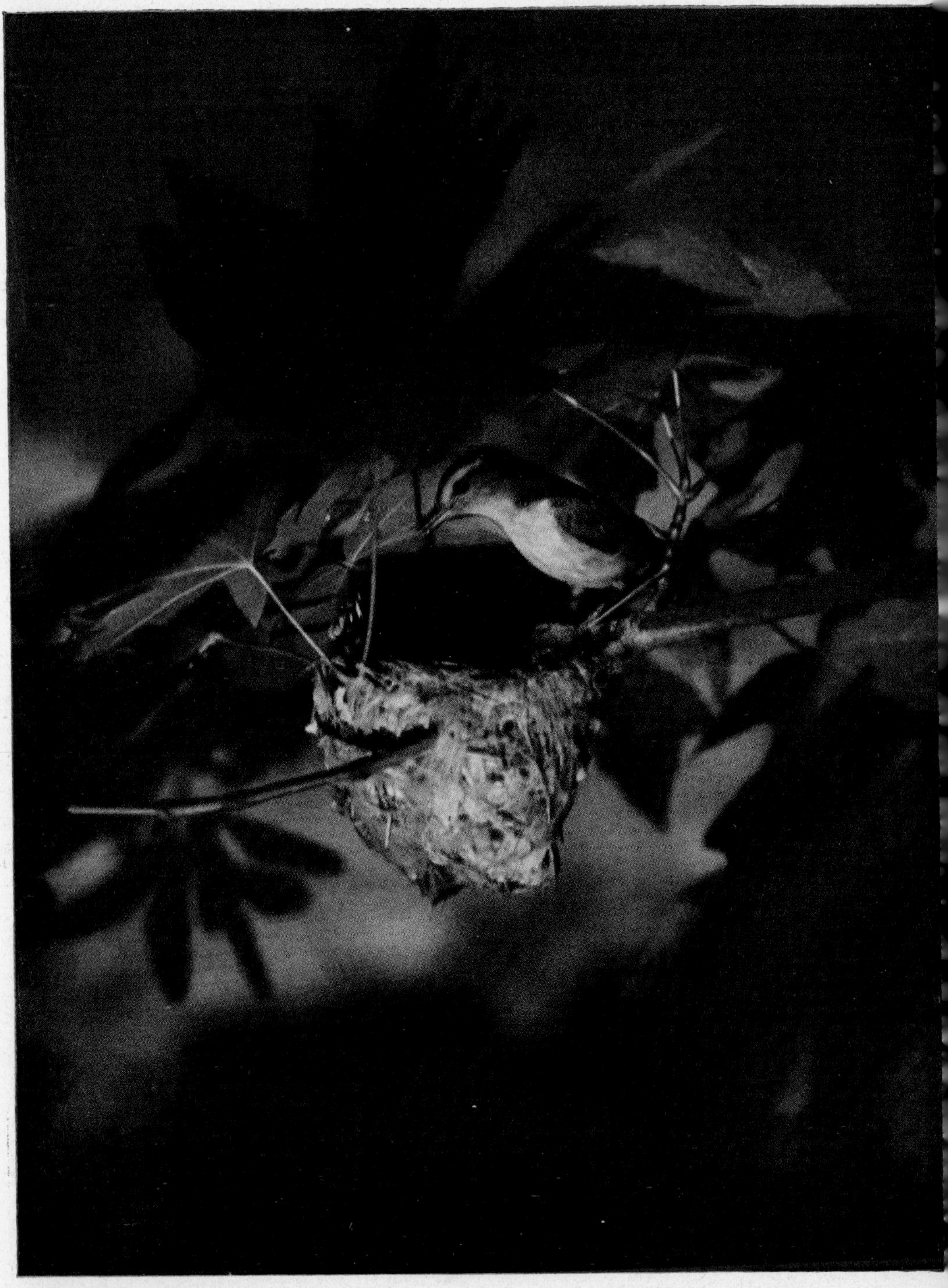

WESTERN WARBLING VIREO (*Vireo gilvus swainsoni*). Length: 5 to 6 inches. Male and female: above greenish gray; whitish below. Head palely striped. Range: breeds from Canada south to Mexican border. Winters in Tropics. Voice: a languid warble. Call-note is a wheezy querulous *twee.*

R. T. Congdon

near to me had uttered the song. It seemed to come from far off in the woods. But, no! This time I watched it sing. And that is how I met my first Black-throated Green Warbler.

Since then I have read many interpretations of the song. A common one is *zee-zee-zee-zee-zu-zwee*. Another is *ree-to tee-tetee to-tay*. A more liberal interpretation gives it the words: *trees, trees, murmuring trees*. But until this day, my ears are still satisfied with the notes as I wrote them years ago.

Of course, every individual does not sing exactly the same. Indeed, each male seems to have at least two different songs, but one of them is always as I have written it, or at least close to it. Indicative of the male Black-throated Green's passion for singing is an observation made by Mrs. Margaret M. Nice. During a period of seven hours, she recorded 1,680 songs of this bird. At another time, she clocked him at 379 songs during the first hour of singing in the morning. She ventured that "A really typical day should have resulted in well over three thousand songs."

The male Black-throated Green Warbler (4½ to 5¼ inches) has a bright yellow face framed by a solid black throat and upper breast. His back, wings and tail are olive-green. White outer tail feathers and two white wingbars complete his field marks. Females are similar but duller, having much less black in the throat.

A compact, deeply-cupped nest is placed generally against the trunk of a tree, supported by one or two branches. Conifers are preferred but that is not essential. In a hemlock forest, I found one nest in yellow birch and another in rhododendron. The four eggs are finely spotted. Incubation is the female's job, but the male assists in feeding the young. Only one brood is raised in a season.

The Black-throated Green Warbler is distributed generally over eastern North America, north to Newfoundland and Athabasca, and west to the Plains. In winter it occurs from Mexico to Panama, and is casual in the West Indies.

Wayne's Warbler *(D. v. waynei)*, a subspecies, is indistinguishable in the field. It is a resident bird in its restricted range in the swamps along the South Carolina coast.

GOLDEN-CHEEKED WARBLER

(Dendroica chrysoparia)

Restricted in range to the Edwards Plateau of Central Texas, the Golden-cheeked Warbler (5 inches long) is the only Warbler of that locale with yellow cheeks and black throat. It has no yellow on the breast, and its back is solid black. The female is like the male except that her back is olive green.

The Golden-cheeked Warbler prefers cedar trees and builds its nest in a hole in the tree. The four eggs are white, speckled with brown. The song is high pitched and hurried, given as *tweeah, tweeah, twee-sy*.

HERMIT WARBLER

(Dendroica occidentalis)

The male Hermit Warbler is conspicuous for his bright yellow head and face, with a black throat and dark back. The underparts are white. The female has a whitish or dusky throat, but her coloring is otherwise similar. The size is 4½ to 5 inches.

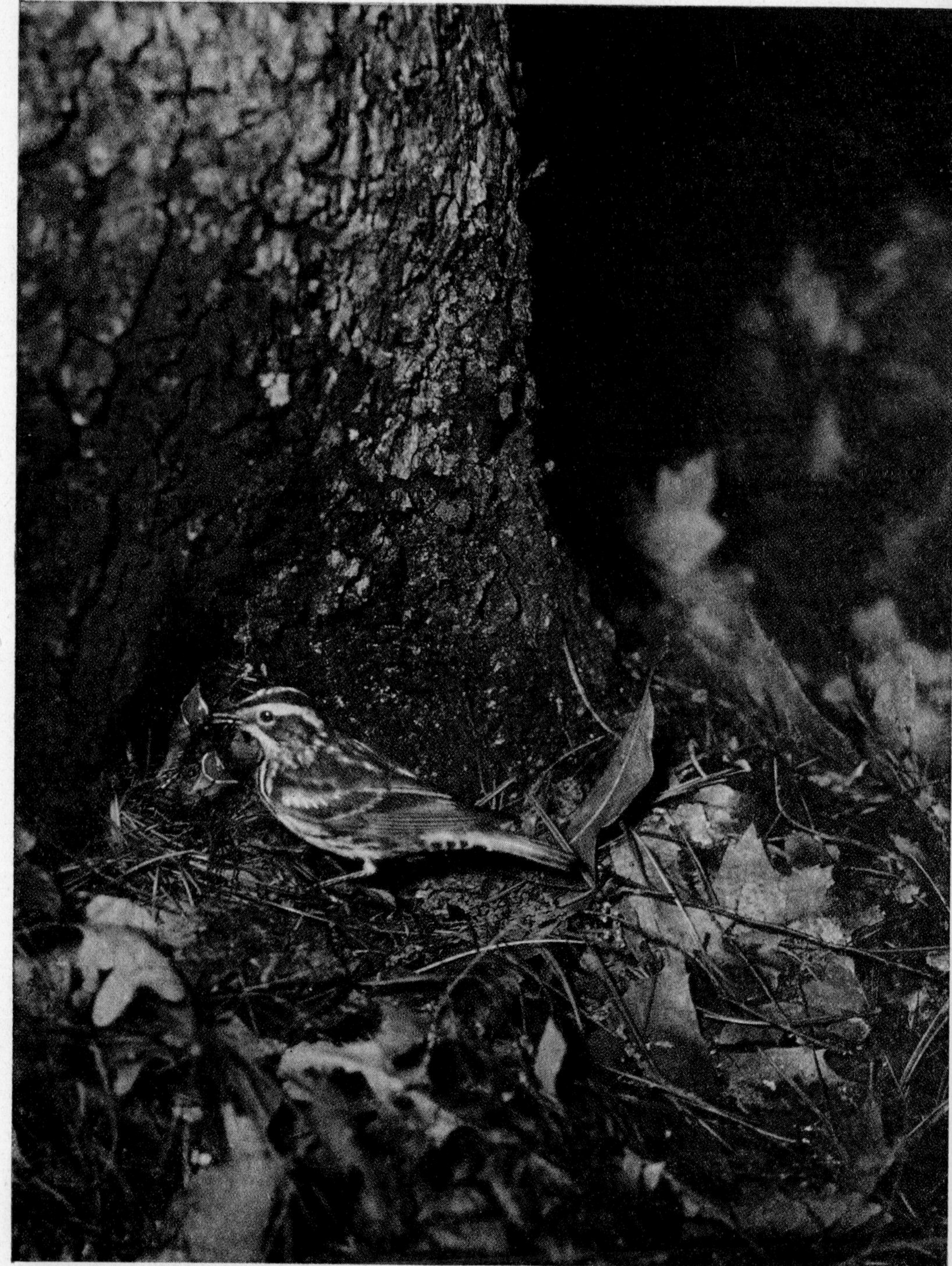

MALE BLACK AND WHITE WARBLER (*Mniotilta varia*). Length: 5 to 5.5 inches. Male: black and white striped upperparts; more finely streaked on sides. Pure white below. Female: pure white throat, not so black above as male. Range: eastern North America, occasional in migration to Colorado, Wyoming and Montana; occasional also in California. Voice: high, thin, *tisi, tisi, tisi, tisi, tisi, tisi, tisi, tisi, tisi.*

Hal H. Harrison

A bird of the coniferous forests of the west, it has a trick of hanging upside down at the end of a twig which is characteristic. Its song is composed of three high two-syllabled notes followed by two quick lower notes. It builds its nest in tall pines and lays grayish white eggs which are spotted around the broad end with brown or lavender. It breeds from Washington,

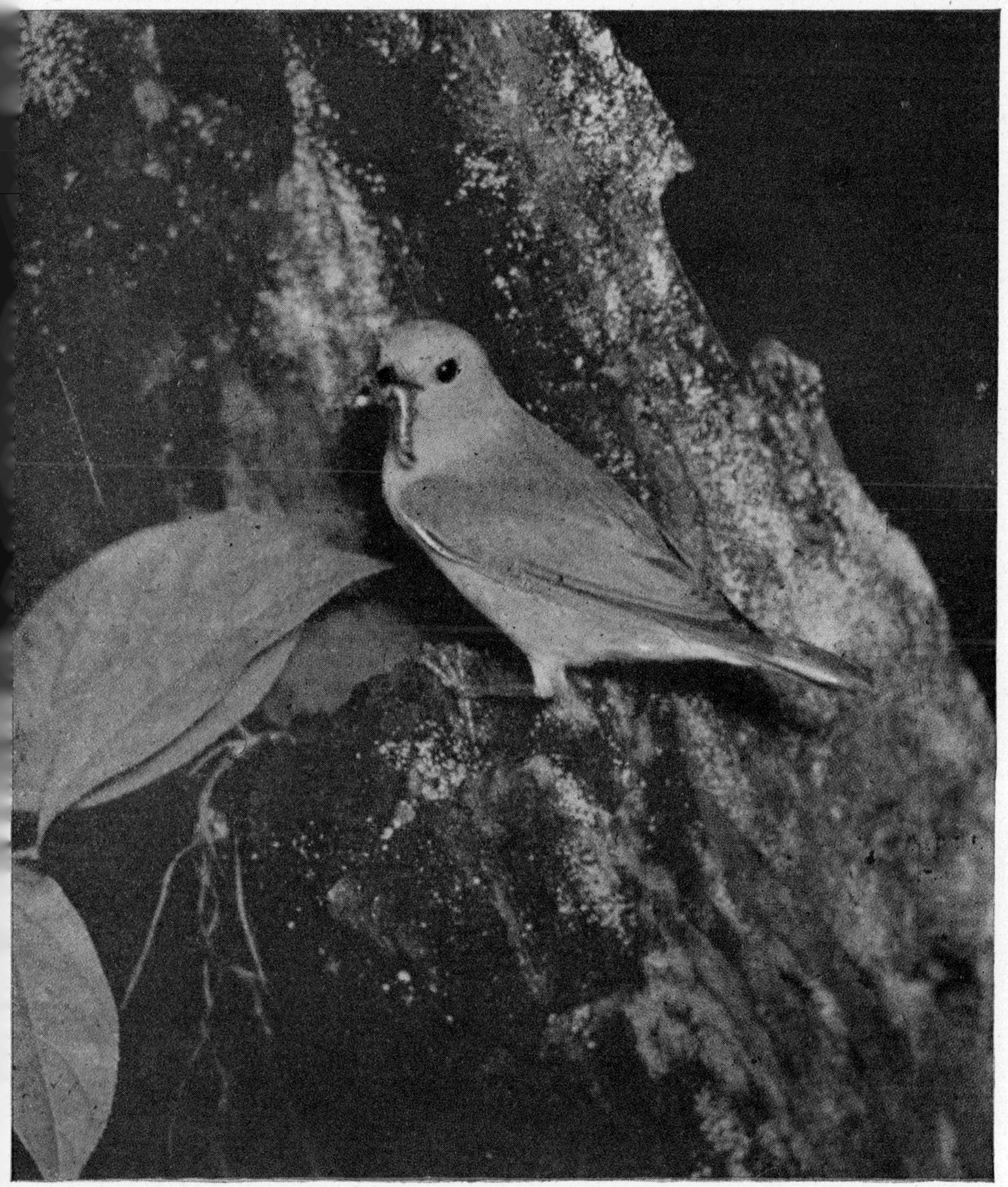

PROTHONOTARY WARBLER (*Protonotaria citrea*). Length: 5.5 inches. Male and female: yellow head and breast. Body yellowish green. Wings blue gray. Female duller than male. Range: river swamps from Minnesota, Michigan, New York, and New Jersey, south to central Florida and Gulf Coast; winters in Central and South America. Voice: song on one pitch, *tweet, tweet tweet tweet tweet.*
Samuel A. Grimes

CERULEAN WARBLER (*Dendroica cerulea*). Length: 4 to 5 inches. Male: upperparts grayish blue and black; underparts white. A *narrow black ring* crosses the upper breast. Legs and feet, dark blue. Female: blue gray and olive green above, and whitish below. Has white line over the eye and two white wingbars. Range: breeds from central New York, southern Ontario, southern Michigan, Minnesota and Nebraska to northern parts of Gulf states. Winters in South America. Voice: rapid, buzzy notes on one pitch, followed by a longer note on a higher pitch: *zray zray zray zray zreeee.*

Rudolph Hindemith, American Museum of Natural History

and British Columbia to California, and migrates through southern California, Nevada and Arizona.

CERULEAN WARBLER

(Dendroica cerulea)

One of the pleasantest memories of spring Warbler "waves" in the eastern states is that of entering a deciduous woodland fresh with unfolding leaves on a May morning to find the trees literally swarming with Cerulean Warblers. Their abundance is made known quickly by their songs—a series of rapid wiry notes all on one pitch, ending in an ascending trill that trails off somewhere beyond the range of human ears. In migration, Ceruleans (4 to 5 inches) often feed low where one may revel in the heavenly blue of the male's back, and where the dusky band across the white breast is so conspicuous.

Females follow later to build their nests high in the trees (very often oaks) and far out on the limbs, much in the manner of Wood Pewees. Female Ceruleans are blue-gray and olive above, white below, with white wing-bars and a line over the eye.

In its breeding range, the Cerulean barely reaches southern Ontario. The Ohio River Valley is its center of abundance, but it occurs as far west as southeastern Nebraska and south to the northern part of the Gulf States. Eastward it ranges to central New York and southward west of the Appalachians. It winters in South America.

BLACKBURNIAN WARBLER

(Dendroica fusca)

No bird that I have wanted to photograph in natural color has eluded me quite as completely as the Blackburnian Warbler. To date, I have not even found its nest, although I am sure that on many occasions it was right above me.

I do not feel the least bit apologetic about the matter either, for I believe that an element of luck will be necessary before I shall ever record in Kodachrome that flaming orange head and throat against the bird's contrasting black and white body. My lucky day will be the day I find a low nest, a condition that the Blackburnian usually avoids. When I say that I have stood underneath a nest, I mean that somewhere in the top of a virgin hemlock towering 100 to 150 feet above my head, this tiny bird had built its tiny nest. My friends have suggested everything from helicopters to "sky hooks" for reaching the Blackburnian at home.

Among my acquaintances are a number of persons whose ears record the songs of most birds but are incapable of catching the extremely high-pitched song of the Blackburnian. At best the song is not forceful, but is a thin, wiry utterance that Saunders aptly writes as *tsita-tsita-tsita-tsita zzzzzzz.* The ending *z's* are very high pitched and go up and up until they trail off into nothing.

It is an interesting coincidence that the bird's appropriate name of Blackburnian (black body with a "burning" head) should have been the name of the man who discovered it—Blackburn. It is one of the so-called "hemlock Warblers," and is likely to be found in the same habitat as the Magnolia, the Black-throated Green, the Parula, and the Canada Warblers.

The Blackburnian Warbler is 5 or 5½ inches long. The female in spring is similar to the male, but paler and with the flaming red replaced by orange. In the fall both sexes are paler, with yellow replacing the more intense red or orange, and with distinctive yellow stripes on the head making them easy to recognize.

YELLOW-THROATED WARBLER

(Dendroica dominica)

In swamp forests, bottomlands of big timber, and in pines and oaks generally, but particularly where Spanish moss is abundant, the Yellow-throated Warbler *(D. d. dominica)* is at home in the southeastern states. Its breeding grounds extend from Florida to Maryland along the coastal plain.

BLACKBURNIAN WARBLER AT NEST *(Dendroica fusca)*. Length: 5 to 5.5 inches. Male in spring: black and white with *flaming orange* around the head and throat. Female: paler. Autumn birds: more yellowish orange. Distinctive clean-cut yellow head stripings. Range: breeds in evergreen woods from central Manitoba to Minnesota, Michigan, and southern New England, and in Appalachians to north Georgia. Migrates through eastern United States. Winters in South America.
Samuel A. Grimes

YELLOW-THROATED WARBLER (*Dendroica dominica*). Length: 4.5 to 5.5 inches. Male: upperparts gray; underparts yellow and white. Forehead, cheeks and part of crown black. Wings are double-barred with white. Female and immature: plain olive brown, with rich yellow throat, white belly and buffy yellow breast. Range: breeds from southern Labrador, Quebec and Alberta, to Florida and Gulf coast; winters from Louisiana and Florida north to North Carolina. Voice: distinctive song, a rapid *witchity-witchity-witchity-witchity-witch,* or *witchity-t-witchity-ta-witchity-ta-witch.* Note, a husky *tchep.*

Rudolph Hindemith, American Museum of Natural History

Its pattern and coloration are distinctive and the bird (4½ to 5½ inches long) is not likely to be confused with others. The upperparts are gray with two white wingbars; cheeks, forehead and sides of throat are black; throat and upper breast yellow, belly white; sides with black streaks. A white stripe over the eye becomes yellow on the lores (the area between bill and eye). The female is like the male.

In the Mississippi valley, from southern Wisconsin and southern Michigan south to the Gulf occurs a subspecies of the Yellow-throated, the Sycamore Warbler (*D. d. albilora*). The "*albilora*" identifies it, for if one is close enough, it may be seen that the line over the eye of the Sycamore is entirely white; the yellow lore is absent.

GRACE'S WARBLER

(Dendroica graciae graciae)

The western counterpart of the Yellow-throated Warbler is Grace's Warbler, a breeding bird of the mountainous, yellow pine regions of southwestern Colorado, central and eastern Arizona, and New Mexico. Throughout the year, both adults and young may be identified by their gray cheeks

GRACE'S WARBLER (*Dendroica graciae graciae*). Length: 4.5 inches. Male and female: upperparts gray streaked with black. Yellow throat. Has two white wingbars, yellowish line over the eye and black stripes on the sides. Range: breeds in pine forests on high mountains of southwest Colorado, central and eastern Arizona and New Mexico. Voice: a repetitious *cheedle, cheedle, che che che che* ending in trill.

Rudolph Hindemith, American Museum of Natural History

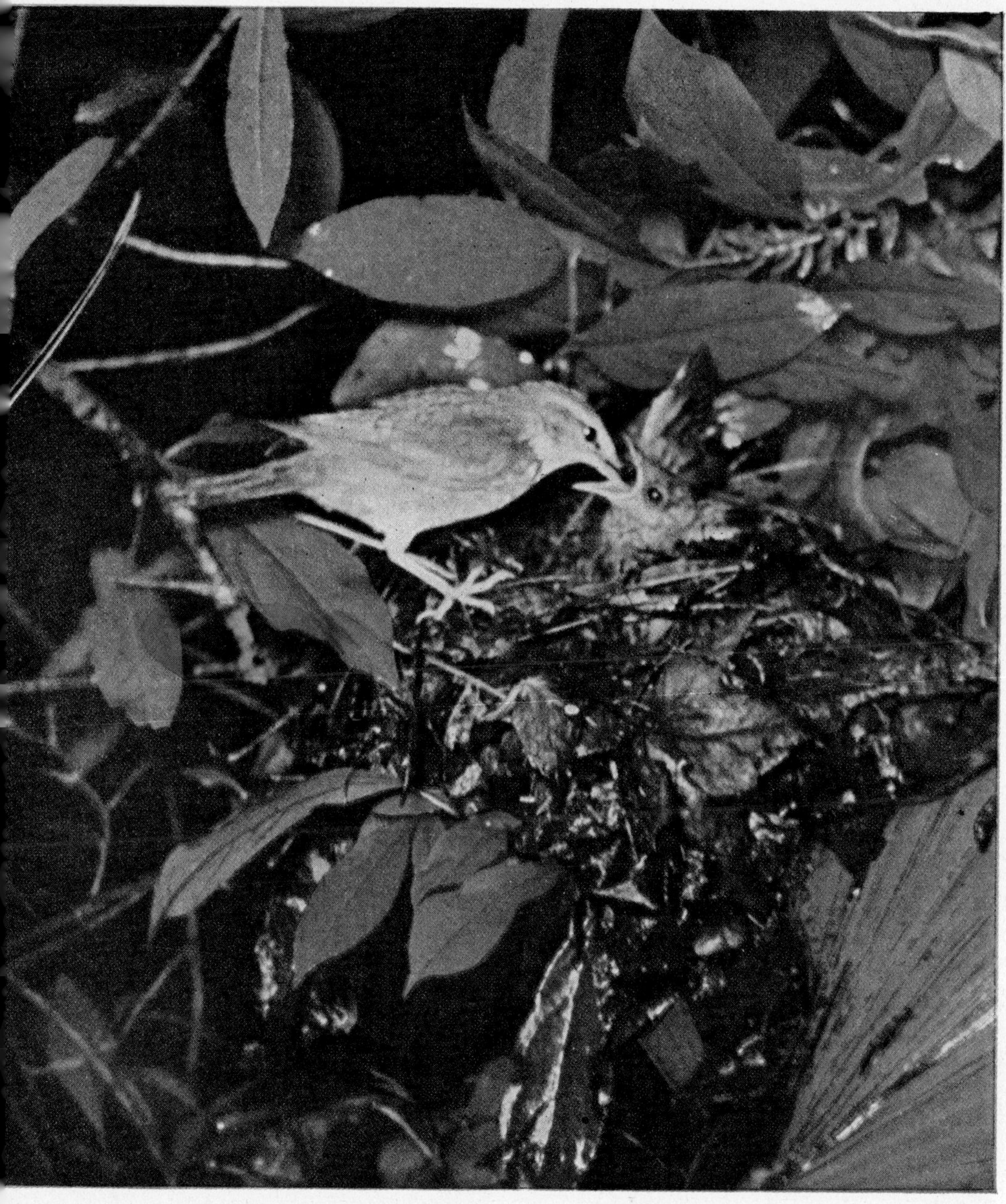

SWAINSON'S WARBLER (*Limnothlypsis swainsonii*). Length: 5 inches. Male and female: upperparts olive brown, dingy white below. Prominent white stripe over the eye. Range: breeds from Maryland, Virginia, Indiana and Oklahoma, south to Florida and Louisiana. Winters in Jamaica and Yucatan. Voice: short song; two slurred notes, two low notes, and one high one.
Samuel A. Grimes

and back, in combination with a yellow throat. The underparts are white and the bird, which is 4½ inches long, has two white wingbars. Peterson describes its song as "a repetitious *cheedle cheedle che che che che,* ending in a chippy-like trill." It is distinguished from Audubon's Warbler by the lack of black on its breast and yellow on its rump.

CHESTNUT-SIDED WARBLER

(Dendroica pennsylvanica)

Color Plate Page 344

It was at the nest of a Chestnut-sided Warbler that I had one of the most exciting experiences that I have ever enjoyed while watching wild birds. The principal character in the drama was not this tiny bird (5 inches) with the yellow crown and chestnut colored sides, but a female Cowbird that paid an early morning visit to the nest of this Warbler.

It was dawn on the morning of May 25th. My camera equipment was in place at the nest of a Chestnut-sided which contained two eggs of the Warbler and one of a Cowbird. Hoping the Cowbird would return to lay another egg, I waited in a blind thirty feet away. I held a battery with which I could operate the camera by remote control. From past experiences, I knew that it was in the dim light of dawn that the Cowbird always made her clandestine visit.

I had guessed right! At 4:29 she appeared in a tree overhead. At 4:32 she flew to the ground in back of the nest which was built in a wild currant bush three feet from the ground. At 4:34 she stood on the rim of the nest. My finger was tense as I prepared to push the release button. Now I waited only for her to sit in the nest. But this Cowbird had other plans. Suddenly she reached into the cup and pierced a Warbler egg with her bill. Slowly she raised it above the rim of the nest.

My finger pressed the releases. Flash went the camera! And the only color picture ever taken of a Cowbird stealing an egg from the nest of another bird was taken. The Cowbird flew off in the woods, carrying the stolen egg in her bill. The photograph showed that she had pierced the egg with the tip of both mandibles with her beak wide open. From past observations, I knew she would eat that egg, shell and all.

The song of the Chestnut-sided Warbler is one that is often confused with the songs of several other Warblers, such as the Redstart, the Yellow and the Hooded. It is described as similar to that of the Yellow Warbler, but more emphatic. A clearly enunciated ending to the song, interpreted as *wee-chew* is slurred downward. Translated into words, a number of phrases are suggested, such as *sweet, sweet, sweet, I'll switch you,* and *we wish to meet Miss Beecher,* and *dis-dis-dis-dismiss you.* A shorter utterance is given as *see Mister Beecher.*

The Chestnut-sided Warbler should be confused with no other bird, except possibly the Bay-breasted Warbler, the only other Warbler with chestnut sides. The Bay-breasted also has a chestnut throat and a dark crown. The female Chestnut-sided is similar to the male, but duller and with less chestnut. In fall plumage, the best field marks are the white underparts, wingbars, eye-ring, and greenish yellow back. Very little chestnut, if any, is evident in the fall.

Along roadsides, margins of woods, hillsides of sprout growth, and thickets of briars and bushes are nesting sites for the Chestnut-sided Warbler. The nest, a loosely built cup of grasses and weed stalks, is always placed low in a bush. The four white eggs are spotted with brown. It is a member of that group of birds that thrives best in cut-over land, birds that arrive when the timber is cut and the forest-dwelling birds leave.

The Chestnut-sided breeds from Newfoundland, southern Quebec, central Ontario, central Manitoba, and central Saskatchewan south to northern New Jersey, northern Georgia, northern Ohio, Illinois, southern Missouri, and eastern Nebraska. It winters from Guatemala to Panama.

BAY-BREASTED WARBLER AND YOUNG *(Dendroica castanea)*. Length: 5 to 6 inches. Male *in spring:* upperparts buffy olive, black and chestnut. Underparts, chestnut and buff. Large spot of pale buff on the side of the neck. Female: more washed out. Male and female, autumn: olive green above with two white wingbars, dingy buff below. Range: spruce forests from Gulf of St. Lawrence and central Manitoba south to New England and Adirondacks. Migrates through eastern United States. Winters in Panama and Colombia. Voice: a high, thin *teesi teesi teesi* on one pitch.
Allan D. Cruickshank, National Audubon Society

BAY-BREASTED WARBLER

(Dendroica castanea)

Another beautiful Warbler of the Canadian fauna that we in the United States must view hurriedly in the spring as it passes through the states and on to nest north of our border is the Bay-breasted. Again in the fall, if we are watchful, we may detect it in drab plumage associating with other Warblers which are difficult to identify.

In spring the Bay-breasted (5 to 6 inches long) is outstanding with its chestnut throat, upper breast, and sides. A large buffy spot on each side of the neck is conspicuous. Females are much duller. In the fall, some of the adults show traces of chestnut on the sides, but otherwise are plain olive-green above and buffy below.

The song of the Bay-breasted Warbler is reminiscent of the songs of the Black-poll and the Black and White Warblers. It is soft and high pitched, a single note repeated with rising and falling inflection.

BLACK-POLL WARBLER

(Dendroica striata)

On a morning in late May in eastern Pennsylvania, I watched a small flock of migrating Black-poll Warblers feeding in the tree tops. As they sang, I made the following notes regarding the song: "A ringing trill, rising in volume and then falling, but remaining monotone; does not spiral; lacks the buzzy quality of many Warbler songs; is rather Chipping Sparrow-like; phrases deliberate, and not run together."

The Black-poll is a breeding bird of the north, even to the limit of trees. In the east, it ranges no farther south than the Catskills and is rarely found

BLUE-WINGED WARBLER *(Vermivora pinus)*. Length: 4.5 to 5 inches. Male and female: olive green above, lemon yellow below. Yellow face. Black mark through eye. Wing has two white bars. Range: Minnesota, Michigan and New England to Kansas, Missouri, Delaware and Georgia. Migrates via Gulf States to Central America. Voice: *bee-bzzzz.*
Fred Bashour

below 4,000 feet elevation. In the west, it is a spring migrant only, east of the Rockies, in Colorado, Wyoming, and Montana. It winters in South America, and the greatest distance between its summer and winter ranges is at least 5,000 miles.

This striped gray Warbler (5 to 5½ inches long) with the conspicuous black cap is more likely to be confused with a Chickadee than another Warbler, but it lacks the latter's black throat. The Black and White Warbler has a striped, not solid, crown, and its creeping habits are diagnostic. The female in spring lacks the black cap, and is greenish above and white below, streaked with black. In the fall, both sexes are greenish above and dingy yellow below, with faint streaking, and two white wingbars. They are almost impossible to differentiate and identify positively.

PINE WARBLER

(Dendroica pinus)

Color Plate Page 346

The name Pine Warbler was a happy and appropriate choice of names for this rather inconspicuous little yellow bird, for it spends its life in pine trees, forced away from them only during spring and fall migrations when it may be found in deciduous foliage. The pine woods of Manitoba, Michigan, Ontario, and New Brunswick, south to east-central Texas, the Gulf states, and Florida are the summer home of the Pine Warbler. In winter it is found among

NASHVILLE WARBLER (*Vermivora ruficapilla ruficapilla*). Length: 4.5 to 5 inches. Male and female: upperparts gray and olive green, underparts yellow. White eye-ring. Range: Gulf of St. Lawrence to Connecticut, New Jersey, West Virginia, Illinois and Nebraska. Migrates through Gulf States; winters in Central America. Voice: two-parted song, *seebit, seebit, seebit, seebit tititititititititi.*

Fred Bashour

BLACK-POLL WARBLER *(Dendroica striata)*. Length: 5 to 5.5 inches. Male in spring: a striped gray warbler with *a solid black cap*. Female in spring: less heavily streaked, lacks black crown patch; greenish gray above and white below. Range: breeds in timberline in Canada south to northern Michigan, northern Maine and mountains of New York, Vermont and New Hampshire. Migrates through eastern United States. Winters in South America. Voice: a thin, mechanical *zi-zi-zi-zi-zi-zi-zi* becoming slightly louder and more emphatic in the middle, and softening toward the end.

Chicago Natural History Museum

the pine trees of the southern states where in some localities it is a resident.

The male's upperparts are dull yellowish green; the underparts are brighter, more decidedly yellow, with faint dusky greenish streaks on the sides; the wings are dusky with two prominent white bars. The female is similar but duller, being mostly whitish underneath. In the autumn the females and immature birds are grayish above and whitish below, with two white wingbars, another of the species in which autumn identification is so different. The birds are 5 to 5½ inches long.

The song of the Pine Warbler is a Junco-like or Chipping Sparrow-like trill, but sweeter than the songs of those birds. It nests high in pine trees, usually on a horizontal limb. Bark strips, pine needles, and fine grasses are used. The eggs are grayish white spotted with reddish brown.

Two races occur: Northern Pine Warbler *(D. p. pinus)* and the Florida Pine Warbler *(D. p. florida)* which show no field differences.

KIRTLAND'S WARBLER

(Dendroica kirtlandii)

Kirtland's Warbler is one of North America's rarest birds. Its breeding range is confined to the jack pine region of a few counties in north-central Michigan. Its entire known breeding range is an area estimated at 100 miles long and 60 miles wide. From its chosen habitat has come another name, "Jack Pine Warbler."

This tail-wagging Warbler, which is 5¾ inches long, is grayish with black stripes above; yellow beneath. The breasts and sides are spotted or streaked with black. The male sports a black mask. Two white wingbars help distinguish it from the similar Canada Warbler. Its song is unusually loud and low-pitched for this genus, being rather like the Northern Waterthrush or House Wren.

PRAIRIE WARBLER

(Dendroica discolor)

Although the Northern Prairie Warbler *(D. d. discolor)* is listed as "common from Florida to New England, and from Nebraska and Kansas to the Atlantic," I have found that condition of "common" to be very localized. Certainly the Prairie Warbler does not breed throughout all parts of that extensive range, and by no means is it a bird of the prairies as its name would imply. It is a shy little yellow bird of the brushy hillsides, oak and pine barrens, and sprout growth generally. A southern relative, the Florida Prairie Warbler *(D. d. collinsi)* is a resident of the mangrove tangles of the Florida coast.

The field marks of the Prairie Warbler (4½ to 5 inches) are its yellowish green upperparts marked with faint reddish brown spots; lemon yellow underparts, the sides of the neck and body with broad black streaks; tail with extensive white patches on all but the middle feathers; sides of the head yellow with two black facial stripes, one through the eye and one below it. Its tail-wagging habit is always a good field mark. The female is similar. In the fall immature birds are pale yellow below with indefinite streaking, and lack any wingbars.

The song of the Prairie Warbler is described as a thin *zee zee zee,* ascending a chromatic scale, similar to the Parula but more distinct.

The eggs of this bird usually number three to six and are glossy white marked by specks and spots.

PALM WARBLER

(Dendroica palmarum)

If you see a little brown and yellow bird (5 to 5½ inches long) with a chestnut cap feeding on the ground during migration, and if it has the habit of flicking its tail up and down, you are looking at a Palm Warbler. If the bird is bright yellow below, it is a Yellow Palm Warbler *(D. p. hypochrysea)*; if it is pale yellowish-white below (except the under-tail coverts which are bright yellow), it is a Western Palm Warbler *(D. p. palmarum).* In fall plumage, the eye line is white in

KIRTLAND'S WARBLER AT NEST *(Dendroica kirtlandii).* Length: 5.75 inches. Male: upperparts, bluish gray with prominent black streaks on the back. Face has black 'mask'. Underparts, light yellow with dark streaks on flanks and sides of breast. Female: duller, and lacks mask. In fall, face sides and upperparts are brown. Range: eastern United States in the north central part of the lower peninsula of Michigan in an area about 100 miles long and 60 miles wide. Winters in Bahamas. Voice: starts with three or four staccato notes, continues with quick ringing notes on a higher pitch, and ends abruptly.

B. W. Baker

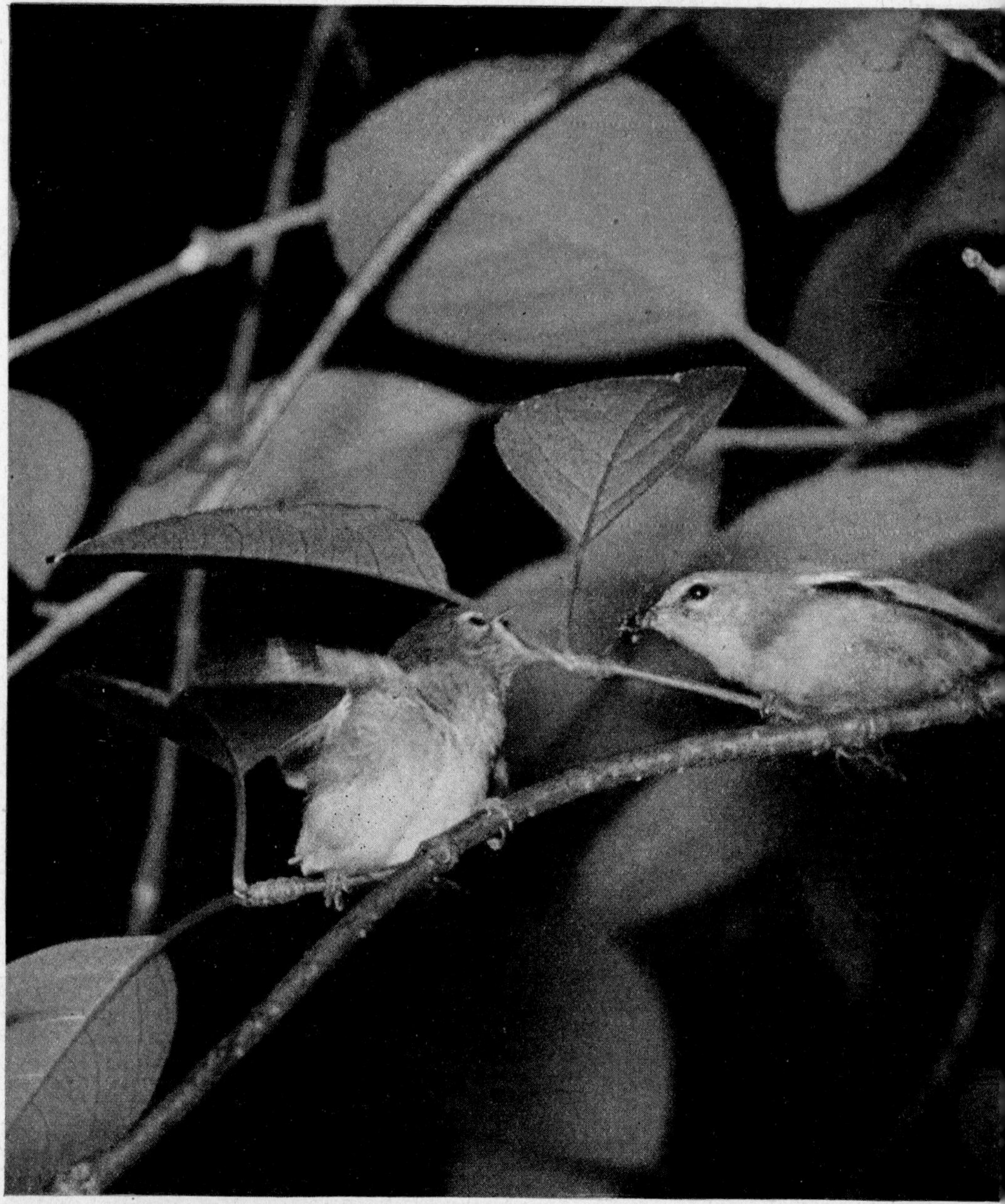

PARULA WARBLER (*Parula americana*). Length: 4.25 to 4.75 inches. Male and female: bluish gray above, yellow throat and breast. Greenish patch on back. Two prominent white wingbars. From below dark band crossing breast is visible. Female lacks this and is duller throughout than male. Range: breeds from Gulf of St. Lawrence and central Canada south to Florida, Gulf Coast and Texas; winters in Florida and the Tropics. Voice: buzzy rattle or trill which ascends scale, *zeeeeeeeeeee-up*. Also *zh-zh-zh-zheeeee*.
Samuel A. Grimes

the Western Palm, yellow in the Yellow Palm.

The Yellow Palm ranges westward to Ontario and southward to southern Nova Scotia, New Brunswick and Maine. It winters from southern Florida and Louisiana southward. The Western Palm is a more western form, found chiefly west of the Appalachian mountains. In autumn, it migrates on the Atlantic slope.

On its breeding grounds in the spruce-tamarack bogs of the northern woods, the Palm Warbler builds its nest in a hummock of moss or sedge. The song is a Junco-like trill.

OVENBIRD

(*Seiurus aurocapillus*)

Color Plate Page 347

The first time I succeeded in tracing the loud, ringing song of *teacher, teacher, Teacher, TEACHER,* to the little Warbler that delivered it from a low limb of a maple tree in a sunny woodland glade, I was amazed that such a dainty creature (5½ to 6½ inches) could possess such a powerful voice. If the Ovenbird had been twice its size, the song would still have seemed too loud for the singer.

The bird's entire manner changed when it realized that the privacy of its musical studio had been invaded. It flew to the ground, walked through the ferns on little pink legs, and jumped to a moss covered log. Here it stopped to survey me and to throw a few well chosen *chirps* in my direction.

Now I could see why the Ovenbird is also called the Golden-crowned Thrush, for through its crown runs a bright orange-brown stripe, neatly edged in black. The back is olive-brown and its white breast is streaked with black, a point that might cause a casual observer to consider it a

YELLOW WARBLER (*Dendroica petechia*). Length: 5 inches. Male: entirely yellow with faint chestnut red streakings on chest. Female: similar to male but lacks streakings. Range: breeds from Canadian tree limits to Georgia, Missouri and Oklahoma. Winters in Tropics. Voice: cheerful song, *tsee-tsee-tsee-tsee-ti-ti-wee* or *weet weet weet weet tsee tsee.*

Hal H. Harrison

PRAIRIE WARBLERS AT NEST *(Dendroica discolor)*. Length: 4.5 to 5 inches. Male and female: upperparts olive green, underparts yellow, with black streaks confined to sides. There are two black marks on face, one through the eye, and one below. Immature birds lack wingbars, and streaking of underparts is indistinct. Range: breeds from Florida north to Massachusetts, and New York, and west to eastern Nebraska. Winters from Florida to West Indies. Voice: a rising, thin *zee zee zee zee zee zee zee zee*.
Ralph E. Lawrence, National Audubon Society

Thrush. Like a tiny chicken, putting its head forward with each step, the Teacher-bird tip-toed to the end of the log, jumped to the ground and disappeared among the ferns, the trilliums and the geraniums of its woodland home.

Although I have found many nests of the Ovenbird, rarely have I found one by actually setting out to find it. Most of the nests have been found accidentally, by flushing the tight-sitting female as she incubated or brooded. The behavior of a surprised female is always the same. She flutters from the nest with wings and tail dragging as though she were mortally wounded. In the case of a predator that has come upon the nest suddenly, I daresay this ruse often works to advantage in luring it away.

It is from the shape of its nest, carefully concealed on the forest floor, that the Ovenbird gets its name. Like an old-fashioned Dutch oven, it is domed over the top with the opening on the side. The entrance is often a mere slit in the grasses and dead leaves used in construction. The five eggs are spotted with reddish brown. Incubation requires about twelve days, and like many other ground-nesting birds, young Ovenbirds leave the nest when only seven or eight days old.

The Ovenbird is a very common victim of the Cowbird. As many as seven eggs of this parasite have been found in a single nest. In his life-history study of the Ovenbird, Dr. Harry W. Hann found from one to four Cowbird eggs in twenty-two of a total of forty-two nests with eggs. In one summer, I studied seven nests of the Ovenbird on a ninety-acre tract, six of which were parasitized by the Cowbird. A total of twelve Cowbird eggs were laid in these six nests. The same summer, I was able to take the only color picture ever taken of a Cowbird laying her egg in an Ovenbird's nest. The laying occurred at dawn (4:58 a.m.) on June 1st.

In the summer the Ovenbird ranges from northern Ontario and the Gulf of St. Lawrence south to Kansas, Arkansas, northern Georgia, and eastern North Carolina. It winters from Florida and the Gulf coast south to South America. There are two geographical subspecies which show no differences.

NORTHERN WATER-THRUSH

(Seiurus noveboracensis)

I have a tremendous respect for the ability of the Northern Water-Thrush to hide its nest, for, although I have searched repeatedly in swamp forests and bogs where singing males abound, I have yet to find my first nest. It is a different story with the Louisiana Water-Thrush, a more southern relative of this Warbler, for I have found many nests of this species, along woodland streams in dank ravines.

Although the two species never nest in the same habitat it is well to remember that the Northern Water-Thrush has the yellowish eye line while the Louisiana's is always white. Another field mark is the unspotted throat of the Louisiana.

The name of "Thrush" applied to this bird, although descriptive of its woodland habits, is confusing in placing the species where it belongs—in the Warbler family. Its wild call has been well interpreted as *hurry, hurry, hurry, pretty, pretty, pretty,* although

MAGNOLIA WARBLER *(Dendroica magnolia)*. Length: 4.5 to 5 inches. Male and female: upperparts black with yellow and white patches. Underparts yellow striped with black. From above tail is tipped with wide white band. In fall: brown above, yellow below. Range: Canada to Minnesota, Michigan, Massachusetts, and in Appalachians to Virginia. Winters in Central America. Voice: song, *weeta weeta weetee*, or *weeta weeta weeta*.

Hal H. Harrison

perhaps Peterson's *chew-chew-chew* is more accurately descriptive of the ending, which drops rapidly in pitch.

The Water-Thrush is 5 to 6 inches long, solidly brown on the back and heavily striped on the breast which is tinged with yellow. It has the habit of bobbing like a Sandpiper.

NORTHERN WATER-THRUSH (*Seiurus noveboracensis*). Length: 5 to 6 inches. Male and female: upperparts dark brown with conspicuous *light stripe over the eye,* and sandy-colored underparts *heavily streaked* with *black*. Range: Canada down through northern central America, east to New York and south to the mountains of West Virginia. Voice: distinctive song, *chew-chew-chew* (*twit twit twit twee twee twee chew chew chew*) rapid, lowering in pitch at the end.

Rudolph Hindemith, American Museum of Natural History

Two races of this Warbler are recognized: Northern Water-Thrush (*S. n. noveboracensis*), which breeds from northern Ontario and the Gulf of St. Lawrence south to southern Ontario, New York, and in the mountains to West Virginia; and Grinnell's Water-Thrush (*S. n. notabilis*) which breeds from the limit of trees in western Canada south to western Montana, and northwestern Nebraska, northern Minnesota, northwestern Michigan, and east to northeastern Ohio and northwestern Pennsylvania.

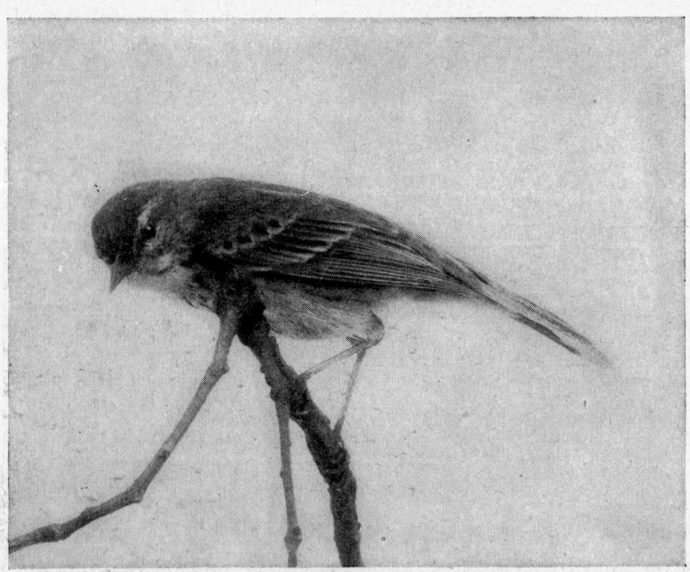

PALM WARBLER (*Dendroica palmarum*). Length: 5 to 5.5 inches. Male and female: upperparts grayish olive, with *chestnut red* crown (obscure in fall and winter), underparts yellow and whitish, with chestnut streaks. Range: breeds from Gulf of St. Lawrence, south to Maine and northern Minnesota; migrates throughout eastern United States; winters from Louisiana to Florida, and occasionally north along coast to Massachusetts. Voice: a series of weak notes *thi, thi, thi, thi, thi, thi.*

Chicago Natural History Museum

LOUISIANA WATER-THRUSH

(*Seiurus motacilla*)

Color Plate Page 351

It was a blustering raw day in mid-April. My hike had led me along the banks of a flood-swollen stream in a little valley in western Pennsylvania.

Trillium spikes were spreading their curled leaves over the hillsides. Hepaticas were in full bloom. Red maple trees were covered with blossoms.

Suddenly from far ahead of me up the narrow ravine came the wild, ringing call of the bird for which I had been searching. It was the spring song of the Louisiana Water-Thrush, not a Thrush at all, but a dainty little Warbler also called a Water Wagtail. There is something joyous and exhilarating in that song on an April morning when spring no longer hides her return. It is a song for which I listen each year as eagerly as for the soft warbling of the Bluebird.

But to hear the song is not to see the bird, as many hikers have discovered after chasing this "song" up and down a dark, woodland glen with hardly a glimpse of the singer. To catch up with it is to find a little brown bird with a streaked breast and a white eye-line, teetering like a Sandpiper from one wet rock to another. Like the Ovenbird, also a member of the genus *Seiurus*, the Louisiana Water-Thrush walks rather than hops.

Shady, stream-fed ravines are its northern home. Here the male establishes his territory early in the spring. Here, in late April, or early May, his mate will select a little nook along the bank among the exposed roots of a tree or under a mossy ledge. In this carefully hidden spot, she will place a foundation of dried leaves and mosses onto which will go the nest of coarse grasses. Four to six creamy eggs speckled with brown are laid.

One spring I was fortunate enough to discover the female the day she started to build her nest—April 25th. It was completed May 3rd. One egg a day was laid until six were laid. Incubation required exactly 13 days. The young were in the nest 10 days, leaving on June 1st.

A later migrant in the spring is the Louisiana Water-Thrush's close relative, the Northern Water-Thrush *(Seiurus noveboracensis noveboracensis)* and its closely related western form, Grinnell's Water-Thrush *(S. n. notabilis)*. The latter two cannot be told apart in the field, but both can be distinguished from the Louisiana Water-Thrush by the yellow eye line and the rather yellowish underparts. The songs are different, too; the Northern lacking much of the wild ring of the Louisiana. In all cases the

CONNECTICUT WARBLER *(Oporornis agilis)*. Length: 5.25 to 6 inches. Male and female: gray-hooded head; foreparts, slate gray; upperparts, olive; underparts, yellow. Round white eye-ring. Range: bogs from Manitoba to central Minnesota and northern Michigan, winters in South America. Voice: an Oven-bird-like *beecher beecher beecher beecher beech.*

Rudolph Hindemith, American Museum of Natural History

sexes are alike in plumage. The Louisiana is slightly larger, measuring 6¼ inches.

While the Louisiana Water-Thrush is invariably attracted to streams of running water, it is my experience that the Northern Water-Thrush prefers wooded swampland and isolated pools in heavily wooded areas. I found this species abundant in a rhododendron bog, a place one would never look for the Louisiana.

In summer, the Louisiana Water-Thrush ranges from Massachusetts, southern Ontario, southeastern Minnesota, and eastern Nebraska south to central South Carolina, northern Georgia, southern Alabama and northeastern Texas. Although a few Northern Water-Thrushes winter in Florida, the winter range of all members of the family is generally Mexico south to Colombia and the West Indies.

One of the most curious habits of the Louisiana Water-Thrush is its practice of laying a pathway of leaves leading from the nest which form a doormat, sometimes a foot long.

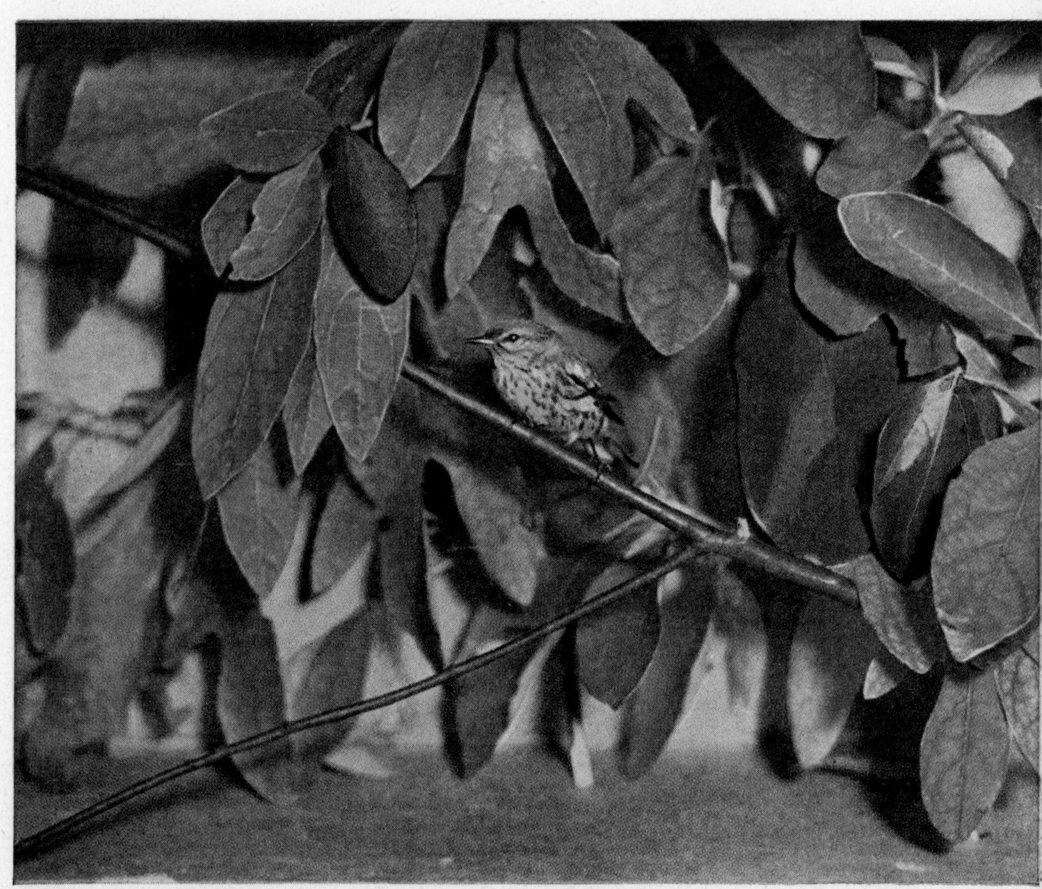

CAPE MAY WARBLER (*Dendroica tigrina*). Length: 5 to 5.5 inches. Male: blackish crown with chestnut patch about the eye and cheek. Grayish back streaked with black. Large white patch in the wing. Yellow underparts, narrowly striped with black, yellow head and rump. Females and immature: lack chestnut cheeks and are duller throughout. Dim patch of yellow behind the ear. Range: across Canada to Nova Scotia and south through Maine and New Hampshire. Migrates through eastern United States; winters in West Indies. Voice: high *seet seet seet seet* repeated four or more times.
Hal H. Harrison

KENTUCKY WARBLER

(Oporornis formosus)

Color Plate Page 354

MOURNING WARBLER (*Oporornis philadelphia*). Length: 5 to 5.75 inches. Male: bluish gray head and neck; back greenish brown, apron of black crepe on upper breast where hood meets yellow abdomen. Female: similar to male, but with head, neck and breast grayish brown. Range: Manitoba and Gulf of St. Lawrence throughout mountains of northeastern America to West Virginia. Winters in Central and South America. Voice: song, *chirry, chirry, chorry, chorry;* last two notes, low.

Rudolph Hindemith, American Museum of Natural History

If you are able to distinguish the song of the Kentucky Warbler from that of the Carolina Wren, you should have no further trouble identifying this richly colored yellow bird with the black sideburns or whiskers. The two look nothing alike, but the loud, clearly - whistled *turtle, turtle, turtle,* notes are very similar. To some, the Kentucky's song is reminiscent of the Ovenbird's *teacher* song but the former is delivered in a monotone. I have known a few bird watchers to confuse the *purty, purty, purty,* song of the Cardinal with the refrain of the Kentucky Warbler but careful listening will aid here.

Although otherwise a very shy and suspicious bird, the male is a persistent singer. Of this fact, Dr. Frank M. Chapman writes: "On one occasion at Englewood, New Jersey, I watched a male for three hours. During this period, with the exception of five interruptions of less than forty-five seconds each, he sang with the greatest regularity every twelve seconds. Thus, allowing for the brief intervals of silence, he sang about 875 times, or some 5,250 notes. I found him singing, and when I departed he showed no signs of ceasing."

The Kentucky Warbler (5½ inches) haunts the bushy swamps, boggy woodlands, and the dark, damp tangles. There it forages for food, and there it nests. Were it not for its song, many watchers no doubt would pass it by unnoticed. The nest is hidden carefully near the ground, a rather bulky structure of dead leaves, grapevine bark, rootlets, and grasses. Four or five finely speckled white eggs are laid.

Although the black head markings of the male are generally darker than those of the female, I was unable to distinguish between the sexes when I took the natural color picture on page 354. This nest was hidden beneath the broad leaves of a mandrake or May-apple.

In the fall, the Kentucky Warbler is seldom seen. The southern movement gets underway in August. Quietly the birds head toward their winter home in Mexico, Central and South America, staying close to the ground in the underbrush, passing through the states practically unnoticed. The Kentucky nests from the Gulf States north to southwestern Nebraska, southern Wisconsin, northern Ohio, and rarely to the lower Hudson Valley.

CONNECTICUT WARBLER

(Oporornis agilis)

If you live in the Mississippi valley and wonder why you never see the Connecticut Warbler in fall migration; or, if you live in the Atlantic coast states and wonder why you never see the Connecticut Warbler in spring migration, it is because the bird travels one way in the spring and the other way in the autumn. But the Connecticut is such a shy secretive bird, that one might be in the path of its migration and still miss it.

Like its close relative, the Mourning Warbler, the Connecticut wears a gray hood. The former, however, also shows a conspicuous black mark on the breast, absent in the Connecticut. The Mourning Warbler also lacks the Connecticut's white eye-ring. The Nashville is similar except for a yellow, not a gray, throat.

The Connecticut Warbler is at home in the summer in the tamarack and spruce bogs from Manitoba south to central Minnesota and northern Michigan. Its nest is on the ground, sunk into moss, or under a clump of grass. In the winter, the Connecticut is found in northern South America from Brazil to Colombia.

MOURNING WARBLER

(Oporornis philadelphia)

Alexander Wilson called it the Philadelphia Warbler, and the quiet retiring manner of the Mourning Warbler with its gray Quaker-like garb encircling the head and neck, might well be compared with the plain folks of early Philadelphia. Unlike the very similar Connecticut Warbler, the Mourning Warbler lacks an eye-ring, and the male has a black scarf where the yellow underparts meet the breast. This black mark is absent in the female Mourning, but the female Connecticut shares the white eye-ring with her mate. The Mourning Warbler measures 5 to 5¾ inches in length.

Although far from common, the Mourning's shyness makes it appear more rare than it actually is. It skulks in dense thickets, seldom leaving the low growth except to sing from a bush or tree. The female builds her large nest of dead leaves, fibers, grasses, and hairs on or near the ground. The location chosen is usually in rank vegetation bordering a bog or marsh, or in briar tangles. The two-parted song is loud and throaty, beginning with several two-note phrases and ending with two or more lower notes uttered rapidly.

The Mourning Warbler's breeding range is essentially eastern, occurring from the mountains of West Virginia, Pennsylvania, and New York, central Minnesota and Michigan, north to Manitoba and northwestern Ontario. It winters in Central and South America.

MACGILLIVRAY'S WARBLER

(Oporornis tolmiei)

The western counterpart of the more eastern Mourning Warbler is the Macgillivray's Warbler, which breeds from Canada south to central California, Arizona and northern New

Mexico, and from the Pacific Coast to southwestern South Dakota.

Although similar to the Mourning Warbler with its slate-gray hood that encircles the head and neck, and its yellow belly and olive back, the Macgillivray's Warbler (4¾ to 5½ inches) has a white eye-ring and a grayer breast. Its song is two-parted. The first phrase of three notes is delivered in a higher pitch than the latter phrases of two notes. Translated into words, the song seems to say: *sweet-sweet-sweet, sugar-sugar.*

YELLOW-THROAT

(Geothlypis trichas)

Color Plate Page 358

That nervous little Wren-like Warbler with the black domino mask across his black eyes is the Yellow-throat. If his mask is not enough to remind you of Hallowe'en and masquerades, he will help by singing his characteristic song *witchity, witchity, witchity.*

The male Yellow-throat wears his black mask throughout the year, but the female has no sign of a mask. She is plain olive-colored above with a yellow throat and breast (lighter than the male's) and a white belly. Immatures resemble the female. The birds are 4½ to 5½ inches long.

With suitable tangles and tall grasses for nesting, the Yellow-throat may come into the garden to build its home, but more often we find it in the marshes, damp bottomlands, and the weed patches along the roadsides. I have found the nest deep in a swamp, carefully hidden in the leaves of a skunk cabbage. Again, I have found it on a dry mountainside, hidden in laurel. The natural color photograph on page 358 was taken at the latter nest.

Wherever it is found, the Yellow-throat is a bird of the ground. Its nest, a bulky structure of grasses, strips of bark, and rootlets, is never very high. The four eggs are white with spots and specks. The female alone incubates, but the male is attentive to the young. Unlike most Warblers, the Yellow-throat is said to have two broods each season, the second occurring in July.

Nine geographic races of this Warbler are recognized throughout its range from southern Canada to southern California, Texas, and Florida. Four are eastern (Maryland, Northern,

MACGILLIVRAY'S WARBLER *(Oporornis tolmiei)*. Length: 4.75 to 5.5 inches. Male and female: olive above, yellow below, with a slate gray hood encircling head and neck, and white eye-ring. Range: breeds from Canada south to central California, central Arizona, and north New Mexico; migrates into Mexico. Voice: a rolling chant, *chiddle, chiddle, chiddle, turtle, turtle,* or *chiddle-chiddle-chiddle, wick-wick.*

Rudolph Hindemith, American Museum of Natural History

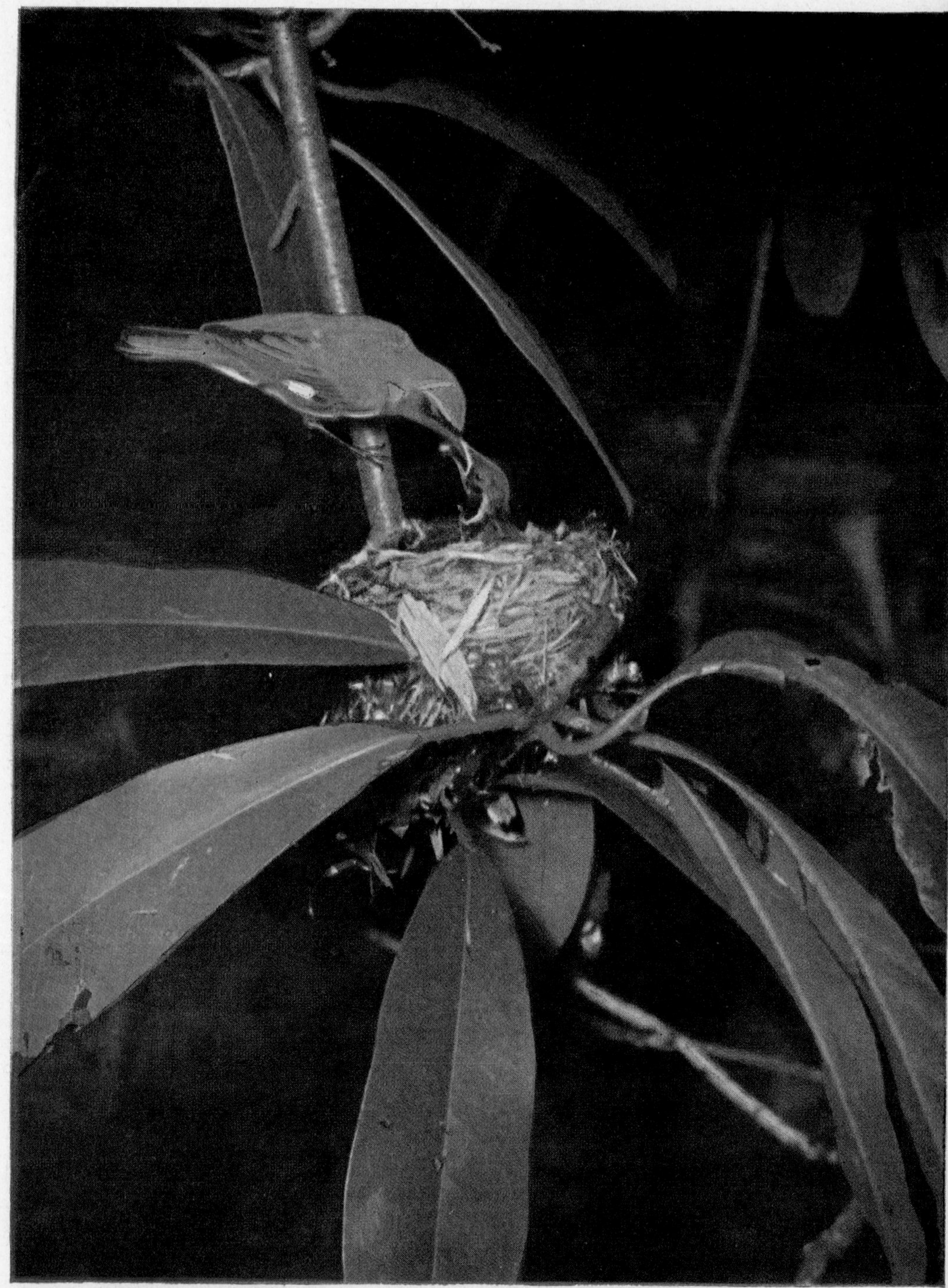

MALE BLACK-THROATED BLUE WARBLER FEEDING YOUNG (*Dendroica coerulescens*). Length: 5 to 5.5 inches. Male: blue gray above, black sides; belly and breast white. Females: very plain, brownish olive upper parts; olive yellowish underparts. Light blue over the eye, small white wing-spot. Range: breeds from northern Minnesota and southern Quebec to southern Minnesota, Ontario and Massachusetts. Winters at Key West and in West Indies. Voice: husky *zur zur zur zreee* or *I am lazy*.

Hal H. Harrison

AUDUBON'S WARBLER *(Dendroica auduboni)*. Length: 4.75 to 5.25 inches. Winter male and female: upperparts gray streaked with black; underparts black and white; yellow rump. Male in spring: slate gray above, heavy black breast patch shaped like inverted U. Throat, crown, and side patches yellow. Distinctive white wing patches. Female in spring: brown instead of gray of male. Lacks wing patch. Range: breeds from Canada south to mountains of California, Arizona, and New Mexico. Winters in Pacific States and lower Rio Grande Valley, Texas. Voice: loose two-parted song, *seet-seet-seet-seet seet-trrrrr*. Note, a loud *tchip*.
Harry L. Crockett

Athens and Florida Yellow-throats) and five are western (Western, Sonora, Salt-Marsh, Brownsville, and Tule Yellow-throats). It winters from southern United States to Costa Rica and Haiti.

RIO GRANDE YELLOW-THROAT

(Chamaethlypsis poliocephala poliocephala)

The Mexican Ground-chat, or Rio Grande Yellow-throat is larger (5½ inches) and quite different from its northern relative. Its bill is thicker and strongly curved downward. The male has a very limited black spot between the eye and bill. While the female does not have the black on the face, her larger size and lack of white on the underparts distinguish her from the female Yellow-throat.

The Rio Grande Yellow-throat is limited to the lower Rio Grande Valley where it builds its nest off the ground in clumps of coarse grass. The four eggs are creamy white marked with brown. Its song is short and cheerful, rather like that of a Bunting.

YELLOW-BREASTED CHAT

(Icteria virens virens)

Color Plate Page 359

I remember well my first adventure with a Yellow-breasted Chat, the larg-

LONG-TAILED CHAT AT NEST *(Icteria virens auricollis)*. Length: 6.5 to 7.5 inches. Male and female: olive brown above with bright yellow throat and breast and white belly. White spectacles are prominent. Range: breeds from Washington and Montana to Mexico; winters in Mexico. Voice: various harsh or whistled notes in series, with long pauses between series, somewhat suggestive of the Mockingbird.

Eliot F. Porter, National Audubon Society

est member of the Wood Warbler family. It occurred many years ago at a nest I found concealed carefully in an elderberry bush along a river bank. It contained four white eggs, spotted with rufous. The birds were shy and made no fuss while I examined the nest. Indeed, only at a distance was I able to identify the white-spectacled bird with the brilliant yellow breast.

Then I made one of the many mistakes that I made regularly while learning to take pictures of wild birds. I set up my remote control camera equipment and focused on this nest with eggs. As I learned later, pictures of adult birds at the nest should not be attempted until the young are fairly well grown, or, when the adults' instinct to return to the nest to feed is greater than the instinct of fear aroused by the camera nearby.

Two and a half hours later, I packed up the equipment and went home, hot, disgusted, out of patience, and quite disturbed over my failure. At home I checked through a reference book and came to a picture of a Yellow-breasted Chat captioned as follows: "One of the shyest of North American birds. The only photograph of a Yellow-breasted Chat on its nest." I felt better!

My second encounter came years later. Much film had run through my camera during the intervening years. On that day, working at a nest containing two youngsters in a wild grape tangle, I shot twenty-two pictures in eleven hours. During the first two hours that I was in the blind some forty feet from the nest, the birds refused to pose, but with those two hungry babies as decoys, the adults finally gave in.

Late that day, when I finished my twenty-second picture, "North America's shyest bird" hardly bothered to get out of my way as I packed up the equipment. By that time I was one of the family!

No one can fully appreciate the Chat until he has witnessed the courtship antics of this Warbler. Here, indeed, is birdland's clown. His song is "out of this world," for there is nothing with which to compare it. Listening to it early one May morning, I wrote the following impressions: the alarm call of a Wren; a series of nasal *quacks;* a fresh fellow whistling at a passing girl; a fog horn; and a chuckling, high-pitched laugh. If you can put all that into one song, you have the love voice of the Yellow-breasted Chat.

Various phrases of his song are often delivered while he leaps into the air, and, with legs and tail dangling awkwardly, he flaps and clowns his way to another singing perch.

The male and female Yellow-breasted Chat, which are 7 or 7½ inches long, are similar, olive green above, with a bright yellow throat and breast. The belly is white. The white "spectacles" around the eyes are unmistakable.

Chats are found throughout the greater part of the United States. They migrate to Mexico and Central America for the winter. In the west, the Yellow-breasted Chat is replaced by a subspecies, the Long-tailed Chat (*I. v. suricollis*).

LONG-TAILED CHAT

(Icteria virens auricollis)

In the low valley country from southern British Columbia, Montana and North Dakota south to Mexico breeds the western counterpart of the Yellow-breasted Chat (*Icteria virens virens*), called theLong-tailed Chat. Ornithologists tell us that the latter has a longer wing, tail and bill, than the eastern race, but be that as it may, it has the same eccentric song and is just as much of a clown as the Yellow-breasted Chat.

The Chat is the largest of the Warblers. If it were not for its vivid yellow color, one might be tempted to think of it as a small Thrasher. Its love of the underbrush, its curved bill, long tail, and even its song all remind one of the Mimic Thrushes.

The upperparts of the long-Tailed Chat are grayish olive green and the white of the cheek region extends further than does that of the Yellow-breasted Chat but location is a better guide to recognition.

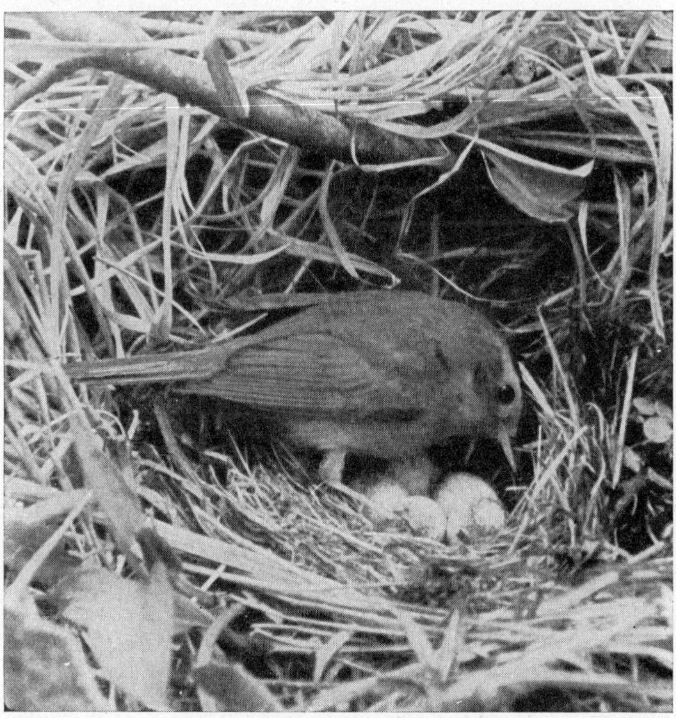

PILEOLATED WARBLER AT NEST (*Wilsonia pusilla*). Length: 4.25 to 5 inches. Male: upperparts yellowish olive with *round black cap.* Female and immature: small, plain birds, olive green above and bright yellow below with no distinctive markings. Range: Canada south to southwestern United States. Voice: a series of dry notes, all on one pitch; *chi-chi-chi-chi-chit-chit-chit* becoming louder and faster towards the end.

Alfred M. Bailey, National Audubon Society

PAINTED REDSTART *(Setophaga picta picta)*. Length: 5 inches. Male and female: black with *large white patches* on the wings and tail, and a *large bright red patch* on the breast. Range: higher mountains of central and southern Arizona and New Mexico and southward over higher districts of Mexico. Voice: song, a repetitious, *weeta-weeta-weeta wee*, or *weeta weeta, chilp, chilp, chilp*. The note is a ringing Finch-like *clee-ip*.
Ross and Florence Thornburg

RED-FACED WARBLER

(Cardellina rubrifous)

A western Warbler, the Red-face (5¼ inches) has a gray back and a bright red face and breast. Its head has a black crown, and the nape and rump are white. Its underparts are whitish.

Limited to the mountains of southwestern New Mexico and southeastern Arizona, the Red-face is the only Warbler found in that section with a red face. Its song is a sweet typical Warbler's song. Its home is among the spruces and other conifers.

HOODED WARBLER

(Wilsonia citrina)

Color Plate Page 361

I walked quietly through a Pennsylvania woodland early one morning in late May. The sunlight broke through the maple leaves overhead and fell in shattered fragments upon the rhododendrons around me. Suddenly, one of those bits of sunlight moved. I stopped dead in my tracks. Slowly the binoculars came up to my eyes. I picked out a spot of gold and in my glasses I found my first Hooded Warbler.

One would never suspect that such a brilliantly feathered gem could be so hard to see, but here I found natural camouflage plus eruptive markings neatly hiding my bird. The black hood of the male encircles the head and neck forming an onyx frame for the startling yellow face and forehead. The underparts are yellow, too, but the back is olive. The bird is 5 to 6 inches long.

A moment later, I saw his mate. She suffered from comparison and looked almost drab beside his golden majesty, being olive above and yellow on the forehead and underparts. But she was alarmed. I noticed instantly her characteristic habit of swishing her tail open and shut, exposing the lighter colored outer tail feathers with each flicking motion. Her alarm note was a loud, metallic *chip,* not unlike that of the Louisiana Water-Thrush or even the Cardinal.

This nervous reception could mean only one thing—a nest nearby. To find it was a task requiring great patience, and it took me over an hour in a hiding place some distance away to follow her finally in my glasses to the correct spot. The nest was hidden carefully under the broad leaves of a rhododendron. It was a tiny cup of grasses and weed stalks on a foundation of dried leaves. It contained four white eggs finely speckled with brown and purple.

I followed this nest until the young left. I learned that the male is a devoted father and not a bit camera-shy. The female, however, never ceased to be nervous when I was near. During my studies, I listened for hours to the male's simple song. He sang as he fed, and to me, he seemed to repeat: *ta-weet, ta-weetee-you*. Years later, when I heard my first Magnolia Warbler, I was struck by the similarity between its song and the song of the Hooded Warbler.

To the late Dr. Frank M. Chapman, the Hooded Warbler was a particular favorite. "To my mind there is no Warbler to which that much misused word 'lovely' may be so aptly applied. Its beauty of plumage, charm of voice, and gentleness of demeanor, make it indeed not only a lovely, but a truly lovable bird."

In our northern states, I have always found the Hooded Warbler in low, woodland cover, often in moist locations such as ravines and river bottoms. In the south, the bird is commonly found in forested swamps where dense tangles hide its movements.

In the winter, the Hooded Warbler ranges from Mexico to Panama. Migrating north in the spring, it reaches the United States by a flight across the Gulf of Mexico. It breeds from Con-

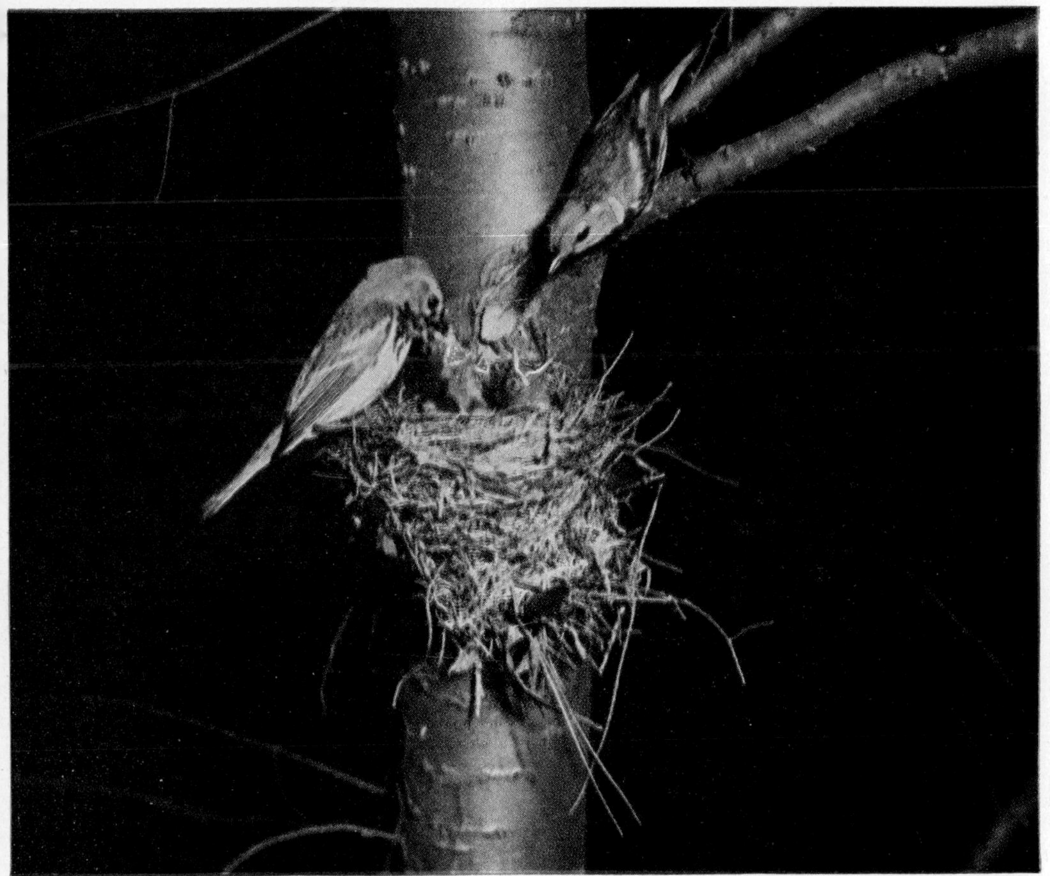

BLACK-THROATED GREEN WARBLERS, FEMALE AT THE NEST, MALE ON LIMB ABOVE (*Dendroica virens*). Length: 4.5 to 5.25 inches. Male: bright yellow face; upperparts olive green; black throat, upper breast and sides of breast. White abdomen. Female: similar to male but chin and throat usually pale yellowish and black, broken by whitish spots. Range: Canada to Minnesota, Ohio and New Jersey, and Long Island. Also from Virginia to South Carolina. Winters in Mexico and Central America. Voice: zoo zee zoo zoo zee or zee zee zee zoo zee, song, sung in a dreamy manner.

Hal H. Harrison

necticut, central New York, southern Michigan, northern Iowa, and Nebraska south to Florida and the Gulf States, west to Louisiana.

CANADA WARBLER

(Wilsonia canadensis)

Color Plate Page 364

No writer has been able to catch in words the sprightly song of the Canada Warbler. It is rippling, bubbling, clear, and sweet, but entirely uncertain and greatly varied.

Saunders writes of the song: "a variable twittering, high-pitched group of ten or fifteen notes, no two successive notes on the same pitch. The pitch and time are irregular with no definite fixed form or rhythm."

There seems to be no other Warbler's song with which the Canada's can be compared, although some field observers detect certain phrases that suggest the Yellow-throat's *witchity*. One negatively helpful point is that the song lacks the buzzing or husky notes of many of the Warblers.

This song, and the songs of the Chestnut-sided Warbler and the Redstart, were the most difficult for me to learn of all Warbler songs. The difficulty is to tie the right bird with the right song. Nothing helps more than repeated experiences in seeing the bird and hearing it sing at the same time.

Sight identification of the Canada Warbler (5 to 6 inches) presents none of the difficulties of song identification. The male's startling yellow breast makes a beautiful background for a necklace of short black spots and stripes. This, combined with a plain gray back and a prominent yellow eye-ring, makes identification positive. The female is similar, but the necklace is faint, so much so that at a distance it seldom can be detected at all. Her yellow breast is unmistakable.

The Canada Warbler is sometimes called the Canada Flycatcher because it often feeds in the manner of a Flycatcher, darting out from its perch to snatch a luckless insect. The catch is made with a sharp click of the bill, also a Flycatcher trait. Thayer described the bird as "a sort of mongrel between a Dendroica, an American Redstart, and a true Flycatcher."

I spent a happy summer with Canada Warblers. I found them abundant in a rhododendron bog where they had as their neighbors the Black-throated Blue Warblers, and the Grinnell's Water-Thrushes.

Two nests that I found were buried deep in leafy liverwort *(Bazzania trilobata)* in rotted stumps. The opening to the nest through the liverwort was so small that it was difficult to see the four white, rufous-speckled eggs. Two other nests were hidden in the sides of mossy banks along woodland trails, both in damp locations. In this habitat, I found them associated with Slate-colored Juncos whose nests were placed in identical locations.

With young in the nest, the adults become quite noisy and excited when approached. The alarm note, delivered incessantly at that time, is a loud *chip*. Nests are much easier to find when they contain young, for the birds lose the reserve that characterizes them earlier in the season. The *chipping*, however, often occurs some distance from the nest.

The summer range of the Canada Warbler extends from Newfoundland westward to the Rocky Mountains and southward along the Appalachians to northern Georgia. It migrates to South America for the winter.

WILSON'S or PILEOLATED WARBLER

(Wilsonia pusilla)

A yellow Warbler with a bluish black cap is a Wilson's Warbler *(W.p. pusilla)* in eastern United States, but in western United States it is one of two races of the Wilson's—the Northern Pileolated Warbler *(W.p. pileolata)* or the Golden Pileolated Warbler *(W.p. chryseola)*. Which of the western two you observe depends largely upon where you find it. The Pileolated of the Pacific coast from British Columbia to southern California is the Golden Pileolated, while the northern race is the one most likely to be encountered from northern Alaska south into eastern Oregon and California to mountainous New Mexico and Texas. The birds appear alike in the field.

But wherever you find it, the Wilson's or the Pileolated is a busy little Warbler (4½ to 5 inches long) crammed full of energy. At times, its manner of feeding is quite suggestive of a Flycatcher, while at other times it gleans its food in accepted Warbler-fashion among the leaves. The females may or may not show the black cap. Immature birds never do. Then they appear as perfectly plain birds, olive above and yellow below.

AMERICAN REDSTART

(Setophaga ruticilla)

Color Plate Page 368

My first sight of a male Redstart came to me just as I had read about it in all the bird books—a flaming black and orange torch flickering down through the leaves on shafts of sunlight. It was late in May in a woodlot of young maples. I spied him high in a tree, darting out in Flycatcher-fashion to snare passing insects. One victim must have eluded him, for he came fluttering through the sun-spangled leaves, fanning his tail, spreading his wings, displaying his brilliant plumage "in a manner to set at defiance all laws of aggressive coloration." Down he came like a blazing tropical butterfly, only to swoop upward suddenly, and perch near his mate.

I had not noticed her before, but that seemed excusable when I had studied her protective coloration of olive-brown, yellow and white. She is olive-brown above and white below, and shows yellow in the wings and tail in flight. Although a nervous little sprite, she lacked his verve and dash. But what a lovely pair of birds! Little wonder that the Cubans call the Redstart "Candelita," which Dr. Chapman interpreted as "the little torch that flashes in the gloomy depths of the tropical forests."

During years afield, my experience with the Redstart's song has been paralleled by the experience of many other bird watchers. It is not a song that I can tie to, like the *witchity* of the Yellow-throat; the wild ring of the Louisiana Water-Thrush; the squawk of the Chat; or the *teacher* of the Ovenbird. I must stop and listen carefully while I eliminate the Yellow Warbler, the Hooded Warbler and the Chestnut-sided Warbler.

Roger Peterson offers interpretations for two songs of the Redstart, which are commonly alternated, making an excellent field aid. They are: *tsee tsee*

CHESTNUT-SIDED WARBLER (*Dendroica pensylvanica*). Length: 5 inches. Male and female in spring: yellow crown, chestnut colored sides, olive yellow above; underparts, white. Male and female in autumn: olive green above and white below; white eye-ring and two wingbars. Range: Canada to Nebraska, Illinois, Ohio, New Jersey, Tennessee and west South Carolina; winters in Central America. Voice: emphatic *I wish to see Miss Beecher* or *please please please to meetcha.*
Hal H. Harrison

tsee tsee tsee-o and *teetsa teetsa teetsa teetsa teet.* The Redstart's repertoire includes many variations, however, and these will often delay identification.

It was during a brisk June shower that I found my first Redstart's nest twelve feet from the ground in a fork of a young birch. The female was incubating four speckled eggs in a compact, felted cup of plant down, grapevine bark, and cobwebs. The male does not share in the incubation, but he is very attentive to the young. Indeed, while photographing these birds, I have watched the male Redstart come to the nest with food while I worked with the camera a few feet away.

A noteworthy characteristic of this Warbler is the fact that the males do not acquire adult plumage until the end of their second summer. First-year males are similar to the females but may have a few black feathers to distinguish them. They breed in this first year plumage, causing uninformed observers to believe they have watched a female Redstart singing. The bird is 4½ to 5½ inches long.

Redstarts, like most Warblers, have only one brood. In the summer, they range from northern British Columbia to Newfoundland, and south to Utah, Oklahoma, and northern Georgia. They winter in the West Indies and northern South America.

PAINTED REDSTART

(Setophaga picta picta)

Not many of us have ever seen a Painted Redstart, but after admiring the color paintings made of this gorgeous Warbler, one often wonders if he would not be well repaid for his trip into the mountains of southern Arizona or southwestern New Mexico or the Chisos Mountains of the southwestern corner of Texas where he might see it, study it, and perhaps photograph it in natural color.

What a beautiful splash that large patch of red on the breast would make in Kodachrome! The black and white body would serve as ideal background material for the brilliant coloring. And since the sexes are similar, the chances for pictures would be more than doubled! And what is more, the nest is easily accessible. It is placed on the ground. Dreams for color photographers!

WEAVER FINCHES

Family Ploceidae

Birds of the Old World, the Weaver Finches are known in the United States only by two introduced species, among the least attractive members of the family. The name of Weaver Finch comes from the elaborately woven nests which some members of the family construct. Although the birds are generally Sparrow-like, some males are very handsome, particularly among the African and Asiatic species.

ENGLISH SPARROW

(Passer domesticus)

Color Plate Page 369

It was a dark day in the lives of all true American Sparrows when that European importation, the Weaver Finch, was named an English Sparrow. From that day on, unrecorded thousands of little songsters have fallen dead with air rifle pellets in their hearts.

PINE WARBLER *(Dendroica pinus)*. Length: 5 to 5.5 inches. Male: upperparts olive green with two white wingbars; underparts lemon yellow, palely streaked breast, bright yellow on throat. Female: dull colored male. Immature and fall female: grayish above with two white wingbars. Underparts dingy white. Range: Canada to northern Michigan, Florida and Gulf States. Winters in southern United States north to southern Illinois and Virginia. Voice: loose musical trill.

Samuel A. Grimes

OVEN BIRD AT NEST (*Seiurus aurocapillus*). Length: 5.5 to 6.5 inches. Male and female: upperparts olive brown, with light orange patch on crown; underparts straw color speckled with black. Range: Massachusetts, Ohio, Wisconsin, and Nebraska south to Gulf of Mexico. Voice: a rasping hiss, *kschh*.
Hal H. Harrison

Because the English Sparrow is afforded no protection in the United States, all little brown birds must suffer. Typical of the attitude of legions of boys throughout the country was the answer I received once from a misinformed lad who had just shot a Song Sparrow. "What's the difference?" he asked, "It's just a Sparrow!"

I would suggest that the way to correct that situation is not to hope that all the boys with air rifles will change suddenly, but rather, to make it a legal violation to shoot song birds. Let those who are having trouble with English Sparrows control them legally as they would any other obnoxious creature, but let us not continue to persecute any species by affording it no sanctuary.

Like most maligned creatures, English Sparrows are not as black as they are pictured. They do very little damage, especially in the cities where they are most abundant. Many city children who delight in throwing crumbs to the birds, would never see a bird at all if these hardy little beggars did not accept their hospitality. Objectionable at times are their flocking habits in trees, vines, and about city buildings.

English Sparrows were first introduced in America in 1850 when eight pairs were released in Brooklyn. Others followed, and within fifty years, the

English Sparrow, also called House Sparrow, had spread to every corner of the United States and Canada. Their success is due largely to the fact that they are not seasonably migratory, but that they are hardy, adaptable, and most omnivorous.

Today, the English Sparrow's greatest enemies are the automobile and the Starling; the former because it has replaced the horse which furnished the bird with its greatest food supply in spilled grain, stable refuse, and manure; and the latter because its hole-nesting habit makes it highly competitive for nesting sites.

Openings in the eaves of buildings, holes in trees and telephone poles, openings in old brick walls, bird houses, and similar places are nesting sites for English Sparrows. They begin to nest in March and usually have three broods.

In the spring, the male (5 to 6½ inches long) acquires his nuptial plumage—a large black bib under the chin, and chestnut markings on the head and wings. This spring attire comes as the gray feather tips of the winter plumage are worn away, not as a result of a molt. The birds molt only once a year—in late summer. Females are plain.

The courtship antics of the male are familiar to many. With wings drooping, tail held high, and black chest thrown out, he invites the female to accept him. Sometimes, several males are observed courting the same female. This causes quite a furor, and much fluttering, strutting, and chirping ensues.

EUROPEAN TREE SPARROW

(Passer montanus montanus)

A European species introduced around St. Louis in 1870, the European Tree Sparrow has become naturalized in that region. It resembles the male English Sparrow somewhat; both sexes are alike, with a black throat patch and a large black spot behind the eyes. However its crown is chestnut color, not gray as is the English Sparrow's. A white collar almost surrounds the neck, and the wings are marked with two white bars. Its habits are like the English Sparrow, but it is more lively and is found more in trees.

MEADOWLARKS, BLACKBIRDS, and ORIOLES

Family Icteridae

This entirely American family consists of a group of quite different birds which defy classification in a convenient family name. Neither in their habits, coloration, songs, or even in their physical structure do they resemble one another. The family name is derived from the Greek word for Oriole.

BOBOLINK

(Dolichonyx oryzivorus)

Color Plate Page 373

"This flashing, tinkling meteor bursts through the expectant meadow air, leaving a train of tinkling notes behind." Thus Thoreau described the fluttering flight song of the Bobolink, a song that bubbles and tumbles in a series of rollicking notes. The bird is anything but Blackbird-like, but then Bob-lincoln is used to being contradictory as far as his family is concerned.

In its color pattern, the male Bobolink reverses things. Most birds are colored lighter below than above. The Bobolink (6½ to 8 inches long) is black beneath and largely white above with buffy head patches. It is the only member of the Blackbird family with pointed tail feathers.

The Bobolink's summer and winter life is a sort of Dr. Jekyll and Mr. Hyde existence. Before leaving the northern meadows, the male changes all its feathers, the new plumage resembling that of the female—yellowish-buff with dark stripes on the head and upperparts. Thus in late summer, Bobolinks start their migration which takes them as far south as Brazil and Argentina, nearly 5,000 miles south of the northern breeding grounds. As they pass through the southern states, they are no longer Bobolinks; they are Reedbirds, or Rice-birds.

In the role of Rice-bird, the Bobolink is a Dr. Jekyll to many southerners because of the damage the bird is said to do, but the Bobolink's role in the north during the summer is a most beneficial one. Its diet is composed largely of harmful insects.

Nesting occurs on the ground in the meadows over which the male sings his famous song. Nests are grassy cups, well hidden in dense vegetation. The eggs are gray, heavily spotted with reddish brown.

MEADOWLARK

(Sturnella magna)

Color Plate Page 376

In the northern states, bird watchers have a select group of migratory birds which they can depend upon to announce the end of winter and the advent of spring. This group, which generally arrives during the first half of March, often when spring seems to be the most remote thing in the world, in-

WESTERN MEADOWLARK *(Sturnella neglecta)*. Length: 8 to 10 inches. Male and female: upperparts streaked with pale chestnut, black and buff, bright yellow breast crossed by a black V. Outer tail feathers white. Range: breeds from Canada south to Mexico; winters from Washington and Montana, south. Voice: variable song of seven to ten notes, flute-like, gurgling and double-noted.
Rudolph Hindemith, American Museum of Natural History

cludes the Robin, Bluebird, Redwing, Killdeer, Phoebe, Flicker, Mourning Dove, and Meadowlark.

The last is not a Lark. It is a Blackbird, just as Orioles, Bobolinks, and Cowbirds are Blackbirds, although their names do not betray their relationship. The Meadowlark is a chunky brown bird of the open fields and meadows, 9 to 11 inches long, characterized by a fluttering-sailing-fluttering flight, and conspicuous white outer tail feathers. The bright yellow breast crossed with a broad crescent or V is not always a good field mark due to the bird's habit of keeping its ground-colored back turned to an intruder in its domain.

I have always thought that the classic interpretation of the Meadowlark's song, "spring o' the year," was more wishful thinking than an accurate description of the clearly whistled notes. Closer to what the Meadowlark seems to say, I think, are four notes delivered in two phrases, each note on a different pitch and delivered slowly, thus: *tee-you, tee-year*.

A grass nest, domed over the top and carefully hidden in dense cover, is the Meadowlark's home. The four or five white eggs are spotted with reddish brown. Two broods are usual, I believe.

Breeding range of the eastern species *(S.m. magna)* occurs north to New Brunswick, southern Quebec, and central Ontario, south to Florida, the Gulf Coast and New Mexico; west to eastern Minnesota, western Nebraska, northwestern Texas, and north central Arizona. In winter it retires south of southern New Jersey, the Ohio valley and Kansas.

Three subspecies of the eastern race are recognized: Southern Meadowlark *(S.m. argutula)*; Rio Grande Meadowlark *(S.m. hoopesi)*; and Arizona Meadowlark *(S.m. lilianae)*.

WESTERN MEADOWLARK

(Sturnella neglecta)

If it were not for its characteristically different song, the Western Meadowlark would present quite a problem to bird watchers in the central prairie states where its range overlaps that of the Eastern Meadowlark. True, the western species is paler, and the yellow of the breast extends into the cheeks, but these distinctions are difficult to ascertain in the field, the

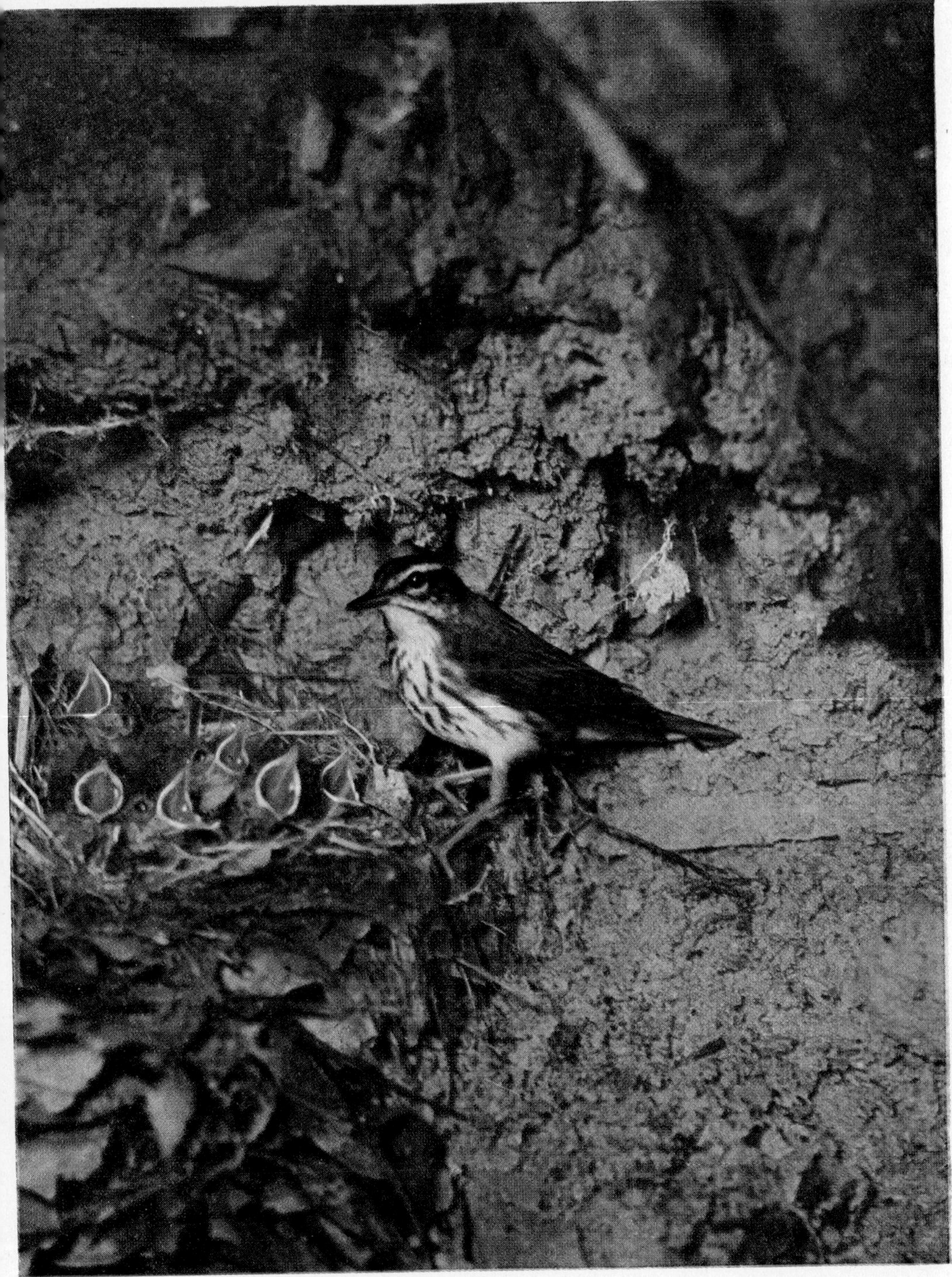

LOUISIANA WATER-THRUSH (*Seiurus motacilla*). Length: 6.25 inches. Male and female: grayish olive above; darker on crown; white underparts streaked with grayish olive. Light stripe through eye. Range: breeds from New England, Ontario, Minnesota and Nebraska to South Carolina, Georgia, Louisiana and Texas; winters in Central America. Voice: musical ringing song; three whistles and a jumble of twittering notes.

Hal H. Harrison

song being the bird watcher's salvation.

The Eastern Meadowlark has a clear, whistled song; the Western Meadowlark's utterance is a flutelike melody of six or more notes. West of the Great Plains and from Canada to Mexico, the Western Meadowlark lacks competition from its eastern relative, and its loud warbling song is a delightful part of the western countryside.

In habits the western and eastern species are alike.

YELLOW-HEADED BLACKBIRD

(Xanthocephalus xanthocephalus)

Color Plate Page 378

Unlike many drab denizens of the western marshes that live their quiet lives unseen, the Yellow-headed Blackbird is one to attract attention immediately. His gaudy head, throat, and breast of orange-yellow are startling against a contrasting background of jet-black on the belly and upperparts. Only a prominent white epaulet on each wing breaks the black framing. There is just no other bird with which it can be confused. Even the females are distinctive with yellow on the throat and upper breast. They are smaller and browner than the males, which are 9 to 11 inches long. Their note is a low *cack*.

Although associating with their relatives, the Red-winged Blackbirds, in the marshes, the Yellow-heads go off by themselves to nest in select colonies. Like the Red-wings, these birds hang their woven basket-like nests in the marsh vegetation where they lay three to five grayish or greenish eggs spotted and splotched with brown. Before the young can fly, they often leave the nest to climb about in the tule. Here many of them fall victims to predators.

Following the breeding season, Yellow-headed Blackbirds join others of their kind in huge flocks that wander over the pastures and fields, feeding on grain and weed seeds. In the evenings they return to the marshes to roost. In the fall, they associate with Red-wings, Brewer's Blackbirds and Cowbirds. Like other Blackbirds, the Yellow-head walks, but its gait has been described as a "pompous strut."

The Yellow-headed Blackbird breeds from

ORCHARD ORIOLE—MALE AT NEST (*Icterus spurius*). Length 6 to 7.25 inches. Male: fore and upperparts, black; underparts, chestnut. Young males have greenish cast, and a black throat patch. Female: above, yellowish olive green; underparts dull canary yellow, tinged with olive on sides and flanks. Range: eastern United States, breeding west to western Texas, occasionally in eastern Colorado and eastern Wyoming.

Samuel A. Grimes

British Columbia, the southern Mackenzie, central Manitoba, and northern Minnesota, south to Mexico and east to Wisconsin and Indiana. It winters south to Mexico.

AUDUBON'S ORIOLE (*Icterus graduacauda auduboni*). Length: 8 to 9.25 inches. Male and female: a yellow body, with foreparts, wings and tail black, and with yellowish back. Range: lower Rio Grande Valley. Texas, occasionally to San Antonio. Voice: a series of low whistled notes of a human quality disconnected with half-tones. Sweet with suggestion of sadness.
Chicago Natural History Museum

RED-WINGED BLACKBIRD

(Agelaius phoeniceus)

Color Plate Page 379

Spring announces her return to the north in myriad ways.

Skunk cabbages pop up like brownies in a muddy marsh; the woodland floor is blanketed with spring beauties, and through the bare trees a mourning cloak butterfly tries its wings; the din of spring peepers rises from the ponds; fern fiddleheads push through brown blankets of dead leaves; Bluebirds warble from the fenceposts along the roadside; yes, March is here at last!

Down in the marsh where the cattails have waved so long in the winter winds, a chorus rises at twilight, bringing joy to those who love the out-of-doors. During the day, a little band of hardy Red-wings has arrived from the south, and from the tip of the highest cattail, "pretty Red-wing" spreads his shiny wings in the setting sun and pours out his joyous song, *Oka-leeee!* To us, the intruders in his recently acquired sanctuary, he extends a disgruntled *check.*

It will be another week or possibly two before the drab females, looking for all the world like overgrown Sparrows (7½ to 9½ inches) will join the jet-black males, whose "shoulders" flash with gaudy red epaulets edged in buff or yellow. The courtship consists of much bowing and much flashing of epaulets as well as much chasing.

After territories are established, each male guards jealously his chosen corner. Sometimes, the Red-wing permits two or more females to nest in his homeland, and since the males assist with feeding the young, polygamy works a hardship on them. The females do all the incubating, however.

Although marshes are favored nesting sites for Red-wings, they sometimes place their deep cups in meadow grass, low bushes, and trees. I found a colony once that favored evergreen trees surrounding a lake. The nests are expertly woven and hung to surrounding vegetation. This habit of hanging the nest to growing vegetation often causes it to be tilted or even crushed.

Pale blue is the background color for the four eggs which are scratched and scrolled with black, brown, and lavender. They are not unlike the eggs of Orioles.

Young Red-wings at first look like the females. After the fall molt, however, young males can be told by their orange shoulder patches. These remain orange throughout the next season, so first-year males may be distinguished instantly from the red-shouldered oldsters.

In the fall, Red-wings gather in tremendous flocks, roosting in the marshes at night, feeding and traveling south by day. By November, most Red-wings have arrived in the southern states for the winter.

The eastern Red-winged Blackbird is divided into a number of geographic forms. West of the Rockies, the Bi-colored or California Red-wing males *(A.p. californicus)* have plain red shoulder patches with no edging, while the Tri-colored Red-wing males *(Agelaius tricolor)* show a clear white edging along the shoulder patch.

The eastern Red-winged Blackbird is distributed throughout the eastern United States to Florida and west to the Rockies.

KENTUCKY WARBLER *(Oporornis formosus)*. Length: 5.5 inches. Male and female: upperparts olive green; underparts yellow. Broad black side-burns from eye down to throat. Range: breeds from Gulf States north to Nebraska, Wisconsin, Ohio and lower Hudson Valley; winters in Mexico and Central America. Voice: rolling chant, *tory-tory-tory-tory* or *churry-churry-churry-churry*
Hal H. Harrison

TRICOLORED RED-WING

(Agelaius tricolor)

Generally similar to the common Red-wing, the Tricolored (7½ to 9 inches) is limited in range to the valleys of California and Oregon between the mountains and the coast. The male has a white edge to the red wing patch rather than yellow. The female is blackish above and dark gray underneath.

The Tricolor is extremely gregarious, nesting in large colonies. It builds its nest in alders and willows, laying four or five light buff eggs, which are marked with a brownish circle around the large end, and numerous spots. Its voice is much harsher than the common Red-wing, but its persistent joyfulness in the gloomy swamps makes up for this.

SCOTT'S ORIOLE, MALE AND YOUNG *(Icterus parisorum)*. Length: 7.25 to 9.25 inches. Male: lemon yellow oriole with black head, back, wings and tail. Female: above, olive greenish; underparts greenish yellow on breast and abdomen. Grayish cheeks. Range: desert country of southern California, Nevada, southwest Utah, Arizona, south to central New Mexico and western Texas. Voice: rich, variable whistled notes.

George M. Bradt

ORCHARD ORIOLE

(Icterus spurius)

Like a young male Redstart in the Warbler family, it takes a young male Orchard Oriole in the Blackbird family an extra year to "grow up." While most male song birds acquire adult plumage in the spring following their hatching, a few birds, like the Orchard Orioles resemble the female during their second summer. The young Orchard is female-like except for a prominent black chin and throat, absent in the female. Not until the third summer does the youngster take on the gay colors of the adult.

Those "gay" colors however, are not nearly as flashy as the black and orange of the Baltimore Oriole, a more common relative. Adult male Orchards (6 to 7¼ inches) have black heads, backs, wings, throats, and tails with dark chestnut rump patches and underparts. The female is greenish above and yellow below, with two white wingbars.

This species is found in orchards and shade trees, especially in the south central states where it is most abundant. It rarely reaches the Canadian border during the breeding season, preferring the southern states to western Texas and occasionally to Colorado and Wyoming.

AUDUBON'S ORIOLE

(Icterus graduacauda auduboni)

Within the range of the Audubon's, or Black-headed, Oriole (lower Rio Grande Valley of Texas) no other Oriole combines a black head with a yellow back; all other males have black backs. The female is similar to her mate. The birds are 8 to 9 inches long.

Like many other birds of the lower Rio Grande Valley, the Audubon's Oriole is a Mexican bird that reaches the northern extremity of its range in the United States. It has been found casually as far north as San Antonio. It is a resident bird, building its hanging nest in mesquites. Its song is a pleasing whistle.

HOODED ORIOLE

(Icterus cucullatus)

Color Plate Page 383

Sennett's Oriole *(I.c. sennetti)*, the Arizona Hooded Oriole *(I.c. nelsoni)* and the California Hooded Oriole *(I.c. californicus)* are Mexican Hooded Orioles that reach the United States in southern California, Arizona, New Mexico and Texas. Sennett's is confined entirely to the lower Rio Grande Valley in Texas.

The "hood" is an orange crown, nape, neck, and upper back, the only Oriole so marked. The bird, which is 7 to 8 inches long, is largely orange throughout with a black throat patch, forepart of back, wings, and tail. The female is olive and yellow, similar to the female Bullock's. The latter has a whitish belly while Sennett's and the Arizona Hooded are entirely yellow on the belly.

The species winters in Mexico.

SCOTT'S ORIOLE

(Icterus parisorum)

The lemon-yellow and black Scott's Oriole is the only Oriole so colored throughout its range along the Mexican border from California to Texas and north to southern Nevada and southwestern Utah. Other species (Hooded and Bullock's) of the same region are orange.

The male has his head, back, wings, and tail black, and yellow underparts. The female is greenish above and greenish yellow beneath, with two white wingbars. The immature male has a black throat. The bird is 7 to 8 inches long.

The richly whistled song of Scott's Oriole, ringing through the deep canyons of the southwest, is reminiscent of the song of the Western Meadowlark. The Scott's nests near the ground, often in yucca.

BALTIMORE ORIOLE

(Icterus galbula)

Color Plate Page 386

In a world so ever-changing as ours, it is a source of comfort and refuge to know that among the constantly-dimming memories of childhood associaions, the birds are forever loyal and dependable. Friends die, move away, change their personalities and grow old in the process, but the birds never change at all from the way we knew them when we were youngsters. They look the same, they sing the same, they act the same. Indeed, if I did not know better, I would swear they were exactly the same birds.

The old elm near the river where the Baltimore Oriole sang each May, is gone. Someone thought it cast too much shade, and it was felled. But I remember so vividly the brilliant flash of orange and black among the leaves, and the awe-struck lad that listened to the Oriole's mellow, clear, low-pitched whistle.

Next May, when I listen again to a Baltimore Oriole far from the site of that boyhood elm, the bird will look exactly the same, and although the song may vary, it will still carry the unmistakable timbre of my Oriole of years ago. I grow old, but to my eyes and ears, the Oriole is timeless.

English colonists in what is now Maryland named this member of the Blackbird family an Oriole. It was a misnomer, however, for the European Oriole for which it was named, is an entirely different bird. Skins that were sent to England indicated that this Oriole wore the orange and black ancestral color of Lord Baltimore. Thus, Linnaeus named it the Baltimore Oriole.

Although not at all drab, the female Baltimore Oriole does not match her mate's brilliance. On her, yellow replaces his bright orange underparts, and her back is brown instead of black. Any prestige she may have lost because of quieter coloring, she has more than gained back in her reputation as the master nest builder of all song birds. The low-hanging basket of the Baltimore Oriole is woven skillfully with strings, fibers, weed stalks, horsehair, and similar materials, and is hung high in a tree at the end of a swaying limb. The Baltimore Orioles are 7 to 8 inches long.

The four to six eggs are scrawled with black in typical Blackbird markings. Young Orioles are noisy in the nest during their last few days of confinement, and many nests previously hidden are discovered at that time. Orioles raise only one brood a year.

RUSTY BLACKBIRD (*Euphagus carolinus*). Length: 8.5 to 9.5 inches. Male in spring: black with whitish eye, dull greenish on head, little iridescence. Female in spring: grayish. Adults and immature in autumn: rusty, with closely barred underparts. Range: breeds in Canada and northern United States; winters south to the Gulf of Mexico and west to the Rockies. Voice: a harsh *cack*. Song is high and squeaky with several lower gurgling musical notes.
Chicago Natural History Museum

YELLOW-THROAT (MALE) *(Geothlypis trichas)*. Length: 4.5 to 5.5 inches. Male: olive green above; forehead and face wear black mask. Throat and breast yellow, dull yellow abdomen. Females and immature birds: plain olive brown; rich yellow throat; paler yellow breast and *white belly*. Lacks mask. Range: Canada to Florida and Gulf Coast. Winters from Louisiana and Florida to North Carolina. Voice: distinctive rapid song, *witchity-witchity-witchity-witch* or *witchity-ta-witchity-ta-witchity-ta-witch*. Note, a husky *tchep*.

Hal H. Harrison

Unlike most gayly colored birds, such as the Tanagers, Buntings and many of the Warblers, the male Baltimore Oriole does not lose his bright plumage in the fall molt. He goes south just as brilliantly clad as when he arrived in the spring. The southern trip ends in Central America and south to Colombia where he spends the winter. The breeding range of the bird extends from southern Canada almost to the Gulf and west to the Rockies and southern Texas. It is also found in Nova Scotia. No subspecies have been recognized.

BULLOCK'S ORIOLE

(Icterus bullockii bullockii)

Color Plate Page 390

Bullock's Oriole is to the west what the Baltimore Oriole is to the east, replacing the Baltimore west of the Rockies. Only from the eastern slopes of the Rockies to Texas, Kansas, Nebraska, and South Dakota, do the ranges of the species overlap. The two may be distinguished instantly by the solid black head of the male Baltimore. The Bullock's male (7½ to 8½ inches) has a black crown with orange cheeks.

YELLOW-BREASTED CHAT (*Icteria virens virens*). Length: 7 to 7.5 inches. Male and female: upperparts greenish brown with disconnected white eye-ring. The throat and breast are bright yellow with white belly. Range: Massachusetts, central New York, southern Ontario, Michigan and southern Minnesota, south to Florida and Gulf of Mexico; winters in Central America. Voice: song, composed of clear repeated whistles alternating with harsh notes and soft *caws*. Single notes, *whoit*, or *kook*.
Hal H. Harrison

A large white wing patch in the Bullock's is diagnostic. Throughout much of its range, Bullock's is the only Oriole. The females are greenish above, with yellow tails and underparts, and two white wingbars.

The nest of Bullock's Oriole is very similar to the long, pendant basket of the Baltimore, woven of fibers, bark and horsehair. It is often hung in cottonwood trees along streams, irrigation ditches and river bottomland. Sycamores and willows are also favorite nesting trees.

After the breeding season, the males take on duller plumage, caused by edgings of gray on the new feathers. Young males of this species do not acquire full adult plumage for several years, appearing at first like females with black throats. In the winter, Bullock's Oriole will be found in Mexico and Central America

The Bullock's song is a typical Oriole rendition, a series of gurglings and chuckles, often delivered as double notes. Its call is a sharp *skip*. His wholesome gay song goes well with his dashing color.

A California race, Ridgway's Oriole (*I.b. parvus*), has recently been recognized.

BRONZED GRACKLE (*Quiscalus versicolor*). Length: 11 to 13 inches. Male and female: body uniform bronze color. Chest varies from greenish blue to brassy green coloring, and is iridescent. Long wedge-shaped tail. Range: interior of North America, west to Rocky Mountains. Voice: song, discordant; harsh note, *chack*.
Hal H. Harrison

RUSTY BLACKBIRD

(Euphagus carolinus)

One will look in vain to find anything "rusty" about a Rusty Blackbird as flocks of these white-eyed birds move northward to their boreal breeding grounds in the spring. But in the fall, when adults and young traverse ancestral migration routes through eastern North America, one may note the tinge of rust color on the margins of the feathers.

In early spring, travelling with Redwings, Cowbirds and Grackles, the Rusties may be distinguished easily as all black birds of average size (8½ to 9½ inches) with white eyes. Females are white-eyed, but their plumage is slate-colored. Grackles, which also have white eyes, are larger and have long, boat-shaped tails. In the west, the Rusty generally breeds north of the range of the similar Brewer's Blackbirds.

Rusty Blackbirds should be looked for in the vicinity of swamps and sloughs, although during migration they often feed in open fields. Their note is a *chuck*. Their song is a squeaking, unmusical utterance, which reminds one of a hinge that needs oil. They winter chiefly in southern United States.

The Rusty Blackbird eats beetles and other insects, and weed seeds.

BREWER'S BLACKBIRD

(Euphagus cyanocephalus)

Color Plate Page 391

An eastern bird watcher on a field trip in the western states might believe he had found a race of dwarfed Bronzed Grackles when he comes across a flock of white-eyed black birds whose plumage shows purplish on the head and greenish on the body.

But that very evident smaller size (8 to 9½ inches), about the size of a

Red-winged Blackbird, distinguishes these birds as Brewer's Blackbirds, common residents of the pastures, fields, parks and ranches.

The vocal utterances of the Brewer's would not distinguish it readily from the Grackles, for it, too, has a squeaky note that sounds as if a drop of oil would improve it. Its call is a sharp *check*. Characteristic of this bird is its habit of walking with wings drooped.

Female Brewer's are brownish-gray with brown eyes. They may be distinguished from female Red-wings by the lack of streaks in the plumage, and from female Cowbirds by the longer bill, darker plumage, and greater size.

Brewer's Blackbirds are common about corrals of ranches where they feed on the ground among the livestock. In cities, they will be found in the parks. This species is generally colonial in its nesting habits, several pairs choosing a tree, a thick bush, or even some tussocks of grass on the ground for their nests of sticks and grasses. They lay four to six greenish or grayish eggs, splotched with brown.

Brewer's breeds from Canada south to California and northern Arizona, New Mexico, and Texas. During migration Brewer's Blackbird is distributed occasionally to Iowa, Wisconsin, Illinois, Missouri, Louisiana and even extends to South Carolina. It winters south into Mexico to Guatemala. However it is a resident bird over much of its range.

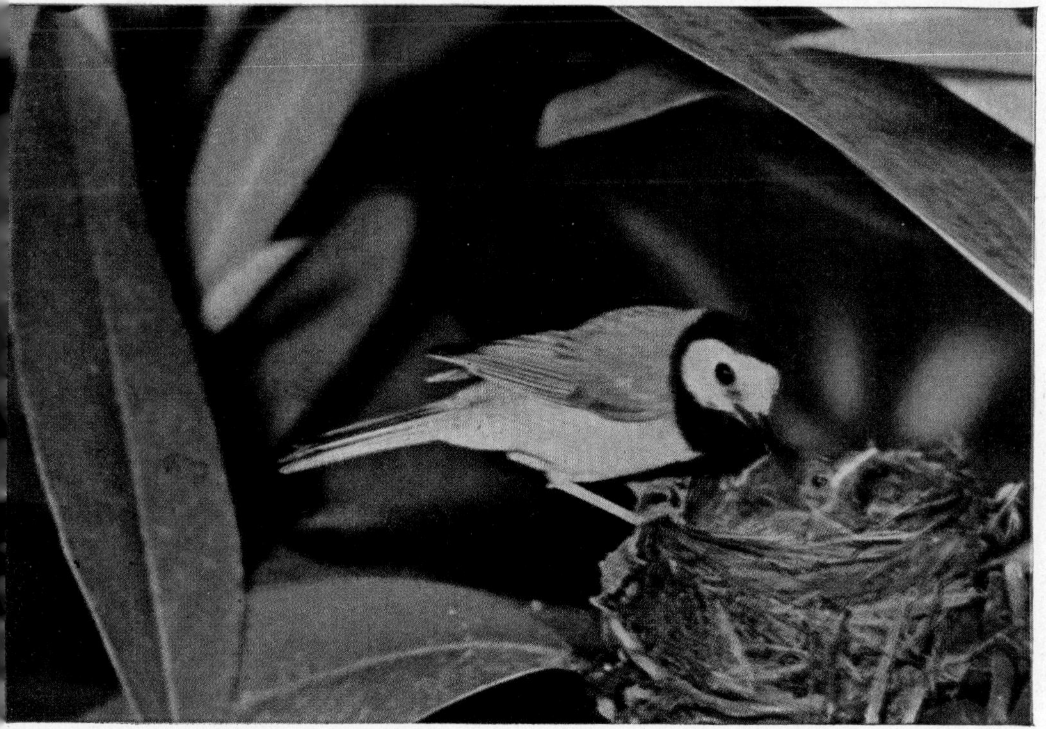

HOODED WARBLER (*Wilsonia citrina*). Length: 5 to 5.75 inches. Male: bright yellow face encircled by black hood. Back olive greenish brown. Lower breast and abdomen yellow. Female: plain olive above, bright yellow on forehead and underparts. No distinctive marks. Range: breeds from Rhode Island, New York and Michigan south to Gulf of Mexico; winters in Central America. Voice: a whistled song *weeta wee-tee-o*.

Hal H. Harrison

BOAT-TAILED GRACKLE

(Cassidix mexicanus)

Color Plate Page 393

The strutting "Jackdaw" of the south is a handsome fellow. Along the coastal beaches, oyster bars, salt marshes, and lakes, the Boat-tailed Grackle, a large edition (16 to 17 inches long) of the Purple Grackle, shines with green and purple iridescence in his blue-black plumage. But only the males are so endowed. The female Boat-tailed Grackle is a plain brown bird about four inches smaller than her pompous mate. Her crown and hindneck are sepia-brown; the rest of her upper parts are dull brown.

"Jackdaw" is a misnomer, for the Boat-tail is an entirely different bird from the European Jackdaw. Indeed, it might be mistaken occasionally for a Fish Crow, with which it sometimes feeds, but its long keel-shaped tail should identify it easily. The Boat-tail is partial to water. Not only do the birds feed in wet areas, but the females usually nest close to water.

Boat-tailed Grackles are most decidedly polygamous, and colonies of nesting birds are the rule. The females receive little or no help from their mates so far as domestic duties are concerned, for soon after nesting begins, the males desert the colonies and flock together. They are joined later by the females and the young on the wing.

A *chuck* or *check* is the common note of the Boat-tail. The song is a series of more or less harsh *churrs* and *chucks* in a variety of tones.

The Jackdaw ranges along the coast through the South Atlantic and Gulf states from Delaware to Florida and westward to eastern Texas. It occurs inland in Florida.

PURPLE GRACKLE

(Quiscalus quiscalus)

Color Plate Page 396

A beautiful bird with a bad reputation. That's the Grackle!

Along the Atlantic coast and east of the mountains, it is the Purple Grackle *(Q.q. stonei)* that is accused of robbing other birds' nests and stealing large quantities of grain and domestic fruit. In Florida it is the Florida Grackle *(Q.q. quiscalus)*. West of the Alleghenies and across the country to the Rockies, it is the Bronzed Grackle *(Quiscalus versicolor)* that receives the condemnation.

The Purple Grackle, also called Crow-Blackbird, is a black bird 11 to 13 inches long, with a long tail which it creases in the middle by depressing the central feathers. This "keeled" tail is conspicuous in flight. The Grackle's beautifully iridescent plumage is purple and green in sunlight, but in dull light, the bird is plain black. Females are duller and less iridescent.

Grackles are gregarious throughout the year. Not only do they flock together by the thousands in the fall and winter, feeding and roosting together, but in the spring and summer they nest together in small colonies. The tops of tall evergreens are preferred nesting sites, although they sometimes nest in bushes and deciduous trees.

Grackles are pompous-looking birds as they walk stiffly about in search of food. The straw-colored eyes, set in dark plumage, give the impression that the bird is staring coldly at an intruder.

Although quite unsuccessful in uttering anything remotely musical, the Grackle is a persistent singer. What comes from its throat is about as musical as a rusty hinge on a barn door.

And that is what it sounds like. The call note is a husky *chuck*.

BRONZED GRACKLE

(Quiscalus versicolor)

At this writing, the matter of a clear definition of species in the genus *Quiscalus* is still unsettled in the minds of many ornithologists. The Bronzed Grackle, the Grackle found in New England and west of the Allegheny Mountains, westward to the foothills of the Rockies, is now considered a full species. Until recently, however, it was listed as a subspecies of the Purple Grackle and was named *Quiscalus quiscalus aeneus*.

Although the bronze-colored back of the Bronzed Grackle is cited as an identifying field mark to distinguish it from the Purple Grackle, which has a purplish back, I do not feel that this is of any use to a bird watcher unless the observation is made under most favorable circumstances—a situation not ordinarily encountered in the field. In addition, where their ranges overlap, the Bronzed Grackle and the Purple Grackle intergrade, resulting in a hybrid with broken iridescent bars on its back. These are commonly called Ridgway's Grackles, but they have been given no recognition as yet by the American Ornithologists' Union (A.O.U.). Undoubtedly, as scientists study these species, the classifications will be changed.

His nest is similar to the Purple Grackle in its bulkiness, and site; in fact; the habits and characteristics of the Bronzed Grackle are so similar to those of the Purple Grackle that what has been written of the Purple may well suffice for the present species.

COWBIRD

(Molothrus ater)

Color Plate Page 397

No one alive today has ever seen the nest of our common Cowbird. It builds none. Perhaps it did generations ago, but today the Cowbird, also called Cow Blackbird, Cow Bunting and Tick Bird, is parasitic upon other birds. It lays its eggs in their nests, and then leaves the hatching and raising of its offspring to less irresponsible foster parents. Often it chooses the nests of birds smaller than itself, but not always.

A companion and I spent a summer studying this interesting member of the Blackbird family. We took some revealing photographs of the female in the act of laying her eggs in the nests of other birds, such as the one on page 397. We learned that she invariably lays her egg at dawn before her host returns to the nest to lay its own egg for that day. We caught the Cowbird red-handed at the nests of a Song Sparrow (see illustration), Indigo Bunting, Red-eyed Vireo and Ovenbird. Her arrival, furtively and slyly executed, was close to 4:30 a.m., E.S.T., in each case.

Many believe that the young Cowbird is the only one to survive in a parasitized nest; that the young of the foster parents are crowded out or starved. This is rarely true. In most cases, the young of the host thrive along with the Cowbird. Indeed, in the nest of a Wood Thrush, we discovered that the young Thrushes were larger than the young Cowbird on nest-leaving day.

When the Cowbird lays more than one egg in the nest of a smaller bird (as many as five have been found), then the lives of the smaller youngsters are jeopardized. Strange as it may seem,

CANADA WARBLERS AT NEST, MALE ON LEFT, FEMALE ON RIGHT (*Wilsonia canadensis*). Length: 5 to 5.75 inches. Male and female: plain gray upperparts, bright yellow below. Male has black short stripes encircling breast; in female and immature birds this is faint or not at all. All have yellow eye-ring. Range: Canada to Minnesota, Michigan, New York, northern New Jersey and in mountains to northern Georgia; winters in South America. Voice: Confused mixture of musical notes.
Hal H. Harrison

most birds tolerate this encroachment; a few resent it.

Although many disagree with me, I have always defended the Cowbird as a grand example of natural adaptation for survival. This female, with apparently no instinct for building a nest of her own, has found a way to propagate her kind through parasitism. We humans call it "chisling." I'll bet Mother Nature has a better name for it!

The female Cowbird is uniformly grayish brown. The male is more conspicuous. He is our only black bird with a coffee-brown head. In April and May, a female with several males courting her is not an unusual sight. A typical courtship gesture is for the male to spread his wings and bow low before the female. A few gurgling notes serve as a love song. The call note is a *chuck*. The birds are 7 to 8 inches long.

The name "Cowbird" came from the birds' affinity to cattle which they follow to glean insects thus stirred up. The bird's diet is economically beneficial and includes many harmful weed seeds. When bison roamed the prairies, the Cowbird was then known as the Buffalo Bird.

Cowbirds spend the winter in the southern states and Mexico. They travel north and south in large flocks, often in company with Red-wings and Grackles. The Cowbird ranges throughout the United States and southern Canada, except in the southeastern corner and in the high mountains. Geographic forms include: Eastern Cowbird *(m.a. ater)*; Nevada Cowbird *(M.a. artemisiae)*; and the Dwarf Cowbird *(M.a. obscurus)*.

RED-EYED COWBIRD

(Tangavius aeneus aeneus)

Color Plate Page 400

Although the Red-eyed Cowbird of southern Texas (north to San Antonio) is a different looking bird from the common Cowbird, it still has that family trait of laying its eggs in the nests of other birds.

The male (6½ to 8¾ inches) has a glistening black coat (no brown head as in the common Cowbird) and a ruff on the back of his neck, quite conspicuous during the breeding season. The red eye is not a good field mark at a distance. Females are duller and not gray like female common Cowbirds. They are smaller than the males and have less conspicuous neck ruffs.

A close relative, the Bronzed Cowbird *(T.a. milleri)* sometimes wanders into Arizona from its home in Mexico. There is little or no field difference apparent.

TANAGERS

Family Thraupidae

The Tanagers are birds of temperate and tropical America, distinguished for the most part by the fact that the males wear red to a considerable extent. The females are usually greenish or yellowish, like the female Orioles, but much more sluggish in their habits. The Tanagers have a thick, rather conical bill, with the tip of the upper mandible curved downward. Their nests are shallow, saucer-like affairs, rather loosely constructed. The diet of these birds is mainly insectivorous.

WESTERN TANAGER

(Piranga ludoviciana)

Color Plate Page 401

Bird watchers from northern British Columbia, the Mackenzie River, and southwestern South Dakota, south to the mountains of western Texas, southern Arizona, and southern California are in the favored area where the Western Tanager nests. Yellow and black, with a crimson face, the male has no rival with which he may be confused. Seen against the dark green of an evergreen forest, where nesting occurs, the male is a conspicuous and beautiful creature. In the autumn he loses his red coloring. The birds are 6¼ to 7 inches long.

The female Western Tanager, like her relative, the female Scarlet Tanager, is dull in comparison, greenish above and yellowish below. Two white or yellowish wingbars set her apart, however.

The male's call is a double note, *chee-tik.* His song is Robin-like in form, hoarser, and made up of a repetition of short phrases uttered with rising and falling inflections. Easterners hearing this song will be reminded of certain notes of the Scarlet Tanager.

During the winter, Western Tanagers will be found in Mexico and Central America.

SCARLET TANAGER

(Piranga olivacea)

Color Plate Page 404

If wild birds could talk, Tommy would have told you he was a dead male Scarlet Tanager the afternoon in June when he had flown across the highway in front of a speeding automobile. It was only a matter of minutes until the next car would snuff out his little life as he lay there unconscious.

But luck was with Tommy that day. The next car happened to be that of a doctor who loves birds, and the sight of the brilliant red Tanager with the jet-black wings and tail caused the busy surgeon to stop. It was his afternoon away from the hospital, so he took a busman's holiday.

While the bird was still unconscious, he set the broken leg and the broken

HEPATIC TANAGER (*Piranga flava*). Length: 7 to 7.5 inches. Male: flame red body, dark ear patch, blackish bill. Female: upperparts, dull olive greenish, underparts yellowish olive. Range: breeds in mountains of Arizona, New Mexico and western Texas. Voice: song made up of short phrases. Note, a single *chuck*.
Rudolph Hindemith, American Museum of Natural History

wing. Both were fastened securely to the bird's body with thread so that they could not be moved. When Tommy (that was the doctor's name for him) came to, he was resting in a special little box in the kitchen of the doctor's home enjoying real solicitation.

Under this professional care, the broken leg and wing healed and were finally unbound. Then Tommy had to learn to fly again. Special exercises were prescribed. A special diet of hard boiled eggs and ripe bananas with a host of insects collected at night around the porch light kept the bird well fed. Tommy got well.

I heard this story twenty-three days after the accident. That day I visited the doctor in his home. There I saw him step into the kitchen and call, "Come on, Tommy!" and then I saw one of the shyest of all wild birds fly from his perch and alight on the doctor's finger. Completely unafraid, the beautiful bird sat there as the man stroked his plumage.

Late in the summer, Tommy was taken into the country, far from town, and given his freedom. I wonder how he fared on his autumnal migration flight to Colombia or Bolivia in South America.

The next summer, I found the nest of a Scarlet Tanager fourteen feet from the ground in a wild crabapple. The female had laid three eggs, and a Cowbird had assisted the clutch by depositing one of her own, making four

COOPER'S TANAGER (*Piranga rubra cooperi*). Length: 7 to 7.5 inches. Male: bright rose red *all over*, no crest. Female: olive above, deep yellow below. Range: breeds chiefly along river-bottoms in southeast California, southern Nevada, southern and central Arizona, southern and central New Mexico, and western Texas. Voice: song made up of short phrases. Note, *chick-tuk*, or *chick-i-tuck*.
Rudolph Hindemith, American Museum of Natural History

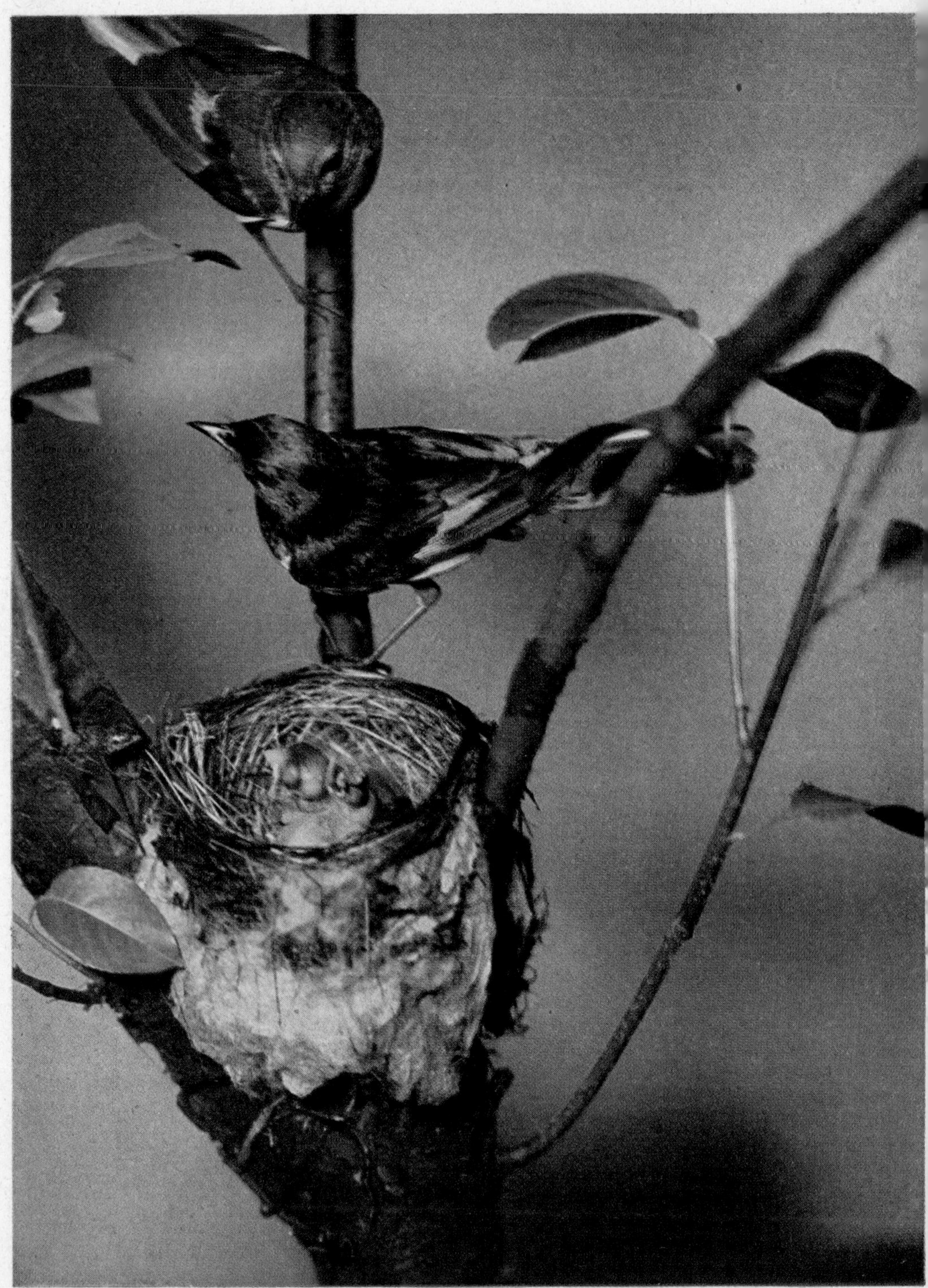

MALE AND FEMALE AMERICAN REDSTART (A WARBLER) (*Setophaga ruticilla*). Length: 4.5 to 5.5 inches. Male: upperparts glossy black. Bright orange patches on wings and tail. White underparts. Throat and upper breast black. Female: brownish olive above, white below, yellow wing and tail patches. Immature male: much like female. Range: breeds in eastern United States and northwest to Washington. Voice: two alternated songs *tsee tsee tsee tsee tsee tsee tsee-o* and *teetsa teetsa teetsa teetsa teet.*

Hal H. Harrison

ENGLISH SPARROW (*Passer domesticus*). Length: 5 to 6.25 inches. Male: reddish brown upperparts streaked with black; grayish white underparts. Deep gray crown and chestnut nape. White cheeks and black throat. Female: dull brown above and dingy white below. Range: throughout the United States and Canada.
Hal H. Harrison

in all. The Tanager eggs were lovely, pale greenish blue with rufous markings, but the nest was nothing to brag about—just a loosely constructed little platform of twigs and rootlets with a lining of grasses.

To the uninformed, the first sight of a female Scarlet Tanager is always a shock. She wears no red at all, but is plain olive-green, just as protectively colored as her mate is conspicuous. But the male sports this fiery plumage only in the spring and summer, for he emerges from the August and September molt almost as drab as the female, except that he retains the black wings and tail. Scarlet Tanagers are 6½ to 7½ inches long.

The song of the Scarlet Tanager has been described well as "a Robin with a sore throat," a hurried, hoarse caroling. The alarm note is a distinctive low *chip-chur*.

Scarlet Tanagers nest from Saskatchewan and Nova Scotia, south to eastern Kansas and Virginia, and in the mountains to Georgia. They winter in South America.

HEPATIC TANAGER

(Piranga flava)

In the oaks and pines of the mountains that overlook the deserts of western Texas, New Mexico, and Arizona, the Hepatic Tanager spends its summers. It is a brick red bird 7 to 7½ inches long, that may be distinguished from the Cooper's Tanager by its gray cheeks, grayish back, and dark bill. The female Hepatic Tanager is dark above and yellowish below.

Although the ranges of the Hepatic and Cooper's Tanagers overlap, Cooper's prefers the low stream bottoms, while the Hepatic is found in high woodlands. Its song is Robin-like in form like the Cooper's; its call note is a single *chuck*.

Two races are recognized: the Hepatic Tanager *(P. f. hepatica)*, and the Eastern Hepatic Tanager *(P. f. dextra)*. There are no field differences.

SUMMER TANAGER

(Piranga rubra rubra)

An all red bird without a crest, found in the summer from New Jersey to Nebraska, and southward to Florida and the Gulf states, is sure to be a Summer Tanager. The red Cardinal has a black face and a crest. The Scarlet Tanager has jet black wings and tail. The female Summer Tanager may be distinguished from the female Scarlet Tanager by the lack of dusky wings, present in the latter. The Summer Tanager is 7 to 7½ inches long.

T. Gilbert Pearson describes the call note of the Summer Tanager as *which-a-too*. Dr. Chapman interprets it as *chicky-tucky-tuck*. Its song is Robin-like, but clearer than the hoarse notes of the Scarlet Tanager.

The Summer Tanager winters in Central and South America.

SUMMER TANAGER AT NEST *(Piranga rubra rubra)*. Length: 7 to 7.5 inches. Male: bright rose red *all over*, no crest. Female: olive above, deep yellow below. Range: breeds in woodlands and groves from Florida and Gulf of Mexico north to southern New Jersey, southern Iowa, central Illinois, etc. Winters in Central and South America. Voice: note, a staccato *pi-tuck*, or *pik-ituck-ituck;* song, a clear whistled caroling made up of short phrases of two or three notes.

Alfred M. Bailey, National Audubon Society

COOPER'S TANAGER

(Piranga rubra cooperi)

Along the river bottoms of southeastern California, southern Nevada, Arizona, and New Mexico, east to western Texas, a western representative of the eastern Summer Tanager makes its summer home. It is the Cooper's Tanager, and like its eastern counterpart, it is rosy red all over. It is a bit larger than the Summer Tanager (7 to 7½ inches), has a longer bill, and rosier underparts. The female is olive above and deeper yellow below.

The only bird with which the Cooper's might be confused is the mountain-inhabiting Hepatic Tanager, but the latter is darker and has gray cheeks and a grayish back. Although its coloring is somewhat like the Cardinal's, it does not have a crest.

The song of Cooper's Tanager is like the Hepatic Tanager, but its call note is a two- or three-syllable note similar to the Western Tanager's, written according to Peterson as *chick-tuk* or *chick-i-tuk*, somewhat similar to the notes of the Western Tanager.

FINCHES

Family Fringillidae

The Finch family, the largest family among the birds, contains the Grosbeaks, Finches, Sparrows, and Buntings. All are distinguished by their strong conical bills which enable them to eat seeds, the major food for all the family. They do eat some insects, however. Most of the members of the family are drably colored, although some of the male Finches wear very bright coloring. Of the twelve hundred-odd species belonging to this family throughout the world, some two hundred are known to the United States.

CARDINAL

(Richmondena cardinalis)

Color Plate Page 405

One treasures his bird experiences as so many jewels strung on a necklace of memories. The jewels, strange to say, are not events of great magnitude, but are, on the contrary, moments of lasting impression that may occur to a bird watcher entirely unheralded. Several come to mind instantly: the Hermit Thrush's song at twilight; the sky dance of a Woodcock; sweeping hordes of migrating Swallows feeding over a marsh; the sweet warble of spring's first Bluebird; wild Geese in a perfect V in the sunset; the pendulum dance of a love-struck Hummingbird; and the scarlet flash of a Cardinal.

To many a northerner, that red flash from the shrubbery to the feeding station has been the happy start of innumerable winter days. For as far north as the Cardinal now ranges, there it remains throughout the year. Originally a bird of the south, the Kentucky Cardinal, or Virginia Redbird, has pushed its way northward until now it is a resident of the lower Hudson valley, northern Ohio, Indiana, Illinois, and South Dakota. In the south, it ranges from the Atlantic coast to southern Arizona.

The male Cardinal is a master whistler with a vast repertoire. The first warm days of late February and early March are tuning up time, and when April's sunny days arrive, the Redbird is in rare form. His whistle is loud, clear, and melodious. One song may be written: *what cheer! what cheer; whit-whit-whit-whit.* Another is *purty, purty, purty, purty.* Still another is *cue, cue, cue.* Unlike most female birds, the female Cardinal's song rivals that of her mate. Her singing season begins later and ends earlier, however.

A red Finch, smaller than a Robin (8 to 9 inches), with a conspicuous crest and black face is a good thumbnail sketch of a male Cardinal. The female is brown with patches of red in her wings, tail, and crest. Both adults have red beaks, typical grosbeaks,

BOBOLINK *(Dolichonyx oryzivorus)*. Length: 6.5 to 8 inches. Male in spring: black below and largely white above. Female and fall birds: body yellowish buff with upperparts streaked with brown. Range: Quebec to West Virginia, west to Illinois. Winters in southern South America. Voice: melodious song starting low and rising. Sung in flight.
Fred Bashour

strong and heavy. Young Cardinals resemble the female, but have dark beaks.

Throughout the winter Cardinals are found in mixed flocks. At this time they are easily attracted to feeding stations by sunflower seeds, corn, and mixed seeds. In March, the flocks break up into mated pairs, and nesting is underway by mid-April. The home site chosen is often in garden shrubbery, porch vines, thickets, briar patches, small trees, and evergreens.

The nest is of twigs, stems, strips of grapevine bark, and leaves, lined with grasses and rootlets. Three (sometimes four) spotted eggs are incubated twelve days. The male never incubates. The young are in the nest from seven to eleven days. At one nest that I studied, they left on the eighth day. The male helps feed the young, and while the female is incubating, he often feeds her. When his mate starts a new nest, the male usually takes full charge of the first fledglings. In the southern states, as many as four nestings a season are not uncommon.

The geographic races of the Cardinal include the following: the Eastern Cardinal *(R. c. cardinalis)*, the Florida Cardinal *(R. c. floridana)*, the Louisiana Cardinal *(R. c. magnirostris)*, the Gray-tailed Cardinal *(R. c. canicauda)*, and the Arizona Cardinal *(R. c. superba)*.

The Cardinal is a great enemy of many important insect pests such as the cotton worm. His food habits, along with his song, and brilliant appearance add to his strong appeal for us.

PYRRHULOXIA

(Pyrrhuloxia sinuata)

Color Plate Page 408

If you would know the ever changing moods of the Pyrrhuloxia, a gray Cardinal of the arid regions of Texas, Arizona, and New Mexico, then watch its crest. That flaming red adornment is a fleeting guide to its emotions as it raises and lowers it, now quickly, now slowly, sometimes loosely, sometimes stiffly, and so on, indicating alertness, curiosity, boredom, fear, annoyance, and the gamut of emotions through which a bird must go from minute to minute. Few birds are so expressive of their emotions.

The Pyrrhuloxia reminds one constantly of its more widely distributed relative, the Cardinal, although there is no reason to confuse the two. The male Pyrrhuloxia (7½ to 8 inches) has a red breast, but its gray back identifies it instantly from the Cardinal. The bill is short, yellow, and Parrot-like. The Cardinal's bill is red. The gray back and yellow bill of the female distinguishes her from the brown backed female Cardinal.

The song of the Pyrrhuloxia is a cheery whistle, much like that of the Cardinal, but not as loud nor as pure. It utters the *what-cheer* notes of the Cardinal as well as a clearly whistled *queet, queet, queet.*

The typical form of the bird is named the Texas Pyrrhuloxia *(P. s. sinuata)* while the western form, which ranges into southern Arizona, is named the Arizona Pyrrhuloxia *(P. s. fulvescens)*.

LAZULI BUNTING WITH YOUNG *(Passerina amoena)*. Length: 5 to 5.5 inches. Male: head and upperparts turquoise blue; rufous band across breast and sides; white belly and wingbars. Female: brownish above, dull buff below, with some dull greenish blue on wings and tail. Range: breeds in the western United States from Canada to southern California and northern New Mexico; winters in Mexico. Voice: a high typical Finch song which has been rendered *Come! come! come! heeeer, quick! quick! quick! quick!*

A. M. Bailey and R. J. Niedrach

ROSE-BREASTED GROSBEAK

(Pheucticus ludovicianus)

Color Plate Page 410

My one and only attempt at taxidermy occurred when I was a boy in grade school, and to my undying shame, it cost the life of one of America's most beautiful birds—a male Rose-breasted Grosbeak. The advertisements told me how simple it was to stuff birds (after so many easy lessons at so much for the course). Before enrolling, however, I thought it might be well to experiment. That's when the singing male Grosbeak dropped from his perch with a pellet from an air rifle in his already crimson breast.

Within an hour, all the glamour of taxidermy had disappeared, and into the family garbage can I dropped the torn, bloodstained feathers of the once lovely bird. I can still remember the feeling of remorse that came over me as I gave up in sickening disgust. But the experience has served me well in the intervening years, for the only shooting I have done since then has been with my camera. Could I ever have learned to mount a Grosbeak to look like the one I "shot" for the natural color picture on page 410?

The male Rose-breasted Grosbeak is unmistakable, a black and white Finch about the size of a Cardinal (7 to 8½ inches), with a shield-shaped rose breast tapering to a rose streak down the middle. The bird's tremendous beak looks like a great white nose. In flight, its wings seem to be twirling, an illusion caused by the rapid movement of the black wings with their large white spots. The bird's delicate pink wing underlining is noticeable in overhead flight.

The female is unbelievably drab beside her mate. She has been aptly described as "an overgrown Sparrow." She is heavily striped above, brown-streaked below, with white spots on the wings, and a white line over the eye. Like the female Cardinal, the female Rose-breasted Grosbeak sings a Robin-like song.

Young birds resemble the female, but the males show rose under their wings. As they mature, they develop traces of rose coloring in their breasts. First year males show considerable brown in the wings and tail. In the fall molt, adult males retain their black wings and tail, but otherwise resemble the female. A trace of pink often remains in the breast.

Rose-breasted Grosbeaks nest in bushes and trees in woodlands, orchards, gardens, and parks. The nest is a thin, curved structure of twigs and dried weed stalks, lined with finer materials. The four eggs are greenish blue, speckled and spotted with chestnut and shades of brown. They resemble the eggs of the Scarlet Tanager. Unlike most brightly colored birds, the male Rose-breast shares in incubation and even sings while on the nest.

The song of the male is a long broken warble, similar to the song of a Robin, but sweeter and more varied. It also resembles the Scarlet Tanager's song, but lacks its hoarseness. The call note is an unmistakable metallic *kink*.

The breeding range of the Rose-breasted Grosbeak is northern United States and Canada, from Nova Scotia and New England westward to the Dakotas, and then northward to Great Slave Lake; in the mountains south to northern Georgia. It migrates through the southern states to the Gulf of Mexico, crossing to its winter home in southern Mexico, Central America, and northwestern South America.

BLACK-HEADED GROSBEAK

(Pheucticus melanocephalus)

Color Plate Page 411

What the Rose-breasted Grosbeak is to the east, the Black-headed Grosbeak is to the west. Not only is this true because of distribution, for each species is unknown in the other's range, but it is true because of the very similar habits of the two. Even the well known habit of the male Rose-breasted Grosbeak incubating the eggs and brooding the young is duplicated in the west where the Black-headed Grosbeak does

EASTERN MEADOWLARK (*Sturnella magna*). Length: 9 to 11 inches. Male and female: light brown body streaked with chestnut, black and buff. Large black crescent patch on upper breast. Rest of underparts bright yellow. Prominent patch of white on each side of the short tail. Range: Canada throughout northeastern America, west to Nebraska. Winters in southern United States. Voice: song two musical whistles, *tee-yah, teeyair.*
Samuel A. Grimes

the same. The songs of the two are similar, and their feeding habits are alike.

Indeed, the only important breach that definitely separates them, besides distribution, is the entirely different plumage, which would seem to indicate that climatic environment had created two different looking birds.

The male is black headed, with an orange-brown breast, a chestnut colored nape, and conspicuously marked black and white wings. Several white spots occur on the outer black tail feathers. The black and white wing and tail pattern, and the cinnamon colored rump are conspicuous when the bird is in flight. The female is generally brown with light lines over the eye and through the crown. Her underparts are orange-brown. The Black-headed Grosbeak is 6½ to 7¾ inches in length.

VARIED BUNTING *(Passerina versicolor)*. Length: 4.5 to 5.5 inches. Male: dark plum color which looks black at a distance, crown of head blue, with bright red patch on nape. Female: plain gray brown, lighter below. Range: breeds in lower Rio Grande Valley. Voice: a typical Finch song, distinctly phrased.
Rudolph Hindemith, American Museum of Natural History

The Black-headed Grosbeak often becomes quite tame and sociable, especially around parks, camps, public picnic grounds, and other places where visitors throw feed for them on the ground.

Two forms of this bird are recognized in the west: the Rocky Mountain Grosbeak *(P. m. maculatus)* and the typical Pacific coast race, the Black-headed Grosbeak *(P. m. melanocephalus)*. There are no field differences.

BLUE GROSBEAK

(Guiraca caerulea)

Color Plate Page 414

Although the Blue Grosbeak ranges throughout the southern part of the United States from the Atlantic to the Pacific, it is not a common bird anywhere. It is a bird of the open country, delighting in the grown-over fields, borders of woodlands, pasture lands, and tangles of briars and weeds. In the east, it breeds as far north as Maryland, and in the west, as far as central California. It winters south to Central America.

Like the Indigo Bunting (which see), the Blue Grosbeak is not always blue. In unfavorable light, it looks positively black. It has been suggested that under these circumstances it might easily be mistaken for a male Cowbird, although the huge beak is quite conspicuous. Seen favorably, the Blue Grosbeak (6½ to 7½ inches) is deep blue with black wings and tail, each wing bearing two chestnut bars. The female is brown with pinkish cinnamon wingbars.

"Big Indigo's" song is a melodious warble. To some observers it is reminiscent of the Purple Finch's song. It reminds me more of the Rose-breasted Grosbeak's song, although not as sweet nor mellow. The alarm note is a *spink*.

The loosely constructed nest of weeds and grasses, often lined with horsehair, is usually placed in low shrubbery or small trees. The three or four eggs are pale bluish white.

Three geographic forms of the Blue Grosbeak are recognized; the Eastern Blue Grosbeak *(G. c. caerulea)*, the Western Blue Grosbeak *(G. c. interfusa)*, and the California Blue Grosbeak *(G. c. salicaria)*.

INDIGO BUNTING

(Passerina cyanea)

Color Plate Page 415

Fond memories of boyhood days along a dusty country road in midsum-

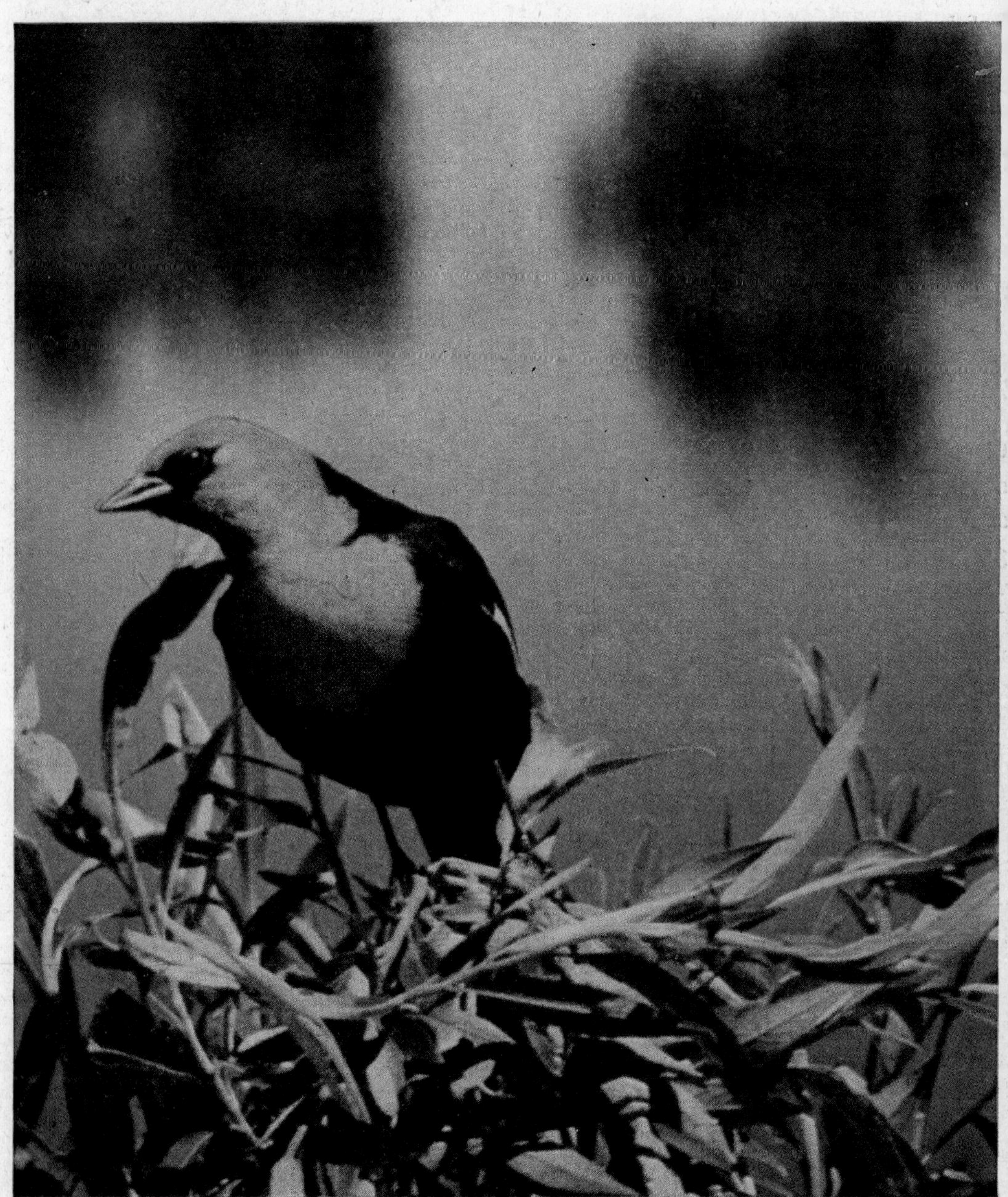

YELLOW-HEADED BLACKBIRD *(Xanthocephalus xanthocephalus)*. Length: 9 to 11 inches. Male: glossy black body with white patch on wings, which shows when bird is in flight; and yellow head, throat and breast. Female: browner than male, with breast streaked with white and most of yellow restricted to chest and throat. Range: western North America from Manitoba to Nebraska; winters from Louisiana to Mexico. Voice: a low rasping song.

William L. & Irene Finley

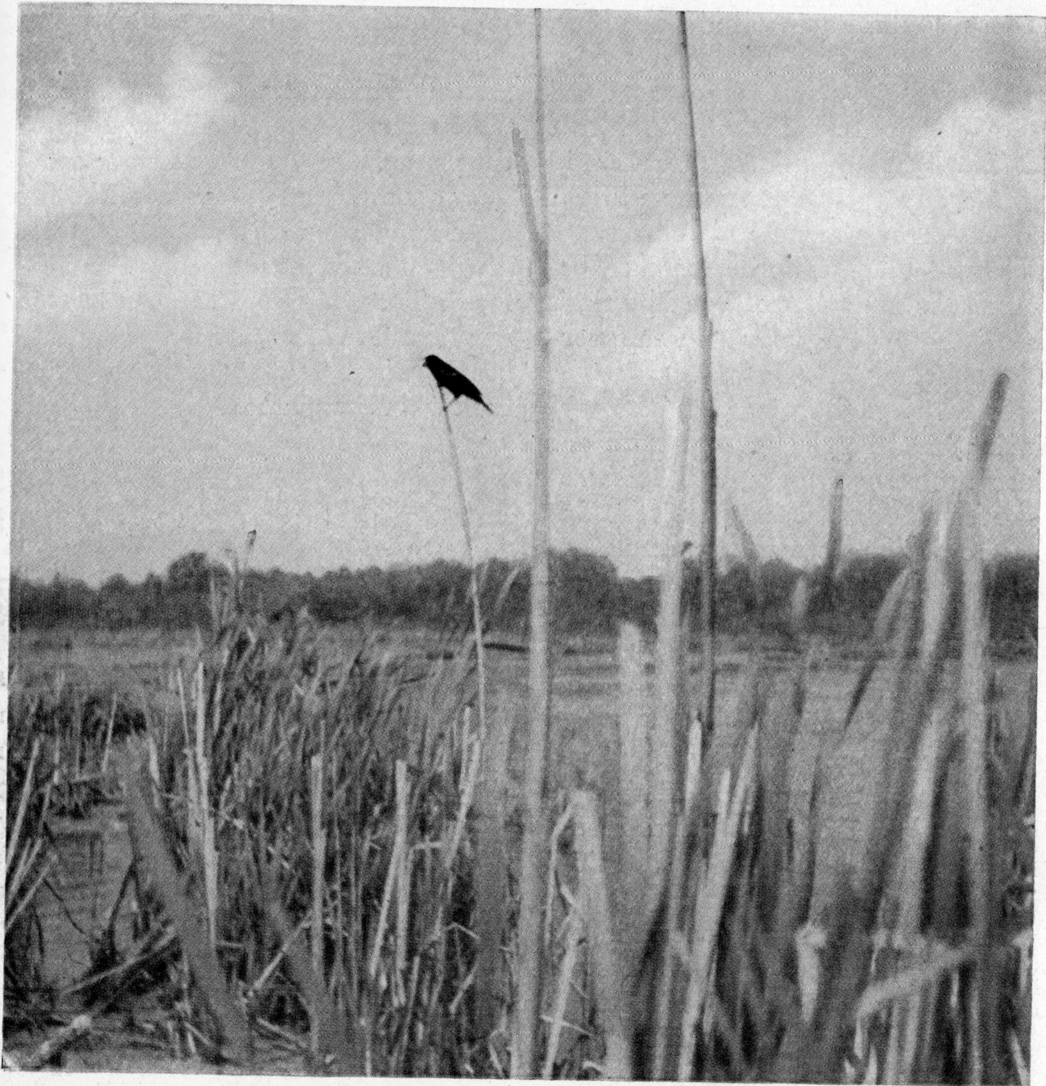

RED-WINGED BLACKBIRD (*Agelaius phoeniceus*). Length: 7.5 to 9.5 inches. Male: black with red patches at wing bends. Immature male: brown, but with red patches. Female: brownish body with lighter underparts streaked with dark brown. Range: Nova Scotia, Quebec and Ontario south to Florida and Texas. Winters in southern United States. Voice: song, a gurgling, *konk-la-reee* or *o-ka-leeee*, the last note high pitched and trembling.
Hal H. Harrison

mer are recalled vividly when I listen to the *sweet-sweet* high-low song of the Indigo Bunting. How well I remember the hot afternoon in July, many years ago, when I saw my first Indigo Bird perched on the top branch of a roadside apple tree, singing his paired notes in a high pitched voice.

On a rainy afternoon some days later, I heard my bird again near the same apple tree. I looked in vain for a bright blue bird, for that day a dark brown, almost black, bird was singing his song. It was then I learned that blue birds are not always blue, but it was not until years later that I learned why this is so.

In the drizzling rain, the Indigo Bunting's feathers were wet and incapable of reflecting the light that ordinarily makes them appear blue; for blue, green, and purple birds are really brown birds whose feathers are covered with a thin transparent coating that catches light rays and refracts them in such a way as to produce those bright colors. Many times I have observed a "brown" Indigo Bunting perched between the sun and me. The Bluebird's back also appears brown in unfavorable light.

The Indigo Bunting (5¼ to 5¾ inches) is a Finch, but not until one learns to recognize the drab Sparrow-like female does one fully realize it. She has no distinctive markings at all, except a slight wash of blue on the shoulders and some very faint streaks on the breast. The young are more heavily streaked beneath than the female, which they resemble.

Excepting possibly the Red-eyed Vireo, no other summer bird sings so persistently as the Indigo. All day long, from May until early August, he sings from the tree tops and the telegraph wires. Not until the molt occurs in late summer is he silent. When the molt is over, the Indigo Bunting looks brown in any light, for he has lost his gay blue feathers, all but just a few inconspicuously placed in his drab plumage. In this attire, the Indigo Bird leaves in October for its winter home in Central America and Panama.

While on its breeding range from New Brunswick south to central Georgia and west to North Dakota and central Texas, the Indigo Bunting has two broods, each in a different site. The nest is built of grasses laid on a foundation of dead leaves, often in briar patches, and sometimes in bushy second growth. Invariably the nest is well hidden. Incubation of the four bluish white eggs requires twelve days. The young are in the nest for ten or twelve days. The female alone handles all the nesting duties, except for occasional visits from the male bringing food to the young.

In the southern states where the Indigo's range coincides with that of the Blue Grosbeak, the two may be confused. The Grosbeak's larger size (the size of a Tanager), its two chestnut-brown wingbars, and its heavy grosbeak will distinguish it.

LAZULI BUNTING

(Passerina amoena)

The Lazuli Bunting of the western states is another of the gorgeous birds about which color photographers have restless dreams. The head, neck, rump, and upper tail coverts of the male are turquoise blue. In other light, they seem Nile blue. Across the chest, just below the blue, runs a band of chestnut, and below this is a white belly. Two white bars adorn the dark wings. The female? Just a nondescript little brown bird 5 to 5½ inches long, without streakings or any outstanding field marks except two pale wingbars.

Easterners find in the song and habits of the Lazuli Bunting a western counterpart of their own Indigo Bunting. The Lazuli is a close relative of the Painted Bunting, another bird that answers a Kodachrome photographer's fondest dreams.

VARIED BUNTING

(Passerina versicolor)

As in the case of its close relative, the Painted Bunting, colors were literally thrown at the Varied Bunting when its plumage was created. With its combination of purple wings, blue crown, bright red nape, and plum colored underparts, no other bird is even slightly similar to it except the gaudy Painted Bunting which sports a bright red breast. The female Varied Bunting is plain gray-brown, lighter on the breast, without any markings of any sort. She is grayer than the female Indigo Bunting which is inconspicuously marked. The Varied Buntings are 4½ to 5½ inches long. Their song is similar to the Painted Bunting, but less warbled.

The two races of this Bunting, which are indistinguishable in the field, breed in the mesquite thickets of the lower Rio Grande Valley in Texas. They are the Varied Bunting *(P. v. versicolor)* and the Beautiful Bunting *(P. v. pulchra)*.

PAINTED BUNTING

(Passerina ciris)

Color Plate Page 419

The Painted Bunting always looks to me like a little Sparrow (5¼ inches) that had hopped into a half dozen pots of Easter egg dye. When he hopped out of the last one, his plumage was a patchwork of blue, green, violet, and red above, with a lot of red underneath. The female missed most of the dye pots, for she shows only green above and yellowish green underneath.

DICKCISSEL *(Spiza americana)*. Length: 6 to 7 inches. Male: gray, brown and black streaked above, with yellow breast and black bill. Female: like the male, but much duller in color. Range: breeds in the plains from western Ohio and south to Texas and Alabama; winters in South America. Voice: its name, *Dick-ciss-ciss-ciss,* repeated constantly.

Frank N. Wilson, National Audubon Society

Like the male Redstart in the Warbler family, the first-year males of the Painted Bunting are similar to the female except for some bluish feathers on the head. When adult plumage is acquired, the male wears his bright colors the year 'round.

The range of the Eastern Painted Bunting *(P. c. ciris)*, or Nonpareil, is restricted during the breeding season to the south Atlantic and Gulf states. In the east, it nests only from southern North Carolina to central Florida, and west to southern Kansas. While most individuals go south of the United States in winter, some remain in Florida. A western race *(P. c. pallidior)* breeds from central Oklahoma to southeastern New Mexico, wintering south of the border.

The quiet and retiring manner of the Painted Bunting has gained for it a reputation of being shy. It does spend much of its time in the dense thickets and bushy borders of woodlands where it may be overlooked easily. On the other hand, I have a friend in southern Florida who feeds the Painted Bunting throughout the winter at his garden feeding station.

This species' habits are similar to those of the Indigo Bunting. Thick bushes or small trees are usually chosen as the site of the compactly woven nest of grasses, weeds, strips of bark, dead leaves, and rootlets. The three or four eggs are white with reddish brown marks.

Although the Nonpareil's song resembles that of the Indigo Bunting, it is inferior in quality, being a sweet musical warble.

DICKCISSEL

(Spiza americana)

"Little Meadowlark" is just as appropriate a common name for the Dickcissel as the one it bears, for the first describes its appearance and *dickcissel* interprets its song. Still another common name, Black-throated Bunting, is also appropriate, for this Mississippi valley Bunting (6 to 7 inches) is black throated, with a yellow breast and brown back. A reddish brown patch at the bend of the wing is a field mark of both sexes. The female is like a pale English Sparrow. In fact, careless observers may mistake either sex for an English Sparrow. The Dickcissel is somewhat larger, however.

The Dickcissel is a bird of the prairies and grassy meadows, ranging from southern Texas and Mississippi to Minnesota and North Dakota. Formerly, it ranged commonly into the eastern section of the United States, but today it is a rare straggler east of the Mississippi valley.

EVENING GROSBEAK

(Hesperiphona vespertina)

Color Plate Page 418

For my first sight of a flock of Evening Grosbeaks, I made a hundred mile trip on a January day when the thermometer never went above zero. I drove to the little oil town of Titusville in northwestern Pennsylvania to find a flock of nineteen males and six females feeding in a garden.

Evening Grosbeaks are rare in Pennsylvania, even as winter visitors, so bird watchers for miles around went to Titusville that year to have their first view of these lovely golden birds of the north. The Titusville bird lovers held them at their feeding stations until April by making great quantities of sunflower seeds always available.

For a long time, the Grosbeaks returned to Titusville every other year, indicative of the erratic movements for which they are noted. Finally, they came in 1947, repeating their 1946 visit, so their annual return is now anticipated.

Evening Grosbeaks are the size of the more common Rose-breasted Grosbeak, about the size of a Starling (7½ to 8½ inches), but chunky and short tailed. The male has a yellow forehead, black crown, olive-brown back, yellow underparts, and black wings and tail except for the secondary feathers of

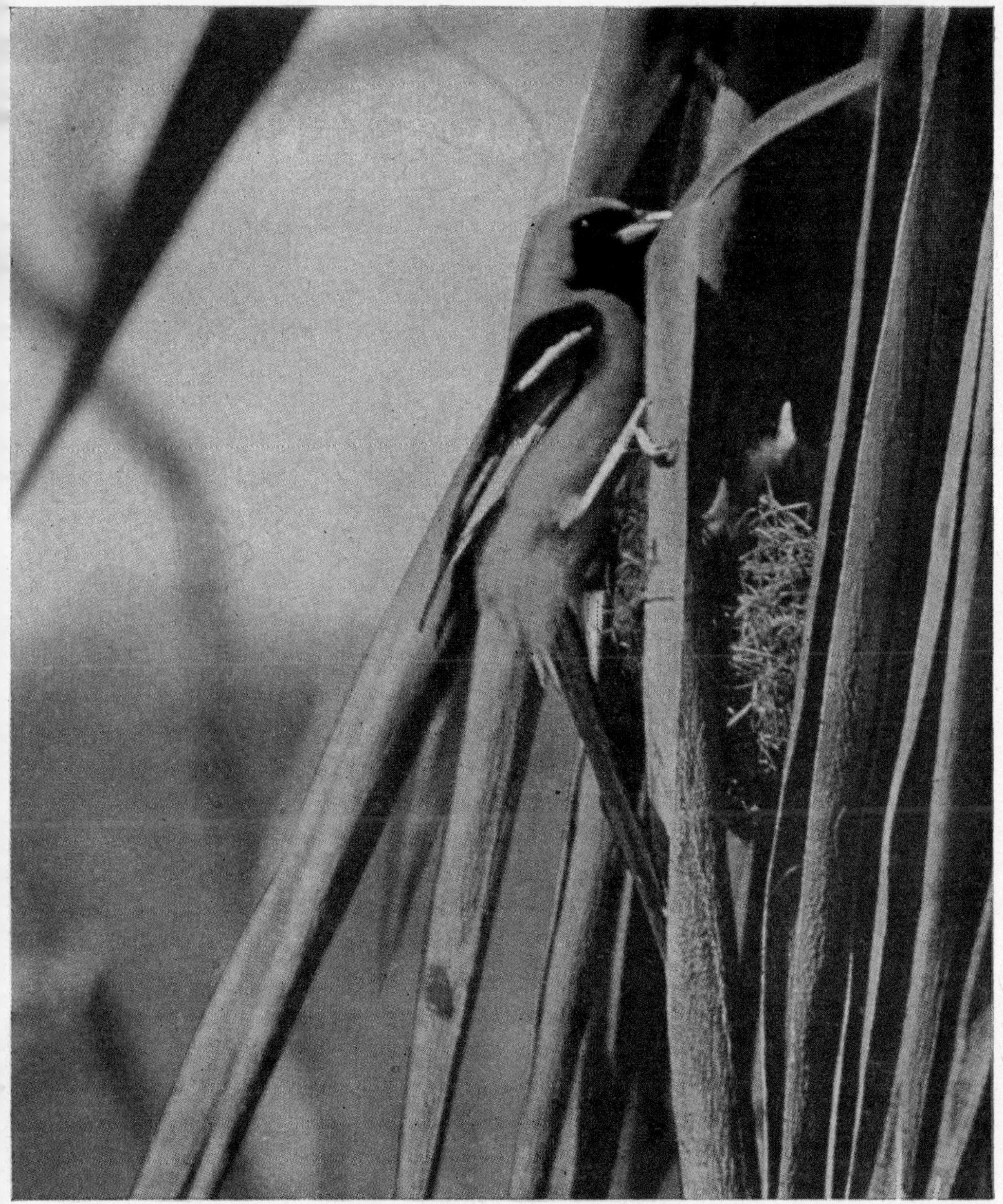

SENNETT'S HOODED ORIOLE (*Icterus cucullatus*). Length: 7 to 7.75 inches. Male: black throat, wings, upper back and tail. Body and head deep yellow orange. Wings double-barred with white. Female: olive back, yellowish olive underparts. Immature male: similar to female, but has black throat of male. Range: breeds in lower Rio Grande Valley, Texas. Voice: song which is mixture of notes and whistles, *chut chut whew whew.*
Samuel A. Grimes

the wings which are snow white. The female is grayish, tinged with yellow. Both birds have large white beaks.

The chirping notes of the Evening Grosbeak remind me of the notes of the common English Sparrow, but more harsh and shrill. While feeding, the birds chirp constantly. They also fight constantly over the possession of a feeding tray. One bird will devote its entire time to the task of chasing others from a tray which it dominates and which may contain enough food and enough room for a dozen other birds.

Because it resembles the Hawfinch of England, the Evening Grosbeak is often referred to as the American Hawfinch. Its generic name is from the Greek, Hesperides, "Daughters of Night," who dwelt in the western sunset. It was named by Cooper in 1825, following its discovery by Schoolcraft in 1823. It was misnamed by these early ornithologists who thought it sang only at sundown. And while it was formerly regarded as distinctly a bird of the Canadian northwest, its breeding range extends east to Michigan. Its winter range includes all of New England and south irregularly to Maryland, Kentucky, and Missouri.

The summer home of the Evening Grosbeak is the fir and spruce forests of the north. The loosely woven nest is placed high in a conifer, the shallow cup lined with fine rootlets. The three or four greenish eggs are lightly blotched with brown.

A western form of the Evening Grosbeak is the California, or Western, Evening Grosbeak *(H. v. brooksi)*, which may be distinguished from the eastern form by its darker, duskier coloration.

CALIFORNIA PURPLE FINCH (*Carpodacus purpureus californicus*). Length: 5.25 to 6 inches. Male: rosy-red brightest on head and rump. Female: heavily striped brown with broad white line over eye. Range: breeds on the Pacific Coast from British Columbia south to California. Winters from Oregon to southern Arizona. Voice: a dull, metallic *tick* or *pit*. Song, a lively warble lower in pitch than the house finch.

Rudolph Hindemith, American Museum of Natural History

PURPLE FINCH

(Carpodacus purpureus)

Fortunate indeed are those bird watchers who have been able to attract a flock of Purple Finches to their winter feeding stations with generous quantities of sunflower seeds; fortunate, for they have at their very window one of the most strikingly colored of North American birds. Raspberry or old rose is nearer the color of the male than purple, and the coloring is brightest on the head and rump, with the breast conspicuously splashed with it. The female, poor soul, is a brown striped Sparrow with a white eye line.

The similarly colored Pine Grosbeak might be confused with the Purple Finch (5½ to 6 inches) were it not for the fact that the former is half again as large. The Pine Grosbeak also has two conspicuous white wingbars. Redpolls might be confusing, but they have red foreheads and streaked crowns. Young Purple Finches of both sexes resemble the female for more than a year, but the young males sing well in this plumage. Peterson describes the song as a fast, lively warble, and the note a distinctive dull metallic *tick* or *pit*.

CASSIN'S PURPLE FINCH (*Carpodacus cassinii*). Length: 6 to 6.5 inches. Male: rosy red with brown wings, back and tail. Prominent squarish red crown patch. Female: back olive gray, streaked with black stripings, underparts white. Range: breeds in high mountains from Canada to northern Arizona and New Mexico. Winters in valleys of same regions. Voice: a typical Finch warble.
Rudolph Hindemith, American Museum of Natural History

The breeding territory of the Purple Finch lies in northern United States and Canada as far west as northwestern British Columbia. It is partial to small conifers. In the west, the California Purple Finch (*C. p. californicus*), a subspecies of the Eastern Purple Finch (*C. p. purpureus*), breeds in the Transition Zone of the Pacific states from Canada to Mexico, and east to the Cascades and Sierra Nevadas.

CASSIN'S PURPLE FINCH

(Carpodacus cassinii)

Although similar in appearance and in habits to the more widely distributed Purple Finch, the Cassin's Purple Finch may be distinguished from that race by its larger size (6 to 6½ inches) and its paler breast and rump. Cassin's is the only Purple Finch in the Rockies, but its range overlaps that of the California Purple Finch in the mountains of the Pacific states. Its song is similar to the California Purple Finch. It breeds in the high mountains and winters in the lowlands.

HOUSE FINCH

(Carpodacus mexicanus)

Color Plate Page 422

Considering the House Finch's bad reputation as a destroyer of fruit in many parts of the west, especially California, it is surprising to learn that seven-eights of the bird's diet is composed of seeds, mostly from weeds. However, the House Finch's abundance in certain fruit-growing areas justifies its being considered a nuisance on many occasions.

Those not confronted personally with its fruit-destroying habit are free to enjoy this red-headed Linnet's lovely plumage, its cheery musical song, and its sociable ways. In the west, it replaces the English Sparrow of the east as a dooryard bird. As one accustomed to the latter, I feel that my western friends are getting the better bargain.

The House Finch (5½ inches long) resembles the Purple Finch with its bright red breast, forehead, and rump, but the coloring of the male Purple Finch is more rose than red. The striped underparts of the male House Finch are its best field mark, however. The female is striped, grayish brown above and whitish below.

Except during the mating season which begins in April, House Finches are found in flocks, feeding about the dooryard, the towns, and the countryside from central Texas and western Kansas to California and Oregon. They nest in a variety of locations, but are particularly partial to nooks and crannies about buildings where they place bulky nests. Their song is typical.

Three subspecies are recognized: the Common House Finch *(C. m. front-*

BALTIMORE ORIOLE (FEMALE) *(Icterus galbula).* Length: 7 to 8 inches. Male: brilliant orange body, black head, throat, upper back, wings and tail. Wing feathers edged with white. Sides of tail orange. Female: upperparts olive brown, yellowish below, with two white wingbars. Range: breeds from Nova Scotia, Ontario and Manitoba to Georgia, Louisiana and southern Texas. Winters in Central America. Voice: a whistled piping song.

Hal H. Harrison

alis), the San Clemente House Finch *(C. m. elementis)*, and the San Luis House Finch *(C. m. potosinus)*. There are no field differences.

EUROPEAN GOLDFINCH *(Carduelis carduelis britannica)*. Length: 5.5 inches. Male and female: tawny brown body, black tail and wings, bright red patch about base of bill and broad yellow band crossing wing. Range: naturalized in Bermuda; small colonies established in southeast Long Island. Voice: song, liquid, suggesting canary note, *swit-wit-wit*.

Rudolph Hindemith, American Museum of Natural History

SHARPE'S SEEDEATER

(Sperophila morelleti sharpei)

A very small Finch (3¾ to 4¼ inches) with a short stubby thick bill, Sharpe's Seedeater is found in the lower Rio Grande Valley. The male is black above and white below. The wings and tail are black, and the wings are much marked with white. The female is brown on the back and yellow-brown below. Her wings have two yellowish bars.

The song is surprisingly loud for such a tiny bird and extremely sweet, consisting of repeated high notes followed by several at a lower pitch. The nest is built in small shrubs, and the four or five eggs are blue-green spotted with brown.

PINE GROSBEAK

(Pinicola enucleator)

Color Plate Page 423

Whether or not many easterners will see Pine Grosbeaks next winter will depend upon how successfully the conifer trees of the north bore their fruits this autumn. If the spruce and hemlock cones fail to mature in normal abundance, then we may expect Pine Grosbeaks to move south in search of food. Such an influx occurs in the northern states about every five to ten years, although stragglers may be seen almost any year.

The Pine Grosbeak is the largest of the Grosbeaks (9 to 9¾ inches), considerably larger than the Purple Finch or the Crossbills with which it might be confused. The male has a rose colored head, breast, and rump. The wings and tail are black, with two white bars crossing each wing. The females are generally grayish, the rose of the male being replaced by olive-green in the female.

To see the Pine Grosbeak on its nesting grounds, one would have to visit the boreal forests of Canada or the high mountains of New Hampshire in the east; the Rocky Mountains south to New Mexico in the west; or the central Sierra Nevadas in California. In summer the bird avoids the lowlands.

Its song is a sweet, melodious Grosbeak-like warble. Peterson describes the characteristic call as "*tee-tee-tew*, remarkably like the cry of a Greater Yellow-legs."

GRAY-CROWNED ROSY FINCH *(Leucosticte tephrocotis)*. Length: 5.75 to 6.75 inches. Male: dark brown body with pinkish wash on wings, rump, tail and lower abdomen. Dark brown breast and light gray patch on the back of the head. Black bill. Female: duller than male and gray crown patch inconspicuous. Range: breeds from northwest Montana into Canada. Winters to the Cascades and south to Utah and Colorado. Voice: high, chirping, twittering notes.
Ruth and H. D. Wheeler, National Audubon Society

Seven forms of the Pine Grosbeak are recognized throughout its range, but differences among them are so slight that field identification is impossible.

EUROPEAN GOLDFINCH

(Carduelis carduelis britannica)

Introduced in Hoboken, New Jersey in 1878, the European, or British, Goldfinch, a larger species (5½ inches) than our native Goldfinches, has established itself in small colonies in the region of New York City. Early in the present century, the birds showed a decided decline in numbers, and it has been only in comparatively recent years that any increase has been noticed. The birds are still very localized in their range, and breeding records are rare.

The bright red faces and broad yellow wing bands of the tawny brown adults distinguish them from any native birds. The sexes are similar. The song is more reminiscent of a Canary than of the native birds.

GRAY-CROWNED ROSY FINCH

(Leucosticte tephrocotis)

One must have alpine inclinations to study the Rosy Finches, for their favorite haunts are the snow capped peaks above the timber line in the western mountains.

The Gray-crowned Rosy Finches are brown Sparrow-like birds 5¾ to 6¾ inches long, with a pinkish wash on the rump and wings. A light gray patch on the back of the head is this species' best field mark. The similar Black Rosy Finch has a black body. The Brown-capped Rosy Finch is quite similar, but it lacks the conspicuous gray head patch. The voice of the Gray-crowned consists of chirpings like the English Sparrow.

His food consists mainly of insects blown by the winds to the mountain tops, where he lives.

The geographic races of the Gray-crowned Rosy Finch are: Hepburn's Rosy Finch *(L. t. littoralis)*, the Gray-crowned Rosy Finch *(L. t. tephrocotis)*, the Sierra Nevada Rosy Finch *(L. t. dawsoni)*, Aleutian Rosy Finch *(L. t. griseonucha)*, the Pribilof Rosy Finch *(L. t. umbrina)*, and the Wallowa Rosy Finch *(L. t. wallowa)*. Hepburn's Rosy Finch has a much more extensive rosy crown; otherwise there are few field differences.

BLACK ROSY FINCH

(Leucosticte atrata)

The Black Rosy Finch is limited in its breeding range to the high mountains of Idaho, northern Utah, and western Montana. It is very similar to the Gray-crowned Rosy Finch, except that its body is blackish instead of chestnut, resulting in a handsome little bird 6 inches long, the size of a Sparrow. The female is grayish brown where the male is black. Its voice is a high pitched chirping.

Like the other Rosy Finches, it nests in crevices in the rocks above the timber line, and feeds on insects and seeds that have been blown up by the winds. In the winter it is found southward to Colorado.

BROWN-CAPPED ROSY FINCH

(Leucosticte australis)

Similar to the preceding two species, the Brown-capped Rosy Finch breeds in the high mountains of Colorado, and winters in the valleys of Colorado and south into New Mexico. Its body is a lighter brown than the Gray-crowned, and it has no light gray patch on the back of its head. The crown is dark brownish black. It is like the other Rosy Finches in song and habits.

HOARY REDPOLL

(Acanthus hornemanni exilipes)

We were watching a a large flock of Redpolls foraging among the sand dunes along the New England coast. Their low rattling calls pleased us as they flew about from one weed patch to another. Suddenly someone sighted an individual much whiter than the others. It had a white rump and the body streaking was quite faint. We had found a Hoary Redpoll, another visitor from the Arctic tundra, but much less common than the Redpolls with which it flocks.

Identification of a Hoary Redpoll is always risky unless the bird is seen side by side with the Common Redpoll. However, this favorable condition often prevails. It is somewhat smaller, 4½ to 5½ inches, and whiter looking.

REDPOLL

(Acanthus flammea)

A lone Redpoll in the United States is unusual. So gregarious are these little Arctic waifs that they invariably visit us during the winter in flocks, often numbering hundreds. They are sociable

HOARY REDPOLL *(Acanthus hornemanni exilipes)*. Length: 4.5 to 5.5 inches. Male and female: similar to common Redpoll but smaller and whiter. The rump is white without streakings. Range: subarctic, very rare winter visitor to Montana. Voice: similar to Redpoll.
Rudolph Hindemith, American Museum of Natural History

with other species, too, feeding and flying regularly with Goldfinches, Crossbills, Siskins, and Evening Grosbeaks. In flight, the birds utter a soft *chut, chut,* conveying to the listener a rattling sound.

The bright red forehead and black chin patch are the Redpoll's best field marks. Other characteristics are its streaked grayish brown upperparts, pinkish breast and rump, white abdomen, and streaked sides. The female lacks the pinkish wash on the breast and rump. The birds are 5 or 5½ inches long.

The two races of the Redpoll that reach the northern states in winter nest from Alaska and Quebec to Alberta and the Gulf of St. Lawrence. Most regular and abundant is the Common Redpoll *(A. f. flammea)*. Much less frequent is the Greater Redpoll *(A. f. rostrata)* which is somewhat larger than the other, darker, and larger billed.

PINE SISKIN

(Spinus pinus pinus)

Color Plate Page 425

If ever there was an erratic bird, it is the Pine Siskin, also called Pine Finch and Pine Linnet. A coniferous forest may actually swarm with Siskins during one winter, then for years a Siskin may not be seen again in that place. The winter movements are more ir-

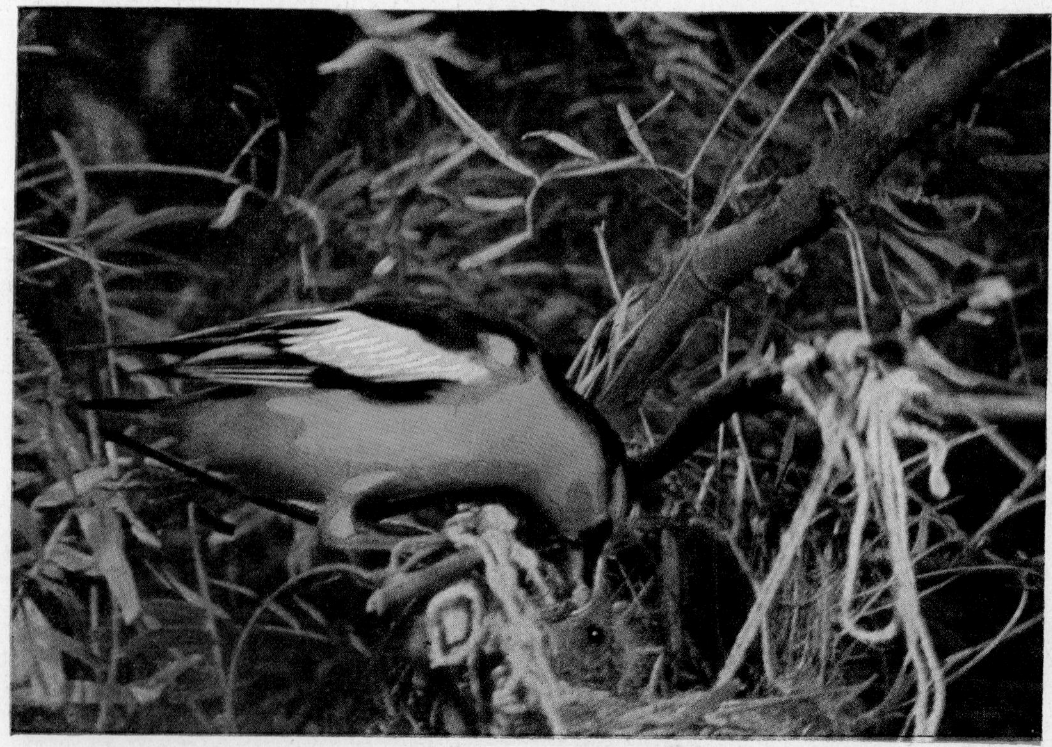

BULLOCK'S ORIOLE *(Icterus bullockii bullockii)*. Length: 7.5 to 8.5 inches. Male: bright orange body. Jet black upper back, crown, throat and line through eye. Black wings marked with white, and black center to tail feathers. Female: upperparts grayish olive. Blackish throat. Underparts whitish yellow. Range: breeds in western United States, east to Kansas, winters in Mexico. Voice: a succession of accented double-notes, with piping notes inserted.

Fred Bashour

BREWER'S BLACKBIRD (*Euphagus cyanocephalus*). Length: 8 to 9.5 inches. Male: body entirely covered with shiny greenish black, turning purplish-black on the neck and head. Has a white eye. Female: has dark eye, and brownish gray body. Range: western North America from Canada to California. Winters from Washington and Montana south to Mexico. Voice: a harsh, wheezy song, *que-ee*, or *ksh-eee*. Notes, a harsh *check*.
Harlan E. Eckler

regular than the summer range of the bird, although it is difficult to foretell where Siskins will choose to make their nests any season.

Generally, these heavily streaked little brown birds (4½ to 5 inches) so reminiscent of Redpolls and Goldfinches, breed throughout the coniferous forests from the Atlantic to the Pacific and in the mountains, as far south as North Carolina in the east and southern California in the west. It winters south to the Gulf.

In summer, Siskins are identified easily from the more brightly colored Goldfinches, but in winter it is the heavy streaking above and below that sets them apart. In flight, the yellow wing and tail patches are evident. The Siskin does not change its plumage with the seasons. The American Pine Siskin is identical in coloring with the Tarin, or European Siskin, of the Old World, but it is an entirely different species.

Found feeding among the hemlocks, pines, or spruces, a flock of Siskins looks like so many brown-streaked Sparrows. Their songs and calls are like the Goldfinches, but lower pitched. A *see-a-wee* call is very similar to that of the Goldfinch. Unlike the latter bird, however, Siskins are often attracted to winter feeding stations where they appear in company with other northern visitors like the Redpolls, Evening Grosbeaks, and Tree Sparrows.

REDPOLL ON NEST (*Acanthus flammea*). Length: 5 to 5.5 inches. Male: streaked gray brown bird with *bright red* cap on the forehead and a *black* chin, and pink breast. Female: similar to male but underparts buffy or whitish. Immature: no red on crown. Range: northern portions of Northern Hemisphere. In winter south to more northern United States. Voice: *chug* or *chet-chet* most characteristic note.

William H. Carrick

GOLDFINCH

(Spinus tristis)

Color Plate Page 428

"Wild Canary" is certainly a well chosen name for the Goldfinch. It looks like a Canary, and it sings like a Canary. When a flock of these bright yellow birds with black wings, black caps, and black tails swoops down on a bed of ripening cosmos, bachelor buttons or coreopsis, one would swear that someone left the big cage door open at the Canary farm. The female is dull greenish yellow, with dark wings and conspicuous wingbars. The birds are 5 to 5½ inches long.

How delightful to listen to the low *swee-swee* notes of a carefree band of these golden birds as they flit from one flower stalk to another in the summer sunshine. They seem to have not a care in the world as they bound hither and yon in undulating flight, singing, feeding, and finally wooing and nesting as the season grows late.

Long, long after most wild birds have gone to housekeeping, indeed, after many have finished, the Goldfinch annually earns for itself the title of "the last bird to nest." When the thistle ripens in July and August, these happy bands of Finches break up into mated pairs, and nesting territories are established.

Then, as the female builds her dainty cup of down and grasses in the crotch of a tree, as she incubates her three to six pale bluish white eggs, far overhead her mate flies in great wide circles. The downward plunge of each undulating swoop is marked by his sweet love call of *per-chic-o-ree*. What a devoted lover! As he sings to his mate, who wears the drab plumage that he, too, will adopt when winter comes, he remembers to bring dainties for her to eat throughout her hot days on the nest.

When the young have hatched, the male joins the female in feeding them. Even then, he flies to her occasionally with a particularly fine morsel that he wishes her to have for her own. The young are fed by regurgitation, largely on partly digested vegetable matter.

One becomes so fond of this lovely bird that it is always a shock to learn that its nest is ill kept and unclean. A Goldfinch's nest may be identified long after the young have left by the thick ring of excrement that remains piled around the edge of the cup.

As soon as the young are on the wing, usually in September, the birds again join in cheery bands to roam the countryside and harvest the autumn weed seeds. Many move southward in the fall; others winter in the north. On a Christmas bird census in western Pennsylvania one year, I found two flocks totaling 89 birds. They were feeding on the seed balls of the sycamore trees. Both sexes look very much alike at this time, but by careful observation the males may be distinguished by their darker wings and yellow shoulder patches.

Folks who enjoy birds in their gardens can bring more Goldfinches to their grounds by a method I have found highly successful. Since Goldfinches are fond of thistle seeds, I buy large quantities from my dealer and place them in small flower pots nailed to the tops of sticks. The sticks may be placed conveniently about the garden, and the seeds will serve as a magnet for these golden birds.

The Goldfinch feeds largely on birch seeds, buttonbush and weed seeds in winter. In summer it subsists on weed seed plus many injurious insects.

Throughout the summer Goldfinches are resident in most of the United States except the Gulf states. The common Eastern Goldfinch *(S. t. tristis)* is replaced in the Rocky Mountains by the Pale Goldfinch *(S. t. pallidus)*, and on the Pacific coast by the Willow Goldfinch *(S. t. salicamans)*. This latter form is somewhat smaller and paler, with less white in the wings.

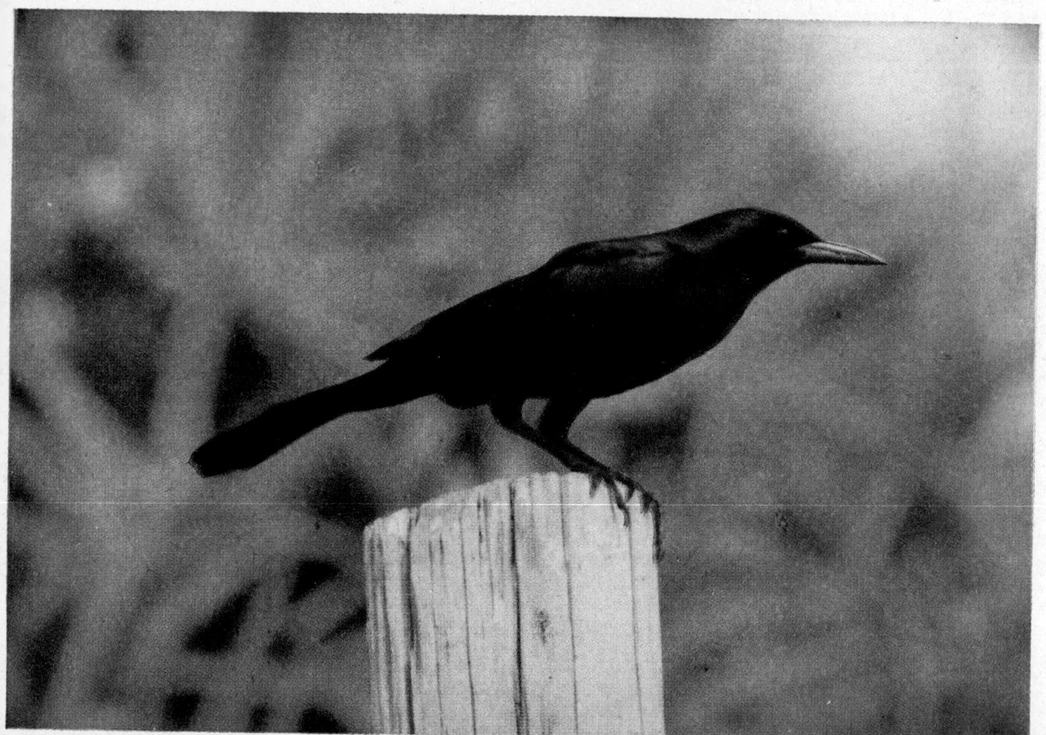

BOAT-TAILED GRACKLE *(Cassidix mexicanus)*. Length: male, 16 to 17 inches; female, 12 to 13 inches Male: jet black body with long, wide *keel-shaped* tail. Female: brown. Range: near salt water from Delaware to Florida and west to Texas. Voice: harsh *check check check.*

Helen Cruikshank

LAWRENCE'S GOLDFINCH (*Spinus lawrencei*). Length: 4 to 4.5 inches. Male: dark gray bird with touch of yellow on the throat and rump and broad yellow wing base. It has a black patch on the forehead and chin. Female: similar to male but without black face patch. Range: breeds in central and southern California, west of Sierras; winters in southern California and Colorado River Valley. Voice: call-note, *tink-oo;* song, clear, long-sustained canary-like warble.
Laidlow Williams, National Audubon Society

GREEN-BACKED or ARKANSAS GOLDFINCH

(*Spinus psaltria*)

Color Plate Page 429

All male western Goldfinches may be distinguished from the widely distributed Common Goldfinch by the color of their backs. While males of the Common Goldfinch, including the Willow Goldfinch *(S. t. salicamans)*, a Pacific coast race, have bright yellow backs in breeding plumage, the male Arkansas (4 inches) have black backs. In winter, when the bright yellow of the Common Goldfinch changes to brownish and the black cap disappears, the male Arkansas Goldfinch retains its black cap. The females are similar, although the female Arkansas Goldfinch has a more greenish back.

The Arkansas Goldfinch *(S. p. psaltria)* may be distinguished from its more western form, the Green-backed Goldfinch *(S. p. hesperophilus)* by the olive-green back of the latter species.

The song of the Arkansas Goldfinch is like the Canary's, but less sustained than the Common Goldfinch. The notes, according to Peterson, are very distinctive; "a sweet plaintive *tee-yee* (rising inflection) and *tee-yer* (dropping inflection)."

The Arkansas Goldfinch breeds from Oregon and Utah through southern California and Arizona, and winters into Mexico.

LAWRENCE'S GOLDFINCH

(*Spinus lawrencei*)

The black chin of Lawrence's Goldfinch (4 to 4½ inches), a bird of the hot dry areas of southern California, identifies it from all other Goldfinches. Although similar to the Green-backed Goldfinch, its gray head in combination with a black cap and chin, and a yellow throat are diagnostic. The wings are crossed with broad yellow bars. The female is similar to the male, but without the black face mask. Unlike the other Goldfinches, this species does not change its plumage with the seasons.

In regard to the song of this species, Ralph Hoffmann writes: "The notes of the Lawrence Goldfinch bear a general resemblance to those of the other Goldfinches, but among its call notes is a harsh *kee-yerr,* unlike any notes of the other two [Willow or Green-backed]. The song is lower in pitch and rougher, with occasional harsh phrases."

RED CROSSBILL

(Loxia curvirostra)

Color Plate Page 432

The crossed mandibles of a Crossbill are indicative of the bird's highly specialized food habits—that of feeding extensively on the seeds of coniferous trees. These are extracted from their cones after the Crossbill has inserted its closed bill into the cone and then forcefully opened it, the action tearing off the scales that protect and hide the seeds. The food is then removed with a scooplike tongue.

The male Red Crossbill (5¼ to 6½ inches) is brick-red with a carmine rump. The wings and tail are dusky brown. Females and young are grayish olive, streaked with brown, and yellowish on the rump and breast. Young males show considerable variation in transition plumage, many appearing rather orange. The song is a warble which resembles the Finches. The notes are a harsh *pip-pip-pip.*

The movements of the Red Crossbill are erratic, especially in winter when flocks may appear suddenly in conifers far south of their usual range. The bird is at home in the summer in evergreen forests from central Alaska and Nova Scotia, south to the northern edge of the United States, except on the Pacific coast, the Rocky Mountains, and the Appalachians, where it breeds further south.

Eight geographic races of the Red Crossbill are recognized throughout its extensive range.

WHITE-WINGED CROSSBILL

(Loxia leucoptera leucoptera)

During an invasion of White-winged Crossbills in a hemlock forest in western Pennsylvania in February, 1941, I made the following notes: "I stood directly under a hemlock that was being attacked by the entire flock. On me and around me came a continual shower of cones until the snow-covered ground was thick with them.

WHITE-WINGED CROSSBILL *(Loxia leucoptera leucoptera).* Length: 6 to 7 inches. Male: bright rose pink with black wings and tail, the wings with two broad white bars. Female: grayish with yellowish rump; wings and tail dark slate gray with white wingbars like male. Range: breeds in Canada south to northern United States; winters irregularly south to Nevada, Illinois and Virginia. Voice: a sweet *wheet,* single or repeated. The song is a clear whistled twittering trilling on varying pitches.

Rudolph Hindemith, American Museum of Natural History

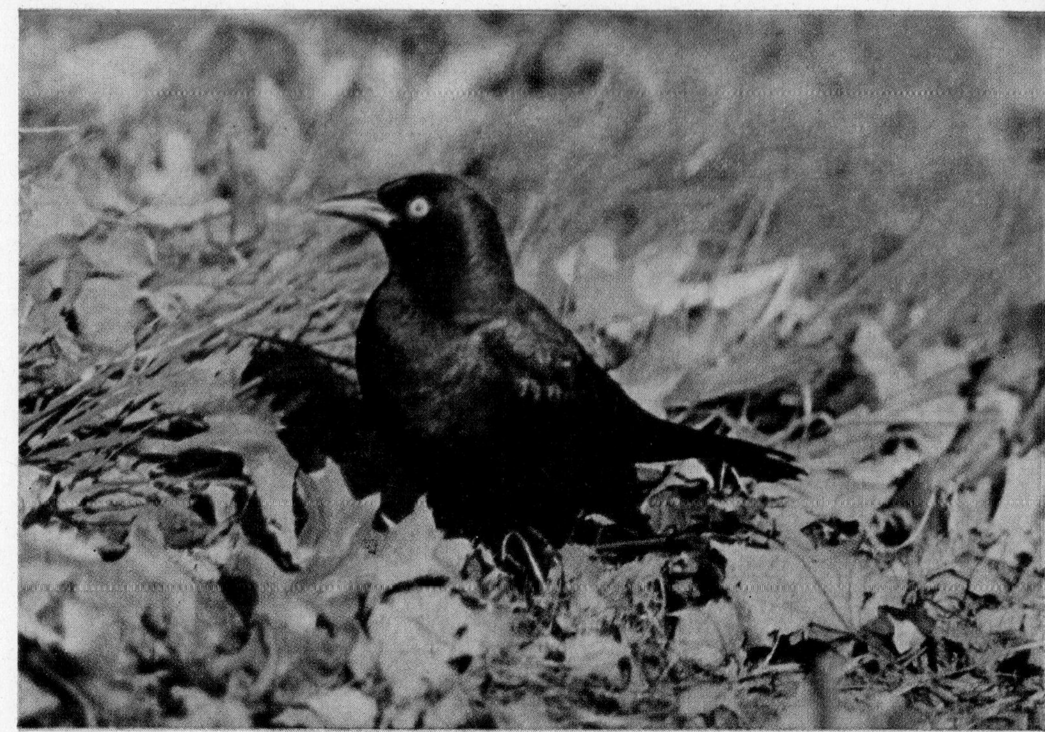

PURPLE GRACKLE *(Quiscalus quiscalus)*. Length: 11 to 13 inches. Male: iridescent purplish black with long wedge-shaped tail. Female: smaller and duller than male. Range: breeds from southern New England and southern New York, south to Florida and southern Louisiana. Winters in southern United States north to New Jersey. Voice: song, rasping note, *chuck*.
Helen Cruikshank

The birds were very nervous and kept moving from tree to tree. In flight, and often while feeding, they kept up a continual chattering, reminding me of a flock of Goldfinches. Watching these gorgeous raspberry colored birds cracking open cones while they hung like little parrots from the terminal branches of snow-laden hemlocks was a sight I shall long remember."

The male White-winged Crossbill (6 to 6¾ inches) is pinkish red with black wings and tail. Two broad white bars cross each wing. Females resemble female Red Crossbills, but the white wingbars are distinctive. The habits of this species are similar to the Red Crossbill.

Their voice is a *chif-chif*, or a sweet *peet*, according to Peterson. He describes the song as "a succession of low trills on different pitches."

White-winged Crossbills breed in the coniferous forests of Alaska and Canada to the limit of trees. Occasionally they nest in the high mountains of New England and New York state. Like Red Crossbills, their winter movements to the south are erratic.

TEXAS SPARROW

(Arremonops rufivirgatus rufivirgatus)

The Texas Sparrow (5½ to 6 inches), also known as the Green Finch, is a bird of very restricted range in the chaparral areas of southern Texas and northern Mexico. Its uniform olive-green upperparts make it

COWBIRD, COMMON OR EASTERN (*Molothrus ater*). Length: 7 to 8 inches. Male: iridescent black, except for chestnut brown head and neck. Female: brownish gray body. Range: from Canada to Mexico. Voice: *glug-glug-gleee* or *klug-tseeee*, with high-pitched last note.
Hal H. Harrison

appear more Finch-like than Sparrow-like. The underparts are light with a buffy area on the breast and sides. Two brown stripes traverse the crown lengthwise. The female is similar to the male.

GREEN-TAILED TOWHEE

(Chlorura chlorura)

Brush covered mountainsides where trees are not distributed heavily are the favorite haunts of the Green-tailed Towhee, a ground-loving bird 6¼ to 7 inches long that ranges in the summer from south-central Montana and central Oregon, south to west-central Texas and southern California. It winters from western Texas and southern California south into Mexico.

Regarding the bird's habits in New Mexico, Florence Merrian Bailey writes: "The Green-tailed Towhee, or Red Top, as he is sometimes called, finds his food largely by scratching over the ground in Towhee fashion under sagebrush, oak brush, or chaparral. Here his mewing call may often be heard, and glimpses may be caught of him, a glint of green, a rufous cap, and white chin, as he shifts from one part of this thicket to another or pitches down with head lowered and tail widespread. When startled, I have seen him throw his long tail over his back and raise his crown till it glowed red in the sun; then vanish. He also runs over the ground with his tail over his back. When not disturbed, he will sing from the top of a juniper or other lookout in plain view."

The sexes are alike, with an olive-green back, gray breast, a ruddy crown, and white throat.

TOWHEE or CHEWINK

(Pipilo erythrophthalmus)

Color Plates Pages 433 and 436

The names of many birds are poorly chosen, but not the Towhee. It belongs to the small group of birds that have been named for their songs, like the Chickadee, Phoebe, Whip-poor-will, Bob-white, and Killdeer. The Towhee calls its name, but it slurs the first part. It sounds like *t'whee*. From its other common call of *che-wink*, it has gained the name of Chewink. Because it looks a bit like a Robin and spends much of its time on the ground, some call it the Ground Robin, although it is really a large Sparrow (7½ to 8¾ inches).

On its territory during the nesting season, the Towhee delivers its real song from the top of a bush or low tree. With its tail hanging limp and its head thrown back, the bird utters a musical three-syllabled song which can readily be interpreted as *drink your teeeeeeeee*. The third syllable is given in a quavering voice.

Identifying features of the male Towhee are its black head, bill, throat, upper breast, upperparts, wings, and tail. The sides of the body are rich chestnut. White in the wings and in the corners of the long rounded tail is diagnostic. Females are the same pattern, but brown where the male is black.

Young birds, during the summer, look like large slender Sparrows, streaked below, but are recognizable for the characteristic white markings on the wings and tail.

Red-eyed Towhee is the name of the eastern species *(P. e. erythrophthalmus)*, the first name coming from the red-eyed adults. Young Towhees have brown eyes. If you happen to be in Florida and suddenly discover a Towhee with white eyes, you have found a subspecies *(P. e. alleni)*. Anatomically, the White-eyed Towhee is smaller and has less white in the wings and tail. The iris of the eye is brownish yellow or yellowish white, often described as "straw" color, instead of red as in the commoner species. Its call is higher pitched and more wheezy than its relative, the Red-eyed. The White-eyed Towhee breeds from North Carolina to Florida.

If you see a Red-eyed Towhee during the nesting season in Alabama, you are looking at an-

TEXAS SPARROW *(Arremonops rufivirgatus rufivirgatus)*. Length: 5.5 to 6 inches. Male and female: upperparts olive green. Two broad dull brown stripes on the crown. Narrow ring of dull white around the eye; underparts whitish. Range: southern Texas north to Corpus Christi. Voice: a series of dry notes all on one pitch.
Rudolph Hindemith, American Museum of Natural History

other subspecies, the Alabama Towhee *(P. e. canaster)*. This one has less white in its tail, although such a slight difference is of little consequence in the field.

GREEN-TAILED TOWHEE *(Chlorura chlorura)*. Length: 6.25 to 7 inches. Male and female: ground dwellers. Plain *olive green* back, *rufous* crown and conspicuous white throat; breast gray, underparts, white and gray. Range: breeds in mountains from central Oregon and south central Montana, south to southern California, southeast New Mexico, and Texas, west to Cascades and Sierras; winters from southern California, southern Arizona and western Texas, south into Mexico. Voice: mewing note like a kitten, song opens with one or two sweet notes and ends in long burry notes; *weet-chur-cheeeee—churrrr*. Has dry burr in the long notes.
Rudolph Hindemith, American Museum of Natural History

The Red-eyed Towhee is decidedly eastern in its range, reaching only to the edge of the Great Plains where it is replaced by the Spotted Towhee and its subspecies. The differences among all of these are so slight that they are of little use in field identification.

Towhees are ground-loving thicket birds. They are not birds of the doorstep, but their appearance in tangles and busy parts of the garden may be expected. The noise made by Towhees scratching for food among the dead leaves on the ground is loud. Indeed, one is often led to believe that some large animal is at work when this bird is throwing the leaves about so energetically. Characteristic of this foraging is the Towhee's ability to scratch with both feet at the same time. It is quite a trick to throw both feet back at the same time, and still bring them forward fast enough to keep from falling down.

The first nest of the season is usually on the ground, the second in a low bush or tree. The structure is built of dried leaves, stems, and grasses, a rather bulky affair. The four to six white eggs are finely dotted all over with reddish brown.

The Towhee feeds mainly on insects and seeds, and some wild berries.

The breeding range of the Red-eyed Towhee is from southern Manitoba, southern Ontario, and southern Maine, south to central Kansas and northern Georgia. It winters from the Gulf of Mexico north to Lake Erie and southern New York, although its appearance in the extreme northern part of this winter range is decidedly casual. Occasionally it reaches Massachusetts.

SPOTTED TOWHEE

(Pipilo maculatus)

The common Red-eyed Towhee of the east is replaced in the west by a race of birds known as Spotted Towhees (7 to 8¼ inches). The two species are similar, but the Spotted Towhee has more white on the tail and the back is spotted with white. Its voice is a buzzy trill.

RED-EYED COWBIRD (*Tangavius aeneus aeneus*). Length: 6.5 to 8.75 inches. Male: black body with prominent ruff on sides of neck, and with red eyes. Female: smaller ruff and body dull blackish color. Range: southern Texas north to San Antonio.
Ross and Florence Thornburg

Known in different localities by different names, such as Spurred Towhee, Oregon Towhee, Large-billed Towhee, Nevada Towhee, and Arctic Towhee, these subspecies are indistinguishable in the field. As a race, they breed from Canada to Mexico, and from the Great Plains and western Texas to the Pacific. They winter in the Pacific states and from Arizona and New Mexico southward.

BROWN TOWHEE

(Pipilo fuscus)

Of the seven geographic races of the Brown Towhee that occur in western United States, those that inhabit the Pacific states are indistinguishable in the field, while the Cañon Towhee *(P. f. mesoleucus)*, a breeding bird of western Arizona, New Mexico, southern Colorado, and western Texas is somewhat different in appearance.

The Pacific races are 8¼ to 9½ inches long, dull grayish brown, with reddish brown under tail coverts, and faintly streaked buffy breasts. The Cañon Towhee, in addition, has a light rufous crown and a central breast spot.

Concerning this species, Hoffmann asks: "Can even a bird lover become enthusiastic over a Brown Towhee—a plain brown bird that hops stolidly in and out of brush heaps about farm buildings, with no bright colors, no attractive song, and no tricks or manners of especial interest?" Concerning its song, Hoffmann writes: "The commonest note is a rather emphatic *chip*. The song is a feeble imitation of the

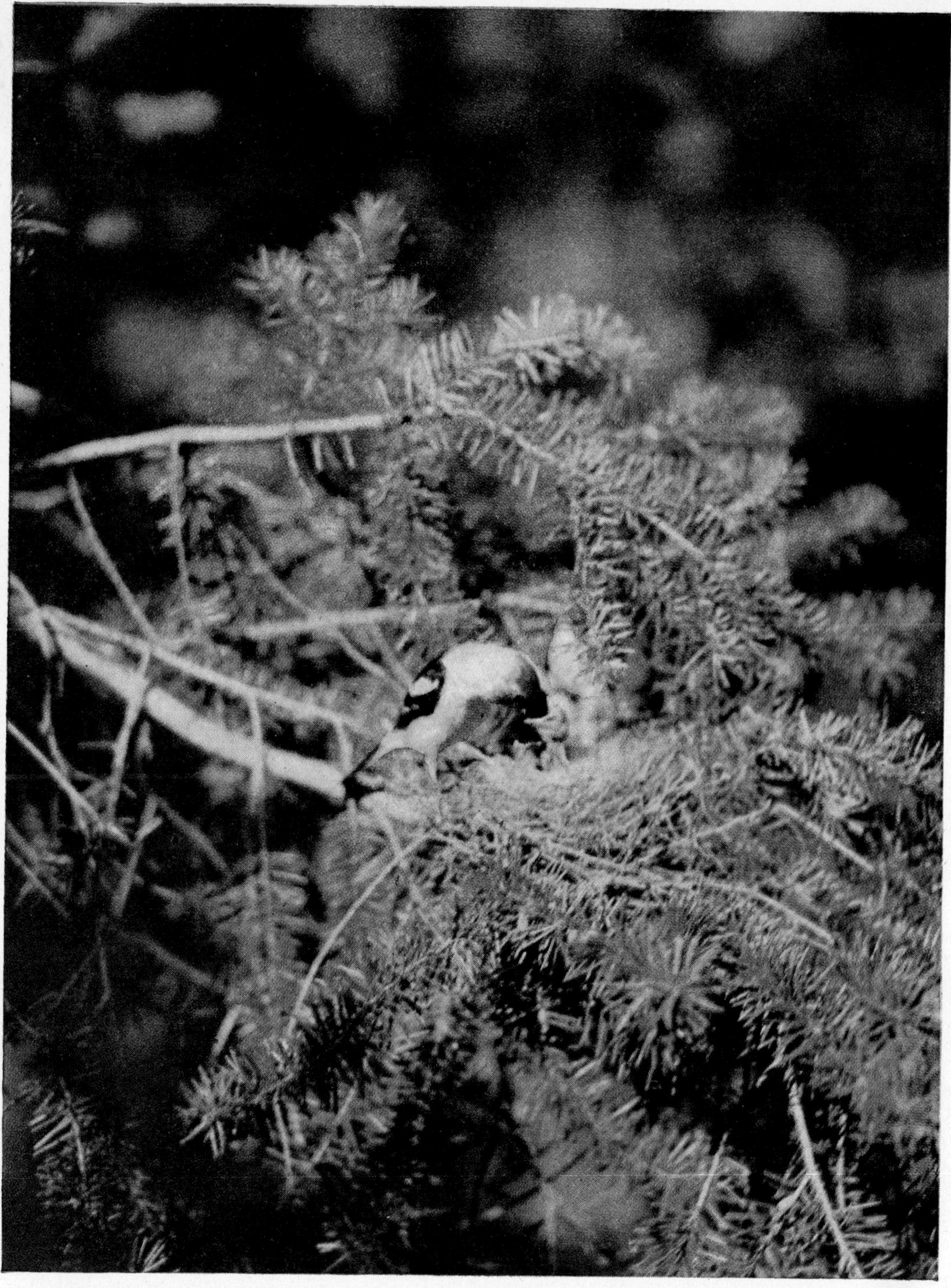

WESTERN TANAGER (*Piranga ludoviciana*). Length: 6.25 to 7 inches. Male: upperparts, black; wing patches and rump bright yellow. Head and neck brilliant orange red; rest of underparts, bright yellow. Female: upperparts olive green, back and shoulders grayish; yellowish wingbars; pale yellowish underparts. Range: Canada to southern California, Arizona, New Mexico and western Texas; winters in Mexico. Voice: song made up of short phrases. Note, a dry *pi-tic* or *pit-i-tic*.

R. T. Congdon

Wren-tit's fine crescendo performance. It suggests the syllables *tsip tsip tsip tsip churr churr churr*, given without much animation, and not freely uttered even in the height of the breeding season.

SPOTTED TOWHEE (*Pipilo maculatus*). Length: 7 to 8.25 inches. Male: entire head and upperparts, black with several rows of white spots on back and wings. Sides are *Robin-red;* abdomen, white. Female, similar to male, but with dusky brown head. Range: breeds from Canada to Mexico and from Great Plains and western Texas to the Pacific. Winters in Pacific states and from Arizona and northern New Mexico, south. Voice: a drawn-out, buzzy trill, *chweeeeeeee.*
R. T. Congdon

ABERT'S TOWHEE

(Pipilo aberti)

The Towhee of the southwestern deserts, Abert's Towhee ($8\frac{1}{4}$ to 9 inches) is best distinguished by its browner appearance and black patch at the base of the bill. Its underparts are buffy brown, darkening to tawny reddish on the underside of the tail.

It builds its nest in dense thickets near streams, usually within five feet of the ground. The nest is large and carelessly made. The two to four eggs are pale blue, finely spotted with dark brown and black. Its voice is like the Brown Towhee. In winter Abert's Towhee is found southward to Lower California and Mexico.

BROWN TOWHEE (*Pipilo fuscus*). Length: 8.25 to 9.5 inches. Male and female: dull gray brown with rather long tail. *Pale rusty* under tail and tail coverts. Streaked buffy throat. Range: southwest Oregon, California, Arizona, New Mexico, southern Colorado and western Texas. Voice: same as Abert's Towhee; song, a rapid *chiuk-chiuk-iuk-iuk-iuk-iuk-iuk-iuk*, often ending in a trill.
Ross and Florence Thornburg

LARK BUNTING

(Calamospiza melanocorys)

A small black bird with large white patches on its wings, seen during the summer throughout the Great Plains, is certainly a Lark Bunting, commonly called a White-winged Blackbird. Since it is a Finch, this common name is confusing, although most descriptive. The larger Bobolink shows much more white above, mostly on the back.

Not only in appearance, but in change of plumage, the male Lark Bunting (5½ inches) resembles the Bobolink. In the autumn, it trades its jet-black feathers for the streaked brown plumage of the female. In winter, Lark Buntings flock together from Arizona and Texas southward into Mexico. Their song is a sweet trill; their note a soft *hoo-ee.*

A bird of the ground, the Lark Bunting nests on the ground, sinking its cup of grasses and weedstalks into an indentation where it is protected by overhanging vegetation. Four or five plain pale blue eggs are usual.

IPSWICH SPARROW

(Passerculus princeps)

This bird was so named because the first specimen was taken on the sand dunes of Ipswich, Massachusetts, in 1868. It was twenty-six years later before ornithologists discovered its breeding grounds on Sable Island, Nova Scotia, where it is the only breeding land bird.

This species is a large (6 to 6¼ inches), pale edition of the Savannah Sparrow, and to some taxonomists, it appears to be more of a subspecies of that bird than a full species of its own but its isolation in breeding tends to intensify the differences.

Bird watchers have an opportunity to study the Ipswich Sparrow in winter when it migrates to the mainland and scatters along the outer beaches south to Georgia.

SAVANNAH SPARROW

(Passerculus sandwichensis)

While driving along a state highway in marsh country in northwestern Pennsylvania, I suddenly became conscious of an insect-like song in a road-

ABERT'S TOWHEE AT NEST *(Pipilo aberti).* Length: 8.25 to 9 inches. Male and female: upperparts dull unmarked grayish brown with *black* patch around the base of the bill. Entire underparts buffy brown. Range: deserts of southeastern California, southern Nevada, southwestern Utah, southern Arizona, and southwestern New Mexico. Voice: song, a rapid *chink-chink-ink-ink-ink-ink-ink.* Often ends in trill. Note, a metallic *chink.*
Eliot Porter

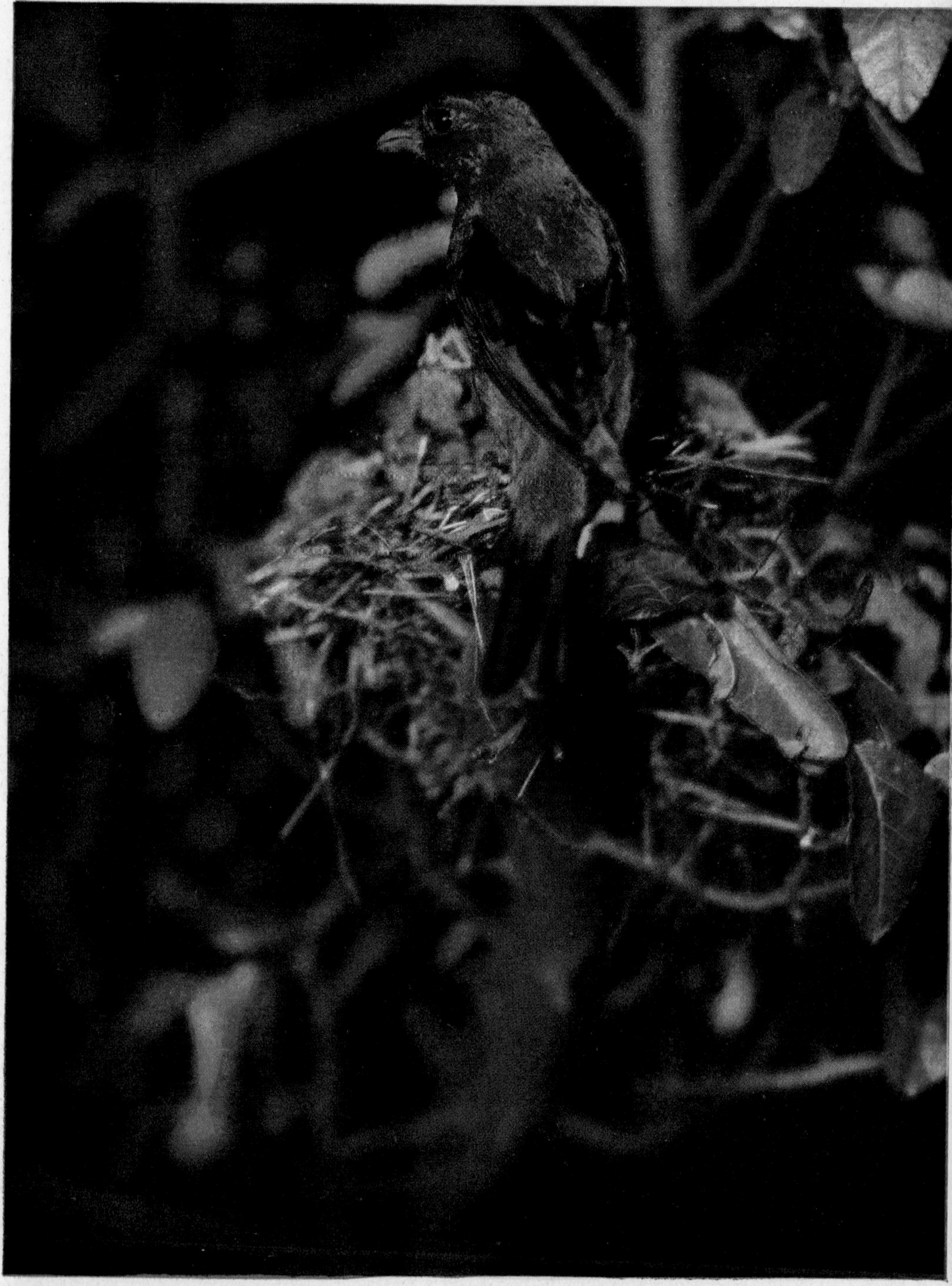

MALE SCARLET TANAGER (*Piranga olivacea*). Length: 6.5 to 7.5 inches. Male: bright scarlet body with black tail and wings. Female, immature, and winter male: olive green above, yellowish below, brownish or blackish wings. Range: Canada south to South Carolina, Georgia, Alabama, and Kansas; winters in South America. Voice: a low *chip-burr*. Song, four or five short nasal phrases.
Hal H. Harrison

MALE CARDINAL ON PINE TREE (*Richmondena cardinalis*). Length: 8 to 9 inches. Male: entire body bright red, except for grayish red back, wings and tail, and black patch from upper throat surrounding red bill. The head is crested. Female: olive grayish head and body. Bill patch is slate gray. Bill, head crest, wings and tail, dull red. Underparts pale yellowish brown. Range: eastern United States from southeastern New York, west to Iowa, south to Florida and eastern Texas. Voice: song, a series of whistles; *what-cheer, cheer cheer,* or *whoit, whoit, whoit.*

Hal H. Harrison

LARK BUNTING (*Calamospiza melanocorys*). Length: 5.5 to 7.5 inches. Male in spring: black with white wing patches. Females, immature and males in autumn: grayish brown with white streaking on breast; usually some indication of wing patch. Range: breeds on the prairies east to Minnesota and Nebraska; winters in Mexico. Voice: a cheery, sweet *hoo-ee*. Song is a rich sweet trill.
Rudolph Hindemith, American Museum of Natural History

side field. It went *sip-sip-sip-sweeeeeee-sreee.* I stopped my car and listened. It was consistently five notes; three short ones, an insect-like buzz, and the last note ascending and cutting off suddenly. It was a Savannah Sparrow, and I found it singing from the top of a weed stalk.

A bird carrying food indicated a nest, but it required over two hours of patient observation to locate it on the ground, carefully hidden by overhanging weeds and grasses. The birds never flew directly to the nesting site nor left directly from it. Invariably they would alight and take off some distance away, walking to and from their home.

The head markings and the slightly forked tail of the Savannah are its best field marks, for the breast is streaked like many other members of the Sparrow family. A wide yellowish line over the eye and a narrow whitish one through the center of the crown are diagnostic. The bird measures $4\frac{3}{4}$ to 6 inches long.

The Savannah, with its many geographical races, breeds from Alaska to Labrador, and southward to New Jersey, Indiana, and northern New Mexico. It winters south of its breeding range.

Bird watchers who frequent the tidal marshes of southern California from Santa Barbara to San Diego encounter Belding's Sparrow (*P. s. beldingi*), a subspecies until recently considered a separate species. Although the Savannah Sparrow inhabits the drier areas, the two are found in close proximity.

The heavy dark understreaks of the Belding's are considered its best field mark in distinguishing it from the Savannah. It is also darker than the Large-billed Sparrow with which it also associates and with which it is very likely to be confused. It will require considerable practice on the part of the bird student to name these three species. In the east it need only be differentiated from the Sharp-tailed Sparrow.

LARGE-BILLED SPARROW

(Passerculus rostratus)

Although the Large-billed Sparrow lives in the salt marshes of southern California, it is also found in the streets and along the wharves of the coastal towns. It is similar to Belding's Sparrow, but is much paler and browner in color and does not have the black markings on wings and back. In size it is about the same, 4¾ to 5¾ inches. Its breast is streaked with brown. However, its best identification is the bill, which is longer and heavier than that of Belding's.

The Large-billed Sparrow breeds along the coast from Santa Barbara southward.

GRASSHOPPER SPARROW

(Ammodramus savannarum)

Color Plate Page 437

I wonder how many persons have heard the song of the Grasshopper Sparrow and have never seen the bird. Indeed, I wonder how many persons even knew they were listening to a bird at all. Whether it sounds like a grasshopper or not is questionable, but that it sounds exactly like the buzzing of some insect there is no doubt. The song is distinctive, and once it is learned, the bird watcher will be surprised to discover how common this bird really is.

Old pastures and grassy meadows, offering ample ground cover, are the places to look for the Grasshopper Sparrow, or, rather, to listen for it. Like others of the ground - inhabiting sharp tailed tribe of Sparrows, the Grasshopper skulks away when an intruder appears, and it is not always an easy matter to see the bird distinctly or for any length of time. I have found that my automobile, parked at the side of a field, is unnoticed by the bird, and my best observations have been made from this vantage point.

A clear view of the bird shows it to be small (5 to 5¼ inches), but with a large flat head, out of proportion to its body. The underparts are unstreaked, differentiating it from the similar Henslow's Sparrow (which see) but are buffy on the breast and flanks. Its tail is ridiculously short.

The nest of the Grasshopper Sparrow, like the nest of the Henslow's, is seldom found, even by field ornithologists. It is so cleverly built (domed on the top with a small, inconspicuous opening in the side), so well hidden in tall grasses, and the adults are so wary about approaching or leaving it, that one may well be proud of his find when the home is discovered.

Four geographic races are recognized: the Eastern Grasshopper Sparrow *(A. s. pratensis)*, the Western Grasshopper Sparrow *(A. s. perpallidus)*, the Florida Grasshopper Sparrow *(A. s. floridanus)*, and the Arizona

IPSWICH SPARROW *(Passerculus princeps)*. Length: 6 to 6.25 inches. Male and female: large, pale sandy-colored bird. In spring it has pale yellow line over the eye. Range: breeds on Sable Island, Nova Scotia; winters in dunes and at edge of salt marshes along coast south to Georgia. Voice: a dreamy, lisping *tsit, tsit-tsit-, tseeee-tsaaay.*

Rudolph Hindemith, American Museum of Natural History

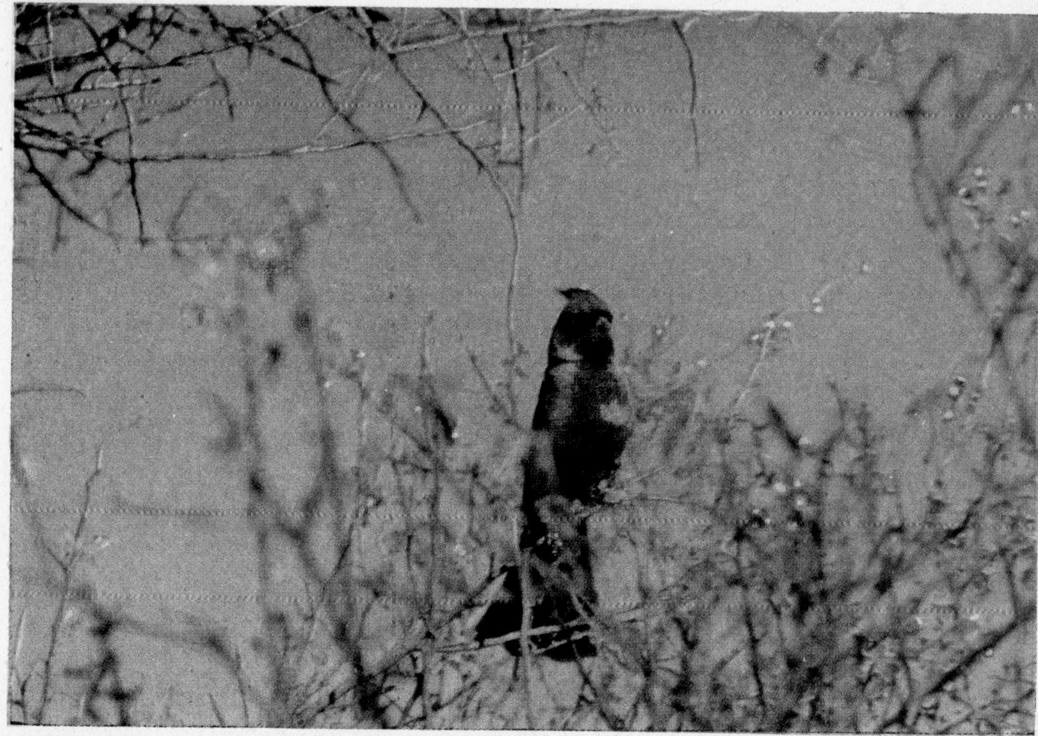

PYRRHULOXIA *(Pyrrhuloxia sinuata)*. Length: 7.5 to 8.25 inches. Male: gray back, rose colored breast and crest. Almost parrot-like bill. Females: gray back, yellow breasted with touches of red, in wings and crest. Range: southern Arizona, southern New Mexico and western and southern Texas. Voice: song, a clear *quink quink quink quink quink* on one note.
William L. and Irene Finley

Grasshopper Sparrow *(A. s. ammolegus)*. There are no field differences.

BAIRD'S SPARROW

(Ammodramus bairdii)

Baird's Sparrow, which closely resembles the Savannah Sparrow, is a breeding bird of the western prairies from Minnesota to Saskatchewan and central Montana. It migrates through eastern Wyoming, Colorado, Arizona, and New Mexico, and winters from central Texas, and probably southern Arizona, south into Mexico.

The head of this species is ochre or buffy and marked similarly to that of the Savannah Sparrow, but the central head stripe is broad and ochre. In the Savannah, this stripe is narrowed and light. The bird is 5 to 5 1/2 inches long. The song is said to resemble that of the Savannah (which see) but contains more warbling notes and is less insect-like.

LECONTE'S SPARROW

(Passerherbulus caudacutus)

On the prairie marshes from Great Slave Lake south to the Mississippi Valley, Leconte's Sparrow makes its summer home. This elusive little (5 inches) brown, sharp tailed Sparrow is similar to Henslow's Sparrow, but the yellow-brown throat and breast distinguish it from that species. It resembles the Grasshopper Sparrow, too, not only in appearance, but in its insect-like buzzy song, but the streaked sides eliminate the Grasshopper. A buffy eye-line and a whitish stripe through the crown are also characteristic.

Leconte's Sparrow winters in the southern United States.

BAIRD'S SPARROW *(Ammodramus bairdii).* Length: 5 to 5.5 inches. Male and female: light breast crossed by *narrow band of fine black streaks.* Head yellow brown streaked with black. Underparts white. Tail deeply forked. Range: breeds in dry upland prairies from southwest Saskatchewan to North Dakota and northwest Minnesota. Migrates through plains to Mexico. Voice: song often begins with three or four musical *zips* and ends with trill on lower pitch.
Rudolph Hindemith, American Museum of Natural History

HENSLOW'S SPARROW

(Passerherbulus henslowii)

Color Plate Page 440

The Henslow's Sparrow is a species that eludes many bird watchers for a long time. I know from experience. Although I had it pointed out to me long ago during fall migration, it was not until recent years that I was able to stop my car suddenly while passing an open meadow and announce quite proudly to the other occupants, "There is a Henslow's Sparrow singing in that field."

LECONTE'S SPARROW *(Passerherbulus caudacutus).* Length: 5 inches. Male and female: upperparts, pale grayish, streaked with darker gray, black and brown. Underparts, whitish, streaked with black. Has bright buffy-ochre eye-line, throat and breast, and pinkish brown collar. Range: Saskatchewan and Manitoba to North Dakota and northwest Minnesota, migrates to Mexico. Voice: three or four musical zips and ends with trill on a lower pitch.
Chicago Natural History Museum

Until one learns to recognize the insect-like hiccoughing that the bird utters as its song, he will discover that finding the Henslow's Sparrow by sight alone is almost a hopeless task. But when that quick little *chis-lick* note is associated with the bird, it will become unmistakable, for no other bird has such a song.

The *chis-lick* interpretation is my own.

Other writers hear it as *flee-sic, tsi-lick,* or *tee-wick.* A friend of mine, listening to the same bird that said *chis-lick* to me, heard *sa-link.* Regardless of the interpretation, it is the shortest song uttered by any song bird. And it is surprising how far those thin penetrating double notes will carry.

When the singer is located, he will be seen on his perch atop a mustard weed or a small bush. There he throws back his head, utters his quick song with a deliberate jerk, and then waits for inspiration to deliver another one. All day long he sings, and according to other observers, all night long too, if the spirit so moves him.

The bird itself is just as plain as its song. It is 4¾ to 5¼ inches long, short tailed, large headed, has a chestnut back with black spots, reddish brown wings, and dull white underparts with the breast and sides streaked with black. A greenish cast about the head and neck may help identify it. The bird is often confused with the Grass-

ROSE-BREASTED GROSBEAK (*Pheucticus ludovicianus*). Length: 7 to 8.5 inches. Male: upperparts blackish brown. Wings and tail black spotted with white, lower back, white. Bright rosy red triangle shaped patch on breast. Underparts whitish. Female: brown replaces black of male bird; breast and back streaked with dark brown. White line over eye and through center of crown. Prominent white wingbars. Both sexes have large bill. Range: Canada south to Kansas, Missouri, Ohio and New Jersey south to northern Georgia. Winters in Central and South America. Voice: mellow warble. Note, a sharp *kick* or *eek*.

Hal H. Harrison

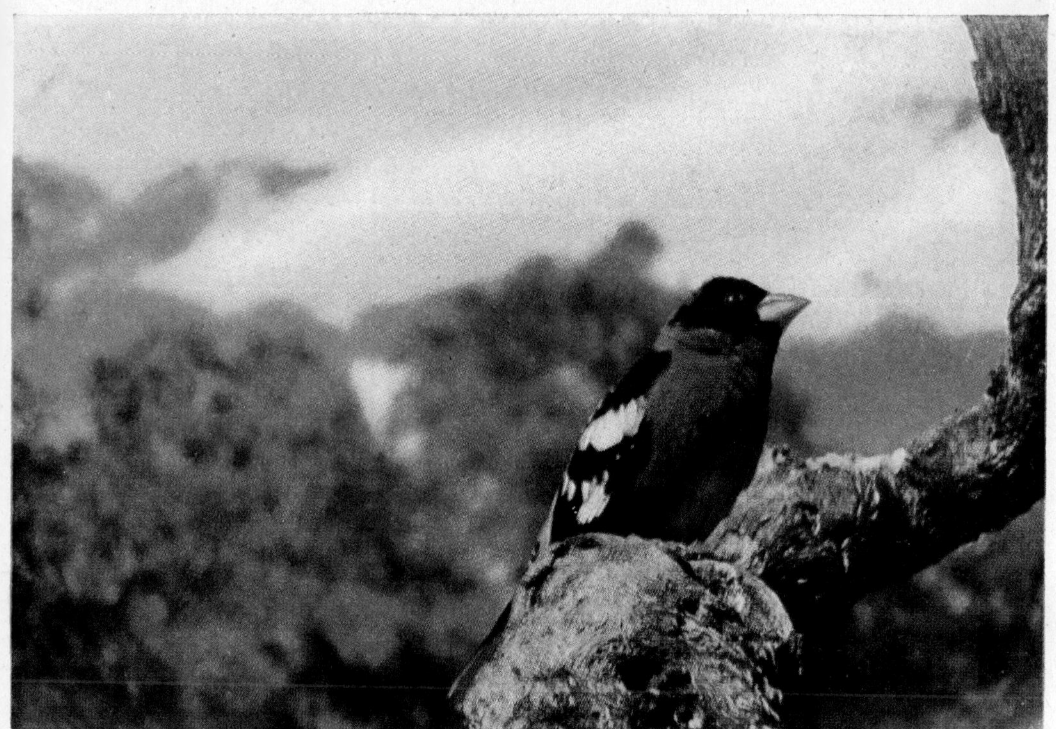

BLACK-HEADED GROSBEAK (*Pheucticus melanocephalus*). Length: 6.5 to 7.75 inches. Male: upperparts black and tawny with strongly marked black and white wings, rusty breast and yellow abdomen. Female: brown with crown streaked with tawny, underparts yellowish light brown Range: Canada south to Mexico. Voice: rising and falling song. Note, a sharp *ik* or *eek*.
Ross and Florence Thornburg

hopper Sparrow with which it associates, but the latter, in adult plumage, has a plain breast. The different songs are the best field points, however. The Grasshopper's song is a prolonged insect-like buzz.

The nesting habits of the Henslow's and the Grasshopper Sparrows are so much alike, and the eggs are so similar, that I was unable to identify my first nest when I found it. Males of both species sang continually in the meadow in which the nest was hidden. The incubating female left the nest long before I arrived in the area, probably at a warning note from the ever alert male. She hurried through the grasses for quite some distance before taking flight, making identification most difficult.

The nest, a cup of grasses hidden beneath an overhanging weed stalk, contained four white eggs spotted with reddish brown. Not until there were young in the nest, and the adults could be observed from a nearby blind, was I able to identify the birds positively as Henslow's.

Henslow's Sparrows nest in colonies, several pairs occupying the same grassy meadow. They are quite localized throughout their range, however. Their habit of avoiding detection by running through the grasses rather than taking flight is characteristic.

The Eastern Henslow's Sparrow *(P. h. susurrans)* and the Western Henslow's Sparrow *(P. h. henslowi)* breed from New York and southern New Hampshire to Ontario and South Da-

SAVANNAH SPARROW AT NEST *(Passerculus sandwichensis)*. Length: 4.75 to 6 inches. Male and female: breast heavily streaked, *yellow stripe* over the eye, and shorter forked tail than Song Sparrow; a whitish stripe through the crown, and pale pink legs. Range: breeds from Canada south to central California, Nevada, Colorado, and north New Mexico. Winters in Pacific states, Arizona, New Mexico and Texas. Voice: a dreamy, lisping *tsit-tsit-tsit-tseeee-tseeee.*
Hal H. Harrison

kota, south to northern Texas and northern Virginia. Both races winter in southeastern United States.

SHARP-TAILED SPARROW

(Ammospiza caudacuta)

The Sharp-tailed Sparrow is a little mouselike bird of the salt marshes, ranging along the Atlantic coast from the Gulf of St. Lawrence to Virginia, and in certain geographic forms, in inland prairie marshes from Great Slave Lake south to Minnesota and South Dakota.

Sharp-tails are difficult to observe as they are shy and very apt to conceal themselves in the marsh grass when an intruder enters their territory. They are low-flying birds, and when they alight, they do so suddenly by dropping into the grass. They prefer to run rather than fly when disturbed.

The best field mark of the Sharp-tail which is 5 to 6 inches long, aside from its very characteristic habits, is a gray ear patch surrounded by ochre-yellow on the face. It is large headed and short tailed, buffy below, with sharply defined dark breast streakings. The Seaside Sparrow, with which it might be confused, lacks the ochre-yellow face markings.

In winter the Sharp-tail is found

SHARP-TAILED SPARROW *(Ammospiza caudacuta)*. Length: 5 to 6 inches. Male and female: *ochre-yellow face* which surrounds gray ear patch. Upperparts brownish, olive green, marked with gray and white; wing bend is yellow, throat and abdomen, white. Range: salt marshes along coast from Virginia to Gulf of St. Lawrence. In winter its range is from New Jersey to Florida along the coast. Voice: a hissing, *tuptup-sheeeeee* song.
Rudolph Hindemith, American Museum of Natural History

along the Atlantic coast to Florida, and west along the Gulf to Texas.

Five geographic races are recognized at this time, based generally on coloration, but recognition is very difficult.

DUSKY SEASIDE SPARROW (*Ammospiza nigrescens*). Length: 5.5 to 6.5 inches. Male and female: upperparts, blackish olive gray, underparts heavily streaked with black. Range: salt marshes around Merritt Island, in vicinity of Titusville, Florida. Voice: a buzzy *cut-a-zheeeeeee*.

Rudolph Hindemith, American Museum of Natural History

SEASIDE SPARROW

(Ammospiza maritima)

Color Plate Page 442

So attached to their favorite habitat are the Seaside Sparrows that one need never look for them elsewhere. As the name indicates, the birds live by the sea, where they are common inhabitants of the salt marshes and surrounding vegetation.

Bird watchers have difficulty seeing this bird. It is ground-dwelling, and keeps out of sight much of the time. The male may be observed occasionally as he mounts to the top of a grassy perch to utter his loud buzzing which ends in a low pitched trill, trailing off at the end. The song is similar to that of the Sharp-tailed Sparrow with which it associates and with which it is often confused.

Check carefully these field marks of the Seaside: the yellow line before the eye, the white streak along the jaw, a white throat area, and dusky streaked underparts. It is olive-gray above, dingier than the Sharp-tailed Sparrow and lacking the yellowish brown face markings of that species. In size it is about the same as the Sharp-tail, 5½ to 6½ inches.

The Seaside breeds along the Atlantic and Gulf coasts.

DUSKY SEASIDE SPARROW

(Ammospiza nigrescens)

Florida bird watchers have their own private little bird in the Dusky Seaside Sparrow, for it is found only in a restricted range of not more than twenty-five miles in length in the salt marshes about Merritt Island and on the mainland around Salt Lake, near Titusville. It is abundant in that area and is nonmigratory.

It is the size of the northern Seaside Sparrow, but its upperparts are black or blackish brown, and its underparts are heavily streaked with black. Its local name is Black and White Shore Finch, or just Black Shore Finch.

CAPE SABLE SEASIDE SPARROW

(Ammospiza mirabilis)

Another Seaside Sparrow of very limited range, the Cape Sable is found only in the salt marshes at Cape Sable,

Florida, an area of about three square miles. It is the only Seaside Sparrow to be found in southern Florida, and is distinguishable by the greenish cast of its upperparts and the whiteness of its underparts.

While it has only recently been admitted as a species, the isolation of its range has made for a relatively quick intensification of its characteristics, thus illustrating a process which has produced most of the varying species.

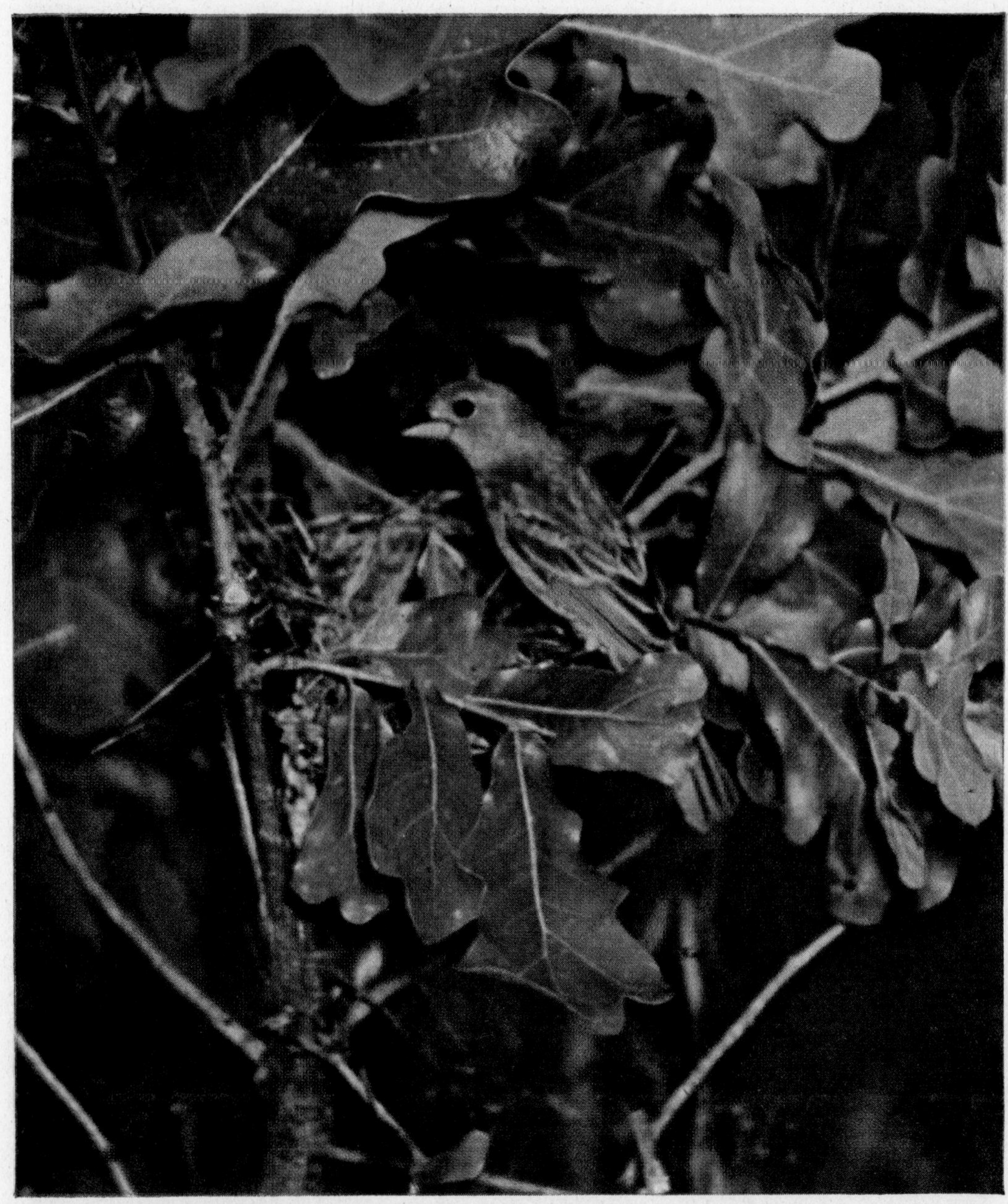

BLUE GROSBEAK (*Guiraca caerulea*). Length: 6.5 to 7.5 inches. Male: deep blackish blue body; two broad chestnut bars on blackish wings. Female: brown body, two tan wingbars, and clay-colored underparts. Range: California, southern Nevada, Colorado, Arizona, New Mexico, and western Texas. Voice: a warbling song. Note, a sharp *pink*.

Samuel A. Grimes

FEMALE INDIGO BUNTING AT THE NEST (*Passerina cyanea*). Length: 5.25 to 5.75 inches. Male: whole body deep ultramarine blue. Female: plain brown with paler underparts striped with grayish brown. Range: New Brunswick, Ontario, and North Dakota, south to central parts of Gulf States. Winters in Cuba and central America. Voice: a lively, high-pitched song, with well-measured phrases at different pitches.

Hal H. Harrison

VESPER SPARROW

(Pooecetes gramineus)

Color Plate Page 443

Like its habitual associate, the Prairie Horned Lark, the Vesper Sparrow is a bird of the wide open fields where a lack of vegetation, rather than an abundance of it, is desired for its nesting site. The bird's own natural camouflage, and the likeness of its nestlings to the ground into which the nest is sunken, makes the wind-swept fields ideal habitat for the Vesper.

The bird is shy and retiring, and were it not for its fine voice and its one unmistakable field mark, the flashing white outer tail feathers, it would certainly escape detection on many occasions. A pale, streaked Sparrow 5½ to 6½ inches long aptly describes this Grass Finch or Bay-winged Bunting as it is also called. The chestnut patch on the wing at the shoulder, which gave it the latter name, is not always conspicuous. It is noticeable in the natural color picture on page 443, but at a distance in the field, it cannot be relied upon. Its eye seems to be circled by white.

One forgets the Vesper's nondescript appearance when he hears the sweet

WESTERN LARK SPARROW AND YOUNG *(Chondestes grammacus)*. Length: 5.5 to 6.25 inches. Male and female: *black fan-shaped* tail with much white in the outside *corners. Chestnut ear-patches*, a striped crown and a white breast with a single, dark central spot. Immature: finely streaked breast and lacks central spot. Range: breeds from Canada to Mexico except in humid northwest coast belt, winters from northern California and southern Mexico, south. Voice: a variable song of clear notes and trills with buzzing passages occasionally.

Ruth and H. D. Wheeler, National Audubon Society

song that it utters from a fence post, a telegraph wire, or the top of a bush. It reminds one of the Song Sparrow's voice, but is still distinctive. Its rendition starts with two pairs of clear notes (sometimes three), the second pair higher than the first. The rest of the song is a musical trill. Should it be confused with the Song Sparrow's song, it is well to remember that the song of that bird opens with three repeated single notes, followed by a musical trill.

RUFOUS-CROWNED SPARROW (*Aimophila ruficeps*). Length: 5 to 5.75 inches. Male and female: upperparts buffy brown, sharply streaked with black; underparts, grayish white. The black whisker mark on each side of the throat, and the *rufous red cap* distinguish this bird. Range: southeastern Arizona. Voice: a variable series of notes, some musical, some buzzy, starting with three notes, *sweet, sweet, sweet.*

Rudolph Hindemith, American Museum of Natural History

In his immortal "Wake-Robin," John Burroughs paints a lovely word sketch of the Vesper Sparrow. He writes:

"His song is most noticeable after sundown, when other birds are silent; for which reason he has been aptly called the Vesper Sparrow. The farmer following his team from the field at dusk catches his sweetest strain. His song is not so brisk and carried as that of the Song Sparrow, being softer and wilder, sweeter and more plaintive. Add the best parts of the lay of the latter to the sweet vibrating chant of the Wood Sparrow [Field Sparrow] and you have the evening hymn of the Vesper bird—the poet of the plain, unadorned pastures. Go to those broad, smooth, uplying fields where the cattle and sheep are grazing, and sit down in the twilight on one of those warm, clean stones and listen to this song. On every side, near and remote, from out the short grass which the herds are cropping, the strains rise. Two or three long silver notes of peace and rest, ending in some subdued trills and quavers, constitute each separate song. Often you will catch only one or two of the bars, the breeze having blown the minor part away. Such unambitious, quiet, unconscious melody! It is one of the most characteristic sounds in nature. The grass, the stones, the stubble, the furrow, the quiet herds, and the warm twilight among the hills, are all subtly expressed in this song; this is what they are at last capable of."

Some writers have expressed the song in words as *oh, oh, see, see, what a pretty little bird I be.*

Three races of the Vesper Sparrow are recognized: the Eastern Vesper Sparrow (*P. g. gramineus*), the Western Vesper Sparrow (*P. g. confinis*), and the Oregon Vesper Sparrow (*P. g. affinis*). This latter species is somewhat larger and paler and more gray, with light breast streaks. The bird ranges across the continent from coast to coast, as far north as southern Canada in summer, and to the Gulf coast in winter.

EVENING GROSBEAK (*Hesperiphona vespertina*). Length: 7.5 to 8.5 inches. Male: upperparts olive brownish; dusky around head and breast becoming yellower toward rump. Bright yellow forehead patch. Wings are black with large white patches. Female: gray. Both sexes have extremely large whitish bill. Range: western United States from Canada to California. Winters in nearby lowlands and south to southern California. Voice: short, uneven warble. Note, a ringing chirp, *cleer* or *clee-ip*.
Hal H. Harrison

LARK SPARROW

(*Chondestes grammacus*)

Color Plate Page 446

It has been predicted that someday bird watchers of the Atlantic coast states may come to know the lovely Lark Sparrow as a common bird of that area; that like the Prairie Horned Lark, the Lark Sparrow will extend its range eastward over the Alleghenies.

Until that time, only bird enthusiasts of the central and western states may enjoy this trim Sparrow (5½ to 6¼ inches long) with the white and chestnut head stripes, chestnut cheek patches, white breast with a dark central spot, and the dark rounded tail with the white corners.

Ridgway describes the song of the Lark Sparrow as "one continued gush of sprightly music, now gay, now melodious, and then tender beyond description—the very expression of emotion." The bird's sweet melody is often broken by a buzzy *churr* note.

The Eastern Lark Sparrow (*C. g. grammacus*) breeds in the Mississippi valley east of the Great Plains from southern Ontario, Minnesota, and southern Saskatchewan, south to Texas and east to northwestern West Virginia. It winters on the Gulf coast.

West of the Great Plains to the coast (except in the humid northwest), and from Canada to Mexico, one finds the lighter colored Western Lark Sparrow (*C. g. strigatus*).

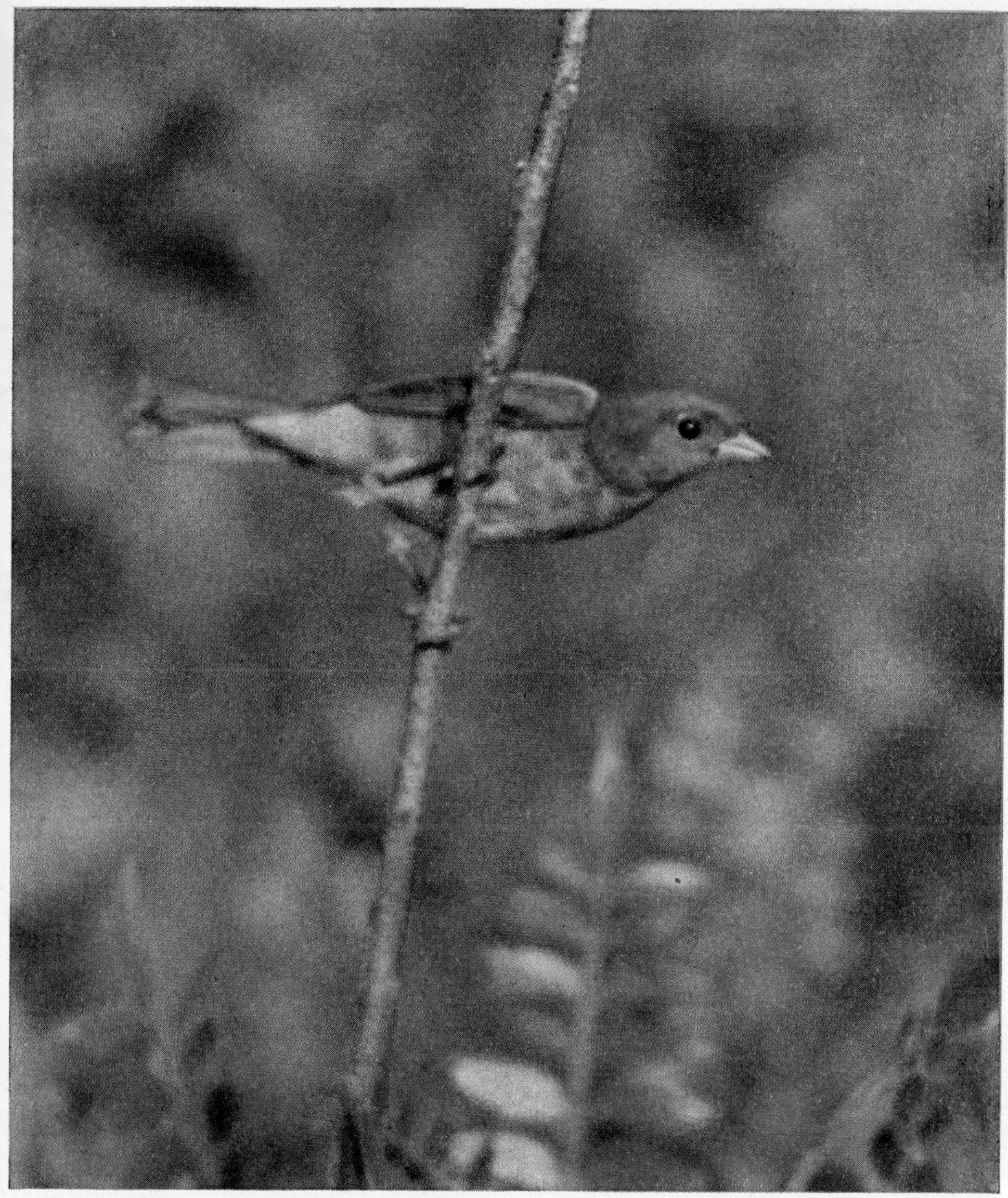

PAINTED BUNTING *(Passerina ciris)*. Length: 5.25 inches. Male: blue head and neck, green back and shoulders, red rump and tail coverts, red eye-ring and underparts. Female: upperparts and tail, olive greenish, underparts yellow. Immature: grayish brown above, underparts grayish buff. Range: southern United States from Gulf States to North Carolina and west to Arkansas. Winters from Florida to tropics. Voice: a pleasant warble.
Samuel A. Grimes

RUFOUS-WINGED SPARROW

(Aimophila carpalis)

A rare localized Sparrow, the Rufous-wing is found in the Santa Catalina mountains in Arizona. It is about 5 inches long. The upperparts are buff-brown with black streaks. The grayish crown is streaked with rufous, and marked by a conspicuous gray line

CASSIN'S SPARROW *(Aimophila cassinii)*. Length: 5.25 to 5.75 inches. Male and female: plain grayish Sparrow; underparts dingy white, with no markings. Upperparts obscurely marked with brown, and breast is unmarked. Range: breeds in southeast Nevada, western Oklahoma, southeast Colorado, Arizona, New Mexico, and western and southern Texas. Voice: quite sweet song; one or two short opening notes, a high sweet trill and two lower notes; *ti, ti, tseeeeee tay tay.*

Rudolph Hindemith, American Museum of Natural History

through the middle. The underparts are whitish. The most conspicuous mark is the rufous shoulder patch on the wings.

Rufous-winged Sparrows feed in small flocks and in habits rather resemble the Chipping Sparrow. The song is like that of the Song Sparrow.

RUFOUS-CROWNED SPARROW

(Aimophila ruficeps)

Look for the Rufous-crowned Sparrow in mountainous slopes and foothills where small bushes and cacti abound in southern California, through Arizona and New Mexico, to western Texas. The rufous crown distinguishes this species from all other Sparrows within its range except the Chipping, but it lacks the black line through the eye that characterizes the latter. Black stripes bordering the throat are excellent field marks for the Rufous-crowned, which measures between 5 and 5¾ inches.

There are a number of geographic races of this bird in the western states, including the more widely distributed Scott's Sparrow *(A. r. Scotti)*. There are no obvious field differences between the subspecies.

PINE WOODS SPARROW

(Aimophila aestivalis aestivalis)

In the dry, open pine forests of Florida and southeastern Georgia, where the dense scrub palmetto flourishes, we find the shy little Pine Woods Sparrow, well named for its favorite habitat.

Although an abundant resident bird in Florida, its range is severely restricted to that region, and particularly to the dense cover afforded by the palmetto. The bird is about the size of a Song Sparrow (5¾ inches), brown headed, buffy below, with no streakings in the underparts.

The song of the Pine Woods is an attractive musical offering. Indeed, Dr. Chapman considered this Sparrow superior to the Hermit Thrush in purity of tone and execution of its song. Howell states that "the reedlike tones are sweet and clear, suggesting the song of the Bewick's Wren, but somewhat stronger and of richer quality."

Closely related to the Pine Woods Sparrow is the grayer Bachman's Sparrow *(A. a. bachmanii)*, also called the

Southern Pine Finch, which breeds from the Gulf states north to southern Indiana, southern Ohio, and central Virginia. A third race is the Illinois Sparrow *(A. a. illinoensis)* which ranges in southwestern Indiana and southern Illinois to southern Mississippi and eastern Texas.

BOTTERI'S SPARROW

(Aimophila botterii botterii)

Botteri's Sparrow is a dingy, nondescript Sparrow of southern Arizona and the lower Rio Grande Valley. Its back and wings are gray, streaked and spotted with brown and black. The underparts are plain dingy white. Cassin's Sparrow, which is found in the same area is grayer, and Botteri's Sparrow has a browner tail. The song is very different, being a sweet tinkling, almost constant, and somewhat Canary-like. It lives in tall overgrown grass and builds its nest on the ground.

CASSIN'S SPARROW

(Aimophila cassinii)

Cassin's Sparrow, a breeding bird of open country from Kansas and Nevada southward to Texas and Mexico, is such a nondescript creature that one would like to pass it off as "just another Sparrow." I am afraid that it will be of little help to the bird student to state that the Cassin's sandy-brown back is gray-streaked, and that the bend of the wing shows a trace of yellow. It is paler than similarly marked Sparrows, but that, too, is a comparative description. In size, too, it is about average, 5¼ to 5¾ inches.

Mrs. Bailey found it interesting, however, and she writes: "When you pass through their country while the birds are in full spring song, one by one the hidden songsters spring up perhaps twenty feet into the air, when, with wings outspread and heads uplifted in a rapture of song, they give themselves to the air, floating slowly down as they sing." In this respect they are like a Skylark.

BELL'S SPARROW AT NEST *(Amphispiza belli)*. Length: 5 to 5.5 inches. Male and female: gray birds with *single dark breast spot* and *dark marks on the side of the throat*. Whisker stripe is solid and unbroken. Range: California west of Sierras, and along coast. Voice: song, four to seven notes forming a jerky but somewhat musical phrase which is rapidly repeated two or three times.
James Murdock, National Audubon Society

HOUSE FINCH *(Carpodacus mexicanus)*. Length: 5.5 inches. Male: upperparts brownish gray with red breast, stripe over eye, rump and forehead. Has ashy white underparts and sides streaked with gray. Female: upperparts grayish brown, underparts whitish streaked with gray. Range: southeast Washington, Oregon, southern Idaho, southern Wyoming into Mexico. Voice: bright, lengthy song, sometimes ending in harsh *wheer* or *che-urr*.
Alfred M. Bailey

DESERT or BLACK-THROATED SPARROW

(Amphispiza bilineata)

Color Plate Page 450

In the Sparrow family, where misidentification of species is an everyday occurrence among bird watchers, it is refreshing to find a member of the family as clean-cut and distinctive as the beautiful songster of the desert—the Black-throated Sparrow.

A jet black throat and chin, a white line over the eye, a white malar line, and a black tail with white corners (conspicuous in flight) are the best field marks. The sexes are similar.

The sweet trilling of the Black-throated Sparrow is a common voice of the desert. It sings gaily from the top of a bush, black throat thrown out, uttering its cheerful melody. Peterson describes it as a sweet "*cheet cheet cheeeeee* (two short, clear opening notes and a fine trill on a lower or higher pitch." The bird is average size, about 5 inches long.

The Black-throated Sparrow *(A. b. bilineata)* and the Desert Sparrow *(A. b. deserticola)* are indistinguishable in the field. The former is an eastern race with a range extending from western Kansas through Texas and across the Rio Grande. The race as a whole breeds in the deserts of California, Nevada, Utah, to southwest Texas and winters south from southeastern California, Arizona, and Texas.

PINE GROSBEAK *(Pinicola enucleator)*. Length: 9 to 9.75 inches. Male: rosy red color with two white wingbars, and slate-colored tail. Female: smoke-gray, head and rump washed with yellow, and also having wingbars. Immature male: similar to female but head and rump touched with red. Range: high mountains from Canada to California and east to Arizona and Nevada. Voice: pleasing song; call, a whistled *tee-tee-tew*.

Alfred M. Bailey

BELL'S SPARROW

(Amphispiza belli)

In the hot sagebrush country of southern California, west of the Sierra, lives a little grayish brown Sparrow 5 to 5½ inches long, with a dark tail, a central breast spot, and a black "whisker" mark on each side of its face. When it flies from the ground to the top of a desert bush, it jerks its tail nervously. Its name is Bell's Sparrow.

During the breeding season, Bell's Sparrow is not likely to be confused with any other Sparrow, except the Lark Sparrow which shows considerable white in the tail and has chestnut head stripes. In winter, when the Sage Sparrow, now a subspecies, joins the Bell's Sparrow in southern California, it is difficult to distinguish the two. To name the Sage Sparrow, one must see a paler bird with the black "whisker" marks broken into a chain of dark streaks. In Bell's, this mark is solid and continuous.

However, the best distinction between the two is the breeding range. Bell's Sparrow prefers brush covered hillsides, and the Sage Sparrow lives in the flat sagebrush country.

WHITE-WINGED JUNCO

(Junco aikeni)

The White-winged Junco might well be described as a Slate-colored

WHITE-WINGED JUNCO (*Junco aikeni*). Length: 6 to 6.75 inches. Male and female: gray bird with gray back. Usually has two white wingbars and a lot of white in tail. Range: breeds in southeast Montana, eastern Wyoming, west South Dakota, and northwest Nebraska. Winters from Black Hills to southern Colorado and northern New Mexico. Voice: a loose, musical trill.
Rudolph Hindemith, American Museum of Natural History

Junco with two white wingbars, except that sometimes the bird lacks these distinctive marks. Then it is most difficult to determine that the White-winged is larger (6 to 6¾ inches) and paler, and that it has a greater amount of white in the tail (one additional feather on each side of the tail is white). Its song is a trill, similar to the other Juncos.

The breeding range of the White-winged is limited however, and we find it in summer in the Black Hills of South Dakota, southeastern Montana, northwestern Nebraska, and northeastern Wyoming. It winters from its breeding grounds south to Texas and New Mexico, and east to Nebraska and Kansas.

SLATE-COLORED JUNCO

(*Junco hyemalis*)

Color Plate Page 451

From the vast spruce forests of the Maine wilderness, from the peaks of New England's highest mountains, from the cool, damp coniferous forests of the Canadian provinces, and from the pine and hemlock highlands of the Appalachian plateaus, gay chattering bands of Slate-colored Juncos come each autumn to spend the winter close to our homes.

These are the "snowbirds" that come each day for the seeds we place for them and their hardy companions, the Tree Sparrows. We recognize the Junco's field marks: a gray vest, sharply cut off by an abrupt line where the white underparts begin; white outer tail feathers that flash on and off as the birds fan their tails in flight; and a characteristic *'tsip* note spoken among themselves as they feed. They are 6 to 6½ inches long. In distinction to the Snow Bunting, they are called Black Snowbirds.

The females are distinguishable among the dark gray males, for their backs are brownish and their vests are less sharply marked. Throughout the day, they come and go from the feeders. Sometimes they seek a more varied diet from the nearby fields, the waste places where weed seeds are abundant, and along the roadsides where grit is found.

Thus they spend the long winter, roaming the countryside in carefree flocks from Nova Scotia and New York, westward to Washington, and south to Florida and the Gulf states. In April they become restless. A more vigorous male will sing a few bars from his sweet trilling song, a trill very

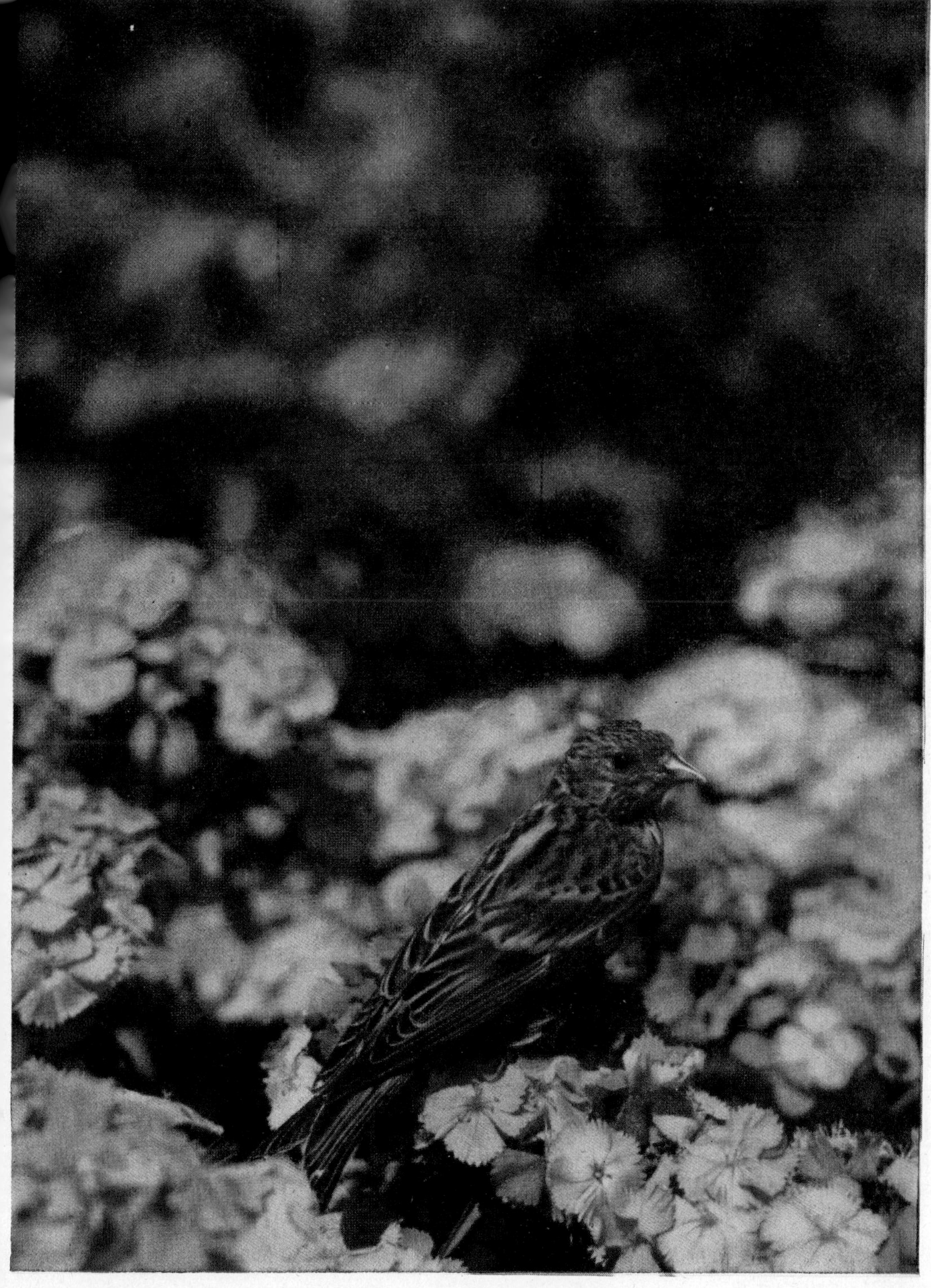

PINE SISKIN (*Spinus pinus pinus*). Length: 4.5 to 5 inches. Male and female: upperparts grayish brown heavily streaked with dark brown and black. Flash of yellow in wing and tail. Underparts grayish white thickly streaked with black. Range: western United States. Voice: call, *clee-ip, clee-ip* or *chlee-ip;* also *tit-i-tit* and *shreeeee.*

William L. and Irene Finley

similar to that of the Chipping Sparrow, but shorter, faster, and more musical. Soon they are gone, to be seen no more until falling leaves fill the autumn days.

PINK-SIDED JUNCO (*Junco oreganus mearnsi*). Length: 6.2 inches. Male and female: brownish back, gray head, broadly pinkish sides. Range: southern parts of Montana and Idaho, north of Wyoming; winters through Wyoming and Colorado. Voice: typical Junco, loose, musical trill.

Rudolph Hindemith, American Museum of Natural History

One summer I followed the Juncos to their summer home in a pine and hemlock forest. Here each day I heard them sing their sweet, simple trill; and here I found them friendly, too, as they had been in my garden the winter before. Table crumbs thrown in the dooryard of our cabin attracted twittering bands of them, still talking among themselves, seeming to repeat *true, true, true* in unpretentious fashion.

OREGON JUNCO (*Junco oreganus*). Length: 5 to 6 inches. Male: neck and upper breast, dark slate gray. Reddish back, black head. Female: grayer head, pink or brownish sides. Range: northwestern America. Winters through Pacific States and Rocky Mountains to Mexico. Voice: a loose, trembling trill all on the same pitch.

Ruth and H. D. Wheeler, National Audubon Society

All of the seven nests I found were hidden carefully on the slopes of mossy banks along woodland roads or forest trails. That the Junco has at least two broods each season was evident from the fact that in June I found young out of the nest, nests with eggs, and nests under construction.

If the adult birds had not helped me, I am sure I would not have found as many nests as I did. Their loud *clicks* and their evident nervousness when an intruder was within a short distance of their hidden treasures, were certain signs of nests or young. Even with this assistance, it was not always easy to locate instantly the deep cupped grassy nest in lush moss covered banks. The Junco is an artist at concealing this rather large and bulky structure.

Young Juncos out of the nest have the fabled ostrich habit of hiding their heads in holes in the ground. Often I watched a little one attempt to hide among the mosses while its entire body and little white tail feathers were fully exposed.

Geographic races of this Junco are: the Carolina Junco *(J. h. carolinensis)*, the Boreal Slate-colored Junco *(J. h. hyemalis)*, and the Cassiar Junco *(J. h. cismontanus)*.

OREGON JUNCO

(Junco oreganus)

Ornithologists recognize eight geographic races of the Oregon Junco, but the bird watcher will be unable to distinguish them accurately in the field. As a species, the Oregon Junco has an extensive breeding range in western North America, nesting as far north as Yakutat Bay, Alaska. In the United States, the species nests in northwestern Montana, northern Idaho, Washington, Oregon, and in California as far south as San Diego County. It winters through the Pacific states, the Rocky Mountain tablelands, and south into Mexico.

The Oregon is a mahogany backed Junco 5 to 6 inches long, with a black head, neck, and chest. Like the Pink-sided Junco, it has rusty sides, but the Pink-sided may be distinguished by its gray head and dull brown back. The female Oregon Junco has the mahogany back less sharply defined, and is grayer.

Russet-pink sides and breast are the identifying marks of the Pink-sided Junco *(J. o. mearnsi)*, formerly considered a full species. It is a breeding bird from southwestern Saskatchewan through the Rockies to northern Wyoming and southern Idaho. The sexes are similar in this species, both have gray heads and dull brown backs.

GRAY-HEADED JUNCO

(Junco caniceps caniceps)

Color Plate Page 454

Eastern bird watchers never have "Junco trouble." If you see a Junco in the eastern part of the United States, it is a Slate-colored Junco, and that is that! If you see a Junco in the western part of the United States—well, you

RED-BACKED JUNCO *(Junco coniceps dorsalis)*. Length: 5.5 to 6.5 inches. Male and female: gray sides, bright rufous back. Black upper mandible of bill. Range: mountains of Arizona and New Mexico, spreading southeastward in winter as far as western Texas and northern Mexico. Voice: lively, musical song.
Rudolph Hindemith, American Museum of Natural History

may not be so sure of your identification. There are fourteen different species and subspecies of western Juncos listed in the A. O. U. Check-List of North American birds.

The Gray-headed Junco shown in the natural color plate on page 454 breeds in the Rocky Mountains of Wyoming, Colorado, Utah, Nevada, and northern New Mexico. It is 5½ to 6 inches long.

The Gray-headed may be confused with its subspecies, the Red-backed Junco *(J. c. dorsalis)*. The combination of ashy gray sides and bright rufous back distinguishes it from all others. The Gray-headed is darker gray with a whiter belly than the Red-backed, but if you are close enough to see the bill, identification can be positive. The bill of the Gray-headed is entirely pink, while the upper mandible of the Red-backed is black. Another useful point for field identification is the fact that the Red-backed Junco does not occur north of Arizona and New Mexico.

The Red-backed Junco was formerly considered a separate species, together with the Arizona Junco.

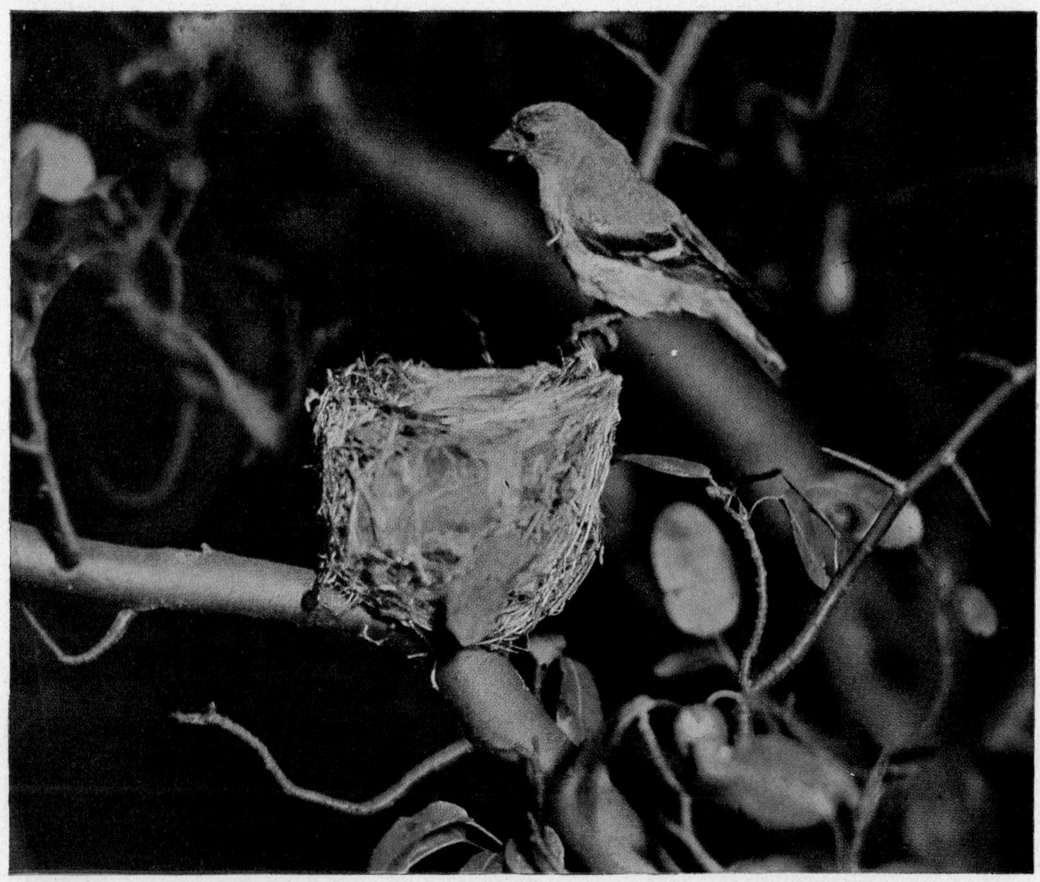

FEMALE GOLDFINCH (*Spinus tristis*). Length: 5 to 5.5 inches. Male in summer: bright yellow, crown, forehead, wings and tail black. Female in summer, and both sexes in winter: dull olive yellow with blackish tail and wings streaked with white, and grayish white underparts. Range: Newfoundland to northern Georgia and west to southern Oklahoma. Winters from southern Canada to Gulf Coast. Voice: clear, canary-like song, long sustained. Flight song; *ti-dee-di-di.*

Hal H. Harrison

ARKANSAS GOLDFINCH (*Spinus psaltria*). Length: 4 inches. Male: upperparts olive greenish, wings and tail blackish. Black cap; underparts, yellow. Female: upperparts olive greenish; black in male more grayish; underparts light olive yellow. Range: from Colorado, New Mexico and Texas, south to Mexico. Voice: sweet notes *tee-yee*, and *tee-yer*. Canary-like song.
Fred Bashour

ARIZONA JUNCO

(*Junco phaeonotus palliatus*)

The Red-backed Junco, so similar to the Gray-headed Junco, was considered a distinct species from the latter until recently. Now the two are placed in the same group, while the Arizona Junco, which was formerly assigned to the same genus as the Red-backed, now stands alone.

All three, however, are difficult to distinguish in the field. By the color of the eye and the bill one may distinguish the Red-backed from the Arizona. The Red-backed, which breeds in the high mountains of New Mexico and northeastern Arizona, has an eye with a brown iris and a bill with a flesh colored lower mandible. The Arizona Junco, a resident bird in the mountains of southeastern Arizona, has a bright yellow iris and a yellow lower mandible. The upperparts of the Arizona are ash gray except for a reddish brown back. The chest and sides are ashy white.

TREE SPARROW

(*Spizella arborea*)

Color Plate Page 455

Like the merry tinkling of tiny sleigh bells in the snow, a flock of Tree Sparrows whispered little jingles among themselves as they foraged for weed seeds in the garden on a cold morning in January. Bright, brisk, and full of energy, these "Winter Chippies" were intent on filling their crops after the energy-sapping freeze of the long winter night.

Against a background of pure white snow, the birds showed to good advantage. Chestnut caps were bright and clean, and the lone central black breast spot stood out like a badge on the plain grayish breast of each bird. The two white bars on each dusky brown wing was another point for accurate field identification. The sexes are similar, and the bird is 6 or 6½ inches long.

In a neglected corner of the garden, the birds seemed delighted with the dried stalks of pigweed or lambs-quarter *(Chenopodium album)*. The seeds clung tenaciously to the stalks as the Sparrows fluttered about them actually knocking them to the ground where they gathered them in the snow. This performance reminded me of Professor Beal's now famous statement regarding the diet of the Tree Sparrow. This renowned authority on the food of birds declared that in the state of Iowa, alone, the winter Tree Sparrows consumed 875 tons of weed seeds each year.

Tree Sparrows are winter visitors in the United States. They return in late October and November from their breeding grounds in the tundra of northern Canada. Throughout the winter, they inhabit the northern states from the Atlantic coast west to the Cascades, and south to Virginia, Kentucky, northern Arkansas, central Texas, New Mexico, northern Arizona, and Nevada.

Warm April days send the wintering flocks of Tree Sparrows north to nest beyond the limit of trees. Before they leave us, however, the similar Chipping Sparrow, Field Sparrow, and Swamp Sparrow have started to return from the south. The best field mark of the Tree Sparrow is always its large central breast spot, for the other three chestnut-capped Sparrows have plain breasts.

Although strains of the Tree Sparrow's song may be heard while the bird is in migration, the song is heard at its best by the inhabitants of the far north. It is described as a Canary-like warble, sweet but metallic, and varying in pitch and length.

Few, indeed, are those who have seen an occupied nest of the Tree Sparrow. It is usually placed on the ground, but may be anchored in a low bush. It is made of grasses and weed stems, neatly lined with feathers. Five or six eggs are laid. They are said to resemble closely the eggs of the Song Sparrow. Nesting does not occur until June, thus only one brood is attempted. Young Tree Sparrows, true to the family tradition, have streaked breasts, but after the fall molt, they make their first journey to the United States in the same plumage as their parents.

Two races of the Tree Sparrow are recognized: the Eastern Tree Sparrow *(S. a. arborea)* and the Western Tree Sparrow *(S. a. ochracea)*. The western race is slightly paler than the other.

CHIPPING SPARROW

(Spizella passerina)

Color Plate Page 457

If you have a garden of average size, you surely have a pair of Chipping Sparrows as your guests each summer. They are such domestic little birds, so insistent upon making their home at your very doorstep, and so fond of the insects and weed seeds that they find in your yard, that they seldom go far afield in search of a summer residence.

The Chipping Sparrow is such an unassuming little bird (5 to 5½ inches) that perhaps you have missed it entirely. Never does it make any bid for attention except when it sings its loud, musical trill, a string of *chips* repeated on one pitch and delivered so rapidly that they run together. The alarm note is a single *chip*.

There are two other Sparrows with which the Eastern Chipping Sparrow *(S. p. passerina)* might be confused: the Field Sparrow and the Tree Sparrow, both of which, like the Chipping Sparrow, wear a chestnut head cap. The Tree Sparrow can be eliminated quickly, however, for its plain gray breast is broken by a single center dot of black, while the breasts of the other two species are entirely plain. The fact that the Tree Sparrow is a winter resident in most of the states and is gone during the summer nesting of the other two, also helps to place it.

Between the Chipping Sparrow and the Field Sparrow, there are two principal field differences: the Field Sparrow has a pink bill, the Chipping Sparrow has a black bill; and the Field Sparrow has no eye line at all, while

YOUNG WESTERN CHIPPING SPARROWS (*Spizella passerina*). Male and female: very small clear gray-breasted Sparrow with a bright *rufous cap*, a *black line* through the eye, and a *white line* over it. Immature birds: in summer are finely streaked below; in winter are more buff than adults with a striped crown. Range: breeds from Canada to southern California, central Arizona and New Mexico; winters from southern California, southern Arizona and central Texas south into Mexico. Voice: dry chipping rattle or trill all on one pitch.

Ruth and H. D. Wheeler, National Audubon Society

MEXICAN CROSSBILL *(Loxia curvirostra)*. Length: 6.14 inches. Male: crossed bill tips, dull brick red body. Female: grayish olive, yellowish on rump and underparts. Immature: heavily striped with dark gray, whitish beneath. Range: from Wyoming to Guatemala and from Colorado west to Nevada. Voice: warbled song, note *pip pip* or *pip pip pip*.
Ross and Florence Thornburg

the Chippy has a white line above the eye and a black line through the eye. As its name indicates, the Field Sparrow is a resident of the brushy fields and pastures. The Chipping Sparrow seldom goes far from human habitation. The song of the Field Sparrow differs somewhat, being a rather melancholy series of sweet little notes, lacking the ringing sound of the Chippy's voice.

For its nesting site, the Chipping Sparrow chooses the lower branch of a tree, often an apple tree; the well hidden center of an evergreen, particularly arbor vitae and juniper; a hedge; the shelter of thick vines over a porch or trellis; or some similar place in the garden or close to the house where it is protected.

The nest is a tiny cup of grasses and rootlets invariably lined with hair, usually horse hair. Lawrence H. Walkinshaw analyzed a Chippy's nest and found the following: a lining of 752 horse and human hairs, an inner lining of 182 rootlets, and an outer cup of 145 pieces of grass, larger rootlets, and tumble weeds. The total number of pieces in the nest was 1079.

The three or four tiny eggs are a lovely shade of bluish green with a wreath of black spots around the larger end. They are incubated eleven days, mostly by the female. The young are in the nest only a short time, leaving seven or eight days after hatching. Young Chippys can fly quite well at two weeks. Unlike their parents, they have streaked breasts and no caps.

The western form of the Chipping Sparrow *(S. p. arizonae)* might be confused with the similarly marked Rufous-crowned Sparrow, for both of them have red caps and unstreaked breasts. The latter, however, has a black "whisker" mark on each side of the throat. It also lacks the black line through the eye that characterizes the Chippy. The Western Chipping Sparrow breeds from the Pacific coast to central Arizona and New Mexico.

The two races of the Chipping Sparrow breed across the continent and winter throughout the Gulf states and Mexico.

CLAY-COLORED SPARROW

(Spizella pallida)

In bushy grasslands east of the Rockies to the prairies of the upper Mississippi valley, one may look for the Clay-colored Sparrow, a shy, inconspicuously colored little bird, closely related to the Field and Chipping Sparrows. It is clear breasted like its relatives, but lacks the reddish crown. In the Clay-colored the crown is streaked, and a dark bordered brown cheek patch is characteristic. It is 5 to 5½ inches in length about the same as the other two.

MALE AND FEMALE RED-EYED TOWHEE AT THEIR NEST *(Pipilo erythrophthalmus)*. Length: 7.5 to 8.75 inches. Male: head, throat, back, wings, upper breast and tail, glossy black. White lower breast and abdomen, reddish sides. In flight white tail-patches show. Female: dusky brown replaces black in male. Range: eastern United States from Maine to Florida. Winters from Gulf of Mexico to Lake Erie. Voice: song, *drink-your-teeeeee*. Call, *chewink*.

Hal H. Harrison

The song of the Clay-colored Sparrow, as described by Walkinshaw, is "a very unimpressive *scree-scree*. Sometimes only one of these notes is given; again there are two or more, up to six." The song also has been described as "a thin, rasping, cicada-like buzz." (Pough)

BREWER'S SPARROW

(Spizella breweri)

"Sage Chippy" is a common local name for the Brewer's Sparrow, a summer resident of the sagebrush country and the mountain slopes from British Columbia to southern Arizona and western Texas. It does resemble the well known Chipping Sparrow, but its streaked head and back, and its long, deeply notched tail sets it apart from other desert Sparrows.

The song of the Brewer's Sparrow is a Canary-like trilling. It is a small bird, measuring only 5 inches.

FIELD SPARROW

(Spizella pusilla)

Color Plate Page 460

The little brown Field Sparrow that sings from morning until night in the busy pastures and neglected fields seems so melancholy and forlorn. It's the sad little song that makes me think so. From the top of a huckleberry bush or a thorn tree it pours out the mournful trill.

It might be mistaken for the song of the Chipping Sparrow, but that bird's simple trill is more sprightly and more ringing. The Field Sparrow's song gets underway with several little notes delivered slowly and on the same pitch. Then, the phrases are accelerated until the song ends in a rapidly repeated trill. It has been written well as *he-ew, he-ew, he-ew, hew hew, hew, hew, he, heeeu*. A friend of mine refers to the bird as "weeps," for to her, the bird's song is a prolonged weeping.

If the Field Sparrow is sad, it must be very sad,

CLAY-COLORED SPARROW AT NEST *(Spizella pallida)*. Length: 5 to 5.5 inches. Male and female: clear breasted gray Sparrow with *light stripe* through center of crown and a brown ear patch. Immature: distinctly striped crown, without much reddish brown. Range: prairies of north central United States, west to eastern Montana, eastern Wyoming, and eastern Colorado, winters from southern New Mexico and southern Texas, south. Voice: a rasping insect-like *zi-zi-zi-zi-zi*.
Samuel A. Grimes

BREWER'S SPARROW (*Spizella breweri*). Length: 5 inches. Male and female: upperparts chiefly grayish brown streaked with black. Underparts dusky white. Crown finely streaked with black. Range: breeds in Great Basin and Rocky Mountains' sections from Canada south to New Mexico and Arizona and west to Pacific Coast. Voice: long, musical buzzy trills on different pitches.
Rudolph Hindemith, American Museum of Natural History

for it sings this forlorn refrain constantly. Hot afternoons do not deter it in the least, and as evening shadows creep across the pasture, its melancholy music seems all the more sad as one hears it in the hush of twilight.

Somewhere near her mate's singing perch in the busy pasture, the female Field Sparrow sits on her four spotted eggs in a neatly constructed little cup. The nest is firmly woven of tiny grasses, often lined with hair. It is well hidden close to the ground in a low bush, a clump of weeds, or even on the ground.

The bird is naturally shy, and unlike its close relative, the Chipping Sparrow, it shuns human habitation for its summer haunts. Despite its retiring nature, I have found the bird quite easy to photograph. The natural color picture on page 460 was taken a few minutes after the camera was focused on the nest with eggs. The birds seemed entirely oblivious to the camera three feet away. It was operated by remote control from a blind thirty feet away but they did not seem to be bothered by the setting up of the blind or the coming and going.

I have never known young birds to leave the nest so soon after hatching as Field Sparrows. Working one summer with a companion on a bird-banding project, I found that unless the young were tagged before they were six days old that we ran the risk of losing them. After the first week, a nest full of young Field Sparrows was sure to "explode" the moment it was disturbed. Once out of the nest, the young never return to it. To prove that point, try to put them back someday.

The Field Sparrow's (5¼ to 6 inches) best field marks are its pink bill, clear breast, and the brownish wash on its sides. For a complete discussion of the field marks of the Sparrows with red caps, see the text on the Chipping Sparrow.

In spring migration, the Field Sparrow arrives in the northern states ahead of the Chipping Sparrow. Indeed, in two different years, I found little bands of Field Sparrows wintering in western Pennsylvania. Usually it winters in the southern states.

The two races, the Eastern Field Sparrow (*S. p. pusilla*) and the Western Field Sparrow (*S. p. arenacea*) breed west to the Rockies, but are not found on the Pacific coast. The western form is generally like the eastern, but grayer and paler above, and with less brown on the breast.

WHITE-EYED TOWHEE (*Pipilo erythrophthalmus alleni*). Length: 7.5 to 8.75 inches. Male: head, throat, back, wings, upper breast and tail, glossy black. White lower breast and abdomen; reddish sides. Has only two outer tail feathers conspicuously tipped with white. White iris of eyes. Female: similar to male but brown replaces black of male. Range: from South Carolina to Florida. Voice: southern drawled *shrink* or *zree*. Song, *cheet, cheet, cheeeee.*
Helen Cruikshank

WORTHEN'S SPARROW

(Spizelli wortheni)

Probably only accidental in the United States, Worthen's Sparrow is a Mexican bird that has been found in southern New Mexico. It is like a Chipping Sparrow, but lacks the eye stripes. It has a conspicuous white eye-ring and a pinkish or ruddy bill.

BLACK-CHINNED SPARROW

(Spizella atrogularis)

Its limited range in the brush covered mountain slopes of California, Arizona, and New Mexico precludes any possibility of the Black-chinned Sparrow becoming a favorite among bird watchers, but its sweet, plaintive song and its unusual color pattern strongly recommend it. The bird's back is reddish brown, the head and underparts are gray, and the bill is flesh colored and is completely encircled by a black chin patch. It is 5 to 5½ inches long. The immature birds lack the black patch.

Four geographic races are recognized: the Mexican Black-chinned Sparrow *(S. a. atrogularis)*, the California Black-chinned Sparrow *(S. a. cana)*, the San Francisco Black-chinned Sparrow *(S. a. caurina)*, and the Arizona Black-chinned Sparrow *(S. a. evura)*. There are no field differences.

GRASSHOPPER SPARROW (*Ammodramus savannarum*). Length: 5 to 5.25 inches. Male and female: upperparts mixed gray, buff, brown and black. Whitish underparts unstreaked. Pale stripe through center of crown. Range: breeds in eastern United States from New Hampshire to Georgia. Winters from North Carolina and Illinois to Gulf of Mexico. Voice: two songs, an insect-like buzzing and *pi-tup-zeeeeeee.*
Fred Bashour

HARRIS'S SPARROW

(Zonotrichia querela)

Harris's Sparrow is a large Sparrow, 7 to 7¾ inches long, of the Mississippi valley, breeding in the region west of Hudson's Bay to Illinois and the Dakotas, and migrating in winter south to Texas.

It is brown on top, streaked with black. The top and back of the head, the throat, and bib are jet black. The wings show two distinct white bars. The bill is bright pink.

The bird builds its nest on the ground at the base of a small tree or shrub, or in a bed of moss. Three to five eggs are pale green, heavily spotted with brown. The song of Harris's Sparrow varies but most usual is a plaintive three notes. It feeds on the ground, scratching for seeds and insects.

WHITE-CROWNED SPARROW

(Zonotrichia leucophrys)

Color Plate Page 461

For most of us, the sweet plaintive song of the White-crowned Sparrow must remain forever a melody unheard. We are privileged twice each year to see it, an aristocratic looking and aristocratic acting Sparrow, traveling to and from its breeding range in the far north, but its song is saved for summer days in the Canadian wilderness and in the Rocky mountains.

While other Sparrows enjoy the company of mixed flocks traveling in migration, the White-crown remains aloof, moving over ancestral routes alone, or in small bands of its own kind. Even when joined by other Sparrows in feeding areas, this stately bird is off by itself, shunning the association.

The White-crowned Sparrow migrates about two weeks later than its close relative, the White-throated Sparrow, with which it is often confused. The latter has a conspicuous white throat and a yellow patch between the bill and the eye, both absent in the White-crown which has a pearl gray breast. Although both birds have black and white striped crowns, the fluffy, dome shaped head of the White-crown is distinctive from the flatter crown of the other species. For closer checking, the bill of the White-crown will be found to be reddish brown. The bird is 6½ to 7½ inches long.

Some observers have detected snatches or phrases of the White-crown's song while in migration, but only those who have listened to the bird in its summer home have heard the full, rich melody. Dr. George M. Sutton describes it as "composed of soft, rich whistles which have a plaintive character, similar to that of the well known White-throat's 'peabody' song, with an additional rough undertone between the first and the latter parts of the song."

BLACK-CHINNED SPARROW AT NEST (*Spizella atrogularis*). Length: 5 to 5.5 inches. Male and female: upperparts rusty brown, head and underparts gray and white, with a *black chin patch*. Black patch encircles flesh colored bill. Immature: lacks black patch and has unmarked gray head and breast. Range: breeds in southern New Mexico, Arizona and locally in southern California. Voice: song, a series of notes on about the same pitch; starts with several high, clear notes and ends in trill, *sweet, sweet, sweet, weet, trrrrrr*.

James Murdock, National Audubon Society

Gambel's Sparrow *(Z. l. gambelii)* is a western race that may be identified in the field, provided the bird watcher is able to note that the white eye line starts from the bill instead of from the eye as in the White-crowned Sparrow. Or, to say it another way, the lores (area between the bill and eye) are black in the White-crowned, and white in the Gambel's.

Three other subspecies occur in the Pacific coast area: Nuttall's Sparrow *(Z. l. nuttalli)*, the Puget Sound Spar-

GOLDEN-CROWNED SPARROW (*Zonotrichia coronata*). Length: 7.2 inches. Male and female: upperparts grayish brown, underparts dull whitish gray. *No white line over eye* and a *golden yellow stripe* through center of crown. Immature: without lateral black stripe, and crown yellowish olive, flecked with dark gray. Range: Louisiana, Wisconsin, Illinois, New Jersey and Massachusetts.
Rudolph Hindemith, American Museum of Natural History

row (*Z. l. pugetensis*), and the Oregon White-crowned Sparrow (*Z. l. oriantha*). The songs of the various races vary, and Peterson gives a transcription of each.

GOLDEN-CROWNED SPARROW

(*Zonotrichia coronata*)

A breeding bird of Canada and Alaska, the Golden-crowned Sparrow is a winter bird in Oregon and California, west of the Sierras. In migration it is found through Washington, and casually in Nevada and Colorado.

This winter visitor is best described as a White-crowned Sparrow with a dull orange-brown crown. It lacks the white eye line of the latter species also. Its size is about the same, 6 to 7 inches. Its plaintive whistled song is three-parted, each note an interval lower than the one it follows. Ralph Hoffmann states that the notes are "to the tune of 'Three Blind Mice,' more poetically rendered *Oh dear me.*"

WHITE-THROATED SPARROW

(*Zonotrichia albicollis*)

It depends upon where you live as to what the lovely White-throated Sparrow says to you in its song.

LINCOLN'S SPARROW AT NEST (*Melospiza lincolnii*). Length: 5.25 to 6 inches. Male and female: upperparts brownish, finely streaked with brown, black, gray and dark brown. Broad band of creamy buff across breast. Range: from boggy spots in Newfoundland to Maine and northern New York. Winters from northern Mississippi and southern Oklahoma, outh to Gulf. Voice: sweet gurgling song, starting low, rising abruptly, and dropping at the end.
Alfred M. Bailey, National Audubon Society

HENSLOW'S SPARROW (*Passerherbulus henslowii*). Length: 4.75 to 5.25 inches. Male and female: upperparts mixed chestnut, black and white. Striped olive head and reddish wings. Underparts are whitish. Range: breeds from Ontario, New Hampshire, and New York, south to North Carolina, West Virginia and Texas; winters in southeast United States. Voice: a jerked *tsi-lick*.
Hal H. Harrison

If you are a Canadian, living where most of these birds choose to nest, you will probably interpret the song as *Sweet Canada, Canada, Canada*. If you are a staunch New Englander, living where a few of them nest, you will declare that it sings *Old Sam Peabody, Peabody, Peabody*. But Dawson, the famous Ohio ornithologist, declared that "the bird does not utter anything remotely resembling Peabody when in Ohio."

But whatever it says and where it says it, the song of the White-throated Sparrow is one of the loveliest of all bird songs, not because of any complicated warblings or difficult carolings, but just for its own sweet simplicity. I shall long remember a sunny morning in late April, sitting alone on a hillside surrounded by sweet scented trailing arbutus blossoms, listening to the whisperings of a little block of White-throats foraging in a briar patch below me. A more peaceful setting I shall never know.

John Burroughs found one flaw in the song of the White-throat, which, he claimed, kept it from ranking first among bird singers. In "Wake-Robin," Burroughs states: "Its song is very delicate and plaintive—a thin, wavering, tremulous whistler, which disappoints one, however, as it ends when it seems only to have begun. If the bird could give us the finished strain of which this seems only the prelude, it would stand first among feathered songsters."

The distinct white throat patch, the yellow mark between the bill and eye, and the flatter shaped head of the White-throated Sparrow (6½ to 7 inches) will distinguish it instantly from the similar White-crowned Sparrow. Adults of both species have the black and white head stripes, however. Migration of the White-throat through the northern states occurs about two weeks earlier than that of the White-crown, although later in the spring both will be found moving north together. The White-throat often sings enroute to its nesting grounds, but the White-crown is usually silent.

For those fortunate to find the White-throat in its summer home, a nest should be looked for on the ground, often in a mossy hummock, but sometimes in a low bush. The nest is of grasses, mosses, and rootlets. The four or five pale greenish blue eggs are speckled with rufous brown.

The breeding range of the White-throated Sparrow is generally more southern than that of the White-crown, although the center of density is in Canada. The White-throat, however, is often found in summer in the Adirondacks, Maine, and mountainous regions of New England. The White-throat is more eastern than its relative, breeding only east of the Rockies. It occurs in California as a winter visitor, however. In the east and central states, it winters from the Ohio valley and Massachusetts south to the Gulf of Mexico. It may occur in winter in any area in northern United States.

FOX SPARROW

(Passerella iliaca)

Color Plate Page 465

In a number of ways, the Fox Sparrow is distinctive. It is one of the largest of the Sparrow tribe (6¾ to 7½ inches); to many it is the handsomest of all the Sparrows; and its sweet, melodious song, heard completely and in best voice only on its breeding grounds in the Canadian forests, is declared to be the number one song among all the Sparrows.

To most of us in the United States, the Fox Sparrow is a migrant to be watched for eagerly each spring and fall. It is not easy to find, for this streaked-breast bird with the rich reddish tail is shy and prefers to feed in the thickets and the wooded ravines. In Towhee-fashion, little flocks of Fox Sparrows forage among the dried leaves, scratching with both feet at the same time, making quite a commotion.

During its passage through the United States, the Fox Sparrow may be confused with the Hermit Thrush, which migrates about the same time. However, the Thrush is not as chunky and its breast is spotted, not streaked.

Of the sixteen geographic races of the Fox Sparrow in the United States, only one, the Eastern Fox Sparrow *(P. i. iliaca)*, is found in eastern North America. Variations in plumage and color designate the various subspecies. A gray phase and a brown phase of this Sparrow are recognized. The western races all lack the rich brown coloring of the typical eastern variety.

The western species breeds in the high mountains from Canada to southern California west of the Rockies; the eastern species breeds from northern Canada to the Gulf of St. Lawrence.

SEASIDE SPARROW *(Ammospiza maritima)*. Length: 5.5 to 6.5 inches. Male and female: upperparts dark olive gray; underparts, white. Short yellow line before the eye and white streak along the jaw. Range: salt marshes from Massachusetts to Florida and west along Gulf of Mexico to Texas. A few winter north to Long Island. Voice: *cutcut, zhe'*-eeeeeee song. Note, *chack*.
Fred Bashour

LINCOLN'S SPARROW

(Melospiza lincolnii)

For a bird whose general range is given as "North America at large," the Lincoln's Sparrow is certainly a little known species. Although its breeding range is chiefly north of the United States, the Lincoln's Sparrow must be much commoner in migration throughout the country than any of us suspect.

In the spring, the Lincoln's is a rather late migrant, and while the woods and fields are swarming with other birds of conspicuous colors and songs, it often slips past us and is gone before we can add it to our list of birds observed. In the fall, migrating with flocks of other Sparrows, it again passes us by unless we are most alert and on the watch for it.

Lincoln's Sparrow is smaller (5¼ to 6 inches) than a Song Sparrow which it resembles closely. It has a shorter tail, but its most distinguishing field mark is a buffy band across its narrowly streaked breast. The olive color of the sides of the head is an identifying aid if it can be detected. The song of the Lincoln's is said to suggest the bursting, gurgling notes of the House Wren.

SWAMP SPARROW

(Melospiza georgiana georgiana)

Color Plate Page 468

Unlike the friendly little Chippy, the ubiquitous Song Sparrow, the melancholy Field Sparrow, or the beautifully voiced Vesper Sparrow, the shy little Swamp Sparrow is one member of the family that the bird watcher must look for patiently.

Not that it is uncommon, for in its favorite haunts, it is abundant, but if ever a bird could be called mouselike, it is this dweller of the open cattail marshes and the wet grassy fields. It is most retiring from the public eye, and, although you may be familiar with the loud sweet trill that marks the male's territory, you are by no means sure of a view of him because you have identified the song. If he spies you first, he is likely to plunge from his low perch into the rank marsh grass where he will skulk until the coast is clear again.

This mousey characteristic makes the finding of the Swamp Sparrow's nest a much more difficult task than finding nests of birds like the Song Sparrow or Field Sparrow that will sit close until flushed. The Swamp Sparrow slips quietly from its nest before the intruder gets close, creeps into the surrounding vegetation, and retreats noiselessly to a safe distance. The sight of the nest, then, comes by accident rather than by any help from the owners.

VESPER SPARROW AT NEST *(Pooecetes gramineus)*. Length: 5.5 to 6.5 inches. Male and female: grayish brown upperparts streaked with black; white underparts. Has chestnut colored patch at the bend of the wings. Range: Gulf of St. Lawrence to North Carolina, Kentucky, Missouri and Nebraska; winters to Florida and Gulf coast.

Hal H. Harrison

McCOWN'S LONGSPUR; MALE AT NEST (*Rhynchophanes mccownii*). Length: 6 inches. Male and female: brownish gray streaked with black. Spring male: forehead and patch on breast, black, tail largely white. Hind-neck gray. Crown black with a white line over the eye. Range: northern Great Plains. Winters in plains from Kansas to Texas. Voice: flight song, clear sweet warbles.
A. Dawes Dubois, National Audubon Society

row is on its nesting grounds in the northeastern and central states, there is little reason to confuse it with the Chipping Sparrow and the Field Sparrow, which also have reddish head caps, for the latter two are rarely found in the same marshy habitat with the Swamp Sparrow. Rather, one finds it in constant association with the Song Sparrow, but the heavily streaked breast of that bird distinguishes it instantly from the plain gray breasted Swamp Sparrow. The smaller size (5 to 5¾ inches) and the shorter tail of the Swamp Sparrow are also diagnostic. I have never thought that the white

Many of the nests of this bird that I have found have been anchored in dead cattail stalks. Others were in tall marsh grass. One, which I thought at first was a Song Sparrow's nest (the eggs of the two species are practically indistinguishable), was hidden by weeds on the ground on a bank bordering a marsh. What made me doubt that this was a Song Sparrow's nest was that no matter how often I passed that way, I never flushed a bird from the nest, yet the eggs were always warm. I waited patiently at a distance and finally brought the hesitant little Swamp Sparrow into my binoculars.

During the summer while the Swamp Spar-

LAPLAND LONGSPUR AT NEST (*Calcarius lapponicus lapponicus*). Length: 6 to 7 inches. Male and female: upperparts light brownish streaked with blackish. Underparts white. Two white wingbars; males have a varying amount of reddish on necks and napes. In spring, both sexes acquire a black throat. Range: northern Arctic regions. South to Texas in winter. Voice: a dry rattle followed by a whistle '*ticky-tick-teu*'.
W. H. Carrick

throat of the Swamp Sparrow was much help in identification unless the observer was quite close.

In migration and on its winter range in the southern states, the Swamp Sparrow is not confined to a marshy habitat. It is seen often with flocks of other Sparrows in brushy fields and pastures. In fall and winter, its head cap is streaked.

SMITH'S LONGSPUR (*Calcarius pictus*). Length: 6.5 inches. Upperparts streaked with buff, brown and black. Tail edged with white. Spring male: white spot on cheek in center of black ear patch triangle. Range: Arctic, migrates south through plains to Texas. Voice: a dry rattle followed by a whistle, '*ticky-tick-teu*'.
Rudolph Hindemith, American Museum of Natural History

The song of the Swamp Sparrow is very much like that of the Chipping Sparrow, but is a louder, more musical trill. A fairly constant rule would be—if you hear a Chipping Sparrow in a marsh, it's a Swamp Sparrow. Along with the sewing-machine-rattlings of the Long-billed Marsh Wrens and the chucks and *oka-leeees* of the Redwings, the song of the Swamp Sparrow is a typical voice of the summer marshes; a voice that brings pangs of nostalgia when remembered on a cold blustering January day in Pennsylvania.

SONG SPARROW

(Melospiza melodia)

Color Plate Page 469

On the first warm days of late winter when the sun at last breaks through the northern smog, there is one harbinger of spring that mounts to the top of the lilac in our garden and proclaims joy to the world. It is the little Song Sparrow whose beautiful song belies its drab appearance.

Perhaps it's because bird songs have been a memory for so many months, or perhaps he really is one of our grandest songsters, but the spring lay of the Song Sparrow, when winter still holds us in its icy grip, is certainly a melody to stop the most disinterested passer-by.

We have a Song Sparrow in our Pennsylvania garden all winter. At the feeding station it must vie with English Sparrows, but it is always aloof, never mingling with these immigrants, but nudging them away should they get in its road as it feeds. In February it starts to sing. Perched on the top of the lilac, tail lowered, head thrown back and upward at a 45 degree angle, he renders his liquid melody. Over and over he starts his song with three identical notes, followed by several trilled short notes in a variety of pitches.

Folks often try to interpret into words what the Song Sparrow offers in his music. The "bird lady" of my town once told me that to her the Song

LARK SPARROW *(Chondestes grammacus)*. Length: 5.5 to 6.5 inches. Male and female: brownish gray streaked with blackish; white underparts. Chestnut crown and ear region. The white breast has a single dark central spot. Black fan-shaped tail with white corners. Young birds lack central spot. Range: southern Ontario, Minnesota and southern Saskatchewan south to Texas and Louisiana, east to Ohio and northwest West Virginia; winters in Gulf states. Voice: a broken song consisting of clear notes and trills.

Alfred M. Bailey

Sparrow sang, *Sweet, sweet, sweet, as ever it may be*. A member of our Audubon Society interpreted it as *Peace, peace, peace, be unto you my little children*. Thoreau's journal entry for June 22, 1853 reads: "The Song Sparrow is said to be imitated in New Bedford thus: *Maids, maids, maids . . . hang on your tea kettle . . . ettle, ettle, ettle, ettle*."

I remember an April walk along a country road bordered by shrubby meadows and a meandering creek. Song Sparrows were on their territories, and the Song Sparrow population was so dense that about fifty feet along the road represented the average frontage for a single territory. Suddenly, one songster mounted to a small bush and started to sing. Like so many jumping jacks, Sparrows appeared for as far as I could see, each mounting to a singing perch and declaring its territory too. A dozen or more birds were singing at once. Then, just as suddenly, all was silent. The birds returned to their feeding. But let one bird again take the initiative, and a dozen more popped up from the ground to join the chorus. Seemingly they needed only one bird's urging to start them all singing.

Early nests that I find are invariably on the ground, usually hidden under clumps of dried grasses, or secluded in weed stalks. Second and later nestings are in low bushes, garden shrubbery, berry patches, and even in vines on porch trellises. The four eggs are green-

PINE WOODS SPARROW (*Aimophila aestivalis aestivalis*). Length: 5.75 inches. Male and female: gray, widely streaked with chestnut brown, dingy buff wash across the unmarked breast. Range: Florida, Gulf coast and Texas north to Maryland, southwestern Pennsylvania, southern Ohio, central Illinois and southeastern Iowa. Winters north to North Carolina. Voice: a variable song, *seeeeee, slipslipslipslipslip.*
Samuel A. Grimes

ish white, blotched heavily with brown.

The heavy streaks and the central spot on the breast of a Song Sparrow distinguish it from most other Sparrows. The Savannah's streaks are fainter and it shows yellow head markings and a forked, not rounded, tail. The Song Sparrow's habit of pumping its tail while in flight is an excellent field mark. Its size varies from 5 to 6¾ inches.

The Song Sparrow, in all of its twenty-seven geographic forms, enjoys the widest distribution of any native North American bird. It breeds from Alaska to Mexico and from the Atlantic to the Pacific. Although most Song Sparrows are migratory to some degree, many remain in the north as permanent residents.

McCOWN'S LONGSPUR

(Rhynchophanes mccownii)

The gray nape of the neck on McCown's Longspur (6 inches) is its best field mark. All other Longspurs have chestnut or brown napes. The Mc-

Cown's shows a black forehead and black breast patch. The bird with which it is most likely to be confused is the Chestnut-collared Longspur (which see), which occupies the same range over much of its breeding grounds in the Great Plains west to eastern Montana, Wyoming, and northeastern Colorado.

In the winter the male resembles the Sparrow-like female. It can then be distinguished from the Chestnut-collared by the white T on its dark tail. All the other Longspurs have triangular or wedge-shaped tail marks.

LAPLAND LONGSPUR

(Calcarius lapponicus lapponicus)

The best known of the Longspurs is the Lapland, which breeds in the Arctic and winters in the United States through the central states to Texas, and along the Atlantic coast to South Carolina. In the winter, this Longspur is often found in company with Snow Buntings and Horned Larks, foraging together on the coastal beaches or on the prairies. The Lapland is the only common Longspur east of the Great Plains.

SNOW BUNTING *(Plectrophenax nivalis nivalis)*. Length: 6 to 7 inches. Male in summer: white, with black back, shoulders, wing coverts and center tail feathers. Female in summer: white; upperparts streaked with black. Male and female in winter: black parts become rusty in color. Range: breeds in the Arctic; winters south to northern United States and down the Atlantic Coast to North Carolina. Voice: a tinkling whistled *tee* repeated at intervals. When disturbed, a harsh *beez-beez*. They also have a musical purring note.
A. A. Allen, National Audubon Society

As we see it in the northern states in winter, the Lapland Longspur (6 to 7 inches) has a brown back, streaked with black; light underparts with the abdomen streaked with brown; two white wingbars; and the nape of the neck faintly chestnut. The black throat and breast and the bright chestnut nape are acquired in the spring. The Lapland has the darkest tail of any of the Longspurs, all the others showing more white.

Its voice is a dry rattle, sometimes followed by a whistle.

A western race, the Alaska Longspur *(C. l. alascensis)* winters south to northwestern United States. It is accidental in California. The Alaska is identical with the Lapland for practical field purposes.

SMITH'S LONGSPUR

(Calcarius pictus)

From its nesting grounds in the far north, the Smith's Longspur moves south to winter in the Great Plains from Kansas to Texas. In the breeding plumage that it wears in its Arctic home, Smith's Longspur is quite distinct from its close relative, the Lapland Longspur, having a triangular black ear patch with a spot of white in the middle, but in winter plumage the two are easily confused. The buffy underparts and the slender, more pointed, bill of the Smith's are considered its best field marks. They are about the same size, 6½ inches.

CHESTNUT-COLLARED LONGSPUR

(Calcarius ornatus)

Color Plate Page 472

The strikingly marked Chestnut-collared Longspur is a bird of the wide open spaces, breeding in the Great Plains west to Montana and eastern Wyoming, and wintering through the southwest into Mexico. Its breeding range extends farther east than its close relative, the McCown's Longspur, although the nests of the two are found on the same prairies over much of their range.

The Chestnut-collared is the smallest Longspur (5½ to 6½ inches). In summer the male is solid black below, except for a white throat. The crown is black, and the nape of the neck is chestnut. Diagnostic is the white tail with a triangular black wedge at the end. McCown's Longspur has a black T at the end of its white tail. The nape of the neck of the McCown's male is gray, not chestnut, and only the breast is black. The Sparrow-like females and young of the two species are similar, but the McCown's are unmarked underneath while the Chestnut-collared are streaked.

With its black underparts and lighter back, the Chestnut-collared Longspur might be described loosely as a small Bobolink. Its fluttering nuptial flight adds credulity to the comparison. Some observers have likened its song to that of the Western Meadowlark.

Nests are placed on the ground on open prairies with very little attempt at concealment. The four eggs are greenish spotted. Males do not incubate, but sing close by, an aid in locating the nest.

SNOW BUNTING

(Plectrophenax nivalis nivalis)

Like big flakes of snow driven across the fields by a bitter, biting wind, the Snow Buntings fly and forage together through our long northern winters. Birds of land's last outpost on the Arctic tundra, they move southward in the fall to invade the Atlantic coast south to North Carolina and inland across the northern states through the Great Plains to Wyoming and Oregon.

No other song bird is as white. In overhead flight, they show none of the brown that streaks the white upperparts, and they appear pure white. Horned Larks, Longspurs, and Pipits are often their winter companions, but these are all darker birds and should not be confusing.

Regarding the voice of the 6 to 7 inch long "Snowflake," John Burroughs wrote: "Its twittering call and chirrup coming out of the white obscurity is the sweetest and happiest of all winter bird sounds. It is like the laughter of children. The fox-hunter hears it on the snowy hills, the farmer hears it when he goes to fodder his cattle from the distant stack, the country schoolboy hears it as he breaks his way through the drifts toward the school. It is ever a voice of good cheer and contentment."

DESERT OR BLACK-THROATED SPARROW *(Amphispiza bilineata)*. Length: 4.75 to 5.25 inches. Male and female: gray upperparts, underparts white. Jet black throat and white face stripes. Range: desert country of southwestern United States; winters from California, Arizona and Texas, south. Voice: a sweet song, *cheet cheet cheeeeeeee.*

Samuel A. Grimes

RECOGNITION CHARTS

In the following charts, the American land birds covered in this book have been segregated by size and coloration as an aid in identification. For instance, if one sees a black and white bird the size of a Robin, the chart indicates that this may be a Kingbird, or one of several Woodpeckers and Sapsuckers. Then, by turning to the text on these particular birds, one can eliminate those which are out of the question geographically, and thus narrow the possibilities to one or two birds which may be studied carefully to arrive at the identification. No attempt has been made to be specific in the coloring patterns; only the color which is obvious to a casual observer has been listed.

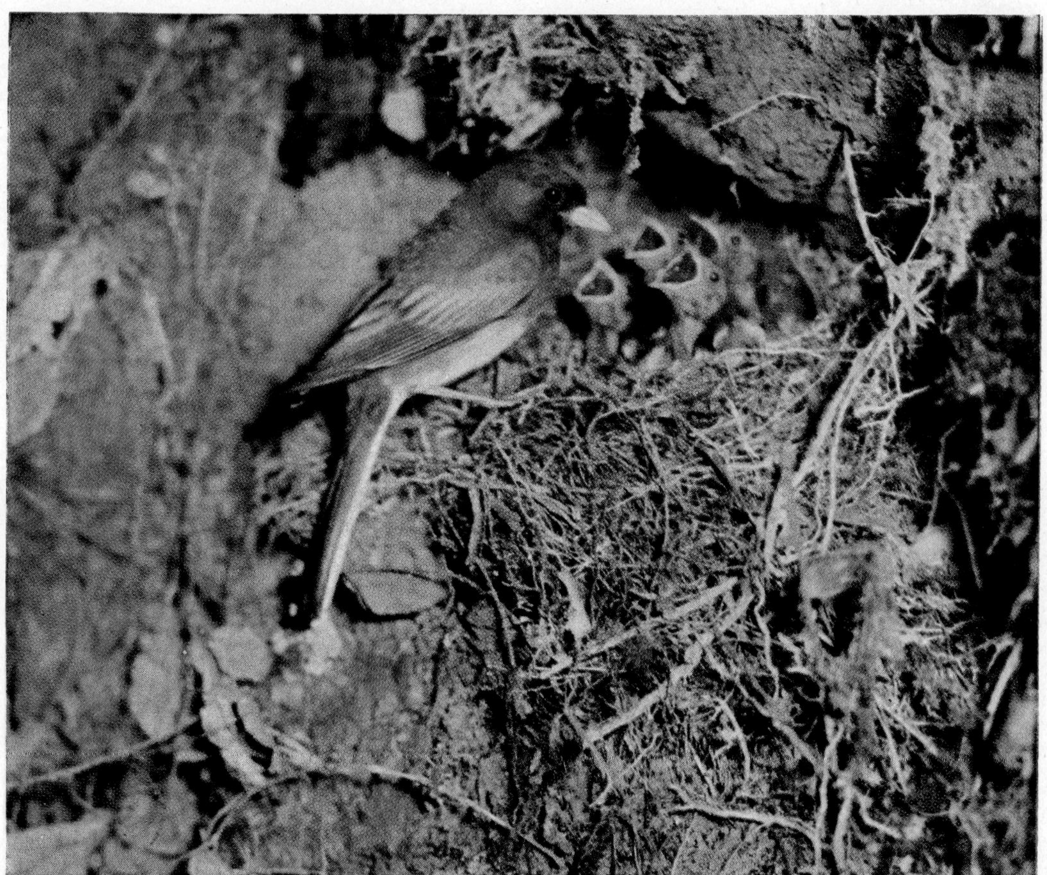

SLATE-COLORED JUNCO AT NEST (*Junco hyemalis*). Length: 6 to 6.5 inches. Male and female: upperparts throat and breast dark slate gray. Abdomen white. Range: breeds in Canada and Alaska, winters south to Colorado, New Mexico and south to southern California. Voice: song, a simple trill.

Hal H. Harrison

17 INCHES AND LARGER
(Size of Crow and larger)

BLACK

Crow
Fish Crow
White-necked Raven
Raven
Ivory-billed Woodpecker
Pileated Woodpecker
Black Vulture
California Condor
Turkey Vulture
Audubon's Caracara
Everglade Kite
Western Red-tailed Hawk
Swainson's Hawk (2 color phases)
Short-tailed Hawk (2 color phases)
American Rough-legged Hawk (2 color phases)
Harris's Hawk
Mexican Black Hawk
Ferruginous Rough-leg
Zone-tailed Hawk
Gyrfalcon (black or white—2 color phases)

BLACK AND WHITE

Yellow-billed Magpie
American or Black-billed Magpie
Swallow-tailed Kite

WHITE

Snowy Owl

GRAY

Krider's Red-tailed Hawk
American Goshawk
Red-tailed Hawk
Harlan's Hawk
Sooty Grouse
Spotted Owl
Richardson's Grouse
Oregon Dusky Grouse
Florida Red-tailed
Sennett's White-tailed Hawk
Mexican Goshawk
Marsh Hawk
Barred Owl
Great Gray Owl
Dusky Grouse

BROWNISH GRAY

Wild Turkey
Sage Grouse or Sage Hen
Florida Red-shouldered Hawk

BROWN

Great-horned Owl
Golden Eagle
Prairie Falcon
Greater Prairie Chicken
Ring-necked Pheasant
Red-shouldered Hawk
Northern Red-shouldered Hawk
Bald Eagle
Ruffed Grouse
Sharp-tailed Grouse
Chachalaca
Barn Owl

BROWN AND WHITE

Road-runner

GREEN

Thick-billed Parrot

14 to 17 INCHES
(Size of Grouse)

BROWN

Willow Ptarmigan (summer)
Spruce Grouse (female)
Short-eared Owl
Boat-tailed Grackle (female)
Lesser Prairie Chicken
Band-tailed Pigeon
Hawk Owl

BLACK

Rock Ptarmigan (summer)
Boat-tailed Grackle (male)

GRAY

Spruce Grouse (male)
Aplomado Falcon
Broad-winged Hawk
White-tailed Kite
Long-eared Owl
Franklin's Grouse
Duck Hawk
Cooper's Hawk
Mississippi Kite

WHITE

Rock Ptarmigan (winter)
Willow Ptarmigan (winter)

10 to 14 INCHES
(Size of Flicker)

BLACK

Bronzed Grackle
Groove-billed Ani
Purple Grackle
Smooth-billed Ani
Lewis's Woodpecker

BROWN

Sharp-shinned Hawk
Yellow-billed Cuckoo
Upland Plover
Merrill's Pauraque
Red-shafted Flicker
Chuck-will's-widow
Black-billed Cuckoo
Mourning Dove
Flicker
Mearn's Gilded Flicker
Santa Cruz Jay
Steller's Jay
Sennett's Thrasher
Richardson's Owl
Killdeer
Bobwhite
White-winged Dove
California Quail
California Jay
California Thrasher
Crissal Thrasher
Woodcock

GRAY-HEADED JUNCO (*Junco caniceps caniceps*). Length: 5.5 to 6 inches. Male and female: unstriped gray sides with bright rufous back, and white abdomen. Flesh colored bill. Range: Rocky Mountains, winters south to Mexico. Voice: loose trill.
Alfred M. Bailey

BROWN (cont'd)

Mountain Quail
Wilson's Snipe
White-fronted Dove

GRAY

Rock Dove
Scissor-tailed Flycatcher
Clark's Nutcracker
Palmer's or Curve-billed Thrasher
Scaled Quail
Maynard's Cuckoo
White-crowned Pigeon
European Partridge
Canada Jay
LeConte's Thrasher
Arizona Jay
Ringed Turtle Dove
Chinese Spotted Dove
Red-billed Pigeon

BLUE

Florida Jay
Pinon Jay
Pigeon Hawk
Blue Jay
Belted Kingfisher

GREEN

Green Jay
Coppery-tailed Trogon
Carolina Paroquet

TREE SPARROWS ON LOG (*Spizella arborea*). Length: 6 to 6.5 inches. Streaked gray, rusty and black upperparts. Gray underparts. Round black spot in the center of the breast, bright *red-brown cap*, and white wingbars. Upper mandible of bill is dark; yellow below. Range: Canada south to Kansas, Arkansas, and South Carolina. Voice: sweet variable song. Note, *tseet;* feeding note, *teeler* or *teelwit*.
Hal H. Harrison

RUFOUS

Sparrow Hawk
Brown Thrasher

8 to 10 INCHES
(Size of Robin)

BLACK

Hairy Woodpecker
Williamson's Sapsucker
White-headed Woodpecker
Rusty Blackbird
Arctic Three-toed Woodpecker
California Woodpecker
Brewer's Blackbird

BLACK, AND YELLOW OR ORANGE

Audubon's Oriole
Yellow-headed Blackbird

BLACK AND WHITE STRIPED

Red-bellied Woodpecker
Gila Woodpecker
Red-cockaded Woodpecker
Eastern Kingbird
Yellow-bellied Sapsucker
Golden-fronted Woodpecker
American Three-toed Woodpecker
Red-naped Sapsucker
Red-breasted Sapsucker

BLACK AND CHESTNUT

Towhee or Chewink

BLACK AND RED

Tricolored Red-wing
Red-winged Blackbird
Red-headed Woodpecker

BROWN

Bendire's Thrasher
Sulphur-bellied Flycatcher
Couch's Kingbird
Burrowing Owl
Mearn's Quail
Western Meadowlark
Abert's Towhee
Arizona Woodpecker
Derby Flycatcher
Crested Flycatcher
Inca Dove
Meadowlark
Brown Towhee

BROWN AND RUST

Robin

RED OR RUST

Cardinal
Screech Owl (Red phase)
Pine Grosbeak

GRAY

Spotted Screech Owl
Gambel's Quail
Stephen's Whip-poor-will
Texas or Lesser Nighthawk
Ash-throated Flycatcher
Loggerhead Shrike
Townsend's Solitaire
White-rumped Shrike
Northern Shrike
Gray Kingbird
Western or Arkansas Kingbird
Screech Owl (gray phase)
Whip-poor-will
Nighthawk
Coues's Flycatcher
Cassin's Kingbird
Sage Thrasher
Varied Thrush
Mockingbird
Catbird
Mexican Crested Flycatcher

YELLOW

Long-tailed Chat

OLIVE GREEN

Pine Grosbeak

CHIPPING SPARROW *(Spizella passerina)*. Length: 5 to 5.5 inches. Male and female: upperparts gray, rusty and black striped; underparts gray. Has black line through eye, white line over it and a bright rufous cap. Young birds have finely streaked underparts in summer. Immature in winter have striped crown and are buffier than adults. Winter adults are browner. Range: eastern America from Canada to Gulf States; winters in southern United States. Voice: a dry rattling song. Note, a short *chip*.

Hal H. Harrison

6 to 8 INCHES
(Size of Oriole)

BLACK

Black Swift
White-throated Swift
Cowbird
Vaux's Swift
Red-eyed Cowbird

BLACK AND BROWN

Orchard Oriole
Spotted Towhee (male)
Red-eyed Towee (male)

BLACK AND WHITE

Nuttall's Woodpecker
Bobolink
Ladder-backed Woodpecker
Rose-breasted Grosbeak

BLACK, WHITE AND CINNAMON

Black-headed Grosbeak

BLACK, YELLOW OR ORANGE

Hooded Oriole
Western Tanager
Bullock's Oriole
Scott's Oriole
Baltimore Oriole

BLACK AND RED

White-winged Crossbill
Scarlet Tanager

BROWN

Poor-will
Eastern Phoebe
Say's Phoebe
Olive-sided Flycatcher
Red-eyed Towhee (female)
Horned Lark
Western Wood Pewee
Gray-cheeked Thrush
Wren-tit
Gray-crowned Rosy Finch
Wheatear
Flammulated Screech Owl
Saw-whet Owl
Fox Sparrow (streaked)
McCown's Longspur (streaked)
Xanthus's Becard (female)
Cassin's Purple Finch (female, also streaked with black)
Veery
Wood Thrush
Cactus Wren
Spotted Towhee (female)
Rose-breasted Grosbeak (female)
Wood Pewee
Hermit Thrush
Western Bluebird
Pipit
Louisiana Water-thrush
Ferruginous Pygmy Owl
Ground Dove
Harris's Sparrow (streaked)
Lapland Longspur (streaked)
Cedar Waxwing
Blue Grosbeak (female)
Smith's Longspur

BROWN, AND YELLOW OR ORANGE

Baltimore Oriole
Dickcissel

GRAY

Black-whiskered Vireo
Pygmy Owl (gray phase)
Olivaceous Flycatcher
Dipper or Water Ouzel
Xanthus's Becard
White-winged Junco
Ipswich Sparrow
Pyrrhuloxia (female)
Elf Owl (gray phase)
Russet-backed or Olive-backed Thrush
Bohemian Waxwing
White-throated Sparrow (streaked)
Sprague's Pipit
Tufted Titmouse
Cape Sable Seaside Sparrow

GRAY AND RED

Red-backed Junco
Pyrrhuloxia (male)

GRAY AND WHITE

Slate-colored Junco

GRAY, STREAKED

White-crowned Sparrow
Golden-crowned Sparrow
Gambel's Sparrow

BLUE

Coahuila Cliff Swallow
Barn Swallow

BLUE AND WHITE

Mountain Bluebird

BLUE AND BLACK

Blue Grosbeak

BLUE AND RUST

Eastern Bluebird

RED OR RUST

Hepatic Tanager
Cooper's Tanager
Elf Owl (red phase)
Summer Tanager
Cassin's Purple Finch

GREENISH

Western Tanager (female)
Yellow-green Vireo
Bullock's Oriole (female)
Alder Flycatcher
Gray Flycatcher (greenish gray)
Texas Kingfisher
Scarlet Tanager (female)
Green-tailed Towhee
Wright's Flycatcher
Yellow-breasted Chat
White-winged Crossbill (female)

OLIVE AND BLACK

Evening Grosbeak

WHITE

Snow Bunting

4 to 6 INCHES
(Size of Song Sparrow)

BLACK

Chimney Swift
Brown-capped Rosy Finch
Rivoli's Hummingbird
Lark Bunting

BLACK AND WHITE

Long-billed Marsh Wren
Black and White Warbler

BLACK AND ORANGE

American Redstart (male)
Lawrence's Goldfinch
Green-backed or Arkansas Goldfinch
Magnolia Warbler

BLACK AND WHITE AND RED

Painted Redstart

BLACK AND GRAY

Chestnut-collared Longspur

FIELD SPARROW (*Spizella pusilla*). Length: 5.25 to 6 inches. Male and female: upperparts streaked with rusty and black; lower parts gray. Chest, pale pinkish brown. Pinkish bill. Range: eastern North America west to the Great Plains. Winters in southern United States north to Illinois and New York. Voice: a clear sweet song, starting slowly, rapidly developing into a trill.
Hal H. Harrison

BLACK, GRAY AND WHITE

Carolina Chickadee
Black-capped Chickadee
Mexican Chickadee
Audubon's Warbler
Mountain Chickadee

BLACK AND BROWN STREAKED

Desert or Black-throated Sparrow
Worthen's Sparrow
Song Sparrow
Purple Finch (female)
Cassin's Sparrow
Short-billed Marsh Wren
Lincoln's Sparrow
House Finch (female)
Swamp Sparrow
Chipping Sparrow
Lark Sparrow
Sharp-tailed Sparrow
Vesper Sparrow
Grasshopper Sparrow
European Tree Sparrow
Brewer's Sparrow
Clay-colored Sparrow
Rufous-crowned Sparrow
Botteri's Sparrow
Baird's Sparrow
Indigo Bunting (female)
English Sparrow

WHITE CROWNED SPARROW (*Zonotrichia leucophrys*). Length: 6.5 to 7.5 inches. Male and female: pearly gray breast, light underparts, dark with streaks of brown above. Puffy high crown, striped with black and white. Immature: buffier, head striped with dark red-brown and light buffy brown, pinkish bill. Range: Canada, migrates through Mississippi Valley, winters mainly from Ohio Valley to Gulf of Mexico. Voice: clear song, ending in hoarse trilled whistle.

George M. Bradt

BROWN

Indigo Bunting (male)
Redpoll
Pine Siskin
Large-billed Sparrow
Rufous-winged Sparrow
Leconte's Sparrow
Brown Creeper
Black-chinned Sparrow
Northern Water-thrush
Canon Wren
Bachman's Sparrow
Winter Wren
Ovenbird
Rough-winged Swallow
House Wren
Chestnut-sided Warbler
Varied Bunting (female)
European Goldfinch
Savannah Sparrow
Henslow's Sparrow
Belding's Sparrow
Dusky Seaside Sparrow
Carolina Wren
Bell's Sparrow
Pine Woods Sparrow
Oregon Junco
Rio Grande Yellow-throat
Chestnut-backed Chickadee
Vermilion Flycatcher
Field Sparrow

BROWN (cont'd)

Buff-breasted Flycatcher
Bewick's Wren
Bank Swallow

BROWN AND YELLOW

Palm Warbler

BROWN, BUFF AND WHITE

Worm-eating Warbler
Arizona Junco
Hudsonian, Acadian or Brown-capped Chickadee

OLIVE

Swainson's Warbler
Seaside Sparrow
Western Flycatcher
American Redstart (female)
Hooded Warbler
Lawrence's Warbler
Tennessee Warbler
Olive Warbler
Black-capped Vireo
Hutton's Vireo
MacGillivray's Warbler
Red-eyed Vireo
Golden-cheeked Warbler
Hammond's Flycatcher
Red Crossbill (female)
Texas Sparrow
Least Flycatcher
Yellow-throated Vireo
Bay-breasted Warbler
Bachman's Warbler
Blue-winged Warbler
Nashville Warbler
Townsend's Warbler
White-eyed Vireo
Yellow-throat (yellowish olive)
Bell's or Least Vireo
Orange-crowned Warbler
Yellow-bellied Flycatcher
Warbling Vireo

OLIVE AND BLACK

Black-throated Green Warbler

OLIVE AND BLUE

Blue-headed Vireo

GRAY

Hermit Warbler
Mourning Warbler
Lucy's Warbler
Virginia's Warbler
Cape May Warbler (tiger-like underparts)
Verdin
Brown-headed Nuthatch
Yellow-throated Warbler
Plumbeous Gnatcatcher
Philadelphia Vireo
Myrtle Warbler
Red-breasted Nuthatch
Connecticut Warbler
Gray Vireo
Gray-headed Junco
White-breasted Nuthatch
Brewster's Warbler
Golden-winged Warbler
Rock Wren
Colima Warbler
Plain Titmouse
Bush-tit
Ruby-crowned Kinglet
Bridled Titmouse
Grace's Warbler
Black-throated Gray Warbler
Black-throated Blue Warbler

GRAY (cont'd)

Pygmy Nuthatch
Pigmy Nuthatch
Beardless Flycatcher
Red-faced Warbler
Kirtland's Warbler (black striped)
Plumbeous Vireo
Black-crested Titmouse
Black-poll Warbler

GRAY AND YELLOW

Canada Warbler

GREENISH

Acadian Flycatcher
Prothonotary Warbler
Broad-tailed Hummingbird
Buff-bellied Hummingbird
Prairie Warbler
Pine Warbler
Blue-throated Hummingbird
Painted Bunting (female)

WHITE

Hoary Redpoll

RED

Purple Finch
House Finch

BLUE

Lazuli Bunting
Cliff Swallow
Parula Warbler
Cerulean Warbler
Tree Swallow
Blue-gray Gnatcatcher
Sennett's Warbler

GREEN AND PURPLE

Violet-green Swallow

YELLOW

Wilson's or Pileolated Warbler
Goldfinch
Kentucky Warbler
Yellow Warbler

VARIED COLORS

Painted Bunting
Varied Bunting

4 INCHES AND UNDER
(Size of Hummingbird)

GREEN

Ruby-throated Hummingbird
Costa's Hummingbird
Allen's Hummingbird
Broad-billed Hummingbird
Lucifer Hummingbird (female)
Black-chinned Hummingbird
Anna's Hummingbird
Calliope Hummingbird
Golden-crowned Kingbird

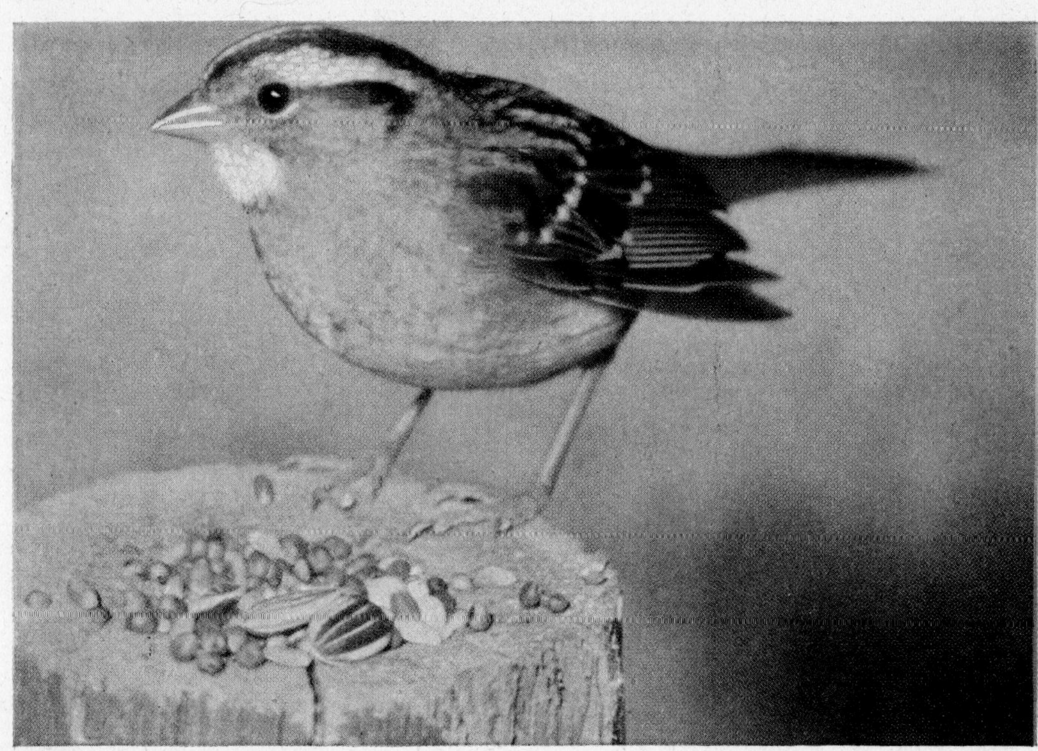

WHITE THROATED SPARROW (*Zonotrichis albicollis*). Length: 6.5 to 7 inches. Male and female: rusty-brown upperparts streaked with black. White and gray underparts. White throat patch and yellow spot between bill and eye. Range: Canada to Minnesota, New England and northeast Pennsylvania. Winters from Ohio Valley and Massachusetts south to Gulf of Mexico. Voice: wistful, clear song opens on one or two clear notes and follows with three quavering notes of different pitch.
Hal H. Harrison

RUST

Lucifer Hummingbird (male) Rufous Hummingbird

BLACK AND WHITE

Sharpe's Seedeater

BROWN

White-eared Hummingbird

DISTRIBUTION CHARTS

In these distribution charts an attempt has been made to divide the American land birds covered in this book into geographical listings. Some birds are found widely distributed over most of the United States; others are localized to a greater or lesser extent. Some birds are seen only in spring and fall migration through the United States. While this listing makes no claim to be exhaustive or definitive, it should be an aid in eliminating for identification purposes those birds which are a geographical impossibility in a particular section.

BIRDS FOUND THROUGHOUT MOST OF THE UNITED STATES

Blackbird, Red-winged
Bobolink
Bobwhite
Bunting, Indigo
Cardinal
Chat, Yellow-breasted
Chickadee, Black-capped
Cowbird
Crow
Dove, Rock
Flicker
Flicker, Northern
Flycatcher, Crested
Flycatcher, Olive-sided
Goldfinch

FOX SPARROW (*Passerella iliaca*). Length: 6.75 to 7.5 inches. Male and female: upperparts gray striped with brown or entirely chestnut. Underparts white spotted heavily with chestnut. Bright rufous red tail. Range: from Canada to Gulf of St. Lawrence in spruce belt. Winters from Massachusetts to Gulf of Mexico. Voice: a melodious song.

Fred Bashour

THROUGHOUT UNITED STATES (cont'd)

Hawk, Cooper's
Hawk, Marsh
Hawk, Red-tailed
Hawk, Sparrow
Killdeer
Kingbird, Eastern
Kingfisher, Belted
Martin, Purple
Meadowlark
Mockingbird
Nuthatch, Red-breasted
Nuthatch, White-breasted
Owl, Barn
Owl, Great-Horned
Owl, Long-eared
Owl, Screech
Owl, Short-eared
Pipit
Robin
Siskin, Pine
Sparrow, Chipping
Sparrow, English
Sparrow, Grasshopper
Sparrow, Henslow's
Sparrow, Lark
Sparrow, Song
Sparrow, Vesper
Swallow, Bank
Swallow, Barn
Swallow, Cliff
Swallow, Rough-winged
Tanager, Summer
Thrasher, Brown
Thrush, Hermit
Thrush, Russet-backed or Olive-backed
Towhee or Chewink
Vireo, Blue-headed
Warbler, Bay-breasted
Warbler, Yellow
Water-thrush, Louisiana
Woodpecker, Downy
Woodpecker, Hairy
Woodpecker, Pileated
Wren, Bewick's
Wren, House
Wren, Long-billed Marsh
Yellow-throat

NORTHEAST

Blackbird, Rusty
Crossbill, White-winged
Crow, Eastern
Dove, Mourning
Eagle, Northern Bald
Flycatcher, Alder
Flycatcher, Least
Flycatcher, Yellow-bellied
Gnatcatcher, Blue-gray
Goldfinch, European
Goshawk, American
Grackle, Purple
Grouse, Canada Ruffed
Grouse, Canada Spruce
Grouse, Eastern Ruffed
Grouse, Oregon Dusky
Grouse, Spruce
Kingfisher, Eastern Belted
Owl, Northern Barred
Snipe, Wilson's
Sparrow, Eastern Field
Sparrow, Eastern Fox
Sparrow, Eastern Tree
Sparrow, Ipswich
Sparrow, White-throated
Swallow, Tree
Thrush, Gray-cheeked or Alice's
Veery, or Wilson's Thrush
Vireo, Northern Blue-headed
Warbler, Black-throated Green
Warbler, Golden-winged
Warbler, Myrtle
Warbler, Nashville
Warbler, Palm
Warbler, Pine
Warbler, Yellow Palm
Water-thrush, Northern

EAST

Blackbird, Eastern Red-winged
Bluebird, Eastern
Cardinal, Eastern
Chickadee, Acadian
Chickadee, Carolina
Chuck-will's-widow
Cowbird, Eastern
Crow, Fish
Cuckoo, Black-billed
Cuckoo, Yellow-billed
Eagle, Bald
Flicker, Yellow-shafted
Goldfinch, Eastern
Grackle, Boat-tailed
Grackle, Bronzed
Grackle, Ridgway
Grosbeak, Eastern Blue
Hawk, Broad-winged
Hawk, Eastern Pigeon
Hawk, Eastern Red-tailed
Hawk, Eastern Sparrow
Hawk, Sharp-shinned
Hummingbird, Ruby-throated
Jay, Blue
Junco, Slate-colored
Kinglet, Eastern Golden-crowned
Lark, Prairie Horned
Nighthawk
Nuthatch, Brown-headed
Oriole, Baltimore
Oriole, Orchard
Ovenbird
Owl, Barred
Partridge, European
Pewee, Wood
Phoebe, Eastern
Plover, Upland
Sparrow, Bachman's
Sparrow, Clay-colored
Sparrow, Eastern Chipping
Sparrow, Eastern Grass-hopper

EAST (cont'd)

Sparrow, Eastern Henslow's
Sparrow, Eastern Lark
Sparrow, Eastern Vesper
Sparrow, European Tree
Sparrow, Illinois
Sparrow, Leconte's
Sparrow, Savannah
Sparrow, Seaside
Sparrow, Swamp
Starling
Swift, Chimney
Tanager, Eastern Hepatic
Tanager, Scarlet
Thrasher, Brown
Thrush, Wood
Titmouse, Tufted
Towhee, Red-eyed
Vireo, Eastern Warbling
Vireo, Mountain Blue-headed
Vireo, Philadelphia
Vireo, Philadelphia Warbling
Vireo, Red-eyed
Vireo, White-eyed
Vireo, Yellow-throated
Warbler, Black and White
Warbler, Blackburnian
Warbler, Black-throated Blue
Warbler, Blue-winged
Warbler, Brewster's
Warbler, Cerulean
Warbler, Chestnut-sided
Warbler, Connecticut
Warbler, Hooded
Warbler, Kirtland's
Warbler, Magnolia
Warbler, Mourning
Warbler, Northern Pine
Warbler, Northern Prairie
Warbler, Parula
Warbler, Prothonotary
Warbler, Sycamore
Warbler, Tennessee
Warbler, Wayne's
Warbler, Wilson's
Warbler, Wilson's or Pileolated
Warbler, Yellow-throated
Whip-poor-will
Woodcock
Woodpecker, Red-bellied
Woodpecker, Red-headed
Wren, Carolina
Wren, Eastern House
Wren, Ohio House
Wren, Short-billed Marsh

SOUTHEAST

Ani, Smooth-billed
Bluebird, Florida
Bunting, Painted
Cardinal, Florida
Cardinal, Louisiana
Crow, Florida
Crow, Southern
Cuckoo, Maynard's
Eagle, Southern Bald
Flicker, Southern
Flycatcher, Acadian
Flycatcher, Southern Crested
Grackle, Florida Purple
Hawk, Florida Red-tailed
Hawk, Little Sparrow
Hawk, Short-tailed
Jay, Florida or Scrub
Kingbird, Gray
Kite, Everglade
Kite, Mississippi
Kite, Swallow-tailed
Meadowlark, Southern
Mockingbird, Eastern
Nuthatch, Gray-headed
Owl, Florida Barred
Owl, Florida Burrowing
Pigeon, White-crowned
Red-Shoulder, Florida
Red-Shoulder, Insular
Sparrow, Cape Sable Seaside
Sparrow, Dusky Seaside
Sparrow, Florida Grass-hopper
Sparrow, Pine Woods
Sparrow, Sharp-tailed
Towhee, Alabama
Towhee, White-eyed
Turkey, Eastern Wild
Turkey, Wild
Vireo, Black-whiskered
Vireo, Key-West White-eyed
Warbler, Bachman's
Warbler, Florida Pine
Warbler, Florida Prairie
Warbler, Kentucky
Warbler, Swainson's
Warbler, Worm-eating
Woodpecker, Florida Pileated
Woodpecker, Ivory-billed
Woodpecker, Red-cockaded
Woodpecker, Southern Pileated
Wren, Burleigh's Carolina
Wren, Florida

NORTHERN UNITED STATES

Bunting, Snow
Catbird
Chickadee, Brown-capped
Creeper, Brown
Finch, Aleutian Rosy
Finch, Purple
Flycatcher, Northern Crested
Grosbeak, Rose-breasted
Grouse, Gray Ruffed
Grouse, Hoary Ruffed
Grouse, Hudsonian Spruce
Grouse, Nova Scotia Ruffed
Grouse, Ruffed
Gyrfalcon
Hawk, Rough-legged
Hawk, Duck
Hawk, Harlan's
Hawk, Pigeon
Hawk, Red-shouldered
Jay, Alaska
Jay, Canada
Junco, Boreal Slate-colored
Kinglet, Ruby-crowned

SWAMP SPARROW (*Melospiza georgiana georgiana*). Length: 5 to 5.75 inches. Male and female: upperparts brown streaked with black; white throat and reddish cap; gray underparts. Immature birds in first winter are streaked and have no red on the crown. Range: from Canada to West Virginia and west to Nebraska. Winters from southern New England to Gulf of Mexico. Voice: a slow, sweet trill.

Hal H. Harrison

NORTHERN UNITED STATES (cont'd)

Lark, Horned
Lark, Northern Horned
Longspur, Alaska
Longspur, Lapland
Longspur, Smith's
Owl, Great Gray
Owl, Hawk
Owl, Richardson's
Owl, Saw-whet
Owl, Snowy
Pheasant, Ring-necked
Ptarmigan, Rock
Ptarmigan, Willow
Raven
Raven, Northern
Redpoll
Redpoll, Common
Redpoll, Greater
Redpoll, Hoary
Redstart, American
Redshoulder, Northern
Sapsucker, Yellow-bellied
Shrike, Northern
Sparrow, Field
Sparrow, Fox
Sparrow, Harris's
Sparrow, Lincoln's
Sparrow, Tree
Vireo, Northern White-eyed
Warbler, Black-poll
Warbler, Canada
Warbler, Cape May
Warbler, Northern Parula
Waxwing, Bohemian
Wheatear
Wren, Winter
Woodpecker, American Three-toed
Woodpecker, Arctic Three-toed
Woodpecker, Northern Pileated

SOUTHERN UNITED STATES

Becard, Xanthus's
Caracara, Audubon's
Dove, Eastern Ground
Dove, Ground
Falcon, Aplomado
Flycatcher, Vermilion
Grosbeak, Blue
Paroquet, Carolina
Vireo, Southern White-eyed
Vulture, Black
Warbler, Southern Parula

SONG SPARROW ON NEST *(Melospiza melodia).* Length: 5 to 6.75 inches. Male and female: brown and black streaked upperparts; white streaked with black lower parts. Large central spot on breast. Range: breeds from Gulf of St. Lawrence to coastal North Carolina, southern Virginia, northern Georgia, southern Illinois, and Missouri; winters from Massachusetts, Lake Erie and Iowa south to Gulf of Mexico. Voice: a variable musical song, *sweet, sweet, sweet, sweet,* etc.
Hal H. Harrison

NORTHWEST

Crossbill, Red
Crow, Northwestern
Finch, Black Rosy
Finch, Gray-crowned Rosy
Finch, Hepburn's Rosy
Finch, Pribilof Rosy
Finch, Wallowa Rosy
Flicker, Boreal
Flycatcher, Gray
Grosbeak, Evening
Grouse, Franklin's
Grouse, Richardson's
Grouse, Sitka
Hummingbird, Rufus
Jay, Black-headed
Jay, Oregon
Jay, Steller's (Cyanocitta stelleri)
Jay, Steller's (C.s. stelleri)
Junco, Oregon
Junco, Pink-sided
Junco, White-winged
Pigeon, Band-tailed
Ptarmigan, White-tailed
Sparrow, Oregon Vesper
Sparrow, Oregon White-crowned
Sparrow, Puget Sound
Sparrow, Western Tree
Thrush, Varied

NORTHWEST (cont'd)

Vireo, Red-eyed
Warbler, Orange-crowned
Warbler, Townsend's

WESTERN

Blackbird, Brewer's
Blackbird, Tri-colored Red-winged
Blackbird, Yellow-headed
Bluebird, Mountain
Bluebird, Western
Bunting, Lark
Bunting, Lazuli
Bush-tit
Bush-tit, California
Bush-tit, Coast
Bush-tit, Lead-colored
Chachalaca
Chat, Long-tailed
Chickadee, Colombian or Cascade Brown-headed
Chickadee, Hudsonian
Chickadee, Mountain
Chicken, Attwater's Prairie
Cowbird, Nevada
Creeper, Rocky Mountain Brown
Creeper, Sierra Nevada Brown
Creeper, Tawny or California Brown
Crow, Western
Cuckoo, California
Dickcissel
Dipper, or Water-Ouzel
Dove, Western Mourning
Eagle, Golden
Falcon, Prairie
Finch, Brown-capped Rosy
Finch, California Purple
Finch, Cassin's Purple
Finch House
Flicker, Northwestern
Flicker, Red-shafted (Colaptes cafer)
Flicker, Red-shafted (C.c. collaris)
Flycatcher, Hammond's
Flycatcher, Western
Flycatcher, Wright's
Gnatcatcher, Western
Goldfinch, Arkansas
Goldfinch, Green-backed
Goldfinch, Pale
Goldfinch, Willow
Goshawk, Western American
Grosbeak, Black-headed
Grosbeak, California or Western Evening
Grosbeak, Pine
Grosbeak, Rocky Mountain
Grosbeak, Western Blue
Grouse, Dusky
Grouse, Sage or Sage Hen
Grouse, Sierra
Grouse, Sooty
Hawk, Black Pigeon
Hawk, Red-bellied
Hawk, Swainson's
Hawk, Western Pigeon
Hawk, Western Red-tailed
Hummingbird, Allen's
Hummingbird, Black-chinned
Hummingbird, Broad-tailed
Hummingbird, Calliope
Jay, Gray
Jay, Nevada Crested
Jay, Pacific Canada
Jay, Pinon
Jay, Queen Charlotte
Jay, Rocky Mountain
Jay, Santa Cruz
Jay, Woodhouse's
Junco, Gray-headed
Kingbird, Cassin's
Kingbird, Western or Arkansas
Kingfisher, Western Belted
Kinglet, Western Golden-crowned
Magpie, Black-billed
Meadowlark, Western
Nutcracker, Clark's
Nuthatch, Black-eared
Nuthatch, Nevada
Nuthatch, Pygmy
Oriole, Bullock's
Oriole, Scott's
Owl, Burrowing
Owl, Coast Pygmy
Owl, Flammulated Screech
Owl, Northern Spotted
Owl, Pygmy
Owl, Spotted
Pewee, Western Wood
Phoebe, Say's
Pigeon, Red-billed
Poor-will
Poor-will, Dusky
Poor-will, Nuttall's
Ptarmigan, White-tailed
Pyrrhuloxia, Arizona
Quail, Mountain
Quail, Plumed
Quail, Valley
Raven, American
Rough-leg, Ferruginous
Sapsucker, Natalie's
Sapsucker, Northern Red-breasted
Sapsucker, Red-breasted
Sapsucker, Red-naped
Sapsucker, Williamson's
Shrike, Loggerhead
Shrike, Northwestern
Shrike, White-rumped
Solitaire, Townsend's
Sparrow, Baird's
Sparrow, Brewer's
Sparrow, Cassin's
Sparrow, Desert
Sparrow, Gambel's
Sparrow, Golden-crowned
Sparrow, Sage
Sparrow, Scott's
Sparrow, Western Chipping
Sparrow, Western Field
Sparrow, Western Grass-hopper
Sparrow, Western Henslow's
Sparrow, Western Lark

WESTERN (cont'd)

Sparrow, Western Vesper
Sparrow, White-crowned
Swallow, Violet-green
Swift, Black
Swift, Vaux's
Swift, White-throated
Tanager, Cooper's
Tanager, Western
Thrasher, Crissal
Thrasher, Sage
Thrasher, Western Brown
Thrush, Northern Varied
Thrush, Pacific Varied
Thrush, Western Olive-backed
Titmouse, Plain
Towhee, Brown
Towhee, Green-tailed
Towhee, Spotted
Turkey, Merriam's
Vireo, Bell's or Least
Vireo, Bell's (V. belli belli)
Vireo, Cassin's
Vireo, Hutton's
Vireo, Plumbeous
Vireo, Western Warbling
Warbler, Alaska, Myrtle
Warbler, Audubon's
Warbler, Black-throated Gray
Warbler, Caleveras
Warbler, Golden Pileolated
Warbler, Grace's
Warbler, Hermit
Warbler, Lucy's
Warbler, MacGillivray's
Warbler, Northern Pileolated
Warbler, Virginia's
Warbler, Western Palm
Water Thrush, Grinnell's
Waxwing, Cedar
Woodpecker, California
Woodpecker, Northern White-headed
Woodpecker, Nuttall's
Woodpecker, Western Pileolated
Woodpecker, White-headed
Wren, Canon
Wren, Rock
Wren, Western House
Wren-tit
Wren-tit, Coast
Wren-tit, Ruddy

SOUTHWEST

Ani, Groove-billed
Blackbird, Bicolored or California Red-winged
Bluebird, Chestnut-backed
Bunting, Beautiful
Bunting, Painted
Bunting, Varied
Bush-tit, Lloyd's
Cardinal, Arizona
Cardinal, Gray-tailed
Chickadee, Chestnut-backed
Chickadee, Mexican
Condor, California
Cowbird, Bronzed
Cowbird, Dwarf
Cowbird, Red-eyed
Creeper, Mexican or Sierra Madre Brown
Dove, Inca
Dove, Chinese Spotted
Dove, Mexican Ground
Dove, Ringed Turtle
Dove, White-fronted
Dove, White-winged
Finch, Common House
Finch, San Clemente House
Finch, Sierra Nevada Rosy
Flicker, Gilded
Flicker, Mearn's Gilded
Flycatcher, Ash-throated
Flycatcher, Beardless
Flycatcher, Buff-breasted
Flycatcher, Coues's
Flycatcher, Derby
Flycatcher, Mexican Crested
Flycatcher, Olivaceous
Flycatcher, Scissor-tailed
Flycatcher, Sulphur-bellied
Gnatcatcher, Black-tailed
Gnatcatcher, Plumbeous
Gnatcatcher, Plumbeous (*P.m. melanura*)
Gnatcatcher, Sonora
Goldfinch, Lawrence's
Goshawk, Mexican
Grosbeak, California Blue
Grouse, Mount Pinos
Hawk, Desert Sparrow
Hawk, Mexican Black
Hawk, Sennett's White-tailed
Hawk, Zone-tailed
Hummingbird, Anna's
Hummingbird, Blue-throated
Hummingbird, Broad-billed
Hummingbird, Buff-bellied
Hummingbird, Costa's
Hummingbird, Lucifer
Hummingbird, Rivoli's
Hummingbird, White-eared
Jay, Arizona
Jay, Blue-fronted
Jay, California
Jay, Coast
Jay, Couch's
Jay, Green
Jay, Long-crested
Junco, Arizona
Junco, Red-backed
Kingbird, Couch's
Kingbird, Mexican
Kingfisher, Texas
Kite, White-tailed
Magpie, Yellow-billed
Meadowlark, Arizona
Meadowlark, Rio Grande
Mockingbird, Western
Nighthawk, Texas or Lesser
Nuthatch, Pygmy
Nuthatch, White-naped
Oriole, Audubon's
Oriole, Hooded
Oriole, Arizona Hooded
Oriole, California Hooded
Oriole, Sennett's
Owl, California Pygmy
Owl, California Spotted
Owl, Elf
Owl, Ferruginous Pygmy
Owl, Mexican Spotted
Owl, Spotted Screech
Owl, Texas Barred
Parrot, Thick-billed

CHESTNUT-COLLARED LONGSPUR (*Calcarius ornatus*). Length: 5.5 to 6.5 inches. Male: solid black breeding plumage except that throat and nape of neck are chestnut. Female and winter male: Sparrow-like, except for large amount of white on tail. Range: From Canada to Kansas and Minnesota. Winters from Nebraska to Mexico. Voice: Feeble, but musical song.
Alfred M. Bailey

SOUTHWEST (cont'd)

Pauraque, Merrill's
Phainopepla
Phoebe, Black
Poor-will, Desert
Poor-will, Sonora
Pyrrhuloxia
Pyrrhuloxia, Texas
Quail, Arizona Scaled
Quail, California
Quail, Catalina
Quail, Chestnut-bellied Scaled
Quail, Gambel's
Quail, Olathe
Quail, Scaled
Raven
Raven, White-necked
Red-Shoulder, Texas
Redstart, Painted
Sapsucker, Southern Red-breasted
Seedeater, Sharpe's
Sparrow, Arizona Black-chinned
Sparrow, Arizona Grass-hopper
Sparrow, Belding's
Sparrow, Bell's
Sparrow, Black-chinned
Sparrow, Botteri's
Sparrow, California Black-chinned
Sparrow, Large-billed
Sparrow, Mexican Black-chinned
Sparrow, Nuttall's
Sparrow, Rufous-crowned
Sparrow, Rufous-winged
Sparrow, San Francisco Black-chinned
Sparrow, Texas
Sparrow, Worthern's
Swallow, Coahuila Cliff
Swallow, Sonora Rough-winged
Tanager, Hepatic
Thrasher, Bendire's
Thrasher, Brownsville
Thrasher, California
Thrasher, Curve-billed
Thrasher, Desert
Thrasher, Leconte's
Thrasher, Palmer's or Curve-billed
Thrasher, Palmer's (T.c. palmeri)
Thrasher, Sennett's or Long-billed
Titmouse, Black-crested
Titmouse, Bridled
Towhee, Abert's
Towhee, Canon
Trogon, Coppery-tailed
Verdin
Vireo, Arizona
Vireo, Bermuda White-eyed
Vireo, Black-capped

SOUTHWEST (cont'd)

Vireo, Gray
Vireo, Least
Vireo, Rio Grande White-eyed
Vireo, Stephen's
Vireo, Texas
Vireo, Yellow-green
Warbler, Black-fronted
Warbler, Colima
Warbler, Golden-cheeked
Warbler, Olive
Warbler, Red-faced
Warbler, Sennett's
Whip-poor-will, Stephen's
Woodpecker, Ant-eating
Woodpecker, Arizona
Woodpecker, Cactus
Woodpecker, California
Woodpecker, Gila
Woodpecker, Golden-fronted
Woodpecker, Ladder-backed
Woodpecker, Lewis's
Woodpecker, Southern White-headed
Woodpecker, Texas
Wren, Cactus
Wren, Lomita
Wren, San Bernadine
Wren-tit, Gambel's
Wren-tit, Pallid
Yellow-throat, Rio Grande
Road-runner

GREAT PLAINS REGION

Chicken, Greater Prairie
Chicken, Lesser Prairie
Grouse, Sharp-tailed
Hawk, Krider's Red-tailed
Hawk, Richardson's Pigeon
Longspur, Chestnut-collared
Longspur, McCown's
Pipit, Sprague's

AMERICAN BIRDS IN MIGRATION

FOUND IN EASTERN UNITED STATES GOING SOUTH

Cuckoo, Black-billed
Cuckoo, Yellow-billed
Flycatcher, Yellow-bellied
Warbler, Blackburnian
Warbler, Palm
Warbler, Yellow Palm

CROSSES GULF STATES AND FLORIDA, GOING SOUTH

Flycatcher, Alder
Nuthatch, Red-breasted
Swallow, Bank
Warbler, Bachman's
Warbler, Golden-winged
Warbler, Hooded

MIGRATES THROUGHOUT MOST OF UNITED STATES GOING SOUTH

Chat, Yellow-breasted
Grosbeak, Rose-breasted
Hawk, Harlan's
Pipit
Sapsucker, Yellow-bellied
Sparrow, Fox
Sparrow, Lincoln's
Tanager, Summer
Warbler, Bay-breasted
Warbler, Cape May

CROSSES UNITED STATES FROM WEST TO EAST

Warbler, Orange-crowned
Warbler, Western Palm

MIGRATES THROUGH SOUTHWESTERN STATES

Hummingbird, Rufous
Sparrow, Baird's
Sparrow, White-crowned
Warbler, Black-poll
Warbler, Golden Pileolated
Warbler, Hermit

MIGRATES THROUGH WESTERN STATES

Owl, Burrowing
Sparrow, Gambel's
Sparrow, Golden-crowned
Sparrow, Harris's

MIGRATES THROUGH NORTHERN UNITED STATES TO EUROPE AND AFRICA

Wheatear

RANGE OF AMERICAN BIRDS IN WINTER

WEST, and SOUTH INTO MEXICO

Junco, Oregon
Longspur, Chestnut-collared
Pigeon, Band-tailed
Sapsucker, Natalie's
Sparrow, Baird's
Waxwing, Cedar

SOUTHWEST

Finch, Black Rosy
Finch, Brown-capped Rosy
Finch, Hepburn's Rosy
Flycatcher, Vermilion
Hawk, Richardson's Pigeon
Junco, White-winged
Mockingbird, Western
Phoebe, Say's
Sparrow, Gambel's
Sparrow, White-crowned
Thrush, Pacific Varied
Towhee, Spotted
Warbler, Audubon's
Warbler, Townsend's

WEST

Hawk, Black Pigeon
Longspur, Smith's
Sparrow, Golden-crowned
Sparrow, Harris's
Waxwing, Bohemian

NORTHWEST

Longspur, Alaska

NORTH AMERICA

Gyrfalcon
Hawk, American Rough-legged
Hawk, Cooper's
Hawk, Sharp-shinned
Kinglet, Ruby-crowned
Longspur, Lapland
Owl, Great Gray
Owl, Hawk
Owl, Richardson's
Owl, Snowy
Ptarmigan, Willow
Redpoll
Redpoll, Common
Redpoll, Greater
Sparrow, Eastern Tree
Sparrow, Tree
Wheatear

NORTHERN UNITED STATES, south

Lark, Northern Horned
Lark, Prairie Horned
Owl, Long-eared
Owl, Saw-whet
Shrike, Northern
Sparrow, Ipswich
Wren, Short-billed Marsh

SOUTHERN UNITED STATES, south

Blackbird, Rusty
Bunting, Lark
Catbird
Cowbird, Eastern
Grackle, Bronzed
Hawk, Marsh
Hawk, Pigeon
Pipit
Sparrow, Chipping
Sparrow, Eastern Grass-hopper
Sparrow, Eastern Lark
Sparrow, Field
Sparrow, Leconte's
Sparrow, Savannah
Thrasher, Brown
Vireo, Blue-headed
Vulture, Turkey
Warbler, Alaska Myrtle
Warbler, Black and White
Whip-poor-will
Wren, Long-billed Marsh

SOUTH AMERICA

Cuckoo, Black-billed
Cuckoo, Yellow-billed
Flycatcher, Olive-sided
Hawk, Duck
Kingbird, Eastern
Martin, Purple
Nighthawk
Plover, Upland
Swallow, Bank
Swallow, Cliff
Vireo, Eastern Warbling
Vireo, Red-eyed
Warbler, Blackburnian
Warbler, Black-poll
Warbler, Cerulean

NORTHEAST

Bunting, Snow
Grosbeak, Evening

SOUTHEAST and SOUTHEAST, south

Chuck-will's-widow
Cowbird
Flicker, Boreal
Gnatcatcher, Blue-gray
Goshawk, American
Killdeer
Meadowlark
Ovenbird
Owl, Short-eared
Sparrow, Eastern Chipping
Sparrow, Eastern Henslow's
Sparrow, Henslow's
Sparrow, Sharp-tailed
Sparrow, Western Henslow's
Swallow, Tree
Thrush, Wood
Vireo, White-eyed
Warbler, Black-throated Blue
Warbler, Myrtle
Warbler, Orange-crowned
Warbler, Palm
Warbler, Parula
Warbler, Pine
Warbler, Yellow Palm
Warbler, Yellow-throated

MEXICO, south

Blackbird, Brewer's
Blackbird, Yellow-headed
Bunting, Painted
Flycatcher, Acadian
Goldfinch, Arkansas
Grosbeak, Rose-breasted
Hawk, Broad-winged
Hawk, Mexican Black
Hawk, Swainson's
Hawk, Western Pigeon
Hummingbird, Ruby-throated
Hummingbird, Rufous
Jay, Long-crested
Kingbird, Western

MEXICO, south (cont'd)

Oriole, Arizona Hooded
Oriole, Bullock's
Oriole, California Hooded
Oriole, Hooded
Oriole, Sennett's
Rough-leg, Ferruginous
Sparrow, Eastern Vesper
Sparrow, Vesper
Sparrow, Western Vesper
Swallow, Barn
Swallow, Rough-winged
Swallow, Violet-green
Tanager, Western
Towhee, Green-tailed
Vireo, Yellow-throated
Warbler, Black-throated Green
Warbler, Blue-winged
Warbler, Hooded
Warbler, Magnolia
Warbler, Nashville
Water-thrush, Louisiana

CUBA

Warbler, Bachman's

CENTRAL AMERICA, south

Bunting, Indigo
Flycatcher, Alder
Pewee, Wood
Thrush, Veery or Wilson's
Vireo, Philadelphia
Warbler, Chestnut-sided
Warbler, Golden-winged
Warbler, Mourning
Warbler, Prothonotary
Warbler, Tennessee
Warbler, Yellow
Yellow-throat

WEST INDIES

Kingbird, Gray
Redstart, American
Sapsucker, Yellow-bellied
Warbler, Cape May
Warbler, Swainson's

BIRDS OF LIMITED RANGE

RIO GRANDE VALLEY REGION

Chachalaca
Dove, White-fronted
Flycatcher, Derby
Jay, Green
Kingbird, Couch's
Oriole, Audubon's
Oriole, Sennett's
Owl, Ferruginous Pygmy
Pigeon, Red-billed
Seedeater, Sharpe's
Sparrow, Botteri's
Thrasher, Brownsville
Thrasher, Sennett's or Long-billed
Vireo, Rio Grande
Warbler, Sennett's

SOUTHWESTERN DESERTS

Bush-tit, Lead-colored
Falcon, Aplomado
Gnatcatcher, Plumbeous
Hawk, Swainson's
Rough-leg, Ferruginous
Thrasher, Crissal

WESTERN MOUNTAINS

Chickadee, Mountain
Finch, Gray-crowned Rosy
Flycatcher, Buff-breasted
Flycatcher, Olivaceous
Flycatcher, Sulphur-bellied
Goldfinch, Pale
Grosbeak, Pine
Grouse, Dusky
Grouse, Richardson's
Grouse, Sooty
Hawk, Western Pigeon
Hummingbird, Broad-billed
Hummingbird, Calliope
Hummingbird, Rivoli's
Hummingbird, White-eared
Jay, Black-headed
Jay, Blue-fronted
Junco, Arizona
Nuthatch, Pygmy
Ptarmigan, White-tailed
Sapsucker, Natalie's
Sapsucker, Southern Red-breasted
Sapsucker, Williamson's
Sparrow, Rufous-crowned
Sparrow, Rufous-winged
Solitaire, Townsend's
Thrush, Northern Varied
Thrush, Western Olive-backed
Trogon, Coppery-tailed
Turkey, Merriam's
Vireo, Gray
Vireo, Plumbeous

WESTERN PRAIRIES

Caracara, Audubon's
Falcon, Prairie
Grouse, Sage or Sage Hen
Hawk, Swainson's
Sparrow, Baird's
Sparrow, Western Grasshopper

GREAT PLAINS

Chicken, Greater Prairie
Chicken, Lesser Prairie
Grouse, Sharp-tailed
Hawk, Krider's Red-tailed
Hawk, Richardson's Pigeon
Longspur, Chestnut-collared
Longspur, McCown's
Pipit, Sprague's

SOUTHEASTERN PRAIRIES

Sparrow, Florida Grasshopper

SOUTHWESTERN DESERTS

Dove, White-winged
Flicker, Mearn's Gilded
Flycatcher, Mexican Crested
Gnatcatcher, Plumbeous
Hawk, Swainson's
Poor-will, Desert
Quail, Arizona Scaled
Quail, California
Quail, Chestnut-bellied Scaled
Quail, Gambel's
Quail, Olather
Quail, Scaled
Raven, White-necked
Tanager, Hepatic
Thrasher, Bendire's
Thrasher, Leconte's
Towhee, Abert's
Verdin
Woodpecker, Cactus
Wren, Cactus

WESTERN COAST

Flicker, Northwestern
Hawk, Red-bellied

EASTERN COAST

Eagle, Northern Bald
Eagle, Southern Bald

SOUTHEAST MOUNTAINS

Vireo, Mountain Blue-headed

INDEX

In this index the common colloquial and regional names for birds have been handled in one sequence with the ornithologically correct names. In each case, a *see* reference directs the reader to the correct name. This listing does not pretend to be exhaustive, but it does contain those names most often used. An asterisk (*) denotes an illustration.